A HISTORY OF EARLY VEDĀNTA PHILOSOPHY

A History of Early Vedānta Philosophy

Hajime Nakamura

TRANSLATED INTO ENGLISH BY
TREVOR LEGGETT, SENGAKUL MAYEDA,
TAITETZ UNNO AND OTHERS

Part One

MOTILAL BANARSIDASS PUBLISHERS
PRIVATE LIMITED
DELHI

First Edition: Delhi, 1983
Reprinted: Delhi, 1990

ISBN: 81-208-0651-4

Also available at:
MOTILAL BANARSIDASS
Bungalow Road, Jawahar Nagar, Delhi 110 007
Chowk, Varanasi 221 001
Ashok Rajpath, Patna 800 004
24 Race Course Road, Bangalore 560 001
120 Royapettah High Road, Mylapore, Madras 600 004

PRINTED IN INDIA
BY JAINENDRA PRAKASH JAIN AT SHRI JAINENDRA PRESS, A-45 NARAINA INDUSTRIAL AREA, PHASE I, NEW DELHI 110 028 AND PUBLISHED BY NARENDRA PRAKASH JAIN FOR MOTILAL BANARSIDASS PUBLISHERS PVT. LTD., BUNGALOW ROAD, JAWAHAR NAGAR, DELHI 110 007.

In Memory of
THE LATE DR. HAKUJU UI
and my Parents

PREFACE

The purpose of the present work is to trace the development of early Vedānta philosophy before Śaṅkara. Fairly well known to the academic world is the Vedānta philosophy of Śaṅkara and his successors, but pre-Śaṅkara Vedānta has been little explored and this work aims at filling the gap. It will be published in three or four volumes.

The Japanese original of this work was my doctorate thesis submitted to the University of Tokyo in 1942. From 1936 to the end of 1941 I was engaged in post-graduate research at the University under the guidance of the late Dr. Hakuju Ui, finally submitting a thesis, entitled "A History of Early Vedānta Philosophy", on pre-Śaṅkara Vedānta philosophy, which was accepted by the University in 1943. Just after World War II it was difficult to arrange publication, but it finally appeared in four volumes, published respectively in the years 1950, 1951, 1955 and 1956.

After that I made some piecemeal English translations of certain sections, some of which appeared in foreign journals, but there seemed not much possibility of completing the task. However Professor Daniel H. H. Ingalls urged me to make a complete translation into English, and was kind enough to recommend the project to Harvard-Yenching Institute, whose director Professor John Pelzel generously interested himself in the matter. In 1967 and 1968 the Institute offered a grant towards the work of translating.

After one abortive effort, I asked Professor Taitetsu Unno of the University of Illinois (now Smith College, Mass.) to supervise a translation team consisting of the following scholars :

Mr. Clifford Miyashiro
Mr. Robert Wargo
Mr. Ryushin Uryūzu
Mr. Masao Kodani

Citations of original texts were checked, and often re-translated, by Dr. Sengaku Mayeda, then head of the research section of the Suzuki Foundation, who completed this part of the work in 1970.

I had also had some correspondence with Mr. Trevor Leggett of England who had made some translations of parts of the work for his own interest. Mr. Leggett came to Japan in 1975, and using his knowledge of both Sanskrit and Japanese went over the whole manuscript during his four months stay, in regular consultation with me.

I count myself fortunate that with the help of the above-mentioned scholars I have been able to bring the task to completion, though it has been an exacting one, almost amounting to a new work, with some chapters being re-written in English.

For many years Messrs Motilal Banarsidass have expressed their desire to publish the English translation; on my periodic visits to India every two or three years I discussed it with them, and in January 1976 in Delhi, we finalized the last details.

I wish to express my sincere gratitude to those I have mentioned and also the many others, too numerous to list by name, who have kindly given me their collaboration in various points. This all too brief acknowledgement must suffice to express a deep appreciation of their generosity with time and trouble.

The manuscript was checked finally by Mr. Trevor Leggett. I am greatly indebted to him as well as to other scholars whose names are mentioned in the preface.

March 1976, Tokyo | Hajime Nakamura

Some portions of this work were formerly published in English, mostly in foreign journals, as follows (—They are mentioned in the same order as they appear in this work):—

1. The particular Nature of the Vedānta. (*Kavirāj Abhinandana Grantha*, Lucknow : Akhila Bhāratīya Saṃskṛta Pariṣad, 1967, pp. 159-165.)
2. The Circumstance of the Formation of the Vedānta School. (*Science, Philosophy and Culture. Essays Presented in Honour of Humayun Kabir's Sixty-second Birthday*, ed. by K. Satchidananda Murty and Others, Bombay : Asia Publishing House, 1968, pp. 184-193).
3. Upaniṣadic Tradition and the Early School of Vedānta as Noticed in Buddhist Scripture. (*Harvard Journal of Asiatic Studies*, Vol. 18, 1955, Nos. 1 and 2, pp. 74-104).

4. The Vedāntic Chapter of Bhavya's Madhyamakahṛdaya. (*Brahmavidyā. The Adyar Library Bulletin.* vol. XXXIX, 1975, pp. 300-329).
5. The Tibetan Text of the Madhyamaka-hṛdaya-vṛtti-Tarkajvālā (Dbu-maḥi sñiṅ-poḥi ḥgrel-pa rtog-ge ḥbar-ba). (*Indo-Iranian Journal,* Vol. II, 1958-Nr. 3, Mouton & Co., the Hague, Holland, pp. 181-190).
6. The Vedānta as Presented by Bhavya. (*Journal of the Oriental Institute,* M. S. University of Baroda, Baroda. Dr. Benoytosh Bhattacharya Memorial Number, Oriental Institute, Baroda. Vol. XIV Nos. 3-4, March) (June, 1965, pp. 287-296).
7. The Vedānta Thought as Referred to in the Texts of Bhavya). (*Professor Hiriyanna Birth Centenary Commemoration Volume,* Mysore : University of Mysore, 1972, pp. 174-176).
8. A Note on Pre-Śaṅkara Vedānta Philosophy—The Vedāntic, Portions of the Tattvasaṁgraha by Śāntirakṣita—. (*proceedings of the Okurayama Oriental Research Institute, Yokohama,* Vol. 1, 1954, pp. 1-13).
9. Vedānta Philosophy as Seen from the Scriptures of Early Jainism (*Journal of the Oriental Institute,* Baroda, Oriental Institute, Vol. VIII, No. 2, Dec. 1958, pp. 148-155).
10. The Vedānta as Noticed in Mediaeval Jain Literature. (*Indological Studies* in Honor of W. Norman Brown, American Oriental Society, 1962, New Haven, Conn. pp. 186-194).
11. The Vedāntic Thought as Represented in the Dharma-śāstra and the Arthaśāstra. (*Science and Human Progress, Essays in Honour of late Prof. D. D. Kosambi Scientist, Indologist and Humanist,* Bombay : Popular Prakashan, 1974, pp. 137-153).
12. Vedānta Philosophy in Philosophical and Religious works. *Umesha Mishra Commemoration Volume* (Allahabad, Ganganatha Jha Research Institute, 1970), pp. 47-64.
13. The Historico-Social Attitude of the Brahma-Sūtras. (*Charudeva Shastri Felicitation Volume.* Delhi : Charu Deva Shastri Felicitation Committee, 1974, pp. 373-378).
14. Early Vedāntic scholars subsequent to the Brahma-sūtra. (*Studies in Indo-Asian Art and Culture. Acharya Raghu*

Vira Commemoration Volume, vol. I, edited by Perala Ratnam, New Delhi : The International Academy of Indian Culture, 1972, 165-170).

15. Bhartṛhari the Scholar. (*Indo-Iranian Journal*, vol. IV-1960, Nr. 4, pp. 282-305).
16. Tibetan Citations of Bhartṛhari's Verses and the Problem of his Date. (*Studies in Indology and Buddhology*, Presented in Honor of Professor S. Yamaguchi, Kyoto, Hozokwan Publishing Company, 1955, pp. 122-136).
17. Bhartṛhari and Buddhism (Kshetresa Chandra Chattopadhyaya Felicitation Volume, pt. 2: *Journal of the Ganganatha Jha Kendriya Sanskrit Vidyapeetha*, Allahabad, vol. XXVIII, Jan.-April, pts. 1-2, 1972, pp. 395-406.
18. Buddhist Influence upon the Vākyapadīya (Ganganatha Jha Centenary Volume, *Journal of the Ganganatha Jha Kendriya Sanskrit Vidyapeetha*, Allahabad, vol. XXIX. pts. 1-4, 1973, pp. 367-88.
19. The Chapter of the Self. Translated into English by Trevor Leggett (Trevor Leggett: *The Chapter of the Self*, London: Routledge and Kegan Paul, 1978, pp. 159-165)
20. The Concept of Brahman in Bhartṛhari's Philosophy (*Journal* for Research of the Kuppuswami Research Institute, 1982), pp. 135-150.

The thought of Śaṅkara was formerly discussed by myself in English in foreign journals as follows :

1. Approaches to the Upaniṣads : Swami Nikhilananda's *The Upanishads*. (In *Philosophy East and West*. vol. XI Number 4, January, 1962, pp. 245-253).
2. Conflict between Traditionalism and Rationalism : A Problem with Śaṅkara. (In *Philosophy East and West*, vol. XII, No. 2, July, 1962, pp. 153-161).
3. A review of V. M. Apte's *Brahma-sūtra Śāṅkara-bhāṣya*. (In *Journal of the American Oriental Society*, vol. 81, No. 2, April-June, 1961, pp. 141-142).
4. Practice of Selfless Action. (In *The Integral Philosophy of Sri Aurobindo, A Commemorative Symposium*, edited by Haridas Chaudhuri and Frederic Spiegelberg. London, George Allen and Unwin Ltd. 1960, pp. 223-230).

5. An Interview with Śaṅkarāchārya. (*The Jagadguru*, compiled by V. Raghavan, Madras, Jayachandra, June 1965, pp. 55-70).
6. Meditation in Śaṅkara, (*The Journal of Religious Studies*, vol. VII, No. i, Spring 1979, pp. 1-18).
7. Weisheit und Erlösung durch Meditation. Ihr Sinn in der Philosophie Schankaras (*Munen Muso. Ungegenständliche Meditation. Festschrift für Pater Hugö M. Enomiya-Lasalle S.J.zum* 80. *Geburtstag*. herausgegeben von Günter Stachel. Mainz : Matthias- Grünewald-Verlag, 1978, S. 52-63.)

ABBREVIATIONS

AAA. Abhisamayālaṃkārāloka, edited by Unrai Wogihara.
ABhI. Annals of the Bhandarkar Institute, Poona.
AKV. Abhidharmakośavyākhyā, edited by Unrai Wogihara.
Ait. Up. Aitareya-Upaniṣad.
Ān. (Ānandaj.) Ānandajñāna.
A. N. Aṅguttara-Nikāya.
AnSS. Ānandāśrama Sanskrit Series (Poona).
ApDhS. Āpastamba-Dharma-Sūtra.
Aufrecht : Bodl. Cat. Th. Aufrecht : Catalogus Codicum MSS. Sanscriticorum Bibliothecae, Bodleiane, Oxonii 1859-64.
Aufrecht : CC. Th. Aufrecht : Catalogus Catalogorum 1891; II, 1896; 1903.
AV. Atharva-Veda.
Avadānaśataka. ed. by J. S. Speyer (BB, III), St. Pétersbourg 1902-1909.
BB. Bibliotheca Buddhica (Leningrad).
BCAP. Bodhicaryāvatārapañjikā (B. I.).
BCAP. ed. by Poussin. Louis de La Vallée Poussin : Bouddhisme, p. 297ff.
BEFEO. Bulletin de l'École Francaise d'Extrême Orient.
Belvalkar : ŚSG. S. K. Belvalkar : An Account of the different existing Systems of Sanskrit Grammar, Poona 1915.
Belvalkar : Lectures. S. K. Belvalkar : Shree Gopal Basu Mallik Lectures on Vedānta Philosophy, Part 1, Poona 1929.
BenSS. Benares Sanskrit Series.
Bhag. G. Bhagavadgītā. (Commentaries on it are cited from the edition by Wāsudev Laxmaṇ Shāstrī Paṇsikar, NSP.).
Bhāgavata-Purāṇa. Le Bhāgavata Purāṇa on histoire poétique de Krichṇa, traduit et publiés par M. Eugéne Burnouf, t. I—III, Paris 1840-47. t. IV et V publiés par M. Hauvette-Besnault et. P. Roussel, Paris 1848 et 1898.
Bhāmatī. The Brahmasūtra-Śāṅkarabhāṣyam with the commentaries Ratnaprabhā, Bhāmatī and Nyāyanirṇaya, ed. by Mahādeva Shāstri Bākre (NSP.), second edition, Bombay 1909.

Bhāskara ad BS. Bhāskara : Brahmasūtra-bhāṣya (ChowkhSS, 1903, 1913, 1915).

BI. (.........Bibl. Ind.) Bibliotheca Indica.

Br. Brāhmaṇa.

Bṛhad. Up. Bṛhadāraṇyaka-Upaniṣad.

Bṛhad. Up. Vārttika. Sureśvara : Bṛhadāraṇyaka-Upaniṣad-Bhāṣya-Vārttika (Ān SS, No. 16).

BS. Brahmasūtra.

BSOS. Bulletin of the School of Oriental Studies, London University.

BSS. Bombay Sanskrit Series.

Bodhisattvabhūmi. Ed. by Unrai Wogihara.

Buddhacarita. The Buddhacarita, edited by E. H. Johnston (Panjab University Oriental Publications, No. 32).

Caraka-saṃhitā, ed. by Moti Lal Banarsi Das, Lahore 1929.

Catuḥśatikā, ed. by Haraprasad Shastri, Memoirs, Asiatic Society of Bengal, Vol. III.

Chānd. Up. Chāndogya-Upaniṣad.

Chowkh SS. Chowkhambā Sanskrit Series (Benares).

Dasgupta : H I Ph. S. Dasgupta : History of Indian Philosophy, 5 Vols.

Deussen : AGPh. P. Deussen : Allgemeine Geschichte der Philosophie.

Deussen : SV. P. Deussen : System des Vedānta, Leipzig 1883.

D. N. Dīgha-Nikāya.

ERE. Encyclopaedia of Religion and Ethics, edited by James Hastings.

Farquhar : Outline. J. N. Farquhar : An Outline of the Religious Literature of India, Oxford 1920.

Ghate : the Vedānta. V. S. Ghate : the Vedānta. A Study of the Brahma-sūtras with the Bhāṣyas of Śaṃkara, Rāmānuja, Nimbārka, Madhva and Vallabha (Government Oriental Series, Class C, No. 1.), Poona 1926.

GK : Gauḍapādīya-Kārikā (ĀnSS, No. 10)..

GOS. Gaekwad's Oriental Series, Baroda.

Guha : Jīvātman. Abhayakumar Guha : Jīvātman in the Brahma-sūtras, published by the University of Calcutta 1921.

Hopkins : GEI. Hopkins : The Great Epic of India, New York 1901.

HOS. Harvard Oriental Series, ed. by Ch. R. Lanman.

IHQ. The Indian Historical Quarterly, ed. by Narendra Nath Law. Ind. Ant. Indian Antiquary.

Jacob : Concordance. Colonel G. A. Jacob : A Concordance to the Principal Upanishads and Bhagavadgītā, 1891.

JAOS. Journal of the American Oriental Society.

JASB. Journal of the Asiatic Society of Bengal.

JBRAS. Journal of the Bombay Branch of the Royal Asiatic Society.

JORM. Journal of Oriental Research Madras.

JRAS. Journal of the Royal Asiatic Society of Great Britain and Ireland.

Kauṣ. Up. Kauṣītaki-Upaniṣad.

KF. O. Böhtlingk : Sanskrit-Wöterbuch in Kürzerer Fassung, St. Petersburg 1879-89.

Laṅk. The Laṅkāvatāra-sūtra, ed. by Bunyiu Nanjio.

MadhyK. Mūlamadhyamaka-Kārikās (Mādhyamika-sūtras) de Nāgārjuna avec la Prasannapadā, commentaire de Candrakīrti, publiée par L. de la Vallée Poussin (BB. IV, St. -Petersbourg 1913.

Māṇḍ. Up. Māṇḍūkya-Upaniṣad.

Mahābhāṣya. The Mahābhāṣya ed. by F. Kielhorn (BSS. Nos. 18-22, 26, 28-30), 1906 ff.

Masson-Oursel : Esquisse. Paul Masson-Oursel : Esquisse d'une Histoire de la Philosophie Indienne, Paris 1923.

MAV. Madhyāntavibhāga.

MAVṬ. Madhyāntavibhāga-Ṭikā, ed. by Susumu Yamaguchi.

Max Müller : ASL. F. Max Müller : A History of Ancient Sanskrit Literature, London 1859.

MBh. Mahābhārata (Bombay Edition).

Mhvyut. Mahāvyutpatti, ed. by Unrai Wogihara.

Mit. Mitāksharā, A Gloss on Śri Gauḍapāda Āchārya's Māṇḍūkya Kārikās, ed. by Paṇḍita Ratna Gopāla Bhaṭṭa (Haridās Sanskrit Series, No. 1), Benares 1910.

M. N. Majjhima-Nikāya.

MSA. Mahāyāna-Sūtrālaṅkāra, édité par Sylvain Lévi (Bibliothéque de l' École des Hautes Études, t. 159), Paris 1907.

Muṇḍ. Up. Muṇḍaka-Upaniṣad.

Mvṛ. Madhyamakavṛtti (........MadhyK. ......1)

MW. Sir Monier Monier-Williams : A Sanskrit-English Dictionary, Oxford 1899.

Naiṣkarmyasiddhi, ed. by G. A. Jacob, BSS. No. 38, 1.

NSP. Nirṇaya Sāgara Press (Bombay).

Nyāyabinduṭīkāṭippaṇī, ed. by Th. Stcherbatskoi (BB, XI), St. Petersburg 1909.

Nyāyabhāṣya. ĀnSS, No. 91, 1922.

Nyāyamañjarī. Viz SS. No. V, 1895.

Nyāyasūtra. W. Ruben : Die Nyāyasūtras, Leipzig 1928.

Oldenberg : LU. H. Oldenberg - Die Lehre der Upanishaden und die Anfänge des Buddhismus, Göttingen 1915.

Pañcapādikā. VizSS. Vol. II, 1891, 1892.

Prameyakamalamārtaṇḍa. NSP. 1912.

Prapañcahṛdaya, ed. by T. Gaṇapati Sāstrī (Triv SS. No, 45), 1915.

Prasthānabheda ĀnSS. No. 51, 1928.

Proc. I (II, III) OC. Proceedings and Transactions of the First (Second, Third) Oriental Conference.

PW. O. Böhtlingk und R. Roth : Sanskrit-Wörterbuch nebst allen Nachträgen, St. Petersburg 1855-75.

Radhakrishnan : I Ph. S. Radhakrishnan : Indian Philosophy, 2 Vols, London 1923, 1927.

Ṛ. V. Ṛg-Veda.

Ś. Śaṅkara.

SaddhP. Saddharmapuṇḍarīka, edited by Unrai Wogihara and K. Tsuchida.

Śaṅkara ad BS. Śaṅkara : Brahmasūtra-bhāṣya (ĀnSS. No. 21) 1900.

Śaṅkara's Bhāṣyas on Upaniṣads are cited from the ĀnSS. editions.

Saṃkṣepaśārīraka. ĀnSS. No. 83.

Sarvasiddhāntasaṃgraha, ed. by Prem Sundar Bose, Calcutta 1929.

Śat. Br. Śatapatha-Brāhmaṇa.

SBE. Sacred Books of the East (Oxford).

Schmidt : Nachträge. R. Schmidt : Nachträge zum Sanskrit-Wörterbuch in kürzerer Fassung von Böhtlingk, Leipzig 1924-8.

Schrader, Diss. F. O. Schrader : Über den Stand der indischen Philosophie zur Zeit Mahāvīras und Buddhas, Strassburg 1902, Diss.

SDS. the Sarvadarśanasaṃgraha of Sāyaṇa-Mādhava, ed. by Vasudev Shastri Abhyankar (Government Oriental Series, No. 1), Poona 1924.

SHA. Sitzungsberichte der Heidelberger Akademic der Wissenschaften, Philosophische-historische Klasse.

Siddhitraya. Chowkh SS. No. 36, 1900.

Ślokavārttika. Chowkh SS. 1898-99.

S. N. Saṃyutta-Nikāya.

SPA. Sitzungsberichte der Preussischen Akademie der Wissenschaften in Berlin.

Śrībhāṣya. ed. by Vasudev Shastri Abhyankar (BSS, No. 68), Bombay 1914.

Śvet. Up. Śvetāśvatara-Upaniṣad.

Tait. Ār. Taittirīya-Āraṇyaka.

Tait. Saṃh. Taittirīya-Saṃhitā.

Tait. Up. Taittirīya-Upaniṣad.

Tattvasaṃgraha. Tattvasaṃgraha of Śāntarakṣita with the Commentary of Kamalaśīla, ed. by Embar Krishnamacharya, 2 Vols. (GOS, No. 30), Baroda 1926.

Thibaut : VS. G. Thibaut : The Vedānta-sūtras (SBE. Vols. 34, 38).

Triṃśikā. Deux Traités de Vasubandhu, Viṃśatikā (La Vingtaine) accompagnée d'une explication en prose et Triṃśikā (La Trentaine) aveclacunae commentaire de Sthiramati, publié par Sylvain Lévi, Paris 1925.

Triv SS. Trivandrum Sanskrit Series.

TT. Taisho Tripiṭaka, ed by J. Takakusu and K. Watanabe, Tokyo.

Up. Upaniṣad.

Upadeśasāhasrī. Minor Works of Śaṅkarācārya, ed. by Hari Raghunath Bhagavat, Poona 1925 (pp. 295-350).

Vajr. Pr. Vajracchedikā-Prajñāpāramitā-sūtra, ed. by F. Max Müller in "Buddhist Texts from Japan", Anecdota Oxoniensia, Aryan Series, I, 1, 1881.

Vāj. Saṃh. Vājasaneyi-Saṃhitā.

Vakyap. Vākyapadīya, ed. with the commentary of Puṇyarāja and of Helārāja (Ben SS.), 1887-1907, 1928-1937.

Vedāntasāra. [O. Böhtlingk : Sanskrit Chrestomathie. Commentaries on it are cited from G. A. Jacob's edition, NSP.]

Vedārthasaṃgraha. The Vedārthasaṃgraha, with the gloss

called Tātparyadīpikā by Sudarśanasūri, ed. by S. Sum. P. S. Rama Misra Sastri (Reprint from the Pandit), second edition, Benares 1924.

Viṃśatikā, cf. Triṃśikā.

Viṣṇusahasranāmabhāṣya. Minor Works of Śaṅkarācārya, pp. 505-584.

Vivekacūḍāmaṇi. Minor Works of Śaṅkarācārya, pp. 219-271.

Viz. SS. Vizianagram Sanskrit Series.

Walleser : DAV. Max Walleser : Der ältere Vedānta. Geschichte, Kritik und Lehre, Heidelberg 1910.

Weber : HIL. A Weber : History of Indian Literature, London 1892.

Winternitz : GIL. M. Winternitz : Geschichte der indischen Literatur, 3 Bde, Leipzig 1908-1920 .

Winternitz : HIL. M. Winternitz : History of Indian Literature, tr. by Mrs. S. Ketkar and revised by the author, Vol. I, Calcutta 1927.

WZKM. Wiener Zeitschrift für die Kunde des Morgenlandes.

Yogabhāṣya. ĀnSS. No. 47, 1932.

Yogavāsiṣṭha. NSP.

ZDMG. Zeitschrift der Deutschen Morgenländischen Gesellschaft.

ZII. Zeitschrift for Indologie und Iranistik.

Pāli texts are cited from the editions by the Pāli Text Society.

Numbering in this English version is the same as in the Japanese original text. Those readers who read Japanese or Chinese will find it easy to refer to the materials. Those footnotes which have been newly inseıted in the English version are mentioned with "dashes."

CONTENTS

PART I
THE SIGNIFICANCE OF EARLY VEDĀNTA PHILOSOPHY

CHAPTER I
INTRODUCTION

The Vedānta tradition has a great significance in the intellectual history of India, and it is the representative philosophy which forms the principal current of thought in that country. The philosophy of Vedānta has been handed down through the ages in the blood of the Indian people; it is inseparable from the soil of this great Asian subcontinent.

India is a huge and extraordinary country which claims a land space equal to all of Europe, excepting Russia, and it has embraced a mixture of heterogeneous races since ancient times, thus providing for the growth of diverse and complex cultures throughout its rich history. In India there live today approximately 574 million people, speaking standard languages and local dialects which are said to be of more than 700 varieties. Even when we consider this astonishing fact concerning language alone, we can readily understand the variegated and multiform civilization that has matured on this land. Consequently, the philosophical thought that has evolved over a period of more than 3,000 years through the contributions of countless thinkers is extremely complex and suggestive, and it cannot be summarized in a single frame of reference. People frequently jump to some over-simple conclusion and state that Indian philosophy has such and such a characteristic. But anyone who has even a passing knowledge of the history of Indian thought can immediately present counter-evidences. In its long history, the basic patterns of the various opposing types of world-view which confront each other in Western philosophy or Chinese thought can be found in almost identical form. The philosophers of India engaged in heated controversies from the respective standpoints of materialism and spiritualism, idealism and realism, rationalism and nominalism, hedonism and asceticism, conservatism and liberalism, theories of self and of non-self, claims for logic and for intuition. The history of Indian philosophy is the uninterrupted and continuing narrative of such opposing and contradictory systems of thought. Modern studies on this complicated history commenced with the introductory works of Henry Thomas Colebrook, F. Max Muller, and Paul Deussen, and they were followed by more technical studies, conducted by specialists in various disciplines and attaining a high scholarly level especially in recent years, but the introductory studies on philosophers and their works are far from complete, due to the complexity, volume and number of the principal literature. In fact, even the names of the various schools and religious sects, let alone their classification, are not completely clear. And the scientific studies of basic texts can be said to be barely in their preliminary stages. The attempt, therefore, to define some common characteristic of all shades of Indian philosophy confronts formidable problems. Indian philosophy, so-called, is nothing more than a general descriptive term to cover variegated, heterogeneous systems of thought, a historical product of countless thinkers of various racial and cultural origins advocating mutually opposing views, criticizing each other and sometimes synthesizing diverse strands of thought. It is almost impossible to reach a final decision on what constitutes "Indian philosophy."

In spite of this complexity which defies any easy summarizing of its major presuppositions, if we were asked to name the representative thought of India, we would not hesitate even for a moment to assert that it is Vedānta philosophy. No other form of thought has left such a decisive and enduring impression on the whole of Indian culture. In every age there were many thinkers and schools which opposed Vedānta philosophy, but none could ever amass enough social support and influence to counter the impact of Vedānta. Although the Sāṃkhya philosophy was relatively influential at one time, it did not spread as widely as Vedānta, and Mahāyāna Buddhism, even in its flourishing period, was predominant in only one segment of Indian society. We may thus conclude that the leading and principal tradition in the history of Indian philosophy has been Vedānta philosophy.

As an independent philosophical movement, Vedānta originated before the appearance of Śākyamuni Buddha and is found in the Upaniṣads, and as a scholastic tradition it has continued without interruption to affect constantly the other systems of thought. The Sāṃkhya system was often combined with Vedānta philosophy, a fact which is prominent especially in the great epic, *Mahābhārata*, the sacred Purāṇas, and the Sāṃkhya literature of later ages. The Mīmāṃsā school developed with the same socio-historical background as that of the Vedānta, and, although it maintained opposition to the Vedānta school in the Medieval Period, it reverted to its original alliance in later ages.[1] Even Jainism, which was rejected as heterodox by the orthodox Brahmanical schools, incorporated Vedāntic ideas in the Medieval Period.[2] The prevalence of Vedānta thought, furthermore, is found not only in philosophical writings but also in various forms of literature, such as the epics, lyric poetry, drama, and so forth, and it also forms the basis for the thinking of jurists, medical practitioners, grammarians, and others.[3] What is especially worthy of attention is that the Hindu religious sects, the common faith of the Indian populace, looked to Vedānta philosophy for the theoretical foundations for their theology.[4] The influence of Vedānta is prominent in the sacred literatures of Hinduism, such as the various Purāṇas, Saṃhitās, Āgamas, and Tantras. Many commentaries on the fundamental scripture of Vedānta, the *Brahmasūtra*, were written by the founders or leading scholars of the various sects of Hinduism, and they are transmitted to this day as documents indispensable in the respective sectarian traditions.[4] If we were to interpret the appellation 'Vedānta school' in its widest sense, the sects of Hinduism, at least in their philosophical aspects, would be included in it. Even apart from its relationship to Hinduism, the tradition of Śaṅkara, which is the least sectarian of the Vedānta sub-schools, maintains the central position in the philosophical world of modern India, and it has transmitted many important works to this day. The majority of the traditional and conservative scholars in India today, called Pandits, are students of Vedānta, and an overwhelming number belong to the lineage of Śaṅkara—five-sixths of all Pandits, according to some authorities.[5]

The leaders who initiated the renaissance of Indian culture and the reform of Indian society in order to throw off the political and economic subjugation of India by British rule have more or less advanced along the lines of Vedānta thought. The most powerful movements to reform Hinduism since the beginning of the 19th century have been the Brahma-Samāj and the Ārya-Samāj. A Vedānta colouring is prominent in the creeds of both the churches, and the Upaniṣads and Vedānta works were seriously studied by their leaders. Swami Vivekananda, who won acclaim throughout the world as a new type of spiritual leader, also stands in this tradition; and the two outstanding figures of modern India, Rabindranath Tagore and Mohandas Karamchand Gandhi, reflect the same tendencies in their thinking. In spite of the fact that these men were all stimulated and heavily influenced by Western civilization, their fundamental standpoint was consistently Vedāntic in nature.

Although Indian thought is extremely diverse and complicated, Vedānta philosophy stands supreme as regards social and intellectual influence, especially in the modern period. It has had a determining effect on the ways of thinking of all Indians, transcending racial distinction, class status, degree of education, and so forth. And the outstanding characteristic of the history of Indian philosophy is the fact that Vedānta has been such a powerful and predominant intellectual force.[5]

The fact is, however, that the philosophy of the Vedānta school has yet to be fully examined from a historical viewpoint. The research on Vedānta in the 19th century disregarded almost completely historical changes and developments, and it regarded Śaṅkara (first half of 8th century) as its foremost representative. Scholarly research seems to give the impression of having concentrated solely on the translation and interpretation of his principal work, *Brahmasūtrabhāṣya*.[6] This was followed by attention directed to Rāmānuja, who represents a different lineage within the same tradition, and then the ideas of Madhva, Vallabha and others were introduced, but it did not go beyond giving a general outline of the thoughts of the various founders within Vedānta. These studies consist of discussions on certain special aspects of Vedānta history, and are inadequate as inquiries into the history of thought. Scholars realized this weakness of past research, and they proceeded to investigate the works and ideas of thinkers other than the founders of the Vedānta subschools, but the vastness of its scope made it almost impossible to complete a comprehensive and integrated study.

In recent years, however, Professor S. Dasgupta of India traced the development of Indian philosophy and published an integrated history of the major movements. His magnum opus, *History of Indian Philosophy*, enumerates the names of many Vedānta scholars and the titles of their works in chronological order and discusses their ideas in rather detailed outline. Professor Dasgupta's achievement is a landmark in Indological studies, especially in the present situation which lacks even an adequate outline of the names of Vedānta scholars and their writings. The work is also very valuable as a reference work for scholars, for it makes wide use of source materials difficult to obtain and manuscripts which are still unpublished. But from the standpoint of the history of thought or the history of philosophy, the work is wanting in the sense that it fails to go beyond an introduction to the works of ancient scholars and their philosophical contents.

While Professor Dasgupta's contribution to the study of Vedānta philosophy is epoch-making, we notice that he begins his discussion with Śaṅkara, and of the thinkers before him, he mentions only Gauḍapāda and that very briefly. The tendency of the contemporary academic world is to concentrate mainly on the period after Śaṅkara, and this trend is especially evident in Indian scholars. But the opinion of the present writer is that to omit the consideration of pre-Śaṅkara Vedānta thought and focus attention only on subsequent developments is a major defect in the historical approach to philosophical studies. However well one studies the history of thought after Śaṅkara, the results will be very incomplete if its relationship to pre-Śaṅkara Vedānta philosophy is neglected. Generally speaking, Indian systems of thought have the tendency to revere unduly the writings of the ancients, and the Vedānta school in particular is characterized by the tendency to take ancient scriptures and writings as absolutely authoritative. That the pre-Śaṅkara scholars and literature were held sacrosanct by later Vedāntins is evident from the fact that the thinkers after Śaṅkara frequently make allusions to them. Although their works are almost all lost today, this does not mean that pre-Śaṅkara scholars can be disregarded. What happened was that due to the popularity of the writings of scholars such as Śaṅkara, Sureśvara and others, the works of earlier scholars were in recent times gradually neglected and soon all the manuscripts were dispersed and lost. Consequently, the clarification of their names, writings, and ideas is a minimum pre-condition for the scientific study of the complete history of Vedānta. The history of philosophy after Śaṅkara would be incomplete and imperfect, if the pre-Śaṅkara period were to be discarded, because the proper evaluation of the original contributions of later Vedānta philosophers can be made only when it is viewed in the light of past developments. (This work proposes to show that what has been hitherto considered as unique and original contribution of Śaṅkara or his successors was in reality existent much earlier among Vedāntic thinkers.)

Thus, unless we clarify the history of Vedānta philosophy before Śaṅkara, we can neither write the general history of Vedānta nor fully comprehend modern and contemporary Indian thought in which Vedānta philosophy assumes a central role. In this work, the period before Śaṅkara will be called "Early Vedānta Philosophy" for the sake of convenience. When our study on this early period reaches a tentative conclusion, then we may be able to understand correctly the historical significance of such great scholars as Śaṅkara and Rāmānuja. It may as a result necessitate revision of our ideas concerning their contributions to Vedānta philosophy.

The Vedānta school claims the Upaniṣads as its principal scriptures and utilizes the *Bhagavad-Gītā* as an important source of ideas. A considerable amount of research has been conducted on these works, and today their textual reading and interpretation, as well as various other kinds of analysis, have been fairly well done. These works however do not belong solely to Vedānta, for they are revered by all Brahmanical schools, albeit as of varying degrees of importance. In our research, therefore, they will not be our main concern but will be referred to whenever necessary. The principal subject matter for us is the Vedānta school and its philosophical thought between the formation of these scriptures and the appearance of Śaṅkara.

These scriptures were compiled approximately several centuries[7] before the beginning of the Christian era, and it is generally said that about a thousand years elapsed until the time of Śaṅkara.

What, then, was the situation of the Vedānta school during the long period from the appearance of these scriptures to the age of Śaṅkara? Who were the scholars that appeared during this interval? Such a historical problem has not been fully investigated in the past, but surely these scriptures were neither forgotten nor abandoned during the thousand years between the Upaniṣads and Śaṅkara. Originally these scriptures were not put down in writing but were orally transmitted from master to disciple, both of whom thus committed them to memory. With oral tradition, there must not be even a single break in the teacher-pupil line. Since the scriptures were taught in Sanskrit and since the daily language of both teacher and student was this same Sanskrit, they must have easily understood the contents of the scriptures, mastered the doctrines completely, and immersed themselves in philosophic reflection and thought. If some sort of communal life was pursued by the intellectuals engaged in such philosophic activities, the formation of a distinctive movement or school was inevitable, and the people belonging to such a group must have had differences of opinion and of scriptural interpretations which consequently led to disputations. There is a definite history of more than a thousand years before Śaṅkara in the evolution of this school, but the actual position of that period remains unclarified.

This work proposes to examine that neglected history of early Vedānta as comprehensively and thoroughly as possible.

Now, in writing our history of early Vedānta philosophy we must provide precise answers to two preliminary questions:

(1) What is "Vedānta Philosophy" ?

(2) What is the chronological range covered by the term "Early" ?

In the next two chapters we shall attempt to answer these two questions. We shall begin by first discussing the latter question.

Notes

1. For example, Laugākṣi Bhāskara (in the former half of 17th century) incorporated the Vedāntic thought at the end of his work *Arthasaṃgraha.*
2. This will be discussed in Part II, chapter II of this work.
3. This will be discussed in Part II, Chapter III.
4. This will be discussed in Part IV.

5. M. Winternitz: *Geschichte der indischen Litteratur*, III, S. 432, Anm. 2. Cf. Thibaut : *Sacred Books of the East*, XXXIV, Introduction, p. XV.

6. E. Windisch : *Geschichte der Sanskrit-Philologie*, S. 196.

7. The dates of the Upaniṣads are discussed in the following chapter. The *Bhagavadgītā* is believed to have been composed in the second century B.C. (cf. Winternitz: *History of Indian Literature*, vol. I, p. 437).

CHAPTER II

THE CHRONOLOGICAL DIVISIONS OF EARLY VEDĀNTA

INTRODUCTION

The present work, as a study of the history of "early Vedānta philosophy," should first determine what is the chronological span covered by the word "early."

The Vedānta being a systematic philosophy based upon the Upaniṣadic canon, it is clear that the Upaniṣads must have acquired authority as sacred texts before its rise. Vedānta therefore *could not have existed earlier than the Upaniṣads.* So the date of origination of the Upaniṣads can be taken as the earliest limit for the formulation of Vedānta. Of course there is the question whether or not the Upaniṣads attained canonical authority immediately, or whether sometime, and if so how much time, elapsed before they did so. This too will be included in the present field of enquiry. But in any case, unless we can first make a general estimate of the period of composition of the Upaniṣads, no chronological distinction of "early Vedānta philosophy" will be possible. This is what will be done in Part I.

The other limit of "early Vedānta" is roughly that it should be before Śaṅkara, who thus marks its later limit. Of course in this book we shall refer to Śaṅkara and his successors as occasion warrants, but the work centers on what preceded him. His date has been a knotty point much debated among Indologists for a good many years, but unless it is clearly determined, there can be ultimately no clear meaning to the expression "early Vedānta." This point will therefore be taken up in the second Part.

In determining the date of Śaṅkara, we shall have to examine and collate the dates of numerous philosophers who have been taken to have some relation with him, and the dates of these various others will be discussed as well.

PART ONE

THE PERIOD OF THE COMPOSITION OF THE UPANIṢADS

SECTION I

THE OLD UPANIṢADS

Sub-Section I The Relative Date Order of the Old Upaniṣads. After the Upaniṣads became known in the West, many Indologists simply held to a vague notion that the principal Upaniṣads were composed before Buddhism, and for a good time no thoroughgoing examination of the dating and order of composition of the many extant Upaniṣads was undertaken. It was Paul Deussen who succeeded in making a general classification and determined a date order for the principal Upaniṣads.[1] He examined closely the style, language, content and parallel passages in fourteen Old Upaniṣads, and divided them into three groups, with the following date order :

I. The Upaniṣads of the Early Period (Chiefly Prose)

Bṛhadāraṇyaka (Particularly I-IV)	*Chāndogya*
Taittirīya	*Aitareya*
Kauṣītaki	*Kena*

II. The Upaniṣads of the Middle Period (Poetry)

Kāṭhaka	*Īśa*
Śvetāśvatara	*Muṇḍaka*
Mahānārāyaṇa	

III. The Upaniṣads of the Late Period (Poetry)

Praśna	*Maitrāyaṇa* (or, *Maitri*)
Māṇḍūkya	

The listed order of these fourteen Upaniṣads represents the order of composition as well.

Deussen maintained that though there are newer and older strata to be distinguished within the larger Upaniṣads themselves, still if each Upaniṣad is taken as a single unit, then the order of composition is roughly as above. His order was thereafter accepted almost as it stood by many scholars.

Keith, however, opposed Deussen's chronological order, holding that the *Aitareya* is the oldest of the Upaniṣads, and must have been composed at the latest about 600 or 550 B.C. His analysis[2] is as follows:

Chapter II, 1-3, II. 4-6, and III in the *Aitareya-Āraṇyaka* have each become Upaniṣads, and of them II.1-3 and II.4-6 may probably be older than the *Bṛhadāraṇyaka*, with Chapter II.1-3 being much older. His reasons are:

(1) The doctrines in this *Āraṇyaka* are chiefly allegorical explanations of eulogistic verses (*uktha*) in praise of the officiating priests in rituals and as such connected with the Brāhmaṇas. Philosophical discussions are few in number and unclearly stated; they are thus in all probability earlier than the precise philosophical argumentations of Yājñavalkya.

(2) Parts of II.4-6 show traces of an advance in thought when compared to earlier parts. That is, the *ātman*, whose fundamental nature is here determined as wisdom (*prajñā*), is contrasted with *puruṣa, prāṇa*. The mode of thought here is of greater intellectual clarity than that of the earlier sections, although not up to the level characteristic of Yājñavalkya's teachings. Specifically:

(a) The Āraṇyaka doctrines do not teach the notion "the knowing subject cannot be known." This kind of idea appears only in later Upaniṣads (e.g. *Ait. Ār.* III.2, 14,19);

(b) The idea that only the *ātman* is true and all else is unreal, is not in evidence;

(c) No theory of liberation is mentioned. Śaṅkara and Sāyaṇa interpret "the one who knows the true meaning of the teaching will become immortal" in II.4-6 as referring directly to liberation, the two things should be distinguished.

(d) Transmigration is taught in *Bṛhadāraṇyaka* IV.4,5, but still not referred to in the *Aitareya-Upaniṣad*. Probably it was believed that human beings not yet enlightened die again and again, as the Brāhmaṇas say. The expression *yathāprajñaṃ hi sambhavāḥ* in the *Aitareya-Āraṇyaka* II.3.35 does not refer to transmigration, but can better be interpreted as, "For their experiences are according to their measure of intelligence." This is, in brief, the case which Keith put forward.

The disagreement was a stimulus to the world of scholarship. However, though it could be maintained, following Keith, that the *Aitareya-Upaniṣad* had been composed before the dialectics of Yājñavalkya in the *Bṛhad-Āraṇyaka-Upaniṣad*, it is impossible to go on to the conclusion that it was composed earlier than any part of the *Bṛhad-Āraṇyaka-Upaniṣad*. From the point of view of arranging in stages of development of the thought, it can certainly be said that the doctrines of the *Aitareya-Upaniṣad* are primitive and should be placed before the profound philosophical ideas found within the *Bṛhad-Āraṇyaka-Upaniṣad* but it is hardly to be concluded directly that therefore it must have come first *chronologically*. Especially as the results of linguistic analysis, as will be shown later, make the *Aitareya* later than either *Bṛhad-Āraṇyaka* or *Chāndogya-Upaniṣads*. And so Keith's hypothesis has not been generally accepted, and most scholars[3] have adopted the Deussen chronology almost as it stands.

Notes

1. Deussen : *A.G.Ph.*, I.2.S.22 *f.* Deussen adds that he published a chronological theory of the same import in *Transactions of the Third International Congress for the History of Religions*, II, Oxford, 1908, pp. 19-24.

2. A. B. Keith, *JRAS*, 1906, p. 492 ff. Keith discussed in detail his theory that the *Aitareya* is the oldest Upaniṣad, in his *Aitareya-Āraṇyaka*, Intro., p. 41 ff. His reasons for placing it earlier than the *Bṛhadāraṇyaka-Upaniṣad* were already stated [for the most part] in the former article.

3. A. Hillebrandt : *Aus Brahmanas und Upanisaden*, Jena, 1921, S. 170; Anm., 23. H. Jacobi : *Die Entwicklung der Gottesidee bei den Indern und deren Beweise für das Dasein Gottes.* Bonn und Leipzig, 1923. (Trans. into Japanese by Ryūjō Yamada and Kazuo Itō, *Indo Kodai Shinkan Shi*, pp. 10, 320) M. Winternitz : *GIL.*, Bd. I, S. 205 f. Junjiro Takakusu and Taiken Kimura, *Indo Tetsugaku Shūkyō Shi*, p. 294, passim. Further, Hume : *The Thirteen Principal Upaniṣads*, has also arranged the 13 most ancient Upaniṣads in virtually the same chronological order as Deussen; although he does not include the Mahānārāyaṇa here, taking it to be a work of the later centuries, while the *Śvetāśvatara*, he holds, was formulated notably later than Deussen had supposed. That is, his arrangement is : *Bṛhad, Chānd., Tait., Ait., Kauṣ., Kena, Īśa, Muṇḍ., Praśna, Śvet., Maitri.*

Sub-Section II Criteria for Dating

After Deussen's investigations there has thus been fairly general agreement among scholars (except for Keith's individual view) as to the chronological sequence of the Old *Upaniṣads*, but from Deussen onwards, no one has been able to come to any definite conclusions as to what centuries B.C. these Upaniṣads were composed. That is to say, there has been for the most part agreement as to the sequence of composition of the *Upaniṣads* relative to each other, but to their actual dating, opinion has been divided into many divergent lines of thought. The large majority of scholars of Indology place their date of composition long before the rise of Buddhism,[1] while there are those who assert on the contrary that even the most ancient of the Upaniṣads cannot be traced back to the sixth century B.C.[2] To tackle this problem, some standard criterion must be sought which can reliably determine the periods of the Upaniṣads, but the Upaniṣads themselves are lacking in positive clues. Many personal names appear in the Upaniṣads, but their dates are completely unknown; furthermore, though the same names appear in the Buddhist and the Jaina Canons, since it cannot be finally concluded (i.e. determined by comparison of the contexts) that these names refer in fact to the same individuals, they can not serve as suitable criteria. Unless the problem is to be given up as hopeless, the following two methods may be worth considering as possibly giving some clues.

(1) To find out whether the language and style of the earlier Upaniṣads are of the period before or after the grammarian Pāṇini; and

(2) To clear up the relation of these Upaniṣads with other schools of thought.

I. *Linguistic Investigation*

The Old Upaniṣads in their entirety were written in Sanskrit, although the form of their language is by no means in accord with the rules of Pāṇini's *Grammar.* Composed of course primarily in classical Sanskrit, the Upaniṣads of the early period still do show particular features of the Vedic language, while colloquialisms and the influence of the Epics also can be found in some Upaniṣadic writings. It can be supposed that the existence of minute divergences from the rules of Pāṇini's *Grammar* would make it possible to determine whether the date of an individual Upaniṣad was before or after Pāṇini.

This idea, which from a purely linguistic standpoint marks the first substantial contribution to the determination of the dates of the Upaniṣads, was the focus for the investigations of Otto Wecker (Otto Wecker : *Der Begrauch der Kasus in the älteren Upaniṣad—Literatur verglichen mit der Kasuslehre der indischen Grammatiker*. Beiträge zur Kunde der indogermanischen Sprachen, herausgegeben von Ad. Bezzenberger und W. Prellwitz, III (1906), p. 1 ff., 177 ff). Wecker carried out a thoroughgoing inquiry into case usage in the Old Upaniṣads; collating them with the rules of Pāṇini's *Grammar*, he divided the Upaniṣads into four chronological groups which were to show their relative sequence of composition. His results are as follows:

1. The Upaniṣads *Bṛhadāraṇyaka*, *Chāndogya* and *Kauṣītaki* are prior to Pāṇini , and furthermore they were perhaps composed in that order.
2. The Upaniṣads *Aitareya, Taittirīya,* and *Kaṭha* are perhaps earlier than Pāṇini.
3. In the absence of any evidence to the contrary, the *Kena* and *Īśa* Upaniṣads may be presumed to be earlier than Pāṇini.
4. The Upaniṣads *Śvetāśvatara* and *Maitrāyaṇa* were composed later than Pāṇini.

The next development was the work of Kirfel which centred on the extraordinary development of the employment of compound words in Sanskrit. (Willibald Kirfel: *Beiträge zur Geschichte der Nominalkomposition in den Upaniṣads und im Epos,* Bonn 1908, Diss.) The elegant literary style of later centuries called "kāvya" was much addicted to the use of compounds, but they had passed through a fairly long process of development before that. Kirfel analysed the compound words found in several parts of certain Upaniṣads and the Epics, testing them individually against the rules and prohibitions of the three great grammarians (Pāṇini, Kātyāyana and Patañjali), and arriving at the following results:

1. There is no doubt that the *Bṛhadāraṇyaka-Upaniṣad* was composed prior to Pāṇini.

2. The Upaniṣads *Praśna, Muṇḍaka,* and *Kaṭha* were already composed by the time of Pāṇini. That is, they were already in existence in 400-300 B.C.

3. The *Śvetāśvatara-Upaniṣad* is later than Pāṇini.

4. The *Rāmopākhyāna* and *Lokapālasabhākhyāna* sections of the *Mahābhārata* Epic, and the second and third kāṇḍas of the *Rāmāyaṇa* Epic, both at least in their present form, were composed after Patañjali (c. 150 B.C.) and perhaps later than the Christian era.

Fürst, drawing on the results of his two predecessors, carried out further research on the early Upaniṣads by considering in a similar way the rules of phonetic change (*saṃdhi*) and suffix change of nouns and verbs (A. Fürst : Der Sprachgebrauch der älteren Upaniṣads verglichen mit dem früheren vedischen Perioden und dem des klassischen Sanskrit. *Zeitschrift fur vergleichende Sprachforschung auf dem Gebiete der indogermanischen Sprachen,* begründet von A. Kuhn, XLVII, 1915, p. 1-82).

His results were as follows :

1. The three Upaniṣads *Bṛhadāraṇyaka, Chāndogya* and *Kauṣītaki,* are definitely prior to Pāṇini.

2. The Upaniṣads *Aitareya, Taittirīya, Kaṭha* and *Muṇḍaka* are in all likelihood prior to Pāṇini.

3. It is possible that the *Śvetāśvatara* and *Mahānārāyaṇa* Upaniṣads are posterior to Pāṇini.

4. The date of the *Īśa* and *Kena* Upaniṣads, in relation to Pāṇini; is uncertain.

What is to be noted here is that the conclusions of three separate investigators, using three separate criteria, are in general agreement. It is therefore easy to suppose that their results are very reliable. However conclusions as to dates based solely upon linguistic facts are not necessarily beyond question. It might be that a certain Upaniṣad has consciously made use of archaisms, in which case there would be the danger of mistakenly concluding it to be ancient although its actual date of composition might be late.

In the same way, caution should be exercised in considering the arguments which attempt to establish the dates of composition by the criterion of metre. Oldenberg for example asserted that since the metres of the Kāṭhaka-Upaniṣad are stylistically the same as those of Brāhmaṇa literature, and more archaic than those of the *Dhammapada* of the Pali scriptures, at least the principal sections of the *Kāṭhaka* Upaniṣad must have been composed before Buddhism (H. Oldenberg : *Buddha* S. 58) "Das altindische Ākhyāna" *ZDMG* Bd. XXXVIII, 1883, S. (54-86). Rather it is perhaps more probable that the Upaniṣads, due to their claim to authority as a part of the Vedic sacred canon, resorted to the archaic metre, while Buddhism, as a newly emergent religion appealing to the hearts of the general masses, employed a new metre in the production of its sacred verses. Thus chronological conclusions reached solely on the basis of these facts are highly tenuous.

It is therefore necessary, as a matter of course, that chronological theories based upon such linguistic investigations be checked by cross comparison with arguments formed from other conceptual standpoints. The merits of such linguistic investigation may then be admitted in the following aspects only : (1) It has become clear that the theories on the dates of formulation broadly postulated from Deussen on are corroborated by researches in the history of language; to the extent that there is no counter-evidence from other quarters, the sequential relation of the dates of the Upaniṣads is then essentially indubitable.

(2) Pāṇini did not originate the grammar of a dead classical language, but rather instituted his rules based upon how the language was actually in use at the time.[3] For this reason alone, in the absence of concrete points of reference, it is difficult to determine what would in fact constitute a "pre-Pāṇini composition" of an Upaniṣad. Post-Pāṇini compositions, on the other hand, have Pāṇini as a ground for linguistic studies, as established point of reference from which to proceed. It is on this basis that this discussion of the Old Upaniṣads composed after Pāṇini rests.

What remains to be determined, however, is how much earlier than Pāṇini can we trace back those Upaniṣads that are thought to have been composed before him. As this cannot be settled by linguistic studies, other points of view must be considered. In this regard, the question of relation with other contemporary streams of thought will be considered.

II *Relation with Other Schools of Thought*

Among the schools of Indian philosophical thought, it is the relation of the Sāṃkhya school to the Brahminical tradition of the Upaniṣads that is perhaps the most dynamic as well as definite. Sāṃkhya theories appear in varying degrees in the three compositional periods of the Upaniṣads. As regards the early period, scholars have discussed the hypothesis that the Chāndogya-Upaniṣad VI. 4, which takes all existence as being constituted of three essential elements, is the forerunner to this notion in Sāṃkhya philosophy.

From the middle period on, the influence of Sāṃkhya philosophy appears conspicuously in the Old Upaniṣads, where a prevalence of Sāṃkhya thought as well as corresponding modes of Sāṃkhyan expression and technical terms is in evidence.[4] But as to whether these were adopted from Sāṃkhya established as an independent school, or whether they were developments within Vedānta, of Sāṃkhya-like ideas, is a point on which scholars are so divided in their views that no real conclusion can be reached. Looking at the Sāṃkhya ideas in the Śvetāśvatara-Upaniṣad and the Maitrāyaṇa-Upaniṣad it may well be thought that they were taken in directly from the system of a Sāṃkhya now already established as a school, but that is limited to conjecture and nothing further can yet be determined. This is something which remains to be investigated. The early history of Sāṃkhya is itself so obscure, and so much research remains to be done in this important field itself, that it is a very weak evidence for the date of the Upaniṣads.

Similarly, the accounts of Yoga in the Upaniṣads are of little use in the determination of dates. The ideas of the Nyāya-Vaiśeṣika mark virtually no change from those of the Upaniṣads.

The history of the orthodox Brahmanic tradition is exceedingly uncertain; outlines of its historical development cannot be clarified by using only the materials within this tradition. In marked contrast the main outlines of the history of Buddhism have been established on the basis of the accounts of its communication with China, the translation of its sūtras, etc.

So it is possible that the history of India in the ancient and middle period can, in many instances, be clarified by means of materials related to Buddhism. Therefore, to determine the dates of the Upaniṣads, it is proper that the problem of the relationship with Buddhism be investigated.

The prevalent theories concerning the dates of the formation of the Vedas have been calculated by scholars, as an inference taking as their basis the dates of the life of the founder of Buddhism, Gotama the Buddha. Thus, in absence of the knowledge of the relationship with Buddhism, the theory of the dates of the Vedas in general could not be formulated.[5] The relation with Buddhism, consequently, must be regarded as crucial to the dates of the Upaniṣads as well.

In view of this fact, researches, initially in linguistics, have been conducted which try to locate the peculiar features of Buddhistic Sanskrit and of Pāli in the Upaniṣads.[6] While some results have been presented, one cannot immediately conclude, however, that they can be regarded as definitely sharing the influence of Buddhistic Sanskrit or of the Pāli language. Changes in suffixes which are difficult to interpret both by the grammar of the Vedic language and by the grammar of classical Sanskrit have frequently been found already in the Old Upaniṣads (such as the *Bṛhadāraṇyaka* and the *Chāndogya*). Scholars such as Böhtlingk regarded all of these as clerical errors. In order to make them easier to read, he revised them completely according to the rules of Pāṇini's *Grammar*, and subsequently published them. It cannot be said, however, that this is the correct method for studying literature.

Rather, some strange linguistic expressions in the Upaniṣads should be interpreted as a reflection of the colloquial language employed by the masses of that time. Similarly, the extraordinary declensions which can be found in the Upaniṣads of middle and late periods were influenced, in much the same way, by the colloquial languages of that time; but this amounts only to an assertion that that colloquial languages occasionally resembled Pāli and Buddhist Sanskrit. Since comparative researches can only be conducted upon the surviving literature of the orthodox Brahmanic schools and of Buddhism, because the folk literature of the colloquial languages of that time has been almost completely lost, one immediately and simply infers that there is the influence of Pāli. However, since the colloquial words comparable to the Pāli of that time exist in unusually great numbers alongside the

Pāli, and may, in fact, have actively been used, one cannot immediately conclude, merely on the basis of declensions which resemble those of Pāli and Buddhist Sanskrit, the evidence of a Buddhist influence. Moreover, terms similar to Buddhist words can also be found in the Ancient Upaniṣads.[7] However, since these should be regarded as the precursors of usages in Buddhism and should not be interpreted as the influence of Buddhism, they are, accordingly, of no direct use in the determination of dates. Consequently, more concrete clues must be sought.

With reference to the relationship with Buddhism, we shall first take up the problem of the Kāṭhaka-Upaniṣad, a work whose origin was assumed by the great majority of Indologists to be prior to the rise of Buddhism.[8] In this regard Professor Stcherbatsky once took up the problem of the following passages of this Upaniṣad (IV.14;15), inferring within it a reference to an idea of Buddhism precursory to the Buddha which may subsequently have been rejected as a heretical theory.[9]

(14) "Just as the rain water runs down the steep paths of the mountains in different directions, so does he, who looks at the Dharmas as different, run after them."

> *yathodakaṃ durge vṛṣṭam parvateṣu vidhāvati,*
> *evaṃ dharmān pṛthak paśyaṃs tān evānudhāvati.*

(15) "Just as pure water which is poured into pure water becomes the same (pure) as it is, so, O Gautama, the *ātman* of the sage who has knowledge becomes (pure)."

The meaning of *dharmas* in this case is problematic; that is, the meaning in this passage does not signify the meaning of *Dharma* in the Vedic Literature in general, yet to conclude that it refers to the *dharma* of Buddhism is of course a forced interpretation which has no other examples in literature. (Śaṅkara interpreted the word *dharma* as meaning *ātman*, commenting *dharmān āṭmano bhinnān pṛthak paśyan.* Further, although the *dharma* in *Gauḍapādīya-kārikās* IV.1; 10, 46, 53, 81, 91, 92, 96, and 99, also has a Buddhistic meaning, Śaṅkara interpreted it similarly as *ātman.*) Geiger has already noticed this fact;[10] and Stcherbatsky later asserted as follows :

"What emerges from the passage of the *Kaṭhopaniṣad* cited above is that there was a doctrine opposed to the reigning soul-theory, that it maintained the existence of subtle elements and separate elements (*pṛthag dharma*), and that such a doctrine, in the opinion of the author, did not lead to salvation. Śaṅkara, in his commentary, agrees that Buddhism is alluded to, but, very bluntly, he interprets *dharma* as meaning here individual soul. As a matter of fact, dharma never occurs with this meaning in the Upaniṣads. Its occurrence in the *Kaṭhopaniṣad*, leaves the impression that it is a catchword referring to a foreign and new doctrine, some *anātma-dharma* theory... Thus it is, that the fundamental idea of Buddhism—a plurality of separate elements without real unity—had its roots in the primitive speculations of the Upaniṣads. At the time when a new conception of the Soul was elaborated in Brahmanical circles, some kind of the pre-Buddhaic Buddhism, under which we understand the *anātma-dharma* theory, must have been already in existence. This time is the epoch of the *Kaṭhopaniṣad*, which, as Professor Jacobi points out, might also be the time of pre-Jinistic Jainism, the time of Pārśvanātha, i.e. the eighth century B.C."[11]

Stcherbatsky's inference is acceptable as far as it goes, but there are two mistaken premises in his assertion :

(1) He has determined in advance that the general assumption of Indian scholars that the *Kāṭhaka Upaniṣad* had been formulated prior to Buddhism, is a confirmed theory, and (2) he has assumed that the idea of the Sarvāstivādin which expounds the distinctness of the *dharmas*, was, in that form, a genuine theory of Śākya-muni. That the latter is mistaken goes without saying; and that the former is nothing more than mere conjecture has not yet been sufficiently demonstrated. The theory of Stcherbatsky, accordingly, cannot be adopted as it stands, nevertheless, as I have already mentioned, the "dharma" here is undoubtedly of Buddhistic usage. In the Chinese translation of the *Āgamas*, the *sūtra* which records a dialogue between an itinerant monk (*paribbājaka*), Vaccha, and the Blessed One, contains passages which possess the same conception as the above two stanzas; "Vaccha again said, 'Gautama, I wish now to tell you a parable. I beg you to listen to what I have to say.'

The Buddha said to him, 'Tell me as you like.'

Just as the heavy rain, which falls from the heavens, follows down water currents and pours into the great ocean, so too is your *dharma* (teaching); receiving the rain of the *dharma* (teaching) of the Buddha in the long night, men and women, adults and children, as well as the decrepit and aged, all reach *nirvāṇa.* Excellent, indeed, is Gautama ! Excellent, indeed, is the wonderous *dharma* (teaching) ! Excellent, indeed, is the one who can penetrate the *dharma* (teaching) of the Buddha !" (Separate Translation, *Saṃyuktāgama,* Vol. X, TT. II. 446c.) "Vaccha said to the Buddha, 'Just as the heavy rain, which falls from the heavens, follows down water currents, so too are the *dharma* and *vinaya* of Gautama; following water currents (of the *dharma* and *vinaya*), monks and nuns, laymen and laywomen, young men and young women, all go toward *nirvāṇa* and are rapidly carried into *nirvāṇa*" (Ibid., Vol. XXXIV, TT. II. 247a).

If an instance which corresponds to this is taken from the Pāli texts, the words of the itinerant monk Vaccha who praises the *dharma* of the Buddha, though rain water is not referred to, may be cited from the *Mahā-vaccha-gotta-suttanta* (MN. No. 73): "Just as the Ganges river turns toward the great ocean, and flows to the great ocean, and inclines toward the great ocean, and, touching the great ocean, peacefully abides in it, so does, Gotama, your order which is composed of laymen and monks, turn toward nibbāna, flow toward nibbāna, incline toward nibbāna, and, touching nibbāna, peacefully abide in it. How great you are, O Gotama, how great you are, O Gotama. Just as you, O Gotama, raise up the fallen, uncover the covered, teach the path to those who are lost, and bring a torch in the darkness so that the person with eyes should see the form-color, so too *has the dhamma been shown by means of various expedients* by you, Gotama, (*anekapariyāyena dhammo pakāsito*)."[12]

Just as the rain waters fallen to the ground run down in different directions, but in the end enter the great ocean, in this manner, although the Buddha taught various dhammas, one can after all enter nibbāna no matter upon which one of those he relies, and one must not regard these dhammas as different. If the previously quoted passage in the *Kāṭhaka Upaniṣad* should be interpreted in conformity with this, it would be easy to understand its import; and thus it perhaps follows that it is more suitable than any of the interpretations of the European scholars to the present ? Again, the fact, too, that Śaṅkara's commentary is incorrect, would itself be clear. The previously noted passage, accordingly, was a passage of the Buddhist canon rewritten and inserted here by the author of the *Kāṭhaka-Upaniṣad.* Since in the writings of the *orthodox Brahmins* there are hardly any other instances of this particular usage of the term "dharma," this fact would be more than verified. Furthermore, it would be clear also that its contrary is impossible. In addition, the fact that the above two passages invoke a strange awareness by their existence in the *Kāṭhaka-Upaniṣad* could also be satisfactorily explained by means of this supposition. It can be thought, of course, that the word "dharma" in this *Upaniṣad* does not mean the "teaching" but rather that the meaning of "thing" was loosely attached to the term by the author; the fact, however, that its author depends upon the above simile, using the word "dharma" and without employing any other word which means "thing," should be interpreted likewise as the influence of Buddhism.

Further Resemblances between the *sūtra* on the itinerant monk Vaccha and the *Kāṭhaka-Upaniṣad* exist in other points. In the story of the *Kāṭhaka Upaniṣad* the deity Yama (the god of death) allowed Naciketas to select any three boons he so desired, Naciketas wished first that his father pacify his anger toward him and become a person of tempered heart and good will, secondly that he be instructed in the ritual fire which leads men to the heavenly world; and in fulfilment of third boon, he desired the following :

"There is this doubt about a person who is dead—some people say, 'He exists.' and others, 'He does not exist.' I would like to know this, instructed by you. This is the third of my boons" (*Kāṭhaka-Up.* I.1.20)

Thereupon the god of death was startled and told him to give up thinking about that alone; but as Naciketas earnestly entreated him and would not relent, the god of death finally disclosed this secret. That secret was the teaching of *ātman.* It is, however, not a one-sided conclusion as to whether a human being exists or not after death. (The existence of the *ātman*, however, is strongly emphasized.)

Now, the story of Naciketas's receiving the three boons from the god of death had already appeared in *Taittirīya-Brāhmaṇa,* III.11.8.1-4. Among these three boons, the first and the second correspond closely to those of the *Kāṭhaka-Upaniṣad,* but the third in contrast, is "vanquishing of re-death" (*punarmṛtyor apaciti*). When he sought for the third boon, the god of death gave him the "fire of Naciketas" (*Nāciketa agni*). The *Brāhmaṇa* thereupon concludes : "He truly has vanquished re-death by means of it. The person who constructs the altar of the fire of Naciketas will vanquish re-death." Here, therefore, as in the *Brāhmaṇas* in general, the surpassing and conquering of re-death (that is, the repeated death in the other world after death in this world is only mentioned as *a wished-for fact*. Virtually no philosophical speculation on the problem of life after death has been advanced. The *Kāṭhaka-Upaniṣad*, however, while inheriting the skeleton of this story, *changed its contents into a philosophical argument*. It can be thought then that the expression of such speculation in this *Upaniṣad* must have been influenced by the evolution of philosophical speculation among Indians of that time.

Of interest in this regard, is the fact that a central problem in the *Kāṭhaka-Upaniṣad* also became one of the central problems in the *sūtra* which was taught to the itinerant monk Vaccha. That is, we see in the *Aggivacchagotta-sutta*[13] (*MN*. No. 72) that when Vaccha sought for various explanations of metaphysical problems from the Buddha, the Buddha is believed to have taught the following :

'You, O Gotama, you, O Gotama, are you of the opinion that "the *Tathāgata*[14] exists after death. This is truth; all else is false" ?'

'O Vaccha, I do not have the view that "the *Tathāgata* exists after death. This is truth; all else is false." '

'You, O Gotama, you, O Gotama, do you have the view that "The Tathāgata does not exist after death. This is truth; all else is false" ?'

'O Vaccha, I do not have the view that "The Tathāgata does not exist after death. This is truth; all else is false." '

Again, in a later passage, the following is said :

"[Vaccha says,] 'In what place is the bhikkhu who has such a liberated mind reborn ?'

'O Vaccha, it is not appropriate to say that he is reborn.'

'O Gotama, is he then not reborn ?'

'O Vaccha, it is not appropriate to say that he is not reborn.' "

Thereafter this meaning has been expounded in detail. Thus, it is clear that since the Buddha also considered one-sided judgment, whether affirmative or negative, to be a fallacy, and taught the dharma which accords to the absolute truth. his solution to this problem is very similar to that of the *Kāṭhaka-Upaniṣad.* Such an idea is expounded in various passages[15] throughout the early Buddhist scriptures and is not rare; however it is worthy of note that this idea is likewise expounded in the above-mentioned *sūtra* of Vaccha.

Moreover, in the *Kāṭhaka-Upaniṣad,* the god of death immediately answered Naciketas's question concerning the problem of life after death as follows :

"On this problem even the gods had doubts formerly. Truly, it is not easily known. This *Dharma* is subtle.

O Naciketas, select another boon. Do not make me suffer. For my sake, abandon this (boon)" (I.21).

> *devair atrāpi vicikitsitam purā na hi sujñeyam aṇur eṣa dharmaḥ /*
> *anyaṃ varaṃ Naciketo vṛṇīṣva mā moparotsīr ati me*[16] *sṛjainam / /*

The *dharma*, in this instance, also has a buddhistic significance.[17] After discussing the problems concerning life after death, the above *sūtra*, which was taught to the itinerant monk Vaccha, teaches the same :

"O Vaccha. This dharma truly is exceedingly deep, difficult to see and difficult to understand; it is tranquil, excellent, beyond logic; and subtle; it can be known only by the wise man. It is difficult to be known by you who have different views, who follow different faiths, who embrace different interests, who practice differently, and who act differently.

> *gambhīro hi ayaṃ vaccha dhammo duddaso duranubodho santo paṇīto atakkāvacaro nipuṇo paṇḍitavedanīyo, so tayā dujjāno aññadiṭṭhikena aññakkhantikena aññarucikena aññatrayogena aññathācariyakena* (*MN. I, p. 487.*)

Furthermore, that the truth is subtle and extremely difficult to see, was also taught in very old *gāthās* (stanzas) in the Buddhist scriptures. For example, there is a verse which indicates Śākyamuni's mental state in which a hesitation to preach the *dharma* to men immediately after he had attained buddhahood is revealed.

"It is not necessary for me to teach now that which I have achieved by suffering and travail. This *dhamma* is not easily understood by those who are overcome with greed and anger (*nāyaṃ dhammo susaṃbuddho*). It goes against the usual current of the world, is subtle, deep, difficult to see, and minute (*nipuṇaṃ gambhiraṃ duddasaṃ aṇuṃ*).

Those who are defiled by greed and are covered by a mass of darkness cannot see (it) ' (SN. Vol. I, p. 136).

Thus, if one takes into account the resemblance in the thought, the method of expression, and the order of the presentation and solution of the problem, the conclusion follows that the *Kāṭhaka-Upaniṣad* must have been influenced by the Buddhist Scriptures.[18] The reason, however, why the *sūtra* taught to the itinerant monk Vaccha, among a great number of early Buddhist sūtras, has particularly a deep relation with the *Kāṭhaka-Upaniṣad*, is unknown and must await future investigation.

The question of whether or not the soul exists after death seems to have been a common problem throughout the intellectual world during the time of the Buddha. Six prominent heretical philosophers (the so-called 'Six Masters') who lived approximately during the same period as the Buddha took up this problem. It is particularly the skeptic Sañjaya Belaṭṭhiputta who held, according to a tradition, the theory which most resembled the *Kāṭhaka-Upaniṣad* in its treatment. His doctrine is thought to have been called "the argument as difficult to grasp as a *slippery* eel (*amarāvikkhepa*)", since he did not give a conclusive answer whenever he was asked a metaphysical question, but, instead, gave an answer whose real meaning was difficult to grasp as was vague and obscure. The following passage which describes one of his theories is cited in the *Sāmaññaphala-sutta* in the Pāli scripture:

"If you should ask whether there is another world, and if I should think that there is another world, I would answer you that there is another world. However, I do not think thus. I do not think that it is so. I do not think the contrary. I do not think that it is not so. I do not think that it is not the case that it is not so.

"If you should ask whether there is not another world . . .(the following is the same as the preceding passage).

". . .(omitted). . .

"If one should ask whether the *Tathāgata* exists, does not exist, both exists and does not exist, neither exists nor does not exist after death, . . .(The following is the same as the preceding passage)."[19]

Various divergent theories, accordingly, existed on this problem in the time of the Buddha, and they had been arranged in conformity with a set form of this nature. The *Kāṭhaka-Upaniṣad* was also faintly influenced by such a tendency in the intellectual sphere, and was also thus chronologically later than it. Since the resemblance, however, with the sūtra on the itinerant priest of the Vaccha tribe is particularly remarkable, the formulation of the *Kāṭhaka-Upaniṣad* must be thought to have surely been after the rise of Buddhism.

Oldenberg once asserted that at least the first half of the *Kāṭhaka-Upaniṣad* was formulated before Buddhism.[20] His reasons were that the story in which the deity of death tries to tempt the seeker after truth, Naciketas, and make him indulge in the pleasures of this world, should be compared with the story of Māra who afflicted Śākya-muni before he attained the enlightenment; and that the outline of that story was still in the process of formulation and had not been completed in the *Kāṭhaka-Upaniṣad*. Because the story of the temptation by the deity of death, however, cannot be found elsewhere in the Vedic literature, it would be far more rational to think rather that they made up such a story under the influence of the Buddhist Scriptures. It is a fact that the features of Māra in the Buddhist Scriptures are by far more complete; and because there is nothing in the works by the pure orthodox Brahmanic line, even in later centuries, which is on such a large scale as in the Buddhist Scriptures, the mere fact that the narration is simple does not necessarily demonstrate that it is earlier chronologically. Again, the features of Māra, which appear in the various *gāthās* which manifest the oldest stratum, even in the same early Buddhist sacred texts, are extremely artless and simple (Cf. *Saṃyutta Nikāya*, Vol. I.) And the attitude of Naciketas, especially, who tried to throw away his own life in order to hear the truth, brings to mind the attitude of the seekers after the path who appear in the Buddhist Scriptures.[21]

As an example which resembles the Upaniṣad on this point, we can cite *Jātaka* No. 537, the *Mahāsutasomajātaka*. According to it, when Prince Sutasoma, prepared to throw away his life, taught the *dharma* to a cannibal (porisāda), the latter was seized with delight throughout his entire body and promised to grant four boons (*vara*) to the prince, saying: "Ask whatever you desire." After the prince had first wished for three special boons in succession, he thereupon wished as the final boon that the cannibal would give up eating human flesh. The cannibal refused, saying that he could grant anything but that; but, overcome by the earnest persuasion of the prince, he finally gave up eating human flesh. The above is the gist of the story, and here Prince Sutasoma, throwing away his life, realized the *dharma*. This Jātaka story has a remarkable resemblance in its narrative construction to the *Kāṭhaka-Upaniṣad.* There must have been some contact culturally on some points among the poet-writers who composed the two works. To throw away one's life and seek the *dharma* is a virtue emphasized in the Buddhist Scriptures in particular.

Further, the plot in which the ascetic accepts the ethical *dharma* as a special boon from gods, also appears elsewhere in other stories in the Buddhist Scriptures. According to the *Kañha-Jātaka* (No. 440), for example, Śakra tries to give Brahmin Kañha a boon desired by the latter. Kañha thereupon wanted this as his boon : "I wish that my conduct shall be without anger, without hate, without greed, and without yearning"; and it is said that he received this boon from Śakra.

Judging from the several vestiges such as were pointed out above, we can no longer close our eyes to the fact that throughout the entire *Kāṭhaka-Upaniṣad* the traces of the influence of early Buddhism are remarkable. It can also be thought, of course, that the opposite assumption, that these special features first appeared in the *Kāṭhaka-Upaniṣad* and were finally developed in early Buddhism, is perhaps also possible. These particular characteristics, however, have appeared but little in over 3000 years of the history of Brahmanism; and their appearance in the *Kāṭhaka-Upaniṣad* is a completely sudden and exceptional phenomenon. It seems thus more likely that the *Kāṭhaka-Upaniṣad*, influenced by the Buddhism of the early period and the new streams of thought of that time, came to show anomalous characteristics as an orthodox Brahmanic work.

Now, even in the *Kāṭhaka-Upaniṣad* in particular, the first part (*I Adhyāya*) was composed very early, and the second part was later appended to it;[22] if the first section of the *Kāṭhaka Upaniṣad* thus came to be influenced by early Buddhism, it must have been composed after Buddha entered Nirvāṇa. Because the entrance into Nirvāṇa of the Buddha was c. 386 B.C.[23] the first half of the *Kāṭhaka-Upaniṣad* must have been composed in the middle of the fourth century B.C. at the earliest. And since the latter half, i.e., Part II, moreover, must have been composed later, one could say that the same *Upaniṣad* was composed from the middle to the latter half of the fourth century B.C., that is, from 350 to 300. It might perhaps be even later than that. Now it happens that according to the results of the linguistic investigations previously noted, the *Kāṭhaka-Upaniṣad* may have *perhaps* been formulated prior to Pāṇini; and since it is an established theory in the academic world that Pāṇini lived c. 350 B.C., there seems at first glance a contradiction. While that may be so on the face of it, Pāṇini's *Grammar* in fact was concerned to extract and enumerate the rules of the language current at that time; and since even if the *Kāṭhaka-Upaniṣad*, composed as an Upaniṣad, is taken to have been formulated in the same period, it would be quite natural that it employed archaic modes of expression and phraseology, so that there is no objection at all even if it is regarded as being formulated later than Pāṇini. In that wide land of India, men of either the same period or immediately after Pāṇini cannot be assumed to have made their compositions according to all the rules of Pāṇini's *Grammar*. Again, it has become an established theory in the academic world that the date of Pāṇini is c.350 B.C., but the grounds for this argument are extremely flimsy,[24] and it can rather be held without objection that he is later than that. Prof. Ui has supposed that the *Kāṭhaka-Upaniṣad* was composed somewhere around 300-200 B.C.,[25] and it is a very probable hypothesis; at least, no data exist which could be a counter-evidence. Thus if one should accept tentatively the date of Pāṇini, admitted in general by the academic world, the date of composition of the *Kāṭhaka-Upaniṣad* would be c. 350-300 B.C.; and if one should ignore that one may think that its date is 350-200.

Further, there are also scholars[26] who think that since the *Kāṭhaka-Upaniṣad* has quoted passages from the *Bhagavad-Gītā*, it was formulated later than the *Gītā*; but actually one should rather take it that the *Gītā* adopted passages from the *Kāṭhaka-Upaniṣad*.

Thus, we can say that we here have acquired one foundation stone in the determination of the dates of the Upaniṣads.

Since the *Kāṭhaka Upaniṣad* is the oldest composition[27] among the Old Upaniṣads of the middle period, as has been equally admitted by scholars, the Old Upaniṣads of the middle period and the late period must have been formulated later than it.

First of all, the *Śvetāśvatara-Upaniṣad* was formulated later than the *Kāṭhaka-Upaniṣad*, and it has also been thought that it was composed even later than the early Buddhist sacred texts.[28] Moreover, since it was composed later than Pāṇini according to the linguistic researches previously noted, its date should be considered to be roughly 300-200 B.C. or even later. Two verses from the *Śvetāśvatara-Upaniṣad* are quoted consecutively in the *Abhidharmamahāvibhāṣā-śāstra*,[29] which, as Hsüan Tsang has reported, was compiled under the aegis of King Kaniṣka (reigned c. 100-150 A.D.) during the Kushana Dynasty. The historical reliability of this tradition has been a subject of debate in the most recent researches,[30] but at all events, it is perhaps certain that it was compiled prior to (or at the same time as) the appearance of Nāgārjuna. There is no doubt, accordingly, that this Upaniṣad was formulated earlier than that, and it can be thought that the actual date must be traced back to an ancient age, very much earlier. Further, the fact that some of the phrases in the *Śvetāśvatara-Upaniṣad* have been quoted in almost their original form in the *Mahābhārata*, becomes collateral evidence in view of the above chronological theory.[31]

Again, that the *Maitrāyaṇa-Upaniṣad* was influenced by Buddhism, and was formulated later than the rise of Buddhism, is an established theory agreed upon by scholars.[32] It was written in prose similar to that of the early Upaniṣads; the special features of the Vedic literature are no longer found in its prose; it reminds one of classical Sanskrit literature, both in language, diction, and contents. The influence of Sāṁkhya philosophy is also remarkable. Because this Upaniṣad was not quoted even once in the Commentary on the *Brahma-sūtra* by Śaṅkara,[33] it has frequently been wondered whether it may perhaps be a work of later centuries. However, since there are a few passages in the *Mahābhārata* which appear to be based upon expressions from this Upaniṣad, the entire *Maitrāyaṇī-Upaniṣad* must have been formulated prior to that.[34] The *Mahābhārata* was formulated for the most part in its present form in the fourth century A.D.,[35] and since it has been supposed that most of it was composed before the second century B.C.,[36] the period in which the *Maitrāyaṇī-Upaniṣad* was formulated, accordingly, it can justly be thought to be before then.

Further, I shall discuss in more detail the *Māṇḍūkya-Upaniṣad* later, but as it was formulated later than the *Maitrāyaṇa-Upaniṣad* and was influenced by the thought of *Śūnyatā* of Mahāyāna Buddhism,[37] it can perhaps be thought to be a composition from before the Christian era. Since Śaṅkara, in his *Commentary on the Brahma-sūtra,* did not quote or refer to the *Māṇḍūkya-Upaniṣad* even once,[38] although this Upaniṣad must have been formulated by that time, it probably had not been regarded particularly highly as yet. At any rate, that the last two Upaniṣads were not quoted by Śaṅkara can be thought to relate to the fact that these two were composed comparatively late among the Old Upaniṣads.

I have above examined successively the Upaniṣads in which traces of exchange of thoughts with other schools is remarkable; the determination of the dates of the conservative and vedāntic Upaniṣads, on the contrary, is quite difficult, even of those formulated later than the *Kāṭhaka-Upaniṣad.* The two Upaniṣads, *Muṇḍaka* and *Praśna,* may probably be thought to have been formulated in a period not too distant from that of the *Kāṭhaka-Upaniṣad,* if we go upon the results of the linguistic research previously noted. Deussen counted the *Muṇḍaka* among the middle period Upaniṣads, and classified the *Praśna* with the late period Upaniṣads;[39] it cannot be said, however, that since one is written in verse, it is ancient or since the other is written in prose, it is later. It is impossible to find a great chronological interval between the two. Again the opinions of scholars on the *Mahānārāyaṇī-Upaniṣad* are by no means in agreement; and since Deussen and other scholars have classified it with the early period Upaniṣads and other scholars have thought that it is newer than any of the other Old Upaniṣads,[40] it is now impossible to conclude which view is by far the most correct.

Now, if one should determine in this way the approximate dates of the Old Upaniṣads of the middle and late periods, it becomes a problem why the influence of Buddhism cannot be found in the majority of the Ancient Upaniṣads of the middle period. That the influence of Buddhism cannot be found, however, does not enable one to affirmatively demonstrate that they were composed earlier than early Buddhism. The wide diffusion of Buddhism throughout India in general was after King Aśoka, but even in the period prior to him, the steadfast vitality of the Brahmins in the farms and mountain villages could not be superseded, and India was never completely converted to Buddhism. It can be thought that the Brahmins still continued to lead the populace in the villages of the farms and mountains, and compiled their own sacred canon completely without relation to Buddhism. Accordingly, even if the influence of Buddhism cannot be found in the early Upaniṣads, and puerile expressions were occasionally used to expound inferior ideas, there is no necessity that one must think that their dates of formulation are ancient. That is, Buddhism and orthodox Brahmanism differed in their social background upon which they were supported and gradually developed progressing side by side. Understood in this way, the facts are easily explained.

Notes

1. E.g., Max Müller (*ASL.*, p. 313) places the period of the sūtras at c. 600-200 B.C., and says that the Āraṇyakas (including the Upaniṣads) belong to a period earlier than that. Radhakrishnan (*Ind. Phil.*, Vol. I, p. 142), places the dates of the Upaniṣads at c. 1000-300 B.C., and Belvalkar (*Lectures*, pp. 44-45) regards the formulation of almost all the Ancient Upaniṣads as 1250-500 B.C. All Indian scholars have a tendency to think that the dates of the Upaniṣads are ancient.
2. Hopkins, *JAOS.*, XXI, 1901, p. 336. Further, Rapson (*Ancient India*, p. 181) considers that the Buddha was a person of 563 to 483 B.C., and that the oldest Upaniṣads were formulated c. 600 B.C.
3. Otto Wecker : *Der Gebrauch der Kasus in der älteren Upaniṣad-Literatur*, p. 206.
4. R. E. Hume : *The Thirteen Principal Upaniṣads*, pp. 8-9; R. Garbe : *Sāṁkhya Philosophie*[2], p. 21. *Anm.*; p. 28 f.
5. Cf. Winternitz : *HIL.*, I, p. 290 f.
6. Cf. R. E. Hume : *op. cit.*, pp. 6-7.
7. Cf. R. E. Hume : *op. cit.* Further, H. Oldenberg (*Die Lehre der Upanishaden*, p. 131, Anm., I) says that *pratibuddha* is also a Buddhistic expression.
8. See, for example, H. Oldenberg : *Die Lehre der Upanishaden*, pp. 288-89; O. Straus : *Die Indische Philosophie*, p. 64. Keith (*Buddhist Philosophy*, p. 138), says that this Upaniṣad is older than any of the early Buddhist sacred canon.
9. Th. Stcherbatsky : *Central Conception of Buddhism* [Susil Gupta (India) Ltd., 1961], p. 58 ff.

10. Magdalene and Wilhelm Geiger (*Pāli Dhamma.* München, 1920, p. 9) also took the example of *dharma* as an expression in the buddhistic sense in the *Kāṭhaka-Upaniṣad,* and citing the passages IV. 14, II.13, and I. 21, translated IV. 14 as follows : "Wer so die Dinge (Objekte, Erscheinungen) einzeln betrachetet, läuft hinter ihnen her nach allen Richtungen," d. h. er kann sich nicht auf das Reale konzentrieren.

11. Stcherbatsky : *op. cit.*, pp. 58, 62. Further, Jacobi : *Die indische Philosophie,* says that the same opinion is expressed in "Das Licht des Ostens."

12. *MN.*, Vol. I, p. 493. The quotation from the Pāli literature below has been cited in reference to the Japanese translation in the *Tripiṭaka of the Southern Tradition.*

13. *MN.*, Vol. I, p. 483 f.

14. Tathāgata has been translated as "thus come," but it is by no means a word of Buddhism only. In the *Āyārañga-sutta* of the sacred canon of Jainism, "the sacred one" is called *tathāgaya bhikkhu* (i.e., *tathāgata bhikṣu*). Professor Ui has frequently translated it as "the true person."

15. A problem similar to this has been repeatedly discussed in the *Saṁyutta-Nikāya* 44 (*avyākata-saṃyutta*) also. For data on this problem in the sacred canon of early Buddhist, see further, Dr. Watsuji, *Genshi Bukkyô no Jissen Tetsugaku,* p. 135; and Professor Watanabe, *Butsuda no Kyōsetsu,* p. 195.

16. Although the original phrase has *mā,* it has been revised to *me* following Bohtlingk.

17. Oldenberg : *LU.*, p. 192. Further, Stcherbatsky (*Central Conception.*, p. 68, n. 1), interpreted this *dharma* as "an element, but a subtle and immortal one"; and Geiger, *op. cit.*, translated it as "dieser Gegenstand." But it rather means either "law" or "creed."

18. Further, a construction equivalent to the two verses previously noted of the *Kāṭhaka Upaniṣad* can also be found in the final salutory verse of the *Saṁyutta-Nikâya*44 (*Avyākata-saṃyutta*) which is given as follows :

O River, the word of the victor (brimming over with) the waters of the eight-branched (sacred) path which splash out from the rocky mountains of the ten powers and which reach, in the end, the great ocean of Nirvāṇa, carry (us) along ! (*based upon the translation* by Shundō Tachibana, *Nanden Daizōkyō,* Vol. 16a, p. 137).

This also is set forth in poetry, after *the problem of the existence or non-existence after death* of the Thus-come has been taken up.

19. Hakuju Ui; *Indo Tetsugaku Kenkyū,* Vol. II, pp. 362-363.

20. Oldenberg : *op. cit.*, pp. 288-89.

21. That the story of Naciketas is congruent in spirit with the *Jātaka,* Rhys Davids (*Dialogues of the Buddha,* Vol. II, p. 162) also asserted. In particular, the story of the child from the snow mountain who abandoned his body in order to hear the last half of the verse from Rākṣasa (the devil) (*Daijō-honsho Shinji-kangyō,* Vol. 1; *Daihantsu-nehan-kyō,* Vol. 14), is famous even in China and Japan.

"If I could hear the verses full of deep meaning, even if I should hear them from the mouth of a slave-servant, I would serve him with deep respect,

O Lord of Men. For truly I do not feel satisfied in my knowledge of the true *dharma*" (*Mahāsutasomajātaka*, v. 48) *Jātaka*, Vol. V, p. 485.

In the works of Brahmanism, on the other hand, e.g., in the famous story of the chaste woman, Sāvitrī, in the *Mahābhārata*, it is recounted that Sāvitrī, facing the deity of death Yama, fervently wished as the final and most important gift for herself, that he restore the life of her husband, and finally succeeded; but here the attitude of the chaste woman distressed with concern for the body of her husband is the principal theme; and the attitude of one who tries to hear the universal *dharma* valid for all men is completely unrelated.

22. Oldenberg: *op. cit.*, p. 351, *Anm.*, 127; J. Rawson: *The Kaṭha Upaniṣad*, Oxford, 1934, Intro., pp. 48-49.

23. According to H. Ui, "A Discussion of the Date of Buddha's Demise," in *Indo Tetsugaku Kenkyū*, Vol. II. Although it might be that the dates given by the same doctor will be moved somewhat earlier or later by future research, since all the ancient sūtras and treatises of the schools in India, however, have handed down the date of Buddha's demise as about 100 years previous to the ascension of King Aśoka, it can be thought that these approximate figures probably cannot be moved. (Further, that the date of the Buddha's demise was 100 years prior to King Aśoka, was asserted already in the Tokugawa Period by Nakamoto TOMINAGA in his *Shutsujō* Kōgō, using the *Daichido-Ron*, the Chinese version of the *Mahāprajñāpāramitā-upadeśa-śāstra*. Recently the date of the Buddha was discussed by myself in detail, and I was led to the conclusion that his date is approximately 463-383 B.C. (Hajime Nakamura: *Indo Kodaishi*, i.e. History of Ancient India, vol. II. (Tokyo: Shunjusha Press, 1966), pp. 409-37.

24. This theory of the dates of Pāṇini is based upon the account in the *Kathāsaritsāgara* composed in the 12th century, that is, over *a thousand and several hundred years* after Pāṇini, and a great deal of trust cannot be placed in this account of the story as historical data. The logical grounds, accordingly, for placing the date of Pāṇini at c. 350 are extremely flimsy. However, since Pāṇini's *Grammar* refers to things Greek (*Yavanānī*), which are derived from the Greeks (*Yavana*), it is perhaps difficult to set the dates of his life earlier than that; and it is possible, rather, to move them down to a later century. That is, since the contacts between the Indians and the Greeks arose after the expeditions of Alexander to India, it has been a common argument in the academic world up to now to say that the dates of Pāṇini cannot be traced back earlier than that (Cf. Otto Böhtlingk : *Pāṇini's Grammatik*, Einleitung; Winternitz : *GIL.*, III, p. 383).

To be sure, scholars who oppose such a popular theory and who try to place the dates of Pāṇini's life in a far more ancient period, have also appeared very recently (E.g., Belvalkar: *Systems of Sanskrit Grammar*). He asserts that the contacts between the Indians and Greeks had occurred since quite ancient times. One cannot, however, conclude that this is clearly so by the sources in India. The Indians are referred to only in the sources from Greece and Iran (see, for example, the data given in Winternitz: *GIL.*, III, p. 383, *Anm*: Poussin: *Dynasties*, p. 365; Rapson: *CHI*, I, p. 674 f., etc.). Furthermore, instead of regarding the form of the word *Yavana* as a direct derivation from the Greek word *Iāones*, the opinion has been held that it should rather be regarded as a derivation passing through the ancient Persian language. Even if it should be taken as such, however, it can be thought that this term was diffused in general by the Persian translators whom Alexander had brought with him, as A. Weber (*HIL.*, p. 220, Cf. A. Weber: *Die Griechen in Indien*, Berlin: 1890, p. 5) has asserted. Especially insofar as the grammarians like Pāṇini could bring forth the things Greek *as grammatical examples*, the Greeks must have been regarded as *a tribal and social opposition* among the Brahmins who were chiefly at the leadership level of the farm villages. Accordingly, it will still be difficult to displace the popular theory held to the present; but since the problems of the dates of Pāṇini and *Yavana* are important, I hope that they will be discussed further in the academic world.

25. H. Ui: *Indo Tetsugaku Shi*, p. 148. Further, cf. *Indo Tetsugaku Kenkyū*, Vol. I, p. 135. Hopkins also regards the Upaniṣads, *Kāṭhaka*, *Śvetāśvatara* and *Maitrī* as formulations of the fourth century B.C. (*JAOS*, 1901, p. 336).

26. S. Radhakrishnan, *IPh.*, Vol. I, p. 142.

27. In the *Kāṭhaka Upaniṣad*, especially in the early section, traces of the thinking and narrations similar to those on the Brahman can be found (Oldenberg: *op. cit.*, p. 203).

28. Oldenberg: *op. cit.*, p. 289. However, there are scholars who consider that the majority of these were formulated prior to Buddhism. E.g., Strauss: *Die indische Philosophie*, p. 64.

29. *Abhidharmamahāvibhāṣā-śāstra*, Vol. 200 (TT. XXVII.999m). Cf. *Śvet. Up.* III.8; 7 (Cf. the present work, Part II, Chap. I., Sect. 3ff.).

30. Cf. Benkyō Shiio. *Bukkyo Kyoten Gaisetsu*, p. 75 ff. Taiken Kimura, *Abidatsumaronsho no Kenkyū*, pp. 202-257.

31. Hopkins : *GEI.*, p. 28.

32. Oldenberg: *op. cit.*, p. 205; O. Strauss: *Die indische Philosophie*, p. 64; Winternitz: *HIL.*, Vol. I, p. 238.

33. Deussen: *SV.*, p. 33.

34. Hopkins: *GEI.*, p. 33 ff. Prof. Naoshirō Tsuji has recently placed this Upaniṣad after 200 B.C. (*Gengo Kenkyū*, Vol. 74, p. 21).

35. Winternitz: *HIL.*, Vol. I. p. 475.

36. Hopkins: *ERE.* Cf. the item on *Mahābhārata*.

37. The concept of the fourth realm (*caturtha*) was perhaps influenced by the *Śūnyatā* of Mahāyāna Buddhism.

38. Deussen: *SV.*, p. 32 ff.

39. Deussen: *AGPh.*, I, 2, pp. 24-25.

40. Hume: *Thirteen Principal Upaniṣads*, p. 5, n. 21. H. Ui, *Indo Tesugaku-shi*, p. 151.

Further, R. Zimmerman (*Die Quellen der Mahānārāyaṇa Upaniṣad*, Leipzig, 1913. Diss.) says that since this *Upaniṣad* frequently quotes passages from the middle period Upaniṣads, even if it should belong to the middle period, it must perhaps be placed towards the end of that period. Again, because of the fact that the influence of Sāṁkhya theories in this *Upaniṣad* is remarkable, it has been reckoned among the sectarian Upaniṣads (*Die Sāṁkhya-Philosophie*², p. 26, *Anm*).

III. *The Chronological Relation of the Early and Middle Period Upaniṣads*

What were the dates of the Upaniṣads composed prior to the *Kāṭhaka* ? Clues no longer exist which might be used to determine their dates of composition, so that we can do no more than make vague guesses. Restricting ourselves to their relative chronological order, scholars agree that the *Bṛhad-āraṇyaka* and the *Chāndogya*, the greatest even in size, were composed earliest, and reveal the special features of the Brāhmaṇas in their language, style and content. That the *Bṛhad-āraṇyaka* is the oldest of these two, is accepted by scholars in general; and it has also been remarked that the Mādhyandina School's tradition on the *Bṛhad-āraṇyaka* shows an older structure than that of the Kāṇva sect.[1]

Again, the two Upaniṣads, *Bṛhad-āraṇyaka* and *Chāndogya* were themselves not composed at one time, but several texts, formed and handed down over a long period, came to be grouped together as one, at some time taking on their present form. We see that the *Bṛhad-āraṇyaka-Upaniṣad* is made up of three sections : Madhu-Kāṇḍa ("Honey Section" i.e. Adhyāya I-II); The Yājñavalkya-Kāṇḍa ("Yājñavalkya Section" i.e. Adhyāya III-IV); and the Khila-Kāṇḍa ("Appended Section" i.e. Adhyāya V-VI); and the dialogue with Yājñavalkya, in almost identical words, has been included in both II.4 and IV.5. Judging from this fact, it seems that the different sections (Kāṇḍa) were originally compiled separately, the first two being later combined into one; and with the Khila-Kāṇḍa being appended to them, the present form of this Upaniṣad came into existence. And it can be thought that the dialogues with Yājñavalkya, for example, represent a newer, more developed, layer. Other passages must have been composed earlier than it. The view of Deussen, which held that the thought of Yājñavalkya was the most ancient thought in the Upaniṣads'[2] has been rejected by scholars in general today. As the Yājñavalkya dialogues are in a highly sophisticated form of presentation full of skilful touches, it would be proper to think that they were composed later than the other passages. And since older and newer texts exist side by side in each section (Kāṇḍa) to carry out a full investigation into the history of the composition of the original work, one must consider each Upaniṣad by analysing it section by section. And one should discuss the order of composition and the sequential relation of each section. Belvalkar and Ranade[3] conducted this kind of minute and analytic research along the right lines; but I shall not go into such detailed problems here but simply remark that as complete works the *Bṛhad-āraṇyaka* and the *Chāndogya Upaniṣads* are the oldest.

Next after these, the oldest are the *Aitareya, Kauṣītaki*[4] and *Taittirīya Upaniṣads,* which can be taken as earlier than the rise of Buddhism; but the theories as to the sequential relation of the dates of these three are not unanimous. Since new and ancient layers exist alongside each other in these three Upaniṣads also the problem becomes that of the relative chronological sequence of separate passages one by one; and the very attempt to determine the relation of chronological sequence of one Upaniṣad as a complete work with another Upaniṣad as a complete work might be almost impossible. There are few positive clues for the determination of the dates of the *Kena* and *Īśa* Upaniṣads, because they are so short, and they can be taken as either prior to early Buddhism or of the same period. Deussen held that the *Īśa* was influenced by the *Kāṭhaka*,[5] but we cannot give immediate assent to that. Since it can be regarded as merely anticipating the theistic idea, it probably was formulated late among the early period Upaniṣads. Again, it has generally been thought that as the first half of the *Kena-Upaniṣad* was written in poetry and the latter half in prose, it represents a transition to the middle period Upaniṣads.

Positive grounds for asserting that the early period Upaniṣads above must have been composed prior to early Buddhism do not exist; but when one compares them with the various Upaniṣads of the middle and late periods, there are remarkable differences to be found in various points, and one cannot but admit that there is a considerable gap in terms of dates between the earlier Upaniṣads of the middle and later periods and the *Kāṭhaka-Upaniṣad.*

The dates of the former, accordingly, must be thought to be surely prior to early Buddhism. Therefore let us contrast the special features of difference to be found between the early and middle period Upaniṣads, and even in the same Upaniṣad.

(1) The Old Upaniṣads of the early period are portions of

the Brāhmaṇas, and the Āraṇyakas, as I shall set forth later. It seems, accordingly, that the dates of composition of the Old Upaniṣads of the early period are for the most part close to the dates of their Brāhmaṇa or Āraṇyaka, and were probably not much later than they. The Upaniṣads of the middle and late periods, on the contrary, have been handed down as separate and independent of the Brāhmaṇas and the Āraṇyakas, and although they have been handed down as belonging to Vedic Schools, no internal and necessary connection with some particular schools is apparent.[6] It can be thought, accordingly, that the dates of composition of these were considerably later than those of the Brāhmaṇas and the Āraṇyakas.

(2) The language and syntax of the early period Upaniṣads closely resemble those in the Brāhmaṇas or Āraṇyakas in which they have been inserted. All these sentences are simple, composed in a somewhat stilted and archaic prose, and with their own peculiar elegance. The style is mostly prose, but here and there interspersed with poetry. (Only the first half of the *Kena Upaniṣad* is in poetry, and it has been thought that it is the latest of the early period Upaniṣads.) As against this, however, the Upaniṣads of the middle period (apart from the *Praśna*), after the *Kāṭhaka*, were composed in elegant and beautiful prose, with traces of the art of the poet to be found in them. The language and sentence-structure, therefore, differ markedly from those of both Brāhmaṇas and Āraṇyakas. Again, the particular features of the Brāhmaṇas or Āraṇyakas are hardly to be found in the prose of the *Praśna-Upaniṣad*.

(3) The early period Upaniṣads frequently refer to rituals similar to those in the Brāhmaṇas, and have also many allegorical similes similar to those of the Āraṇyakas; but these are extremely few in the middle period Upaniṣads.

(4) Various word-usages and modes of expression frequently employed in the Brāhmaṇas and the Āraṇyakas exist in the early period Upaniṣads, but in general neither the word-usages nor the modes of expression peculiar to the middle period Upaniṣads can be found. In the middle period Upaniṣads, on the contrary, typical word-usages and modes of expression used to express the thoughts of the Vedānta are repeated everywhere; the usage of compound words has now been perfected; and there are instances

also where passages of the Upaniṣads of the early period have been inserted unchanged.

(5) Brahman and Ātman, together with the ideas of transmigration, Karma and liberation, which have been generally taken as the central concepts[7] in the Upaniṣads, were in the process of development in the early period Upaniṣads and still not definite philosophical concepts; but in the middle period Upaniṣads they are already treated as definite and generally accepted concepts or thoughts.

(6) Despite the fact that the corpus of the early period Upaniṣads is large, the technical terms of general Indian philosophy are relatively little used in them. In the middle period Upaniṣads a great number of technical terms appear on the stage for the first time. For instance, technical, terms like *cetanā, cetas, caitanya, cit, avyakta, ahaṁkāra, karaṇa, kārya, kriyā, tanu* (flesh), *deha, dehin, dravya, nivṛtti, pariṇāma, prakṛti, pratyaya, phala* (result), *mokṣa, śakti, sarvaga, sarvajña, sūkṣma, hetu,* which are used by all the Indian philosophical schools, appear for the first time in the middle period Upaniṣads.[8]

(7) Thoughts or expressions suggestive of the Sāṁkhya philosophy are extremely rare in the early period Upaniṣads, but the influence of the thought of the Sāṁkhya and the Yoga is remarkable in the Upaniṣads of the middle and late period, especially in the *Kāṭhaka, Śvetāśvatara,* and *Maitrāyaṇa Upaniṣads*.

Since such a remarkable difference in content thus exists between the early period Upaniṣads and the middle period Upaniṣads their respective dates of formulation must have been well apart in time. That is, the period in which the early period Upaniṣads were produced can be thought to be far earlier than the period in which the middle period Upaniṣads were composed in verse by the religious poets.

This is also substantiated by other facts. Both the grammarians Kātyāyana, in his commentary, and Patañjali, in his *Mahābhāṣya,* cite the name of the great scholar Yājñavalkya who appears in the *Śatapatha-Brāhmaṇa;* and Patañjali refers to the *Yājñavalkāni, Brāhmaṇāni.*[9] Thus by the time of Kātyāyana, the *Śatapatha-Brāhmaṇa*, which perhaps includes also a part of the *Bṛhad-āraṇyaka Upaniṣad,* had not only been already composed, but had also attained the authority of a Brāhmaṇa scripture

And it can be thought that the Old Upaniṣads of the early period were perhaps formulated prior to the appearance of the etymologist Yāska. Since the mode of expression in Yāska's work on etymology, the *Nirukta*, belongs to the period between the language of the Vedas and the language prescribed by Pāṇini's *Grammar*, it has commonly been said that Yāska was prior to Pāṇini.[10] Now, it has been agreed that various words which are presented in the *Nirukta*, in particular the meaning or interpretation of the technical terms of linguistics, are identical with those appearing in the *Aitareya* and the *Kauṣītaki* Brāhmaṇas and the *Chāndogya Upaniṣad*, etc.[11] Yāska neither directly referred to nor directly quoted, these sacred works; but judging from the above-mentioned fact, it may perhaps be no great mistake to think that they had been composed earlier than Yāska. It is difficult to determine the dates of Yāska; but, at any rate, there is no doubt that the Ancient Upaniṣads of the early period were composed considerably earlier than Pāṇini.

Such an inference can also be justified from what has been recorded by the Vedānta scholars of the early period. Vedānta scholars prior to Jaimini and Bādarāyaṇa, i.e., Bādari, Kāśakṛtsna, Kārṣṇājini and Ātreya, were of the same period in which the various *Kalpa-sūtras* continued to be produced; Āśmarathya is of the same period as Pāṇini; Kāśakṛtsna was before Kātyāyana; and Auḍulomi was prior to Patañjali.[12] Now, we see from the *Brahma-Sūtra* that all these scholars have discussed the purport of passages of the *Bṛhad-āraṇyaka* and *Chāndogya* Upaniṣads, but have no concern with the other Upaniṣads. It can be thought, therefore, that the period in which these scholars lived was at least after these two Upaniṣads had been compiled for the most part and had further attained the status of the sacred canon. And, therefore, these two Upaniṣads would surely have been composed several hundreds of years earlier than the Vedānta scholars cited here.

The next problem is the period in which the various *Kalpa-sūtras* were produced, together with the period in which Pāṇini, Kātyāyana, and Patañjali lived. Max Müller previously fixed the date in which the sūtras were produced at 600-200 B.C. Following the accounts in the collection of stories, *Kathāsaritsāgara* composed in the 12th century A.D., he assumed that the grammarian Kātyāyana lived in the second half of the fourth century B.C., and identifying him with the Kātyāyana who is the author of the *Kalpa Sūtra*, he took this as a fixed point and roughly estimated the dates of other scholars from it; thus he made the beginning of the Sūtra period about 600 B.C., and its end about 200 B.C., namely about three generations after Kātyāyana.[13] His theory later has been accepted in the academic world; but as the accounts in the *Kathāsaritsāgara* itself cannot be relied upon as historical data as they stand, there is room for doubt whether the grammarian Kātyāyana is the same person as Kātyāyana, the author of the *Kalpa Sūtra*. The figures given by Max Müller, accordingly, are exceedingly unreliable. I think, however, that his early limit of the Sūtra period may be adopted for the most part. One of the reasons is that since the present form of the *Āpastamba-dharma-sūtra* was compiled roughly 300-250 B.C., or later,[14] there would be no objection to putting the general *Kalpa Sūtras* substantially prior to that. Again, it is generally accepted now that Pāṇini lived c. 350 B.C.,[14] the grammarian Kātyāyana c. 250 B.C., and Patañjali c. 150. The grounds used to establish these dates are exceedingly flimsy; if one should take these postulated dates to be mistaken, it would be a question of moving them to somewhat later centuries. And since the Vedānta scholars previously mentioned lived in about this period (or earlier), the dates of their lives would be around the center of the third century B.C. In that case, since various parts of the *Bṛhad-āraṇyaka* and the *Chāndogya Upaniṣads* would have been formulated several hundreds of years earlier, even if many sections in these two Upaniṣads had not been compiled then in their present form, it must still be thought that these two Old Upaniṣads were formulated prior to early period Buddhism.

As I shall discuss further later,[15] the Greek Megasthenes, who came to India c. 300 B.C., gave an account of the thought of the Brahmins of India of that time; and in it, he recorded not only the ideas of the Old Upaniṣads, but also new ideas which do not appear in them. One must suppose therefore that the Old Upaniṣads of the early period at least were produced far earlier than the coming of Megasthenes.

We see throughout the sacred texts of both early Buddhism and early Jainism that the intellectual worlds of that time were highly developed in splendid rivalry, but that among the ideas which can be seen in the early period Upaniṣads, not a few are extremely puerile and artless, and some are common to the beliefs of primitive races in general. The supposition, accordingly, that the early period Upaniṣads had been formulated far earlier than early Buddhism and the Jain sacred scriptures, has adequate grounds. Because the middle period Upaniṣads had been influenced by the general philosophical world, their ideas are remarkably advanced, and their philosophical terminology also is abundant.

If one asks, however, how much of a chronological interval there was between the early period and the middle period Upaniṣads, there is no evidence whatsoever now which could settle that problem. The theories of the dates of the Upaniṣads by scholars, accordingly, are no more than mere assumptions. Since the *Kāṭhaka-Upaniṣad,* however, was formulated in a period not too distant from that of the Buddha, it must be thought that the early period Upaniṣads were surely prior to the Buddha. And one can conclude that the *Bṛhad-āraṇyaka* and the *Chāndogya Upaniṣads,* in particular, must be traced back to a much earlier period than that of the Buddha.

Notes

1. Fürst: *Kuhn's Zeitschrift*, XLVII, 1915, pp. 20; 60. (I am indebted for this information to the late Prof. Hisao Sakai.)

2. Deussen: *AGPh.*, I, 2. p. 208 ff.

3. Belvalkar and Ranade: *History of Indian Philosophy*, Vol. II; Belvalkar: *Lectures*, pp. 44-45.

4. Since the *Kauṣītaki-Upaniṣad* has some internal connection with the *Kauṣītaki-Brāhmaṇa*, Keith has asserted that it was formulated later (Keith: *Aitareya Āraṇyaka*, Intro., p. 41, n. 2).

5. Deussen: *AGPh.*, I, 2, p. 24.

6. Cf. Max Müller, *ASL.*, p. 122, n. 1.

7. E.g., the word "transmigration" (*saṁsāra*) does not appear in the Ancient Upaniṣads of the early period, but first appears in the *Kāṭhaka-Upaniṣad.* Again, the word *mokṣa*, which means "(spiritual) liberation," was first employed in the *Śvet. Up.* VI. 16; *Maitrī-Up.* VI. 20, 30, 34; and the words *mukti* (*Bṛhad.* III. 1. 3, 4, 5, 6), *vimokṣa* (*Bṛhad.* IV. 3.14, 15, 16, 33), *vipramokṣa* (*Chānd.* VII. 26.2), *atimukti* (*Bṛhad.* III.1.3-6), *atimokṣa* (*Bṛhad.* III.1.6), were used to express a concept close to (spiritual) liberation in the early period Upaniṣads. Accordingly, "transmigration" and "liberation" had not yet become clear philosophical concepts in the early Upaniṣads.

8. Written by Hermann Jacobi, trans. by Yamada and Ito, *Indo Kodai Shinkan-shi*, pp. 33-34.

9. Vārttika 4 under IV.2.66; *Mahābhāṣya* on IV.2.66.

10. B. Liebich: *Zur Einführung in die indische einheimische Sprachiwissenschaft*, II. Historische Einführung und Dhātupāṭha: *SHA.*, 1919, pp. 28-29.

11. B. Liebich: *op. cit.*, pp. 8-18.

12. Cf. the present work, Vol. II, Part III, Chap. I.

13. Max Müller, *ASL.*, pp. 239-45; 300 ff.

14. Cf. the present work, Part II, Chap. II, Sect. 3.

Albrecht Weber placed the date of Pāṇini later than Böhtlingk and supposed : "We have, in Pāṇini's work itself, a very weighty argument which goes to show that the date to be assigned to him can by no means be so early as Böhtlingk supposes (about B.C.350). For in it Pāṇini once mentions the Yavanas" (Albrecht Weber : *The History of Indian Litrature* (London : Kegan Paul, Trench, Trübner and Co. 1892), pp. 220 f.

15. Cf. the present work, Part II, Chapter IV.

IV. *Conclusion*

I now set out the results of the foregoing study as follows :

I. Early Period Upaniṣads (Prior to the Buddha) First Period

Bṛhad-āraṇyaka *Chāndogya*

Second Period

Aitareya *Kauṣītakī* *Taittirīya*

Third Period

Kena *Īśa*

II. Middle Period Upaniṣads [After the Buddha (roughly 466-386 B.C.)]

Kāṭhaka	350-300
Muṇḍaka	,, ,,
Praśna	,, ,,
Śvetāśvatara	,, ,,

III. Late Period Upaniṣads

Maitrāyaṇī (i.e., *Maitrī*)	200-? ?
Māṇḍūkya	00—200 A.D.

The above list follows for the most part the order of composition. That is, it is in order of dates. Strictly speaking, one ought to discuss the order of composition of each of the parts of an individual Upaniṣad. It can be said that the above is the approximate order, only if one is merely indicating the order of composition of the individual Upaniṣads taken as single units, and without entering any such detailed discussion. Some parts of an Upaniṣad cited late in the list given above may have been formulated earlier than some parts of an Upaniṣad cited earlier. Such detailed analysis must await future investigation.

In addition to these, there exist further some parts of the Vedic *Saṁhitās* which came to be regarded as Upaniṣads in later centuries; but since these do not have an important significance as Upaniṣads, I shall omit them here.[1]

Notes

1. Cf. A. Weber: *HIL.*, pp. 52, 108. See further the present work, this Part, Chap. II, Sect. 1.

SECTION II THE DATES OF THE FORMULATION OF THE NEW UPANIṢADS

We have considered above the dates and order of formulation of the 13 or 14 Old Upaniṣads which have been admitted by scholars to be ancient; and while these Upaniṣads thus differ both in their dates of formulation and in the degree to which they have been regarded as important, they are important materials for history of thought of Ancient India, inasmuch as they were composed in the ancient period. Upaniṣads, however, are not limited to this period alone. They were being composed without interruption even afterwards. There are, in addition to these, over 200 on which the appellation "Upaniṣad" has been bestowed, and that are extant today.[1] I shall call these by the generic name "New Upaniṣads." These New Upaniṣdas are supposed by most scholars to belong to their respective Vedic schools, but the actual relation with the Vedic schools is obscure, and the classificatory relation of the one and the same Upaniṣad has been handed down differently and variously by tradition.[2] These New Upaniṣads usually have been classified as belonging to the *Atharva-Veda*, and are comprised under the name *Atharva Upaniṣad*, but internal connection between them is difficult to find. Furthermore, because the Saṁhitās of the *Atharva-Veda* have a character which differs somewhat from that of the Saṁhitās in the other three Vedas, it was most natural to think that it was connected with the Upaniṣads formulated in later centuries.

These New Upaniṣads were written either in prose or in a mixture of prose and poetry, and have also been partially written in the *ślokas* of lyrical poetry. And they were not necessarily handed down as one and the same recension, but there are cases in which the Upaniṣads with the same name have been handed down in several recensions.[3] We find that all of them are comparatively brief, and that the principal theme is usually uniform. In many places they have been influenced by the philosophy or religion of later centuries; and there exist those which are closer to the Purāṇas and the Tantras than to the Vedas. Their contents are many and diverse, and one cannot readily make a simple division of them, but Weber, who was the pioneer in the research on the New Upaniṣads, classified them into three general divisions:[4]

I. Those which study the fundamental nature of the *ātman.*

II. Those which teach the means and methods to be *united with the ātman* by means of the practice of Yoga.

III. Those which are markedly sectarian, and which expound the worship of either Śiva or Viṣṇu.

Deussen, again, selected 39 of the most widely known of the Upaniṣads which have been called the appendices of the *Atharva-Veda*, and classified them into the following five groups according to their contents.[5]

I. Pure Vedānta-Upaniṣads (Nine) [*Muṇḍaka, Praśna, Māṇḍūkya*], *Garbha, Prāṇāgnihotra, Piṇḍa, Ātma, Sarvopaniṣatsāra, Gāruḍa.*

II. Yoga-Upaniṣads (Eleven)
Brahmavidyā, Kṣurikā, Cūlikā, Nādabindu, Brahmabindu, Amṛtabindu, Dhyānabindu, Tejobindu, Yogaśikhā, Yogatattva, Haṃsa.

III. Saṃnyāsa-Upaniṣads (Seven)
Brahma, Saṃnyāsa, Āruṇeya, Kaṇṭhaśruti, Paramahaṁsa, Jābāla, Āśrama.

IV. Śiva-Upaniṣads (Five)
Atharvaśiras, Atharvaśikhā, Nīlarudra, Kālāgnirudra, Kaivalya.

V. Viṣṇu-Upaniṣads (Seven)
Mahā, Nārāyaṇa, Ātmabodha, Nṛsiṃhapūrvatāpanīya, Nṛsiṃhottaratāpanīya, Rāmapūrvatāpanīya, Rāmottaratāpanīya.

This classification is by no means exact. For example, since the Upaniṣads which have taught the knowledge of the Brahman have also mainly taught Yoga as their method of practice, these span both (I) and (II); and since some Yoga-Upaniṣads teach the worship of Viṣṇu, they can be classified in either (II) or (V). This classification, accordingly, cannot be said to be perfect; but as it is convenient, it has come to be utilized by many scholars. Other Upaniṣads not cited above could presumably be included somewhere among the five divisions above. Winternitz has further established that in addition to the five divisions above, there are also the Upaniṣads of the Śākta School.[6]

Classifications by scholars in this way are by no means in agreement, and the contents of the New Upaniṣads are highly complicated and diverse, even if understood in this way. We see that the dates of formulation of these New Upaniṣads are completely indefinite—there are those which are so old that they may be thought to have originated shortly after the Christian era, and there are those which were first composed in the 10th century or later. It is held, however, that among them, the *Jābāla, Paramahaṃsa, Subāla, Garbha, Atharvaśiras,* as well as the *Vajrasūcikā* and others, were formulated comparatively early.[7]

Notes

1. A. Weber (*HIL.*, p. 155, n.) says that he can count 235 which have been entitled "Upaniṣads." Among these, however, it might be that the same Upaniṣad has been given different names.
2. Winternitz: *HIL.*, I, pp. 241-42.
3. *Ibid.*, I. p. 241.
4. Weber: *op. cit.*, p. 156 ff.
5. Deussen: *Sechzig Upaniṣads*, p. 543.
6. Winternitz: *op. cit.*, I, p. 240.
7. *Ibid.*, I., p. 240.

An article on "The Dates of Formulation of the Upaniṣads" was already published in the *Tōyō Gakuhō*, Vol. 31, p. 211 ff; 355 ff.; but following suggestions and criticisms by scholars, I revised and expanded it.

SECTION III THE EARLY LIMIT OF THE EARLY VEDĀNTA SCHOOL

The Vedānta school is the school which is devoted to the Upaniṣads. That is, it is the scholarly tradition of men who devoutly follow Upaniṣads already established as a sacred canon and of generally accepted authority, who have constructed a philosophical theory based upon them. The Vedānta having thus arisen after the Upaniṣads became established as sacred canon, it must be later than the Upaniṣads. Still, more than two hundred of the Upaniṣads were composed at very late periods, whereas the Vedānta school was already in existence long before them. So the Vedāntins prior to that, believed in and accepted as sacred canon a lesser number of Upaniṣads. *So the later the Vedāntins, the greater the number of Upaniṣads which they accepted as sacred canon.*

Taking Śaṅkara first, we find he has quoted as sacred canon all the Old Upaniṣads except the *Māṇḍūkya* and the *Maitrāyaṇī*, and has also quoted frequently as canonical authority the section of the Brāhmaṇas called *rahasya* (secret doctrine), and the *Jābāla* and *Paiṅgi Upaniṣads*, together with some Upaniṣads whose names have been lost and which have not been handed down to modern times.[1] Again, Rāmānuja (11th century) has quoted all the Old Upaniṣads, except the *Māṇḍūkya*, and in addition the Upaniṣads *Jābāla, Garbha, Cūlikā, Mahā, and Subāla*. It is notorious that Madhva of the 13th century, furthermore, has quoted an unusually large number of strange works which he called Vedic sacred Scriptures. And the *Muktikā-Upaniṣad*, composed at a late date enumerates the names of 108 Upaniṣads.

Thus the later the century, the greater the number of Upaniṣads which are taken as canonical authority; and conversely, the more ancient the period, the fewer the Upaniṣads which are so taken. What then was the position in the first period of Vedānta ?

The view which finds special significance in the Sacred Upaniṣads and seeks to follow them devoutly can, I think, be traced back to the Old Upaniṣads of the middle period. That there must have been a considerable chronological gap between the Upaniṣads of the early period and those of the middle period, I have already shown in the preceding section; and during that interval, the Upaniṣads of the early period would have been compiled once for all in their present form, and their authority as sacred works established. As I shall set out later,[2] the Upaniṣads of the middle period clearly state that they find a special significance in the "Vedānta," and that they themselves are based upon it. Because the poets who composed the Old Upaniṣads of the middle period had no longer any concern with rituals, and must have differed also in their social lives from the authors of the early period Old Upaniṣads, I think that we can recognize that there were now Vedāntins devoted to the Sacred Upaniṣads. And their lines of doctrinal transmission have continued unbroken for over two thousand years down to the present day. That is, Sacred Upaniṣads were further compared and commentaries and systematic interpretations of them were composed by men who belonged to such traditional lines. Accordingly, not only did the Vedānta students follow the early period Upaniṣads as sacred canon, they were also continually producing Upaniṣads and they ascribed canonical authority to these as well. *The history of the composition of the Upaniṣads is exactly the same as the history of the Vedānta school.*

To take up the problem of the rise of the Vedānta school, therefore, we have to trace it back at least to the period of the middle-period Old Upaniṣads. And the period in which the composition of the middle-period Old Upaniṣads began, that is, from the time of the Buddha and Mahāvira, must be re-discovered in what remains of the Vedānta school and the historical changes in its philosophy. Considerable research has been accumulated so far on the texts and thoughts of the Old Upaniṣads, but the purpose of the present work is to clarify how the Vedānta school brought about the development of the peculiar philosophical thought which specially follows the Upaniṣads, and how its ideas actually came to be developed.

Notes

1. Deussen: *SV.*, p. 32 ff.
2. Cf. the present work, Part I, Chap. III, Sect. 5.

PART TWO

THE DATES OF ŚAṄKARA AND CONTEMPORARY PHILOSOPHERS

If as already proposed we tentatively limit "philosophy of the early period Vedānta" to the Vedānta philosophy in the period prior to Śaṅkara, then after the dates of the composition of the Upaniṣads, we must necessarily come to some definite view as to the dates of Śaṅkara. However, since his dates must be determined by taking into consideration also his relation to the dates of other philosophers, they will be considered together with the dates of the famous philosophers of that time. In the following, section A will carefully go into the theories advanced hitherto on the dates of Śaṅkara,[1] together with the arguments for them; and in section B, I shall set out my own theory.

Notes

1. I have examined mainly the theories set out in Winternitz (*GIL.*, Bd. III, pp. 434; 651) and Belvalkar (*Lectures*, pp. 209-216), and the subsequent theories.

M. Krishnamachariar: *History of Classical Sanskrit Literature* 1937, pp. 321-322, has referred to some additional literature, of which some items have not been accessible to me, but since they apparently are not particularly concerned with the dates of Śaṅkara, I think that what is cited below will have exhausted all the important theses.

A. A Critique of Past Argument on the Dates of Śaṅkara

SECTION I. THE TRADITIONAL THEORY OF THE ŚĀṄKARA SCHOOL

That the period of Śaṅkara was probably around the eighth century has been assumed by scholars in India since early days,[1] but the thesis published by K. B. Pathak in the *Indian Antiquary* XI (1882, pp. 174-175), was the initial cause of active debate about Śaṅkara's dates among scholars of Indian studies.

He pointed out that the vague arguments for the dates of Śaṅkara proposed by scholars previously did not get beyond mere conjecture, and in seeking a basis for them in the material transmitted in the Vedānta school, he found and published an original manuscript made up of three leaves. Both title and dates of the work of which this is a manuscript are obscure, but since the invocatory verse in the beginning is dedicated to the teacher Śaṅkara, it probably should be regarded as a work of the Śāṅkara school. According to it, Śaṅkara was born in the year 710 of the Śaka era, and in Śaka 742 "returned to Śiva" (*Śivatām agāt*), that is, died. Converting these dates to the western calendar, he would have been born in 788 and died in 810. As precise figures were thus obtained, it attracted unusual attention in academic circles. It should be further noted that the year of birth, 788, coincides with the year of birth of Śaṅkara which appears in the work *Āryavidyāsudhākara*,[2] according to which Śaṅkara was born in the village of Kālapī in the region of Kerala in the year 3889 of the Kali period (Kaliyuga), i.e. in the year 845 of the Vikrama era, which according to the western reckoning would be 788.[3] Again, it is recorded in the work *Śaṅkaramandārasaurabha* also, in exactly the same way, that he was born in the year 3889 of the Kali period. As the accounts in the works thus agree, and because the dates presented by Pathak have been thus reinforced, almost all Indologists today have adopted these figures.[4]

Nevertheless, this theory holds that as Śaṅkara was born in 788 and died in 810, he would have ended a youthful career at the age of 32,[5] in which case, the question arises whether, since he left behind an unusually large number of voluminous works, he could have actually completely written all of them before he was 32. It strikes one that in view of the massive corpus of his works, death at the age of 32 is perhaps a little too early. Burgess therefore raised the doubt that either the year of birth or the year of death in the above dates may be mistaken, or that these figures indicate neither the year of his birth nor the year of his death, but indicate respectively the beginning and end of the years of his actual period of activity.[6]

At any event, he is to be taken as having lived long enough to have been able to leave behind such a great number of works, either the year of his birth or the year of his death cited above must be moved. One group of scholars (like Keith and Macdonell), therefore, accepted the year of the birth of Śaṅkara as it stands, and tried to shift the year of death forward. They interpreted the sentence, "he returned to Śiva," in the manuscript discovered by Pathak, as meaning not that "he passed away," but that Śaṅkara, attaining enlightenment, was mystically united with Śiva and entered on a new spiritual activity; that Śaṅkara himself had a fairly long life; and that the actual year of his demise was perhaps in the middle of the ninth century.[7] Opposing this, however, the erudite Indologist Bühler considered shifting the birth-date of Śaṅkara back, maintaining that the "Birth of Śaṅkara" (*Śaṅkarodaya*) in the year corresponding to 788 A.D. in the manuscript above does not mean the birth of the flesh, but birth in a spiritual sense (that he entered a new life as an ascetic), that such expressions are found frequently among the Buddhists, the Vaiṣṇavas and the Śaivas, and that such examples also exist in works of that time.[8]

At any event, no matter which interpretation one adopts, the outcome is that Śaṅkara lived roughly from the eighth century to the ninth century. As the argument of dates presented thus by Pathak cites precise figures, it seems to be very well supported and has been adopted by almost all Indologists. Examination of the manuscript which was the evidence for his demonstration, however, shows that it can never be fully reliable.

The only clear fact is that the manuscript discovered by Pathak was written by scholars of the Śaṅkara line; neither has it been accepted as authoritative in the Śaṅkara sect, nor is its authorship clear. Since it describes the rise and tradition of the teachers of both the Rāmānuja sect and the Madhva sect, and as it is likely that Madhva lived from 1197 to 1276, this manuscript must certainly be later than the 14th century. It is impossible, accordingly, that we give complete credence to such an account in an anonymous manuscript some later century. Again, the *Āryavidyāsudhākara* briefly describes the ritual which should be performed by orthodox Brahmins, together with an outline of the doctrines of the philosophical school, and introduces also the doctrines of both the Madhva sect and the Vallabha sect; and since furthermore it refers to the *Śaṅkaradigvijaya*[9] of Mādhava, it cannot be before the latter half of the 16th century at the earliest. Accordingly it was composed after more than 800 years had elapsed from the time of Śaṅkara, and so no more can we accept unconditionally the account in this work.[10] And even if the account in the manuscript discovered by Pathak concurs with the accounts in the *Āryavidyāsudhākara* and the

Śaṅkaramandārasaurabha, since such a tradition on the birth-year of Śaṅkara was formulated in later centuries and can be thought to have been adopted in these works, the coincidence of these accounts cannot necessarily demonstrate the accuracy of their contents.

Of course, one cannot doubt the authority of these accounts merely because they are accounts in works of later centuries. If the argument for the dates recorded in them did not contradict all the other historical facts, there would be, of course, no objection to admitting them; but since they do contradict several historical facts as will be set forth in the latter half (*B*) of this section, the theory of dates presented by Pathak is no longer absolutely reliable by any means, and I shall point out that it can be superseded by other more cogently demonstrative arguments.

As a further argument for the dates of Śaṅkara based upon the tradition of the Śāṅkara school, there exists the theory of S. V. Venkateswara.[11] Reckoning from the account in the *Śaṅkaradigvijaya*, written by Mādhava, of the star which appeared at the time of Śāṅkara's birth, and taking as a basis in praise of the goddess *Devī* which is traditionally written by Śaṅkara, he has argued that Śaṅkara lived from 804-897, and takes the account of the tradition of the teachers of the Śaṅkara sect called the *Jagad-gururatnamālā-stava* as corroborating evidence. The grounds for his argument, however, are very flimsy. It has frequently been doubted whether the *Śaṅkaradigvijaya* is really a work by Mādhava;[12] and it has frequently been argued that its account is unreliable. Again, it is not clear whether or not the aforesaid poem either is an authentic writing of Śaṅkara. And since this argument for his dates also contradicts other historical facts, we cannot admit it either.[13]

Again, it is recorded in the work *Darśanaprakāśa* composed in 1638 A.D. that Śaṅkara "entered the cave" in 642 of the Śaka era, i.e., 720 A.D.; but because this too is an account in a work of recent centuries, unless it can be confirmed on other certain grounds, it cannot be accepted as it stands.

Notes

1. Cf. Jas. Burgess: "The Date of Śaṅkarācārya," *Ind. Ant.*, XI (1882),, p. 263; A. Weber: *HIL.*, p. 51.

2. Deussen: *SV.*, Anm. 23; *Āryavidyāsudhākara by Yajñeśvara Cimaṇa* (The Punjab Sanskrit Series. No. 3, 1923), p. 123.

3. Belvalkar: *Lectures*, pp. 211-212.

4. Winternitz: *GIL.*, III, p. 434; Dasgupta: *HIPh.*, I, p. 429; II, p. 112; C. M. Duff: *Chronology of India*, p. 69; R. W. Frazer: *A Literary History of India*, p. 325; V. S. Ghate: *ERE.*, Vol. XI, p. 185; Bühler: *Ind. Ant.*, Vol. XIV (1885), p. 64, and *SBE.*, Vol. XXV, p. cxi; Weber: *Indische Studien*, XIV, p. 353; Belvalkar: *Lectures*, pp. 209-217.

5. According to the *Keralotpatti*, however, his death was at the age 38.

6. Jas. Burgess, *Ind. Ant.*, XI (1882), p. 263.

7. A. B. Keith: *Aitareya Āraṇyaka*, Intro., p. 11; Macdonell: *Sanskrit Literature*, p. 402; J. N. Farquhar: *Outline*, p. 171.

8. Cf. the correspondence of Bühler to Garbe (R. Garbe: *Sāṃkhya Philosophie*², p. 157, *Anm.*, 2).

9. *Āryavidyāsudhākara* (Punjab Sanskrit Series, No. 3), p. 123.

10. Although Deussen (*SV.*, Anm., 23) has cited the account of the *Āryavidyāsudhākara* as his only source, he hesitated to go on to adopt immediately these dates, and has recorded vaguely that Śaṅkara lived from c. 700-800.

11. S. V. Venkateswara: *The Date of Śaṅkarāchārya*, *JRAS.* (1916), pp. 151-162.

12. Kurt Klemm ("Mādhava, sein Lehrer und seine Werke," *Gurupūjākaumudī*, p. 41 ff.) does not count the *Śaṅkaradigvijaya* as a work by Mādhava.

13. Cf. Farquhar: *Outline*, p. 171, n. 3; Keith, *The Karma-Mīmāṃsā*, p. 16.

SECTION II. THE ARGUMENT FOR ŚAṄKARA'S DATES BASED UPON THE *Keralotpatti*

Even before the article by Pathak was published, studies on the dates of Śaṅkara had already been put forward in the academic world. F. W. Ellis, in his article in which he introduced the language of Malayālam,[1] translated selected portions of the contents of the work on history, the *Keralotpatti*, one of the important books written in that language. This work recorded the history of the country of Kerala on the western shores of southern India; and according to it, Śaṅkara was born in the year corresponding to 400 A.D., taught the *dharma* by travelling about each region of India as a wandering priest, and passed away at the age of 38.[2] Since these dates, as Ellis himself has commented, err in that they are too early, when compared together with other historical circumstances, they cannot be adopted as they stand.

W. Logan was later led to the conclusion that Śaṅkara had lived in the first quarter of the ninth century, basing it on the account in the *Keralotpatti* which says that a war broke out during the reign of King Perumāl and that Śaṅkara was born at that time.[3] Looking at his argument, however, besides the fact that historical researches on the dates of King Perumāl are founded upon very weak grounds, we also feel a great caution in regard to any argument for the dates of Śaṅkara based in general upon the *Keralotpatti*.

The *Keralotpatti* was written in the Malayālam language and the Malayālam language was formulated originally around the ninth century as an offshoot of the Tamil language. It was influenced and reformed by the Brahmin culture around the 17th century, and borrowing a great number of Sanskrit words, came to produce various literary works. It is said that the *Keralotpatti* was first written in Sanskrit and later translated in the Malayālam language;[4] nevertheless, it is not a very ancient work, for it refers to the invasion by the Muhammedans.[5] Schomerus says that, while this work did gather together the oral traditions from of old, it was nevertheless formulated in the 17th century, and its contents are highly legendary.[6] Accordingly, it probably cannot but be said that the attempt to determine the dates of Śaṅkara based upon such a work of later centuries written in a Dravidian language, is highly unreasonable. Since it has been generally handed down that Śaṅkara was a native of the region of Kerala, the *Keralotpatti*, even if it is a work of later centuries, still would presumably perhaps have reported the actual historical facts on Śaṅkara; however the date of Śaṅkara, described in it is remarkably far removed from the actual Śaṅkara. It is explained in the *Keralotpatti* that even a Śūdra can finally attain liberation by the teaching of Śaṅkara; but Śaṅkara himself never expounded a teaching for the Śūdra, and moreover, as the monasteries of the non-dualistic monistic sect, the traditional line of Śaṅkara, admitted only Brahmins and refused entrance to any other social ranks until the time of *Madhusūdana-sarasvatī*,[7] the *Keralotpatti* cannot have faithfully transmitted the figure of Śaṅkara, the author of the *Brahmasūtrabhāṣya*.

Notes

1. F. W. Ellis, "Essay on the Malayālam Language", *Ind. Ant.*, VII (1878), p. 275 ff.
2. *Ind. Ant.*, XIII, p. 95 f.
3. W. Logan: "The Date of Śaṅkarāchārya," *Ind. Ant.*, XVI (1887), pp. 160-161.
4. Cf. Ellis: *op. cit.*, p. 286.
5. *Ibid.*
6. H. W. Schomerus: *Die Dravidischen Literaturen* (Die Literatur Indiens, herausgegeben von H. von Glasenapp). p. 318.
7. J. N. Farquhar: "The Organisation of the Sannyasis of the Vedānta," *JRAS.*, 1925, pp. 479 ff.

SECTION III. THE ARGUMENT FOR ŚAṄKARA'S DATES BASED UPON THE LEGENDS OF NEPAL

J. F. Fleet, who had a detailed knowledge of the history of India, inferred the dates of Śaṅkara from legends of Nepal.[1] The *Vaṃśāvali*, a history of Nepal, says that at the end of the reign of King Vṛṣadeva in the Sūryavaṃśi Dynasty, or within several months after his death, Śaṅkara visited Nepal. Now, since King Vṛṣadeva lived c. 630-655 A.D. according to the research by Fleet, Śaṅkara, accordingly, lived during the middle of the seventh century. However, the account in the history *Vaṃśāvali*, which gives the story, is very difficult to rely on, and it has recorded many events which are not actual historical facts.[2] Since the compilation of this work was completed only in the 19th century,[3] one probably cannot but say that a determination of the dates of Śaṅkara based upon it rests upon extremely flimsy grounds. Moreover, no evidence whatever exists for concluding that this particular account dealing with Śaṅkara is true; and further there are differing views on the dates of King Vṛṣadeva.[4]

Notes

1. J. F. Fleet: "A Note on the Date of Śaṅkarāchārya," *Ind. Ant.*, XVI (1887), pp. 41-42.
2. Fleet has also admitted this. Garbe has criticized this work as "Märchen" (Garbe: *Sāṁkhya Philosophie*², p. 157, *Anm.*, 2).
3. Banarsi Das Jain: "Die Literaturen des nördlichen Indien," (*Die Literaturen Indiens*, hrsg. von H. von Glasenapp. p. 235). We see from Daniel Wright: *History of Nepal, translated from the Parbatiyā*, 1877, a translation of the *Vaṃśāvali*, that the same work has also recorded events of c. 1850 A.D.
4. Cf. Fleet: *op. cit.*, Further, B. Indraji has maintained that King Vṛṣadeva lived c. 260 A.D. (*Ind. Ant.*, XIII, 1884, pp. 412; 427).

SECTION IV. THEORIES WHICH TRY TO TRACE BACK FROM THE DATE OF THE *Saṃkṣepa-śārīraka*

The *Saṃkṣepa-śārīraka* by Sarvajñātman is a summary description, in verse, of the doctrines of the non-dualistic monistic school, and is an important work of the school. Sarvajñātman was also a pupil of Sureśvara,[1] and succeeded him as head of the school of non-dualistic monism.[2] Thus if one could establish the dates of Sarvajñātman, by tracing backwards from them one could get a general idea of the dates of Śaṅkara. The first who turned his attention to and discussed this was R. G. Bhandarkar.[3] His argument is as follows:—Sarvajñātman, in the concluding verse of the *Saṃkṣepa-Śārīraka*, has recorded that this work was written in the reign of King Manukulāditya.[4] This word "Manukulādiṭya" can be interpreted as "the sun (āditya) of the Manu tribe." The problem then arises as to which king it refers to. The kings of the Cālukya Dynasty designated themselves as belonging to the Manu tribe (Mānava-gotra). Now, kings of this dynasty whose names end in *'āditya* are either Vikramāditya I (Śaka Era 601, i.e., reigned until 679 A.D.), or Vikramāditya II (Śaka Era 669, i.e., reigned until 747 A.D.). Since Sarvajñātman was a pupil of Sureśvara and a grand-pupil of Śaṅkara, if the "*Āditya* of the Manu tribe" referred to Vikramāditya I, Śaṅkara would have lived at the end of the sixth century, and if it referred to Vikramāditya II, he would have lived c. 680.

To determine which of these two possible cases one should adopt, one must rely upon other sources. Scholars have been adopting the one which accords with their own position.[5] In any case, Bhandarkar's supposition itself is extremely weak as evidence. Opposing Bhandarkar's theory, Bühler has made, in summary, the following criticisms :[6] The assumption that "*Āditya* of the Manu tribe" probably refers to a king of the Cālukya Dynasty is perhaps correct; but the deduction that the name of that king either was Āditya or ended in = āditya is not correct. There are examples to prove the point. Further, the Second Cālukya Dynasty, restored in the 10th century, was also designated as descended from Manu. The description in the end of the *Saṃkṣepa-Śārīraka*, accordingly, is completely without force for determining the dates.

Notwithstanding this statement by Bühler, later scholars did not give up this lead, but tried to pursue it still further to arrive at some conclusion. A. Balakrishna Pillai has conjectured that since the name "Manukulāditya" has been found on rock-inscriptions discovered in the southern tip of the region of Travancore (978 A.D.), Sarvajñātman lived in that period and was associated with that area.[7] Again, S. V. Venkateswara identifies the King as Rājakesarivarman Āditya I (880-907 A.D.) who was King Cola.[8] And D.R. Bhandarkar has identified this king with Vimalāditya of the Cālukya Kingdom.[9] Hiriyanna, on the other hand, takes this king to be Chêramān Perumāl.[10]

Since the scholars thus differ from one another about which king exactly "*Āditya* of the Manu Tribe" refers to, no established theory exists yet. As a result, neither have the dates of Sarvajñātman been established. In this situation Dasgupta,[11] taking instead the argument for the dates of Śaṅkara presented by Pathak as a basis, has reckoned that the dates of Sarvajñātman are roughly 900 A.D.; but since we have now found that basis itself to be doubtful, his argument on dates has, for us, very little meaning. As I have already pointed out, however, since Sarvajñātman was a pupil of Sureśvara and, accordingly, corresponds to a grand-pupil of Śaṅkara, it can be taken that even if the dates of Śaṅkara and Sureśvara were moved back or forward, an interval of about two generations, i.e., nearly 60 years, can be placed between Sarvajñātman and Śaṅkara. This is the sole warranted conclusion.[12]

Notes

1. Sarvajñātman himself has saluted his own teacher Deveśvara in both the eighth verse and the final verse of the *Saṃkṣepa-śārīraka*, and Deveśvara is Sureśvara (*idānīṃ sākṣāt svaguruṃ Sureśvarācāryam abhipūjayanti.* —Rāmatīrtha ad v. 8). The theory which takes these two men as separate persons cannot be established. Further, see Dasgupta: *HIPh.*, Vol. II, p. 111.

2. Cf. S. V. Venkateswara: "The Date of Śaṅkarācārya", *JRAS.* (1916), p. 161.

3. R. G. Bhandarkar: *Collected Works*, II, pp. 14-15 (i.e., the Report on the Search for Sanskrit Manuscripts during the Year 1882-83).

4. *Saṃkṣepa-śārīraka*, IV, 62.
Śrī-deveśvarapādapaṅkajarajaḥsaṃparkapūtāśayaḥ/
sarvajñātmagirā'ṅkito munivaraḥ Saṃkṣepaśārīrakam/

cakre sajjanabuddhimaṇḍanam iḍam rājanyavaṃśye nṛpe
śrīmaty akṣataśāsane Manukulāditye bhuvaṃ śāsati//

5. E.g., K. T. Telang (*JBRAS.*, XVII, 1889, pp. 78-79) says that this refers to Vikramāditya I.

6. *Ind. Ant.*, XIV (1885), p. 64.

7. A. Balakrishna Pillai: "The Date of Sarvajñātman and Śaṅkarācārya," *Ind. Ant.*, L (1921), pp. 136-137.

8. *JRAS.* 1916, p. 156. Cf. "The Date of Śaṅkarācārya," *Ind. Ant.* (1914), p. 238.

9. D. R. Bhandarkar: "Can We Fix the Date of Śaṅkarācārya More Accurately?" *Ind. Ant.*, XLI (1912), p. 200.

10. *Ind. Ant.*, LV, 1926, p. 19.

11. Dasgupta: *HIPh.*, Vol. II, pp. 111-112.

12. *Saṃkṣepa-śārīraka*, IV, 14, refers to the theory of "Those who attain liberation" (*muktikovidāḥ*), and the commentary by Puruṣottamamiśra says that it refers to "The authors of *Iṣṭasiddhi*" (*Iṣṭasiddhi-kārādyaḥ*). Since the *Iṣṭasiddhi* is a work by Vimuktātman (1200 A.D.), if one were to accept this gloss, Sarvajñātman would have lived after the 13th century, as was, in fact, maintained by T. R. Chintamani (*JORM.*, Vol. III, 1929, p. 50).

However it is likely that Puruṣottamamiśra made his comment as he did because the view as to "those who attain liberation" in his text was identical with that of Vimuktātman, and it does not seem correct to conclude, on the basis of this commentary, that the *Saṃkṣepa-śārīraka* is a work of later centuries.

SECTION V. THE ARGUMENT FOR ŚAṄKARA'S DATES BASED UPON HIS RELATION WITH HINDUISM

S. V. Venkateswara, as already mentioned, reckoned from the *Śaṅkaradigvijaya* the account of the star at the time of Śaṅkara's birth and asserted that Śaṅkara lived from 805-897; and, as corroborating evidence for his demonstration, he has also tried to establish from Śaṅkara's relation with Hinduism,[1] that he lived in the ninth century. The gist of his argument is as follows:

(1) Since Śaṅkara has referred in his own works to Tirujñāna-Saṃbandha, Sundaramūrti Nāyanār, sages of the Śaiva sect, he lived after them. Now, according to the traditional theory of the Malayālam region, the latter lived c. 825 A.D.

(2) Although the Āḷvars, as for example, Śaṭagopa and Tirumaṅgai, sages of the early period of the Vaiṣṇava sect, attacked the Śaiva sect, the Sāṁkhya school and Buddhism, they referred neither to non-dualistic monism (Advaita) nor to Śaṅkara, (The Āḷvārs are of the eighth century). Nāthamuni of the 10th

century and Yāmuna of the 11th century, however, did attack the theories of Śaṅkara. It should be taken, accordingly, that Śaṅkara lived sometime in the ninth century. This was Venkateswara's thesis.

First of all, let us look at the reasons for (1). In his own work, the *Brahma-sūtra-bhāṣya*, Śaṅkara never once expounds the worship of Śiva, but refers mainly to the worship of Viṣṇu.[2] Thus if Śaṅkara praises a sage of the Śiva sect in one of his other works, the authenticity of that work becomes suspect. It is impossible, accordingly, to base dates related to Śaṅkara upon the accounts here presented.

In connection with (2), even if some cases should have been found in which some Vaiṣṇava works should have attacked the theory of non-dualistic monism, we need not necessarily take them for attacking the theories of Śaṅkara. As I shall discuss in more detail later in this section, the theory of non-dualistic monism had been vigorously promulgated prior to Śaṅkara. On the other hand, just because the Āḷvārs (usually reckoned as 12 men) did not refer to the theory of Śaṅkara, one cannot conclude that Śaṅkara was chronologically later. In the early period, the non-dualistic monistic school which was the precursor of the Śaṅkara line, and the religious movement of the Vaiṣṇava sect centering round the Āḷvārs, were two parallel streams of thought with no relation to each other. Not a few of the original Āḷvārs were of either Śūdra or of outcaste birth, and were venerated by the men of lowly station whom they taught. The non-dualistic monistic school, accordingly, which appealed to and obtained the support of the upper stratum of society, was completely different in its social and class standpoints. Therefore, though the theory of non-dualistic monism had been followed from the extremely remote past, yet since the religious movement of the Āḷvārs in the early period had absolutely no relation and no traffic with the level of society which continued to support the theory of non-dualistic monism, it did not try strongly to attack that theory. However, while the Śaṅkara school progressively gained strength those who drew spiritual life from the followers of the Āḷvārs also came to form a great brotherhood : both schools began to feel a spiritual and social pressure from each other, and it seems that Nāthamuni finally came to attack the theory of Śaṅkara.

Therefore one cannot but say that the attempt to determine the dates of Śaṅkara from his relation with the writings of Hinduism is exceptionally uncritical.

Notes

1. S. V. Venkateswara : "The Date of Śaṅkarācārya," *Ind. Ant.*, Vol. XLIV (1915), p. 164; *JRAS.* (1916), pp. 154-155.

2. [Additional note: This problem has been thoroughly discussed in my article published in "*Essays in Honour of Dr. Hakuju Ui.*"] (Tokyo : Iwanami Press, 1951), pp. 331-372.

SECTION VI. THE ARGUMENT FOR THE DATES OF ŚAṄKARA BASED UPON THE PROPER NOUNS IN THE *Brahma-sūtra-bhāṣya*

There is no room for doubt that the *Brahma-sūtra bhāṣya* of Śaṅkara is an authentic work. Since the determination of whether or not the great number of works generally ascribed to Śaṅkara are really his authentic works comes down, in the final analysis, to the problem of whether or not they were composed by the author of the *Brahma-sūtra-bhāṣya*, and because the arguments for the dates of Śaṅkara based upon other sources have all resulted in failure, it can probably be said that the only remaining way to determine the dates of Śaṅkara is by taking the proper nouns in the *Brahma-sūtra-bhāṣya* as a clue. This method was first adopted by Telang.[1]

(1) *The Theory of Telang*

In the *Brahmasūtrabhāṣya* Śaṅkara refers to large cities such as Srughna,[2] Mathurā, Pāṭaliputra etc.

"Now, supposing the Avayavī material, together, subsists in every Avayava of the material (Dravya) of the cause, one by one in a series, then it would be that while it operates in one place it could have no operation in another place. Devadatta while he is living in Srughna cannot on the same day be living in Pāṭaliputra also." (on II.1.18. vol. I, pp. 477-478. *Brahma-sūtra Śāṅkara-bhāṣya*, translated into English by V. M. Apte, Bombay: Popular Book Depot, 1960, p. 318).

"It is possible to say of a man, who, after going to Mathurā from Srughna proceeds from Mathurā to Pāṭaliputra, that he goes from Srughna to Pāṭaliputra" (On IV.2.5. vol. II, p. 505. Apte's translation, p. 817).

However the city of Pāṭaliputra had been destroyed by a flood in the middle of the eighth century A.D.,[3] and the city of Mathurā had fallen into ruins when Hsüan-tsang made a trip in India in the seventh century A.D. Therefore the date of Śaṅkara should be sought for in the period prior to these events.

Moreover, Śaṅkara refers to the coronation of King Pūrṇavarman :

"Certainly it is ordinary experience that a limitation can be attached to existent things such as fields and houses, but not so in the case of non-existent things. For by attaching some such limit as "before the coronation of Pūrṇavarman, the king was the son of a barren woman" one cannot (in fact) attach to the son of a barren woman, who is not perceptible (i.e. who is unreal), any such limit (i.e. predicate) as that he was formerly a king, or is at present a king, or will become a king" (on II. 1.18. Vol. I, p. 479).

Thus (according to Telang) Śaṅkara must have lived about the same time as King Pūrṇavarman. Now since Hsüantsang refers to King Pūrṇavarman, Śaṅkara lived prior to Hsüantsang.[4]

With the above-mentioned two passages as his most important reasons, Telang concluded that Śaṅkara lived in the latter half of the sixth century.

But this too can never be a conclusive basis for establishing the dates of Śaṅkara, because it cannot be maintained that these names refer to contemporary facts. Taking first King Pūrṇavarman, even though Śaṅkara does refer to King Pūrṇavarman, he is citing the name of a king as an example chosen at random, whose relation to the dates of Śaṅkara is quite obscure. As Pathak has pointed out,[5] exactly the same example as this one cited by Śaṅkara is cited in the *Saṃkṣepa Śārīraka*,[6] except that there King Yudhiṣṭhira is taken as the subject. But we could not say that the author Sarvajñātman was of the same period as Yudhiṣṭhira, and similarly we cannot conclude that Śaṅkara is of the same period as King Pūrṇavarman.

Again, Telang asserts that the cities Pāṭaliputra and Mathurā were not in existence in the middle of the eighth century. But evidence survives which indicates that the city of Pāṭaliputra was in existence in the end of the ninth century, as in S. V. Venkateswara's refutation of the point.[7] Again, according to the survey by Pathak,[8] scholars later than Śaṅkara, such as Vidyānanda, Vācaspatimiśra, Somadeva and Amitgati, have referred to the city of Pāṭaliputra. Thus since it turns out that Telang's thesis cannot be established, it is not accepted today by Indologists in general.

I would myself think that one should give a different interpretation to the fact that names of cities like Pāṭaliputra are referred to by Śaṅkara. The cities of Pāṭaliputra, Mathurā and Srughna were frequently employed by the orthodox Brahmin scholars from ancient time as *examples to indicate places unusually far apart.* The grammarian Patañjali, for example, says in the *Mahābhāṣya.*[9]

na khalv apy ekam anekādhikaraṇastham yugapad upalabhyate,
na hy eko Devadatto yugapat Srughne bhavati Mathurāyāṃ ca ||

And the *Sāṁkhya-sūtra* (I.28) also has the following :

na bāhyābhyantarayor uparañjyoparañjaka-bhāvo' pi, deśavyavadhānāt, Srughnastha-Pāṭaliputrasthayoriva.

In these examples, the point is the same as in those of Śaṅkara. So Srughna and Mathurā, not to mention Pātaliputra, were perhaps important cities during the time of Patañjali in *the second century B.C.*; and despite the fact that these cities later fell into decay, the citing of their names as an example to indicate two places unusually far apart was traditional among scholars of India. And even in the later period, scholars, disdaining to cite the newly arisen cities as examples, went on quoting names of cities already destroyed, and preserved only in the scholarly tradition of the orthodox Brahmins. Thus Śaṅkara also is simply reproducing the hackneyed examples originally current among the orthodox Brahmin scholars of nearly 1000 *years* prior to his time; and whether or not cities like Pāṭaliputra were actually in existence in his time was of no concern for Śaṅkara as a scholar. It must be said that the arguments of both Telang and those of the scholars who opposed him have been completely mistaken on this point in their treatment of the accounts of Śaṅkara.

We cannot but say, accordingly, that the attempt to determine the dates of Śaṅkara by relying upon the proper nouns in the *Brahma-sūtra-bhāṣya* has resulted in complete failure. At the same time, however, we have gained a valuable harvest from the failure itself. That is the fact that Śaṅkara, in commenting upon the sacred canon and upon those works whose authority is derived from them, relied as much as he could, upon examples employed in the writings of the sages from the ancient past, instead of taking the actual circumstances of his times. To mention Srughna and Mathurā as example of cities far apart is an attitude which has little relation to the time in which the author lived,—at least, insofar as he ignored the contemporary situation in which he lived, but resorted to examples mentioned in ancient classical works. This attitude is more out of the usual than mentioning "Kamakura" and "Kyoto" today. We can here find in Śaṅkara a classicist attitude which ignores the political, cultural and intellectual vicissitudes of the contemporary world, and seeks to venerate only facts of remote antiquity. And this is also at the same time a tendency prevalent throughout the whole of the Vedānta philosophy, as we shall see.

Telang has further enumerated various reasons besides the above argument to show that Śaṅkara lived in the latter half of the sixth century; but none of these are acceptable today. As corroborating evidence, Telang says that "there is the account in the work on history and biography, the *Kongudêśarājākaḷ*, in the *Mackenzie Collection*, that Śaṅkara converted Trivikramadeva Cakravartin I to Śaivaism; and since this king lived in the sixth century, Śaṅkara also lived in the sixth century"; but Taylor's researches have made it clear that this does not refer to Śaṅkara.[10] Again, he regarded the commentary (*Bhāṣya*) by Gauḍapāda on the *Sāṁkhya-sūtra* as identical with the *Suvarṇa-saptati-śāstra*; and he regarded Gauḍapāda as identical with the author of the *Māṇḍūkya-kārikā* (the teacher of the teacher of Śaṅkara); he then tried to use these as corroborative evidence in the determination of Śaṅkara's dates. But this argument, too, cannot be entirely accepted today. He further has taken as corroborative evidence the account by Mādhava in the *Śaṅkaradigvijaya* which holds that Śaṅkara lived in the same period as the six men, Bāṇa, Mayūra, Daṇḍin, etc., but, as we have already stated we cannot immediately accept the account in that work as it stands.

(2) *The Theory of D. R. Bhandarkar*

D. R. Bhandarkar, following the same idea as Telang, took it that the personal Name "Balavarman," which comes in II.4.1 and IV.3.5 of the *Brahma-sūtra-bhāṣya,* refers to a historical personage who lived at the same time as Śaṅkara, and that he may be the same person as the Balavarman which can be seen in the inscription of Govinda III (reigned 767-785) of the Rāṣṭrakūṭa Dynasty.[11] However, we see that there are only the following passages in the commentary by Śaṅkara :

"A comparison is possible only where there is similarity; for example, as in 'Balavarman is like a lion" (on II.4.1. vol.II, p. 97).

"Accordingly, even in ordinary life, guides give directions like 'You go from here to Balavarman's place. Then go to Jayasiṃha. And then go to Kṛṣṇagupta.' " (on IV.3.5. Vol. II, p. 532).

The "Balavarman" given here in these passages does not point to a historical personage, but is quoted merely at random as an example of a personal name. This is exactly as in English where "John", "Kenneth", etc. frequently appear as examples. It is conceivable that "Balavarman" was probably a common man's name in India at the time.

Thus we again have to say that the attempt to determine Śaṅkara's dates on the basis of the proper nouns in the *Brahma-sūtra-bhāṣya* has resulted in a complete failure.

In the above we have classified into six general types and examined one by one the various logical grounds which have been brought forward to determine the dates of Śaṅkara; and it has become clear that none of them can be used to reach a definite conclusion. Does it mean, then, that the inquiry is doomed to complete failure ?

One cannot but say that unfortunately in the present situation no clear determination of actual dates of the life of Śaṅkara, the year he was born, the year he finished his studies, the year he died, is possible. To state exactly what year Śaṅkara was born and what year he died may well never be possible. Be that as it may, to form a rough estimation of the dates of Śaṅkara is not impossible at all. What is the method ? Among the philosophers before and after Śaṅkara there were many whose dates are quite exactly known. Accordingly, if one could establish the temporal relation between the dates of these philosophers and Śaṅkara, the dates of Śaṅkara should themselves become clear.[12] Attempts on these lines have already been made, namely to fix the date of the writing of the *Saṃkṣepa-śārīraka* and from that to know the dates of Śaṅkara; but inasmuch as even after much debate by scholars, the date of the *Saṃkṣepa-śārīraka* could not be fixed, the attempts have resulted, in the last analysis, in failure. We shall now again bring forward certain grounds, and discuss this problem thoroughly. At the same time, this research will establish also the dates of the philosophers related to Śaṅkara.

Notes

1. K. T. Telang : "The Date of Śaṅkarācārya," *Ind. Ant.*, XIII (1884), p. 95 ff.

2. Srughna is frequently referred to in the *Mahābhāṣya*. It has been said that Srughna is either the Sehranpour or the Sugh of today (A. Weber: *Indische Studien*, XIII, pp. 378, 377, Anm., 3).

3. The vicissitudes as well as the destruction of the city of Pāṭaliputra have been discussed in details in K.T. Telang: *Mudrārākṣasa by Viśākhadatta* (*BSS.*, XXVII), Introd., p. 22 ff.

4. Telang has repeatedly discussed this in detail in his articles, "Pūrṇavarman and Śaṅkarācārya" (*JBRAS.*, XVII, 1889, p. 63 ff).

5. Pathak, *JBRAS.*, 1894, p. 236.

6. *Viśeṣaṇānām asati pravṛttir na dṛśyate kvāpi na yujyate ca,*
Yudhiṣṭhirāt prāg abhavan narendro vandhyāsutaḥ sūra itīha yadvat.
—*Saṃkṣepa-śārīraka*, III. 200.

7. *JRAS.* (1916), p. 153.

8. Pathak, *JBRAS.* (1894)., p. 235.

9. *Mahābhāṣya*, on I.2.64, under Vārttika 48 (p. 244).

10. According to T. R. Chintamani: "The Date of Śrī Śaṅkarācārya and Some of His Predecessors, " *JORM.*

11. D. R. Bhandarkar: "Can We Fix the Date of Śaṅkarācārya More Accurately ?" (*Ind. Ant.*, XLI, 1912, p. 200). Cf. R. Narasimhachar, "Śaṅkarācārya and Balavarmā," *Ind. Ant.*, XLII (1913), pp. 53-55, for criticism of this.

12. The previously mentioned essay by Chintamani has the same plan and discussion as my own which follows. Among the materials presented in his essay, only those which are incontrovertible have been used below.

B. The Determination of the Dates of Śaṅkara and Contemporary Philosophers

In order to determine roughly the dates of Śaṅkara by the method which I have mentioned above, we must establish properly earlier and later limits. I shall therefore first of all consider the lower limits of that period.

SECTION I. THE RELATION BETWEEN ŚAṄKARA AND THE PHILOSOPHERS AFTER HIM

(1) *The Relation between Śaṅkara and the Dates of Vācaspati-miśra and Bhāskara*

For the later limits of the period of the life of Śaṅkara, we must first consider the dates of Vācaspati-miśra. A great and erudite scholar of his generation, Vācaspati-miśra wrote commentaries on the important works of all the philosophical schools; and in the field of Vedānta learning also he has written a commentary, the *Bhāmatī*, on the complete *Brahma-sūtra-bhāṣya* of Śaṅkara. This, which is a sub-commentary upon Śaṅkara's own commentary *from beginning to end*, is the oldest of the extant sub-commentaries. There is no doubt, therefore, that Śaṅkara lived prior to Vācaspati-miśra. What then were the dates of Vācaspati-miśra ? And how much further back from them must be traced the dates of Śaṅkara ? That is now the problem.

According to what Vācaspati-miśra has recorded in the verse in the end of his own work, the *Nyāyasūcīnibandha*, he could have written this work in 841 A.D.[1] This date is exceedingly important as one of the fixed points by which to determine the dates of several personalities in the history of Indian Philosophy of the middle ages. And the accuracy of the date recorded by Vācaspati-miśra can be confirmed from other directions. In his great work, the *Nyāyamañjarī*, Jayanta-Bhaṭṭa has referred to Vācaspati-miśra. Śaktisvāmin, the great-grandfather of Jayanta-Bhaṭṭa, was the prime minister of King Lalitāditya (c. 753), and furthermore, a work by his son Abhinanda, *Kādambarīkathāsāra* was extant c. 900 A.D., so that we must suppose that Jayanta-Bhaṭṭa lived c. 850-900 A.D., and that Vācaspati-miśra was somewhat prior to that.[2] Accordingly, there can be no objection to taking the year in which the *Nyāyasūcīnibandha* was written as established.

In the last verse of the *Bhāmatī* Vācaspati-miśra has enumerated the titles of his own works; and this may, for the most part, be taken as the chronological order of his works. Thus, he apparently first wrote works related to the two Mīmāṁsā, next shifted to an investigation of the Nyāya, and then wrote commentaries on works of the Sāṁkhya and Yoga, and finally composed the *Bhāmatī*.[3] In that case, the writing of the *Bhāmatī* was after the year 841, and it would not be far wrong to take it for the time being as c. 850.

Now, in his *Bhāmatī* he referred to theories in other sub-commentaries on either the *Brahma-sūtra* or Śaṅkara's *Brahma-sūtra-bhāṣya* and in not a few passages, rejected them. We see in the *Vedāntakalpataru* (a work by Amalānanda in the 13th century), which is a commentary on the *Bhāmatī*, that it says that in certain passages of the *Bhāmatī*[4] he refuted the theory of the *Pañcapādikā* of Padmapāda. Padmapāda was a direct disciple of Śaṅkara, and in his work, the *Pañcapādikā*, he has commented on only the first four sūtras of Śaṅkara's *Brahma-sūtra-bhāṣya*. May one then suppose that there was an interval of at least two generations (nearly 60 years) between the time when Vācaspati-miśra wrote the *Bhāmatī* and the period of activity of Śaṅkara ? If this supposition should be correct, the period of activity of Śaṅkara must be placed prior to 790.

Relying again upon the account of the *Vedānta-kalpataru* in the same way, we see in the *Bhāmatī* that there are refutatory passages at least at ten places, according to what I myself have checked, in which Vācaspati-miśra has rejected the views in Bhāskara's *Brahma-sūtra-bhāṣya*.[5] We see from a comparison of the wording of these passages in the *Bhāmatī* with the phrases in Bhāskara's *Brahma-sūtra-bhāṣya* that they frequently are highly congruent, and the account in the *Vedāntakalpataru*, therefore, seems to be fairly reliable, insofar as this point is concerned. In that case, Bhāskara was earlier than Vācaspati-miśra, and if one considers that there was a separation of over a generation between them, it must be said that Bhāskara was surely earlier than 820.

The dates of Bhāskara can also be further ascertained from other points. The Jain scholar Prabhācandra, in his great work the *Prameyakamalamārtaṇḍa* (a commentary on the *Parīkṣāmukha* by Māṇikyanandin), has attacked and censured the Vedānta theory of Bhāskara.[6] Prabhācandra lived c. 800, as I shall later examine. It must be said, accordingly, that Bhāskara lived earlier than that. How many years he can be moved back will be the next problem; but we see from his relation with prior scholars that since it is impossible to put him very much earlier, it can be concluded that Bhāskara was active for the most part during the period 750-800. Since Udayana, a scholar of the Nyāya school in the end of the tenth century,[7] has referred to the Vedānta philosophy of Bhāskara[8] in his work the *Nyāyakusumāñjali*, it was already well known in academic world that Bhāskara was prior to him; but judging from the above facts, it can be known that there was a separation of about 200 years between him and the period of Udayana's activity, and that in the interim the doctrines of Bhāskara had been vigorously studied in the other sects. (It was formerly accepted by the academic world in general that the date of Bhāskara was c. 900;[9] but the notion had no historical basis whatsoever, other than the fact that it had been accepted, following the argument by Pathak, that Śaṅkara lived c. 800, and Udayana, on the other hand, at the end of the tenth century, so Bhāskara's date was vaguely fixed at c. 900, just because he must have lived sometime between the other two.)

If we thus fix the dates of Bhāskara, the next problem will be his relation with Śaṅkara. Not once in his work the *Brahmasūtra-bhāṣya* has Bhāskara referred to Śaṅkara by name, but as he has often attacked the view called *māyāvāda*,[10] and has censured in places Śaṅkara's interpretation of the Sūtras,[11] Śaṅkara must have lived earlier than Bhāskara. In particular, because Yāmuna of the 11th century has recorded in his work, the *Siddhitraya*, that the scholar Śrīvatsāṅka lived between Śaṅkara and Bhāskara, the latter two cannot have been in the same period.)[12] Śaṅkara, accordingly, must be prior to 750. But I shall later examine, when this date is considered in conjunction with the upper limit of Śaṅkara's dates, it is impossible to place it much earlier than that. It can be taken that the dates of Śaṅkara are, very generally, during the period 700-750. After I have dealt with some other aspects, this will be a clear conclusion.

Notes

1. J. H. Woods : "Yoga-systems of Patañjali" (*HOS.*), 1914, p. xxiii See further, Dr. Kanakura, "Tetsujin Vācaspati-miśra," in *Shūkyo Kenkyū*, New Series, Vol. 14, no. 1, p. 64 ff; R. Garbe: *Sāṁkhya-Philosophie*," p. 88, Anm. 4. However, a difficult problem exists when the year recorded by Vācaspati-miśra is interpreted as 841 A.D. In his work, the *Sāṁkhya-tattva-kaumudī* (on 72), he has quoted three verses as *tathā ca Rājavārttikam* ..." Śrībhāratī, in his sub-commentary on the *Sāṁkhya-tattva-kaumudī*, interpreted this as "Bhojarājavārttika" (Woods: *op. cit.*, p. xxii). As this can be thought to be a work by King Bhoja (1018-1060), of Dhārā, Pathak, for example, has concluded that Vācaspati lived in the 11th century, using it as one of his grounds (*JBRAS.*, XVIII, 1894, p. 89). In that case, it would not coincide with the theory of Woods; but Garbe has resolved this contradiction by saying that it refers to King Bhoja (862-882) of a previous period, and that Vācaspati-miśra, accordingly, wrote the *Śāṁkhya-tattva-kaumudī* after 862. Woods, on the other hand, has raised doubts on the tradition that King Bhoja wrote the *Rājavārttika* (Woods: *op. cit.*, p. xxii). As might be expected, it is not clear whether or not King Bhoja did write it; but it can be supposed that, as has frequently occurred in India, the king ordered the scholars to write it, and then said it was his own work (cf. R. Garbe: *Sāṁkhya-Philosophie*², p. 91). [The date of Vācaspatimiśra has been generally admitted as c. 841-850. But recently Paul Hacker proposed his date as c. 970-980 A.D. (*Festschrift Schubring*, S. 169)]

2. Keith: *The Karma-Mīmāṃsā*, p. 15. Keith, following Satis Chandra Vidyabhusana (*History of Indian Logic*, p. 147, n. 3) has interpreted the saying of "ācārya" quoted on p. 312 of the *Nyāya-mañjarī* as the saying of "Vācaspati". Again, the publisher of the *Nyāya-mañjarī* has remarked that the saying of "ācārya" on p. 66 and p. 78 also appears in the *Nyāya-vārttikatātparyaṭikā*. Further, Keith, following the publisher, regards the verse which begins *Yenānumito...* on p. 120 as a quote of the *Bhāmatī*, but this is really a phrase in Bhartṛhari's *Vākyapadīya*, I. 34.

3. Y. Kanakura, *op. cit.*, p. 83.

4. On I.2.26, I.3.17. According to T. R. Chintamani: "The Date of Śrī Śaṅkarācārya and Some of His Predecessors," *JORM.*, III. (1929), p. 45.

5. (a) *Bhāmatī* on *BS.*, I. 1.12 (p. 119, NSP.):
na ca prāṇamayādiṣu vikārārthatvāyogāt svārthiko mayaḍ iti yuktam. *Kalpataru*, on *loc. cit.* (p. 110, *VizSS.*) Bhāskaroktam *āśaṇkyāha—na ceti.*

We see in the commentary by Bhāskara that, on the suffix *maya* as in the above word *ānandamaya*, he rejects the theory which interprets it as meaning "*vikāra*," and understands its meaning as "abundance" (*prācurya*).

(b) *Bhāmatī* on *BS.* I.3.10 (p. 218, NSP.): *ye tu* Pradhānaṃ *pūrvapakṣayitvā 'nena sūtreṇa paramātmaivākṣaram iti siddhāntayanti, tair ambarāntadhṛter ity anena kathaṃ pradhānaṃ nirākriyata iti vācyam* *Kalpataru*, on *Loc. cit.*, (p. 154, VizSS):
Bhāskarastv *asthūlam ity āder varṇeṣv aprāptaniṣedhatvānupapatter adhikaraṇam anyathayām āsa, tad anūdya dūṣayati—ye ty ity ādinā.*

That is, the problem of what "the Indestructible" (*akṣara*) expounded in *Bṛhad. Up.* II.8.8, really refers to, is taken up in *Brahma-sūtra*, I.3.1; and Bhāskara, in his commentary, presents the doubt that:

tatrāyam arthaḥ sāṃśayikaḥ, kim "akṣara"-śabdena pradhānam *ucyate, kiṃ vā brahmeti.*

and regards the theory which interprets the fundamental and original matter (primary cause, *pradhāna*) which is here called "the indestructible," as *pūrvapakṣa*. Vācaspati-miśra, accordingly, rejected the explanation of this kind. Śaṅkara's commentary, on the other hand, has:

tatra saṃśayaḥ kim akṣaraśabdena varṇa ucyate, kiṃvā parameśvara iti/

but Bhāskara has censured the way *pūrvapakṣa* is set up in Śaṅkara's commentary.

(c) *Bhāmatī* on *BS.*, I.4.22. (p. 337):

ye tu Kāśakṛtsnīyam eva matam āsthāya jīvaṃ paramātmano 'ṃśam ācakṣus, teṣāṃ katham niṣkalaṃ niṣkriyaṃ śāntam iti na śrutivirodhaḥ.

Kalpataru, on *loc. cit.* (p. 233) :

Bhāskarasya *matam anūdya dūṣayati—ye tv ity ādinā.*

There is no passage which immediately corresponds to this in the *Bhāskara-bhāṣya* on the *Brahma-sūtra*, I.4.22. However, the theory that the individual self is a part (*aṃśa*) of the supreme Self is referred to in *Brahma-sūtra*, II.3.43, and since not only has Bhāskara for the most part adequately commented upon the *Brahma-sūtra*, but also has admitted generally that his view is that of non-identity and non-difference, it can therefore be said that words of the *Kalpataru* correspond to the thought of Bhāskara. On this fragment, see further the present work, Vol. II, Part II, Chap. I, Sec. 2, "Kāśakṛtsna."

(d) Bhāmatī on BS. II.3.9 (p. 513):

nanu 'nu cāsya kaścij janitā *'ity ātmanaḥ sato 'kāraṇatvaśruteḥ katham utpattyāśaṅkā.*

Kalpataru on *loc. cit.*, (p. 312):

Bhāskaroktaṃ *dūṣaṇaṃ śaṅkitvā bhāṣyam avatārayati—nanu ity ādinā.*

We see in the commentary by Bhāskara that in this *Sūtra* II.3.9, he first rejects the theory of *pūrvapakṣa* in:

śabdasparśādīnāṃ guṇānām upacitāpacitānāṃ dikkālasaṃkhyāparimāṇādīnāṃ cotpattyaśravaṇān nityatvam iti.

This theory of pūrvapakṣa refers to that of Bhāskara, since Bhāskara has argued afterwards that :

ye punaḥ sato brahmaṇaḥ .utpattim āśaṅkā-nirākaraṇārthaṃ sūtraṃ varṇayanti, teṣāṃ nirarthakaṃ sūtraṃ, āśaṅkya—hetvabhāvāt,
"sa kāraṇaṃ karaṇādhipādhipo na cāsya kaścij janitā na cādhipaḥ" (Śvet. Up. VI.9) *iti mantravarṇāt.*

(e) *Bhāmatī* on *BS.* II.3.14 (p. 521): *utpattau mahābhūtānāṃ kramaḥ śruto, nāpyaye, 'pyayamātrasya śrutatvāt.*

Kalpataru on *loc. cit.*, (p. 316):

Bhāskareṇa siddhānte sthitvā annena somya śuṅgenāpo mūlam anviccha ity atra laye 'pi bhūtānāṃ kramaḥ śruta ity uktaṃ, tad ayuktam ity āha— nāpyaya iti.

This, too, is the purport of the content expounded in Bhāskara's commentary (on *BS.* II.3.14).

(f) *Bhāmatī* on *BS.* II.3.14 (p. 521) :

tatra kramabhedāpekṣāyāṃ kiṃ dṛṣṭo 'pyayakramo ghaṭādīnām mahābhūtāpyayakramaniyāmako 'stv, āho śrauta utpattikrama iti viṣaye....

Kalpataru on *loc. cit.* (p. 317):

yac ca Bhāskareṇa 'niyamaḥ pūrvapakṣa ity uktaṃ tad apy ayuktam ity āha— "tatra" iti.

This probably refers to the theory of *pūrvapakṣa* in Bhāskara's commentary. In *Bhāskara-bhāṣya*, it says the following:

bhūtānām utpattikramo 'vagataḥ pralayakramo nirūpyate. aniyamo, *niyamakāriṇaḥ śāstrasyābhāvād iti prāpte ucyate....*

(g) *Bhāmatī* on III.2.41 (p. 669) :

ye punar antaryāmivyāpārāyāḥ phalotpādanāyā nityatvaṃ sarvasādhāraṇatvam iti manyamānā Bhāṣyakārīyam adhikaraṇaṃ dūṣayām babhūvus.......

Kalpataru on *loc. cit.* (p. 390):

atra Bhāskareṇa *pralepe,—Bhāṣyakāramate 'ntaryāmivyāpāraḥ phalotpādakaḥ sa ca saṃnidhimātrarūpa iti nityaḥ sarvajīvasādhāraṇaś cāto na tasyaikaikajīvakarmabhiḥ sādhyatvam iti, tam Bhāṣyavyākhyānenānugṛhṇāti— ye punar iti.*

This may perhaps refer to the following passage in the *Commentary* by Bhāskara (III.2.41):

kecit punar antaryāmivyāpāraniyogaḥ sa phalahetur iti manyante | tad ayuktam | tadvyāpārasya nityatvāt sarvaprāṇisādhāraṇyāc *ca | na kenacid adhikāriṇā 'sau nivartyate | na hi nityasya sādhyatvam upapadyate | savyāpāro hi prayatne puruṣo niyujyate | tasmād asamīcīnam iti |*

(h) *Bhāmatī* on *BS.* III.3.29. (p. 729):

ye tu yadi puṇyam api nivartate, kimarthā tarhi gatir ity āśaṅkya sūtram avatārayanti, *gater arthavattvam ubhayathā duṣkṛtanivṛttyā. ca sukṛtanivṛttyā ca. yadi punaḥ puṇyam anuvarteta, brahmalokagatasyāpiha puṇyaphalopabhogāyāvṛttiḥ syāt. tathāc aitena pratipādyamānagatyanāvṛttiśrutivirodhaḥ tasmād duṣkṛtasyeva, sukṛtasyāpi prakṣaya" iti, taiḥ punar anāśaṅkanīyam evāśaṅkitam.*

Kalpataru, on *loc. cit.* (p. 441):

Bhāskaramatam āha—ye tv iti.

The passage quoted here is almost exactly the same as that in the text of Bhāskara.

yadi puṇyam api nivartate, kimarthā gatir ity āśaṅkyocyate. gater arthavattvam ubhayathā. duṣkṛtanivṛttyā sukṛtanivṛttyā cobhābhyāṃ prakārābhyām. yadi puṇyam anuvarteta, tatphalaṃ anubhūyāvṛttiḥ syāt tataś ca etena mārgeṇa pratipadyamānā imaṃ mānavam āvartaṃ nāvartanta' ity anāvṛttiśruter virodhaḥ syāt. anena pathā gatasyānāvṛttiḥ, aṇuḥ panthā vitataḥ purāṇaḥ tenaiti brahmavit tejasaḥ puṇyakṛc ca' iti vidyākarmākṣiptā gatir viśiṣṭadeśaprāptaye yujyate. (*Bhāskara* on III.3.29, p. 186)

(i) *Bhāmatī* on *BS.* III.4.26 (p. 802):
tasmād yathaiva śamadamādayo yāvajjīvam anuvartante evam āśrama-karmāpy ity asamīkṣitābhidhānam.
Kalpataru on *loc. cit.* (p. 494):
Bhāskaroktam apavadati— tasmād iti.
Kalpataruparimala on *loc. cit.* (*Viz SS.*, p. 654):
vidyāvividiṣayor iva mokṣasyāpi pratibandhakāni karmāṇi santi. tannirāsārtham śamādivat karmaṇām anuvṛttir iti śaṅkā, bhidyate hṛdayagranthir ity ādiśāstrād vidyayaivāvaśiṣṭasakalakarmanivṛttir bhavatīti parihārābhiprāyaḥ.

These passages coincide perfectly with
tasmād yathaiva śamādayo yāvajjīvam anuvartante viduṣām apavargaprāptaye tathāśrama-karmāṇīti nāntarāle parityāgaḥ.
in Bhāskara's *Commentary* (on III.4.26, p. 207),
Bhāskara goes on to refute the theory of Śaṅkara:
yat punaḥ kaiścid ucyate—putraiṣaṇāyāś ca vittaiṣaṇāyāś ca lokaiṣaṇāyāś ca vyuttyāgāya bhikṣācaryaṃ carantīti sarvakarmatyāgavādinī śrutir iti, tad asat.

(j) *Bhāmatī* on *BS.* IV. 3.8. (p. 880):
aprāmāṇikānāṃ bahupralāpāḥ sarvagatasya dravyasya guṇāḥ sarvagatā eva caitanyānandādayaś ca guṇinaḥ paramātmano bhedābhedavanto guṇā ity ādayo dūṣaṇāyānubhāṣyamāṇā apy aprāmāṇikatvaṃ āvahanty asmākam ity upekṣitāḥ.
Kalpataru on *loc. cit.* (p. 514):
atra Bhāskaraḥ pralalāpa. yadi nirguṇāyāṃ vidyāyaṃ gatir anupapannā tarhi sā saguṇāsv apy anupapannaiva. saguṇasyāpi brahmaṇaḥ tadguṇānāṃ ca jñānādīnām ākāśaśabdayor iva vyāpitvād upāsakānām apīhaiva tadbhāvam āpannānāṃ tatprāptau gatyanapekṣatvāt. tatra śrutivaśād-yadi gatiḥ tarhi nirguṇavidyāyāṃ kiṃ na syāt paraprakaraṇe 'pi Muṇḍakādau sūryadvāreṇa te virajāḥ prayānti" (Muṇḍ. I.2.11) *ityādibhir gatyāmnānāt. aṅgīkṛtya ca nirguṇavidyām idam uktam. na tu nirguṇaṃ vastv asti yadvidyā nirguṇā syād. jñānādibhir guṇair brahmāpi bhinnābhinnaṃ saguṇam evety ādi. tatrāha—aprāmāṇikānāṃ bahupralāpā iti.*

Bhāskara, in the *Sūtra* IV.3.13 (14, according to Śaṅkara), refutes the view of Śaṅkara which asserts that "Progress towards the Brahman cannot arise in the man who knows the Nirguṇa Brahman," and there exists a sentence in this passages which nearly agrees with the wording of the *Kalpataru.*

yadi nirguṇāyāṃ gatir anupapannā saguṇāsv api samānā 'nupapattiḥ. tatrāpi brahmaivopāsyate. sarvagatasya ye guṇās sarvagatā eva. yathākāśasya śabdaḥ paramahattvam. ....na nirguṇaṃ vastu vidyate. ....ata eva sarvaśaktitvaṃ. sṛṣṭikartṛtvam ity ete guṇāḥ parasyāsādhāraṇāḥ na kena cit pratiṣeddhuṃ śakyante. guṇakṛtaṃ vā nānātvaṃ ca darśitam. tac cāsmākam na doṣāya, pratyutālaṃkāro, bhinnābhinnātmakavasturūpāvagamāt. ataḥ saguṇabrahmavido 'pi gatir anupapannā, tadbhāvāpatteḥ. ...Muṇḍake ca—sūryadvāreṇa te virajāḥ prayānti (*Muṇḍ* I.2.11) *iti.*

In addition to this, there is further

yathāhuḥ—kāryarūpeṇa nānātvam abhedaḥ kāraṇātmanā.
hemātmanā yathābhedaḥ kuṇḍalādyātmanā bhidā.

in the *Bhāmatī* (on I.1.4. p. 73); and since the above verse has come out in Bhāskara's *Commentary* (p. 18), Chintamani (*JORM*, 1929) holds that it is a quote from Bhāskara; but, as Professor Belvalkar has pointed out, (*Lectures*, p. 215), since it is a *saṅgrahaśloka* quoted from a work prior to Bhāskara, one cannot immediately conclude that the *Bhāmatī* has quoted from Bhāskara's commentary.

6. Cf. the present work, Vol. II, Part II, Chap. II, Sec. 3 and notes.

7. Udayana has clearly recorded in another of his works, the *Lakṣaṇāvalī*, that this work was completed in the year 906 of the Śaka Era (984 A.D.).

8. Aufrecht CC. I, p. 793. See further, Y. Kanakura, "Vedānta no ichi-iryū, toku ni Bhāskara ni tsuite," in the journal *Shisō*, May 1928, p. 160.

9. Farquhar: *Outline*, pp. 221-222, 368.
Dasgupta, *HIPh.*, Vol. III, p. 3.

10. Cf. the present work, Part I, Chap. III, Sec. 4.

11. Cf. the present work, Vol II, Part IV, Chap. II, "Additional Remarks," Sect. 2.

12. *Siddhitraya*, p. 5. Cf. the present work, Part V, Chap. I.
Further, in the *Śaṅkaravijaya*, XV. 80, a work handed down as one by Mādhava, it is explained that Śaṅkara lived at the same time as Bhaṭṭa Bhāskara; but as might well happen, if these two men belonged to nearly the same period, as seen from a later period greatly removed in time, this legend was probably formulated in later centuries.

(2) *The Relation between the Dates of Sureśvara and Śaṅkara*

We shall again examine the dates of the life of Sureśvara as a standard to determine those of Śaṅkara and others. Sureśvara was a direct disciple of Śaṅkara and became the head of that school after him; not only can this fact be found in the genealogies or legends of the tradition of this school; it also has been clearly recorded in his writings.[1] If one were therefore able to learn the dates of Sureśvara, he could form a general estimate of Śaṅkara's dates by tracing back from them. And it probably can be said that an assumption based upon this method is more reasonable than the argument for his dates which traces back from the date of the writing of the *Saṃkṣepa-śārīraka* of Sarvajñātman.

Now, a verse in the *Bṛhadāraṇyakopaniṣad-bhāṣya-vārttika* by Sureśvara has been quoted in the *Aṣṭasāhasrī* (a commentary on

Samantabhadra's *Āptamīmāṃsā*, i.e., the *Devāgamastotra*), by the Jain scholar Vidyānanda.

tad uktam Bṛhadāraṇyakavārttike—
ātmāpi sad idam brahma mohāt pārokṣyadūṣitam /
brahmāpi sa tathaivātmā sa dvitīyatayocyate // (sic) *iti kaścit so'pi na prekṣāvān.*[2]

This coincides with a verse (*Saṃbandha-vārttika*, st. 909. p. 247) in the *Bṛhadāraṇyakopaniṣad-bhāṣya-vārttika*. It is clear, therefore, that Sureśvara was earlier than Vidyānanda.[2a]

In order to determine the dates of Sureśvara, then, one must clarify the dates of Vidyānanda. But as Vidyānanda is referred to in the *Ādi-purāṇa* by the Jain scholar Jinasena,[3] and the *Prameyakamalamārtaṇḍa*, also by a Jain scholar Prabhācandra, was written after the *Aṣṭasāhasrī*, I shall first of all consider the dates of Jinasena and Prabhācandra.

It has been established that Jinasena wrote his *Harivaṃśa-purāṇa* in the year 705 of the Śaka Era, i.e., 783 A.D., and his *Ādi-purāṇa* in 760 of the Śaka Era, i.e., 838 A.D.[4] Since he was probably already an adult when he wrote the *Harivaṃśa-purāṇa*, he must have been born c. 760 A.D., at the latest. Accordingly, he lived from the later half of the eighth century through the early half of the ninth century. This point can also be verified from other sources. Jinasena was a man of about the same period as Amoghavarṣa I,[5] and it is said that he effected the religious conversion of this monarch; Amoghavarṣa I began his reign in 815 and was still reigning in 877.[6] These two, accordingly, were of approximately the same period, but Jinasena was probably somewhat the senior. As he was the teacher of the monarch, it is rather natural that he should have been the elder.

Since Jinasena has referred to Prabhācandra in the *Ādi-purāṇa*,[7] Prabhācandra may perhaps be regarded as his senior in the same period. In that case, Prabhācandra would have lived about c. 800 A.D.[8] Now, since Vidyānanda was a precursor to both Jinasena and Prabhācandra, he cannot but be taken as a man of the latter half of the eighth century. There is further a view which holds that Vidyānanda was a senior to Māṇikyanandin,[9] but as there is also an opposing theory to this,[10] it is quite difficult to determine which of these is true. At any rate, if one considers that Vidyānanda was a man of the later half of the eighth century, it must be thought that both Sureśvara and

Śaṅkara were prior to Vidyānanda. As I shall set forth later, however, a consideration of the chronological relations of the scholars prior to Śaṅkara will show that it is impossible to put a very great interval between Vidyānanda and Sureśvara, and one should probably therefore think that Sureśvara was a man of the middle of the eighth century and that Śaṅkara lived during the first half of the eighth century. This would agree with the dates of Śaṅkara assumed earlier by taking the dates of Vācaspati-miśra and Bhāskara as a standard.

There were formerly many scholars in the Indian academic world who, following in general the theory of Pathak, held that the dates of Śaṅkara were from 788 to 820. but if one were to adopt this view, one could not explain completely the various historical facts cited above. According to the historical facts set forth above, we must shift back the dates of Śaṅkara's life to nearly a century earlier than the prevalent view held in the academic world.[11] It is, however, impossible to shift back his dates to a period earlier than the above. The reason I shall explain in the following Section 2.

Notes

1. It is recorded in the colophon postscript to his *Bṛhad. Up. Vārttika* (p. 207, AnSS.) that he was a pupil of Śaṅkara.

2. Satis Chandra Vidyabhusana: *History of Indian Logic*, p. 187, n. 4; Pathak, *JBRAS*. (1894), p. 228. But in the latter half of the extant edition (AnSS.), it has become:

brahmāpi saṃs tathaivātmā sa dvitīyatayekṣyate.

2a. Vidyānanda referred to Sureśvara. (Nathmal Tātia, A compendium of Vidyānanda's Satyaśāsana-parīkṣā. Reprinted from *Satyaśāsana-parīkṣā*, ed. by Sri Gokulchandra Jain and published by Bhāratiya Jñāna-pīṭha, Varanasi 1964). The original texts cited in this article are not available to me, either. But, if this report is correct it will give an important clue for deciding the date of Śaṅkara.

3. Jinasena, in the *Ādi-purāṇa*, has referred to Akalaṅka, Prabhācandra, and the latter's work, *Nyāya-kumudacandrodaya*, as well as to Pātrakesari: Pātrakesari is another name for Vidyānanda. Again, the *Nyāya-kumuda-candrodaya* is a commentary written by Prabhācandra on the *Laghīyastraya* by Akalaṅka, the teacher of Prabhācandra (cf. R. G. Bhandarkar: *Coll. Works*, II, pp. 272, 280; Pathak, *op. cit.*).

4. Pathak: *op. cit.*, p. 227.

5. In a verse of the *Ādi-purāṇa*, Jinasena has referred to the *Amoghavar-*

ṣanṛpati. Again, Guṇabhadra, a Jain scholar and a pupil of Jinasena, has reported in the end of his work, the *Uttara-purāṇa*, that King Amoghavarṣa was converted by Jinasena (*Collected Works of R. G. Bhandarkar*, Vol. III, p. 94. Cf. p. 105, i.e., "Early History of the Deccan").

6. Cf. n. 5.

7. Cf. n. 3.

8. As it can be known from other grounds that Prabhācandra lived around this period, this has been accepted by scholars in general. (Winternitz: *GIL.*, II, p. 352; Farquhar: *Outline*, p. 404).

9. Pathak says that the *Parīkṣāmukha* of Māṇikyanandin has referred to Vidyānanda (*JBRAS*, 1894, pp. 219-220).

10. Satis Chandra Vidyabhusana: *History of Indian Logic*, p. 188, n. 7.

11. There exist, however, opposing views to the pushing back of Śaṅkara's dates to nearly a century earlier than the prevalent theory of the academic world hitherto. One is the theory of Muni Jinavijayaji. He has examined the works of that great scholar of Jainism, Haribhadra, and has fixed his dates at 707-775 A.D. Following this, he has also referred to the dates of Śaṅkara. According to his assertion, "Haribhadra did not refer at all to Śaṅkara, nor did he cite his theories. If Śaṅkara had lived even a hundred years prior to Haribhadra, it is incomprehensible that Haribhadra would not have referred at all to Śaṅkara or to his writings" (Muni Jinavijayaji "The Date of Haribhadrasūri," *Proc. IOC.*, Poona, Vol. I, 1920, pp. cxxiv-cxxvi. Further, it appears that he has published elsewhere a thesis on the same lines.) This view has also been adopted by other scholars (A. B. Keith: *A History of Sanskrit Literature*, Pref. pp. xxi-xxii). But his grounds are flimsy. Despite the fact that the Vedānta philosophy had already been known to Samantabhadra (c. 600), a Jain scholar, later Jain scholars frequently ignored this philosophy. (Cf. The present work, Part II, Chap. II, Sect. 3). Accordingly, it cannot be said that the Jain scholars after Śaṅkara were necessarily likely to have referred to Śaṅkara.

SECTION II. THE RELATION BETWEEN ŚAṄKARA AND THE PHILOSOPHERS PRIOR TO HIM

(1) *The Relation between Śaṅkara and Dharmakīrti*

The theories of scholars and passages from their works quoted and referred to by Śaṅkara in his voluminous works are not few, but almost all of their dates are unclear and do not have a decisive significance in the consideration of the dates of Śaṅkara's life. It is necessary, however, to note now a phrase quoted from a verse by Dharmakīrti.

In the *Upadeśasāhasrī*[1] (XVIII. 141; 142) of Śaṅkara, there are the following two verses :

anubhūteḥ kim anyasmin syāt tavāpekṣayā vada /
anubhavitarīṣṭā syāt so 'py anubhūtir eva naḥ // 141
abhinno 'pi hi buddhyātmā viparyāsitadarśanaiḥ /
grāhyagrāhakasaṃvittibhedavān iva lakṣyate. 142 //

Pathak says that these two verses quoted the words of "A Buddhist of the Vijñānavāda school" (*vijñānavādin Bauddha*),[2] but perhaps they have been recorded thus in whichever commentary he saw. Now, the latter of these two verses is clearly a quote from the *Pramāṇaviniścaya* of Dharmakīrti.[3]

In the *Upadeśasāhasrī*, again, there is the following verse (143 ab) :

bhūtir yeṣāṃ kriyā saiva kārakaṃ saiva cocyate.

But this too is a famous verse which has been quoted in various philosophical works of India.[4] It was already proposed that this verse might have been quoted from the work of Dharmakīrti[4a] and judging now from the fact that this verse is quoted in this passage after the verse of Dharmakīrti[5] this assumption has been more than ever verified. Now the majority of the works handed down as by Śaṅkara are probably spurious, but since it has been admitted by the academic world in general that the *Upadeśasāhasrī* is his genuine work,[6] the fact can accordingly be known that Śaṅkara regarded Dharmakīrti as the authority for the Vijñānavāda and studied his writings. This point can also be verified by the passages in Śaṅkara's *Brahmasūtra-bhāṣya* which attack the theories of the Vijñānavāda. The views of the Vijñānavāda referred to there do not necessarily coincide with all the Vijñānavāda views in the tradition of Asaṅga and Vasubandhu, but points which are rather close to the views of Dharmakīrti can be found.[7] The *Bhāmatī* of Vācaspati-miśra also, in its commentary on these passages, has quoted a great number of verses of Dharmakīrti. There is no doubt, therefore, that Śaṅkara was later than Dharmakīrti.

At this point the problem next is : what were the dates of Dharmakīrti ? I-tsing, in the fourth chüan of the "Records of the Buddhist Religion," cites the name of Dharmakīrti in a passage referring to the logicians Dignāga, Dharmapāla, and others, and says also that "Dharmakīrti made a further improvement in logic."[8] I-tsing reached the temple at Nālandā towards the end of 673, and perhaps stayed in the Nālandā temple for nearly ten years beginning from 674 or the following year;[9] it can be known that the fame of Dharmakīrti as a logician of that time was unusually high. On the other hand, however, since Hsüan-tsang did not refer to Dharmakīrti at all, it seems that during his stay in India, Dharmakirti's name was not yet well-known to all. Hsüan-tsang was well-versed in Buddhist logic and had so much interest in logic, that he translated into Chinese the *Nyāya-mukha* of Dignāga as well as the *Nyāya-praveśaka* of Śaṅkarasvāmin; but not only did he not translate even one of the many works of Dharmakīrti into Chinese, he also did not even mention his name. Even if one should therefore suppose that Dharmakīrti was alive during the period when Hsüan-tsang was in India, he probably had not as yet attained renown as a scholar. One can accordingly say that the active period of Dharmakīrti was during the years from 634 when Hsüan-tsang left India until 673 when I-tsing entered India.[10]

The assumption of such dates also coincides for the most part with the tradition in Tibet. Tāranātha, in his *History of Buddhism*, says that Dharmakirti was alive during the period of King Sroṅ-btsan-sgam-po.[11] Now this king was born in 617, ascended the throne in 629, married Princess Wên-ch'eng from the T'ang in 641, and, according to T'ang chronicle, passed away in 651.[12] It has accordingly been ascertained from other sources that Dharmakirti lived in the middle of the seventh century.

Further, the Tibetan tradition that Dharmakīrti was a pupil of Dharmapāla has been widely adopted by foreign scholars,[13] though this is exceedingly doubtful. Similarily, Bu-ston, in his *History of Buddhism*,[14] has taken Dharmakīrti as a pupil of Īśvarasena. Again, since Dharmapāla, considered from his relation with Hsüan-tsang, probably lived from 530-561,[15] there exists a great chronological distance between Dharmakīrti and Dharmapāla.

If one should consider in this way that the active period of Dharmakīrti was, for the most part, from 634-673 (or even extending before and after), Śaṅkara's dates must be later than that. The story has been handed down in the *History of Buddhism* by Tāranātha that when Śaṅkara and Dharmakīrti engaged in a logical dispute, the latter was by far the victor; and Śaṅkara finally threw himself into the Ganges river and died. Because of reasons I shall explain later, however, since it is impossible to regard these two as men of the same period, one must say that this amounts to no more than a fanciful story fabricated by Buddhists of later centuries. But I think we may admit that the historical fact exists at the bottom of this legend that Śaṅkara often attacked and condemned the doctrines of Dharmakīrti who had been considered the greatest Buddhist philosopher of that time.[16]

Notes

1. *Śaṅkara's Upadeśasāhasrī*, edited by Sengaku Mayeda (Tokyo: Hokuseido Press, 1973, p. 169). *Minor Works of Shankaracharya*, Poona, 1925, p. 341.

2. K. B. Pathak, *JBRAS*. XVIII, p. 94.

3. *Pramāṇavārttika* II, 354. This verse has also been quoted in *SDS*., II, 206, 207; but Louis de la Vallèe Poussin, in the footnotes in his "Le Bouddhisme d'apes les sources brahmanique," his French translation of Chapter II of *SDS*., says that it coincides with a verse in the *Pramāṇaviniścaya* (Tibetan translation) of Dharmakīrti. This verse is unusually famous in India, and has been quoted in the writings of all the schools. *Prakaraṇapañcikā*, p. 141; *Sarvasiddhānta-saṃgraha* IV, *Sāṃkhyapravacanabhāṣya* on I, 20; *Nyāyaratnākara* (on Ślokavārttika), p. 272; *Nyāyamañjarī*, p. 540.

4. The passage quoted here has been mentioned in the *Prasannapadā*, ed. by Poussin, p. 146, n. 1. Elsewhere, it has been quoted as the words of Vaināśika (Nihilist, a title by which other schools call Buddhism), in the *Tattvavaiśāradī* (on *Yogasūtra*, IV, 20), p. 195 (AnSS).

4a. Dharmakīrti's influence on Śaṅkara is noticed in *Upadeśasāhasrī*, II, 18, 14.

5. Y. Kanakura, *Tetsugaku Zasshi*, 1932, Sept., p. 97.

6. Y. Kanakura, *Vedānta Tetsugaku no Kenkyū*, pp. 306-307; S. Mayeda, "The Authenticity of the Upadeśasāhasrī ascribed to Śaṅkara" (*JAOS*. vol. 85, 1965, pp. 178-196).

7. *Ibid*., p. 221. Further, this is particularly evident in word usage. E.g., *sārūpya* (Vol. I, p. 580, 1.3); *sahopalambha* (Vol. I, p. 583, line 5). When Śaṅkara, attacking Buddhism in particular, says:

> *api ca sahopalambhaniyamād abhedo viṣayavijñānayor āpatati* (on II, 2, Vol. I, p. 580).

he has indeed relied upon a famous phrase in the *Pramāṇaviniścaya* of Dharmakīrti:

> *sahopalambhaniyamād abhedo nīla-tad-dhiyoh.*

8. *TT*. LV. 222c.

9. H. Ui. *Indo Tetsugaku Kenkyū*, V, p. 130.

10. See further, H. Ui, *Indo Tetsugaku Kenkyū*, V, pp. 481-482.

11. A Schiefner: *Tāranātha's Geschichte des Buddhismus*, pp. 184-185; Wassiljew: *Der Buddhismus*, p. 54.

12. Shūkō Tachibana in *Shūkyō Kenkyū*, N.S. vol. XI, No. 4, pp. 120 and 124; vol. XIV, No. 2, p. 124. According to the *Vaiḍūrya-dkar-po*, this king was born in A.D. 627 and married the Chinese wife in A.D. 639 (A. Csoma de Kōrōs: ***A Grammar of the Tibetan Language*, p. 183)** But according to what was told by the late Tanden Kasamatsu, Körös' conversion to the western calender was mistaken, and two years must actually be added to these dates. Again, the year of his death was 698 according to the Tibetan tradition, and 651 according to the T'ang chronicle. The intercourse between the T'ang and Tibet was fairly active at that time, and since the T'ang even went so far as to have Princess Wên-ch'eng marry into the Tibetan royal household, the death of King Sroṅbtsan-sgam-po must have been of great concern for the T'ang also. It can, accordingly, be thought that the record in the T'ang chronicle may perhaps be a certain fact. Chinese chronicles were, generally speaking, accurate with regard to mention of dates.

13. B. Bhattacharya: *Tattvasaṃgraha*, Foreword, p. LXXX; Vidyabhusana: *History of Indian Logic*, p. 306.

14. E. Obermiller: *History of Buddhism*, by Buston, Part II, p. 152.

15. H. Ui, *Indo Tetsugaku Kenkyū*, V, p. 132. (If one, however, considers that Dharmapāla, in his commentary on the *Ālambana-parīkṣā*, the *Kuan-suoyüan-lun-shih*, has referred to Dharmakīrti, as Dr. Kanakura in his *Indo Seishin Bunka no Kenkyū* has indicated, a new problem presents itself. I shall postpone this study until another day).

16. A Schiefner: *op. cit.*, p. 180.

(2) *The Dates of Kumārila in Conjunction with those of Bhartṛhari, Śāntarakṣita, Kamalaśīla, and Maṇḍanamiśra*

Kumārila's life was the exact counterpart of Śaṅkara's. In contrast to the fact that Śaṅkara has been thought to be the greatest philosopher of the Vedānta school, Kumārila has been regarded as the most powerful scholar who actually caused the rise of the Mīmāṁsā philosophy. Because he is a very important figure in the history of Indian thought, and since, if his dates could be determined, the dates of other scholars beginning with Śaṅkara could also be appropriately and clearly prescribed, I shall try to discuss thoroughly his dates in the following.

I shall first examine Kumārila's relations with scholars prior to him and determine the upper limits of his dates. Kumārila, in his work the *Tantra-vārttika*, has quoted a verse from the play *Śakuntalā* by the poet Kālidāsa.[1] As Kālidāsa has been taken as being in the period roughly from 400 to 460, or from 410 to 470, it can accordingly be said that Kumārila is later than 500 A.D. As evidence, however, which can further limit the upper range of his dates, we can cite the fact that, similarly, a verse of the *Vākyapadīya* by Bhartṛhari has been quoted in the *Tantra-vārttika*.[2] Since there can be no doubt that the *Vākyapadīya is*, as I shall discuss in detail later, an authentic work of Bhartṛhari, Kumārila is certainly posterior to Bhartṛhari. In order, therefore, to learn the approximate dates of Kumārila, one must first determine the date of Bhartṛhari.

I-tsing, in the "A Record of the Buddhist Religion," Chüan IV, has recorded in detail some points concerning Bhartṛhari, and says there that "forty years have elapsed since he discarded his human body (i.e., died)."[3] The problem here is : what period of time is the "forty years" based upon ? Calculating on the basis that I-tsing composed the "Records" in 690 or the previous year, scholars have considered that the year of Bhartṛhari's death was 650 or 651; however, since it seems more appropriate to trace back instead from the years in which I-tsing stayed in the Nālandā Temple, calculating back from the beginning period of his stay at the Nālandā Temple (around ten years from 674 or the following year), Bhartṛhari would have passed away c. 630.[4] Similarly, in a passage in the "Records," it moreover says that "he was a contemporary of Dharmapāla," and on the "Prakīrṇaka," Chap. III of the *Vākyapadīya*, it has recorded that "Next, there is the *Pi-na* (Veda), which has 3,000 verses and its commentary has 14,000 verses, the verses being composed by Bhartṛhari and the commentary being produced by the logician Dharmapāla." Since Dharmapāla, as I have already mentioned, lived c. 530-561, it can accordingly be thought that Bhartṛhari was in the period of roughly 530-630. I-tsing has reported that he was a sincere believer in Buddhism, who leaving home for the monastery, returned again to the layman's life, and having returned to the layman's life, again left home for the monastery; thus he alternated seven times between the world and the religious life. And judging from the various works which he left behind, his life was probably of considerable length.

So far was the opinion generally admitted by scholars formerly. However, according to recent studies it is likely that there is some mistake in the number of years that Bhartṛhari died forty years prior to the time when I-tsing stayed in India. As Bhartṛhari's verses are cited by Buddhist writers, we have to take his dates as being approximately 450-500 A.D.[4a]

As Bhartṛhari's dates have been roughly determined in this way, Kumārila's dates will have to be placed in the middle of the seventh century or even later.

First I shall consider the earlier limit of Kumārila's dates. Because some verses of the *Śloka-vārttika* of Kumārila have been quoted and criticized in the works of Sureśvara, Vidyānanda, Prabhācandra and others, Kumārila must be prior to these scholars.[5] However, as grounds for setting back further the earlier limit of Kumārila's dates, we can point to the fact that a great many of the verses of Kumārila's *Śloka-vārttika* have been quoted in the *Tattva-saṃgraha* by Śāntarakṣita.[6] Kumārila was therefore prior to Śāntarakṣita. We must now determine the dates of Śāntarakṣita, together with those of his pupil, Kamalaśīla, who wrote the Commentary (*Pañjikā*) on the *Tattva-saṃgraha.*

I shall consider Kamalaśīla first. His name was translated in China as Lien-hua-chieh (chiai ?), and his work, the *Kuang-shih-p'u-t'i-hsin-lun*, was translated into Chinese; since it was translated by Dānapāla (who came to China in 980) of the Sung Dynasty, I cannot doubt that he lived in the tenth century at the latest. In that case, how far back from this date can he be traced ? As the Chinese material does not give any clues, one must consequently rely upon the Tibetan tradition. According to the *History of Buddhism* by Bu-ston, which is a history of Tibet, and also to the *Dpag-bsam-ljon-bzan*, Kamalaśīla was a pupil of Śāntarakṣita and taught the Tantra for some time in the university at Nālandā; he came to Tibet at the invitation of King Khri-sroṅ-lde-btsan, and at the court of this king engaged in a logical battle and defeated a priest called Abbot Ta-ch'eng (Hva Śaṅ) who had come from China, causing the Abbot Ta-ch'eng to withdraw from Tibet.[7] Again, according to Bu-ston's *History of Buddhism*, the sects classified under the lineage of Chinese Buddhism were extinguished in Tibet at this juncture, and the thought of the Mādhyamikas alone came to be actively pursued. The Abbot Ta-ch'eng, who had been driven out, resented his being defeated in debate, and despatched four assassins who killed Kamalaśīla with their daggers. It is said that this occurred in the later years of King Khri-sroṅ-lde-bstan.[8]

The dates of King Khri-sroṅ-lde-bstan now become the problem. The chronology based upon the account in the

Vaiḍūrya dkar-po, a history of Tibet, that he was born in 728 and died in 786, has been adopted by many western scholars.[9] But Bu-ston's *History of Buddhism* has it that King Khri-sroṅ-lde-bstan died at 69 years of age, so that the traditions in Tibet are by no means in accord. His particulars also appear in the "T'u-po-chuan" (Tibetan Records section) of the *Hsin-t'ang-shu* (New T'ang Chronicles), where they are noted under the name "Ch'i-li-su-lung-la-tsan". According to this account, he was a son of Princess Chin-ch'eng (a woman of Yung-wang Shou-li and adopted daughter of Chung-tsung of the T'ang) who had married in the Tibetan royal family from the T'ang royal family; Princess Chin-ch'eng married in the Tibetan royal family in 710,[10] and King Khri-sroṅ-lde-btsan died in 755.[11] Since the *Hsin-t'ang-shu* was composed by far earlier than the histories of Tibet, and as historical accounts were accurately compiled by the Chinese, we should perhaps give preference to the account in the *Hsin-t'ang-shu*. Thus, since Kamalaśīla died during the later years of this king, it would have been roughly c. 750. The birth-year of Kamalaśīla is not clear, but at any rate, the period in which he flourished may be taken as roughly 700-750.[12]

I shall next consider Śāntarakṣita, the author of the *Tattva-saṃgraha*. He was the teacher of Kamalaśīla and at the same time his senior. His name has been translated into Tibetan as Shi-ba-ḥtsho. It has been said that he was born in the royal household of Za-hor, and it is conjectured that Za-hor may have been a region in Bengal.[13] He, too, was a scholar at the university in Nālandā, but he entered Tibet to promulgate Buddhism. According to Bu-ston's *History of Buddhism*, Śāntarakṣita went to Tibet upon the invitation of the Tibet envoy in Nepal, but because of an anti-Buddhist movement, he was sent back to Nepal for a time, and afterwards was again invited to Tibet. He laboured for the rise and spread of Buddhism and widely extended its following. He then made the prediction that "while no heretic will arise in Tibet, Buddhism will be split into two sects, and doctrinal disputes will arise between the two sects. When that happens, send for my pupil Kamalaśīla. If you do so, the doctrinal disputes will be suppressed, and Buddhism will flourish."[14] Shortly thereafter, it is said that he was kicked by a horse and died. Consequently, since he died before Kamalaśīla entered Tibet, some interval should be posed between the two events, and it may be thought that he was prior to c. 740.

Satis Chandra Vidyabhusana asserted that the year of Śāntarakṣita's death was 762,[15] and Mr. B. Bhattacharya has followed this date in his Preface to the printed text of the *Tattva-saṃgraha*.[16] The grounds for their arguments are as follows :—Śāntarakṣita received the aid of King Khri-sroṅ-ldebtsan and constructed the Sam-ye monastery patterned after the Odantapura (Odantapurī ?) monastery in Magadha. The Sam-ye monastery was the first formal monastery in Tibet and he became the first head there. The year it was constructed corresponds to 749 A.D. according to the history *Vaiḍūrya dkar-po*,[17] and as it is recorded elsewhere, in the history *Dpag-bsam ljon-bzaṅ*, that Śāntarakṣita lived for 13 years after that date, he would, accordingly, have lived until the year 762. While that may be so yet because the *Viḍūrya Dkar-po*, as well as the *Dpag-bsam ljon-bzan*, upon which this argument is based, is an historical work composed in comparatively late centuries, the fact is that it does not suffice to override the account in the *Hsin-t'ang-shu*, an older source, together with that in Bu-ston's *History of Buddhism*. Śāntarakṣita's dates, accordingly, should be said to be somewhat prior to 740, as already stated. There is, however, a difference of only ten years in any case, and to find conclusions based upon completely different sources coinciding closely is a rare occurrence in the history of Indian thought.

Facts which corroborate this conclusion further exist elsewhere. The *Tattva-saṃgraha* by Śāntarakṣita was translated into Tibetan by the Kashmirean scholar Guṇākara-śrī-bhadra in the monastery at Sam-ye; and he has said that the King of Kashmir was a contemporary of King Lalitāditya.[18] Now, King Lalitāditya fought with and defeated King Yaśovarman of Kanauj in 740 or thereabout.[19] The chronological argument can therefore be verified from this point also. It can no longer then be doubted that Śāntarakṣita was active during the first half of the eighth century.

Further, in regard to the year of Śāntarakṣita's birth, Satis Chandra, as well as B. Bhattacharya, have taken it as being prior to the year 705.[20] The reason is that in the *Dpag-bsam ljon-bzaṅ* it has been recorded that Śāntarakṣita was born during the reign of King Gopāla, the founder of the Pāla Dynasty; and since this king reigned until the year 705, the year of Śāntarakṣita's birth must have been prior to that. However, as the dates of that king also are manifestly not certain, and as there are also differing theories,[21] it is impossible to jump to such a conclusion.

Now, we have been able to make, a general estimate of the dates of Śāntarakṣita and Kamalaśīla on the basis of these considerations. If we further take it as a rough assumption that there is usually about 20 years difference of age between teacher and pupil, we can consider that the active periods of these two men were, for the most part as following :—

Śāntarakṣita :	680-740
Kamalaśīla :	700-750

We can now establish in considerable detail the earlier limit of the dates of Kumārila. Since it is a certain fact that the *Tattva-saṃgraha* was written before Śāntarakṣita entered Tibet, the *Śloka-vārttika*, accordingly, must have been studied most vigorously during the middle years of Śāntarakṣita. In that case, one can say that Kumārila could never be prior to c. 720.

The inference as to this date can be verified from other sources also. It is recorded in the beginning of the colophons of the third and sixth of the ten acts in a certain manuscript of the drama *Mālatī-Mādhava*, written by Bhavabhūti, that he was a pupil of Kumārilasvāmin.[22] Bhavabhūti was an author who received the patronage of King Yaśovarman of Kanauj in the early half of the eighth century and lived in his imperial palace.[23] Now, King Yaśovarman fought with and was defeated by King Lalitāditya of Kashmir around 740 A.D.[24] And Bhavabhūti was known by another name, Ubeyaka, and was called Umbeka in the colloquial language; Ubeyaka has been handed down in India in general as a pupil of Kumārila,[25] and his words as a commentator on the doctrines of Kumārila have been quoted in great detail in the *Tattva-saṃgraha-pañjikā* (p. 812) of Kamalaśīla. Consequently, since Ubeyaka had been known as a famous scholar in India before Kamalaśīla went into Tibet, it must be thought that he was prior to 740. Now, while it is true that Ubeyaka was a disciple of Kumārila, he however wrote a commentary on the *Bhāvanāviveka* by Maṇḍanamiśra, who was similarly a disciple of Kumārila;[26] it can be thought that Maṇḍanamiśra was a disciple of Kumārila during the latter's middle years, and Ubeyaka was his disciple during his late years. (As I shall discuss later, Maṇḍanamiśra is a different person from Sureśvara). If we should admit a chronological separation of about 20 years between these three men, and if we then compare them with the upper limit of the dates of Kumārila as mentioned before, we can draw the following conclusion concerning the approximate active periods of these three:

Kumārila :	650-700
Maṇḍanamiśra :	670-720
Bhavabhūti (Ubeyaka):	690-740

Accordingly, the established theory on the dates of Kumārila admitted in general by the academic world to the present day should be pushed back nearly one century.[27] Kumārila has been taken as a contemporary of Dharmakīrti by the Tibetan tradition; and if one regards that as being said in reference to Kumārila's middle years, there should be no objection to regarding this tradition also as a collateral source which corroborates Kumārila's dates.[28]

Notes

1. R. G. Bhandarkar : *Collected Works*, II, p. 110.

2. K. B. Pathak : "Bhartṛhari and Kumārila," *JBRAS*, XVIII (1894), p. 214 f.

3. *TT*.LIV.222c.

4. Hakuju Ui, *Indo Tetsugaku Kenkyū*, V., p. 130.

4a. Citations of Bhartṛhari's verses by Buddhist writers have been made clear. (Hajime Nakamura: Tibetan Citations of Bhartṛhari's Verses and the Problem of His Date, in *Studies in Indology and Buddhology Presented in Honour of Professor S. Yamaguchi*, Kyoto: Hozokan Publishing Co., 1955, pp. 122-136). I shall discuss the problem of his date in detail in Part V of the present work (in a forthcoming volume).

5. Belvalkar : *Lectures*, pp. 209-210.

6. Cf. the Index of Quoted Verses in the Appendix of the *Tattvasaṃgraha*.

7. *History of Buddhism* by Bu-ston, Part II, trans. from the Tibetan by E. Obermiller, Heidelberg, 1932, pp. 191 ff; *Pag Sam Jon Zang*, Part II, ed. by Sarat Chandra Das, Calcutta, 1908, contents, p. xii. See further, Satis Chandra Vidyabhusana; *History of Indian Logic*, p. 327.

About the controversy in the bSam-yas monastery an important study has been published. Paul Demiéville: *Le concile de Lhasa*. Bibliothéque de l'Institute des Hautes Études Chinoises, vol. VII, Paris 1952, I, 177, 183 etc. R. A. Stein : *Une chronique ancienne bSam-yas : sBa-bẓed* (Textes et Documents 1). Paris, 1961, 108 pp. (Publications de l'Institut des Hautes Études Chinoises) Publisher : Adrien-Maisonneuve, 11, rue Saint-Sulpice (Paris VIe)

Detailed sources are found in the following work : Lokesh Chandra : *Mkhas-paḥi dgaḥ-ston.* New Delhi, 1962. 78pp. (Śata-piṭaka series, Indo-Asian literatures, Vol. 9(4), Publisher : International Academy of Indian Culture, J22 Hauz Khas Enclave, New Delhi 16).

8. E. Obermiller: *op. cit.*, Part II., pp. 195-196.

9. A Csoma de Körös: *A Grammar of the Tibetan Language*, p. 183. As has been pointed out already by scholars, however, the conversion to the western calendar by Csoma was mistaken, and one must actually add two years to the figures recorded by Csoma.

10. E. Obermiller: *op. cit.*, p. 196.

11. *Chiu-t'ang-shu*, Chüan 146a. Section of Tibet in "The New Tang Chronicles", vol. 216a.

12. My proposed date for Kamalaśīla has been criticized by Western scholars such as G. Tucci and others, as being too early. P. Demieville's proposal about the date of Kamalaśīla was admitted by Giuseppe Tucci (*East and West*, VIII, n.1. April 1957, p. 109). Morichini suggests emending my proposal by making the date of Śāntarakṣita as 725-785, and the date of Kamalaśīla as 745-795. (*East and West*, vol. 11.1, March 1960, pp. 34ff.) But P. Demieville's studies upon which many Western scholars base themselves are criticized by Shozan Yanagita (*Tsukamoto Commemoration Volume*, p. 882), according to whom the date of Kamalaśīla should be placed in about 750 A.D. Examining Tibetan and Chinese sources in detail, Rev. Shuko Tachibana supports my theory on his date. (*Journal of Indian and Buddhist Studies*, vol. XVI, No. 2, pp. 491-492; 496).

13. B. Bhattacharya: *Tattva-saṃgraha*, Foreword, p. xii.

14. E. Obermiller: *op. cit.*, pp. 187-191.

15. *History of Indian Logic*, p. 323.

16. B. Bhattacharya; *ibid.*, p. xvi.

17. Csoma de Körös: *op. cit.*, p. 183.

18. Satis Chandra Vidyabhusana: *op. cit.*, p. 324.

19. V. A. Smith: *Oxford History of India*, p. 182.

20. Satis Chandra Vidyabhusana: *op. cit.*, p. 323; B. Bhattacharya: *op. cit.*, p. xiv. See further, A. Schiefner : *Tāranātha*, p. 204, on the relation between Śāntarakṣita and King Gopāla.

21. E.g., Smith has pointed out that King Gopāla was elected king of Bengal around 750 (V. A. Smith: *op. cit.*, p. 185).

22. K. B. Pathak, *JBRAS.*, XVIII (1894), p. 88; R. G. Bhandarkar: *Collected Works*, pp. 424-425 (i.e. Preface to the second edition of the *Mālatī-Mādhava*).

Further, Belvalkar ("Rama's Later History," *HOS.*, XXX, Intro., pp. xli-xlii) has questioned the account which holds that Bhavabhūti was a disciple of Kumārila. However, since it is taken as a work by Uṃvekācārya in another passage of that manuscript, if one should admit that Ubeyaka was a disciple of Kumārila, there would be no need to doubt this account.

23. Winternitz: *GIL.*, III, p. 231; B. Bhattacharya: *Tattva-saṃgraha*, Foreword, pp. lxxxiii-lxxxiv; *Rājataraṅgiṇī*, IV. 144.

24. V. A. Smith: *Oxford History of India*, p. 182. Further, Duff, *The Chronology of India*, p.63, says that King Lalitāditya fought with and won a decisive victory over King Yaśovarman probably sometime between 736-747.

25. B. Bhattacharya: *op. cit.*, p. xciii; Belvalkar: *Lectures*, p. 213.

26. B. Bhattacharya: *op. cit.*, p. xciii. This Commentary by Ubeyaka has already been published. Cf. the present work, Part V, Vol. III. Chap 14.

27. The dates of Kumārila have been put at c. 788 by Dasgupta: *HIPh.*, Vol. I, p. 370; in the early half of the eighth century by Farquhar: *Outline*, p. 367; and after the year 700 by Keith: *The Karma-Mīmāṃsā*, p. 11.

28. E. Obermiller: *History of Buddhism by Bu-ston*, Part II, p. 152; A. Scheifner: *Tāranātha's Geschichte des Buddhismus*, pp. 173, 177 f.

(3) *The Determination of Śaṅkara's Dates*

By reason of the considerations in section I, I reached the conclusion that Sureśvara's dates were, at the latest, in the middle of the eighth century or perhaps earlier. It is, however, difficult to regard him as much earlier than the middle of the eighth century. For Sureśvara was posterior to Maṇḍanamiśra. That is, Sureśvara has referred to certain heretical doctrines in his *Bṛhadāraṇyakopaniṣad-bhāṣya-vārttika,* and its commentator Ānandajñāna says that these are doctrines of Maṇḍanamiśra.[1] Now the dates of Maṇḍanamiśra, as already discussed, are approximately from 670-720. In that case, since Sureśvara was posterior to that time, his dates accordingly can probably be regarded as approximately 710-770. And because Śaṅkara was moreover only one generation prior, he probably lived, roughly, 700-750.[2]

Śaṅkara, in his own works, has not cited even once the name of Kumārila, but it has already been pointed out by scholars that there are passages in Śaṅkara's works which refer to and criticize the doctrines of Kumārila.[3] If one were to interpret the dates of these two scholars in the manner discussed above, they would agree nicely with this fact also. In the *Śaṅkara-digvijaya*, said to be a work by Mādhava,[4] both men are taken as contemporaries; but it seems that perhaps insofar as these two scholars had been the two great authorities who had lived in nearly the same period, when viewed from later centuries, biographers of later centuries, emphasizing this point in particular, coined such a legend.

Further, when Sureśvara's dates are determined, it can be said that Sarvajñātman, one generation later, would be in 750-800.

Notes

1. *Bṛh. Up. Vārttika*, IV, 4, v. 796 (p. 1852 ĀnSS.).
2. My proposal to place the date of Śaṅkara in about 700-750 was admitted by L. Renou in his review of this work in Japanese (*Journal Asiatique* 1955, tome CCXLIII, fasc. 2, pp. 249-251) and by Daniel H. H. Ingalls (*Philosophy East and West*, 3, p. 292, n. 2).
3. Cf. the article noted previously by Pathak; Belvalkar: *Lectures*, p. 209.
4. *Śaṅkara-digvijaya* (*ĀnSS*. 22), VII, pp. 61 ff (p. 277), 106 ff. (p. 290).

SECTION III : CONCLUDING REMARKS

In order to determine the dates of Śaṅkara in the foregoing, I have considered in addition the dates of scholars closely related to him : a summary of the results would be roughly as follows :

1. Scholars of the Vedānta School

Bhartṛhari	450-500
Maṇḍanamiśra	670-720
Śaṅkara	700-750
Sureśvara	720-770
Padmapāda	720-770
Bhāskara	750-800
Sarvajñātman	750-800
Vācaspatimiśra	—841—

2. Scholars Outside the Vedānta School

Dharmapāla	530-561
Dharmakīrti	—634-673—
Śāntarakṣita	680-740
Kamalaśīla	700-750
Kumārila	650-700
Bhavabhūti (Ubeyaka)	690-740
Vidyānanda	750-800
Prabhācandra	—800—
Jinasena	—783-838—

Conclusion

By the considerations in Chapter II above, we can conclude the following :

1. The Old Upaniṣads of the early period had already been formulated in substance before Gautama (the Buddha); and shortly thereafter, they came to be looked upon as part of the sacred canon having a particular significance as the Vedānta.

2. The Old Upaniṣads of both the middle and late periods were composed in the period after Gautama; and a great number of New Upaniṣads were, moreover, produced after the Christian Era.

3. The Vedānta school, in its original form, had been formulated already after the early period Upaniṣads had been once completed.

4. Śaṅkara was active during the early half of the eighth century.

5. Accordingly, when one treats the early period Vedānta school prior to Śaṅkara, together with its philosophy, it must be said that its span covers almost 1000 years.

I have clarified above in Chapter II the significance of the "Early Period" in the expression "Early Period Vedānta Philosophy"; in Chapter III which follows, I shall next explain in detail what the "Vedānta Philosophy" is.

In recent years also studies on the date of Śaṅkara have been advanced little by little. According to what I have been told by B. K. Motilal, J. Vorenne's study on the *Mahānārāyaṇa-Upaniṣad*, P. B. Chakravartin's studies on pre-Sāṃkhya are helpful for the problem. In the *Adyar Library Bulletin* articles on his date have been published. But unfortunately they are not available to me. One article referring to Śaṅkara should be mentioned in this connection : Briggs, L. P. : The Genealogy and Successors of Śivāchārya. Suppression of the Great Sacerdotal Families by Sūryavarman I (*BEFEO.*, XLVI, 1, 1952, pp. 177-85).

CHAPTER III

THE SIGNIFICANCE OF THE VEDĀNTA PHILOSOPHY

SECTION I. DEFINITION OF "VEDĀNTA"

Vedānta philosophy means the learning and ideas of the groups of philosophers who not merely revered the sacred Upaniṣads and engaged themselves in interpreting those holy words, but who also pursued philosophical inquiry into their ideas, and came to formulate a number of systematized schools of thought. To set out the historical significance of the Vedānta, the most powerful of the Indian philosophies, it is first necessary to clear up the meaning of the words "Vedānta" and "Upaniṣad".

Vedānta means literally "end of the Veda" or "conclusion of the Veda" (Veda+anta). As the simple words "end" and "conclusion" have themselves different meanings, naturally the word Vedānta will correspondingly vary in meaning.

First of all there is "end of the Veda" as opposed to "beginning of the Veda". In this passage :

"The sacred syllable (*om*) uttered at the beginning of the Veda, and which is established at the end of the Veda."

Yo Vedādau svaraḥ prokto *Vedānte* ca pratiṣṭhitaḥ (*Taittirīya-Āraṇyaka* X, 10, ed. Ān SS No. 36, p. 726 = *Mahānārāyaṇa-Up.* X 8. Atharva Rec.) The word Vedānta refers simply to the end of recitation of the Veda, and it is a special case.

The word generally means "end" of the "Veda" as sacred canon, and specifically indicates the Upaniṣads. The Upaniṣads, constituting the final portion of the Veda in the full sense, as Revealed Sacred Texts (*śruti*), are called the end of the Veda.[1]

To put it in more detail : the structure of the Veda is observed to be four-fold, the "four Vedas" being Ṛg-Veda, Sāma-Veda, Yajur-Veda, and Atharva-Veda. In each Veda the Saṃhitā (main collection) makes up its main part, and in the narrow sense this is sometimes taken as the Veda. The Saṃhitās are collections of hymns, ritual formulae, and spells, and the oldest part of the Vedic corpus. In fact they are the oldest compositions in India. There are explanatory pieces appended to the

Saṃhitās, and these are normally of three kinds: Brāhmaṇas, Āraṇyakas, and Upaniṣads. However, with the separation into schools (śākhā) in the process of transmission, they came to vary a good deal. The Veda transmitted by a particular school is not necessarily completely equipped with all the three. In a particular school, the āraṇyaka may be missing. (In that case, the content of the first part of the Upaniṣad of the school corresponds in general to the missing Āraṇyaka).[2] Again, it frequently happens that the Āraṇyaka and Upaniṣad are not handed down as independent compositions but are included as a section of the Brāhmaṇa, and again it may be that the Upaniṣad is included within the Āraṇyaka.

It is observed that the Upaniṣads recognized as having been composed earliest, the Old Upaniṣads of the first period, make up the last section of a Brāhmaṇa or Āraṇyaka.

I. *Upaniṣads* of the *Ṛg-Veda*
   1. *Aitareya-Upaniṣad* (Of the Śākala School)
      Corresponds to II.4-7 of the *Aitareya-Āraṇyaka* (composed of five *Āraṇyakas*).
   2. *Kauṣītaki-Upaniṣad* (Of the Vāṣkala School)
      Also called the *Kauṣītaki-Brāhmaṇa-Upaniṣad.* Corresponds to III-VI of the *Kauṣītaki-Āraṇyaka* (also called by another name, *Śāṅkhāyana-Āraṇyaka.* Composed of 15 Adhyāyas).

II. Upaniṣads of the *Sāma-Veda*
   3. *Chāndogya-Upaniṣad* (Of the Kauthuma School)
      Corresponds to III-X of the *Chāndogya-Brāhmaṇa* and the *Mantra-Brāhmaṇa* (composed of 10 Adhyāyas). The content of the first Adhyāya of this Upaniṣad is particularly Āraṇyaka-like.
   4. *Kena-Upaniṣad* (Of the Jaiminīya School)
      The *Jaiminīya-Brāhmaṇa* (another name is *Talavakāra-Brāhmaṇa*) is composed of five Kāṇḍas, the fourth Kāṇḍa of which is called he *Jaiminīya-Upaniṣad-Brāhmaṇa,* which corresponds to the Āraṇyaka in other Brāhmaṇas. The *Kena-Upaniṣad* corresponds to IV.18-21 of the *Jaiminīya-Upaniṣad-Brāhmaṇa.*

III. Upaniṣads of the *Yajur-Veda*
   5. *Taittirīya-Upaniṣad* (Of the Taittirīya School)

Corresponds to VII-IX of the *Taittirīya-Āraṇyaka* (composed of 10 Prapāṭhakas).

6. *Mahānārāyaṇa-Upaniṣad* (Of the Taittirīya School) Corresponds to X of the *Taittirīya-Āraṇyaka* (composed of 10 Prapāṭhakas).
7. *Bṛhadāraṇyaka-Upaniṣad* (Of the Vājasaneya School). Although a portion of the *Śatapatha-Brāhmaṇa* of the Vājasaneya school, it has been transmitted by the Mādhyaṃdina and the Kāṇva branch of the same school, a bit differently. That is, in the *Śatapatha-Brāhmaṇa* [of the Kāṇva branch] (which is composed of 17 Kāṇḍas) this Upaniṣad constitutes the final chapter, i.e., the 17th Kāṇḍa,[3] whereas in the *Śatapatha-Brāhmaṇa* [of the Mādhyaṃdina branch,] (which is composed of 14 Kāṇḍas) it corresponds to X.6.4-5; XVI.4-9. (That is, the 14th Kāṇḍa in the Mādhyaṃdina version of *Śatapatha-Brāhmaṇa* became the Āraṇyaka, while the remaining two-thirds then became the Upaniṣad).
8. *Īśa-Upaniṣad* (Of the Vājasaneya School) Has become the last Adhyāya in the *Vājasaneyi-saṃhitā* (composed of 40 Adhyāyas).

There are also some other instances where a portion of a Vedic Saṃhitā has in later centuries come to be regarded as an Upaniṣad.[4] In view of the fact that these omitted Upaniṣads do not bear important significance as Upaniṣads, I shall skip discussing them here. Among these Upaniṣads, the *Mahānārāyaṇa-Upaniṣad* is a later appendage to the *Taittirīya Āraṇyaka*; the others, however, as Upaniṣads belong to the oldest strata, and as such are presumably pre-Buddhist.[5]

The above enumeration of Old Upaniṣads included in the Brāhmaṇas and Āraṇyakas shows clearly the position they occupy in the Vedic literature, and it is clear that these Upaniṣads have their place in the portion which is in fact the *end* (*anta*) of the Vedic sacred canon handed down by each branch-sect. In this sense, because of their position in the texts, the Upaniṣads were termed "the end of the Vedas", that is, the "Vedānta". Further, even among the Old Upaniṣads, there are also those which were not included within either the Brāhmaṇas or the Āraṇyakas, but were handed down as independent works. These are the *Kāṭhaka, Muṇḍaka, Praśna, Śvetāśvatara,*

Maitrāyaṇī, and *Māṇḍūkya* Upaniṣads. Among scholars in India it is generally believed, however, that since these Upaniṣads belong to their respective Vedic Schools,[6] and have been handed down together with the main collections (Saṃhitā) within these schools, they in the same way occupy a position at "the end".

Thus in India the Upaniṣads, belonging as they do to the end of the Vedic sacred canon, are universally termed the "Vedānta". However, we observe instances in the literature of the ancient period where this word was explained as meaning the *Āraṇyakas*,[7] and in some cases scholars have inferred that the word "Vedānta" may indicate the *Āraṇyakas*.[8] On the other hand, in the period when this literature was composed, as the Old Upaniṣads of the middle and late periods were themselves still in process of composition, it is likely that the Upaniṣadic sacred texts were not yet recognized as an independent group of works, but had their significance only as portions of the Āraṇyakas. I have listed above the Old Upaniṣads of the early period included in the Āraṇyakas, matching them with the Āraṇyakas of each school as transmitted to the present day, and it is clear that the Āraṇyakas either are connected with or are included in the tail-end portion of the Brāhmaṇa literature. There is accordingly sufficient reason to assert that in that period (or perhaps more accurately among a group of men of that period) prior to the completion of the Old Upaniṣads, when no special importance was yet attached to Upaniṣads as such, it was the Āraṇyakas which were broadly termed the "Vedānta".

Thus it was the Āraṇyakas that were called the Vedānta during the period when the Upaniṣads were still being composed, and it was when the Old Upaniṣads had been largely completed that the Upaniṣads came to be called the Vedānta. So what was the tail-end portion of the Vedic sacred canon at any particular period, was then regarded as the Vedānta.

The fact that they did occupy the end-portion of the Vedic Scriptural corpus in each branch-school at the same time reveals the *historical* fact that the Upaniṣadic portion was formulated later than the other portions of the Vedas (i.e. the Vedic Saṃhitās and the original Brāhmaṇas). Therefore in the historical sense also they can be called the "end of the Veda". It is for this very reason, i.e. because they occupied the position of end of the sacred Vedas, that the Āraṇyakas were originally called the Vedānta; later, as a great number of Upaniṣads were appended to the Vedas and taken as their tail-end portion, the generic term "Vedānta" came to be applied chiefly to the Upaniṣads. However, to the Indian people of ancient times and of the middle ages, for whom the Vedas, the eternal and indestructible sacred canon of divine revelation, were not of human origin, no concept of historical development had any meaning. It can be taken that the Indian people of a given time, in using the word "Vedānta" were conscious only of the fact that the Vedānta was simply what comprised the final portion of the Vedic sacred canon.

Besides this meaning, however, the word was also used in the sense of "the ultimate meaning of the Vedas" or "the secret principle of the Veda". In these cases there is no connection with the meaning of "final portion of the Vedic sacred canon", but "end" (*anta*) is taken in the sense of "deepest meaning" "ultimate purport" or "secret principle".[9] In the Mahābhārata epic, for example, there is a curse uttered to vanquish an enemy, and it is called "the practice of overcoming as the ultimate purport of the Veda" (*Vedāntasādhana*).[10] Similarly, in early Buddhism one who has completed his spiritual practice (Tathāgata, thus-gone) was called "an adept in the Veda" (*Vedagū*),[11] and was also entitled "he who has attained the ultimate meaning of the Veda" (*Vedāntagū*).[12] In the same way, according to the Vedānta doctrine as was revealed by Bhavya (c. 490-570 A.D.), "Vedānta" is "the attainment of the ultimate in knowledge."[13] Again, Madhva, who advocated a dualistic Vedānta philosophy in later centuries, asserted in his interpretation of the word "Vedānta" in the *Brahma-Sūtra* III.3.1. that it should be understood in the sense of "the settled doctrine of the Veda" (*Vedavinirṇaya*) and should be understood as including not only the Upaniṣads but also the various main collections (Saṃhitās).[14]

Interpretation of "Vedānta" as "the ultimate meaning of the Veda" or "the secret principle of the Veda" is not the same as the previously mentioned interpretation as "the end portion of the Vedas, and the two would presumably be completely different and separate interpretations. In India, however, the two senses were assimilated without the sense of conflict into the one word "Vedānta". That is, the Upaniṣads were understood simultaneously as forming the final portions of the Vedic sacred canon as well as expounding the ultimate meaning of the Veda.

I believe the process was something like this. The Upaniṣads in particular (though the same thing could be said of the Āraṇyakas also) were the parts of the Vedic corpus which were composed at the latest times historically, and were also new in the content of their thinking, and so when each sub-sect came to make its own compilation of the Veda these were naturally inserted at the end. If we put in simple terms, the historical process of a composition of these newer parts of the Veda, we can say that there came a time when the simple and primitive world outlook which appears in the earliest compositions of Indian history, the Vedic hymns and their explanatory texts the Brāhmaṇas, could not satisfy intellectual people generally, and then some thinkers sought after some centre the myriad phenomena or some ultimate principle, or they began to take the rituals ordained in the Veda in a new sense, or came to declare something more important than rituals. When these various new ideas were brought together and edited, they were added on to the already existing Vedic texts, and so the Āraṇyakas and then the Upaniṣads came about. Thus the thinkers who propounded the ideas thus put out could not be satisfied with the general content of the Veda as it stood, but were seeking for some *ultimate meaning* in the Vedic texts.[15] While taking it that the Vedic texts in general did teach truth, yet they had a new idea which transcended it. This is why the Āraṇyakas and Upaniṣads, while they are the "end of the Veda" both in the structure of the Veda in the various sub-sects, and from the point of view of development of ideas, are also collections of various doctrines which claim to expose an ultimate meaning in the Veda.

Looking closely at the history of the ideas, one can easily see how the one word "Vedānta"—as "the end of the Veda"—came to mean both the concluding portion of the Vedas and also the ultimate meaning or ultimate truth of the Vedas, without any sense of conflict between the two interpretations. This dual meaning of Vedānta was a commonplace among Indians in later centuries.[16] It would seem then that these two meanings are a full explication of the word Vedānta.

However, there has been considerable support among Indologists for another interpretation, namely, Vedānta as "the end of the Vedic study". Deussen was perhaps the first who strongly held this view.[17] In his eyes, Vedānta and Upaniṣad were originally colloquial expressions among Vedic students which later were adopted as literary terms. Vedānta originally meant "the termination of the Vedic study". After students had finished the study of the mantras and brāhmaṇas, their masters taught them various secret principles.[18] The instructions on prayers for procreating children in the *Bṛhadāraṇyaka-Upaniṣad* could be given only at the end of the period of student-life. It is in the same sense that Winternitz remarks:[19]

—"We must never forget that the whole of this Vedic literature did not consist of written books, but was only transmitted by word of mouth. What we find in the individual Brāhmaṇas, therefore, and usually call "works" or "books" is nothing but the subject of instructions of various priests' schools. The subject was taught to the pupils within a certain period embracing a number of years during which the pupil had to live with and serve the teacher. The teaching of that which was the most difficult to understand, the mysteries, the mystical and philosophical doctrines, as they are contained in the Āraṇyakas and Upaniṣads, naturally fell into the *end* of this period of instruction."

This argument seems to be very reasonable, although it cannot be called an explanation of the actual origin of the word "Vedānta". It was, to be sure, probably the case that the master did not lightly expose the teaching of the ultimate truth or the mystic doctrine, but rather gave such instructions for the first time only during the final period of Vedic study. This kind of teaching system can generally be found even in the mediaeval religious orders of all countries. Still, such teachings, regarded as mystic doctrine or doctrine of ultimate truth, must have differed considerably even among those in the orthodox Brahmin tradition, according to the intellectual attainments of a particular teacher. And there is no evidence at all to prove that all Brahmins taught the Vedānta section last.[20] On this point the *Code of Manu* itself merely says "Study the Vedas both as mystic doctrine (*rahasya*) as well as ritual learning", but gives no direction in regard to the particular times when they are to be studied.[21] As the Brahmin instructor had to teach the Vedas together with their various subsidiary branches of learning, it is very doubtful whether or not he would have specially postponed instruction on the Vedānta section until the last. In the next place, before the Upaniṣads were established as a portion of the Vedic canon, could not their doctrines have been taught during the final period of study ? The supposition is fully justified and agrees with some passages in the Upaniṣads. Yet the teachings of the Upaniṣads were not imparted just during the final period of study. In fact, many of them were discussions in public halls, conversations between two intimate acquaintances, or between husband and wife. At the very beginning, when such ideas and doctrines were being formulated, no consciousness of the "Vedānta" existed among the persons concerned. So the popular term "Vedānta" must have arisen some time after these doctrines had been inserted into the concluding portion of the Vedic canon.

Alongside with the recitation of Vedic mantras, the recitation of passages of the Upaniṣads seems to have taken place as an actual practice. The *Code of Manu* (VI,83), in the section describing the life of a parivrājaka, the fourth āśrama, enjoins:

> "Let him constantly recite (those texts of) the Veda which refer to the sacrifice, (those) referring to the deities, and (those) which treat of the self (ādhyātmika) and are contained in the Vedānta (the concluding portions of the Veda, i.e. Upaniṣads)"

Winternitz[22] further contends that the Upaniṣads were called Vedānta because they were chanted as a sacred and religious duty at the *very end* of a Vedic recital. But no recitation of Upaniṣadic texts was carried out at the very end, on the occasion of the great religious rites. The religious ceremonies prescribed in the sūtras on rituals have almost no reference to the Upaniṣads. One of the obligations directed by the sūtras to be performed daily by the twice-born castes is the Brahma-yajña, which was the daily recitation from the Vedas, but there is no direction to recite the Upaniṣads at the end. In fact the content of the recitation was left to individual discretion, a few verses from the Ṛg-veda being sufficient, or something from the four Vedas or the brāhmaṇas or even the Purāṇas.[23] It cannot be said, therefore, that the recitation ended with the Upaniṣads. I believe that the definition is best confined to the two meanings presented previously.

With the firm establishment of a Vedānta tradition in later centuries, however, which followed and revered the Upaniṣads.

"Vedānta" came to mean not only the Upaniṣads but now also included the literature such as the *Bhagavad-gītā*, the *Brahma-sūtra*, and commentaries and works related to them.[24] The reference now has come to be to "the general position of the Vedānta school". In relation to the original meaning of Vedānta as explained above, this could be considered as an expanded sense, *Vedānta in the broad sense.* The term Vedānta philosophy is taken by many scholars in modern India in this last sense. That is, it indicates the philosophy of the school of Vedānta (*Vedānta-vādin*), and is thus distinguished from the philosophy of the Upaniṣads. This is now the usual practice, and I shall follow it here.

(It should be noted, however, that the broad sense of "Vedānta" arose comparatively late, and does not appear in the early period of the Vedānta school. Wherever the word "Vedānta", even in the works of Śaṅkara, it indicates chiefly the Upaniṣads, and does not refer to the Vedānta school taken as one of the six orthodox philosophical schools or to the so-called Vedānta philosophy of later times).

Notes

1. Sāyaṇa incorrectly glosses *Vedānte ca pratiṣṭhitaḥ* as *Upaniṣadi pratipādyaḥ*.

The interpretation of the word Vedānta as 'the concluding portion of the Veda' was adopted by the Sāṃkhya school also. In discussing *vidyā* it is said : *Vedānām avasāneṣu paṭhyate.*

(Comm. ad. *Yuktidīpikā*, I, 5), according to Dr. Jikido Nakada, Dr. Kane took the phrase as referring to the Advaitins.

2. E.g., the *Chāndogya-Upaniṣad*, and the *Jaiminīya-Upaniṣad-Brāhmaṇa* are instances of this kind. The contents of the beginning portions of these Upaniṣads substantially correspond to that of the Āraṇyakas.

3. When the whole is divided and numbered in 16 Kāṇḍas, this Upaniṣad corresponds to the *Kāṇvīya ŚBr*. XVI.3-8.

4. E.g., of the forty Adhyāyas of the *Vājasaneyi-Saṃhitā*, the 16th is called the *Śatarudrīya*, the first half (1-16) of the 31st, the *Puruṣa-sūkta*; the 32nd, the *Tadeva*; the beginning (1-6) of the 34th, the *Śivasaṃkalpa-Upaniṣad;* and each is treated as an independent Upaniṣad. Again, the latter half (17-22) of the 31st is called the *Uttaranārāyaṇa*, and this also has a philosophical content. Besides these, it has further been said that the three Upaniṣads, i.e. the *Chāgaleya-Up.*, the *Bāṣkalamantra-Up.*, and the *Ārṣeya-Up.*, whose original Sanskrit manuscripts were discovered during the 20th century (ed. by Adyar Library) should be reckoned among the Old Upaniṣads. Nearly all of these have been included in the Persian translation Oupnek'hat.

5. Cf. the present work, Part I, Chap. II, Sect 1, for a discussion of the dates of composition.

6.

Name of Upaniṣad	Name of Its Branch-School
Kāṭhaka	Caraka-Kaṭha (or, Cārāyaṇīya-Kaṭha) [Black Yajur-Veda]
Maitrāyaṇī	Maitrāyanīya [Black Yajur-Veda]
Śvetāśvatara	Śvetāśvatara [Black Yajur-Veda]
Muṇḍaka	Śaunaka [Atharva-Veda]
Praśna	,, ,, ,, ,,
Māṇḍūkya	,, ,, ,, ,,

7. This holds true with the *Gautama-dharma-sūtra* XIX, 121, in which "Upaniṣad" and "Vedānta" are listed alongside each other, as if the author regarded them as different. In the *Maskari-bhāṣya* there is the comment: *Upaniṣado rahasyabrāhmaṇāni/ Vedāntā Āraṇyakāni.* In one case "Vedānta" meant Upaniṣads and other sacred scriptures. (Kullūka ad *Manu* VI, 94).

8. This line occurs in the *Bhagavad-Gītā* XV 15 as the words of the god Kṛṣṇa: "I am the author of the Vedānta, and the knower of the Veda."

Vedāntakṛd Vedavid eva cāham.

The author of the *Bhagavad-Gītā* accordingly regarded the Vedānta portion as having a special significance distinct from that of the Veda in general. Śaṅkara glossed "author of the Vedānta" as "creator of the tradition of the purport of the Vedānta" (*Vedāntārthasaṃpradāyakṛd*), so he probably regarded the Upaniṣads as the Vedānta. Telang, however, asserted that Vedānta alluded to here is "the latter portion of the Vedas" and refers specifically to the Āraṇyaka (*SBE*. VIII, Intro. pp. 17-18). His reasons are: The *Bhagavad-Gītā* was composed towards the end of the period of active composition of the Upaniṣads. Little chronological separation exists between the two. As proof of this, he cites the passages in the *Bhagavad-Gītā* which are in common with many of the Old Upaniṣads. Therefore, because the Upaniṣads of that time did not have authority as independent sacred canons, it must instead be concluded that the Vedānta mentioned here refers to the Āraṇyakas. Hopkins also endorses Telang's view (*GEI*, p. 93), which seems to have sufficient grounds. The full name of the *Bhagavad-Gītā* is "The Secret doctrines sung by the Divine Lord" (*Bhagavad-Gītā Upaniṣadaḥ*), as such it professes itself to be an Upaniṣad in a certain sense. To contrast, the *Mahābhārata* (I.1.262-263) upholds that the Āraṇyakas are the essence of the Vedic sacred canon:

Bhāratasya vapur hy etat satyaṃ cāmṛtam eva ca /
navanītaṃ yathā dadhno dvipadāṃ brāhmaṇo yathā//262//
Āraṇyakaṃ ca Vedebhyaś cauṣadhibhyo 'mṛtaṃ yathā/
hradānām udadhiḥ śreṣṭho gaur variṣṭhā catuṣpadām//263//

Further, since the *Mahābhārata*. XII.351.1, ff., cites the four names, Sāṃkhya-yoga, Pāñcarātra, Vedāraṇyaka and Pāsupata as the names of existing schools, it is probable that such a school *which in particular thought highly of the Āraṇyaka section* did in fact exist at that time.

It can be thought, accordingly, that in the period during which the epics and sūtras were being produced, the Āraṇyakas, including the earliest

Upaniṣads, or sections similar to the Āraṇyakas, were called "Vedānta". (A conclusion similar to my own has already been mentioned, very briefly in Carpenter: *Theism in Mediaeval India*, p. 185).

9. Examples where *anta* is employed in the sense of "ultimate true view", or "ultimate principle" are *siddhānta, rāddhānta*, etc.

10. *MBh*. XIV.13, 15. Hopkins: *GEI*, p. 94.

11. E.g., *Suttanipāta*. vv. 459, 472.

12. E.g., *ibid*., v. 463. The commentary has interpreted it as *vedānām antaṁ catutthamaggañāṇaṁ gato*. Also *vedāntagū, Vinaya* vol. I, p. 3 Gāthā. Cf. *Udāna* 4, and 5.

13. *rig paḥi mthar phyin pa ni rig byed mthaḥ pa ste* (Tarkajvālā on *Madhyamakahṛdaya*. VIII.1.).

14. Ghate: *The Vedānta*, p. 135.

15. It has been said that the Upaniṣads (Secret Doctrine) are the essence of the Vedas. "*tasya vā etasya yajuṣo rasa evopaniṣat*." (*Śat*. Br.X.3, 5, 12).

16. In the *Muktikā-Upaniṣad* (I.9), the relation between the Vedas and the Vedānta is likened to that between sesame and sesame oil. —*tileṣu tailavad Vede Vedāntaḥ supratiṣṭhitaḥ*.

17. Deussen: *SV*. p. 3. *Anm*. 1.

18. Cf. A. Weber: *Indische Studien*, X. 128; *Chāndogya-Up*. IV.10-15.

19. Winternitz: *HIL*., I, p. 234.

20. The Böhtlingk-Roth Unabridged Dictionary interprets the Vedānta in the case of *Vedāntāvabhṛthāpluta* (*MBh*. II.53.1; VIII.90.114) as "the end of the Vedic study" (cf. s.v. "*Vedānta*" in *PW*.), but here, also, it should be interpreted as "the ultimate meaning of the Vedas" (Hopkins: *GEI*, pp. 93-94).

21. *Mānava-dharma-śāstra* II.140. Cf. the present work, Part II, Chap. III. Sec. 3. In the sūtra literature, it is further laid down that after completion of the study of the Vedas, the teacher should teach the special doctrines included in the Āraṇyakas and Upaniṣads, or special verses like the Śakvarī verses, to a student who carries out special vows (Weber: *Ind. Studien*. Vol. X p. 128). It is not directed, however, that he should be specially taught the Vedānta section of the Vedic literature last.

21' The phrase *vedāntaṃ vidhivac chrutvā* (*Manu* vi, 94) was explained by Kullūka as *upaniṣadādyarthaṃ gṛhasthāvasthāyāṃ yathoktādhyayana-dharmān gurumukhād avagamya*.

22. Winternitz: *HIL*., I, p. 234.

23. A. Hillebrandt: *Ritualliteratur*, p. 75.

24. The *Vedānta-sāra* (1) has: "Vedānta is the Upaniṣads which are the reliable authorities and the *Śārīraka-sūtra*, etc, which supplement them." What is included in this "etc." is a problem, but Rāmatīrtha interprets it as the *Bhāṣya* and so forth, and Nṛsiṃhasarasvatī as the *Bhagavad-Gītā* and so forth. Cf. *Sarvasiddhānta-saṃgraha*. I.22. Further, the following passage, too, may be regarded as an example which interprets the knowledge of the Vedānta school as the "Vedānta": —*Vedānta-Sāṃkhya-siddhānta-brahma-jñānaṃ vadāmy ahaṃ* (*Garuḍa-purāṇa, brahmayajña*. 240, quoted in Guha: *Jīvātman*, p. [12]).

SECTION II. CHARACTERISTICS OF THE VEDĀNTA

As has just been shown, the term "Vedānta" in ancient times sometimes indicated the Āraṇyakas, but later became the name employed as a generic term almost exclusively for the Upaniṣads. What then were the Āraṇyakas and Upaniṣads ? Their special character set the course for a long time of the later Vedānta philosophy and must, therefore, be regarded as extremely important, so I briefly touch on it here.

The Āraṇyakas (forest teachings) are so called because they record secret doctrines to be handed down by the teachers particularly in the forests (*araṇya*), and thus not to be taught in the villages. While their contents are mainly theological explanations of rituals similar to those in the Brāhmaṇas, yet inasmuch as they did not merely present, like the original portions of the Brāhmaṇas, directions on performance of the various forms of sacrifice, but went on into deep philosophical speculations on the significance of the religious ceremonies, they became an intermediate stepping-stone on the passage from Brāhmaṇas to Upaniṣads. Obviously, in view of the fact that almost all the Upaniṣads of the early period were included within Āraṇyakas, it is difficult to draw a precise dividing line between the contents of the Āraṇyakas and those of the Upaniṣads. And when the system of the four periods of life became firmly established as the ideal course of life for a Brahmin, the Āraṇyakas came to be taken as works to be studied by men living in retirement in the forests (i.e. those in their third period).[1]

These Āraṇyakas have some relation to the Vedānta school of later centuries, though a slight one, and the Vedānta school is based chiefly upon the Upaniṣadic canon. It is wellknown that of all the Vedic texts, the Upaniṣads include the most philosophical discussions. The word "*Upaniṣad*" is a noun formed originally by the combination of the prefixes *upa ni* and the root *sad*. Indian scholars from ancient times have also analysed and interpreted its meanings variously, and it is still the subject of vigorous discussion among modern scholars; but it has been mainly taken as meaning "sitting in attendance", "sitting nearby", and also "sitting in secret meeting".[2] That is, it originally referred to the student's sitting near the master to receive instruction; and since the corollary is that participation of others is excluded, it further implied the meaning of a secret meeting and became a concept directly opposed to that of a public meeting (*pariṣad, sampad*). Moreover, since there were verbal exchanges in the secret meetings, the word Upaniṣad is employed throughout India in the derivative sense of "secret meaning", "secret instruction" and "secret doctrine."[3] The final development was the universally accepted title of a body of literature which recorded secret doctrines (especially philosophical doctrines).

(Upaniṣad, as the title of the literature, has sometimes been translated in Japan as "the inner doctrine writings" or okugi - sho, but there is no such translation in the Chinese version of the Buddhist canon.)

As can be seen from the word itself, the basic character of an Upaniṣad is that it is a record of secret teachings given at a meeting in private, with master and disciple sitting facing each other. The Upaniṣads themselves strictly enjoin that the very secret teachings which they expound should be transmitted only to an eldest son or to a most trustworthy and able disciple, and must not be imprudently spoken of or taught to others.[4] Accordingly, even among the Brahmins, the privileged class in ancient Indian society, the Upaniṣads were transmitted in complete secrecy, particularly among the section of philosophical and intellectual culture.

It has been said that the Upaniṣads were originally works clarifying the ultimate meaning of the Vedas as the Vedānta, but the Upaniṣadic "ultimate meaning of the Vedas" was, from the viewpoint of the Vedic canon in general, clearly a new idea, and to the ordinary man of that time appeared as a new and strange teaching. Accordingy, this new idea was passed down from master to disciple in complete secrecy; it remained something whispered in private among the new thinkers, and was never disclosed to the world at large. The thought expounded in the Upaniṣads is the secret teachings which they were afraid to declare in public to the common people of the time. And the fact that these, as secret teachings, had to be kept hidden from the people in general, shows that the teachings of the Upaniṣads differed very much from the general thought of the Vedas, the religious scriptures of the Aryan race of that time.

The Upaniṣads are a collection of the various secret teachings both known to and selected by the Brahmins of the time, and their compilers were undoubtedly orthodox Brahmins devoted to the Vedas; but the expounders of the numerous doctrines in the Upaniṣads were not necessarily only Brahmins. It has frequently been pointed out by scholars that there is a conspicuous influence in them from the thought of the ruling caste of the time. Again, wives[5] and those of humble birth[6] also openly participated in the philosophical discussions quite fearlessly. No matter how lowly the birth might have been, it was accepted that one who spoke the truth had the same qualifications as Brahmins.[7] Accordingly, there are not a few ideas in the Upaniṣads, which from the viewpoint of the ancient orthodox Brahmanism, would appear unorthodox. Here the position of the new thought, revolting against the old thinking, can be found, and for that reason the Upaniṣads had indeed to be treated as a secret teaching. And when the Vedic canon was completely made up into the form extant today, such secret teachings were also compiled and appended on to the tail-end; their special character and significance, however, had already been marked out, and in later centuries they were called by the special name "Vedānta".

In what points, then, do the Upaniṣads differ from the general Vedic canon formulated prior to them ? What are the special features of the thinking of the Upaniṣads ?

Since the Upaniṣads[8] are, as already stated, the collected works of new thinking in the orthodox brahmanic line from before the appearance of the Buddha and continuing after, the currents of thoughts within them are various and manifold and cannot be completely summarized in one generalization; however, if one were to try to find a particular common feature among the various ideas in them, one could say that it is the esteem of the supreme value of knowledge. Previously, the Vedas had ordained, and discussed in detail, the main religious rites to be performed by the Aryans. In other words, they are chiefly concerned with religious behaviour (*karman*). Against this, however, the Upaniṣads regard "knowledge" as important. They say that the religious ceremonies themselves, if performed after *knowing* their true meaning, will have their effects increased and multiplied. And knowledge of the true significance of the religious ceremonies had always been emphasized in the Upaniṣads, inasmuch as it was believed by those who investigated the true significance of the religious ceremonies, that these ancient ceremonies embodied both abstractly and concretely the phenomena of the universe and humanity, and so the metaphysical significance of the universe itself and humanity itself further came to be considered. Speculation in quest of the Absolute was continued for several generations. At the beginning, certain of the items and elements related to the religious ceremonies were regarded as absolute; but finally the thinkers came to assume that the Ātman or the Brahman was the Absolute. Here the philosophy of the Upaniṣads reached its peak. If we were to *know* the Ātman or the Brahman, we could reach the absolute state of acceptance of what life brings in serenity of mind. That is liberation, and it cannot be reached by means of rituals—this was the teaching. Accordingly, all the thinkers in the Upaniṣads regarded knowledge highly, and accepted that it had supernormal mystical powers in it. They believed that unless knowledge, in some sense, controls its objects, it is nothing. And they thought that such knowledge endowed with mystical power should be retained by only a few selected individuals, and should not be transmitted to the people at large. Their regard for their own teachings as a secret doctrine and their reluctance to impart it lightly to others, came partly from the mystical nature of this knowledge. Because this view which stresses knowledge, and the usual view in the Vedas which stresses religious conduct, are mutually opposed, thinkers of later centuries divided the entire Vedic sacred canon into two: the section on rites (*Karma-kāṇḍa*), and the section on knowledge (*Jñāna-kāṇḍa* or *brahma-kāṇḍa*). The former is the section which ordains the actual practices of the rites, and expatiates on their rewards; it corresponds mainly to the Saṃhitās and Brāhmaṇas of the Vedas. The latter is the section which teaches cognition of truth, and refers to the Upaniṣads. While the Upaniṣads are contained within the Vedas, they are nevertheless very different from the thought of the Vedas in general in this point.

Thus the Upaniṣads emphasize knowledge, and cognition of the Absolute in particular, but what is this Absolute which is to be cognized ? On this point, the explanations in the various passages of the Upaniṣads are by no means in accord. In addition to the creator Prajāpati, other things related to the rituals have already been set up as the fundamental principle in the development of the world in the Brāhmaṇa literature; and in the Upaniṣads, still others have been assumed as the fundamental principle. Chief among them are the following :

1. Natural objects such as wind, water, ether, etc.[9] Although these are frequently regarded as the world-principle in the Vedic Saṃhitās, they are no more than merely mentioned in the Upaniṣads.

2. Vital force (*prāṇa*).[10] This was widely regarded in Vedic literature in general as the individual subject or the essential lifeforce of each individual existence, but also at the same time identical with the supreme principle of the myriad existences.

3. Consciousness (*vijñāna*).[11] This is a word meaning individual cognition, but is sometimes proposed as a metaphysical principle, which should be called pure spirit or absolute spirit.

4. *Puruṣa* (the primal man).[12] This word originally meant "man" or "human being", but already in the final period of the *Ṛg-Veda* it was being taken as the fundamental principle which evolves the universe. Again, it was also used in the sense of "the basic substance of the individual person" and "the spiritual self." The more importance given to "puruṣa" as a philosophical concept, the less was its personal significance though that was never altogether extinguished.

5. Being (*sat*).[13] This is particularly stressed in the metaphysics of Uddālaka Āruṇi.

6. Non-being (*asat*).[14]

7. That which is neither being nor non-being.[15]

8. The Unevolved (*avyākṛta*).[16]

9. The Inner Ruler (*antaryāmin*). So-called because it exists latently within the myriad beings and controls them.[17]

10. The Idestructible (*akṣara*).[18]

11. Presiding Deity. This is particularly stressed in the Upaniṣads *Īśa*, *Śvetāśvatara*, etc.

12. Brahman. "Brahman' meant originally the hymns, sacrificial adresses and incantations of the Vedas and, further, the mystical power latent in them, but it finally was taken among the Brahmins who respected the Vedic rituals, as the usual term for the fundamental principle of the world. The word in time lost its original meaning in the Vedānta school to become a technical term used only for the Absolute itself.

13. Ātman. The word "ātman" originally meant "Breath",

but it was also employed derivatively in the sense of "vital force", "body", and further became a word meaning "one's self". As a philosophical concept, it was taken as a technical term meaning "one's ego", "one's self", and further, "soul".

Thus, each one of these many principles has been set up as the world-principle, the Absolute, in the respective passages of the Upaniṣads, where it is asserted that this evolved and brought about the formation of the phenomenal world, and perhaps also maintains and controls the entire world. Because these principles are concepts formally differing from one another, their mutual relations thereupon become a problem, already discussed in the Upaniṣads themselves. But later, in the Vedānta school, they really form a central problem of discussion. At any rate one can say that to assume a unique fundamental principle and to explain the manifold and diverse aspects of the phenomenal world as based upon that principle, is one of the common characteristics of the thought of the Upaniṣads.

These characteristics of thought were inherited by the later Vedānta philosophy, and formed its central topics. And because of differences in opinion on these problems, the various sub-schools within the Vedānta school came to be set up independently in later centuries.

In connection with the differences of opinions on metaphysical problems, it must further be sufficiently noted that there were also differences about practice among the Upaniṣadic philosophers themselves. Among the men who gave instructions on the knowledge of the Absolute, there were, as already mentioned, kings, nobles, and warriors, and alongside them were also those who had come from lowly classes. But the doctrines in the Upaniṣads were set forth and also compiled by the Brahmins chiefly. Even from *the viewpoint of class*, accordingly, those expounders were of varying status. And their actual ways of life were not necessarily similar. The kings and nobles perhaps lived in magnificent castles or mansions, employed many retainers, and may have indulged in a sumptuous life. On the other hand, there were some sages like Raikva, who lived as a wanderer, and suffering from a skin disease. The lives of even the Brahmins who appear in the Upaniṣads were not always similar. Some lived in colossal mansions, maintained many disciples, and instructed on the Vedas, always carrying out the rituals. They married, led a family life, and had wife and children. That is to say, while continuing a life as "head of the house" (*gṛhastha*),[19] they sought after the truth of Ātman, and also instructed others about it. Occasionally, they also became the teachers of kings and nobles. As against these, however, there were also many Brahmins who extolled the life of a wandering mendicant. They renounced their families, severed relations with their wives, relinquished all property, position, and fame, became penniless and propertyless, and plunged into a life of seclusion, becoming friends with the passing clouds and running waters, or wandering.[20] They thought that only in such a life could they actually realize the Ātman. Here one can find remarkable differences in practical life. For example, even supposing the standpoint after one has finished the period as a householder, that one enters on the life of a recluse or a wanderer, it is difficult to find any way to reconcile the concept of practice, which stresses the former, with the concept of practice, which gives absolute significance to the latter.

The Upaniṣads have recorded intact the variances of opinion on the problems of practice, but have not given any conclusion at all. The attempts to come to a conclusion about them later brought about the formulation of many diverse theories on practice within the Vedānta school itself.

Notes

1. Winternitz: *HIL.*, I, p. 234, n.1.
2. Several theories are briefly introduced in Arthur Anthony Macdonell and Arthur Berriedale Keith: *Vedic Index of Names and Subjects* (Delhi etc.: Motilal Banarsidass, 1958), pp. 91-92.
3. Examples in which the word "Upaniṣad" is used in the sense of "a secret significance" or "a secret theory" can be found throughout the general literature of the orthodox Brahmanic line. The word "Upaniṣad" had been employed in nearly the same meaning already in the Brāhmaṇa literature (cf. Macdonell and Keith: *Vedic Index*, s.v. "Upaniṣad"); and the Upaniṣadic canon had also interpreted the word "Upaniṣad" in the same sense as *rahasya* (secret). In the Upaniṣads, phrases such as *ity upaniṣad* and *iti rahasyam*, in the sense of "the foregoing is a secret teaching", frequently appear. The Upaniṣadic canon itself has sometimes been called *rahasya* (*Manu.* II.140, 165; XI.262. Cf. the present work, Part II, Chap. III, Sect. 3.). In addition, secret formulae, secret spells, and secret directions etc. have been called *Upaniṣad* (Winternitz: *HIL.*, I, p. 244, n. 3). In the Buddhist canon, however, *upaniṣad* is employed in a completely different sense (cf. U. Wogihara: *Lexikalisches aus der Bodhisattvabhūmi*, p. 19).

4. *Chānd. Up.* III. 11, 5-6; *Bṛhad. Up.* VI.3.12; *Śvet. Up.* VI,22; *Maitri-Up.*, VI.29.

5. In the *Bṛhad. Up.* III.6, and III.8, because Gārgī, the daughter of Vacaknu, frequently asks the sage Yājñavalkya penetrating questions, he finally says "do not question too much..." Again, in the *Bṛhad. Up.* II.4. and IV.5, Yājñavalkya teaches his wife Maitreyī the philosophical knowledge related to the Ātman.

6. The intelligent Raikva was a wanderer who had been afflicted with a skiñ disease, but because he possessed metaphysical knowledge of the Absolute, he was as arrogant as a king. He was not a Brahmin, but as he possessed the knowledge of Brahman, he was titled "Brāhmaṇa." (*Chānd. Up.* IV. 1-3).

7. *Chānd. Up.* IV, 4 (the story of Satyakāma Jābāla).

8. For the time being, I shall only treat here the Old Upaniṣads.

9. In regards to the canonical grounds one by one, cf. the present work, Part II, Chap. I, Sect. 5, item 2.

10. Cf. the present work, Vol. III, Part VI, commentary note on 1.6 of the *Māṇḍūkya Kārikās.*

11. Cf. the present work, Part II, Chap. I, Sect, 2.

12. Cf. the present work, Part II, Chap. I, Sect. 5, item 2.

13. *Chānd. Up.* VI.2.2.

14. *ṚV.* X, 72, 23; X, 129, 4; *Tait. Up.* II., 7; *Chānd. Up..* III, 19, 1.

15. *Puruṣasūkta* (*ṚV.* X.129). This hymn also came to be regarded later as an independent Upaniṣad.

16. *Bṛhad. Up.* I.4.7.

17. Ibid. III, 7.

18. Ibid. III, 8.

19. When Uddālaka Āruṇi instructed his beloved son Śvetaketu in such philosophical views, he was a householder (*gṛhastha*). (*Chānd. Up.* VI.1) Yājñavalkya had two wives. He instructed his wife Maitreyī on the Ātman *before he left home for the forest.* Again, Satyakāma Jābāla was also a man in lay life (*Chānd. Up.* IV.10). Further in the *Chānd. Up.* VIII.15, a life away from home is not regarded as a necessary prerequisite in order to attain the Brahman.

20. Particularly *Bṛhad. Up.* III.5.1; IV.4.22.

SECTION III. THE CIRCUMSTANCES OF THE FORMULATION OF THE VEDĀNTA SCHOOL

Insofar as it has generally been thought that the Upaniṣads are the works which expound philosophical theories, the "philosophy of the Upaniṣads" is frequently mentioned to such an extent that if one says "Indian philosophy", Western intellectuals in particular will associate it first of all with the Upaniṣads. Again, philosophers, like Deussen who was a great admirer of the Upaniṣads, have expounded a "system" of the thought in the

Upaniṣads. However, an examination of the contents of the Upaniṣads themselves will show that they were never confined to profound philosophical doctrines. All sorts of miscellaneous ideas, injunctions, incantations, theological interpretations, conversations, traditions, and so forth, regarded at the time as secret principles or secret teachings, were assembled and set down without any sequence; and even the sections which do bear on what may be called philosophical thought are really only including that as one of the secret teachings. And since the parts which do specially expound, philosophical thinking in clear and distinct terms are made up mostly of conversations and dialogues between master and disciple, father and child, husband and wife, etc., or else records of debates held in public places, various and diverse philosophical thoughts are expounded in them; but neither is there any record of the speculations of one philosopher, nor is there any collection of the thought of philosophers belonging to a definite philosophical school founded by one person. These sections are no more than mere extracts from the various secret beliefs which many orthodox Brahmins, living over a period of several centuries after the appearance of Śākyamuni, had advocated or adopted; the dates of these thinkers, moreover, differ greatly from one another, and there are not a few cases in which the name of the advocate of a special doctrine has not been clearly recorded. And some among them were not Brahmins, but belonged either to the Kṣatriya class or to the lowest class. Instead of being caught up wholly in the traditional teaching of the Brahmins, they attempted free and independent speculations. Needless to say, therefore accordingly, the thoughts expounded in each part of the Upaniṣads differ greatly from one another.[1] They extend from naive and puerile thoughts, characteristic of primitive people, up to the highest development of philosophical thinking.

In such circumstances, no philosophical school had yet been set up, nor had any fixed doctrine been established. "The Philosophy of the Upaniṣads" is a title like "philosophy prior to Socrates" or "the system of Old Testament ideas". One can see common tendencies, characteristics and historical significances but nothing like a "system" of Upaniṣadic philosophy, is possible at all. If one tries to discover a "system", one can occasionally find some systematic explanations of a sort in the individual conversations or in individual passages out of the Upaniṣadic corpus. These systematic explanations, however, are extremely brief and were never put together in a complex detailed form. Accordingly, the "systems" in the schools of Indian philosophy or later centuries and those of modern Western philosophy are greatly different. The philosophical thought in the Upaniṣads was, after all, a philosophy in the process of formulation; and one cannot say that it is pure, logical and systematic speculation.

Since various philosophical thoughts are thus jumbled together in the Upaniṣads, it seems quite natural that there should indeed be contradictions among the various views. However, in their putting together of the Upaniṣads, the Brahmin scholars avoided any deep examination of these contradictions and differences; in each sub-school, they codified, without additions and in almost the same form, the traditionally accepted secret teachings and philosophical theories into one Upaniṣads, appended this to the last part of the Vedic sacred canon, and conferred upon it the sacred authority of divine revelation. Since the schools who were the compilers probably had already been influenced by the advanced new thought, they perhaps did not accept literally naive and primitive thoughts such as these of the oldest part of the Upaniṣads. By that time, however, this naive and primitive thinking had also been handed down as firmly established doctrine, so much so that it could no longer be completely discarded; so they retained along with the advanced new doctrines, the primitive, naive and puerile ideas as they were, and incorporated them into the sacred canon. And both went on to possess, in later periods, equal authority as sacred revelation *on the same level.*

Many Upaniṣads were compiled in this way in the various Vedic sub-schools; and when later they had to be revered and worshipped as an absolutely authoritative sacred canon of divine revelation, the thinkers of later centuries who revered the Upaniṣads were under the pressure of the need to resolve somehow the contradictions among the various ideas. If theory "A" contradicts theory "B", it is impossible to admit both at the same time. Truth must be only one. Various contradictory philosophical theories have been expounded in the Upaniṣads, but which one ought to be regarded as the teaching which expounds the ultimate truth ? One must first pick out, from among the theories in the Upaniṣads, the true teaching, which can be literally accepted. This was their first task. Yet, even if one determined the true theory in this way, further problems remain. If one were to make any one of the various doctrines of the Upaniṣads the correct theory or the true theory, how ought he to regard the other theories which contradict it ? Since the Upaniṣads are given absolute authority as sacred canon in the orthodox Brāhmaṇic teaching, it could not be allowed that some theories be regarded as true and others as false, for all the theories expounded in them have to be true. If any one of the theories were to be made the true teaching, then what is its relation to the other theories ? Again, why is it that such different and diverse teachings are expounded in the Upaniṣad canon ? The resolution and elucidation of such difficult questions became the second task of the scholars of later centuries who revered the Upaniṣads. And they came to be chiefly engaged in the unificative interpretation of the Upaniṣads.

These students of the sacred canon, as a matter of course, commented upon and explained, one after another, the words and sentences in the Upaniṣads. For them, such efforts were not a particularly difficult task. Why ? As the Brahmin scholars of that time carried out their daily conversations and writings in a Sanskrit which was almost the same as that in the Upaniṣads, they were easily able to understand the significance of the words and phrases in the Upaniṣadic works; all they had to do was to offer commentaries either on some of the obsolete words whose meaning had become unclear by that time, or on the ancient style of the grammar. Because they thus recognized that it was not usually necessary to comment upon each word and each phrase of the Upaniṣads, the scholars of the sacred canon of that time devoted most of their energies to the elucidation of the meaning of individual passages in the Upaniṣads, their connection with other passages, the similarities and differences between all the passages, and to a clear unifying interpretation of the import of the Upaniṣads as a whole. And because research in this sense formed their principal task, the motive of a unifying interpretation behind their intellectual research also influenced the interpretation of each letter and word in the sacred canon; there are not a few cases in which they came to add extremely forced and distorted interpretations on individual passages.[2] Particularly as the Upaniṣads contain various contradictory theories, and because the students of the sacred canon were under the obligation to think that all of them taught the same import, if they were to faithfully interpret and explain the import of a certain passage, they could not but give a far-fetched and strained explanation to the words of other individual passages contradicting it. For to interpret all the passages consistently along a single line and yet to accept all the teachings as they stand, is an impossibility.

Now, an interpretative study of the sacred canon in this sense is possible only where the interpreter himself holds to a particular philosophical view. The demand for a unifying interpretation of the whole body of Upaniṣads, accordingly, gave rise to consciously held distinct and personal philosophical positions among the interpreters of the sacred canon themselves. They then took as a basis certain of the thoughts expounded in various Upaniṣads, and upon them, established philosophical theories of their own, in accordance with these, they then systematized and organized the doctrines of the Upaniṣads. Thus, a Vedānta school arose as an intellectual tradition.

In this way, the men of the Vedānta school took on the task of philosophical interpretation and still more thorough-going elucidation of the various ideas expounded in the Upaniṣads; but when it came to actually carrying out the study, the philosophical position of each thinker was bound to be somewhat different. For instance, one accepted the non-duality of Brahman and Ātman expounded in the Upaniṣads as the ultimate truth, whereas another emphasized the idea of the development in Brahman itself, which is equally taught in the Upaniṣads. This is the kind of difference which appears. Accordingly, depending on the different standpoint, as to which of the various doctrines in the Upaniṣads were accepted as the fundamental truth, there arose automatically corresponding variances among the doctrines of the philosophers belonging to the Vedānta school. Still more refined sub-divisions arose in mutual opposition within the Vedānta school itself, and their protagonists engaged rigorously in lively debates. Although the academic world has hitherto held that the division of sub-schools within the Vedānta school belongs to the period after Śaṅkara, this state of affairs existed long before him. This historical fact will be one of the items investigated in the present work.

Accordingly, even though the Vedānta school followed the Upaniṣads and proclaimed their authority, it took up in regard to the Upaniṣads themselves certain *specific philosophical positions*, so that certain of the various ideas expounded there were held to be important, were emphasized strongly, and were further developed, whereas certain other ideas were completely disregarded and finally forgotten. Other Upaniṣadic ideas, so prominent that it could not be allowed to be disregarded and forgotten, were either combined with the philosopher's own theory and given farfetched and strained explanations, or else rated as of lower value, as either inferior teachings or taught for the sake of the dull. The Vedānta school, therefore, while professing in public to be a reverent follower of the Upaniṣads, in certain instances came in its thinking to differ markedly from the Upaniṣads in general.

In this process, the dialectical exchanges particularly with the philosophical schools of that time must be regarded as having been a very strong factor. The more the Vedānta became established as a school, the more it must have engaged in logical disputes with the contemporary schools. Since the schools which denied the authority of the Vedas as well as of the Vedānta, or the schools which, even if they did not deny this authority, nevertheless thought it of little value and did not accept the thought of the Upaniṣads, came to turn the spearpoint of their attack vigorously against the Vedānta school,[3] the Vedānta school had also occasionally to make positive counter-attacks on the philosophical theories of other schools. For that purpose, it necessarily had to reflect even more deeply upon its own philosophical position, to supplement it with re-considered findings, and to make its systematic structure ever more complete. Its philosophical theories thus were continually influenced by the other schools who were on the attack, came to be remarkably developed, and finally embraced some ideas which were very different from those of its fundamental canon, the Upaniṣads. The influence of thought received from other schools was unusually great, and scholars have already frequently referred to the remarkable influence, in particular, of the philosophy of Mahāyāna Buddhism on the Advaita school of the early period; that of the Sāṁkhya school on the Rāmānuja school, the Nimbārka school, the Vallabha school, and the later Advaita school; and that of the Nyāya-Vaiśeṣika school on the Madhva school. The influence, then, of the thought of other schools can also be found in varying degrees in the Vedānta thinkers of the early period; to make this influence clear is the proposed programme of the present work. Since the Vedānta school itself split up into numerous ramified schools and adopted ideas from the other schools, the history of Vedānta philosophy is really something like a miniature copy or reflection of the entire history of Indian philosophy.

It may then be said that this Vedānta study itself was already a "philosophy" as for example with Śaṅkara. Among his arguments, passages from the Upaniṣads are copiously quoted; but these are chiefly cited as canonical authority in sections which inquire into the actual meaning of the sacred texts, when he is refuting a conflicting theory within the Vedānta school. But when he attacks the ideas of other schools he no longer refers to the Upaniṣadic sacred canon, but mainly engaged in dialectics *in purely logical fashion*. The sacred texts may be quoted as authority among those who accept them as such, but he fully realized that against those who deny their authority, it is pointless to cite them.

This being the character of the Vedānta philosophy, its investigations, while always accepting a close connection with the thinking of the Upaniṣads, still have to proceed tentatively independently of it. And whenever one conducted research on the thought of Śaṅkara in the past, there had been a tendency in the academic world of both India and the West to present the thinking of Śaṅkara alongside that of the Upaniṣads, a corpus embodying ideas a thousand years prior to Śaṅkara; this tendency is very superficial in scholarship.

Further, the schools accepting the Upaniṣads as their sacred texts are by no means limited to the Vedānta school alone. For the schools of the orthodox Brahmin line did in general accept the Vedas as sacred authority, and accordingly more or less acknowledged the authority of the Upaniṣads as one section of the Vedas. The Upaniṣads are actually frequently quoted as sacred authority in the principal works of these schools.[4] For example, the Nyāya school, as well as the Vaiśeṣika school, took a position of pluralistic realism, and is therefore in its philosophical leanings completely different from monistic thought nevertheless, whenever it discusses the Supreme Deity, it frequently quotes passages from the Upaniṣads as authority. Again, we see in the works of later centuries of the Sāṁkhya school that, insofar as it tries to demonstrate that its own theories are based upon the Vedas, it frequently quotes passages from the Upaniṣads. And it seems that such a tendency existed in the Sāṁkhya school from fairly ancient times. Since it is repeatedly asserted in the first sections of the *Brahma-sūtra* that it is not true that some Upaniṣadic passages expound Sāṁkhya theories, there probably did exist at that time some who interpreted passages of the Upaniṣads in terms of Sāṁkhya theories. Since there actually are theories which can be regarded as the sources of Sāṁkhya views, and as there are not a few expository passages especially in Old Upaniṣads of both the middle and late periods, which seem to have perhaps been adopted from Sāṁkhya doctrines, it is not at all strange that the Sāṁkhya school quoted passages from the Upaniṣads as sacred authority for its own theories. The case is the same with the Yoga school also.

Thus while the Upaniṣads were revered as sacred authority by the schools of the orthodox Brahmanic line, schools other than the Vedānta school had previously perfected their respective systems of thought based upon independent philosophical speculation, and adopted passages of the Upaniṣads as their authority only from those sections in the Upaniṣads which coincided with the corresponding ideas within the framework of their own thought-systems. They did not at all try to follow the Upaniṣads in every respect. The Vedānta school on the other hand regarded the Upaniṣads as a whole as absolutely authoritative sacred texts, and, at least superficially, held firmly to the attitude that it must not accept any thought which contradicted them, no matter how slightly. And it has always sought in the Upaniṣads for the sacred authority of any philosophical assertion whatsoever. And while it has been impossible, at times, to find those relied grounds, the Upaniṣads were still to be relied upon. Accordingly, while other schools do not more than refer to passages in the Upaniṣads as merely intellectual corroborating evidence for their own philosophical ideas, the Vedānta school, on the other hand, went progressively on from an interpretative, academic study of the Upaniṣads to consideration of philosophical problems. Theoretical speculation is primary in other schools, with the Upaniṣads trailing along after but it is exactly the opposite in the Vedānta school, at least on the surface.

In this sense, the Vedānta school is that unique school which tries reverently to follow the Upaniṣads as a whole; and conversely, all students who have such an attitude, regardless of their actual thinking, can be counted among those in the Vedānta school. This character is particularly conspicuous in the case of Madhva of the 13th century. Despite the fact that he advocated a philosophical theory very different from the general thinking of the Upaniṣads, since he outwardly professed himself to be an absolutely faithful interpreter of the Upaniṣads, his traditional line has likewise been regarded as a sub-school within the Vedānta school. He has offered very forced interpretations of individual sentences in the Upaniṣads, and just because he was a Vedānta student, he also set forth some far-fetched and strained explanations; someone of another school would never have recognized such a necessity. Despite the fact, accordingly, that the general tendencies of the Vedānta school are extremely complicated and divergent, one may say that in the respect that they have always endeavoured to tie up with the Upaniṣads *in all aspects*, they can sharply be distinguished from other schools. Indeed, it is the Vedānta school which is the only traditional school to inherit and develop the thought of the Upaniṣads.

Notes

1. For actual examples in which theories in the Upaniṣads contradict one another, cf. Ghate: *The Vedānta*, p. 50.

2. E.g., Śaṅkara, the author of the oldest extant commentary on the Upaniṣads, has frequently offered extremely forced interpretations. For an example, cf. Thibaut: *The Vedānta-sūtra, SBE.* XXXIV, Intro., pp. cvii-cxiv.

3. Similarly, even the Mīmāṁsā school, which belongs to the orthodox Brahmanic line and which regards the Vedas as absolute, after Kumārila, attacked the Vedānta philosophy. Cf. the present work, Part II, Chap. III, Sect. 5.

4. Since, however, it is explained in the *Vedāntasāra*, 146 ff., that various schools including the Buddhists and the Lokāyatas have made passages of the Upaniṣads their sacred authority, Hume (*The Thirteen Principal Upanishads*, p. 2) took it as meaning that even the Buddhists and the Lokāyatas regarded the Upaniṣads as sacred texts. But this is not a fact and was probably a forced ascription by Vedānta thinkers of later centuries.

SECTION IV. OTHER NAMES OF THE VEDĀNTA SCHOOL

We shall next survey the names by which the Vedānta school and its doctrines were generally called in India; and, by means of this survey, we shall get new light on its special character.

The original term for the Vedānta school was "Vedānta-vāda," and students of this school have been called "Vedānta-vādin" or "Vedāntin."

Vedānta-vāda : The Böhtlingk-Roth Unabridged Dictionary lists only "*SDS*.XIII.267" as an example of this word, but Bhāskara[1] had already called his own school by this name; and, going back even earlier, the Buddhist Bhavya (sixth century) had referred to *rig byed kyi mthar smra ba* (i.e., *Vedānta-vāda*), *Madhyamaka-hṛdaya*, VIII, 1; 23)

Vedānta-vādin : Similarly, the Böhtlingk-Roth Unabridged Dictionary has it that this designation has appeared only in the *Tattvasamāsa*; Schmidt, in his *Nachträge*, says that it also appeared in the *Yaśastilaka* (II.269.23), a *Campū* written in 959 A.D. by Somadeva, a Jain of the Digambara Sect; Śaṅkara himself, however, who was earlier than these, called the scholars of his own school *Vedānta-vādin*.[2] Much earlier Bhavya called this school *Vedāntavādin*.[3]' The same is true of Bhāskara.[4] These scholars, accordingly, had already *the self-awareness of themselves as Vedānta scholars*. The Jain scholar Mallavādin (eighth century) and the Buddhist scholar Advayavajra (11th Century) also referred to the *Vedānta-vādins*.[5] There are some rare cases in which Mīmāṁsakas are called *Vedāntavādins*. Maṇibhadra, a later Jain scholar, called Jaimini a *Pūrva-Vedānta-vādin*.'[6]

Vedāntin : This designation, on the other hand, seems to have been formulated comparatively late. It seems, according to the Böhtlingk-Roth Unabridged Dictionary, that it had been used generally in India mostly during later centuries. Śaṅkara never used the term in his *Brahma-sūtra-bhāṣya*, and no example of its use exists prior to him in the Vedānta school; but it appears in works by Ānandagiri[7] and Mādhava.[8] And before them, the term had also been cited in the *Yogavāsiṣṭha* (IV, 21, 26) and in the beginning of the drama *Mahānāṭaka*.[9] Further, a term resembling it, *Vedāntika Brahmavedāntavid* was used in the *Vikramacarita*.[10]

Moreover, since the Vedānta school is the school devoted to the Upaniṣads, as already mentioned, it is called *Aupaniṣada, Aupaniṣadika*, and *Upaniṣad-vādin*.

According to the Böhtlingk-Roth Unabridged Dictionary, the word *Aupaniṣada*, as the name of a school, made its appearance in the writings of the Advaita school in extremely late centuries. Śaṅkara himself, however, had already named his own school *Aupaniṣada,*[11] and called the doctrines of his school *Aupaniṣadaṁ*[12] *darśanam*; however he interpreted the term in a broad sense, and called those like Bhartṛprapañca, whose views contradicted his own, "men who call themselves students of the Upaniṣads" (*Aupaniṣadammanyāḥ*).[13] Again, Śāntarakṣita, of nearly the same period as Śaṅkara, called the Vedānta school *Aupaniṣada*, and Kamalaśīla called it *Aupaniṣadika*.[14] Tracing back even further, *Aupaniṣada* has been cited in the *Harṣacarita*[15] by Bāṇa as an independent school alongside other schools. Again, the term *Upaniṣadvādin*, which has the same import, cannot be found in a general Sanskrit dictionary, but Śaṅkara has called himself by that title,[16] and it has appeared twice in the *Bodhicaryāvatāra-pañjikā*[17] by Prajñākaramati also.

Since the Vedānta school takes as its principal mission the exhaustive discussion of Brahman, the central theme of the Upaniṣads, it styles itself *brahma-vāda*, and calls its students *brahma-vādin*. *Brahma-vāda* originally meant "religious discussion" in the Vedic literature, and later was sometimes used in the sense of "discussion on Brahman";[18] but Śaṅkara clearly used it as a technical term to mean the philosophical position of his own school.[19] In some cases, Śaṅkara has also used the word *Brahma-kāraṇa-vāda*[20] (the theory which takes Brahman as the world-cause), which he probably understood in the same sense as the other word. The word *brahma-vādin* in early Vedic literature[21] also meant similarly "he who relates the sacred truths", "Vedic scholar," and "theologian", and even later on was used in such a sense;[22] but with the establishment of the Vedānta school, it came to be taken as a designation for the students of this school. It had already been taken as a name of the students of this school in the *Vāyu-Purāṇa*[23] and in the *Harṣacarita* by Bāṇa,[24] and Bhartṛhari also was called such;[25] Śaṅkara chooses this name frequently more than any other, to refer to the philosophical position of his own school.[26] Now, even the scholars within the Vedānta school who entertained heretical theories are included within the term *brahma-vādin*.[27] Aśvaghoṣa, the Buddhist poet, also called the advocates of Sāṁkhya-yoga theories similar to those of the Vedānta, *parama-brahma-vādin*.[28] Vedānta scholars, even after Śaṅkara, have called in general their own school *brahmavādin*.[29] "Those who follow Brahman").

If *brahma-vāda* and *brahma-vādin* could mean the Vedānta school, then *ātma-vāda* and *ātma-vādin* should also be capable of being a name for the Vedānta school, since ātman is a central concept in the Upaniṣads, on the same level as Brahman. Examples actually exist in which ātman has been used in that sense,[30] but *ātma-vāda* has never been confined to the Vedānta school alone. For example, the *ātma-vādin* mentioned by Śaṅkara,[31] refers rather to the Nyāya-Vaiśeṣika school. And excepting the Lokāyatikas and the Buddhists, the other schools have in fact been included within *ātma-vādin*. Other schools, however, have assumed other metaphysical substances and principles besides the ātman, while the Vedānta school maintains that the ātman alone is the unique substance or the central fundamental principle. Accordingly, whenever one says *ātmaikatva-pakṣa*,[32] or *ātmaikatva-darśin*,[33] he is referring to the Vedānta school, and particularly to the philosophical standpoint of Śaṅkara.

The names mentioned above are applicable to all the sub-schools of the Vedānta school in general, but the systems of Śaṅkara and Gauḍapāda within the Vedānta school can be called in particular *advaita-vādin*,[34] or *advaitin* (non-dualistic monistic school), and their doctrines can be termed *advaita*, or *advaita-vāda* (non-dualistic monism).[35] Striking enough, the Buddhist Vijñānavādins called themselves *Advaitavādinaḥ*.[36] The word *advaita* existed before Śaṅkara;[37] but such a term, as the name of a school, came first to be employed in later centuries,[38] and Śaṅkara himself did not proclaim it.[39] Since he, however, called his own doctrine "the theory of non-difference" (*abheda-darśana*),[40] and clearly called it "the denial of dualism" (*dvaitavādapratiṣedha*),[41] it is in no way unwarranted that men of later centuries gave the appellation "non-dualistic monism" to his doctrine. The doctrines of his system have also sometimes been called in later centuries "absolute non-dualism" (*kevalādvaita*)[42] or "pure non-dualism" (*śuddhādvaita*).[43]

Occasionally the term *advayavādin* also is used.[44] This "non-dualistic monism" or its exponents can also be called *māyā-vāda* or *māyā-vādin*. The most ancient use of this example known at present exists in the *Padma-purāṇa*[45]; occasionally the exponents were called "Māyā-Vedāntins,"[46] and Bhāskara, in rejecting the Śaṅkara theory, called it *māyā-vāda* in his *Brahma-sūtra-bhāṣya*,[47] but Śaṅkara himself never called his theory *māyā-vāda*, and, moreover, none of the thinkers prior to him had ever proclaimed it as their own theory. *Māyā-vāda* may be said to be the idea that only the Brahman is real, and that everything else is completely phantasmagoric or false,[48] but this term is not applicable to Śaṅkara's philosophical theories.[49] Rather, the name is a derogatory term which the men of other systems within the Vedānta school used for the thought of Śaṅkara or to the thought resembling his. Originally, the term *māyā-vāda*, always carried an implication of rejection.[50] In later centuries, however, even the Advaita school came to admit that this designation was adopted as a name of its own theories.[51] Māyā-vāda is sometimes divided into the "ancient māyā-vāda" (*jaran-māyā-vāda*) and the "recent māyā-vāda" (*sākṣān-māyā-vāda*).[52]

Māyā-vāda was vigorously criticized by other sects within the same Vedānta school on the point that its thought resembles that of Buddhist theories. *Māyā-vāda* had already been criticized, as early as the *Padma-purāṇa*, as being an "incorrect teaching" (*asac-chāstra*), as being a theory of "a crypto-Buddhist", and as being "not based upon the Vedas" (*avaidika*);[53] and this view has been inherited by later centuries. Vijñānabhikṣu also frequently discussed the problem of the theory of the "modern proponents of Māyā" (*ādhunika-māyā-vādin, navīna-māyā-vādin*), and commented that they are "crypto-Buddhists" and "a section of the Buddhists," that superficially they are "those who call themselves Vedāntists" (*Vedāntibruva*), but that, actually, this thought is not a Vedānta theory (*na tu tad Vedāntamatam*).[54] He then endeavoured to understand the contents of the *Brahma-sūtra* apart from the Māyā-theory.[55]

Similarities between the Māyā theory and *Buddhist theories*, moreover, have been pointed out by scholars within the Vedānta school. Bhāskara says that the proponents of Māyā are "men who rely upon Buddhist theories" (*Bauddhamatāvalambin*), and who do not agree with the thought of the author of the *Brahma-sūtra*[56]. Again, it has also been said that the non-dualistic theory is an idea which "smacks of Buddhism" (*Bauddhagandhin*).[57] While the influence from Buddhism, and Mahāyāna Buddhism in particular, is remarkable, the scholars of that time had already noticed this fact. Bhāskara says : "Expatiating on the contradictory and groundless māyā-vāda, propagated by the Buddhists, they have misled the world."[58] Padmapāda, a disciple of Śaṅkara, also frequently discussed the reasons why the epistemology of the non-dualistic monist theory differs from the "position of Mahāyāna Buddhism" (*Māhāyānikapakṣa*).[59] Broadly classifying the philosophical schools of Mahāyāna Buddhism, one can assume two groups, Mādhyamaka and Vijñāna-vāda; and the respective resemblances between these two have been noted. Vallabha called the proponents of Māyā "another incarnation of the Mādhyamika itself" (*Mādhyamikasya eva aparāvatāraḥ*);[60] Vijñānabhikṣu, on the other hand, says that one should regard the proponents of Māyā as "a section of the Vijñāna-vādins" (*Vijñāna-vādyekadeśin*).[61] Yāmuna, too, says that the māyā-vāda and the Vijñāna-vāda (of Dignāga, in particular) are essentially identical, and that a difference exists only in the fact that while the latter is "an open Buddhist" (*prakaṭa Saugata*), the former is "a crypto-Buddhist" (*pracchanna Saugata*);[62] and Rāmānuja asserted that the thought of "the crypto-Buddhist who makes a pretence of the Veda-vāda" (*Vedavādacchadma-pracchanna-Bauddha*),[63] that is, Śaṅkara and others, resembles the Vijñāna-vāda, particularly of Dignāga, and that both of them possess common theoretical faults.

Insofar as the non-dualistic monist school of the system of Śaṅkara had thus been designated as "māyā-vāda" by other schools, and had been criticized as being really a Buddhist theory, the thinkers of the non-dualistic monistic school of later centuries, while continuing to admit that there are resemblances with the Buddhist theory, emphasize that there exists a difference between the two. Śrīharṣa, in his *Khaṇḍanakhaṇḍakhādya*, says that while Buddhism asserts the "falsity" (*mithyātva*) of the myriad existences, the Vedānta school teaches the "non-difference" (*ananyatā*) of the myriad existences, and so they are different on this point.[64] It is an undoubted fact that followers of one section of the Vedānta school were, as we have just seen, severely criticized by followers of other systems for their advocacy of theories which were tenets of Mahāyāna Buddhism, and for the remarkable Buddhist influence in their thinking. Such being the case, what Buddhistic influence did the Vedānta school of the early period prior to Śaṅkara receive ? This quite naturally becomes a problem, and is one of the topics to be taken up in the present work.

I have discussed, in the foregoing, the various designations related to the Vedānta school; it is evident that "the Vedānta school," or the names corresponding to it, were formulated and were generally known in a period prior to Śaṅkara. Accordingly, it has become clear that the opinion of a great many scholars who formerly held that the Vedānta school flourished as such for the first time with Śaṅkara, is mistaken. Instead, the Vedānta school itself must have existed in reality from before the time such a name was recorded and handed down in the literature. In what form did it exist ? I shall next enter upon a consideration of that problem in Part II, which follows below.

Notes

1. Bhāskara, on *BS*.II.2.8.
2. Śaṅkara, on *BS*.I.4.22. Vol. I, p. 403, line 16; II, 2, 17.
3. *Madhyamaka-hṛdaya*, VIII, 1.
4. Bhāskara, on *BS*.I.2.22, p. 46.
5. *Nyāyabinduṭīkāṭippaṇī* of Mallavādin, ed. by Stcherbatsky, *Bibliotheca Buddhica* XI, p. 35. Hajime Nakamura, "The Vedānta as Noticed in Mediaeval Jain Literature," in *Indological Studies in Honor of W. Norman Brown*, American Oriental Society, 1962, New Haven, Conn., p. 191.

Bhāskaramatasthita-Vedāntavādimatānupraveśa-prasaṅgaḥ (Advayavajra's *Tattvaratnāvalī* 24, in *Advayavajrasaṁgraha*) Cf. the present work, Part II, Chap. II, Sect. 3.

6. Maṇibhadra's *Laghuvṛtti* on Hemacandra's *Ṣaḍdarśanasamuccaya*, v. 72, Chowkhamba Sanskrit Series, No. 95, 1929, p. 70.
7. E.g., Ānandajñāna, on *GK*., p. 110, line. 13.
8. *SDS*.X, line 145; XIV, line 55.
9. Aufrecht, *Bodl. Cat*., p. 142, b. *Vedāntinaḥ* is mentioned in *Yogavāsiṣṭha* IV, 21, 26. (T. M. P. Mahadevan: *Gauḍapāda*, Madras, 1952, p. 23).
10. Cf. the present work, Part II, Chap. III, Section 6.

11. Śaṅkara, on *BS*.II.2.10, Vol. I, p. 533, line 7. Cf. *Nyāyanirṇaya*, on *BS*.II.2.2.

12. Śaṅkara, on *BS*.II.1.9, Vol. I, p. 447, line 8; II.1.8, Vol. I, p. 443, line 10.

13. Śaṅkara, on *Bṛhad. Up*., p. 328, line 3.

14. *Aupaniṣadika* occasionally means the secret teachings of poetics (*Kāvyamīmāṁsā* I), and also that of erotics (*Kāmasūtra* I, 1, 12). (But the adhikaraṇa named *Aupaniṣadiks* was the 18th Adhikaraṇa which was lost, according to Mr. K. Kamimura).

15. Cf. the present work, Part II, Chap. II, Sect. 6. See further *SDS*. XVI, line 248.

16. Śaṅkara, on *Bṛhad. Up*., p. 297, line 9.

17. pp. 455, 465 (*BI*., ed. by Poussin).

18. E.g., Śaṅkara, on *BS*., Vol. I, p. 339, line 3.

19. Śaṅkara, on *BS*., Vol. I, p. 455, line 1.

20. *Ibid*., p. 455, line 1.

21. Cf. Macdonell and Keith: *Vedic Index*, item on *brahmavādin*. Further, the word *brahmavid* has the same significance.

22. Even in the *Code of Manu* (II.113, IV.91, 199, VI.39, XI.42, 121), for example, it merely calls him by such names as "he who can know the Vedas," "he who recites the Vedas," and "he who teaches the Vedas."

23. Aufrecht: *Bodl. Cat*., p. 56, b.

24. Cf. the present work, Part II, Chap. III, Sect. 6.

25. *Ibid*., Vol. III, Part V, Chap. II.

26. Śaṅkara, on *BS*., Vol. I, pp. 534, line 1; 604, line 10; 605, line 2; 500, line 1, 6; 438, line 14; Vol. II, p. 95, line

27. *kecid Upaniṣadvyākhyātāro brahmavādinaḥ* (Śaṅkara, on *GK*., p. 128, line 20).

28. *Buddhacarita*, XII.42.

29. E.g., Ānandajñāna, on *GK*., p. 182, line 8; *Bhāmatī*, on II.2.28.

30. E.g., by the Jain scholars Abhayadeva, Malayagiri, and others. Cf. the present work, Part II, Chap. II, Sect. 3. See also *Pañcapādikā*, p. 15.

31. Śaṅkara, on *BS*., Vol. II, p. 372, line 6.

32. *Ibid*., p. 95, line 2.

33. *Ibid*., Vol. I, p. 429, line 10.

34. Probably the teaching of Śaṅkara is referred to as *advaitavādinaḥ*. (*Sarvadarśanasaṁgraha*, V. 1.274).

35. Samantabhadra: *Āptamīmāṁsā*, vv. 24, 26, 27. Further, the title of the second chapter of the *Māṇḍūkya-kārikās* is also *advaita*.

Later Buddhists admitted that the *Nirākāravādi-Yogācāra* set forth *saccitta*-advaita-*sākṣātkaraṇa*. (*Tattvaratnāvalī*, 19. H. Ui: *Daijō Butten no* Kenkyū, Tokyo: Iwanami, 1963, p. 5).

36. *Pramāṇavārttikabhāṣya* of Prajñākaragupta, edited by A. S. Altekar Patna, K. P. Jayaswal Research Institute, 1953, p. 606.

37. The term *advaita* is used in *Madhyamaka-hṛdaya*, in a verse after VIII, 76. Its Tibetan version is lacking. The term *advitīya* also is used (*ibid*. VIII, v. 72; cf. *Chānd. Up*. VI).

38. E.g., *SDS.*, VII.96. The word *advaita-vādin* has appeared in Ānandajñāna, on *GK.*, pp. 160, line 5; 165, line 5; 186, line 21; 187, line 4; *Vedāntakalpataru*, p. 310 (*VizSS.*).

39. Such names have not appeared in Śaṅkara's *Brahma-sūtra-bhāṣya*. In his Commentary on the *Māṇḍūkya-kārikās* (p. 99, line 4; 156, lines 9, 11; 194, line 11; 211; line 12), he has called the Vedānta philosophy *advaita-darśana*, but it seems that in this case he means "non-dual intuition" rather than the philosophical theory of "non-dualism" in the narrow sense. Further, the word *advaita-darśin* also exists. Cf. Ānandajñāna, on *GK.*, p. 175, line 24.

40. Śaṅkara, on *BS.*, Vol. II, p. 207, line 10.

41. 35. *Ibid.*, Vol. I, p. 279, line 8. It seems that "dualism" in this case implied the Sāṁkhya school and the Yoga school. *dvaitino hi te Sāṁkhyā Yogāśca nātmaikatvadarśinaḥ* (Śaṅkara, on BS.I, p. 429, line 10).

42. Ghate: *The Vedānta*, p. 23.

43. Ratnaprabhā, on II.1.14 (p. 374, *NSP*), had called the academic standpoint of Śaṅkara *śuddhādvaitaṁ svamatam......* In later centuries, however, the designation *śuddhādvaita* has generally been used in connection with the Vedānta school of Vallabha's system. That is, it can be thus called, because Vallabha understands that the world does not evolve from Brahman by means of Māyā, but evolves from the power of Brahman itself. He does not admit Māyā.

44. According to many dictionaries, *advayavādin* is an appellation of the Advaitins of the Vedānta school, but its sources are not known. It is an appellation of the Buddha, according to the *Amarakośa*.

45. *Padmapurāṇa*, Uttarakhaṇḍa 43 (Aufrecht: *Oxf. Cat.*, p. 14, n. 1). Further, this verse has also been quoted in the *Sāṁkhya-pravacana-bhāṣya* (*HOS.*, Vol. II, p. 16).

46. A recently published anonymous commentary on the *Vaiśeṣika-sūtra* (12th or 13th century) refers to *māyāvedāntins*:

Guṇakarmādikam ekam eveti Māyāvedāntinaḥ|tan na, sarvaikatvasya vyāhatatvāt. (*Vaiśeṣikadarśana of Kaṇāda with an anonymous commentary*. Edited by Anantalal Thakur. Darbhanga: Mithila Institute, 1957, p. 70).

47. Bhāskara, on *BS.*II.1.14 (p. 93 ff.); IV.4.14. Further, Bhāskara has frequently censured the *Brahma-sūtra-bhāṣya* of Śaṅkara. Cf. the present work, Vol. II, Part IV, Chap. II, Additional Remarks, Sect. 2.

48. We see that the item *māyā-vāda* in *KF* has : "die Annahme, dass Alles Täuschung sei, Bez. der Einheitslehre des Vedānta und des Buddhismus." H. Jacobi interprets it as "the Māyāvāda or the doctrine that everything except Brahma is an illusion" (*JAOS.*, 1913, p. 52). Winternitz also says the same (*GIL.*, Vol. III., p. 430).

49. Y. Kanakura, *Vedānta Tetsugaku*, p. 268. Śaṅkara maintained the theory of the empirical reality of the external world. (Paul Deussen: *The System of the Vedānta*, Delhi etc.: Motilal Banarsidass, 1972, p. 55, n. 31; pp. 241-249).

50. Cf. the examples quoted later. Further, works entitled *Māyā-vāda* had been handed down to today in large numbers, but all of them

were written with the intention of *refuting* this doctrine.

Author	Title
Ānandatīrtha	*Māyā-vāda-khaṇḍana*
Pūrṇānanda	*Māyā-vāda-saṁdūṣaṇī* (or, *Māyā-vāda-śatadūṣaṇī*)
Satyanātha (Madhva School)	*Māyā-vāda-paraśu*

On the other hand, no example can be found of a work entitled with this name in the sense of manifestly praising the Māyā-vāda. Further, in a document of donations of the time when King Sadāśivarāya of Vijayanagara donated land to a monastery of the Rāmānuja school, in the year 1478 of the Śaka Era, i.e., 1556 A.D., he called Rāmānuja "the man who has broken the arrogant mind of the Māyā-vādins (*māyāvādimanogarvabheain*)." (*Epigraphia Indica*, IV, 1896-97, p. 15).

51. Ānandagiri says this after he has attacked the theory of non-difference of cause and effect expounded in the Sāṁkhya school.
abhede'pi māyāvāde *naiṣa doṣaḥ kāraṇasya kāryād ananyatvānabhyupagamād* (on *GK.*, p. 164, line 2).

Further, māyāvādimate *kvacid api kārya-kāraṇabhāvasya vastubhūtasyāsampratipatteḥ* (on. *GK.*, p. 169, line 6).

52. It has appeared in the *Śrutaprakāśikā*, a sub-commentary on the *Śrībhāṣya* of Rāmānuja. (Hiriyanna, *JORM.*, 1928, p. 6).

53. Cf. note 38.

Māyāvādam asac-chāstraṃ pracchannaṃ Bauddham eva ca/
mayaiva kathitaṃ, devi, Kalau brāhmaṇarūpiṇe//
....
Vedārthavan mahāśāstram māyāvādam avaidikam/

"Saṁkara's *māyā*-system was declared to be only crypto-Buddhism. (*pracchanna-Bauddha, Madhvavijaya*, i, 51)." (G. A. Grierson, s.v. Madhvas, *ERE.* vol. 8, p. 233a).

54. *Sāṁkhya-pravacana-bhāṣya*, p. 16, lines 5-16; p. 17, line 22; The theories cited as the theory of māyā-vādins in these passages agree with the theory of Śaṅkara and his system. It says that the Māyāvādins teach the five vital airs (*prāṇa* etc.) instead of *tanmātras*, when enumerating the constituent elements of the subtle body, and interprets them as differing from *puryaṣṭaka*, but on this, cf. *Vedāntasāra*, No. 79 ff., Jacob: *The Vedāntasāra*, pp. 100, 170.

55. *Sāṁkhya-pravacana-bhāyṣa*, p. 21, lines 17-18.

56. *ye tu Bauddhamatāvalambino māyāvādinas te 'py anena nyāyena sūtrakāreṇaiva nirastā veditavyāḥ* (Bhāskara, on *BS.*II.2.29).

57. "*mā bhūd bheda iti vadantaṁ Bauddhagandhinam ekadeśinaṁ nirākaroty ākṣeptā* (*Vedāntakalpataru*, *VizSS.*, p. 19).

58. *vigītaṁ vicchinnamūlam Māhāyānika-Bauddhagāthitam māyāvādaṁ vyāvarṇayanto lokān vyāmohayanti*" (Bhāskara, on *BS.*I.4.25, p. 85).

59. *Pañcapādikā* (*VizSS.*), pp. 25, 28. The *Māhābhānikapakṣa* mentioned in *SDS.*XVI, line 464, is probably a clerical error for *Māhāyānikapakṣa*. Here, too, the Buddhist theory has been called thus.

60. Ghate: *The Vedānta*, p. 92.

61. *Sāṁkhya-pravacana-bhāṣya*, p. 16.

62. *Siddhitraya*, p. 19.
63. *Śrībhāṣya*, on II.2.27, p. 494.
64. *Saugata-Brahmavādinor ayaṃ viśeṣo yad ādimaḥ/*
sarvasya mithyātvaṃ brūte, dvitīyas tad-ananyatām//

(Belvalkar: *Lectures*, p. 21, and *The Brahma-sūtras of Bādarāyaṇa with the comment of Śaṅkarācārya*, Part II, Note, p. 98.

cf.

Bhāṣye tatsākṣiti vidhikāṇḍānadhigatatvam uktam/
sarvabhūtasthatvena Bauddhasamayānadhigatiḥ"
(*Vedāntakalpataru*, on B.S.I.1.4, *VizSS*, p. 80).

SECTION V. THE BEGINNINGS OF THE VEDĀNTA SCHOOL

If we take it, then, that the Vedānta school has the special qualities mentioned above, and can limit the date of the early period as discussed already in Chapter II, we have tentatively come to some preliminary conclusions for our investigation of the early Vedānta philosophy. We must next try to trace the historical development of the early Vedānta philosophy from the actual accounts in the literature.

What form the Vedānta school took at the very beginning is anything but clear. But the tendency to regard the *Upaniṣads* as particularly important among the Vedas is already seen to appear in the Old *Upaniṣads* of the middle period. For example, "the men who have determined the meaning through the knowledge arising from the *Vedānta* (*Vedāntavijñānasuniścitārthāḥ*, *Muṇḍ Up.*, III.2.6; *Kaivalya-Up.* 4) and "the highest secret in the Vedānta" (*Vedānte paraṃ guhyaṃ*, *Śvet. Up.* VI.22) are praised with a special earnestness. We can know, accordingly, that, when the Old Upaniṣads of the early period included in the Brāhmaṇas and the Āraṇyakas were produced, and when the Vedic literature of the ancient period was tentatively completed, there were continually appearing in the orthodox Brahmanic intellectual world men who attached particular importance to the special significance and value of the Upaniṣadic portion of the Vedas. As we have already discussed, the *Vedānta* is referred to as distinct from the *Veda* in the *Bhagavad-Gītā* (15.15).[1] Moreover in the New Upaniṣads of later centuries, the word "Vedānta" is cited in *the plural.*

daharaṁ puṇḍarīkaṁ tad Vedānteṣu nigadyate.

"It is called 'a small lotus flower' in the *Vedāntas*."[2] (*Kṣurikā-Up.* 10)

Here, accordingly, the Upaniṣads are undoubtedly referred to as sacred authority.

Since the poets who produced these early Old Upaniṣads and the Upaniṣads after them, thus emphasized the special meaning of the Upaniṣadic sacred texts, one can trace back to this period the intellectual position of the importance of the Upaniṣads. As the Old Upaniṣads of the early period had already been completely composed in the period during which those of the middle period were produced, and as the thought of the former was specially highly regarded in particular, one can here find the very roots of the Vedānta school in its incipient stage.

But how did this germination mature and develop to become later such a great school ? The process cannot, of course, be known from the Upaniṣads, and it is impossible to make it out even from the Vedānta works handed down to the present. In order to find out about this process, it is necessary to collate the accounts of the Vedānta school from among the numerous classical works of the Indian schools, and to elucidate its historical development and its significance for cultural history from these outside sources. I shall therefore treat this problem in Part II which follows.

After that, I shall discuss the three classical works of the pre-Śaṅkara school still extant, i.e., (1) *Brahma-sūtra*; (2) *Māṇḍūkya-kārikā* of Gauḍapāda; and, (3) the works of Bhartṛhari. In each of these three, at any rate, the characteristic Vedānta philosophy is expounded. Furthermore, nearly all the writings of other thinkers prior to Śaṅkara have been lost, but as fragments of their views have been handed down in works of later centuries, I shall collate and examine these, and shall try to discuss them historically by dividing them tentatively into *pre-Brahma-sūtra* and *post-Brahma-sūtra* periods.

Accordingly, the following portion of the present work will be as follows:

Part II : The Vedānta philosophy the Indian Schools Saw.
Part III : Thinkers prior to the *Brahma-sūtra.*
Part IV : *The Brahma-sūtra.*
Part V : Thinking after the *Brahma-sūtra.*

Part VI : The *Māṇḍūkya-kārikā*.
Part VII : The Vedānta Philosophy of Bhartṛhari.
Part VIII : Conclusion.

Notes

1. Cf. the present work, Sect. 1.
2. Cf. *Chānd. Up.*VIII.1; *Maitrī-Up.*. VI. 2.

PART II

THE EARLY-PERIOD VEDĀNTA PHILOSOPHY AS SEEN BY THE INDIAN SCHOOLS

INTRODUCTION

A thousand years is a colossal time in human history; nevertheless, the number of works written in the early Vedānta school, which survived during that long period of time, and are extant today is extremely small, and excluding the Upaniṣadic corpus, it includes only the *Brahma-sūtra*, the *Māṇḍūkya-kārikā*, and the *Vākyapadīya* of Bhartṛhari. One must admit that the historical materials for discovering the circumstances and historical vicissitudes of this school during these long years, are extremely meagre. In the final analysis, accordingly, if we want to clarify the history of this long period, we have no other method than to collect and investigate carefully the great number of fragments of accounts on the Vedānta school, how it was accepted and how it was criticized, in the writings of other thought-systems of that time. Even if we should not be able to know in detail, by such a method, the minute sectarian differences or the individual topics of debate within the Vedānta school, we should be able to grasp the contours of the historical development of the school and make out a general outline of its actual circumstances as a school. While such a study is both significant and meaningful in itself as *a synopsis of the historical development* of the early Vedānta school, it can be regarded additionally as a preparation and foundation for entering upon the examination of the texts belonging to the early Vedānta school itself. In the following, accordingly, I shall first form a general conception of the outline of the development of the early Vedānta school from the outside, based upon materials from other schools; and, having established this basis, I shall examine the classical works and fragments of the school itself.

Now, the classical works of the other thought-systems, when classified roughly, can be divided into the following three:

I. The Buddhist Texts
II. The Classical Writings of Jainism

III. The Cultural and Religious Writings of the Orthodox Brahmanic Systems

This classification is from a religious standpoint. While a great number of literary compositions and cultural writings apart from actual religious and philosophical works exist in India, yet because their authors were mainly believers in either Brahmanism, Buddhism, or Jainism, and as in the end their lives were under the domination of one or the other religion, their writings can tentatively be grouped into one or another of the three classifications given above. Therefore, the following discussion conformably will be divided into three parts. As the Buddhist Canon, among these three, which was composed in about the same period as that of the early Vedānta school, is very rich in data, and has the approximate dates of composition of its individual writings already ascertained, research based upon materials in the Buddhist Canon can probably be said to be the most important.

CHAPTER IV

VEDĀNTA PHILOSOPHY AS SEEN BY THE BUDDHISTS

SECTION I. INTRODUCTION

Among the streams of orthodox Indian thought accepting the authority of the Vedas, the greatest philosophical school would be the Vedānta. And its greatest antagonist among the unorthodox schools was Buddhism. The two are colossal edifices, vying with each other in the spiritual history of India. Of the Vedānta philosophy, though the source of its ideas can be found in the pre-Buddhistic Old Upaniṣads of the early period, the development of vigorous activity as an independent school belongs to comparatively late centuries and is later than the peak of the Buddhist flowering. Moreover as I shall discuss in detail later, quite a few of the Vedānta lines have been greatly influenced by Buddhism, with Buddhist thought pervading them through and through. Those on the Buddhist side, on the other hand, did not regard the Vedānta school as so important. The Buddhists as a whole called those who did not believe in Buddhism the "outer path-farers"—(*tīrthika*); but it seems that the Vedānta school would not have been very influential in the so-called "outer paths", and accounts of it are extremely few even in the large number of Buddhist works. The schools which Buddhists of the time regarded as most important, and which they criticized in their discussions, are the Sāṃkhya and the Vaiśeṣika. These two schools were regarded as typifying the "outer paths".[1] Though Indian writings, apart from the Buddhist scriptures, were not translated as a rule into Chinese, the Sāṃkhya-Kārikās were translated by Paramārtha, and the Vaiśeṣika-daśa-padārtha-śāstra by Hsuan-tsang, and as a result these two schools later attracted the attention of scholars particularly in China and Japan. Whereas the "Vedānta school" under the title is hardly mentioned at all in the Chinese translation of the Buddhist scriptures.[2] No matter how assiduous the search in the voluminous Chinese-translated Buddhist scriptures, the result is disappointing.[3]

In that case, is reference to the Buddhist scriptures completely meaningless in connection with research into the Vedānta school ? By no means; in fact just the opposite. First of all, on the *negative side*, although the Chinese-translated Buddhist scriptures have so copiously introduced the names of schools and criticized so many "outer paths", the fact that they nevertheless do not at all cite the name "Vedānta school" is an important point which should be carefully considered. I shall discuss this later. On the *positive side*, the Buddhist scriptures have moreover an important significance :

1. In examining the works of the thinkers of the early Vedānta, and the fragments of those works which are in most cases all that remain, to collect and study all relevant passages in the light of their relation to Buddhist thought—the attitude towards Buddhism shown by the authors, the existence or non-existence of the influence of Buddhist thought, and the extent of that influence where it exists — would make it possible not only to establish the intellectual position of each of the thinkers but also sometimes to determine their approximate date. In the end, it would be a contribution towards tracing the development of early Vedānta thought. Again, some dates, such as those of Bhartṛhari, have become clear for the first time by the accounts in The Records Of The Buddhist Religion by I-tsing and by other references. While all scholars have indeed been aware of the necessity, in studying the history of Vedānta philosophy, of clearing up its relation to Buddhism, it has been a very difficult undertaking to master the literature of the two thought-systems, so completely different from each other, so that the task has as yet hardly begun.[4] Since it is however a study extremely important for clearly understanding early Vedānta, I want as far as I can to push the investigations further. Since it is more convenient however to examine the early Vedānta literature piecemeal first, I shall defer this study till later.

2. Even though the name "Vedānta *school*" is not cited in the Chinese-translated Buddhist scriptures, the ideas of Vedānta philosophy are frequently mentioned. Again, in the logical works of the late-period Mahāyāna Buddhism — these were not generally translated into Chinese — the Vedānta school (Vedānta-vādin) and the Upaniṣad school (Aupaniṣada, Aupaniṣadika) are clearly mentioned, and are then criticized in minute

detail. Accordingly, if we were to examine such material closely in detail, we could by going over the sources in the Buddhist scriptures develop a summary outline of the history of the development of early Vedānta thought. As the dates of the works in the Buddhist scriptures are considerably better established than those of any other Indian school, the most reliable method of tracing the contours of the pre-Śaṅkara early-period Vedānta philosophy would be to form first a tentative account by means of the Buddhist scriptures. I shall treat this problem in the chapter which follows.

Notes

1. "The Sāṁkhya and the Vaiśeṣika are schools of the outer paths. The Sthaviravāda and the Mahā-sāṁghika schools form the foundation of various Buddhist sects." *Chung-lun-su*, Vol. 9 (*TT*.XLII.132c).

2. In the *Chin-kang-chên-lun*, a work of later centuries handed down with the works of Aśvaghoṣa, the Mīmāṁsā is mentioned as follows, but it is not clear whether it indicates only the ritualistic Mīmāṁsā, or includes the later Mīmāṁsā (*Uttara-mīmāṁsā*), i.e., Vedāntism, as well. "He, too, has false notions; he has understood the four Vedas and the Mīmāṁsā together with the Sāṁkhya and the Vaiśeṣika, as well as the other theories, and has completely mastered them all; he is called a Brahmin." (*Chin-kang-chên-lun*, *TT*.XXXII, 170b).

3. V. A. Sukhtankar says that explicit mention of the Vedānta school is not to be found in the Buddhist scriptures. (*WZKM*., 1908, p. 129).

4. H. Jacobi : "On the Dates of the Philosophical Sūtras," in *JAOS*. XXXI. Hakuju Ui : "Vedānta-kyō no Genryū oyobi Vedānta-gakuha no Seiritsu," in *Indo Tetsugaku Kenkyū*, Vol. I; this article is a study based on the same idea.

SECTION II. EARLY BUDDHISM AND UPANIṢADIC THOUGHT

During the period of Early Buddhism, not only had the greater part of the Vedas been formulated, but the various branches of learning concerned with them had also been extensively pursued. Accounts about this can be found in great numbers in the early Buddhist scriptures. Yet even in these numerous references, the Upaniṣads are not quoted once, and there is no mention of those branches of learning directly connected with the Upaniṣads. Although the Earliest Upaniṣads had been completed prior to Early Buddhism,[1] the fact that they were not cited in particular as Upaniṣads or Vedānta would seem to indicate that for the Buddhists of that time, they had not yet come to be regarded in general as having any outstanding significance in themselves, and were probably merely thought of as being one section of the Vedas. Consequently, even if there were a sect which held the Upaniṣads above all in esteem, it would have been of marginal importance, and could not have been looked upon as an independent school by the Buddhists, at least.

Thus, neither the Upaniṣads nor a Vedānta School are mentioned anywhere in the Early Buddhist scriptures, yet the fact is that the earliest Upaniṣads came into existence before Early Buddhism, and somewhere in that spacious land of India, there must surely have lived some Brahmins who held to ideas like those expounded in the Upaniṣads and who followed the religious ideals and way of life found therein. Accounts can be found in the early Buddhist scriptures of Brahmins who led the life of a wanderer, such as the Upaniṣads eulogize as the ideal. For example, it is reported that a certain Brahmin, "thoroughly conversant with the mantras (i.e., the Vedas)," continually wandered about the country, gaining his livelihood by "picking up fallen grain and eating the fruit of trees," and earnestly desired for himself "that existence which is not existence (e.g., nothingness, *ākiñcañña*)."[2] And the account also has been recorded of another wandering, mendicant brahmin who "fasted in a tomb, performed ablutions three times a day and recited the three scriptures (i.e. the three Vedas)."[3] The Brahmins who thus abandoned wife and children, property, fame, all they possessed, and pursued a life of a wandering mendicant without having any definite place of residence, must have held ideas different in context from those of the great Brahmins who received immense gifts from the wealthy and the kings whenever there was a religious festival, who provided living quarters for their disciples, who lived in grand mansions, and who were accustomed to a life of opulence. Now, since the Buddhist scriptures have recorded that these wandering Brahmins *were conversant with the Vedas*, it would appear that while they did not set a high value on most of the Vedas, i.e., those portions which expound the rituals, they were particularly devoted to and followed those Upaniṣads which praise the itinerant life and which teach the concept of the oneness of Brahman and Ātman. Of course, the life of a wanderer had probably been practised prior to the formulation of the Upaniṣads, as may be noted from the "universal sacrifice" (*sarvamedha*) in which one relinquishes all possessions and dwells in seclusion in mountains or forest, and which was set forth also in the most ancient portion of the Vedic Canon, so that one cannot conclude that just because a brahmin was thoroughly versed in the Vedas and led an itinerant life, he must have necessarily been a follower of the Upaniṣads. It must be said, however, that such a state of peace of mind and independence of fate of the brahmin who has abandoned all material desires and pursues a life typified by floating clouds and flowing waters, was certainly in essential agreement with the teachings expounded in the Upaniṣads.

At all events, accounts of the lives of itinerant brahmins who seem to have been devoted to the Upaniṣads are to be found here and there throughout the early Buddhist texts; furthermore, in this connection, ideas similar to those expounded in the Upaniṣads are also mentioned, before they are controverted.

The idea that the Lord (*issara*) is the creator of the world is cited in several places in the early Buddhist scriptures.[4] The concept of the "Lord" is not well defined at all, but perhaps something like *Brahmā* must have been intended. Since the "Lord" refers to the supreme deity who controls all beings, it is a designation which cannot be applied to the lesser deities. Now, the texts make the Brahmā himself say : "I am Brahmā, am the Great Brahmā, unvanquished vanquisher, the controlling Lord [of the world] who sees everything, Creator [of all], Builder, the Supreme Creator, Master, and the father of those already born and yet to be born." (*Ahaṃ asmi Brahmā Mahābrahmā abhibhū anabhibhūto aññadatthudaso vasavattī issaro kattā nimmātā seṭṭho sañjitā vasī pitābhūta-bhavyānaṃ.*)[5] Although this passage may be found here and there in the early Buddhist texts, neither Śākyamuni nor his disciples created such a concept of Brahmā; there can be no doubt that a section of the people of that time believed such a theory. Those attributes of Brahmā are put forth in the Old Upaniṣads on the Brahman as the creator or the controller of the world, and they were turned into such a stereotyped expression in the early Buddhist texts.[6] Furthermore, the following four properties are attributed to the creator-deity

Brahma:[7] First of all, Brahmā has light (*āloka*) and lustre (*ābhāsa*) as His marks (*nimitta*). Whenever Brahmā appears or comes near, a particular light and lustre appear even among the other gods. Second, He is invisible. Even by the gods who dwell in the world of Brahmā, He cannot be seen. Third, He is unknowable. It is impossible to know His nature. Fourth, He is omniscient. There is nothing which is not known to Brahmā. Now, in the Old Upaniṣads all these attributes are explained as belonging to *Brahman*, the world-principle in the neuter gender, and to Brahmā, the personal god. (On the first, cf., *Chānd. Up.* III.14.7; *Kāṭhaka Up.* V.15; *Muṇḍ Up.* II.2.10; *Śvet. Up.* VI.14; *Maitri Up.* VI.35, 36. On the second : *Kena Up.* I.6; *Kāṭhaka Up.* VI.9.12. On the third : *Kāṭhaka Up.* II.7-9; VI.12; *Kena Up.* I.3; II.3; *Muṇḍ. Up.* III.1.8. On the fourth : *Maitri Up.* VI.38; VII.1; *Muṇḍ. Up.* I.1.9; II.2.7; *Praśna Up.* IV.10; (*Māṇḍ. Up. VI.*)

One can accordingly regard these concepts appearing in the Upaniṣads as being reflected in the Early Buddhist texts. In the Upaniṣads, however, Brahman (neuter gender, Brahma in the nominative case) is largely considered as an impersonal principle; and Brahman (masculine gender, Brahmā in the nominative) is taken alongside of it to be a personal god; in the Pāli scriptures the neuter Brahman does not appear at all,[8] but is exclusively expressed as the masculine Brahmā. One can also say, accordingly, that some differences exist in this respect; however, since there are not a few examples in the Upaniṣads in which Brahman appears as the neuter impersonal principle, and at the same time is thought of as being perhaps similar to the personal god, its particular aspects as an impersonal god had probably strongly impressed the Buddhists of that time.

The idea, then, which took association with such a Brahmā as the ideal, was prevalent among the brahmins of one section at that time. The *Tevijja-suttanta* in the *Dīgha-nikāya* has ably reported on the ideas of the brahmins then, and the brahmins who appear in it regarded "union with the Brahmā (*Brahma-sahavyatā*)" as liberation, and earnestly sought after it. We see in the *Tevijja-suttanta* that the following assertion of the brahmins of that time is reported :

"Truly every brahmin thoroughly versed in the three Vedas has said thus : "We shall expound the path for the sake of union with that which we do not know and do not see. This is the correct path. This path is the truth, and leads to liberation. If one practices it, he shall be able to enter into association with Brahmā.' "

Te vata tevijjā brāhmaṇā evam āhaṃsu : "yaṃ na jānāma yaṃ na passāma, tassa sahavyatāya maggaṃ desema, 'ayam eva ujumaggo ayam añjasāyano niyyāniko niyyāti takkarassa Brahmasahavyatāyāti'."[9]

Again,

"There are several brahmins (e.g.) the Addhariya brahmins, the Tittiriya brahmins, the Chandoka brahmins, and the Bavharija brahmins, who teach various paths. Do all of these paths leading to release truly enable the one who acts according to each to reach association with Brahmā, or do they not ?"

Brāhmaṇā nānā-magge paññāpenti—Addhariyā brāhmaṇā, Tittiriyā brāhmaṇā, Chandokā brāhmaṇā, Bahvarijā brāhmaṇā—atho kho sabbāni tāni niyyānikāni niyyanti takkarassa Brahmasahavyatāya ?[10]

On this problem, the Brahmin gave the answer that, "They all can attain the Brahmā-world." It can be known, accordingly, that in the period of Śākyamuni, all the above-enumerated brahmins of the Vedic schools longed for liberation. It is not likely that brahmins who held such ideas would have regarded the rituals alone as absolute. "Association with Brahmā," then, is frequently expounded in the Early Upaniṣads (*Bṛhad. Up.* I.5.23: *sāyujyaṃ salokatāṃ jayati. Mahānār. Up.* V.3 : *Gacched brahmasalokatām*; and, *Kauṣītaki-Up.* I). Since this Brahmā, then, is taken as "that which we do not cognize and do not see," it corresponds exactly to the concept of Brahman in the Upaniṣadic sagas.[11] Thus from the above passage we see that the fact that the Early Upaniṣads had probably already been formulated in Vedic sub-schools of that time can also be verified from this point. (It should be noted, however, that the sub-schools of the *Atharva Veda* are not cited.)

Besides the concept of Brahmā, other Upaniṣadic ideas can also be seen scattered throughout the early Buddhist scriptures. While it is not the case that Brahman (neuter gender) is clearly mentioned, an idea which sets up an absolute principle corresponding to it has been introduced as one of the "pernicious views" (i.e., mistaken opinions) :

"O Bhikkhus ! At that time Baka, the Brahmā, produced the following pernicious view : 'It is permanent. It is eternal. It is always existant. It is independent existence. It has the *dharma* of non-perishing. Truly it is not born, does not become old, does not die, does not disappear, and is not born again. Furthermore, no liberation superior to it exists elsewhere.' "

Tena kho pana bhikkhave samayena Bakassa brahmaṇo evarūpaṃ pāpakaṃ diṭṭhigatam uppannaṃ hoti : idaṃ niccaṃ idaṃ dhuvaṃ idaṃ sassataṃ idaṃ kevalam idaṃ acavanadhammaṃ, idaṃ hi na jāyati na jīyati na mīyati na cavati na upapajjati, ito ca pan'aññaṃ uttariṃ nissaraṇaṃ natthīti.[12]

The principle expounded here corresponds contextually to the concept of Brahman expounded in the Upaniṣads, but the Buddha is taken to have criticized such a thought : "Truly the Baka Brahmā is covered over with unwisdom (*avijjāgata*)."

Again, the idea which assumes consciousness (*viññāṇa, vijñāna*) as the ultimate principle, was also prevalent at that time. In a passage which Brahmā related to the Buddha, the following is said:

"There is a conciousness which the eye does not see, which does not have boundaries, and which shines in all places. It cannot be perceived even as the earthiness of the earth, cannot be perceived even as the wateriness of the water. ..."

viññāṇaṃ anidassanaṃ anantaṃ sabbatopabhaṃ. taṃ paṭhaviya paṭhavattena ananubhūtaṃ, āpassa āpattena ananubhūtaṃ...[13]

The idea which holds that the absolute is "pure cognition" (consciousness, *vijñāna*) and regards it as identical with the Brahman, had originally appeared already in the Early Upaniṣads.

Since the word "vijñāna" is used with a great number of meanings in the Old Upaniṣads, one cannot discuss it without qualifications; not infrequently, however, "pure cognition" or "pure wisdom" is taken to be essentially identical with the ultimate principle, Brahman.

vijñānam ānandaṃ brahma.—Bṛhad. Up. III.9.28
vijñānaṃ brahma ced veda......Tait. Up. II.5.1
vijñānaṃ brahmeti vyajānād vijñānād dhi...bhūtāni jāyante vijñānena......jīvanti vijñānaṃ prayanti —Tait. Up. III.5.1.

Again, according to the *Maitri-Upaniṣad.* VI.7, "consciousness" manifests various activities in pairs of opposites, and returns to a non-dualistic and undifferentiated state. Such an idea, accordingly, probably is represented here as an expression of Brahmā. Now, the scriptures have recorded that there was no logical attack on nor refutation of this idea directly; the theory on Brahmā was finally overthrown by another method (i.e. refutation by supernatural powers). Although the theoretical reason for such an assumption is not clearly expressed, to set up any kind of a metaphysical principle like "consciousness" was something which early Buddhists were not ready to do. As I shall explain later, this attitude was consistently held by Buddhists until later centuries.

Again, the early Buddhist texts classified the ātman theories of the other schools into several kinds and set up the theory of sixty-two types, but one cannot think that all these theories had actually been held by the intelligentsia of that time. They represent a classificatory method constructed theoretically by Buddhist scholars. It is noteworthy, however, that to classify the "concepts of the self" (*attapaṭilābha*) prevalent at that time into three kinds and to set up a materialistic ātman (*ōḷārika*), a mental ātman (*manomaya*), and a formless ātman (*arūpa*),[14] as is done in the *Poṭṭhapāda-sutta*, has some resemblance to the theory of five sheaths (*kośas*) in the *Taitt. Up.* II.

Further, the theory of the non-functionalists (*akriyāvādins*), who taught the real existence of the ātman, has also appeared in the Buddhist texts; but since it is also mentioned in the Jaina texts, I shall discuss it in Section II of the next chapter. Of the sixty-two views expounded in the Pali *Brahmajāla-suttanta* and in the *Fan-wang-ching* (its Chinese version), none which coincides exactly with Vedānta thought appears.

From our examination above of some of the accounts in the early Buddhist scriptures which seem to have a relation with the Upaniṣadic or Vedāntic thought, we can now derive the following conclusions. During the period which the early Buddhist texts have recorded in writing, no independent school to be called the Vedānta school with a developed and organized philosophical system, had been formulated yet. However, brahmins who devotedly followed the Upaniṣadic doctrines, existed here and there throughout the land; and the various philosophical theories of the Upaniṣads were quite widely disseminated. Consequently those intellectual trends are mentioned in the Buddhist texts, and are rejected as pernicious views.

Notes

1. Cf. the present work, Part I, Chap. II, Sect. I, 1.
2. *Suttanipāta* 976-978.
3. It is likely that in those days Brahmins took a bath three times a day, after which they recited the three Vedas. *Tsa-a-han-ching*, Chüan 9, No. 255. *Taishō Tripiṭaka*, vol. II, p. 63 c, according to the reading of the Sung Yuan, and Ming editions. It is interesting to note that Chinese copyists miscopied the sentences, because in China there did not exist the custom of "taking a bath three times a day".
4. The *Mahābodhijātaka* mentions five masters of doctrine, among whom is included "the master who holds that the Presiding Deity is the cause of the world" (*issarakāraṇavādin*) (*Jātaka* V.228). Again, theories are also cited that "everything done by man is caused by the design of the Lord" *TT*.I.435c), and that pleasure, suffering, non-suffering and non-pleasure which man receives "is caused by the creation of the Presiding Deity" (*Issaranimmānahetu*, *AN*.I.173).
5. *DN*.I.18. Cf. *MN*.I.326-327. See further Hakuju Ui, *Indo Tetsugaku Kenkyū*, III, 104-105.
6. Hakuju Ui (*op. cit.*, pp. 142-147) has demonstrated this in detail.
7. According to H. Ui, *ibid.*, pp. 140-142.
8. Rhys Davids : *Dialogues of the Buddha*, II.298. Further, in the Pali Canon, the word "Brahman," even in compound words, dces not have the meaning of a neuter gender, impersonal world principle, but means only "supreme," "superior," or "purity," (Cf. Yamamoto Kairyū, "Agon ni arawareta gekyō" in the *Nihon Bukkyō gaku Kyōkai Nenpō*, VIII. 270-271.)
9. *DN*.I.239.
10. On the translation of this passage, cf. Yamamoto, *op. cit.*, pp. 260-261.
11. Cf. note 9 *supra*.
12. *MN*.I.326, No. 49. In the Chinese translation of the corresponding sūtra, it has become the following : "Up to this time there exists one Brahmā, who dwells above and gives birth in this way to pernicious views. Here is permanence, here is eternity, here long existence, here is the essential, here the unending dharma, here appears the essential : this appearing essential does not transcend that which is superior, is excellent, and is the greatest." (*Fan-t'ien-ch'ing*, in *Chung-a-han-ching*, ch. 19).
13. *MN*.I.329, No. 49.
14. *DN*.I.195.

SECTION III. SECTARIAN BUDDHISM AND THE UPANIṢADS

The Buddhist community rapidly developed and expanded, receiving the protection and support of King Aśoka after he unified the greater part of India (having ascended to the throne c. 268 B.C.). Thereafter, however, schisms began to appear within the Order, and a great number of the sects found themselves in conflict with others. In the technical treatises which came into existence during this period can be found several passages which refer to the Upaniṣads. Although some of the ideas expounded in the Upaniṣads, as I have considered in the previous section, are reflected in early Buddhist scriptures, these can only be admitted to have a vague resemblance of content; while in the Buddhist treatises of the period of sectarian antagonisms, the passages found in the Brāhmaṇas and Upaniṣads are quoted in nearly the same form as they are in the original. Furthermore, the phase, "The Vedas say", is distinctly recorded in places.

The *Abhidharma-mahāvibhāṣā-śāstra*, the greatest work of the Sarvāstivāda, cites in Book 200, among the 62 views concerning the existence of consciousness in a future life, as a theory of "philosophers who consider the self to be infinite and to have consciousness after death" :

> "Either it exists within the heart, of about the size of a thumb, replete with brilliance and splendour, or it exists within body, corresponding to the size and shape of the body, and is lustrous within and without."[1]

This same view has definitely been set out in the Upaniṣads. Corresponding to the first half of the passages, the following verse is extant :

> "The ātman within is a person (*puruṣa*) of the size of a thumb, and ever dwells within the heart of man."
> (*Kāṭhaka-Up.* VI.17; *Śvet. Up.* III.13)]
> (*aṅguṣṭhamātraḥ puruṣo 'ntarātmā sadā janānāṃ hṛdaye saṃniviṣṭaḥ*).
> "The *puruṣa* the size of a thumb is like unto brilliance and has no smoke." (*Kāṭhaka-Up.* IV.13) (*aṅguṣṭhamātraḥ puruṣo jyotir ivādhūmakaḥ*).
> "That object the size of a thumb has the same aspect as the sun." (*Śvet. Up.* V.8)
> (*aṅguṣṭhamātro ravitulyarūpaḥ*).
> "The *puruṣa* the size of a thumb dwells in the center of the (individual) *ātman*." (*Kāṭhaka-Up.* IV.12)
> (*aṅguṣṭhamātraḥ puruṣo madhya ātmani tiṣṭhati.*)

And the idea referred to the second half, i.e., that the size of the spirit conforms to the size and shape of the body, is famous as an assertion of Jainism in general of later centuries, but it had already been taught in the Upaniṣads.

> "Higher than this is the supreme Brahman, the great, who *exists hidden within all the living species and who conforms in size with (their) bodies (yathānikāyaṃ sarvabhūteṣu gūḍham)*, the unique embracer of all the universe, the presiding deity—if men know it, they will become immortal." (*Śvet. Up.* III.7)

Also in Book 200 of the *Abhidharma-mahāvibhāṣā-śāstra*, there is, as a theory of "the philosophers who hold that the self is infinite and has consciousness after death" :

> "As is stated in the Veda (*ming-lun*), there is the self, the Person (*puruṣa*)—its size is large and broad and its limits are difficult to measure. The colour of its radiance is like the sun; yet, dark and mysterious beings dwell in front of it, so that we are unable to see it. It is necessary to know this self, so that one can cross over and transcend birth and old age, sickness and death; different from this there is no other path for crossing over."[2]

And this corresponds to the next passage. (The "knowledge text" (*ming-lun*) is the phrase used in Chinese versions for translating "Vedas.")

"This great one beyond the darkness, the *puruṣa* (person) possessing the colour of the sun, I know. If men only know it they will transcend death. There is no other path leading to it."

> *Vedāham etaṃ puruṣam mahāntam ādityavarṇaṃ tamasaḥ parastāt,*
> *tam eva viditvā 'ti mṛtyum eti nānyaḥ panthā vidyate 'yanāya.*
> (*Vāj-Saṃh.* XXXI.18; *Tait.-Ār.* III.12.7, III.13.1; *Śvet.Up.* III.8; *Mahānārāyaṇa-Up.* I.12)

The aforementioned theories are also listed in Chapter 130 "Views of the Body," (*Satkāyadṛṣṭi*) of the *Satyasiddhiśāstra*[3] (Chinese *Ch'eng-shih-lun*, composed by Harivarman, c. 250-350 A.D.).

> "A question is asked:—We actually see that the parts of the body, e.g. the hair, nails, are each different. How can the wise man take this to be the self ?
> "The answer is spoken:—There are some who see the spirit as a grain of barley or as a mustard-seed, etc., dwelling within the heart : the spirit of a brahmin is white, that of a

> Kṣatriya is yellow, that of a Vaiśya is red, and that of a Śūdra is black.[4] And in the Vedas it is taught : In the very beginning of the world, the colour of the spirit of the Great Person (*Mahāpuruṣa*) was like the radiance of the sun. If a person knew it, he could cross over birth and death—there is no other path. Of small measure in a small person, large in a large person, it dwells in a cavern within the body. A person who practices meditation can see the aspect of lustre of the spirit within the body, like a string[5] through pure gems."

The theory following "in the Vedas it is taught" is the same as that already given in the *Abhidharma-mahāvibhāṣā-śāstra*. We might also say that the last sentence resembles the next passage.

> "Then when the man who has unified his mind perceives the original essence of the Brahman in this world by means of the truth of the *ātman* which is compared to a lamp-light, he shall know the unborn and steadfast spirit which transcends all essences, and shall be released from all bondage." (*Śvet.-Up.* II.15).

Now, the fact that these passages considered to be theories of the "Vedas" in the *Satyasiddhi-śāstra* coincide for the most part with the *Śvetāśvatara-Upaniṣad,* III.8, III.7, and II.15, and that the contents of the first two verses are combined and quoted *one after the other,* perhaps indicates that not only by the time the *Satyasiddhi-śāstra* came into existence (250-350 A.D.), but also in the period in which the *Abhidharma-mahāvibhāṣā-śāstra* was complied (about 100 to 150 years later), the *Śvetāśvatara Upaniṣad* had already been put together in its present form.

And the idea that the spirit "is like a grain of barley or like a mustard-seed dwelling within the heart" is likewise to be found in the Upaniṣads.

> "This *puruṣa* which lives within the heart consists of mind, has light as its basic quality, and is like a grain of rice or of barley. It is the controller of all, the ruler of all; it directs all whatever there is." (*Bṛhad.-Up.* V.6)

Further, it is also taught in the teachings of the famous Śāṇḍilya (*Śāṇḍilya-vidyā*).[4]

> "This *puruṣa,* existing within the *ātman* (physical body) and consisting of gold, is like a grain of rice or like a grain

of barley, or like a grain of millet, or like the core of a grain of millet." (*Śatapatha-Brāhmaṇa.* X.6.3.2)

Again, nothing like the "spirit of the brahmin is white, that of a Kṣatriya is yellow, that of a Vaiśya is red, and that of a Śūdra is black" is taught anywhere in the Vedas, but such an idea does appear in the epic poems of the orthodox brahmins. For example, one says that the spirit (*jīva*) has six colours, white, yellow, red, blue, gray and black, and of these white is the most excellent, while the others are gradually lower and black is the worst. The fate of the soul is related to its colour.[5] The theory above mentioned of the *Satyasiddhi-śāstra* might have been influenced by this.

As we have seen above, by the time of sectarian splits and divisions in Buddhism, the phrases and verses from the Brāhmaṇas and Upaniṣads were being quoted almost literally from the original sources. In the Early Buddhist texts even, thoughts similar to those of the Vedānta are faintly alluded to and then rejected, but there are no quotations beginning with "it is said in the Vedas." In the next period, on the contrary, not only are the theories presented in the early Buddhist texts quoted in almost exactly the same form as the prototype verse, but in addition, the original passages are mentioned or quoted as "a theory of knowledge texts (the Veda)," or "a theory in the Vedas." We may be appraised, consequently, that the Buddhists of this period had become quite well versed in the scriptures of the orthodox brahmins.

Let us now consider some of the reasons why the passages of the Upaniṣads were frequently quoted in this way. It is quite possible to suppose that one reason was that the then extant Upaniṣads had reached the eminence of being worshipped and followed among the common men of the day. However, it might perhaps have been rather that because quite a few of the orthodox brahmins of the time were converted to Buddhists and became Buddhist priests, the scholars of Hīnayāna Buddhism had the first-hand opportunity to learn the Upaniṣadic sayings as they were originally taught from the lips of the new converts themselves.[6] After all, since the Old Upaniṣads came into being before the advent of the Buddha and from that time on were handed down from master to disciple by word of mouth generation after generation, it would certainly seem that in some region of the land, they had been quite properly studied and memorized. Still, one must not overlook the fact that the very earliest Buddhism developed upon a foundation of the new citizen classes in the recently arisen cities of the time, and was thus limited by such historical and social conditions, the early Buddhists, for example, not evincing a favourable attitude towards Sanskrit, the language employed by the Brahmins, and in many cases the vocabulary of the religious order being the colloquial language. This coincides with the circumstances of early Jainism. But as the Buddhist community progressively developed and several sectarian divisions came into being, a few of the sects made Sanskrit, the traditional cultural language of India, their common language in the religious community, and some of them rewrote their scriptures in Sanskrit. The most influential of the Hīnayāna sects was the Sarvāstivāda, and this sect wrote nearly all of its works in Sanskrit. As a consequence, the scholarly priests in the Buddhist community who had adopted Sanskrit as their daily language were in a far better position to understand the works of the Brahmins, much more so than the other early Buddhist scholars who used only the colloquial languages. Of course, there must have been quite a few others among the Buddhists of the early period who were able to read and interpret Sanskrit, but insofar as they used the common language of the day, they must have somehow had the feeling that Sanskrit was rather *formal and distant* from their everyday language. Scholars of the Sarvāstivāda, on the other hand, were accustomed to employing Sanskrit in their writing and reading, in their conversation and records of everyday living, so that they were able to understand relatively easily the Vedas, and, one feels, must have experienced some pleasure at being able to know their contents. The fact that they could comprehend the Vedas should perhaps be interpreted as being one of the attendant phenomena accompanying the great historical transition which saw early Buddhism, a religion in the very small region of Magadha, come into its own as a religion covering all of India, losing its character as a newly arisen belief of a remote colony, and coming out in the mainstream of Indian culture by means mainly of its employment of Sanskrit.

But it becomes evident from our examination of the materials above that the Buddhists then were merely acquainted with the men who believed in the Upaniṣads and the expressions contained therein, but yet made no references to the great effort of later Vedānta scholars who, confronted with the difficulties of the contradictions apparent in the Upaniṣads, tried to work out some rational and unified way of interpreting them. Lack of reference to this academic tradition which sought to set up systematic and orderly doctrines by seeking out a unified plan of Upaniṣadic thought, would seem to show that such a tendency if it existed at all, was very subdued, and not enough so as to attract the attention of the Buddhists.

In the *Lalitavistara*,[7] a biography of the Buddha which was originally a work of the Sarvāstivādins and which later was adopted by the Mahāyānists, there are mentioned the schools of Sāṃkhya, Yoga, Vaiśeṣika, Hetuvidyā, and Bārhaspatya as contemporary philosophical schools, but there is no mention made of the Vedānta school. Therefore, those Brahmins who were adherents of the Upaniṣads probably believed in the sayings literally. As, for example, in the expressions above like "the size of a thumb," they firmly believed that the *puruṣa* was indeed just exactly the size of the human thumb, and those who, like the later Vedāntists, understood this phrase to contain an abstruse and symbolic meaning, to which were then added their own philosophical interpretations, must indeed have been few.

Now, what thus is recorded as Vedāntic thought of the time, seems to rather be an amalgamation of the thought of both the Vedānta and the Sāṃkhya. The *Buddhacarita* by Aśvaghosa has an account of the story taught by the sage Ārāḍa to Prince Siddhārtha which mentions such ideas as "the ones who meditate on the ātman" (*ātmacintaka*),[8] and "the philosophers of the supreme Brahman" (*paramabrahmavādin*).[9] According to these doctrines, the sphere of liberation is "the imperishable sphere" (*padam akṣaram*)[10] and the "attributeless, permanent, imperishable, Supreme Brahma" (*paramaṃ brahma nirliṅgaṃ dhruvam akṣaram.*)[11] In this respect, some influence of ancient Upaniṣadic ideas, can be found but the thought here expressed as that of Ārāḍa, is more of a mixture of Sāṁkhya and Vedānta philosophy, and coincides with the thoughts expounded in Book XII of the *Mahābhārata*.[12] Consequently, the thought of this period which had general influence throughout the society is perhaps not the Vedāntic school in the narrow sense, but rather philosophical ideas along the lines mentioned above.

At any rate, Buddhists during this period had contact with Vedānta ideas of varying tendencies, and had assumed a positive posture of decisive antagonism towards these concepts. When the Vedāntic thought is referred to in the early Buddhist text, it is by no means always refuted by recourse to logical arguments; rather, the accounts related the recourse to the supernatural powers of the Buddha to break down and overcome the followers of such heretic doctrines. They have yet to take up the question of logical disputation itself. The scholars, on the other hand, of the Sarvāstivāda who compiled the Abhidharma, decisively attacked and refuted the other doctrines by means of logical discourse. And as one example of logical refutation used against Vedānta thought, we should draw attention especially to the attack launched against the concept of "presiding deity (= *Īśvara*)."

Although the concept of "presiding deity" had already been refuted and rejected in the early Buddhist Canon, the great treatise of the Sarvāstivāda, the *Mahā-vibhāṣā-śāstra*, (in its Chinese version)[13] records the following account :

"All that exists is nothing but *puruṣa*, i.e. *pudgala*. All that happens is caused by the transformation of the Self-existent (*Īśvara*). This non-cause is reckoned as the cause by some who observe the religious rules and prohibitions (*śīlavrataparāmarśa*), and should be overcome by the right view about suffering."

(Commentary :) The "this non-cause is reckoned as the cause by some who observe the rules and prohibitions" designates the own (true) nature (*prakṛti*), and "that should be overcome by the right view about suffering' designates its method of treatment (*pratipakṣa*). The detailed explanation is as before.

Question :—How have these views arisen ?

Answer :—They are declared by some outsiders who either are influenced by false ways of thinking, or get pernicious views by meditation, or are misled by evil friends, and that is how these views arise, just as we have learned before. However, nothing (*dharmas*) is caused by *Īśvara*, for things appear gradually and successively (*krameṇa*). If it be said that the whole world comes into existence caused by the transformation of *Īśvara*, then everything should indeed be born at the same instant (*yugapad*). For their causes all exist, and nothing could prevent their not being born. (Cf. *Tattvasaṃgraha*, v. 165). Or if it is said that Īśvara has additional and outside causes so that it can give birth to things, (it) the creator then is not Iśvara, because there are extra causes. (Cf. *Tattva.* v. 159). Or suppose it is said that it is because all dharmas arise in accordance with the desires and pleasures of Īśvara, that they do not suddenly arise. If so, why do the desires and pleasure of Īśvara not suddenly arise ? For Īśvara gives birth to desires and pleasure and there is never anything which can obstruct it. (Cf. *Tattva.* v. 162) Or if it be said that Īśvara needs additional and extra causes in order to give birth to desires and pleasure, then it is not Īśvara. And this again would be a *regressus ad infinitum* (*anavasthā*), for these causes would again require other causes in order to be born. (Cf. *Tattva.* v. 161).

And if it be said that Īśvara gives birth to all dharmas, then because the cause is undifferentiated, the dharmas must also be undifferentiated. (Cf. *Tattva.* v. 136). Or if it be said that Īśvara produces the very first dharma, and afterward, many dharmas are evolved and produced from this dharma, how is it that this dharma can be said to be able to produce many dharmas ? For like Īśvara, its body is one. (Cf. *Tattva.* v. 170).

"And again, all the dharmas which are produced must be eternal, because an effect resembles its cause. (Cf. *Tattva.* v. 138).

"Again, Īśvara itself should not be able to produce these things, for it is eternal like space (*ākāśa*). (Cf. *Tattva.* vv. 140, 147)."

As we may note here, the monistic theistic doctrine that "all and every living thing comes into being by the transformation of 'Īśvara,' i.e. "the presiding deity," is logically refuted. And the Sarvāstivādins, for their part, arrived at the conclusion that such a doctrine is a pernicious theory which should be included within the views of "those who observe the religious rules and prohibitions," having mistaken what is not the true cause for the real cause, and that the way to overcome it is by correctly cognizing the truth of suffering.

Let us now try to express in more detail the import of the above translation. (As we have noted, the same refutation appears without much change in the chapter *Puruṣaparīkṣā* of the *Tattva-saṃgraha* of later days, and for the sake of reference, we shall again append the verse number).

(1) If one holds that everything in the world arises from the presiding deity, the cause of these things should exist latently within that deity. Therefore, when the presiding deity carried out the work of creating the world, all things should have been born at the same time. For no cause exists which would serve as a hindrance to their simultaneous production. Yet in the real world it does not happen that everything is produced and determined at the same time, for a vast range of phenomena are continually and successively being produced. If it were true that all things arise from the presiding deity, such would not be the case as it is (*Tattva.* v. 65).

(2) If one says that "because the presiding deity during the course of its creation of the world needs to rely on another cause in order to complete that process, all things are not brought into being at the same time," the presiding deity is then limited by another cause, and cannot be called the presiding deity (*Īśvara*, i.e., the self-existent, the free one). (*Tattva.* v. 159).

(3) To say that "all things come into being, being based upon the desires of the presiding deity, and so do not arise at the same time," invites the question : "Why is it that these desires of the presiding deity do not arise simultaneously ?" Since it is the ruler of all things, it is also the ruler (controller) of its own desires, and there is not supposed to be anything in existence which could prevent this. (*Tattva.* v. 162).

(4) If one tries to justify the position by the assertion that "all things cannot arise at the same time, because the presiding deity gives rise to its desire to create the world by relying upon some other cause," it cannot be said that this deity is in control of its own desires, and consequently, it cannot be the presiding deity. Furthermore, the cause which it relies upon would have to be based upon another cause and that again would require still another cause, thus the entire argument falls into an infinite regress (*anavasthā*). (*Tattva.* v. 161).

(5) Now, one who holds that the presiding deity causes all things to arise, must if he is a Vedāntist admit that such a presiding deity as the root cause is unique and undifferentiated, all things, as the effect, must also be unique and undifferentiated. Thus the assertion that the differentiated and multifarious elements of the world developed from a unique and undifferentiated principle is clearly illogical. (*Tattva.* v. 136).

(6) The explanation that "the presiding deity, as the world-cause, first produced forth a principle in the remote past, and from this principle a great number of things were brought successively into existence later," raises the question : How could this principle, produced in the very beginning, give rise to a great many other things ? Since that principle, like the same presiding deity, would in itself be unique and undifferentiated, it would be illogical to assume that it could evolve the differentiated aspects of the phenomenal world. (It is possible that what is attacked here is the idea that the world-cause first gave birth to something like the Brahma or the Brahma-egg in the beginning, and at some time, the latter gave rise to the objects in the world). (*Tattva.* v. 170).

(7) The effect must always have a homogeneity and resemblance with its cause. Therefore, since the presiding deity is eternal, the phenomenal world, as its effect, must also be eternal. In effect, it cannot be impermanent. But this assertion is contradicted by our experience of reality. (*Tattva.* v. 138).

(8) Because the presiding deity, the world-cause, is eternal, it will not be able to give rise to anything. This must be the same as in the case of space (*ākāśa*), which also cannot produce anything, since it is eternal. Only something which is impermanent and perishable has the potential to give birth to another thing. (*Tattva.* vv. 140, 147).

We have reproduced above with some elaboration the general import of the verse examined earlier in the Chinese version of the *Mahāvibhāṣā-śāstra.* Up to the present time, the earliest arguments and refutations of the doctrine of spiritualism in Indian history have usually been taken to be those found chiefly in the *Bodhicaryāvatāra* IX.119-126, by Śāntideva (7th century) and those discussed by the Jain scholar, Hemacandra (12th century).[14] We, however, have discovered that long before that time, around the second century A.D., Buddhist scholars in the mountains of Kaśmīr had elaborated detailed speculations in order to refute theistic doctrines. And the arguments there propounded were handed down later among the Buddhists.[15] Prior to Śāntideva, both Maitreyanātha and Asaṅga had already recounted arguments similar to these, and the doctrines of Śāntarakṣita and Kamalaśīla, as pointed out above, also bear a remarkably close resemblance.

Well now, the refutations have taken up in this section coincide with those found in Śāntarakṣita and Kamalaśīla, which we shall list later, and as we see in the explanation of the latter, he is attacking the *Vedavādins*, it might be well to take it that the *Mahāvibhāṣā-śāstra* is also hitting at the Vedavādins and, in a limited sense, the Vedāntists as well (together with the other schools of Hinduism which had adopted that philosophy).

1. *TT*.XXVII.999b. Further, the idea that the size of the soul corresponds to that of the body also is set forth in Book 99 (*TT*.XXVII.997c) and Book 200 (ibid. 999b, 1000c) of the *Mahāvibhāṣā-śāstra.*

2. *TT*.XXVII.999c. The source for this comes from Hakuju Ui, *Indo Tetsugaku Kenkyū*, Vol. I., pp. 174-175.

3. *TT*.XXXII.316b.

3'. The idea that the colour of men differs with soul had already been maintained by the Jainas and the Ājīvikas. (A. F. R. Hoernle, *ERE*. I, p. 262a).

3''. The idea that ātman is like a thread is mentioned in the Sāṁkhya school also. Cf. *Suvarṇa-saptati*, Gauḍapāda's *Bhāṣya* and *Māṭhara-vṛtti*, ad verse 18.

4. The corresponding passage in *Chāndogya-Up*. III.14.3 differs somewhat from this.

"This then is my *ātman* which exists within the heart. Truly smaller than a grain of rice, than a grain of barley corn, than a mustard seed, a grain of millet or the core of a grain of millet, it is my *ātman* which exists within the heart."

5. *MBH*.XII.281.33. Hopkins; *GEL*. 179-180. Further, see Kanakura, *Indo Kodai Seishinshi*, pp. 203-204. And on the phrase, "like a string through pure gems" in the *Satya-siddhi-śāstra*, see the note to v. 18 of the *Sāṃkhya-kārikās*. (The present work, Chap. II, Sect. 6).

6. Prior to the Buddha, the religious texts were handed down primarily by recitation, but after the period of early Buddhism, the general practice in India was to record the words on bark, leaves, bamboo, plates of metal and other objects. (G. Bühler : *Die Indische Paläographie*, S. 3-6). Being now able to look at the scriptures as they had been written down, the Hīnayāna scholars of this period might have been thus enabled to record with some accuracy the Upaniṣadic sayings. Further study on this subject is required.

7. *Lalitavistara*, hrsg. von S. Lefmann, Teil. I, S. 156.

8. *Buddhacarita*, XII.20.

9. *Ibid.*, XII.20.

10. *Ibid.*, XII.41.

11. *Ibid.*, XII.65. Cf. *MBh*. XII.8136.

12. Cf. O. Strauss : *zur Geshichte des Sāṃkhya, WZKM.*, 1913, S.257-275 E. H. Johnston : *The Buddhacarita*, Part II, p. 167 ff (and the footnotes on this section).

13. *TT.* XXVII.993b.

14. Jacobi : *Gottesidee* [Translation in Japanese by Yamada and Itō as *Indo Kodai Shinkanshi* (History of the Concept of God in Ancient India), pp. 66, 184 ff.]

15. In the *Sarvasiddhāntasaṃgraha*, IV.4.22-37, a work attributed to Śaṅkara, a refutation of the concept of presiding deity is presented as one of the Buddhists' views.

SECTION IV. THE MAHĀYĀNA SŪTRAS AND VEDĀNTA THOUGHT

An interesting question is that of the attitude assumed by writers in the Mahāyāna Sūtras towards Vedānta thought. We would have to search a long time, however, in that vast and voluminous compendium of works on the Mahāyāna to find any account which mentions the Vedānta Philosophy. Even passages which discuss the Upaniṣads or refer to their ideas are difficult to come by. In the earliest Mahāyāna Scriptures, e.g., the *Prajñāpāramitā-sūtra*, the *Saddharma-puṇḍarīka-sūtra* and other works, no discussion is made of these heretical theories. This fact is certainly worthy of our attention.

In somewhat later centuries, however, when intercourse had become more frequent with Brahmanic ideas, the Mahāyāna Sūtras clearly refer to the thought of the Upaniṣads and the Vedānta as heretical doctrines. As an example of this, we have at hand an account given in the *Mahāparinirvāṇa-sūtra* (*Nan pen ta pan neih p'an ching*, the Southern Chinese version, Nj. 114) of the Mahāyāna. In this Sūtra, the Tathāgata is said to have originally taught the doctrine of no-self, and while he sometimes spoke of the self, his concept of self "was nothing like the personal self imagined by the ordinary man." Then, this heretical theory is given :

"The self which is presumed by the ordinary man (*pṛthagjana*) and the foolish man (*bāla*) is, in some theories, said to be as large as a thumb, or like a mustard-seed, or like an atom. The self taught by the Tathāgata is completely different from any of these."[1] A similar theory is presented in another passage of the same work:

"Men who are not saints broadly assume that the self has more or less such and such an aspect. as if it were like a weed, or perhaps like a grain of rice, a bean, a thumb, etc. In this way they give birth to various false conceptions, but the symbols of this false thinking are not true."[2]

Again, it is recounted that when the śrāvaka and the pratyeka-buddha of the Hīnayāna asked the general folk about the appearance and state of the self, they were told :

> "It is as large as a thumb, or perhaps it is like a grain of rice, or like a weed. There are those who said that the form of the self dwells within the heart and is as bright as the sun."[3]

These views correspond in general to the tenets of the hermit Śāṇḍilya in the *Śatapatha-Brāhmaṇa* (X.6.3).[4] And while the Upaniṣads frequently refer to the size of the ātman being "as large as a thumb,"[5] the assertion that it is similar to an "atom" appears not only in the Old Upaniṣads,[6] but can also be found in the *Brahma-sūtra* (II. 3. 19-32). It would seem, therefore, that the author of the Mahāyānistic *Mahāparinirvāṇa-sūtra* must have had some knowledge of Upaniṣadic thought.

What offers us a somewhat later, but interesting, account of intercourse with Vedānta thought is the *Laṅkāvatāra-sūtra* (*Ju lang chia ching* in Chinese). This sūtra was formulated comparatively late in the history of Mahāyāna Scriptures. Three versions have been preserved in Chinese translation, and the oldest, the *Lang Chia A Pa To Lo Pao Ching* (four volumes), was translated in 443 during the Sung Dynasty, so that this work must have come into existence, I think, by the end of the fourth century, at the latest. This sūtra contains the doctrines of the fivefold dharma, threefold self-nature, eightfold consciousness and twofold non-self, which are the basic thought of the sūtra itself, but the manner of presentation is confused, and a consistent interpretation eludes us for the moment. Nonetheless, it is quite certain that the concept of *Tathāgata-garbha* is one of the peculiar doctrines that is expounded throughout the entire work. In the sūtra itself, this *Tathāgata-garbha* frequently appears to be regarded as identical with the *ālayavijñāna* of the Vijñānavāda,[7] and is held to be the primal source giving rise to all phenomenal things.

"Oh Mahāmati, the Storehouse of the Thus-come (Tathāgata) is the cause of both good and evil, and is that which creates all living things and pursuits."

tathāgatagarbho Mahāmate kuśalākuśalahetukaḥ sarva-janmagatikartā.[8]

The definition of this Storehouse of the Thus-come is quite similar to that of the Brahman as taught in Vedānta philosophy.[9] The problem now is, what sort of differences exist between the two concepts ? The *Laṅkāvatāra-sūtra* is well-known for its vivid reflection of the state of affairs in the intellectual world of India during that period. It holds, in particular, that Brahman, Viṣṇu, and Īśvara[10] are other names for the Tathāgata, and explains, moreover, its concept of the ultimate state by using the words of Vedānta philosophy. It even says :

"The Supreme Brahma is the ultimate state of existence." (*niṣṭhābhāvaḥ paraṃ brahma*).[11] And in fact the criticism that ultimately both the *Tathāgata-garbha* and the Brahman would be none other than the same principle, seems to have come forth among the Buddhists of the time. In the dialogue between the Bodhisattva Mahāmati and the Buddha we have ample evidence of this occurrence :

"Then the Bodhisattva Mahāmati said to the Buddha : 'Again, the Buddha has expatiated in the Sūtras on the Tahāgata-garbha, even teaching that it is essentially brilliance, and being pure, is the fundamental purity. It is possessed inherently of the 32 marks, exists within all sentient beings, and is like a priceless jewel which has been covered over by some filthy thing. Although it is hidden by the elements (*skandhas*), the spheres (*dhātus*) and abodes (*āyatanas*), and is tainted by the filth of false discriminations like greed, anger and foolishness, it is permanent, steadfast, blissful and eternal—so the Buddha has taught. If this be so, Oh Lord, would not the theory of the *Tathāgata-garbha* be equivalent to *the doctrine of the self held by the outsiders* (*tīrthakara-ātmavāda*) ? The outsiders, too, Oh Blessed One, hold as their doctrine and teaching of the self that 'it is permanent and the agent; separated from all guṇas, it is omnipresent and imperishable (*tīrthakarā api, Bhagavan, nityaḥ kartā nirguṇo vibhur avyaya ity ātmavādopadeśaṃ kurvanti*).' "

To this question, the Buddha replied that he had taught such an idea only for the purpose of leading into Buddhism those who adhered to doctrines of the outsiders.

"The Blessed One said : 'Mahāmati, the doctrine of the *Tathāgata-garbha* which I teach is truly not the same as the theory of self held by outsiders (*tīrthakara-ātmavāda*). But the Tathāgatas, Mahāmati, formed the doctrine of the *Tathāgata garbha* according to the meaning of voidness, reality, Nirvāṇa, unborn, attributeless, desireless, etc., and the Tathāgatas, the Arhats and the Samyak-Sambuddhas, Mahāmati, pointed out the undifferentiated and imageless realm by relying upon the instructions on the *Tathāgata-garbha*, as an introduction in order to lead the foolish man away from his fear of the teaching of selflessness. And, Mahāmati, all the Bodhisattvas and Mahāsattvas of the present and future have formed no attachment in this respect to the self. For example, Mahāmati, just as the potter, by combining his hands, skill, stick, water, cord and labour, can produce many ceramic objects from a lump of fine clay, in the same way, Mahāmati, the Tathāgatas, by combining their wisdom, methods and excellent skill, or by means or the teaching of the (*Tathāgata-*)*garbha* or the doctrine of selflessness, can reveal that the dharmas are selfless so that all aspects of differentiation are ceased, by utilizing these phrases or letters. For this reason, Mahāmati, the teaching of the *Tathāgata-garbha* is not the same as the outsiders' doctrine of the self. Thus, in order to attract those outsiders who adhere to a teaching of self, the Tathāgatas indicate the *Tathāgata-garbha* by means of the teaching on the *Tathāgata-garbha.*—How then (one will think) does the mind of the people who have fallen into the view of a differentiation of an illusory self, and that of the men who have fallen into the realm of the teaching of the three liberations (*vimokṣa*), speedily achieve enlightenment of the supreme truth ? For this purpose, Mahāmati, the Tathāgatas, Arhats and Samyak-Sambuddhas expatiated on the *Tathāgata-garbha*. Therefore, it is not the equivalent of the outsiders' doctrine of self. And thus, Mahāmati, one should now follow (the teaching) of the selflessness (Non-ego) of the Tathāgata and the ('*Tathāgata-*) *garbha*', so that he may put a stop to the views of outsiders."[12]

Even within the ranks of Buddhism, as we have seen in the sentences above, it is evident that there were some who had some doubt about the difference between the thought of the *Tathāgata-garbha* and the Vedānta philosophy (i.e. the Sāṃkhya-Vedānta philosophy). It cannot be denied, in any case, that between the two concepts, there does exist some resemblance in conception.

This can also be said concerning the Vijñaptimātratā philosophy in general. This philosophical system teaches the "evolution of çonsciousness itself" (*vijñāna-pariṇāma*), and this word was also used by the early Vedānta scholars of that period.[13] Consequently, although Śāntarakṣita attacked the Vedānta school, he admitted that their doctrines, when compared with the teachings of the Buddhists, had "only a very small error (*alpāparādha*)."

Elsewhere, we learn that the *Great Sun Sūtra* (*Ta jih ching*, *Mahāvairocana-sūtra*) has recorded some theories of the men who regarded "pure consciousness" (*vijñāna*) as the absolute principle. In the first chapter, *Chu hsin pin*, of this sūtra, thirty types of outsiders are listed, the 16th of which refers to the consciousness theory, held by outsiders. I-hsing, in his *Commentary on the Great Sun Sūtra*, Vol. II, understands this to be : "The saying in the Sūtra, 'or the consciousness,' means that there is one type of people who take this consciousness to be pervasive in all places, from the earth to the water, fire, air and so on. This consciousness pervades and fills all therein."[14] I-hsing refutes this in the following manner :

> "If consciousness or spirit were omnipresent and eternal, it should be able, by itself, to see, hear, perceive and cogitate. Yet, now, what essentially occurs is that by the union of sense-organ and object, we have the birth of consciousness. But in your view the consciousness or spirit has need of nothing else. Again, if consciousness or spirit pervaded the five realms of living beings, how could birth and death recur again and again ? Therefore, we know that it is impossible."

In other words, if the principle of "consciousness" which is being asserted is omnipresent in all things and is also eternal, that consciousness must always be functioning at all times no matter where it is, so that the conscious process should always be arising. Consequently, it cannot be the case that consciousness arises by the contact of our sense-organs with the objects of cognition, such as we experience daily. And if consciousness is omnipresent, it cannot happen that our birth and death, our transmigration, can occur. Thus, what he teaches about consciousness cannot explain the reason why our consciousness and transmigration actually do arise. The idea that *vijñāna* is the absolute principle appears in the Ancient Upaniṣads, and has been already rejected in the earliest Buddhist texts,[15] and it seems again to have here been made the topic of consideration. A thorough investigation of that voluminous corpus of the Mahāyāna should reveal other passages which refer to ideas similar to those of the Vedānta, but it seems more likely that accounts which might be able to clarify directly the history of early Vedānta philosophy are hardly to be expected. It should be adequately noted, however, that the later Mahāyāna Sūtras were composed while struggling against and rejecting, yet at times coming under the influence and persuasion of Vedānta thought.

Notes

1. Southern Recension, *Mahāparinirvāṇa-sūtra*, Vol. VIII. Chap. III (*TT*.XII.618b-c).
2. *Ibid., loc. cit.*, Chapter 12, "The Nature of the Tathāgata," (*TT*. XII.649c).
3. *Ibid., loc. cit.*, (*TT*.XXI.653c). The late Tsukinowa has an article on the ideas of selflessness and the Great-self in the *Mahāyāna-nirvāṇa-sūtra* on these sentences. (Journal, "*Bukkyō kenkyū*," Vol. III, No. 3 (1959, pp. 120-141).
4. Cf. the present chapter, Sect. 3.
5. *Ibid.*, p. 187.
6. Cf. the *Muṇḍ.-Up.* III.1.9, and the *Śvet. Up.* V.8, 9.
7. pp. 221, line 12; 222, lines 6, 9; 223, lines 2, 6, 11; 235, lines 7, 16.
8. p. 221, lines 9-10. Cf. *TT*.XVI.619c.
9. E. g., *Brahma-sūtra* I.1.2, *Vākyapadīya* I.1.
10. *brahmāṇaṁ Viṣṇum Īśvaram* (acc.) p. 192, line 14. (Perhaps a scribal error for *brahmāṇam*).
11. p. 153, line 9. Cf. p. 325.
12. pp. 77, line 13; 79, line 9.
13. Cf. the present chapter, Sect. 6, pp. 379, 391.
14. *TT*. XXXIX.593c.
15. Cf. the present chapter, Sect. 2, p. 183 ff.

SECTION V. THE EARLY MĀDHYAMIKA AND THE UPANIṢADS

Despite the fact that a great number of Mahāyāna *Sūtras* are extant, insofar as there are comparatively few references to the Vedānta thought, and as the chronological order and the dates of their coming into being are still almost entirely unknown, the accounts presented therein, as has already been pointed out, offer relatively little in the way of contributing even indirectly towards the history of Vedānta philosophy. Even so, there nevertheless are innumerable references to Brahmanical thought in the *writings* of the teachers of Mahāyāna, whose dates have been verified to a considerate extent. We may therefore consider their accounts as highly valuable source materials in our elucidation of the history of Vedānta thought.

1. *Nāgārjuna and the Upaniṣads*

The most famous work of Nāgārjuna is his *Madhyamaka-kārikā*, the major concern of which is to criticise the Sarvāstivāda, the Vātsīputrīya, and the Sāmmitīya schools within Buddhism, and the Sāṃkhya and Vaiśeṣika schools outside of Buddhism. No logical discussion is made, however, of the Upaniṣadic thought or Vedānta philosophy, and very little mentions made on the word in the various commentaries (*Akutobhaya, Prasannapadā*, the commentary by Piṅgalanetra, etc.). One feels that, consequently, for Nāgārjuna himself, there was no particular urgency in taking up the Vedānta school as an object of logical criticism, so that whatever influence it had, it must have been very slight.

However, in another work by Nāgārjuna; the *Daśabhūmi-vibhāṣā-śāstra,* there is some treatment of thought which seems to resemble that of the Upaniṣads. In Vol. X, Chapter 22[1] ("Criticism of the Omniscient Person") of that work, he engages in a logical debate on the subject whether or not the Buddha is a man who knows all (omniscient). There, the questioner (refuter) lists several reasons, and asserts that "the Buddha is not omniscient. As one of the reasons, he points out the circumstance that the Buddha is not completely versed in all the Vedas. Nāgārjuna responds to this by answering, "Since the method leading to the liberation of men is not taught in the Vedas, the Buddha did not teach the Vedas, although he knew them well."

"If you say that the Buddha did not teach the Vedas and other heretic scriptures, and therefore was not omniscient, I must now answer that in the Vedas there does not exist a good method for attaining the desired calm; there are only various fallacious doctrines. By all that the Buddha taught, everyone can attain to that wonderful calm. Therefore, although the Buddha did know the Vedas and other scriptures, as these words cannot aid men to attain the desired calm, and thus, he did not teach them."

Hereupon, the refuter asserts that "a method for liberation is also taught in the Vedas."

"It is said : In the Vedas also there are teachings for the desired calm and liberation. In the beginning of the world everything was in darkness and there existed nothing. At first, a Great Person appeared, who was like the sun. If someone sees him, he can cross over death and obstacles, and there are other guidances. Again it is taught, if the body of a person is small, his spirit is small, and if the body of a person is large, his spirit is large. The body forms the abode of the spirit which dwells always therein. If one develops by wisdom and releases the spirit from its bonds, he can obtain release. Thus, we must know that in the Vedas there is calm and release."

The Vedic verse quoted here coincides with the one we quoted from the *Satya-siddhi-śāstra* and examined in an earlier section: it also corresponds to *Śvet. Up.* III.8, III.7, II.15. (See also the *Śvet.-Up.* IV.15, 16 on the latter part of the verse). In reply to this objection, Nāgārjuna answers : "Because the four metaphysical incongruities (*viparyāsa*), i.e., eternality, bliss, self and purity, are taught in the Vedas, liberation by means of the Vedas is also impossible."

"It is answered : This is not the case. For in the Vedas are the four metaphysical anomalies : (1) In the world there is no eternality, yet separate from it, there is an eternal world. This is as to teach that if one once performs the rituals of heaven, he will fall back, if twice, he again falls back, but if a third time, he will not fall back. This is the metaphysical anomaly of there being eternality in the non-eternal. (2) The world is suffering, but they teach that there is an eternal and blissful place. This is the metaphysical anomaly of there being bliss in suffering. (3) Again it is taught, the spirit of the self evolves and becomes a child, and prays to have long life. The child is another body, so how could it be the self ? This is the metaphysical anomaly of there being a self in selflessness. (4) It is taught that the body is pure, supreme and imcomparable, unsurpassed by gold, silver or precious jewels. This is the metaphysical anomaly of there being purity in impurity. The metaphysical anomalies are not true, and not being true, how can there be the desired calm ? Therefore, in the Vedas, there is no method for the desired calm."

The first anomaly on eternality, e.g., the assertion that "there is an eternal world," is frequently used in the Upaniṣads to explain the eternal life of the person who has attained the "world of Brahma (*brahmaloka*)", and perhpas refers to the teaching that once a person reaches there, he no longer dies and returns to this world. (Cf. *Bṛhad.-Up.* VI.2.15; *Chānd.-Up.* VIII.15; *Muṇḍ.-Up.* III.2.6, etc.) The second anomaly concerning bliss, i.e., the idea that "there is a place of eternal bliss," means that the world of Brahma is by far more beautiful, splendid and blissful than this earth, and seems to correspond to the accounts in the Upaniṣads (Cf. *Kauṣ.-Up.* I.3-5; *Chānd.-Up.* VIII.5, 3). Now the third anomaly on the self has some relation to the idea in the society of ancient India which felt that it was important, after giving birth to a child and raising it, to instruct it in performing the ritual for life after death. "By his son alone, the father stands firm" (*Bṛhad.-Up.* I.5.17). While such a thought can be found throughout the general works of the Brahmins,[2] it may in the sentences of Nāgārjuna, refer to the idea of "successful bestowing" (*saṃpatti saṃpradāna*) at the instant of one's death. In the Upaniṣads, there is a prescribed ritual which states that the father, at the instant of his impending death, should call his son to approach the head of his bed, and perform a kind of ritual which symbolizes that the father transfers to his son all his physiological and psychological functions, the father praying for the son's prosperity and happiness, and the son praying for the father's rebirth in heaven (*Bṛhad.-Up.* I.5.17-20; *Kauṣ.-Up.* II.15). As a result of so much esteem for the son, the son is even said to be his ātman (or self). (*ātmā vai putranāmāsi. Śat. Br.* XIV.9.4.26. Cf. *Vedāntasāra* § 147). As for the fourth anomaly, the concept that our body itself is pure, this is not found in the Upaniṣads, but a passage does exist which teaches that one can obtain a pure body :

"He who obtains a body formed from the fire of Yoga,

shall have no disease, no old age and no death." (*Śvet. Up.* II.12)

The opponent, however, asserts that "by means of knowing the Vedas, one can attain liberation."

"It is asked :—It is taught in the Vedas that the one who can know the Vedas becomes pure and peaceful. How can you say that there is no method for obtaining the absolute calm ?"

It is not clear to which passage in the extant Vedas the sentence given above refers, but it seems to be closest in import to the text found in the *Chāndogya Upaniṣad* VII.15. There it is explained that a person who studies the Vedas under a Master, and continues to study and recite them even after returning home as a householder, "will reach the world of Brahman, and will never return (to this world)."

Nāgārjuna refutes this argument by saying that "while there is something taught in the Vedas which resembles liberation, it refers to rebirth as a long-lived god (dīrghāyuṣo devāḥ) and is not the true liberation."

"It is answered :—Although the Vedas teach that he who knows them is peaceful, this is not the ultimate liberation. They think that liberation arises in another body, and teach that liberation is attained by the long-lived gods. Therefore, there is really no liberation in the Vedas.

"And again, it is taught in the Vedas that there are three parts : first, the *mantras* or incantations; second, the *arthavāda* or explanatory passages; and third, the *vidhi* or rules. The *mantras* say, e.g., 'May I obtain a wife, children, cattle and horses, gold and silver and precious jewels !' The *arthavādas* say, e.g., 'You, oh God of Fire (*Agni*), with black head, red neck and yellow body, are always in the five elements of all creatures.' The *vidhis* say, e.g., 'This deed must be performed, and this must not be performed,' just as in the ceremony of the first receiving of fire from the Kṛttikā stars (the Pleiades). But in reality, these *mantras, arthavādas* and *vidhis* do not lead to calm and liberation. Why ? Because the lusting after worldly pleasure, the burning of Kuśa grass and the recitation of formulas have nothing to do with true wisdom. Unless one eliminates afflictions (*kleśas*), how can he have liberation ?"

The central problem of the logical debate given above is this : when the interlocutor (of the opposing school) stoutly maintains that "instructions leading to liberation are also taught in the Vedas," Nāgārjuna replies that "the true liberation is not taught in the Vedas : what is taught amounts to no more than a mistaken conception that liberation consists of being born and attaining long life in a better world in the future." Since the discussion of liberation is found in the Vedas and particularly, the Upaniṣads, the "Vedas" referred to here may justifiably be interpreted as being limited to the *Upaniṣads alone*. And therefore, the Upanisadic doctrine known to Nāgārjuna consisted merely of being reborn in a better world in the future. This fact can also be ascertained from the passages of the Upaniṣads compared one by one with the words of Nāgārjuna in the foregoing. These theories are the inferior teachings in the Upaniṣads and, as can be seen in the standpoint of Śaṅkara later, belong to the "lower knowledge" (*aparā vidyā*). Whereupon we may speculate as follows : During that period, the passages of the Upaniṣads were being faithfully handed down and interpreted and followed in a strictly literal sense; their influence ended here, and there were no thorough-going attempts to formulate a logical and consistent doctrine running through the entire work, such as we have in the Vedānta philosophy to appear later. And therefore, I think we can say that the Vedānta school had yet to assume a definitive form as a true philosophical school.

Further evidence to verify this is also found in the Vedic divisions as mentioned by Nāgārjuna. As we saw above, the brahmin who engaged in debate with Nāgārjuna, divided the entire Vedas in three general parts: the *mantras*, or incantations; the *arthavāda*, or explanatory passages; and the *vidhi*, or rules.

The importance of this fact must not be overlooked. For the construction of each of the four Vedas is divided into two : the Saṃhitās and the Brāhmaṇas. The Saṃhitā consists of *mantras*, the generic term for laudatory chants, ritual formulas and magical phrases. At present, when only the Vedas are mentioned, it is generally taken to mean only the Saṃhitās, as for example, in the case of the Ṛg-Veda, which is the abbreviated title of the *Ṛg-Veda-Saṃhitā*. On the other hand, the Brāhmaṇas are the explanatory literature appended to each of the Veda Saṃhitās, and their contents, according to the Non-dualistic Monistic School of the Vedānta School, are classified into the following three divisions[3]:

1. *Vidhi.* The imperative rules related to the rituals, which control each of the minute regulations for the performance of rituals and ceremonies, the procedural order of the actual performance, the correct usages of the laudatory chants, ritualistic formulas, etc.

2. *Arthavāda* : the supplementary passages on the *vidhi* (*vidhiśeṣa*), which explain the meaning of the laudatory chants and ritualistic formulas, discuss the etymology, explain the origin and secret meaning of the rituals, and interpose here and there myths, legends and ancient stories.

3. *Vedānta* : the Upaniṣads, which have a different nature from either *vidhis* or *arthavādas,* being mainly passages which expound on Brahman. The Vedānta school looks to this portion as its true sacred authority. The Vedānta portion is the Brahmakāṇḍa, while the others are the Karmakāṇḍa.

In regard to the foregoing division, scholars of the later Mīmāṃsā and Vedānta schools worked out extremely subtle and complicated distinctions, and sub-divided them more minutely, but this does not concern us here. We may diagram the classifications given above as follows :

Veda —	Saṃhitā	*mantra*	...karmakāṇḍa
	Brāhmaṇa —	*vidhi*	...karmakāṇḍa
		arthavāda	...karmakāṇḍa
		vedānta	...brahmakāṇḍa

Referring again to Nāgārjuna's discussion of the Vedas, we see that he has completely ignored the "Vedānta," i.e., the Brahmakāṇḍa. Consequently, the orthodox brahmins with whom Nāgārjuna had direct contact, *did not take the Upaniṣads as having a particularly important significance.* In which case, it would be a problem to dètermine under which of the classifications listed above these brahmins subsumed the Upaniṣad portion; perhaps they may have included them either in the *vidhis* or in the *arthavādas.*[4]

From the considerations above, we can now conclude that among orthodox brahmins during Nāgārjuna's lifetime, the tendency to give a particularly high esteem to the Upaniṣads out of all the Vedic texts had yet to appear to any marked degree.

And even allowing that there were some brahmins who were especially devoted to the Upaniṣads, their influence was very slight and had not attracted the notice of Nāgārjuna. Thus, the vast majority of brahmins still interpreted the Upaniṣads literally.

2. Since Mahāyāna Buddhism and Vedānta have a great number of points in common, not only in technical terms and ways of expression but ideologically as well, the intercourse between the two has been a focus of interest. Not a few scholars in the West and in India have thought that Mahāyāna Buddhism had adopted Upaniṣadic views and Vedānta philosophy : from what we have seen above, however, as the brahmins with whom Nāgārjuna was conversant do not seem to have had any particular esteem for the Upaniṣads over other parts of the Veda, it can hardly be supposed that Nāgārjuna was influenced by any Vedāntic thought coming from such brahmins. When, consequently, some identity or resemblance in literary expression does occur between Nāgārjuna's works and those of the Vedānta schools, we must conclude that the Vedānta school had adopted them from Nāgārjuna. The reverse is impossible. Later, in our discussion of the *Māṇḍūkya Kārikās* and the thought of Bhartṛhari, this point will come up very clearly.

Notes

1. *TT*.XXVI. 74b-76.
2. *Atharva-Veda* XI.4.20; *Taittirīya-Brāhmaṇa* III.12.9.7; *Aitareya-Brāhmaṇa* III.13.9; *Manu* IX.8.
3. Classified according to the *Prasthānabheda* of the *Madhusūdana-Sarasvatī*. Cf. H. Ui, *Indo Tetsugaku Kenkyū*, Vol. IV, p. 431 ff.
4. Madhusūdana-Sarasvatī, after emphasizing that some passages of the Vedānta have a nature differing from either the *vidhis* or *arthavāda*, records the following view : "Sometimes, however, the Vedānta (portion of the Veda) is said to be *vidhi* simply for the reason that it teaches something hitherto unknown; but again since it is not a text expressing a command (*vidhi*), but is a group of sentences that is an authoritative source of knowledge, sometimes it is called a "teaching of truth" (*bhūtārthavāda*). Neither of these is objectionable."

2. *Orthodox Brahmanical Thought Mentioned in Āryadeva's Śāstra on Heretic and Hīnayānist Nirvāṇa*

Āryadeva, disciple of Nāgārjuna, directs his special polemical attention towards schools outside of Buddhism; nonetheless, he has seldom referred to the thought of the Vedānta line. In his work, *The Śāstra by the Bodhisattva (Ārya-) Deva on the Explanation of Nirvāṇa by (Twenty) Heretical and Hīnayāna (Teachers) Mentioned in the Laṅkā (-avatāra)-sūtra (T'i-p'o-p'u-sa-shih-lang-chia-ching-chung-wai-tao-hsiao-sheng-nieh-p'an-lun* Nj. 1260), however, both the Upaniṣadic thought and the orthodox Brahmanical ideas are presented in some detail. This work classifies into twenty types, and minutely examines one by one, the arguments enumerated in the *Laṅkāvatāra-sūtra*[1] and related to the concept of Nirvāṇa held by schools outside of Buddhism. It is uncertain whether this work is really by Āryadeva,[2] the disciple of Nāgārjuna, but as it was translated by Bodhiruci (508-535), it must have been composed by the fifth century at the latest. In the following we shall examine the orthodox brahmanical thought presented in this work.

First of all, the theory of the orthodox brahmins who followed the Vedas is introduced as a theory of the Vedavādins.[3]

1. "It is asked:—Which outsiders teach that the Brahmā Deva is the cause of Nirvāṇa ?"

"It is answered : The fourth class of outsiders, the *Vedavādins*, teach that from the navel of the god Nārāyaṇa is born the great lotus flower, and from the lotus is born Brahmā Deva, the forefather of creatures (*pitāmaha*). All living and non-living things are made by Brahmā :[4] from the mouth of Brahmā are born the Brahmins; from his two arms are born the nobility (*kṣatriya*); from his two thighs the Vaiśyas; from his both feet are born the Śūdras. All the earth is a sacrificial place in which are performed acts to bring happiness and merit. All lotus flowers are produced so that they may be used as offerings. Undergoing transformation, it makes the mountains and fields, birds and beasts. Among men, the domestic animals like pigs, sheep, asses and horses, in this world-arena are killed to be offered to the Brahmā Deva, so that man may obtain rebirth in Nirvāṇa, the name of Brahmā's world. And therefore, the Vedavādins teach that Brahmā Deva is said to always be the cause of Nirvāṇa."[5]

Although this account mentions the *Vedavādins,* it would appear that the theory given about is closer to the *Puruṣa-sūkta*[6] in the Vedas. This hymn came into being around the latter period of the *Ṛg-Veda*, which teaches that the gods made puruṣa, i.e. the original man, the object of sacrifice, and, as a result of carrying out the ceremony, all the things in the world evolved from each of its parts.

> "All things of the past and of the future, everything in this whole universe, is none other than puruṣa." (2)
>
> "From the completely burned sacrifice flowed forth the liquid mixture tasting of ghee. All species of living beings which dwell in the sky, in the forests, and in the villages are born from it." (8)
>
> "Horses, too, are born from it, and every beast which has two rows of teeth is born from it. Cattle, too, are born from it, and both goats and sheep are also born from it." (10)
>
> "When puruṣa was cut into small pieces, into how many different portions was it transformed ? What did its mouth become ? What its two arms, what its thighs, and what were its two feet called ?" (11)
>
> "Its mouth became the brahmins, its two arms the Kṣatriyas, its thighs are now the Vaiśyas, and from its two feet the Śūdras were born." (12)
>
> "Candra (the moon) was born from its heart, and Sūrya (the sun) came out from its eye; Indra and Agni (fire) were born from its mouth, and Vāyu (the wind) was born from its breath." (13)
>
> "From its navel arose the world of the sky, and the world of the gods originated from its head. The world of the earth was born from its feet, and the regions from its ear. In the way was this world created." (14)

A cosmogonical myth similar to the above is recounted also in the *Mahābhārata*,[7] where the creation of the world by Prajāpati is told. It, however, does not coincide with the account in Āryadeva's *Śāstra* where the Brahmā Deva is born from the navel of Nārāyaṇa (i.e., Viṣṇu), and the world is constructed from this Brahmā, so that among one section of the religious students of India during that time, some men must have actually lived who taught such a myth of creation based upon the Vedas.[8]

Other Buddhist works[9] have also presented the myth that the lotus flower arose from the navel of Viṣṇu, that Brahmā sits within that lotus, giving birth to "the heavens and earth, and all mankind." Even in the Ancient Upaniṣads, furthermore is there taught the creation of the world from Puruṣa[10] or Brahmā,[11] though these accounts are by no means in agreement with that in Āryadeva's *Śāstra.*

It is also a brahmanical doctrine that the grass, trees, birds and beasts which are killed as sacrifices in the rituals, are born again into a good condition in the future world, and that the men also who perform these ceremonies will receive happiness in a future life. (See, for example, *Manu* V.39, 40, 42; *Viṣṇu Code* 51. 61 ff.; and the *Yoga-Śāstra* II.33 ff.)

Āryadeva has also referred to the creation myth in the Brāhmaṇas.

2. "It is asked :—What class of outsiders teach that the seeing of being and non-being is the cause of Nirvāṇa ?

"It is answered :—The twentieth class of outsiders, the philosophers who hold that in the beginning arose an egg, teach that originally there were no sun, moon, stars, sky or earth, that there was only the great waters. Then a great egg was born, like that of a hen, but of a golden colour all around. When it hatched, it broke into two parts, the upper part making the heavens, and the lower part forming the earth. Between these two parts arose the Brahmā Deva, which is called the forefather of all sentient beings, and which made all animate inanimate things. Thus, these animate and inanimate things fall and disappear into the Brahmā place, which is called Nirvāṇa. And that is why the outsiders, the philosophers of the egg, teach that the great egg gave birth to the Brahmā Deva, who is eternal and is called the cause of Nirvāṇa."

Only water existed in the original state of the universe, after which "a golden egg" arose, and when that hatched, the entire world evolved—this creation myth exists in the ancient Brāhmaṇa literature. (*Śat. Br.* XI, 1, 6, 1-3)"

The creation myth that from the primordial waters[12] a golden egg arose, and from this golden egg the world developed, is also taught in other passages[13] in the Brāhmaṇas, and it also has been held in the Upaniṣads, that the universe evolved from an "egg,"[14] but these do not refer to Brahmā. Now this idea that Brahmā arose from a golden egg, and then caused the entire world to evolve, first appears in the *Mahābhārata*;[15] and in the *Code of Manu* it assumes its most characteristic expression.

"This myriad existence (in the very beginning) was in darkness, was not perceived, had no special marks, was not thought, was not discerned, and was completely fallen into a deep sleep, as it were." (I.5).

"He (i.e., the supreme self) desiring to produce the various kinds of living species (*prajā*) from his own body, thought (thus) and created first of all water. (Next) he placed his seed within the waters." (I.8)

"That (seed) became a golden egg, in brilliance equal to the sun. In that (egg) Brahmā, the forefather of all the world, was himself born." (I.9)

"After staying for one entire year in that egg, such a Blessed One (i.e. Brahmā), by means of thinking about himself (ātman), divided the egg itself into two." (I.12)

"And from those two fragments, he fashioned heaven and earth, and in the space between (heaven and earth), he made the sky, the eight regions and the eternal dwelling place of the water." (I.13)

"He made all the species of living beings as minute portions of himself." (I.16) (*ātmamātrāsu sarvabhūtāni nirmame*).

These verses exist only in the *Laws of Manu*.[16] Consequently it would seem that the author of Āryadeva's *Śāstra* was perhaps using this doctrine of the Manu Code as his source here.

In the same work, again, there are presented also some theories which are found only in the Upaniṣads :

3. "It is asked :—What class of outsiders teach that seeing non-being is the cause of Nirvāṇa ?

"It is answered :—the nineteenth class of outsiders, the philosophers who assert the power of the mouth,[17] teach that space (*ākāśa*) is the cause of everything. In the beginning arose space, and from space arose the wind; from the wind arose fire, and from fire arose warmth; from warmth arose water, and water then froze and made the hard earth. From earth arose all kinds of grass and herbs, and from all these kinds of herbs arose the five grains. From the five grains arose life; therefore, in our theory, it is taught that life is food. In the final period, all returns to disappear in space, which is called nirvāṇa. Thus, the oursiders who advocate the power of the mouth, teach that space is eternal, and call it the cause of Nirvāṇa."

The idea that space is the cause of world evolution, is also found in the *Chānd. Up.* VIII.14; but the theory of "the philosophers who advocate the power of the mouth" given above is in accordance for the most part with the doctrine of world development taught in the *Taittirīya-Upaniṣad* :

"Truly, from this ātman arose space. From space arose the wind. From wind arose fire, and from fire arose water; from water arose earth, and from earth arose vegetation; from vegetation arose food, and from food arose man. Truly, this man (*puruṣa*) consists of the essence of food." (*Tait. Up.* II.1)

"Living things which depend upon the earth, truly all and every one of them arose from food. And they truly exist by means of food. Moreover, they again return to this food (after death). Food, truly, is the highest of (all) the living things."

"(All) the living beings arose from food. And all that has arisen grows by means of food." (*Tait. Up.* II.2)

Then, in the very beginning of the world creation, space arose from Brahmā, from space arose wind, from wind fire, from fire water, from water earth[18]—this order of development is adopted in the *BS.*II.3.1-12. Moreover, food came out from the last-mentioned "earth," so Śaṅkara takes it. And the idea that all living beings exist by means of food, is indeed taught in a great many works of India.[19]

4. "It is asked :—What class of outsiders teach that Nirvāṇa comes about by not seeing a difference between the eternal and transitory ?

"It is answered :—The fifth class of outsiders, the Īśānavādins, hold that the form of the Holy Person (*Bhagavat*) is invisible and omnipresent, and from its formlessness, it can give birth to all living and lifeless things, which is called Nirvāṇa. Therefore those who belong to the Īśānavādins teach this theory, and say that Īśāna is eternal and the cause of Nirvāṇa."

"Īśāna" had already in the Brāhmaṇas been taken as another one[20] of the names for the god Śiva, and is a term which was later inherited also by Hinduism. In the Śvetāśvatara-Upaniṣad, which exalts the god Śiva, a doctrine which corresponds to the one given above is frequently taught :

"He rules all the worlds by his powerful authority. He exists within all men. Having created all living creatures as their protecting deity, he finally withdraws them." (*Śvet. Up.* III.2)

"By that puruṣa, this entire world is filled." (*Ibid.* III.9)

"That which exists higher than this world is formless, and does not suffer. The man who knows it will become immortal." (*Ibid.* III.10)

"He pervades all things, and is bliss (*bhagavat*)." (*Ibid.* III.11)

"You are beginningless and exist pervading all places. All that which is arose from that." (*Ibid.* IV.4)

"His form is not to be seen. No one can see him with the eye. Those men who, through their heart and mind know that he exists thus in the heart, will become immortal." (*Śvet. Up.* IV.20-(var.) *Kaṭha-Up.* VI.9; *Mahānār.* I.11)

The "Holy Person" mentioned in Āryadeva's *Śāstra* perhaps is a translation for *bhagavat.*

5. "It is asked :—What class of outsiders teach that the wind is the cause of *Nirvāṇa* ?

"It is answered :—The third class of outsiders, those who teach that the wind is sacred, teach that the wind can give birth to long-lived living beings; the wind makes all things, and can destroy all things. They say that the wind is *Nirvāṇa.* Thus those who think the wind is sacred teach that the wind is eternal and is the cause of *Nirvāṇa.*"

Since the time of the Ṛg-*Veda*, the god of wind (*Vāyu*) was thought to have been the divinity controlling the natural phenomenal wind and was an important deity alongside other gods such as the sun-god (*Sūrya*), and the fire-god (*Agni*). Even in the Upaniṣads gods of such a character are described but, new thinkers appeared who went a step further and took wind as the fundamental principle of all things. It was taught that "The other divinities, truly, go on their way to destruction, but this does not happen with the wind. This divinity, the wind, is one which never goes to ruin." (*Bṛhad. Up.* I.5.22). And the famous scholarly priest, Yājñavalkya, when asked what the thread (*sūtra*) is which is the principle maintaining the world, answered that it is the wind. "The wind truly is that thread... By the wind, which is the thread, this world, the other world and all existence are held together." (*Bṛhad. Up.* III.7.1-2). And the philosopher Raikva, who spent his life wandering about with no possessions, when asked by King Jānaśruti politely and with due ceremony about his teaching, replied :

"The wind, truly, is the snatcher of all. Verily, when the fire is extinguished, it returns to the wind. When the sun sinks, it returns to the wind. When the moon sets, it returns to the wind, the water dries up, it returns to the wind. For the wind, truly, is that which absorbs all these (deities)." (*Chānd. Up.* IV. 3.1-2)

And he declared that among the gods, that is when described in reference to the universe, the wind is the fundamental principle and when described in regard to the individual substances, breath (*prāṇa*) is the primal function. In both of them, there is *moving air*. (An idea resembling this further appears in the *Jaiminīya-Upaniṣad-Brāhmaṇa* III.i.1, 2[21] and in the *Kauṣ.-Up.* II.12-15).

6. "It is asked :—What class of outsiders teach that the seeing of a certain entity is called Nirvāṇa ?

"It is answered :—The eighteenth class of outsiders, the philosophers who worship water,[22] hold the following theory : Water is the basis of all things. Water can give birth to the heavens and the earth, produce all living and lifeless things. From the Avīci hell below to the *Akaniṣṭha* heaven above, everything is ruled by water. Water can produce things, and water can destroy things, and is called *Nirvāṇa*. Therefore, the outsiders, the philosophers who worship water, teach that water is eternal and is called the cause of *Nirvāṇa*."

The idea that water is the source of all things, is taught in the famous *Nāsadīya-sūkta* (*RV.* X.129), which indicates the highest peak of ancient Ṛg-Vedic philosophical thought, and the theory of "those philosophers who hold that the egg originally gave birth to all," as related above, could be taken as one of the branch-streams of this ideological tendency. In addition, it appears in several places in the Vedic literature (*Kāṭhaka-Saṃhitā* VIII.2; *Vāj, Saṃh.* XXXII.1-*Tadeva-Up.*; *Tait. Saṃh.* V.6.4.2.; *Śat. Br.* VI.8.2.3; XI.1.6.1-16; and, *Tait. Br.* I.1.3.5). The idea gradually disappeared as the Brahmā-ātmā theory developed, but in the Upaniṣads, the Law-books and the Epic Poems, the last traces remain of the thought which regards water as the fundamental principle. (*Bṛhad. Up.* III.6; V.5.1; *Chānd. Up.* VII.10.1-2; *Kauṣ. Up.* I.7; *Kaṭha-Up.* IV.6; *Manu* I.8-11; *MBh.* XII.183, 2-10.)[23]

7. "It is asked :—What class of outsiders teach that all things are created by time, which is called *Nirvāṇa* ?

"It is answered :—The seventeenth class of heretics, the Kālavādins, teach as follows. Time ripens all the elements; time makes all things; and time disperses all things. Therefore, in our doctrine it is taught : Even supposing that one is shot by hundreds of arrows, if his time has not come, he will not die; but if his time has come, he could instantly die by touching a small blade of grass. All things time produces, all things time ripens, and all things time destroys. There is nothing beyond time. Therefore the Kālavādins teach that time is eternal, gives birth to all things, and is called the cause of *Nirvāṇa.*"

The idea that time (*kāla*) is the principle which generates the world, had already been taught in ancient times in the *Kālasūkta* (*AV.* XIX.53), and has always been a concept of the orthodox brahmins. This idea was inherited in the Upaniṣads also;[24] and the later Epic Poems[25] thought that time was one type of divinity which commanded the birth and destruction of all things. Such a concept was later adopted by the Vedānta philosophy also. As we shall discuss later, Bhartṛhari[26] regards time as the principle which causes transformations to arise in the world, while Kamalaśīla, whenever he attacked the *puruṣa* in orthodox brahmanical thought, included within his polemics the theory of "intellectual time (*buddhimān kālaḥ*).[27] Consequently, the concept of "time" postulated by the Kālavādins was not something which made possible the conceptions of before and after, simultaneity, and earlier or later, as was taught as a substance in the Nyāya-Vaiśeṣika School, but was the unique principle which causes generation and transformation to arise in the world.[28] Furthermore, the words quoted in Āryadeva's *Śāstra* above coincide with this verse :

"Time causes living things to mature, and time causes living things to return to destruction. Time is awake in the persons who sleep. Time, truly, is difficult to overcome."

kālaḥ pacati bhūtāni kālaḥ saṃharate prajāḥ /
kālaḥ supteṣu jāgarti kālo hi duratikramaḥ //[29]

The foregoing has been an examination of the coincidence in thought between some theories presented in Āryadeva's *Śāstra* and in the Vedas, particularly the Upaniṣads. And since some theories of Hinduism are also presented by Āryadeva, which have a close connection with these, I shall take the opportunity to examine them now. Firstly, we should note that ideas of the *Bhagavadgītā* are enumerated.

8. "It is asked :—What class of outsiders teach that to see Īśvara, who makes all creatures, is called *Nirvāṇa* ?

"It is answered :—The twelfth class of outsiders, the followers of Māṭhara, say that the adherents of Nārāyaṇa teach that "I make all things. I, among all living things, am supreme. I give birth to the entire world of living and lifeless things. I am the King of Mt. Sumeru, the largest of all mountains. I am the largest ocean of all the waters. I am the grain of all medicines. I am the Muni Kapila of all the sages. If a man with pious heart offers water, leaves, flowers and fruit to me, I shall not lose him, and he shall not lose me.' The Māṭhara masters teach that the adherents of Nārāyaṇa say that "All things are created and produced by me, and when they are dissolved into this principle, it is called Nirvāṇa."

Because "Nārāyaṇa" is another name for the god Viṣṇu, "the adherents of Nārāyaṇa" should refer to the followers of the Viṣṇu sect, or the Vaiṣṇava. In the Viṣṇu sect—not to mention the general orthodox thought in India—, the most important scripture is the *Bhagavadgītā*, in which we can discover many verses corresponding to the above quoted passage.

> "O Son of Kuntī, all living things enter into my original essence (*prakṛti*) when this aeon (*kalpa*) returns to destruction. In the beginning of the aeon, I again create them." (*Bhag.G.*IX.7)
>
> "Taking as base My own original (material) nature, I repeatedly create the entirety of these aggregates of being. As they do not have that power, they rely upon the power of my original nature." (*Ibid.*, IX.8)
>
> "By me, the overseer, the original nature (*prakṛti*) gives birth to the entire world accompanied by both the *things which move* (*animals*) *and those which do not move* (*plants*). O Son of Kuntī, by this causal relation, the world evolves." (IX.10)
>
> "And of the Rudra group of deities, I am the god Rudra. I am the god of wealth among the Yakṣas and the Rākṣasas. And I am the god of fire among the Vasu group of deities. *I am Mt. Sumeru among the highest peaks.*" (X.23)

"And, O son of Pṛthā, know that I am chief lord of prayers (*Bṛhaspati*) among the household priests. I am Skanda (the war-god) of the lords of war, *the great ocean of the lakes and rivers.*" (X.24)

"I am the Bodhi Tree of all the trees. And the Sage Nārada of all the divine sages. I am Citraratha among the Gandharvas. *I am the Sage Kapila among the divine sages who have perfected religious practice.*" (X.26)

"If a man with a devoted mind (bhaktyā) offers to me one leaf, one flower, one fruit, or both hands full of water, I shall accept the offering given with a faithful mind by a person whose heart is devout." (IX.25)

"I am, towards all beings, equal. To me, there is nothing hateful, nor is there anything dear. *If there are any, however, who worship me with a faithful heart, they shall exist in me, and I shall exist in them.*" (IX.29)

In the last two verses, especially, devotion (*bhakti*), the central conception of the *Bhagavadgītā*, is emphasized. Now, in Āryadeva's *Śāstra*, it is recorded that the "adherents of Māṭhara" have handed down this theory of the Vaiṣṇava. Māṭhara, according to several dictionaries of India (*Trikāṇḍaśeṣa*, *Abhidhānacintāmaṇi*, *Anekārtha-saṃgraha*), is another name for Vyāsa.[30] Consequently, this must point to the Vyāsa said to be the author of the *Mahābhārata*, And we note in the *Bhagavatī*, one of the Jaina scriptures, that the historical poems (itihāsa) are called *Māḍhara* in the vulgar language (Prakrit); Albrecht Weber understands this to mean "*die Werke des Māṭhara* (*Vyāsa* ?)."[31] Therefore, not only was the author of Āryadeva's *Śāstra* familiar with the legend that the *Mahābhārata* was a work of Vyāsa, but when he knew it, the *Bhagavadgītā* had already been inserted into the *Mahābhārata*. From this account, we see that the inclusion of the *Bhagavadgītā* in the *Mahābhārata* must have been considerably earlier.

9. "It is asked :—What class of outsiders teach that when the creator and created are united together, this is called Nirvāṇa ?

"It is answered :—The fifteenth class of outsiders, the proponents of Maheśvara, teach as follows : The effect is created by Nārāyaṇa. Brahmā is the cause. Maheśvara has one body and three parts, i.e., Brahmā, Nārāyaṇa, and

Maheśvara. The earth is the foundation. The lord of the earth is Maheśvara. In the three worlds, all the living and lifeless things which exist are produced by Maheśvara. As for Maheśvara itself, space is its head, earth is its body, water is its urine, mountains are its excrement, all creatures are worms in its bowels, wind is its life, fire is its warmth, and merit and demerit are its actions (*karman*). These eight types are the Maheśvara itself. Īśvara is the cause of birth and destruction. All is produced by Īśvara and by Īśvara it is destroyed, and this is called Nirvāṇa. Therefore, the propounders of Maheśvara teach that Īśvara eternally produces all things, and is the cause of Nirvāṇa."

"Maheśvara", is another name for the god Śiva, and is translated in the Chinese as "Great Self-existent Deity". Here the theory presented is of a certain school which worships Śiva. The theory of one body and three spirits (*trimūrti*), which holds that Brahmā, Nārāyaṇa, i.e., the god Viṣṇu, and Maheśvara, i.e., the god Śiva, are three manifestations of the single and supreme reality appears in the latter period of the Epic Poems, and later became a fundamental doctrine of Hinduism.[32] Further, as in the words of Āryadeva's *Śāstra* above, this type of thinking which holds that the supreme deity manifests itself as a person, and that the parts of this deity are the same as the constituent elements of the universe, had already appeared in the Upaniṣads. *Bṛhad. Up.* VI. 4.3; *Chānd. Up.* V.18.2; *Muṇḍ. Up.* II.1.4) The concept of Śiva having "eight manifestations" (*aṣṭamūrti*) appeared already in the Epic Poems (*MBh.*III.49.4, 8)[33], and the poet Kālidāsa also praised Śiva as being of eight manifestations.[34]

On the Buddhist side too, the theory is handed down in the esoteric sūtras that the constituent elements of Īśvara are regarded as identical with the various phenomena of the world.[35]

10. "It is asked :—What class of outsiders teach that the evolution and transformation of the lives of men out of the primary substance is called Nirvāṇa ?

"It is answered :—The ninth class of outsiders, those who hold that all things derive from certain female persons, teach that Maheśvara made eight females. The first is called Aditi, the second Diti, the third Surabhi, the fourth Vinatā, the fifth Kapilā, the sixth Manu, the seventh Ilā, and the eighth Kadrū. Aditi begot the gods; Diti created the demons; Surabhi produced the serpents; Vinatā gave birth to the birds. Kapilā begot quadrupeds; Manu gave birth to men. Ilā produced all kinds of grain; Kadrū gave birth to all kinds of snakes, scorpions, mosquitoes, gnats, flies, fleas, millipedes, centipedes, etc. To know this, is called Nirvāṇa. Therefore, those who teach that all derives from females, say that females are eternal, and are called the cause of Nirvāṇa."

Since this theory also concludes that Maheśvara is the primary cause of world evolution, it might perhaps have been taught by some Śaiva sect. A creation-myth similar to it is also taught in the Epic Poems. In the *Mahābhārata* (I.65), Marīci, the son of Brahmā, is said to have given birth to Kaśyapa, who married the thirteen daughters of Dakṣa, the result being the birth of all the devas, mankind and the animals. These thirteen daughters were Aditi, Diti, Danu, Kalā, Danāyu, Siṃhikā, Krodhā, Pradhā, Viśvā, Vinatā, Kapilā, Muni and Kadrū. The minute details of the birth of these women are recorded, and we note that there are many coincidences with the account given above. Again, according to the *Rāmāyaṇa* (III.14) and the *Harivaṃśa* (170), Kaśyapa weded the eight daughters of Dakṣa, giving birth to all living things. The names of these eight are Aditi, Diti, Danu, Kālikā, Tāmrā, Krodhavaśā, Manu and Analā.[36]

Consequently, while it is true that creation-myths similar to this are merely mentioned in the epics, it is still very interesting that a theory which is in almost complete agreement with the account in Āryadeva's *Śāstra* was handed down by a Jain scholar, Abhayadeva, in the 11th century as a "doctrine of creation" (*nirmitavāda*). (The names of the women mentioned in the passages above translated from the Chinese were derived from Abhayadeva).[37] He has recorded in completely the same form the names of "the eight daughters" and the various things to which they gave birth.

Ten more kinds[38] of heretical doctrines are also presented in Āryadeva's *Śāstra*, but as they do not have any direct connection with the thought of the orthodox brahmins who were devoted to the Vedas, I shall omit them here. From the foregoing we have gathered, rather surprisingly, that the author of this *Śāstra* was minutely versed in orthodox brahmanical thought. However, we have seen in the theories quoted above that while they coincide with those in the Vedas, and, in particular in the Upaniṣads and the *Mahābhārata*, there is nonetheless no explicit reference to Brahman or to ātman, the central concepts of Vedānta Philosophy. Nor is there any mention of the efforts of the scholars who tried to unify and unite the "heretical" doctrines taught in the Vedas (especially the Upaniṣads) and the *Mahābhārata* (particularly the *Bhagavadgītā* included therein), in order to set up a unique system. Not only is no mention made of Vedānta scholars, but the thought of early Vedānta philosophers after the period of the *Brahma-sūtra* is not touched upon either.

As a consequence, we can, I think, draw the following conclusion from these facts.— The brahmins who were in contact with the author of *Āryadeva's Śāstra*, had yet to set up a philosophical system such as we find developed in the later Vedānta. They merely followed some of the special philosophical theories taught in the voluminous Vedic literature, and were only concerned with commenting on and explaining these sacred verses. Even supposing, for example, that somewhere in the Indian society of that time there were scholars or schools which undertook comprehensive and systematic investigations on the entire thought of the Upaniṣads, their influence must have been quite slight, and did not attract the notice of the Buddhists. (Although Āryadeva's *Śāstra* does list the names and present the doctrines of the Vaiśeṣika and Sāṃkhya as schools, and also mentions the *Laṅkāvatāra* itself, in addition to the names of the founders of some of the schools, as Kaṇāda, Kapila, Akṣapāda, Bṛhaspati, and Pāṇini, no name appears which might refer to the Vedānta school in particular or to its philosophers.) Our conclusion, then, is the same as that which we reached when we examined the works of Nāgārjuna.

We should say a word further in this connection : Āryadeva's *Śāstra*, it is true, does quote a number of Upaniṣadic theories as those of *separate teachers*. Thus the author of this work never thought that the passages of the Upaniṣads contain a unified doctrine. He probably accepted as a self-evident fact that the Upaniṣads contain a great number of heterogeneous concepts. It may have been that a good many of the brahmins of the time were emphasizing some one or other of the ideas found in the Upaniṣads.

Notes

1. *Ju-lang-chia-ching*, tr. by Bodhiruci, Vol. VI, Chapter on *Nirvāṇa*. Sanskrit version of the *Laṅkāvatāra-sūtra*, pp. 182, line 15, 184, line 14.

2. I was told that this treatise of Āryadeva was translated into English by G. Tucci in *Toung Pao* XXIV, pp. 16-31, but this was not accessible to me.

3. The word "Vedavādin" appears also in the *Tattvasaṁgraha-pañjikā* ad v. 153. Cf. Vedavāda. (Rāmānuja : *Śrībhāṣya*, ad II.2.27, p. 494). The term *Vedavādin* means in some cases the Mīmāṁsakas. (*Sarvadarśana-saṁgraha*, XII, 1.221.)

4. The idea that Brahmā evolved the whole world is set forth also in *Viṣṇu-purāṇa* I, 2, 58 f.

5. *TT*.XXXII.157 a.

6. *ṚV*.X.90. It also appears in *AV*.XIX.6; *Vāj. Saṃh. Tait. Ār.* III.12.

7. *MBh*.XII.298 (B.296), 5-6 (=10865-10866).

8. The myth that Brahmā is born from the navel of Viṣṇu appears in *Rāmāyaṇa* VII.56.7. (Hopkins : *Epic Mythology*, p. 191.)

9. *Ta-chih-tu-lun* (*Mahāprajñā-pāramitā-upadeśa-śāstra*), Vol. VIII (*TT*.XXV.116a), *Fen-pieh-kung-te-lun* (Nj. 1290), Vol. I (*TT*.XXV.31a.)

10. *Bṛhad.Up.* I.4.1, I.5.2; *Muṇḍ. Up.* II.1.5; *Praśna-Up.* VI.4.

11. *Muṇḍ. Up.*, I.1.1.

12. The Water Doctrine is fully discussed by E. Frauwallner in his *History of Indian Philosophy*, Vol. I (Delhi etc.: Motilal Banarsidass, 1973), pp. 36-41.

13. *Śat. Br.* VI.1.1.8-10.

14. *Chānd. Up.* III.19.103; *Maitri-Up.* VI.36.

15. *MBh.* XII.312.3, XIII.154.16 ff. Cf. Hopkins; *GEI*, pp. 187-188, *Epic Mythology*, p. 191.

16. No similar verses in other works to these verses in the Code of Manu have been given in the "Synopsis of Parallel Passages," G. Bühler's appendix to the English Trans. of the *Manu Code*.

17. Such is the natural meaning of Āryadeva's text. But possibly, as Professor Ingalls has suggested to me, *kou* ("mouth" or "opening") is used here to translate Sanskrit *kha* (="opening", "hole", but also="space," and regularly so in the Upaniṣads). If so, we should translate, "those who assert the power of space."

18. In the *Chānd. Up.* VI.2.4, there is : "Fire is born from food," but the *Brahma-sūtra* (II.3.12) in this case interprets the word for food (*anna*) as earth as a substance.

19. Cf. *Bhag. G.* III.14; *DN.* III, p. 211.—*Sabbe sattā āhāraṭṭhitikā.* "All things are born and exist by food; without food, they die." (*Tseng-i-a-han-ching*, Vol. 42, *TT.* II.778c)

20. R. G. Bhandarkar : *Vaiṣṇavism, Śaivism and Minor Religious Systems* (Strassburg, 1913), p. 105.

21. Oertel, *JAOS*, Vol. XV (1893), pp. 249-251.

22. The "submit to" in the phrase "submit to water" may mean to "observe" or to "worship." The same ideograph appears in the Northern Edition of the *Ta-pan-nieh-p'an-ching* (Nj.113), Vol. 16 (*TT.* XXII.462c), where it says : "For the four months they submit to fire; for the seven days they submit to the wind."

23. On the idea that the concept of primordial water belongs to the orthodox brahmins, see further R. Garbe : *Sāṃkhya Philosophie*[2], S. 23-24.

24. *Maitrī-Up.* VI.14-15. This is listed in the *Śvet. Up.* I.2, VI.1, however, as one of the heretical views. The idea that Time is the principle of change of the world is set forth also in *Ṣaḍdarśana-samuccaya* with Guṇaratna's commentary, pp. 10 ff.

25. *MBh.* XII.223.5 ff, 227-29 ff; *Anugītā.* 45.9 ff.

26. *Vākyapadīya* I, 3; III, 1, 36; III, 7, 42 (p. 201); III, 8, 1 (p. 298).

27. *Tattvasaṁgrahapañjikā* ad v. 170.

28. On Kālavādin, see F. O. Schrader, *Diss.*, S. 17 ff., S. 58 ff. Concerning the accounts extant in Buddhist literature, see Shinko, Mochizuki, *Bukkyō Daijiten* (Buddhist Dictionary), reference under "Jironshi" (Kālavādin). Also, see *Laṅkāvatāra*, p. 184, line 11; *Mvṛ.* p. 159, line 7, 567, line 2.

29. Quoted in the *Madhyamaka-vṛtti*, p. 386, lines 6-7. Cf. Poussin's commentary on this passage. Elsewhere, it appears in Gauḍapāda ad *Sāṁkhya-kārikā* 61, the commentary of the *Suvarṇasaptati* on the same verse, and in Ānandajñāna ad *Bṛhad. Up. Vārttika*, p. 1825. The verse quoted in the Commentary by Bhaṭṭotpāda (Vix.SS.p.9) on *Bṛhatsaṃhitā*, says :

ke 'pi Kālakāraṇikāḥ Paurāṇikāḥ kālaṁ kāraṇam āhuḥ.

30. Cf. the item in *PW* on Māṭhara. Further, the corresponding relationship with the Gītā was already pointed out by Hakuju Ui. (*Tetsugaku Zasshi*, (Journal of Philosophy), 1919, p. 271 ff.)

31. A. Weber, *Über die Fragmente der Bhagavati*, Teil II, S. 248 :— *baisesiyaṃ Buddhasāsaṇaṃ, Kāvilaṃ, Logāyatam Saṭṭhitaṃtaṃ Māḍhara-Purāṇa-vāgaraṇa-nāḍagāī.* Further, in the *Ju-ta-ch'eng-lun* the outsiders are classified as : identical, different, both identical and different, neither identical nor different, and it says :. "All outsiders and Māṭhara have separate doctrines, but these never go outside the four classes" (*TT.*XXXII.40b). In such cases, needless to say, "Māṭhara" does not mean the Māṭhara who wrote the commentary on the *Sāṁkhya-Kārikās.*

32. The word *trimūrti*, however, insofar as the extant Sanskrit literature is concerned, appears in the *Kumārasambhava* of Kālidāsa, and this is the oldest source. It should be adequately noted that the "one body, three manifestations" is clearly mentioned in Āryadeva's *Śāstra*, presumed to be of the same period or prior to the *Kumārasambhava.*

33. According to *Viṣṇu-purāṇa* I, 8, 11-12, also, Śiva had eight sons. They are: Śanaiścara, Śukra Lohitāṅga, Manojava (Hanumat), Skanda, Svarga, Saṁtāna, Budha.

34. Hopkins, *Epic Mythology*, p. 221; M. T. Narasimhiengar, *Kālidāsa's*

Religion and Philosophy, *IA*. 1910, pp. 236-241. Further, as the legend has been handed down in the *Ta-chih-tu-lun*, Vol. VIII (*TT*.XXV.116c), the "eight children" are born from the mind of the Brahmā king, and "the heaven, earth and mankind" are born from these eight children.

35. *Mo-teng-chia-ching* (Nj. 645), Vol. I (*TT*.XXI.402c).

36. Hopkins, *Epic Mythology*, p. 200.

37. F. O. Schrader, *Diss*. S. 56. However, Abhayadeva has taken Sulasā, instead of Kapilā.

38. These ten kinds are not discussed here.

(Further, in *The Questions of King Milinda*, p. 3, among the 19 kinds of learning which King Milinda studied, are given the *Sāṁkhya Yoga Nīti Vaiśeṣikā...Cātubbeda...Hetu*, etc. but there is no reference to either the Mīmāṃsā or the Vedānta.)

SECTION VI. REFERENCES TO UPANIṢADIC IDEAS IN THE EARLY YOGĀCĀRA SCHOOL

The Vijñaptimātratā philosophy is said to have been first set forth by Maitreyanātha (c. 270-350), developed by Asaṅga (c. 310-390), and consolidated and diffused throughout all of India by Vasubandhu (c. 320-400). Now what kind of attitude had these thinkers towards Vedānta thought ?

In books 6 and 7, out of the hundred which comprise the gigantic work *Yogācārabhūmi-śāstra*, ascribed to Maitreya-nātha, there are presented and criticized "the sixteen types of heretical doctrine" prevalent in India up to that time. Despite the fact that his discussion is extremely detailed, he makes no reference to the Vedānta school. The school which held views closest to those of Vedānta was perhaps the *Īśvarādikāraṇavādin*, "those who regard God, etc., as the world-cause."[1] The same passage (space does not permit full quotation), occurs also in a *śāstra* composed by Asaṅga.[2]

What is here taken as the object for criticism, is the theory which asserts that everything in the world is produced by "Īśvara" (=presiding deity), or by Puruṣa. Among a variety of the theory there is, I think, a world-view somewhat like that of the Vedānta which says that from a single and undifferentiated cause, this pluralistic and multifarious world appeared as an evolute. Since these theorists accept that the cause and the effect are heterogeneous, their view was also called a theory of cause being different from effect. Now, the logical grounds that such disputants must have had for assuming a single world-cause, would be as follows : No matter how much man may endeavour to fulfil his desires in this world or the next, he is by no means assured that he will obtain the desired results. Therefore, whether or not man obtains the fruits of his actions, must be thought to depend upon a presiding deity.[3] (A similar argument is set forth in *Nyāya-sūtra* IV.1.1.9 ff.)

Against such an argument, Maitreya-nātha systematically set forth his objections. Since most of his arguments are very similar to those in the *Abhidharma-mahāvibhāṣā-śāstra* noted above and the *Tattvasaṃgraha* to be discussed later, we shall omit examination of them here.

Moreover, in the *Prakaraṇāryavācā-śāstra* [*Hsien-yang-sheng-chiao-lun* (Nj.1177)] by Asaṅga, the 16 types of heretical doctrines are again similarly given, and the theory of *Īśvarādikāraṇa-vādins* is also mentioned, but as it coincides closely with the words and passages in the *Yogācāra-bhūmi-śāstra*, there is no need to re-examine it here.

Again, in the *Mahāyāna-saṃparigraha-śāstra* by Asaṅga there are given five kinds of heretical doctrines based upon a misunderstanding of the first kind of dependent origination (*pratītyasa-mutpāda*) out of the *ālayavijñāna* (storehouse of mental impressions), and one of the five says : "Some adhere to Īśvara as the creator (*nirmāṇa*)" "Some cling to the doctrine that everything is the creation (*nirmāṇa*) of Īśvara." Upon this the famous translator Paramārtha (499-569) comments :

There is but one world-cause, named the Lord (Īśvara). He makes us to do good and evil, and to transmigrate [in the mundane worlds]. Later he causes to arise within us an aversion to transmigration and to wish for liberation from it. If one acquires the knowledge that Īśvara is the world-cause, then one can be freed from all fetters and unite himself with the self of Īśvara.[4]

We see in this passage that Paramārtha here seems to have thought that Īśvara was rather a deity who directs the destiny of the individual. Such an idea has already been taught in several places in the Ancient Upanisads.[5] One can readily find parallels to the above quotation in the Upaniṣads.

Thus, the early Yogācāra scholars, Maitreyanātha, Asaṅga and Vasubandhu presented and criticized the concept of the presiding deity (*Īśvara*) or the *puruṣa* being the world-cause, but were not speaking about any "Vedānta school".

In the *Ratnagotravibhāga*[6] the Vedāntins are not mentioned when it enumerates various heretical doctrines. However, it is likely that the *Tathāgatagarbha* theory was formed under the influence of the Upaniṣadic thought. The unchangeability of the Essence of the *Tathāgatagarbha* is set forth in the *Ratnagotravibhāga* (52) as follows :

"Just as space, being all-pervading,
Cannot be polluted because of its subtle nature;
Similarly, abiding everywhere among living beings
This [Essence] remains unpolluted [by defilements]."

This verse is almost identical to the verse of the *Bhagavadgītā* XIII, 32.[7] Hindu influence is also noticed. 'It is said that the Apparitional Form of the Buddha is like the great Brahmā.'[8]

Notes

1. *Yogācārabhūmi-śāstra* (*Yü-chia-shih-ti-lun*) (Nj.1170), Vol. VII (*TT.* XXX.309.a-c)
2. *Hsien yangsheng chiao lun* (Nj.1177), (*TT.* XXXI, 527a-c) Vol. X.
3. The Īśvara mentioned here need probably not be limited to Śiva alone.
4. *TT.* XXXI.164c. These sentences, not found in Gupta's or Hsüan-tsang's translations, must have been inserted by Paramārtha.
5. E. g., *Kaṭh. Up.*. II.20; 23; *Śvet. Up.* I.6; III.20 etc.
6. Jikido Takasaki : *A Study on the Ratnagotravibhāga* (Roma: IsMEO, 1966), p. 203.
7. J. Takasaki : *The Ratnagotravibhāga*, p. 235.
8. J. Takasaki : *The Ratnagotravibhāga*, op. cit. p. 368. cf. p. 355.

SECTION VII. THE VEDĀNTA PHILOSOPHY KNOWN TO BHAVYA AND DHARMAPĀLA

1. *Introduction*

During the period in which the scholars of the early *Mādhyamika* and *Vijñānavāda* schools lived, i.e. up until c. A.D. 400, the *Vedānta* school, which tried to synthesize and reconcile as a philosophical system the various ideas presented in the Upaniṣads, was not as yet generally known to the Buddhists. Then, when did this school come to the attention of the Buddhists ? The most ancient account in which the term "*Vedānta* school" appears, is, I think, to be found in the works of Bhavya.[1]

It is generally thought that Bhavya (Bhāvaviveka) lived sometime between 490 and 570.[2] He was a senior contemporary of Dharmapāla and a prominent scholar of the Mādhyamika school. Not only did he oppose the Vijñānavāda thought, he also attacked the doctrines of Buddhapālita, who belonged to the same Mādhyamika school as he. From this time on, the Mādhyamika split into two separate schools, that of Buddhapālita which is called the Prāsaṅgika, and that of Bhavya which is called the Svātantrika. Among the works of Bhavya, there is the *Madhyamaka-hṛdaya-kārikā*, on which he himself wrote a commentary called the *Madhyamaka-hṛdaya-vṛtti*, or *Tarkajvālā*. Their Sanskrit originals were lost, but recently the Sanskrit manuscript of the *Madhyamaka-hṛdaya-kārikā* was found. Their Tibetan translation has been handed down in the Tibetan Tripiṭaka. The work consists of eleven chapters. Among them the sixth chapter presents and criticizes the doctrines of the *Sāṁkhya* school; the seventh chapter, those of the *Vaiśeṣika*; the eighth, the *Vedānta*; and, the ninth, the *Mīmāṃsā*. Thus, the *Vedānta, as a separate and independent school*, is here clearly presented in summary and is attacked.[3]

Vedāntic thoughts had often been mentioned and presented previously in Buddhist texts, but no such systematic presentation and discussion can be found in other early Buddhist works. His description of the Vedānta philosophical doctrines, therefore, is extremely important in the sense that it was written by a Buddhist scholar : furthermore, as he is certainly earlier than Śaṅkara by about at least 200 years, his work is an extremely valuable source for the sake of learning the circumstances of the Vedānta philosophy during its early period. After editing the text of the eighth chapter of Bhavya's *Madhyamaka-hṛdaya* I shall examine its contents.

Then we shall take up the Vedānta thought presented in other works by Bhavya, clarify the main features found there, and then, as an appendix, I would like to present some accounts in the works of Dharmapāla, a contemporary of Bhavya.

Notes

1. Scholars have already pointed out that Bhavya's work is the oldest among the Buddhist texts to list the term "Vedāntavādin". (Hakuju Ui, *Indo Tetsugaku Kenkyū*, I.168; Walleser, *Der ältere Vedānta*, p. 15.
2. H. Ui, *ibid*, V. 149.
3. Some of the verses in Chapter Eight have been translated into German by Walleser, *op. cit*, pp. 17-18. The revised edition of the first 16 verses of the *Madhyamaka-hṛdaya* and the *Tarkajvālā*, Chapter Eight, is complete and presented in the *Indo-Iranian Journal*, II (1958) NR. 3, pp. 181-190.

2. *The Vedānta Chapter of Bhavya's Madhyamakahṛdaya*

The eighth chapter of Bhavya's *Madhyamakahṛdaya* deals with the philosophy of the Vedānta school which was current in those days. The Sanskrit text of the portion of the *pūrvapakṣa* was already published by Professor V. V. Gokhale with the text of the Tibetan version edited by myself in *Indo-Iranian Journal*, vol. II (1958), No. 3, pp. 165-80. The Sanskrit Text of the first 16 verses of Chapter Eight contained therein appears below :

The Sanskrit Text of the Eighth Chapter of the *Madhyamaka-hṛdaya*

(1) *Vedāntavādinaḥ prāhur ātmavid durlabho bahiḥ* /
kuta ātmadviṣām mokṣaḥ śūnyasaṃskāravādinām //
(2) *tamaḥparastāt puruṣam mahāntaṃ sūryavarcasam* /
mṛtyum atyeti matimān matvā 'tmānaṃ maheśvaram //
(3) *rukmavarṇaṃ yadā paśyan paśyet kartāram Īśvaram* /
vihāya pāpam puṇyañ ca paraṃ sāmyaṃ tadā 'pnuyāt //
(4) *bhūtam bhavat bhaviṣyac ca sarvam puruṣa iṣyate* /
so 'ntar bahiś ca dūre ca so 'ntike sa ca karmakṛt //
(5) *viśve bhāvās tato jātā ūrṇanābhād ivāṃśavaḥ* /
tasmin pralīnā vidvāṃso nā 'pnuvanti punarbhavam //
(6) *amṛtatvaṃ na martyasya vahneḥ śaityam iveṣyate* /
tasmād amṛtatā 'yuktā 'prabodhāt puruṣe 'mṛte //
(7) *yataḥ paraṃ paraṃ nā'sti yato jyāyān na vidyate* /
aṇīyān nā'pi tenedaṃ viśvam ekena saṃtatam //
de ni phra daṅ rags daṅ ldan /
yaṅ ldan gtso bo dbaṅ sgyur pa //
rab phye ḥdod pahi mthar thug gaṅ /
rnal ḥbyor ji ltar ḥdod par ḥgto //

(Here eight *aiśvarya* or *mahāsiddhi* are referred to. Cf. Vyāsa ad *Yogasūtra* III, 45).

(8) *tasmin sarvāṇi bhūtāni bhavaty ātmaiva paśyataḥ /*
bālapaṇḍitacaṇḍālaviprādīnāñ ca tulyatā //
(9) *ghaṭotpattau vināśe vā nā 'kāśasya tadātmatā /*
tadātmatā 'tmano 'pīṣṭā na dehādyudayavyaye //
(10) *ghaṭākāśavad ekasya nānātvaṃ ced abhedataḥ /*
ghaṭabhedena caikatvaṃ sāmye sarvasya janmavat //
(11) *yathā ghaṭādibhede 'pi mṛdbhedo nā'sti kaś cana /*
(tathaiva dehabhede 'pi nā'tmabhedo 'sti kaś cana //)
(12) *ghaṭākāśe yathaikasmin rajodhūmādibhir vṛte /*
tadvattā na hi sarveṣāṃ sukhāder na tathā'tmanaḥ //
(13) *aprabodhād anātmajñaḥ svapne bhogābhimānavat /*
cinoti karma bhuṅkte ca tatphalaṃ yac chubhāśubham //
(14) *dehasaṃstho 'py asaṃgatvād bhūñjāno nopalipyate /*
rājavat kāmacārī ca pāpenā 'naparādhy asau //
(15) *ekaṃ sarvagataṃ nityam param brahmā 'cyutaṃ padam /*
yogī yuñjāna (āve)tti na tadaiti punarbhavam //
(16) *nityaṃ tad avikalpañ ca yatra vācām agocaraḥ /*
giras tatra prayujyante bhedāpahṛtabuddhibhiḥ//

So far was edited by Prof. Gokhale and published with an English translation. In the Tibetan versions there is between verse 7 and 9 the above-mentioned verse, which is lacking in the Sanskrit manuscript.

Later in 1972 Professor Gokhale came to Japan to give lectures to students of the University of Tokyo. When he left Japan in 1973, he kindly left his handwritten copy of the eighth chapter of the work based upon the manuscript brought over by the late Sankrityayana. I edited it in comparison with the Tibetan version, and with his permission I am going to introduce it with the Tibetan version to the attention of scholars. Collation of various Tibetan versions is not exhaustive. Some printed texts were illegible, and obvious mistakes in Tibetan texts are not mentioned here, which became quite clear owing to collation with the Sanskrit manuscript.

In the following I am going to publish the portion of the *uttarapakṣa*. Numbering of the verses was made according to the Tibetan editions, in which numbering is the same. With regard to Tibetan recensions, I have used mainly the Sde-dge Edition, and whenever occasionally I have utilized the reading in the Snar-thaṅ Edition, this is indicated in the notes. On account of the absence of the Sanskrit original of the *Tarkajvālā* there are not a few places which are difficult to interpret. I have copied Chapter Eight from the two Snar-thaṅ editions in the Tōyō Bunko, Tokyo, but as there were many places which I could not decipher, it was necessary to refer to other editions which were more clearly printed. Fortunately, thanks to the kind assistance of the late Dr. H. Ui, I was able to ask the late Rev. Tokwan Tada of Tōhọku University to check the Sde-dge Edition, and through the good offices of Prof. S. Yamaguchi, to request Dr. Kenshō Hasuba of Otani University to examine the Peking Edition, in order to clarify those unclear passages and to note any differences. With this assistance, I was able to complete, for the most part, the translation of the Sde-dge Edition, but it appeared later that many of the dubious passages had to be rewritten, as I learned from the kind help of my late and respected friend, the late Mr. Kasamatsu. I should wish to express here my profound gratitude to these professors and friends.

The verses of the *Madhyamaka-hṛdaya-kārikās* are preserved separately in the Tibetan Tripiṭaka, and are also included in the *Tarkajvālā*, but it by no means follows that the two are in complete agreement. In the following, I have adopted those readings which seem to be the most appropriate, and have noted whenever there is an important difference between the two. And for those passages of vague meaning, I have given the original in the footnotes.

[18] *atrāpīdaṃ parīkṣante pakṣapātānapekṣiṇaḥ /*
pakṣarāgāvikṛtamatiḥ (?) *sa* [ ] *pi nekṣate //*

Tib. phyogs su lhuṅ ba ma yin pas /
ḥdir ni ḥdi yaṅ ḥdi ltar dpyad //
phyogs la chags pas bsgribs paḥi blos /
ji ltar bden paḥaṅ rtogs mi ḥgyur //

[19] *niṣiddham*[1] *ātmano 'stitvaṃ jagatkāraṇatā tathā /*
atas tad[2]*-darśanān muktir abhūtaiva prakalpitā //*

Abbreviations

P. The Peking Edition
N. The Snar-thaṅ Edition
D. The Sde-dge Edition

1. MS.—*nibaddham.* Tib. bkag-pas na.
2. *tad—ātman.*

Tib. bdag yod pa[1] ni bkag pas[2] na /
ḥgro baḥi rgyu yaṅ de bshin te //
des na de mthoṅ grol ba ni /
mi bden par ni rab brtags ñid //

[20] *satkāyadṛṣṭiḥ sahajā paśūnām apy aśāntaye /*
sarvasaṃkleśamūlatvāt saiva[3] *bhūyo*[4] *vivardhitā //*

Tib. byol soṅ rnams la ḥjigs tshogs lta[5] /
lhan cig skyes yod shi ma gyur //
kun ñon moṅs kun rtsa baḥi phyir /
de ñid khyod kyiś śin tu spel //

[21] *satkāyadṛṣṭyāviṣṭānāṃ mamāhaṃkārakāriṇā /*
[yatobhavi]ka[ḥ] saṃsāro muktir apy[6] *uditā tataḥ //*

Tib. ḥjig tshogs lta la shen pa yi /
bdag ḥdsin bdag gir[7] ḥdsin pa de[8] //
gaṅ las ḥkhor ba ḥbyuṅ bar ḥgyur[9] /
de ñid grol ba yin par smra //

[22] *tad-dṛṣṭau ced bhavec chāntir*
madād iva madātyaye /
ajīrṇāt saṃnipannasya
bhojanāt svasthatā[10] *bhavet //*

Tib. myos par gyur la myos ḥgyur bshin /
de lta ba yis shi ḥgyur[11] na //
śin tu ma shuḥi nad ldan la /
kha zas zos pas phan par ḥgyur //

[23] Sanskrit text is lacking.

Tib. rig byed smra bas bdag de ni /
rnan pa gñis su ḥdod byed de //
lus shes bya ba bciṅs[12] bdag daṅ /
mchog na gnas pa grol baḥi bdag //

1. pa (comm). pas-(Kārikā, D. and N.).
2. pas. (comm). pa-(Kārikā, D. and N.).
3. *sā—satkāyadṛṣṭiḥ.*
4. MS.—*bhūyā*; another emendation is *bhūyāt.*
5. lta. blta—Kārikā, D.
6. MS.—*muktidapy.*
7. gir. gis-P.
8. de. dag-D., P.
9. gaṅ las ḥkhor bar ḥbyuṅ ḥgyur ba (P.).
10. MS.—*svasthatāṃ.*
11. ḥgyur, gyur-Kārikā, D., N.
12. =*śārīra, sa-śarīra, jīvātman.*

[24] *na pareṣṭātmaviṣayād*
yathārthātmeti dhīr matā /
ātmany evaṃ parāmarśā[d][1]
dehādāv ātmadhīr yathā //

Tib. mchog tu ḥdsin pa bdag gi yul /
bdag blo ji bshin don ma yin //
bdag ni ḥdi shes mchog ḥdsin phyir /
lus la bdag gi blo bshin no //

[25] *parikalpitasat[t]vo 'pi kim ātmā kurute tava /*
rūpaśabdādiviṣayāṃ buddhiṃ cetan na yujyate //

Tib. yoṅs su brtags pas[2] yod na yaṅ[3] /
khyod kyis bdag gis ci shig byed //
gzugs daṅ sgra sogs yul rnams la /
bloḥi she na de mi rigs //

[26] *dhiyo rūpādiviṣayā jāyante nātmakartṛkāḥ /*
pratyayāyattajanmatvā(t) sūryakāntād ivānalaḥ //

Tib. gzugs sogs yul la blo dag ni /
byed po bdag ni med kyaṅ skye //
rkyen la bltos[4] paḥi skye yin phyir /
me śel gyi ni me bshin no //

[27] *dhvani[r] varṇātmako yaś ca*
so 'pīṣṭo nātmakartṛkaḥ /
śrāvaṇatvād dhvanitvād vā
tad yathā pratiśabdakaḥ //

Tib. gaṅ yaṅ yi geḥi bdag ñid sgra /
de yi byed po bdag min ḥdod //
mñan byaḥi phyir daṅ sgra yin phyir /
dper na brag ca ji bshin no //

[28] *etena śeṣāḥ pratyuktā gamanāgamanādikāḥ /*
hastapādādivispandalakṣaṇā dehajā[ḥ] kriyā[ḥ] //

Tib. ḥdis ni lus kyi bya ba gshan /
ḥoṅ ba daṅ ni ḥgro ba daṅ //
lag pa rkaṅ pa gyo ba ni /
mtshan ñid lhag ma rnams kyaṅ bkag //

[29] *vyavacchedena saṃjñāyā*
saṃjñānaṃ smaraṇaṃ smṛteḥ /

1. MS.—*parāmarṣā.*
2. pas. pa-Kārikā, D.
3. yaṅ.ḥaṅ-P.
4. bltos-N., P.; ltos-D.

prajñānaṃ ca prakāreṇa
prajñāto vedanaṃ vidaḥ //
Tib. rnam par bcad nas kun śes las /
kun śes dran pa ñid las dran //
so sor rnam par rab śes las /
śes rab ñams su myoṅ las[1] tshor //

[29+1] *na cānyad ātmana[ḥ] kāryaṃ*
svabhāvo nāvadhāryate /
khapuṣpavad atas tasya
na sattāpy avadhāryate //

[This verse is lacking in the Tibetan version of the *Madhyama-kahṛdaya*, but substantially incorporated in the Tibetan version of the *Tarkajvālā* ad v. 29.]

[30] *jñānādeḥ karaṇokteś cet karaṇatvaṃ prasādhyate* /
tadanyakartṛkatvaṃ vā dātṛ[2] *vat tan na yuktimat* //
Tib. śes sogs byed par smra she na /
byed pa ñid du sgrub pa ḥam //
de las gshan paḥi byed po ñid /
gcod byed bshin du rigs ldan min /

[31] *kartari pratyayotpatter*
naiṣāṃ[3] *karaṇatā yataḥ* /
ato [']siddhārthatā hetor
anekāntikatā 'pi vā[4] //
Tib. byed pa po la[5] rkyen ldan shiṅ[6] /
gaṅ phyir byed pa la min pas //
des na gtan tshigs ma grub pa ḥam /
ma ṅes pa ñid yin par ḥgyur //

[32] *jñānādīnāṃ hi kartṛtvaṃ*
kartṛśabdābhidhānataḥ /
devadattaś chinattīti
yathā dṛṣṭātra kartṛtā //
Tib. śes la sogs pa byed po ñid /
byed poḥi sgra yis brjod paḥi phyir //

1. la, D. comm. las—Kārikā, D.; P.
2. MS.—*dātū* (?)*vat*. Tib. gcod byed bshin du (like the one who cuts off).
3. *eṣām*—*eṣāṃ karaṇānām*.
4. MS.—*va*.
5. la—Kārikā, D.; Kārikā, N. ni—N., Comm.
6. shiṅ—Kārikā; D.; P. gyi—D., Comm.

lhas byin gyis ni gcod do shes /
ji ltar byed por mthoṅ ba bshin //

[33] *nirīha eva saṃskārarāśau syāt kartṛvācyatā /*
kāraṇatvād yathā dīpe dīpo dyotayatīti te //

Tib. ḥdus byas phuṅ po byed bral ñid /
ḥdi la byed por brjod bya ste //
byed pa yin phyir mar me yis[1] /
gsal bar byed pa yin pa bshin //

[34] *na mukhyas tattvataḥ kartā*
naiko hi ghaṭakṛd yataḥ /
naupacārikakartṛtvaṃ
[2]dīpāder iṣyate tataḥ //

Tib. yaṅ dag gtso gcig byed po min /
gaṅ phyir gcig gis bum mi byed //
des na mar me sogs byed po /
gdags pa par[3] ni mi ḥdod do //

[35] *cittaṃ rāgādivaśaga[ṃ]*
saktaṃ rūpādigocare /
pratibaddhaṃ[4] [vi(?)]mokṣe ca[5]
duḥkhasaṃsāracārake //

Tib. ḥdod chags sogs kyi dbaṅ phyug sems /
gzugs sogs yul la mṅon shen paḥi //
thar pa mi mthun phyogs kyis phrogs /
ḥkhor paḥi btson rar bciṅs[6] pa yin //

[36] *pāṇyādisamudāyo'yaṃ sa-cittaḥ sattvasaṃjñakaḥ /*
tyāgādicetanotpatter dātetyādi nigadyate //

Tib. lag pa la sogs tshogs pa ni /
sems bcas sems can shes bya ste //
gtoṅ ba la sogs sems ḥbyuṅ ba /
yod pa gtoṅ po la sogs brjod //

[37] *vidyotpattāv avidyādisaṃyojana-nivṛttitaḥ /*
rāgādibandhanān mukto mukta ity abhidhīyate //

1. yis—D., N. yi—P.
2. MS.—*dvīpāder*. Corrected by Tib.
3. par.—P. and N., Kārikā. bar.—D.
4. MS.—*pratibandha*.
5. MS.—*mokṣeva*.
6. btson rar bciṅ, cāraka, imprisoned in the jail, (Sarat Chandra Das: *A Tibetan English Dictionary*, p. 1006).

Tib. rig pa skyes pas ma rig sogs /
kun sbyor ldog par gyur paḥi phyir //
chags sogs ḥchiṅ ba las grol ba /
grol ba śhes ni brjod pa yin //

[38] *ātmani vyomakalpe tu*
sarvam etat sudurvacaḥ /
khapuṣpam astu vāpy ātmā[1]
yady ātmātīva[2] *vallabhaḥ*[3] //

Tib. nam mkhaḥ ḥdra baḥi bdag la ni /
ḥdi dag thams cad brjod par dkaḥ //
gal te bdag la lhag chags na /
nam mkhaḥi me tog bdag ḥdod kyis /

[39] *svabhāvato hi yady ātmā[jñāna-] bhāva itīṣyate* /
na tarhy asyaikatā[4] *yuktā karaṇādi*[5]*-vyapekṣaṇāt* //

Tib. gaṅ phyir bdag ni raṅ bshin gyis /
śes paḥi ṅo bor hdod na ni //
byed pa la sogs bltos paḥi phyir /
de ni gcig tu mi rigs so //

[40] *sati vātmādike jñeye jñānaṃ tan na*[6] *nivartate* /
kṛtārthasyāpi dīpasya dṛṣṭaṃ janma svakāraṇāt //

Tib. bdag sogs śes bya yod pas na /
śes pa ldog par mi ḥgyur te //
don byas zin paḥi mar me yaṅ /
raṅ gi rgyu[7] las skye bar mthoṅ //

[41] *ato jñānodayo yāvat tāvad bījaṃ pracīyate* /
ārāvaprabhavo yāvat tāvat pratiravo yathā //

Tib. ji srid yod la śes ḥbyuṅ ba /
de srid sa bon sogs ḥgyur te //
ji srid sgra ni yod gyur pa /
de srid sgra brñan ḥbyuṅ ba bshin //

[42] *saṃsāraś ca kathaṃ jñasya*[8]
jñānaṃ ca karaṇaṃ vinā /

1. MS.—vāryāte (?)
2. MS.—yadyātīva (?)
3. MS.—vallabhā.
4. MS.—*asyekatā.*
5. MS.—*kāraṇādi.*
6. *tanna.* MS.—*tadva.*
7. *rgyud*—D. Comm.
8. MS.—jñāsya.

sarvadā vāviśiṣṭa [*-tvād*]
[*bandha-*]*mokṣau kutaḥ katham* //

Tib. byed pa med par śes pa ni /
ḥkhor ba ji ltar śes pa yin //
kun tu khyad[1] med yin paḥi phyir /
gaṅ las ji ltar bciṅs daṅ grol //

[43] *na duḥkhenāpi nirmokṣo*
mokṣe 'py ekātmavādinaḥ /
ātmanas tad-ananyatvād[2]
yathoṣṇena vibhāvasoḥ[3] /

Tib. sdug bsṅal las kyaṅ thar min te /
thar daṅ gcig tu smra baḥi phyir //
bdag las de ni gshan min phyir /
ji ltar me daṅ tsha ba bshin //

[44] *līnānutpannabuddhiś ca*
kathaṃ jñaḥ karaṇaṃ vinā /
yathā hi pūrṇakaś chettā
na yuktaḥ[4] *paraśuṃ vinā* //

Tib. ñams daṅ ma skyes pa yi blo /
byed pa med par ji ltar yin //
gaṅ pos gcod par byed pa yaṅ /
sta re med par ji ltar rigs //

[45] *agninā dahatīty ukte*
dahaty[5] *agnir na rādhakaḥ*[6] /
tadvad vetti dhiyety ukte[7]
jñānaṃ vetti, na vaḥ pumān //

Tib. me yis bsreg ces smras pa na /
me yis bsregs kyi byed pas min //
de bshin blo yis rig smras pas /
śes pas rig gi skyes bus min //

[46] *kulālavan na tat-siddhis*
tatsvabhāvo yato na saḥ /

1. khyad. khyab, N., D., P.
2. MS.—*tadatanyatvād. tad=duḥkha.*
3. *vibhāvasu*, fire.
4. MS.—*pūrvakaś cittān na yuktā.*
5. MS.—*na dahaty. na* should be omitted. Tib.
6. byed pas min.—byed pos min (?)
7. MS.—*dhiyer uṅkte.*

neṣṭā dahanavatsiddhiḥ[1]
dāhyābhāve[2] *'gnyasaṃbhavāt* //

Tib. rdsa mkhan bshin du de mi ḥgrub /
deḥi ṅo bo med paḥi phyir //
sred byed bshin duḥaṅ ḥgrub mi ḥdod /
bsreg bya med pas me med phyir //

[47] *na cājño jñaḥ*[3] *kathaṃ kartā*
bhoktā ca sa bhavet tava /
vyomakalpo 'vikalpaś ca
kiṃ kalpyaḥ[4] *kevalāgamāt* //

Tib. gal te mi śes byed po daṅ /
za po khyod kyis śes ci[5] ltar //
mkhaḥ ḥdra rtog pa med pa yaṅ /
luṅ ḥbaḥ shig gis brtags ci bya //

[48] *na cājño jñaḥ*[6] *svabhāvo vā*
niḥsvabhāvo bhaved asau /
niḥsvabhāvaś ca nātmā syād
bandhyātanayavat sa ca //

Tib. mi śes pa ḥam śes dṅos min /
ḥdi ni dṅos po med par ḥgyur //
dṅos med bdag tu mi ḥgyur te /
ḥdi ni mo gśam bu bshin no //

[49] *yat-pīḍānugrahe*[7] *yasya*
na duḥkhā[8] *nugrahodbhavaḥ* /
na tasyātmā hy asau yukto
yathā khaṃ devaśarmaṇaḥ //

Tib. gaṅ la gnod daṅ phan pa las /
gaṅ la gnod daṅ bde mi ḥbyuṅ //
de deḥi bdag tu mi rigs te /
nam mkhaḥ de ba śar maḥi bshin //

[50] *dhyānajñānādi ced iṣṭaṃ*
muktaye 'rthāntarātmanaḥ /

1. MS.—*dahanavadasmin.*
2. MS.—*dahanavadasmin bāhyābhāve hy agnisaṃbhavāt.*
3. MS.—*cājñājñaḥ.*
4. MS.—*kupta* (?).
5. ci. ji—Kārikā, N.; P.
6. MS.—*cājñājñaḥ.*
7. MS.—*pītānugrahe.*
8. MS.—*tadduḥkhā°.*

anātmārthaḥ prayatnaḥ syān
martyaḥ syān amṛtaḥ[1] *katham* //

Tib. ñi tsheḥi bdag daṅ[2] grol bar ni /
bsam gtan śes sogs kyis ḥdod na //
bdag med don la ḥbad pa yis /
śi ba mi ḥchir ji ltar ḥgyur //

[51] *antarātmano 'nyaś cet pratijñā te ca hīyate*[3] /

Tib. ñi tsheḥi bdag ni bdag las gshan /
she na thams cad skyes bu yin //
de ni ñi tshe gñis bdag daṅ /
phyi shes dam bcas ñams pa yin //

[Tr.] 'If you say that the individual *ātman* is different from the (highest) *ātman*, then your assertion that "all is *puruṣa*", "it exists beyond individual essence of duality (*dvaya*)" is hurt.'

[52] *nāntarātmātmano 'nyaś cet pratijñā te ca hīyate*[4] //
bdag las ñi tsheḥi bdag de ni /
gshan min she na dam bcas ñams //
gaṅ yaṅ bdag gi[5] bde sdug sogs /
ḥgro bas mi śes gtso bo min //

[Tr.] If you say that the individual *ātman* is not different from the (highest) *ātman*, then your assertion is also hurt, and also (your assertion that) 'pleasure, pains, etc. of *ātman* is not known by people of the world (*jagat*), and is not the principal one.'

[53] *yadi*[6] *sūkṣmo mahān nāyaṃ*
mahāṃś cen nāsya sūkṣmatā /
na caiko, rūpidharmaś ca
katham ātmany arūpiṇi //

Tib. gal te phra yin ḥdi che min /
chen po yin na phra ba min //
gcig kyaṅ ma yin gzugs kyi chos /
ji ltar gzugs med bdag gi yin //

[54] *na yuktā hasti-dṛṣṭāntād*[7] *ekasyānekarūpatā* /

1. MS.—*syānnamṛtaḥ*.
2. daṅ. gaṅ—D. Comm.
3. MS.—*dīyate*.
4. MS.—*dīyate*.
5. gi. gis—D. Comm.
6. MS.—*ati*°
7. MS.—*yuktādasti dṛṣṭāntād*.

karaḥ karī yato neṣṭaḥ, karādīnāṃ na caikatā //
Tib. gcig ñid du maḥi ṅo bo ru /
glaṅ poḥi dpe ḥdi mi rigs te //
sna ni glaṅ du mi ḥdod phyir /
sna tshogs rnams kyaṅ gcig ñid min //

[55] [1]*sūryādivarno yady ātmā*
syād avarṇaḥ kathaṃ ca saḥ /
neṣṭā palāśa-dṛṣṭāntād
ātmano 'nekarūpatā //
Tib. gaṅ yaṅ bdag ni ñi sogs mdog /
yin na mdog bral ji ltar yin //
bdag de du maḥi ṅo bo yis[2] /
dper na pa la śa mi ḥdod //

[56] *yataḥ palāśo naiko 'sti sarvadā-vikṛtātmakaḥ* /
mūlādayo yato naike, pratyayaiś cāpi bhedinaḥ //
Tib. gcig bu pa la śa med de /
kun tu ḥgyur baḥi bdag ñid daṅ //
ji ltar rtsa ba sogs du mar /
rkyen la sogs pas ḥbyed paḥi phyir //

[57] *jyāyastā*[3] *ca paratvaṃ ca tadanyāpekṣam iṣyate* /
saṃbhavo 'muṣya ca vidher ekatve katham iṣyate //
Tib. gtso bo ñid daṅ dam pa ñid /
de las gshan la bltos nas ḥdod //
gcig ñid yin na tshul ḥdi ñid /
yod par ji ltar ḥdod par bya //

1. *vedāham etaṃ puruṣaṃ mahāntam ādityavarṇaṃ tamasaḥ parastāt* / (*Śvetāśvatara-Up*.-3.8).
= *Vāj. Saṃh.* XXXI. 18 = *Tait. Ār.* 3. 12. 7; 3. 13. 1.
= *Mahānārāyaṇa Up.* 1. 12.
ravitulyarūpaḥ (*Śvet. Up.* 5. 8).
cf. *Satyasiddhiśāstra*, chap. 130 (Taisho, vol. 32, p. 316b.);
Abhidharma-mahāvibhāṣā-śāstra, vol. 200 (Taisho, vol. 27, p. 999b);
Daśabhūmikavibhāṣāśāstra, vol. 10 (Taisho, vol. 26, p. 74b);
Tarkajvālā, 7. 2.
2. yis. yi—Kārikā, N. and D.
3. MS.—*jñayastā*.
cf. *tato jyāyāṃś ca puruṣaḥ* (*Chānd. Up.* 3. 12. 6).
jyāyān pṛthivyā jyāyān antarikṣāj jyāyān divo jyāyān ebhyo lokebhyaḥ (*Chānd. Up.* 3. 14. 3).
yasmān nāṇīyo na jyāyo 'sti kaścana /
(*Śvet. Up.* 3. 9; *Mahānār.* 10. 4).

[58] *dravyaṃ yadi bhaved ātmā*
dravyatvāt sarvago na saḥ /
ghaṭavan nāpi nityaḥ syāt
tena pūrṇaṃ kuto jagat //

Tib. gal te bdag de rdsas yin na /
rdsas yin phyir na kûn khyab min //
bum pa bshin du rtag mi ḥgyur /
des na hgro ba rgyas ci[1] ltar //

[59] *dravyasyādhāratā yuktā dravyaṃ cātmā na yujyate* /
khapuṣpavad ajātatvān nādhāratvaṃ yatas tataḥ //

Tib. rdsas ni rten du rigs ḥgyur na /
bdag ni rdsas su mi rigs te //
nam mkhaḥi me tog ji lta bar /
de bshin ma skyes phyir rdsas med //

[60] *kasmiṃ sarvāṇi bhūtāni*
bhavanty ātmaiva paśyataḥ /[2]
ātmatā 'nātmano[3] *neṣṭā*
yathā 'bhāvasya bhāvatā[4] //

Tib. thams cad byuṅ gyur byuṅ ba daṅ /
ḥbyuṅ ḥgyur bdag med ji ltar mthoṅ //
bdag med bdag tu mi rigs te /
ji ltar dṅos med ṅo bo bshin //

[61] *na bālādyaviśeṣo 'to nirādhāro 'nidarśanaḥ* /
ekatvenātmano 'neka[5]*doṣopaplavasaṃbhavaḥ*[6] //

Tib. byis sogs khyad par med ma yin /
rten med pa daṅ dpe med phyir //
bdag gcig yin na du ma yi /
skyon rnams ḥbyuṅ bar ḥgyur ma yin //

1. ci. ji—Kārikā, N.

2. This half verse is the refutation of the theory set forth in verse 8 of the *pūrvapakṣa* :
tasmin sarvāṇi bhūtāni bhavanty ātmaiva paśyataḥ /
cf. *Taittirīya Up.* 7 :
yasmin sarvāṇi bhūtāni ātmaivābhūd vijānataḥ /
(Śaṁkarānanda's *Dīpikā*)

3. MS.—*ātmatādyātmano*.

4. *'bhāvasvabhāvatā* (?)

5. It is likely that the Tibetan translator took it for *anekadoṣopaplavāsaṃbhavaḥ* /

6. MS.—*naika°*.

[62] *maitrātmā caitrakaraṇaiḥ*[1]
caitrātmavad apīkṣatām /
caitrād abhinnamūrtitvād
deśābhedād athāpi vā //

Tib. tsai traḥi bdag de mai traḥi byed /
mai traḥi bdag giḥaṅ de bshin te //
tsai tra tha dad min dṅos phyir /
yaṅ na yul la dbye med phyir //

[63] *sukhaduḥkhopabhoktā*[2] *ca*
tan[3]*-muktau*[4] *cāpi mucyatām* /
tad[5]*vat(t)ve*[6] *cāpi bandho 'sya*[7]
ta (-d)[8] *duḥkhe vāstu duḥkhitaḥ* //

Tib. bde daṅ sdug bsṅal spyod pa daṅ /
de grol bas kyaṅ grol ba daṅ //
de bciṅs pas kyaṅ bciṅs pa daṅ /
de sdug pas kyaṅ sdug ñid ḥgyur //

[64] *na ghaṭākāśadṛṣṭāntā*[*t*]
sarveṣāṃ tad-[9]*asaṃbhavaḥ* /
ākāśa[*-sya*] *yato*[10]*'siddham*
ekatvaṃ bhavato 'pi[11] *ca* //

Tib. bum paḥi nam mkhaḥ dper bstan pa /
kun la de ni ḥbyuṅ ma yin //
gaṅ phyir nam mkhaḥ gcig ñid du /
khyod kyis[12] de ni ma grub ste //

[65] *rikto*[13] *dravyasya yo bhāvas*
tad ākāśaṃ hi sāṃvṛtam /
gatir gatimatāṃ tatra
so 'vakāśo 'vakāśinām //

1. MS.—*maitrātmacaikatrakaraṇaiḥ.*
2. =Caitra.
3. *tad=sukha-duḥkha.*
4. MS.=°*mukto.*
5. *tad=caitrasya duḥkhaṃ.*
6. *tadbandhe* (?) according to Tibetan versions.
7. *asya=maitrasya.*
8. *tad=caitrasya.*
9. *tad=sukha-duḥkha,* or *bhoga* and *mokṣa.*
10. *yato*—MS. *agrato.*
11. MS.—*bhāvatāpi.* Tib. khyod kyis.
12. kyis. kyi—D. Comm., N. Kārikā.
13. MS.—*mukta*°.

Tib. rdsas kyi ṅo bos gaṅ stoṅ pa /
de ni kun rdsob nam mkhaḥ yin //
de la ḥgro ldan ḥgro ba daṅ /
de ni skabs ḥdod skabs can no //

[66] *nāto 'nāvṛ[ti]r*[1] *ākāśaṃ nāvakāśasya dātṛ ca* /
taddhetūktau tadastitve hetos[2] *tu syād asiddhatā* //

Tib. des na nam mkhaḥ sgrib med min[3] /
skabs sbyin pa yaṅ ma yin te //
de yod gtan tshigs smras pa yis /
gtan tshigs ḥdi yaṅ ma grub ñid //

[67] *nāpi hetv-anupādānān nākāśaṃ bhāva iṣyate* /
bandhyātanayavan nāpi tad ekam eta eva hi //

Tib. rgyu las ñe bar ma byuṅ ba
nam mkhaḥ dṅos por mi ḥdod do //
de ni gcig kyaṅ ma yin te /
mo gśam gyi ni bu bshin no //

[68[*mṛdo ghaṭādirūpāyā mṛjjātīyatayaikatā* /
anyā cānyā ca kuṇḍādāv ato naikatvam ātmanaḥ[4] //

Tib. bum sogs la gzugs kyis rnams ni /
sa yi rigs su gcig na yaṅ //
rdsa sogs gshan daṅ gshan yin ltar /
des na bdag[5] ni gcig ma yin //

The following two lines are inserted in the Tibetan version of the Kārikā text. But this is a citation of a verse setting forth the Vedāntic thought in the *pūrvapakṣa*, and is to be eliminated from the text.

Tib. bdag ma śes śiṅ ma rtogs pas /
rmi lam loṅs spyod ṅa rgyal bshin // (=8.13 ab)

[69] *jñatve saty aviparyāsān neṣṭā*[6] *jñasyābhimānitā* /
ajñatve cāviparyāsān neṣṭā 'jñasyābhimānitā //

Tib. śes ñid phyin ci ma log pas /
śes ḥdi ṅa rgyal mi rigs so //

1. *ākāśam anāvṛtiḥ* (*Abhidharmakośa*, 1. 5;
āvaraṇābhāvamātram ākāśaṃ manyamānasya Saugatasya.
(Śaṃkara *ad Brahmasūtra*, 2. 2. 24)
2. MS.—*heles* (?).
3. min. yin—N. Comm., D.
4. MS.—*ānataḥ*. Tib. des na bdag ni gcig ma yin.
5. bdag. gshan—Kārikā, N.
6. MS.—*naṣṭā*.

mi śes ñid naḥaṅ log med pas /
mi śes ṅa rgyal mi ḥdod do //

[70] *vyomavac cāvikāritvād asaṃgatvād athāpi vā /*
nātmanaḥ kartṛtā yuktā yuktā nāpi ca bhoktṛtā //

Tib. nam mkhaḥ bshin du ḥgyur med phyir /
de bshin chags pa med paḥi phyir //
bdag ni byed por mi rigs la /
za ba por yaṅ mi rigs so //

[71] *kartā cel lipyate nātmā*
kartur iṣṭaṃ phalaṃ katham /
na yukto rājadṛṣṭāntaḥ
pāpabhāg[1] *nṛpatir yataḥ //*

Tib. byed po bdag yin mi gos pa /
byed poḥi ḥbras bu ḥdod ci ltar //
mi dbaṅ sdig daṅ bcas paḥi phyir /
rgyal poḥi dpe ni mi rigs so //

[72] *na caikatā 'dvitīyasya yuktā bāhyā*[2]*napekṣaṇāt*[3] */*
ekatvayogād ekaś ced yogas tasyaiva netaraḥ[4] *//*

Tib. phyi rol la ni ma ltos par /
gcig ñid ṅo bo ñid mi rigs //
gcig ñid daṅ ldan pas she na /
de ni de daṅ ldan ma yin //

[73] *anekaṃ kalpayitvā ced ekatā tad-apohataḥ /*
ekatvaṃ tattvato na syāt kalpanā sāṃvṛtī yataḥ //

Tib. du ma ñid du brtags pa dag /
bsal[6] ba gcig ñid yin she na //
ji ltar brtags[7] pa kum rdsob phyir /
des na gcig de[8] don dam min //

[74] *nityaikatvādirūpeṇa tattvataś cet sa*[9] *vidyate /*
ekādiśabdadhīvṛttir arthe[10] *sati niratyayā //*

1. MS.—*rājadṛṣṭāntūpāpabhāg.*
2. MS.—*pohyā°.*
3. MS.—**kṣaṇāḥ.*
4. MS.—*netannaḥ.*
5. btags, brtags, Kārikā.
6. bsal. gsal, Kārikā.
7. btags. brtags, Kārikā.
8. de. ste, Kārikā.
9. *sa=ātman.*
10. *artha=ātman.*

Tib. rtag daṅ gcig sogs ṅo bo yis /
don dam de yod yin she na //
gcig sogs sgra daṅ blo ḥjug pa /
don yod na ni skyon med ḥgyur //

[75] *ekatvādivikalpāc ca katham asyāvikalpanā /*
vikalpaviṣaye cārthe vācāṃ vṛttir avāritā //

Tib. gcig la sogs par rnam par **rtog** pa /
ḥdi ni ci ltar mi rtog ñid //
rnam par rtog paḥi yul don la /
tshig ḥjug pa ni ma bkag go //

[76] *dhiyāṃ*[1]*[a]viṣayo hy evaṃ*
kathaṃ vā' gocaro girām /
avācyo nirvikalpo[2] *'pi*
vitathaḥ pūrvanītivat //

Tib. ḥdi ltar blo*ḥ*i[3] yul min daṅ /
ṅag gi spyod yul min ci ltar //
brjod med rtog pa med pa yaṅ /
sṅar bstan rigs pas brdsun pa ñid //

[76+1] *buddhyā ced darśanān muktis*
tadbhedāt katham ekatā /
nānātvadhīvat sā ca syād
vitathā pūrvavad grahāt //

Verses through 76+7 are lacking in the Tibetan version.

[76+2] *ajātisamatāṃ yāte*
jñāne 'bhedāt kva darśanam /
adarśanād vimukti(ḥ) syān
muktir vā nāsti kasyacit //

[76+3] *bodhe sati tad*[5] *utpādād ajātisamatā kutaḥ /*
satyabhāvād anutpāde tadvikalpasamo 'pi saḥ[6]*//*

[76+4] *ajātir jātivad dharmas tadabhāve ca sā satī /*
naivātmasamatā tasya yuktā nāpi na tatsthatā //

Cf. *tattvam ādhyātmikaṃ dṛṣṭvā*
tattvaṃ dṛṣṭvā tu bāhyataḥ /

1. MS.—*dhiyāṃ ca.*
2. said of *ātman.*
3. bloḥi, blo yi, Kārikā.
4. rtogs. rtog, Kārikā.
5. *tad=mokṣa.*
6. *saḥ=bodhaḥ.*

tattvībhūtas tadārāmas
tattvād apracyuto bhavet //
Gauḍapādīya-Kārikā 3.38.

[76+5] *ajaś ca ko na bhedo'sti matā yena samarthanam* /
na jātājātayor iṣṭam ajatvaṃ tattvato yataḥ //

[76+6] *khapuṣpāt tad*[1] *abhedaś ced asatpakṣaparigraha...*/
...ṣpatte bhedaś ced advaitaṃ na prasidhyati //

[76+7] *nāto bhāvo na cābhāvo*
na pṛthag nāpṛthak[2] *pumān*[3] /
na nityo nāpy anityaś ca[4]
na buddhir dhvanigocaraḥ

[77] *jñeyasya*[5] *sarvathā 'siddhe*[*r*]
nyāyo buddher agocaraḥ /
dhīgocara-nivṛttau ca
syād girām apy agocaraḥ //

Tib. śes bya ye nas ma grub pas /
blo yi yul du mi rigs so //
blo yi yul las log pas na /
ṅag gi yul las log paḥaṅ yin //

[78] *tāthāgatīm avitathā*(*ṃ*)
matvā nītim imāṃ śubhām /
tasmāj jātaspṛhais tīrthyaiḥ[6]
kṛtaṃ tatra mamāpi [7]*tat* //

1. *tad*=*ātman.*

2. The negation of *ekatva* and *nānātva* is set forth in *Vākyapadīya* 3. 6. 26, 28; p. 172, Benares ed. The negation of *bhāva* and *abhāva* is set forth in *Vākyapadīya* 3. 3. 59; 60; 66; 72. Both argumentations are combined in ibid. 3. 1. 21. These argumentations are set forth repeatedly in Nāgārjuna's *Madhyamakakārikā* and the *Mahāyāna-śraddhotpādaśāstra* traditionally ascribed to Aśvaghoṣa. In the *Saddharmapuṇḍarīka-sūtra*, 2, Gāthā 65, the above-mentioned four ideas are said to be the sources of all the sixty-two wrong metaphysical opinions. The refutation of these four fundamental ideas can be traced in early Buddhism (*Saṃyutta-nikāya* 12. 48; vol. 2, p. 77).

3. *pumān*=*ātman.*

4. MS.—*cāto.*

5. MS.—*jñeya* (?) *sa.*

6. MS.—*tivraiḥ.* But mu stegs pa rnams (Comm.).

7. The similarity in the Mahāyāna and Vedānta teachings was explained away by later Mahāyānists as follows : 'In latter day some remaining teachings of Buddha were stolen by Brahmins who placed them duly in their own treatises.' (The Southern recension of the Chinese version of the *Mahāparinirvāṇa-sūtra*, vol. 16, *TT.*, vol. 12, p. 716c; cf. p. 382a)

Tib. de bshin gśegs paḥi mi brdsun paḥi /
lugs ḥdi dge bar śes nas ni //
de phyir mu stegs ḥdod skyes te /
de la bdag gir byas pa yin //

[79] [*kaḥ*] *śraddhāsyati tāṃ tatra*
pūrvāparavirodhinīm /
atyantātulyajātīyaṃ
maṇiratnam ivāyasaḥ //

Tib. sṅon daṅ phyi mar ḥgal ba yi /
de yi lugs la su shig dad //
śin tu rigs mi gcig paḥi phyir /
lcags las nor bu rin chen bshin //

[80] *deśanāyās tu vaicitryād*
iha[1]*iva*[*ṃ*] *syād ayaṃ nayaḥ* /
ākarṣaṇārtham ekeṣāṃ
śeṣagrāhanivṛttaye //

Tib. ḥdi ltar ḥdi ni lugs ḥdi la /
kha cig dag ni draṅ phyir daṅ //
lhag ma ḥdsin las[2] bzlog paḥi phyir /
sna tshogs dag tu bstan pa yin //

[81] *ajātatā hi bhāvānāṃ svabhāvo 'kṛtrimatvataḥ*[3] /
anapāyitvataś cāsāv ātmety api[4] *nigadyate* //

Tib. dṅos po rnams ni ma skyes ñid /
raṅ bshin bcos ma med paḥi phyir //
ḥdi la ñams pa med pas na /
bdag ces kyaṅ ni brjod pa yin //

[82] *eko 'sāv ekarūpatvād*
bhāvabhede 'py abhedataḥ /
sarva[*gaḥ*] *sarvadharmatvā*[*n*]
nityaś cāpy avināśataḥ //

Tib. tha dad dṅos kyaṅ dbye med phyir /
ṅo bo gcig phyir gcig ñid yin //
kun khyab chos rnams thams cad phyir /
rtag paḥaṅ de yin mi ñams phyir //

1. *iha=buddhaśāsane.*
2. la. las, Kārikā.
3. MS.—*kartṛmatvataḥ.*
4. MS.—*ātmany api.*

[83] *ajātatvād ajāto 'yam*[1]
atu evā 'jarāmaraḥ /
acyutaś cyutyabhāvāc ca
prakarṣatvāt paraṃ matam //

Tib. ma skyes phyir na skye med ñid /
de ñid phyir na rga śi med //
ḥpho ba med phyir ḥdi ḥpho med /
rab mthar thug phyir mchog ñid yin[2] //

[84] *na rūpaśabdagandhādir na bhūmy-agni-jalānilāḥ*[3] /
nākāśa-śaśi-sūryādir na manojñānalakṣaṇaḥ //

Tib. gzugs daṅ sgra daṅ dri sogs min /
sa daṅ me daṅ chu rluṅ min //
nam mkhaḥ zla ba ñi ma min /
yid daṅ śes paḥi mtshan ñid min //

[85] *sarvaś cāsau*[4] *svabhāvatvān*
na sarvaṃ cāvināśataḥ /
tatra kleśādyanutpatteḥ
śuddho 'sau śānta eva ca //

Tib. thams cad ḥdi yin raṅ bshin phyir /
ñams pa med phyir thams cad min //
de la ñon moṅs skye med phyir /
dag pa ḥdi yin shi ñid ḥdi //

[86] *sakalpanāsamāropā*[5]*[d] vācyo 'vācyas tu tattvataḥ* /
sarvathā cāpy avācyatvād ukta eva nirañjanaḥ //

Tib. de ni brtags pas sgro btags nas[6] /
brjod bya yaṅ dag brjod bya min //
ye nas brjod bya ma yin phyir /
ḥdi ni dri ma med ces bstan //

[87] *īdṛśo yady abhipreta ātmā hi bhavatām*[7] *api* /
nāmādi-bahusādharmyān nirdoṣaḥ sopapattikaḥ //

Tib. gaṅ shig ḥdi ltar mṅon ḥdod pa /
khyod kyis bdag kyaṅ yin na ni //

1. MS.—*ajātaś cāyam.*
2. ñid yin. yin ñid—Kārikā, N., D.
3. MS.—°*nilaḥ.*
4. MS.—*sarvasyāsau.*
5. MS.—*samāropa-*°.
6. nas. na, Kārikā.
7. MS.—*tavatām.*

miṅ sogs chos maṅ ḥdra ba la /
skyon med rigs pa daṅ bcas yin //

[88] *nairātmyād eva bhītānāṃ*
bhītyā[1] *tatraiva ca*[2] *sthitiḥ*[3] /
ākāśād iva bhītasya
kva cānyatra sthitir bhavet //

Tib. bdag med ñid kyis ḥjigs pa rnams /
ḥjigs kyaṅ de ñid la gnas te //
nam mkhaḥ ḥjigs par gyur pa dag /
gshan paḥi gnas ḥgaḥ med pa bshin //

[89] *svāgataṃ kriyatām tṛptir*
nātra kaścin na(?) *vāryate* /
buddhānāṃ lokabandhūnāṃ
tattvā-[*mṛtam*] *idaṃ param* //

Tib. saṅs rgyas ḥjig rten gñen rnams kyis[4] /
de ñid bdud rtsi mchog ḥdi la //
ḥdi ni ḥgaḥ yaṅ bkag med pas /
legs par ḥoṅs ṣo ṅoms par gyis //

[90] *api tv ātmā tv akartṛ*[5]*tva-*
bhoktṛtvādi[*r*] *nirāspadaḥ* /
saṃtyajyatām asadgrāho[6]
bhūtadṛk[7] *pratibandhakaḥ* //

Tib. yaṅ dag lta la sgrib med paḥi /
bdag ni byed po za po sogs //
rten med brdsun paḥi ḥdsin pa ni /
des na spaṅ ba kho nar gyis //

[91] *svabhāvājātito 'jātir bhāvānāṃ tattvato matā* /
svabhāvato hy ajātatvād uktaiṣā niḥsvabhāvatā //

1. MS.—*dṛṣṭyā*.
2. MS.—*ca*.
3. The fear of hearing the true teaching on the part of Yogins or philosophers was originally set forth in Mahāyāna scriptures, and was introduced into the Vedānta school. (*Gauḍapādīya-kārikā*, 4. 42. cf. ibid. 3, 39).
4. kyis, kyi, Kārikā, N., D.
5. MS.—*apitvāmatvakartṛ-°*.
6. '*°graho*. Metre requires *grāho*. In Vedānta, however, 'adhesion' or 'understanding by attachment' is called *graha* (not *grāha*). *Gauḍapādīya-kārikā*, 2. 29; 3, 32, 38; 4. 82, 84.
7. MS.—*°drink*.

Tib. dṅos rnams raṅ bshin skye med phyir /
de ñid du na skye med ḥdod //
ṅo bo ñid kyis skye med ñid /
ḥdi yi ṅo bo ñid du bstan //

[92] *nai[ḥ] svabhāvyaṃ ca nairātmyaṃ*
na tadātmā virodhataḥ /
anātmā ced bhaved ātmā
gor abhāvo 'pi gaur bhavet //

Tib. dṅos med ñid ni bdag med pa /
de ni bdag min ḥgal ba ñid //
bdag med bdag tu ḥgyur she na /
ba laṅ min paḥaṅ ba laṅ ḥgyur //

[93] *yataḥ svabhāvābhāvo 'sau*
kathaṃ kartṛ-[tā-bhoktṛ]-te[1] /
dṛṣṭe bandhyāsutasyeha
nākasmāt kartṛbhoktṛte //

Tib. dṅos poḥi ṅo bo med ḥdi ni /
ji ltar byed po za por rigs //
gaṅ phyir mo gśam dag gi bu /
byed po za por ma yin bshin //

[94] *itthaṃ*[2]*bhūtāt kathaṃ janma*
pralayas tatra vā katham /
na vyomakusume yuktā
pralayotpādakalpanā //

Tib. de ltar gyur la skye ji ltar /
de la ñams par ḥgyur ci ltar //
mkhaḥ la me tog med pa la /
ji ltar skye ḥjig brtags pa bshin //

[95] *svabhāvābhāvaviṣayā yāvad buddhiḥ pravartate /*
dhīkalpanāsamāropā[s] tāvad ekādikā[3] *matāḥ //*

Tib. dṅos po med paḥi yul dag la /
ji srid blo ni ḥjug gyur pa //
blo yis brtags[4] pas sgro btags phyir /
de srid gcig la sogs par ḥdod //

[96] *savikalpāvikalpā[ṃ]ś ca*
yadā buddhir nivartate /

1. MS.—*karts...kyate.*
2. MS—*icchaṃ-°.*
3. MS.—*ekāntikā.*
4. brtags—btags, Kārikā.

dhiyām aviṣaye tasmin
prapañcopaśama[ḥ] śiva[ḥ] //

The phrase : *prapañcopaśamaḥ śivaḥ* is found in the salutary verse of the *Madhyamaka-kārikā* of Nāgārjuna.

Tib. rtog bcas rtog pa med pa las /
gaṅ tshe blo ni log gyur pa //
de tshe blo ni yul med phyir /
spros pa ñer **shi shi ba ñid** //

iti Vedānta-tattva-viniścayo 'ṣṭamaḥ paricchedaḥ /

3. *The Vedānta as Presented by Bhavya in his Madhyamaka-hṛdaya* and *Tarka-jvālā*[1]

In the eighth chapter of the *Tarkajvālā*, which is a commentary by the author himself on the *Madhyamaka-hṛdaya*, by Bhavya (c. 490-570) the Vedānta philosophy of his days is described and refuted. Bhavya was a Buddhist philosopher of the Mādhyamika school, and is said to have been the founder of the Svātantrika sub-school of the Mādhyamika school. The chapter, which represents some aspects of pre-Śaṅkara Vedānta philosophy, is very important of the study of the history of the Vedānta school. The arguments used by Bhavya to attack the Vedānta philosophy are highly interesting. Here I should like to point out some of the characteristics of the Vedānta philosophy described in his works, using Bhavya's description as a basis.

In the Vedānta theory described by Bhavya, the Absolute is called Brahman, Ātman, Puruṣa, Īśvara and Maheśvara, all of which are held to be different names for the same fundamental principle. That is, he takes it that all the world principles expounded in the Upaniṣads are the same principle. We learn, accordingly, that those Vedānta scholars known to Bhavya at that time maintained a composite and unified interpretation of the contents of the Upaniṣads.

Now, the Vedānta doctrines of which Bhavya knew are by no means similar, but in fact are variegated and multifarious.

Take the theories on Puruṣa, for example. "Puruṣa," a

noun meaning originally "man" "human being," developed in meaning to become the fundamental principle of the world; but even in the philosophy of later centuries, it was not dissociated from the physical form of man. This is true for Bhavya's account. Puruṣa was, of course, identical with "Īśvara" (v. 3), and "Ātman" (v. 43), and anything that could be said of the Absolute could also be predicated of Puruṣa. He said, for example, that because it surpasses all things, it is "the Great" (*mahat*) (v. 2); as it controls all things, it is called "the god ruling everything (ad v. 15); *Maheśvara*, (v. 2) and "the god who rules all bodies" (dban phyug skyes lu v. 26); it is called "the immortal" (*amṛta*) (v. 6), and liberation is its fundamental nature (v. 43). Yet here as before, he portrays Puruṣa anthropomorphically as having a body similar to that of a human being; he asserts that the individual parts of its body in themselves correspond to the various phenomenal elements of the natural world (ad v. 4). Again, he says that Puruṣa is of gold colour (*Sūryavarcas*, v. 2; *rukmavarṇa*, v. 3), and has inherently the various brilliances of the sun (v. 3; *Sūryādivarṇa*, v. 55). Furthermore, he thought that the place where Puruṣa exists is particular and limited—Puruṣa abides in a dark orbit remote from the orbit of the earth (ad v. 2). He also says that Puruṣa transcending the three spheres of existence exists far away (v. 4). Thus, he portrays Puruṣa very concretely, and there are, in Bhavya's concept of Puruṣa, the remnants of a primitive, *simple and naive* idea.

While Puruṣa is thus a transcendent deity, being one, it also includes the three spheres of existence (ad v. 9. cf. v. 8), and pervades all things (vv. 2, 3, 4). All things in the past, present, and future are none other than Puruṣa; the internal and external, the near and far, are also none other than Puruṣa (v. 4). He says that nothing is other than Puruṣa (v. 43), and that Maheśvara consists of the entire world (v. 2). This idea can also be found in the hymns on Puruṣa in the *Ṛg-Veda*, and was not a new thesis.

Despite the fact that Bhavya frequently employed the word "Puruṣa" in the same sense as Ātman as a philosophical concept, his concept of Puruṣa, whenever he took up this question alone, was still not completely free of a mythological colouring from the remote past. In it were further included child-like speculations.

The fact, then, that an explanation of Puruṣa was thus presented in detail as a Vedānta philosophical theory should be regarded as extremely important in the history of ideas. Vedānta scholars like Gauḍapāda, Bhartṛhari and Śaṅkara, rarely discuss the concept of Puruṣa. It would seem that they thought that Puruṣa was only an ancient mythological concept, and that they did not regard it so highly as a philosophical concept. Since, however, theories on Puruṣa were quite influential during the time of Bhavya, it seems that they ought to have been discussing this one before all else. Both Śāntarakṣita and Kamalaśīla who are later than Bhavya, discuss elaborately the concept of Puruṣa as a theory of the Vedavādins. In the light of this, it would seem that this idea had been vigorously pursued in the intellectual world known to the Buddhists at that time.

It is particularly noteworthy that the concept of Puruṣa presented above has a remarkable resemblance to the concept of the supreme deity in the Śaiva-sect. Here, Puruṣa is portrayed anthropomorphically, with a body similar to that of human beings; and it was asserted that the individual parts of its body in themselves have their respective counterparts in the phenomena and elements of the natural world (ad v. 4). Although this idea had already appeared in the Upaniṣads, the Buddhists presented it as a theory of the Śaiva sect in particular.[2] Again, the fact that Puruṣa is of a golden colour is also expounded in the Upaniṣads which explain the worship of Śiva.[3] This Puruṣa is also called Maheśvara here, and there are many instances throughout Indian religious literature in which this name was used as a title for Śiva. Another interesting fact is that all the Upaniṣads cited here to present the Vedānta theory either teach faith in Śiva, or emphasize the grace (*prasāda*) of the supreme god.[4] In view of these facts, it seems that by the time of Bhavya, a section of the Vedānta school was already worshipping Śiva, and that there existed a particular sect with theistic inclinations which worshipped and followed these Upaniṣads readily related to the theology of the Śaiva sect (*e.g.*, *Īśa*, *Kāṭhaka*, and *Śvetāśvatara*). Bhavya's concept of Puruṣa, then, may have been derived from his knowledge of this sect. And one could suppose that this school formed a tradition different from that of those Vedānta scholars of the *Brahma-sūtra* tradition which emphasized the *Chāndogya-Upaniṣad*.

In this connection, it is also noteworthy that one here finds the idea of sun-worship. Bhavya makes out that Puruṣa is "that which has the brilliances of the sun", that the various colours found in the sun are "the substance of all the gods", and that the fundamental nature of the sun is "the great Īśvara (the great self-existent god)" (ad v. 4).[5] Sun-worship is a form of faith which has been maintained in India without interruption from the time of the *Ṛg-veda.* These Upaniṣads also teach that which exists in the sun and that which exists in the individual bodies (Puruṣa) are really identical (*Tait.-Up.* II.8, III.10). They thought, therefore, that the Absolute Brahman exists in the sun. Apart from this, sun-worship has been of particular influence in Hinduism and the popular faiths of India. Some of the Purāṇas (e.g., *Saura-Purāṇa, Bhaviṣya-Purāṇa* 73) refer to it together with Śiva-worship, and regard Śiva as identical with the sun. And Bhavya may have heard something of the tradition of this faith.

On the other hand, again, it is stated that the Puruṣa is indistinguishable from and completely identical in meaning with the *ātman* as a pure philosophical concept, and I shall next summarize the *ātman* theory presented here. In this theory of ātman, there are traces of an extremely advanced philosophical speculation. As the *ātman* is the original self of every individual soul which cannot be replaced by anything else, no person can be apart from the ātman (v. I). The *ātman* is bound and is also liberated (ad v. I). One ought to say only that it exists (*ātmano'stitvam*, v. 19). And the ātman also has cognition (*jñāna* or knowledge) as its fundamental attribute (ad v. 31; v. 39; ad v. 46).[6] One can also say that it is the subject of cognition (ad v. 39; ad v. 31). As it is the subject of our selves, it cannot be grasped as an object. It is impossible to affirmatively describe its basic essence by words (*vācām agocaraḥ*, v. 16; ad v. 76). The ātman has no form (*arūpin*, v. 53). Actually, the ātman is frequently referred to as "the only one" or "the unique" (*ekatā*, v. 39; *ekatva*, vv. 57; 61; *abhinnamūrtitva*, v. 62; cf. v. 63; *advitīya*, v. 72)

As the One, it exists eternally in time (ad v. 42, v. 74). "The *ātman* belongs to the class of immutable things, and it cannot be split up by any relation whatsoever" (ad v. 6). Again, it exists everywhere spatially (*sarvago* v. 58) Completely filling all bodies, it is the unique *ātman* of all things (ad v. 49). Its characteristics of "eternality," "omnipresence" and "uniqueness" (*ekatva*) are frequently mentioned together v. 61; ad v. 72; ad v. 79). It can also be said to be undifferentiated (v .17; ad v. 75). In some cases, the *ātman* was thought to be a substance (*dravya*) (vv. 58, 59). Because it surpasses everything else, it is also called "the Supreme" (*mchog*) (ad v. 34), "the Principal" (*gtso bo*), "the highest" (*dam pa*) (ad v. 57).

Now, how can ātman as this transcendental Absolute become the subject of the action of individual bodies ?

The Vedānta sect described by Bhavya recognized two kinds of ātman. (1) There is the *ātman* bound by the body, that is, the ātman appearing within the body; and, (2) there is the highest, liberated ātman, that is, the supreme self (tantamount to *paramātman*) (v. 23). The latter corresponds to the Puruṣa described already; the former is generally said to be the individual self (*jīva*) in the Vedānta philosophy, and *all the gods are understood to be individual selves* (v. 12; cf. ad 2, 4). This individual self is the actor who performs good and evil Karma and is also the one who experiences the fruit of its action (vv. 14, 34). The individual self centered within the individual body is sometimes called Puruṣa, and it is said that Puruṣa is the actor and the function within the eyes, etc. (ad v. 30; ad v. 32). The existence of this Puruṣa or *ātman* cannot be perceived by the sense organs (ad v. 33), but the existence of the ātman must be admitted as the subject which integrates its perceptions of the mental processes of the individual body (vv. 25, 28). All mental processes, *e.g.*, sensation, perception, association, memory etc., are really formed by the functioning of the Puruṣa. Human speech and concepts are also produced from the working of the ātman (v. 27; ad v. 30). As to the proofs for the existence of ātman, they follow similar lines as those of the Nyāya-Vaiśeṣika.

Opposed to this, however, is the Supreme Self, the ruler which controls all individual selves. While one must accordingly say that it participates in all actions of individual selves, the Puruṣa or Supreme Self nevertheless, does not itself receive the fruits, good or evil, of its action (ad v. 15). While dwelling within all bodies, it functions with regard to all objects, but it is not staine o defiled by them (vv. 15, 71). And it is completely apart from any defects or faults (*nirdoṣa* v. 87).

Now, individual self, differing with each body, exists in

numerous forms, but the Supreme Self is only one pervasive existence, and does not exist in differentiated forms.

Two illustrations are given in explanation. One analogy likens the individual self to a clay pot and the Supreme Self to the clay. It is said to be similar to the fact that while pots differ from one another as individual objects, the clay from which they are made does not have any differences in its material essence (vv. 12, 67). One cannot, however, directly compare the relation of the Supreme Self to the individual self as one between the material cause and its mutable forms. A further attempt is made to clarify the meaning by an analogy with space. The ātman is frequently compared to space,[7] in which the Supreme Self is likened to the Great Space and the individual self as the space within a pot. The Supreme Self is a unique universal existence, which exists throughout all the individual selves, but never does it receive the fruits of birth and death, pleasure and pain, as does the individual self, nor does it have a transitory, determinate and differentiated nature as does the individual self. It is similar to the fact that while pots are made and destroyed, the space itself which exists within is not produced or destroyed, but is eternal, one and omnipresent (v. 10). In the same way, just as one can establish differences between the Supreme Self and the individual selves, so can one set up differences between various individual selves also. It is not the case that the pleasure and pains of one individual self exert an influence upon another individual self. It is said that this situation is exactly similar to the fact that while the space within one jar may be obscured by dust and smoke, the space in another jar is not obscured thereby (v. 13). We can find the same idea in Chapter III of the *Māṇḍūkya-Kārikā*. As against other theories, the Vedānta theory presented by Bhavya holds that "as the one Great Space divides and becomes the space within numerous jars, so the unique ātman becomes numerous" (ad v. 11). That is, this theory is opposed to the interpretation that the analogy of space means that the ātman evolves. This theory, consequently, adopts the position (or one very close to it) that the individual self and Great Self coincide, that is, the theory of non-dualistic monism. Since, however, no mention is made of ignorance (*avidyā*) or *māyā* as the principle of the temporary appearance of the world, it would seem that although the Māyāvāda of the later Śaṅkara school had not been completely formulated, it was not to be long before its essential strands were to be woven together.

It is not, however, that the non-dualistic monistic view alone is presented here. It is obvious, also, that since it is said that all living species are comprised within the ātman (v. 9), one should admit the seeds of the limited non-dualism (*viśiṣṭādvaita*) of the later Rāmānuja school. Moreover, Bhavya also presents a view that the Supreme Self and the individual self are "neither one or different" (*gsahan daṅ gashan ma yin pa=bhedābheda*) (ad v. 51), and it is worthy of note that such a predication clearly appears. Bhavya, however, divides the view into two, that the individual self *antarātman* is different from the Supreme Self *ātman* and that it is not different, and attacks both of them (vv. 51, 52). As the Mādhyamika School, which admits tentatively the basic principles of formal logic, critically discusses the doctrines of other schools based upon those principles, it seems he could not admit a concept containing the contradiction "neither one nor different" as an affirmative conceptual premise.

We have now learned that several different theories about the relation of the Supreme Self and the individual self were in existence during that era; and, in addition, another view on the ātman is also recorded. According to this : "It has been debated in various ways among scholars whether the ātman is universal existence or whether it only has a size conforming to the body, or whether it is extremely small; but all these opinions merely take up one side of the ātman. It is exactly similar to the parable of the blind men[8] who, feeling the various parts of an elephant, offer many conjectures about its actual body. Both one and many together are but one side of the ātman." (anekarūpatā, v. 54, ad v. 53). It is clear that there the facts of the heterogeneous views on the universe are taken up and reflectively discussed. And since the variations in the opinions about ātman are to be understood as really based upon ātman itself, this philosophical position should rather be regarded as close to that of the *Māṇḍūkya-Kārikā*.

Besides ātman, Brahman also is mentioned (ad v. 17). Although Brahman is taught as being unique, omnipresent, eternal, and the dwelling place of immortality (*acyutaṃ padam*, v. 16), no special explanation is offered beyond that. The appellation "Supreme

Brahman" (*tshaṅs mchog-paraṃ brahma*) (v.16), is cited, but this concept is not contrasted with a concept of "lower Brahman" (*aparaṃ brahma*). "Supreme" here is merely a rhetorical objective with "Brahman". Brahman is also taken to be Īśvara (ad v. 2; ad v. 16). Thus nothing like Śaṅkara's idea of distinguishing two kinds of Brahman was known to Bhavya. Furthermore in the description of Brahman in this passage, Brahman is taken to be different from the cognitive function (*rnam par śes pa-vijñāna*). Later Śāntarakṣita records the theory by which the fundamental essence of Brahman (*ātman*) is the cognitive function[9], and it should be noted that his account differs on this point.

Let us next take up the views on the evolution of the world. Puruṣa, or *ātman*, is the "unique world cause"(vv. 7; *jagatkāraṇatā*, 19), and is the creator (*kartṛ*) of the world (v. 3). The entire world arose from it, just as the silken thread is produced from the body of the silkworm (*ūrṇanābhād ivāṃśavaḥ*, v. 5). Puruṣa itself, however after it has given birth to the entire world, neither changes from its former state nor is completely used up in the process (ad v. 5). This idea was already expounded in the Ancient Upaniṣads, and a similar analogy, that of the thread of the spider, frequently appears in the Upaniṣads. No particularly new idea is thus taught on the evolution of the world, and the position adopted is chiefly that of evolutionism (*pariṇāmavāda*). No explanation on the lines of the Māyā doctrine can be found. In this respect, the theory is quite different from the *Māṇḍūkya-kārikā* in general, and Śaṅkara and others.

While the essentials of his description of the Supreme Self or the Absolute are roughly as above, the Vedānta ideas in Bhavya's work are by no means consistent throughout. Consequently, we can see that prior to the sixth century when Bhavya lived, there existed already differences among various branches within the Vedānta school, and that the thinkers were maintaining among themselves varying theories on the fundamental essence of the Absolute, the relation between the Supreme Self and the individual self, and other problems.

Even in regard to liberation, the theory he represents differs little from the general theory of the Upaniṣads. One obtains liberation by seeing and realising the Puruṣa in its true state (*paraṃ sāmyam...āpnuyāt*, v. 3; v. 19). To see the Puruṣa is

Truth (*tattva*) itself, and no one can ever injure it (ad v. 17). Direct introspection of the Puruṣa is taken as the supreme goal. Liberation is "the highest tranquility (*śānta*)," "the highest state" (*param*) (v. 3 and gloss on it), and is the acquisition of "non-aging and immortality" (vv. 2, 5). In liberation, Puruṣa (=*ātman*) has no activity (ad v. 40), being separated from the sense organs (ad v. 42). As it is separated from all functioning in its state of liberation (ad v. 3), it transcends sinful obstructions and advantageous virtues (*vihāya pāpam puṇyāṁśca*, v. 4), when all evil and good become undifferentiated and equal (*na...viśeṣo, ekatva*, v. 9). There, all differences disappear between fool and sage, lowly and Brahmin, and all becomes of one form (vv. 9, 61), indistinguishably merged into Puruṣa the fundamental principle, with no return to be born into this world filled with its pains and sufferings (vv. 5, 16).

The Vedānta theorists maintain that if one follows the ideas of non-self and momentary destruction of Buddhism one is not able to explain the reasons why bondage and liberation can occur (ad v. 35).

Now, in order to reach this state of liberation, one must think rightly upon, must concentrate his thoughts upon, the Puruṣa or *ātman* (vv. 3, 50; ad v. 16). For that purpose, one must practise meditation or Yoga. The practice of Yoga to see the ātman is given the highest praise (vv. 3, 5, 16; ad v. 17; ad v. 22). The one who completes the yogic practices comes to be endowed with eight kinds of supernormal powers (ad v. 7; ad v. 8).

Judging from this account, the Vedānta scholars of that time accepted a liberation by recognition or knowledge, and grace (*prasāda*) of the Supreme God and devotion (*bhakti*) toward the Supreme God are not emphasized so highly. As already indicated, Bhavya quotes sacred passages from the Upaniṣads which teach faith in Śiva or his grace, but there is no theological account of grace or devotion. Perhaps the early Vedānta scholars whom Bhavya knew taught chiefly Yoga as direct introspection of the Absolute and as the practical method, and as grace and devotion are included within these methods, they were not separately noted by Bhavya. And it seems that among the Vedānta scholars known to Bhavya, no important differences of opinion on the problem of practice existed.

It should be noted, however, that on the question of practice, the Vedānta school which Bhavya reports had endeavoured to destroy the concept of class distinctions firmly maintained by the orthodox Brahmins. It was held that if one were to know the ātman, no matter who he might be, he could obtain the state of liberation; and in that state, all distinction between classes would be reduced to nil (*tulyatā*, v. 9). Although this intellectual trend had already appeared in the Old Upaniṣads,[10] it was still rejected by the orthodox Brahmins, who maintained the position of their own supremacy in all respects. This conservative privileged attitude distinctly appears in the *Brahma-sūtra*. The Vedānta school mentioned by Bhavya, however, opposed this idea, and was universalistic and for the masses, and could endeavour to include all of the castes within its fold, although we are not quite sure whether they did it actually as in the case of Śaṅkara and his followers who did not do it actually. And I hasten to add that this attitude can easily be combined with that of Hinduism, the popular religion of India. Perhaps closely related to this attitude is the fact that in this account by Bhavya, one can dimly discern the tendency to worship Śiva and the sun; and there are ideas in this social position which are also common to those of Buddhism. Some notions of ethical practices in Buddhism might have contributed this factor in the formation of the distinctive features of Vedānta practice.

The topic of the relationship between Buddhism and Vedānta is an important problem. Bhavya offered the view that insofar as the schools outside of Buddhism adopt the theory of tathāgata among their own theories and advocate a doctrine resembling that of Buddhism, the ātman theory of the Vedānta school and the non-self theory of Buddhism are actually identical in content ad v. 87; ad v. 91). He strongly asserted, however, that distinctive differences exist between the two schools (esp. vv. 60, 78, 91; ad v. 79). Buddhists of the late period in general had thought that Buddhism is the only doctrine which ought to be the basis of all philosophical theories, and that the schools outside of Buddhism had secretly stolen Buddhist theories and freely used them as their own doctrines,[11] so that Bhavya also may have gone along with this idea. It should be regarded as important, however, that he emphasized in particular *the differences between Buddhism and the Vedānta theories.* Because the Vedānta school, during Bhavya's time had already taken up to a great extent Buddhist philosophical theories, and had become very close to Buddhist doctrines in respect to its ideas, terminology, methods of expression, etc., and as the similarities and differences between the two schools were discussed in the intellectual world of that day, Bhavya was quite aware of the fact that the Vedānta school held ideas resembling Buddhist doctrines. The problem, therefore, of such expressions as "a crypto-Buddhist", etc., can be traced back to the sixth century when Bhavya was alive.

The Vedānta philosophy presented by Bhavya has, in the main, the features presented above, and taken as a whole, there are no other outstanding traces of an advance in thought to be seen in the Upaniṣadic doctrines. There is no doubt, however, that the Vedānta school, as a philosophical school, had already been firmly established in the intellectual world of that time. It seems that the scholars of this school then mainly endeavoured to synthesize and organize the doctrines taught in the Upaniṣads. For them, accordingly, the sacred Upaniṣads had absolute authority. Bhavya also reports on this attitude (ad v. 48). They were progressing in the direction toward forming a new philosophical system based upon the Upaniṣadic canon. And it is clear that in the various philosophical problems, *the seeds which were to cause sectarian disruptions* in the later Vedānta school itself, had already been planted among the Brahmin scholars of this school during that time. It also seems that the synthesis of the study of grammar and Vedānta philosophy had already begin to be formed during this period.[12]

Notes

1. This section was once published in Journal of the Oriental Institute, Vol. XIV, Nos. 3-4, March-June, 1965, pp. 287-295. But now I have revised it and incorporated Sanskrit words found in the recently discovered manuscript.

2. Cf. *Bodhisattva Ārya Deva's Commentary on the Doctrines of the Heretics, the Hīnayāna and Nirvāṇa in the Laṅkāvatāra-sūtra,* (Hajime Nakamura, Upaniṣadic Tradition and the Early School of Vedānta as noticed in Buddhist Scripture, in *Harvard Journal of Asiatic Studies*, Vol. 18, June 1955, Numbers 1 and 2, pp. 99-101).

3. Eg., *Kaivalya-Up..* II.1.

4. In Chapter VIII of the *Tarka-jvālā*, passages of the Upaniṣads are quoted in eight stanzas. There is one which is unidentified, and of the

others the *Kāṭhaka-Up.* is quoted once, the *Īśa-Up.* once, and the *Śvetāśvatara Up.* five times. Since Īśvara is called Śiva in the *Śvetāśvatara*, and in the *Īśa* there can be found theistic ideas, it is not in the least strange that the word *Īś*(*vara*) should have been interpreted by men of later centuries as another name for Śiva. And the words of the *Kāṭhaka-Up.* II-21 quoted by Bhavya are found in exactly the passage which emphasizes the grace (*prasāda*) of the Supreme Deity.

5. Cf. *Īśvaraḥ sarveṣām bhūtānāṃ gopāyitādityaḥ* (*Nirukta*. III.12).

6. Bhavya mentions, and rejects, the theory that "the essence of *ātman* (*Puruṣa*) is non-cognition (*ajñāna*)" and the theory that "the essence of ātman is not cognition, nor is it non-cognition" (vv. 48, 69), but he may merely have incidentally referred to this in connection with the common doctrine of the Vedānta school that "the essence of ātman is cognition," for the reason that the ātman also cannot be established as something whose essence is different from cognition : and it may not have been that there actually was some who advocated of such a doctrine at that time.

7. Cf. v. 3, ad v. 47, v. 70, among others.

8. *Udāna*, VI, 4. pp. 66-69 (The Pali Text Society edition). The Chinese version of the *Arthavargīya-sūtra*, vol. 1. (*TT.*, vol. 4, p. 178 a-c) The *andhagajanyāya* was commonly resorted to by Brahmin philosophers as well as by Jains. (M. Winternitz : *A History of Indian Literature*, Vol. II, p. 83, n.)

8. *Tattva-saṃgraha* v. 329. Cf. *Gauḍapādīya-Kārikā* III.33, IV. 96, 99.

10. Cf. the *Muṇḍaka-Up.* I 1.5, and the narratives by the poet Raikva and Satyakāma in the *Chāndogya-Up.*

11. "There are some teachings of the Buddha which still remain now. Brahmins have stolen them, and inserted them in various passages of the scriptures of their own." (The *Mahāparinirvāṇa-sūtra* of Mahāyāna, the Southern Version, Vol. 16, *TT*, Vol. 12, p. 716c. Cf. *ibid.* p. 382 a. Chi-tsang: *San-lun-hsuan-i*, ed. by Yensho Kanakura, Iwanami Bunko edition, pp. 26, 161.

12. In the gloss on v. 30, it can be seen that there were several persons who asserted the reasons why the existence of the *ātman* should be posited from the standpoint of the study of grammar.

4. *The Vedānta Thought as Referred to in Other Texts of Bhavya*

This is all there is in the 8th chapter of Bhavya's *Madhyamakahṛdayakārikā* and *Tarkajvālā*, but it should be noted here that some of the Vedāntic theories introduced in the above texts are also mentioned in Bhavya's *Prajñāpradīpamūlamadhyamakavṛtti*, which is a commentary on Nāgārjuna's *Mūlamadhyamakakārikā*; its Sanskrit original has been lost but its Chinese and Tibetan translations are still extant. It refers to the view that Puruṣa is the cause of the universe :

"Again, those who regard Puruṣa as the cause of origination say, 'Because all beings have Puruṣa as their cause.' What does it mean ? Just as threads are woven into a net, just as water comes out of moon-stone, and just as trees sprout their branches and leaves, so do all beings have Him as their cause. What are called past and future, movable and immovable, far and near, inside and outside, are all caused by Puruṣa.'[1]

This view is in accordance with that in the 4th and 5th stanzas of the eighth chapter of the *Madhyamaka-hṛdaya-kārikā*. The similes quoted here are similar to those in the Vedic quotations which appear in Bhavya's commentary on the 17th stanzas of the eighth chapter of the *Tarkajvālā*.[2] Bhavya then introduces another Vedānta theory.

> "There is the following opinion: what is to be asserted by me is only this one *ātman*, which is comparable to space. Discrimination into pots and the like is all provisional (not really true). Since they are provisional, the *ātman* cannot be measured. Therefore the ātman cannot be compared. It is impossible to refute it by any evidence, for the theory is without defect."

The theory mentioned here agrees not only with that of stanzas 10-13 but also with what is asserted in *Māṇḍūkyakārikā* III, 3.

Furthermore, Bhavya refers to the view that *ātman* is the subject of bondage and final release.

> "The *ātman* in bondage and the *ātman* released are not two. Why ? Because bondage and release occur, being based upon the *ātman*, as in the case of the released *ātman*."

This is also mentioned in the commentary on stanza 1.

The fact that the *Vedānta* theories referred to in the two texts are mutually almost in accordance may strengthen the possibility that the two texts are written by one and the same author.

Likewise, Bhavya refers to the *ātman* theory of the *Vedānta* school in his *Ta-ch'êng-chuang-yen-lun*, Fasc. 2.

"If it is said (by non-Buddhists) that the truth is existent as substance, though it is beyond discrimination, it would come to be the same as the concept of the *ātman* which non-Buddhist thinkers assume as the truth, by teaching its name, concept, and discrimination. Although that truth is existent as substance according to them, such distinction as being and non-being is not applicable to the truth, viewed from the standpoint of the highest truth (*paramārtha*) (which Mahāyāna Buddhists assume). It holds true of the *ātman* (which non-Buddhists assume). They think that, although *ātman* is existent as substance, pervading, eternal, being doer and experiencer, it is free from discrimination, since words and conceptualisation cannot be applied to it. Since it is not cognized by the discriminating intellect, it is called "the one free from discrimination." In their teachings they say, 'Since the words do not operate (in regard to it) and the mind does not prove it, it is called *ātman*.' "[3] The *Vedānta* theory quoted above is what is often referred to in the *Tarkajvālā*.[4]

Notes

1. *Prajñāpradīpamūlamadhyamakavṛtti*, Vol. 1 (*TT.*, Vol. 30, pp. 54a).
2. As for its Sanskrit original, see ft. 53 in the previous section.
3. *TT.*, Vol. 30, pp, 275 f.
4. Cf. Bhavya's own commentary on stanzas 17, 75, and 76, of the *Madhyamakahṛdayakārikā*.

5. *The Vedānta Thought Mentioned by Dharmapāla*

As a personage comparable to Bhavya, one must call to mind Dharmapāla. Bhavya was the most outstanding scholar during the early part of the sixth century in the Mādhyamika school, while Dharmapāla is a noteworthy scholar of the Yogācāra school of that period. "The dispute between Dharmapāla and Bhavya" on emptiness and existence has become a famous tradition from ancient times.

In his works Dharmapāla also frequently referred to the ideas of schools other than Buddhism, but unlike Bhavya he does not write a special chapter to attack each school. The Vedānta is, therefore, mentioned only here and there in his works. In fascicule III of his commentary on the *Catuḥśataka*, there is the following view :

> "A group of heretics takes the position that the self pervades everywhere and experiences pleasure and pain; therefore

the self is formless, and actionless, and it can neither go nor come, neither be born nor die together with the body; therefore, it is certain that the inner self pervades everywhere."[1]

"A group of heretics" referred to here admits that the eternal and all-pervading *ātman* is the inner self. Therefore, their idea can be regarded as a forerunner of the thought of Śaṅkara and is very close to the thought *Māṇḍūkya-Kārikā* III (esp. verse 9).

The same idea is also mentioned in the *Vijñaptimātratāsiddhi* by Dharmapāla. The text refers as one of the attachments to the "self", to the following view :

"Some hold that the self always pervades everywhere and is of the same size as space. It accumulates *karman* anywhere and is subject to sufferings."[2]

Then Dharmapāla refutes this view in detail. One cannot say that such a view of oneness of the self belongs necessarily to the *Vedānta* philosophy,[3] but it is certainly an idea prominent there. And the refutation by Dharmapāla follows a similar line to the attack which Bhavya made on theories of the Vedānta. This fact shows that this theory of oneness of the self was being advocated at that time and that Buddhist philosophers criticized it in almost the same manner.

Notes

1. *TT.*, vol. XXX, p. 201 c.

2. The head-noted edition of the Chinese version of the *Vijñaptimātratāsiddhi* vol. I, pp. 3-4.

3. Kyokuga Saheki's head-noted edition of the *Vijñaptimātratāsiddhi* remarks that this is the thought of the Sāṃkhya, the Vaiśeṣika and so forth. The Sāṁkhya and the Vaiśeṣika no doubt advocated such a view of oneness in later days, but it cannot be said that they always taught such an idea. It is generally accepted that they often asserted the plurality of the self, especially in the earlier period.

SECTION VIII. THE VEDĀNTA PHILOSOPHY REPORTED BY ŚĀNTARAKṢITA AND KAMALAŚĪLA

1. INTRODUCTION

After our investigation of the accounts by Bhavya and Buddhapālita, we must now examine the criticism of Vedāntic views by Śāntarakṣita and Kamalaśīla. Śāntarakṣita (or Śāntirakṣita) was active during the period from c. A.D. 680-740,[1] being some 200 years later than Bhavya; yet he must have been, I feel, senior to Śaṅkara. Consequently, the accounts of philosophical argument in his work, the *Tattvasaṁgraha*, are a very valuable sidelight on the early Vedānta philosophy. Properly speaking, in the original Buddhist classics, descriptions related to Vedāntic ideas are comparatively few, when compared with those concerned with other ideas; and in fact among the Sanskrit Buddhist works which have been published so far, (except for the *Madhyamaka-hṛdaya* in the present work exists no other example of a work which gives clearly the names of Vedānta thinkers or Upaniṣad thinkers (*Aupaniṣada*) and criticises in detail their doctrines in this way. In that sense, it should be regarded as extremely valuable.

The *Tattvasaṁgraha* is a voluminous work, consisting of 3646 verses. Kamalaśīla (c. 700-c. 750), a disciple of Śāntarakṣita, wrote a very detailed prose commentary (*Pañjikā*) on it. Both works were discovered and published recently,[2] and attracted the attention of the academic world. (Moreover, both works were translated into Tibetan at a very early date, and at present are included in the Tibetan Tripiṭaka Tanjur).

This work introduces and criticizes from the Mahāyānist point of view various philosophical theories which were well known in the intellectual world of India at that time. It frequently quotes works other than the Buddhist texts. Moreover the theories of other schools which are presented in it are so rich in variety and accurate in their descriptions that it is a valuable source material for the research on the history of Indian thought. Furthermore, the acuteness of the logical method with which the author attacks other schools is a great wonder in the history of Indian philosophy. Throughout the entire works, he consistently employs the method of *reductio ad absurdum* (*prasaṅga*) which reminds one of Nāgārjuna.

The work consists of 23 chapters, two out of which deal with the Vedānta thought. In the sixth chapter "Consideration of *Puruṣa*" (*Puruṣaparīkṣā*), the author makes a sharp attack especially on such concepts as *puruṣa* taught in the Upaniṣads, and on Brahmā or Viṣṇu regarded as the Absolute in schools of Hinduism, though he says that he is refuting the *Vedavādins*. In the seventh chapter, "Consideration of the *Ātman*" (*Ātmaparīkṣā*), he attacks various views of *ātman*, one of which is that of *Aupaniṣadas*. In the following, I would like to translate and examine these two chapters together with the prose commentary by Kamalaśīla. The metrical portion is the text by Śāntarakṣita. (Besides these, Chapter 5 "Consideration of Speech-Brahman" deals with some Vedāntic ideas, but as he attacks especially the thought of Bhartṛhari who is named Bhadrahari in Tibetan texts I would like to translate and investigate that in Part Five, Chapter 2 and in Part Seven of the present work). In translating it, I shall refer to the Sde-dge edition of the Tibetan translation, and correct errors in the Sanskrit edition.[3]

Notes

1. Cf. Part II, Chapter Two, section B of the present work.
2. *Tattvasaṃgraha of Śāntarakṣita with the commentary of Kamalaśīla*, ed. by Embar Krishnamacharya. (GOS. Nos. XXX and XXXI.); translated into English by Gaṅgānātha Jhā, 3 vols., (GOS. Nos. LXXX ff.).
3. Through the courtesy of the late M. T. Kasamatsu I used his photographs of the Sde-gde edition of the *Tattvasaṃgrahapañjikā* which is preserved in Tohoku University, Sendai, Japan.

NEXT-CRITICAL REMARKS ON THE VEDĀNTIC PORTIONS OF THE *Tattvasaṃgraha*

The *Tattvasaṃgraha* of Śāntarakṣita with the Commentary or *Pañjikā* of Kamalaśīla was published in the *Gaekwad's Oriental Series* by Embar Krishnamacharya in 1926, and afterwards the English translation of it was also published by Ganganath Jha in the same series. The work is highly important, in view of the fact that it deals with different philosophical systems of those days, and that it records earlier aspects of many philosophical schools.

Heretofore many researches have been carried on by some scholars upon certain portions of this work, and their results have been published in Western languages. So far as I know, however, the Vedāntic portions of this work have not yet been fully investigated. Of them we would mention the chapter VI, ""Puruṣaparīkṣā" and the chapter VII "Ātmaparīkṣā" (5) ("*Aupaniṣada-kalpita-ātmaparīkṣā*"). These portions are the more important because they present us with some aspects of pre-Śaṅkara Vedāntic philosophy whose sources have been mostly lost and are now so rarely preserved for us. In the following I wish to make some comments upon the original text of these portions. I hope that my few remarks below will aid in reading and study-ing the original Sanskrit text. [For the Tibetan version, I utilized by cour-tesy of the late Dr. T. Kasamatsu the *Sde-dge* edition, a copy of which is preserved in Tohoku University, Sendai, Japan].

VI. *Puruṣaparīkṣā*

O *Pañjikā* ad v. 153, p. 75, *l.* 3 from the bottom of page :

O **Vedavādin.** The word *Vedavādin* is a rather unusual word, but we find some instances of it. Rāmānuja compares *Vedavādin* with *Bauddha* (ad *Brahmasūtras* II, 2, 27, ed. by Vasudev Shastry Abhyankar, Bombay, 1914, p. 494). The *Mīmāṃsakas* can themselves *Vedavādins* (*Sarvadarśa-nasaṃgraha*, XII, *l.* 220, ed Abhyankar). *Vedavādins* in a work ascribed to Āryadeva assert the creation of the world by the God Brahmā (*TT.*, vol. XXXII, p. 157a).

O *Pañjikā* ad v. 154, p. 76, *l.* 4:

ūrṇanābha ivāṃśūnāṃ candrakānta ivāmbhasām /
prarohāṇām iva plakṣaḥ sa hetuḥ sarvajanminām //

This verse is cited also in the Tibetan version of Bhavya's *Tarkajvālā* ad *Madhyamaka-hṛdaya*, VIII, 17. It runs as follows :

de bshin du /
dar gyi srin buḥi snal ma bshin /
chu śel nor buḥi chu bshin du //
rgyo gro yan lag zug rgyu bshin //
de ni lus can kun gyi rgyu //
shes bya ba la sogs pa rigs byed kyi luṅ las mthoṅ baḥi tshad
mas skyes bu mthoṅ ba shes bya ba ni de kho na ñid yin te /

According to this passage, this verse was contained in a Veda (*rigs byed*), perhaps an Upaniṣadic portion of it. In the *Prameyakamala-mārtaṇḍa* (NSP. 1912, p. 17b), a Jain work, this verse is cited in the part refuting the Vedānta doctrine.

The similes of "spider and thread", moon stone "(*candrakānta*) and water", and "trees and buds" are mentioned in another work of Bhavya, i.e., the *Prajñāpradīpa-śāstra*, a commentary upon Nāgārjuna's *Madhyamaka-śāstra*. The original text of the work has been lost, but the Chinese and Tibetan versions are extant and available. The passage runs as follows :

E. Tr.—"Furthermore, those who look upon puruṣa as the cause (of the world) say as follows:—"Puruṣa is the cause of all the worlds. What does this mean ? Just as spiders weave nets with threads emitted by themselves, as *Cāndrakānta*-jewels emit water, and as trees bring forth branches and foliage, even so all the world looks to him as its cause. In the same way, what are called "past" and "future", "movable" and "immovable",, "far" and "near" and "inward" and "outward"—all these have been caused by puruṣa." The Chinese version on the *Prajñāpradīpa*, vol. I, *TT*. vol. XXX, p. 54a).

O *l*.5. : "*puruṣa evaitat sarvaṃ yad bhūtaṃ yac ca bhāvyam*" *iti*.

This is a verse of the *Ṛg-Veda* (X, 90, 2). However, in the *Ṛg-Veda evedam* is *evaitat*.

O v. 155.

l.14: *ṣaṣṭhyantād vatiḥ*.

The suffix, -**vat*, being added after a noun, can denote all cases and numbers of it. Cf. Speyer; *Vedische und Sanskrit-Syntax*, § 118, S. 36.

O *l*.14: *puruṣo janmināṃ hetur notpattivikalatvataḥ* |
gaganāmbhojavat sarvam anyathā yugapad bhavet ||

This is the verse 87 (p. 54) of the *Tattvasaṃgraha* where the first word is *īśvaro* instead of *puruṣo*.

O ad v. 155, p. 76, *l*.18:

kimartham ayaṃ puruṣo jagadracanāvyāpāraṃ īdṛśaṃ karoti.

The purpose of world-creation is discussed in the *Sarvadarśana-saṃgraha*, Government Oriental Series, No. 1, XI, *ll*. 194 ff.

O ad v. 157, p. 76, *l*. 4 from bottom :

kṛpayā parānugrahārthaṃ karoti.

The problem of world-creation out of benevolence is discussed in the *Brahma-sūtras*, II, 1, 34; II, 3, 42.

O v. 157, p. 76, *l*. 4 from bottom :

nārakādiduḥkhitamatvanirvāṇam.

This should be corrected as *nārakādiduḥkhita-sattvanirmāṇam*. Tib.—dmyal ba la sogs pa sdug bsṅal daṅ ldan paḥi sems can sprul bar...

O v. 158, p. 76, *l*. 2 from bottom:

anukampānām should be corrected as *anukampyānām*. Cf. p. 77, *l*. 1. *anukampyasattvābhāvāt*. Tib.—*brtse bar bya ba sems can med paḥi phyir*.

O ad v. 159, p. 77, *l*. 5:

yad eva manuṣyāḥ. This should be corrected as *ye devamanuṣyādayaḥ*. Tib.—lha daṅ mi la sogs pa gaṅ dag.

O ad v. 159, p. 77, *l*. 9:

apekṣyād eva lokasyotpatteḥ. Tib.—*ltos nas lhaḥi ḥjig rten du skye baḥi skye baḥi phyir*' (=*apekṣyu devalokale*] *utpatteḥ*].

O v. 161, p. 77:

krīḍārthā vṛttiḥ.

The doctrine of world-creation for sport is set forth in the *Mahābhārata* (XII, 308, 3: XII, 313, 16), in the poems of Kabir and Nanak (Carpentier : *Theism in Medieval India*, pp. 468; 477), and by later Naiyāyikas (*Sarvadarśanasaṃgraha*, XII, *l*. 156); whereas Uddyotakara refuted it (*Nyāyavārttika*, IV, 1, 21). The *Māṇḍūkya-Kārikā* also repudiates this doctrine (I, 9).

O ad v. 163, *l*. 3 from bottom:

The word *kāraṇa* means not "a cause" but "to make". Tib. byed. pa.

O ad v. 163, *l*. 2 from bottom:

aśaktāvasthāyā aviśiṣṭatvāt.

Tib.—*mi nus paḥi gnas skabs daṅ khyad par med paḥi phyir ro.* The Tibetan translator seems to have taken the word *aśaktāvasthāyā* for an ablative.

O ad v. 163, p. 78, *l*. 2:

Praśastamati. Tib.—*bro gros bzaṅ bo.* The scholar by this name was previously unknown. His opinion is cited with that of Uddyotakara in the *Prameyakamalamārtaṇḍa* (NSP. 1912, p. 75, a). *Praśastamatinā ca*—"*sargādau puruṣāṇāṃ vyavahāro 'nyopadeśapūrvakaḥ, uttarakālaṃ prabuddhānāṃ pratyarthaniyatatvād, aprasiddhavāgvyavahārāṇāṃ kumārāṇāṃ gavādiṣu pratyarthaniyato vāgvyavahāro yathā mātrādyupadeśapūrvakaḥ*" *iti. Uddyotakareṇa ca—bhuvanahetavaḥ pradhānaparamāṇvadṛṣṭāḥ svakāryotpattāv atiśayavad buddhimantam adhiṣṭhitāram apekṣante sthitvā pravṛttes tantur-yādivat.*

O ad v. 163, p. 78, *l*. 8:

anugrahaḥ paraḥ kuryād ekāntasukhitaṃ jagad.

Read *anugrahaparaḥ....* Tib.—*rjes su ḥdsin pa lhur byed pa na ḥgro ba geig tu bde ba daṅ ldan pa byed do.* Cf. v. 156 of the *Tattvasaṃgraha.*

O ad v. 163, p. 78, *ll*. 12-13:

śītoṣṇānvayabhedabhājas tu bhāvā eva hi pratikṣaṇavināśinaḥ kāla iti. Tib.—*graṅ ba daṅ dro ba the dad pa gñis bstan paḥi dṅos po ñid skad cig re re la ḥjig pa ni dus.*

O ad v. 163, p. 78, *l*. 13:

paścāt pratipādayiṣyati.

Cf. The eighth chapter "*Sthirabhāvaparīkṣā*" of the *Tattvasaṃgraha.*

O ad v. 164, p. 78:

svabhāvato vṛttiḥ sargādau.

World-creation as the nature of the Lord.

Cf. Uddyotakara, *Nyāyavārttika*, ad IV, 1, 21, p. 463 (*ChowkhSS*, 1915); H. Jacobi: *Die Entwicklung der Gottesidee bei den Indern und deren Beweise für das Dasein Gottes.* Bonn und Leipzig 1923. *Māṇḍūkya-Kārikā* I, 9.

O ad v. 165, *l*. 6 from bottom:

[*jagatkāraṇasya*] *buddhimattva.*

Cf. *Nyāyavārttika*, ad IV, 1, 21, p. 465. H. Jacobi. op. cit. S. 79, 87 f.

O ad v. 165, *l*. 6 from bottom :

pūrvam evāsmābhiḥ pratipāditam.

Cf. The second chapter, "*Īśvaraparīkṣā,*" of the *Tattvasaṃgraha.*

O ad v. 167, p. 79, *ll*. 3-4:

eṣa niyama iti svahetubalasambhavakṛtaḥ.

Tib. *ṅes pa ḥdi shes bya ba ni raṅ gi rgyu ḥi stobs kyis byas pa ḥo.*

O ad v. 170, p. 79, *l*. 4 from bottom :

tasya grahaṇam....

The lacuna runs as follows in the Tibetan version.

dus kyis ḥbyuṅ ba(s)min par byed /
dus kyis skye dgu sdud par byed //
dus kyis gñid log sad par byed /
dus ni ḥdaḥ bar dkaḥ ba yin //

shes smras pa lta buḥo | "gñid log pa la" shes bya ba ni ḥjig paḥ: dus ḥjig rten na thim pa shes bya baḥi don te | de lta bur gyur pa blo ṅan pas kun tu brtags pa gshan dag kyaṅ sogs pa smos pas bsdu ḥo ||

The verse cited here must be as follows:

kālaḥ pacati bhūtāni kālaḥ saṃharate prājaḥ |
kālaḥ supteṣu jāgarti kālo hi duratikramaḥ ||

This verse is cited very often in such passages as: *Madhyamakavṛtti*, p. 386, *ll.* 6-7 (cf. Poussin's note, 1. c.); Gauḍapāda ad *Sāṃkhya-Kārikā* 61; Suvarṇasaptati ad 61; Ānandajñāna ad *Bṛhad. Up. Vārttika*, p. 1825 (*ĀnSS.*); Bhaṭṭotpala's comm. ad *Bṛhatsaṃhitā* (*VizSS.* p. 9) a treatise ascribed to Āryadeva (*TT.*, vol. XXXII, p. 158a). The Chinese translation of this verse is as follows: "Time produces everything. Time ripens everything. Time destroys everything. Time is unsurpassable." This verse is ascribed to kālavādin. Citing this verse, Bhaṭṭotpala says; *ke 'pi kālakāraṇikāḥ Paurāṇikāḥ kālaṃ kāraṇam āhuḥ.*

O The whole body of the above-mentioned argument in refutation of the world-creation by the Lord had already been set forth in the *Mahāvibhāṣā-śāstra* (*TT.*, vol. XXVII, p. 993 b.).

VII. *Ātmaparīkṣā*

(5) *Aupaniṣadakalpita-ātmaparīkṣā*

O ad v. 328, p. 123, *l.* 1: [vivarta and pariṇāma]

pariṇāma. Tib.—*yoṅs su gyur pa.*

In the verse 128 (p. 67) of the *Tattvasaṃgraha* we find the same word which was rendered into Tibetan as *yoṅs su ḥgyur ba.* The word *vivartate*, (p. 67, *l.* 7 from bottom which is the opening verse of the *Vākyapadīya* of Bhartṛhari) also was translated as *yoṅs ḥgyur pa*, and the word *vivarta* (p. 67, *l.* 5 from bottom) also as *yoṅs su ḥgyur ba.* Thus *pariṇāma* and *vivarta* were regarded as synonymous by ancient Tibetans. This corroborates Dr. Paul Hacker's assertion. (*Vivarta. Studien zur Geschichte der illusionistischen Kosmologie und Erkenntnistheorie der Inder.* Akademie der Wissenschaften und der Literatur. Abhandlungen der Geistes-und Sozialwissenschaftichen Klasse. Jahrgang 1953. Nr. 5)

O vv. 328, 329, p. 123:

From these two verses and the commentaries upon them we can conclude that both Śāntarakṣita and Kamalaśīla took the words *pariṇāma* and *vivarta* as meaning the same thing, namely, "the evolution of the universe from the *ātman.*" This holds true with Bhartṛhari and Śaṅkara also, although later Advaitins (e.g. Madhusūdana Sarasvati) distinguished between the two. In Buddhist literature the origination of the universe is called *vivartate.* (*Abhidharmakośa*, III, verse 93: Hsüan-Tsang's Chinese translation, vol. 12, p. 3 b)

O v. 329:

The word *vijñānapariṇāma* is a term of Buddhist Idealism.

Cf. Sthiramati's *Vijñaptimātratātriṃśikābhāṣya* (ed. by S. Lévi), p. 18, *l.* 2. The Vedāntins, set forth here, use terms of Vijñānavādins. The doctrine of *vijñānapariṇāma* is found in *Gauḍapādīya-Kārikā* IV, 47; 48; 50; 51; 52, and *jñāna* is regarded as essential to, and inseparable from, brahman (ibid. III, 33; IV, 96; 99).

Therefore, we might say that the Vedāntic doctrine which Śāntarakṣita criticized is very similar to that of the *Gauḍapādīya-Kārikās*.

O ad v. 329, p. 123, *l*. 11:

......*avayavinaḥ* / *paramāṇūnāṃ cāsattvāt*.

The word *avayavinaḥ* should go on *asattvāt* and the *daṇḍa* should be deleted, if we take the Tibetan version into consideration.

O v. 330, p. 123:

The word *upalakṣaṇa* means, generally speaking, "implication" or "suggestion". The Buddhist connotation of the word is slightly different. Hsüan-Tsang translated the word as "to observe minutely". (cf. *Bodhisattva-bhūmi*, ed. by Wogihara, p. 83, *l*. 8).

O ad v. 331, p. 124, *l*. 2:

vijñānamātra is the central conception of Buddhist Idealism. This term is used by Sthiramati (*Vijñaptimātratātriṃśikā* v. 28). Hsüan-Tsang translated it as "Consciousness-only" in the above-mentioned verse. However, the meaning of the word *vijñāna* is quite different from that of Śaṅkara. An individual self is called *vijñānātman* by the latter (cf. P. Deussen : *System des Vedānta*, p. 194, Anm. 82). According to Śaṅkara *vijñāna* is synonymous with *manas* and *buddhi*; it is nothing but a mental organ which gives unification to cognitions and actions of an individual (Śaṅkara ad *Brahma-sūtras* II, 3, 32; II, 4, 6, vol. II, p. 108, *l*. 10, ĀnSS). In the *Brahmasūtra* II, 3, 15 also both the opponent and the sūtrakāra take *vijñāna* for an organ of an individual self.

O ad v. 330, p. 123: [The problem of crypto-Buddhists]

alpāparādha. Śāntarakṣita applies this denunciation to the then Vedāntins, believing that their doctrine is near to his but not completely the same. (cf. the similar appellation in *Gauḍapādīya-Kārikā* IV, 43). It means that Śāntarakṣita admitted the similarity of the Aupaniṣada doctrine to Buddhism. Akalaṅka (c. 700—770 A.D.), a Jain scholar, declared that advaita shared the same fallacies with *nairātmyadarśana* (or the *śūnyaikānta* or *kṣaṇika* doctrine) (*Aṣṭaśatī* ad Samantabhadra's *Āptamīmāṃsā* vv. 24-27). Bhavya (c. 490-570 A.D.) said that Vedāntins stole some doctrines of Buddhism and incorporated them into the body of their own doctrine (*Madhyamakahṛdaya* VIII, 78).

de bshin gśegs paḥi mi brdsun paḥi /
lugs ḥdi dge bar śes nas ni //
de phyir mu stegs ḥdod skyes te /
de la bdag gir byas pa yin // (VIII, 78)

brgya la res ḥgaḥ de bshin gśegs-pa ḥjig rten du byuṅ bar gyur ciṅ / des brdsun pa ma yin paḥi gsuṅ rab kyi lugs kyaṅ rab tu bstan nas yoṅs su ṅ-ya ṅan las ḥdas pa yaṅ bstan pa na deḥi lugs de la mu stegs rnams ḥdod pa skyes par gyur nas raṅ gi grub paḥi mthaḥi naṅ du bsres śiṅ lugs ḥdi ni kho bo cag gi yin no shes bdag gir yaṅ byed do // de ni sṅon daṅ phyi mar yaṅ ḥgal baḥi skyon daṅ bcas paḥi grub paḥi mthas ḥdras mthaḥ ḥdres pas rnam par rtog pa yin parmtshon par bya ba yin te /

The similarity and the difference between Vedānta and Buddhism were discussed by Bhavya (ib. VIII, 60, 78, 91 and *Tarkajvālā* ad VIII, 79; 87; 91). So we can assuredly conclude that the accusation of *pracchanna Bauddha* can be traced to days much *earlier* than Śaṅkara.

O ad v. 331, p. 123, *l.* 5 from bottom:
jñānapratibhāsa. Tib.—*śes pa la snaṅ ba.*

O ad v. 331, p. 123, *l.* 5 from bottom:
vicitrāstaraṇapratibhāsavat. Tib.—*gos khra bo snaṅ ba bshin du* (like the appearance of piebald dresses).

O ad v. 331, p. 124, *l.* 1:
tasyaitā iti.
Tib.—*ḥdiḥi ḥdi shes bya la* (=*tasyaiṣā iti* ?)

O ad v. 331, p. 124, *l.* 2:
-°*virodhaś ca*. Tib.—*ḥgal baḥi phyir ro* (=-°*virodhāc ca*).

O ad v. 332, p. 124, *l.* 7:
avasthātṛ jñānam. Tib.—*gnas skabs paḥi śes pa* (=*avasthātṛ-jñāna*).
The Tibetan translator took it for a tatpuruṣa compound.

O ad v. 332, p. 124, *l.* 9:
upalabdhikṣaṇaprāpta. Tib.—*dmigs paḥi mtshan ñid kyir gyur pa.* So the word should be corrected as *upalabdhilakṣaṇaprāpta*. This word is very often used in Dharmottara's *Nyāyabinduṭīkā*. As for *upalabdhilakṣaṇaprāpta*: cf. ad v. 133, p. 69, *l.* 13; ad v. 135, p. 70, *l.* 1 of the *Tattvasaṃgraha*.

O ad v. 332, p. 124, *l.* 11:
kāryaṁ vā. Tib.—*ḥbras buḥi rtags yin graṅ* (=*kāryaliṅgaṃ vā*).
This word is also used in Dharmottara's *Nyāyabinduṭīkā*.

Cf. the *Tattvasaṃgraha*, vv. 147, 148. As for the argumentation here the reader should be reminded of the distinction by Dharmakīrti between *svabhāvahetu* and *kāryahetu*.

O ad v. 332, p. 124, *ll.* 11-12:
na tāvat svabhāvas tathāvidhasya jñānātmanaḥ....

It seems that several sentences have been omitted on account of the failure of a scribe. The original sentences seem to have run as "......*tathāvidhasya kasya cid dharmiṇo 'py asiddhatvena......tathāvidhasya jñānātmanaḥ...*" As the word "*tathāvidhasya*" occurred twice, the scribe seems to have omitted the intermediate part by mistake. Tib.—*de lta bur gyur paḥi chos can ḥgaḥ yaṅ ma grub pas deḥi raṅ bshin ma grub paḥi phyir ro // chos can śes pa tsam grub na yaṅ de la rtag pa ñid kyi bsgrub byaḥi chos kyis ḥgaḥ la yaṅ khyab pa ma grub paḥi phyir ro / ḥbras buḥi rtags kyaṅ ma yin te / rtag pa ni rim daṅ cig car dag gis don byed par mi ḥthad paḥi phyir daṅ / deḥi ḥbras bu ḥgaḥ yaṅ med paḥi phyir daṅ de las tha dad paḥi ḥbras bu gshan khas ma blaṅs paḥi yaṅ phyir ro / des na de lta yin na de lta bur gyur paḥi śes paḥi bdag ñid la sgrub par byed paḥi tshad ma yin la /*

O ad v. 333, p. 124:
bandhamokṣau tataḥ katham. Cf. *Gauḍapādīya-Kārikā* II, 32.

O ad v. 333, p. 124, *l.* 10 from bottom .
yuktimatī. Tib.—*rigs pa daṅ ldan pa ma yin te.* The Tibetan translation is wrong.

O ad. v. 333, p. 124, *l.* 4 from bottom:

yuktā. Tib.—*rigs pa ma yin no.* The Tibetan translation is wrong

O ad v. 333, p. 124, *ll.* 3-4 from bottom:

yathoktam—

saṃkliṣṭā ca viśuddhā ca samalā nirmalā ca |

This is a line from the *Madhyāntavibhāgaśāstra* ascribed to Vasubandhu. Sthiramati comments on it as follows,—

tasmāt saṃkleśaviśuddhikālayoḥ śūnyataiva saṃkliśyate viśudhyate ceti pradarśanārtham āha |

saṃkliṣṭā ca viśuddhā ca |

ity asyāḥ prabhedaḥ | kadā saṃkliṣṭā tadā nirmalety anavabodhāt pṛcchati | kadā saṃkliśyate kadā viśudhyata iti |

sā samalā nirmalā ca |

iti vistaraḥ. (Sthiramati's *Madhyāntavibhāgaṭīkā*, publiée par Susumu Yamaguchi, Nagoya 1934, p. 51). The latter half of the line was restored into Sanskrit by Prof. Yamaguchi, whose conjecture has turned out to be quite correct with respect to wording.

O ad v. 333, p. 124, *ll.* 3-2 from bottom:

saṃkliṣṭā ced bhaven nāsau muktāḥ syuḥ sarvadehinaḥ |
viśuddhā ced bhaven nāsau vyāyāmo niṣphalā bhavet ||

This is *Kārikā* I, 21 of the *Madhyāntavibhāgaśāstra.* Comparing the Tibetan and Chinese versions with each other, Prof. Yamaguchi tentatively restored the Sanskrit text as follows (op. cit., pp. 59-60):

yadi na syāt sa saṃkleśo muktāḥ syuḥ sarvadehinaḥ |
yadi na sā viśuddhiḥ syāt prayatnam aphalam bhavet ||

His tentative restoration is shown to be substantially correct.

Tib. *gal te ñon moṅs ma gyur |*
lus can thams cad grol bar ḥgyur ||
gal te rnam dag de ma gyur |
ḥbad pa ḥbras bu med par ḥgyur || (op. cit., pp. 21-23)

I owe this information to the kind suggestion of Prof. Megumu Honda.

O ad v. 334, p. 125, *l.* 2:

nibandhana. Tib.—*rgyu mtshan.*

O ad v. 334, p. 125, *l.* 3:

sa kevalam āyāsaphala eveti.

Tib.—*de ni ḥbras bu dal ba ḥgaḥ shig tu zad do she bya ba stoṅ pa ni.*

O v. 355, p. 125:

yogābhyāso......aphalaḥ sarva eva ca.

This argumentation was used by Nāgārjuna in the *Madhyamakaśāstra*, XXIII, vv.17; 24; 25. and by Bhavya in the *Madhyamakahṛdaya* VIII, 69.

Sub-Section 1. *An Examination of Puruṣa (Puruṣaparīkṣā)*
A. Translation

Stanza No.

1. Theory of the *Vedavādins* 153-154
2. Refutation
   - (A) General Introduction (There is the same difficulty as with theological theories) 155
   - (B) Detailed Discussion
     - (a) A Criticism of the Loss of Independence 156ab
     - (b) A Criticism of the Theory that Creation is out of Compassion 156cd-159ab
     - (c) A Criticism of the Theory of an Unseen Power in the Living Beings 159cd-160
     - (d) A Criticism of the Theory that Creation is Sport 161-163
     - (e) A Criticism of the Theory that Creation is the nature of the Lord 164-168
     - (f) A Criticism of the Theory that Creation by God is without any idea 169
   - (C) An Application of the Same Method to Viṣṇu, Brahmā, and Kāla (Time) 170

1. *Theory of the Vedavādins*

≪Tib. 190a, Lines 3 ff.≫ [The author] describes the view of the *Vedavādins* by [saying], "Other people..."[1] :

153. Other people, however, whose intellect follows a perverted doctrine assume that *Puruṣa* with qualities the same as those of the Lord (*īśa*) is the cause of the world.

154. It is said that, He possessed a power of knowledge which is not annihilated even at the time of dissolution of everything, and is the cause of all living beings, just as the spider is [the cause] of [its] thread.

They say as follows:—"*Puruṣa* alone is the only cause of the subsistence, creation and dissolution of the whole world, possessed as He is of the excellent power of knowledge which is not annihilated even at the time of dissolution of the world."

Further it is said that:—

"Just as the spider is the cause of [its] thread, just as the moonstone[2] is the cause of water, and just as the fig tree is the cause of the buds, so is He the cause of all living beings."[3] and that :—

> "This Puruṣa is all that has already been and all that is to be." (*Ṛgveda* X. 90. 2).[4]

"With qualities the same as those of the Lord" (*īśasadharmāṇam*) [means] "who has the same qualities as the Lord," since both are the efficient causes (*nimitta*) of origination, subsistence and dissolution of all. But there is this much distinction [between them]: those who assert that the Lord is the cause of the universe (later *Nyāya, Vaiśeṣika* and other schools) think that there are also other causes such as the inherent causes, (samavāyi-kāraṇa), i.e. *ātman* and the like, apart from the Lord, [who is merely the efficient cause], whereas the *Puruṣavādins* think that Puruṣa alone is the cause [of all in every sense]. But both [Puruṣa and the Lord] are equally the efficient causes of origination, subsistence, and dissolution of all. [The compound:] "*durākhyāta-siddhāntānugabuddhayaḥ*" (whose intellect follows a perverted doctrine) is analysed into: *durākhyātasidhāntānugā buddhir yeṣām* ≪Tib. 190b≫. "*Ūrṇanābha*" is "*markaṭaka*" (spider).

2. *Refutation*

(*A*) *General Introduction*

The refutation [of the *Puruṣavādins*] starts with the stanza beginning with "[Entire negation] of Him also":

> 155. Entire negation of Him (=*Puruṣa*) also, as in the case of the Lord (*Īśvara*), should be stated. For why would this (*Puruṣa*) perform activity of this kind (i.e. creation of the world, etc.) ?

[The word] "*īśvaravat*" (as in the case of the Lord...): the suffix-*vat*[5] is based on the genitive case. With regard to this [*Puruṣa*] also such a refutation should be made :—

"*Puruṣa* is not the cause of living beings, because He is (himself) destitute of origination, like a lotus in the sky. Otherwise (i.e., if your assertion is right), everything would be originated at the same time."[6]

And, if the *Puruṣavādins* employ the same arguments as those of the theologians in order to establish the *Puruṣa*, then errors such as failure of proof (*asiddhatā* i.e. "S is M" is not proved) should be pointed out in the same way.

Another kind of refutation is also stated :—"For why...?" People who act deliberately invariably have some purpose; therefore, [the question:] "why does this *Puruṣa* perform the activity of world creation ?" should be asked.

(*B*) *Detailed Discussion*

156. If [they say] that [*Puruṣa* performs the activity of creation] because of being prompted by another, then *Puruṣa* would not have independence (*svatantratā*). If [they say] that [Puruṣa performs the activity of creation] out of compassion, then He would make a purely pleasant world.

157. Further, what kind of compassion could this *Puruṣa* be thought to have, when He creates people afflicted with various sufferings like pain,[7] poverty and anxiety ?

(a) *A Criticism of the Loss of Independence.*

"If" He "is prompted", i.e. to perform the activity of world creation, though [He himself] has no wants, "by another", i.e. by the Lord, etc., then the independence which is claimed for Him is lost.

(b) *A Criticism of the Theory that Creation is out of Compassion.*

"If" He performs the activity [of world creation] out of pity, to do good to others, then He would not fashion the afflicted sentient beings[7a] such as those who are in the hell, but "would make [the world] purely pleasant."

158. Before the world creation, when there are no [sentient beings] to be pitied[8], his pity, which is the reason why *Puruṣa* is conceived to be the creator of the world, could not exist, either.

Furthermore, as there are no sentient beings to be pitied[9] before "*sṛṣṭi*", i.e. the creation (*sarga*); [pity], because of "which" i.e. pity[9a] "this" [*Puruṣa*] is conceived to be "the founder of the world" (*dhātṛ*), i.e. the creator of the world (*sraṣṭṛ*), would not be possible.

159ab And this [*Puruṣa*] could not cause the dissolution of those who are continuously fortunate, "and" if "this" [*Puruṣa*] creates out of compassion, then why does He cause dissolution of those gods and[10] human beings "who are continuously fortunate ?" The meaning is that He should rather cause "the dissolution" only of sentient beings whose individual existence is afflicted with pain and who are destined for ill-fortune.

(c) *A Criticism of the Theory of an Unseen Power in the Living Beings.*

159cd. [Furthermore,] if [He] depends upon their unseen power (*adṛṣṭa*) [for creating the sentient beings endowed with pleasure and pain], *Puruṣa's* independence would be lost.

Moreover, if [it is said] that, depending upon "their unseen power", [*Puruṣa*] created the sentient beings, whom he pities, endowed with pleasure and pain as determined by their past merit or demerit (*dharmādharma*), that is not right because, if so, "the independence which is claimed [*for Puruṣa*] would be lost. ≪Tib. 191a≫.

Moreover, one who has the power, depends upon nothing. Or, if [*Puruṣa*] has not the power, the world is originated in dependence on something else[11] (i.e. merit and demerit). Therefore, it is not accepted that *Puruṣa* is the cause of the world.

160. And why would He depend upon an unseen power which is the cause of pain ? If He is possessed of pity, he should pay no regard to that [unseen power].

Even if He were to depend upon an unseen power, it is not reasonable for a Compassionate One to depend upon an "unseen power" consisting of merit and demerit "which is the cause of pain" but it would be proper for Him to disregard that [unseen power] because He relies on compassion. For the compassionate do not seek to cause others pain, but they act only with a desire to free them from pain.

(d) *A Criticism of the Theory that Creation is Sport.*

161. If He acts from sport, then He would not be the master of that sport, for like a child, He needs accessories with which to sport.

If [it is said that Puruṣa] does not create "out of compassion" but "for the sake of sport", this is not right, either. For then He would not be independent in starting his sport, for [He] "needs accessories" consisting of creation, subsistence and dissolution.

162. Then, if He has the power to make [playthings for Sport],

He would also simultaneously fashion every instrument for the pleasure to be obtained from sport.

163. If He has not the power at the very beginning, He would not come to have it gradually, for an indivisible one cannot have power and not have it [at the same time].

Furthermore, "if" the power which makes the accessories belongs to Him,[12] then He would make them all at the same time. If He has no power "at the very beginning", He would "not" fashion [them] "gradually", for His state of not having the power could not be different[13] [at the beginning and later].

Power and inability in regard to the same thing are two mutually contradictory attributes, and cannot be related to one and the same thing. All the doubtful points concerning theology such as : "why does [the Lord] start such an activity ?" are equally applicable to [*Puruṣa*]. Therefore, what Praśastamati[14] said, namely,

"(1) The Lord acts for the benefit of the others. Just as a sage (*muni*) who has achieved his purpose gives instruction for the benefit of the others,[15] though He cannot have any motive of profit or avoiding loss, so does the Lord act with mercy towards living beings after showing the greatness of his sovereignty. (2) Or, [the Lord acts] since various powers are His nature.[16] Just as, when the time (*kāla*) manifests spring, etc. successively, the transformations of the unmoving (plant) and moving (animal) come about naturally, so is the Lord [naturally] the cause of (a) origination (b) subsistence and (c) dissolution of the living beings, when He manifests the powers of (a) manifestation, (b) favour and (c) collection successively."

This is also refuted by the following argument. For instance, (1) [the assertion] that the Lord acts for the benefit of the others is refuted by this [argument] : "If He is devoted to the benefit [of the living beings],[17] He would make the world purely pleasant" and so on,[18] and (2) against [the assertion] that "[that Lord acts] since various powers are His nature," the following refutation is made :

"[If His] various powers were manifest at the same time, He would bring forth the creation, subsistence and dissolution of the world at the same time. If not, He would be one who does not manifest His powers. Nor (in the later case) can it be maintained that this Lord manifests His powers successively. If the one whose various powers are manifest is different from this (omnipotent) Lord, how can He be the same [called "the Lord"] ?"

With regard to [the assertion] that "when Time manifests spring, etc. successively, there arises the activity successively", there is the following fault: "Time is really a thing which has various distinctions like cold and heat, connection and disjunction, and perishes every moment."[19] This will be explained at another place.[20]

(e) *A Criticism of the Theory that Creation is the Nature of the Lord.*

[The author] suspects that [the opponent] may arrive at Uddyotakara's theory by [saying], "If [His] function [of creation and the like is explained as] due to His own nature..." :—

164. If His function of creation and the like is explained as due to [His] own nature, just as the functions of burning etc. which belong to fire etc. are due to [their] nature alone,

165. If so, everything would be originated from Him at the same time, because the cause with the power to originate them would be existing.

He is really saying : "Bhagavat does not really act for the sake of sport, but just as earth and other elements have just that nature by which they act to produce their effects, so the Lord has [just that nature]."[21] This argument is not reasonable,[22] for all things which owe their existence to Him alone would be created at the same time because there would exist their cause in its full power. It is not reasonable, either, that [His] possession of wisdom would qualify this [and that, therefore, everything would not be created at the same time]. We have previously[23] demonstrated this.

If so, why do the effects of fire and the like not (all) take place at the same time ? Thus [the author] says : "...originated by dint of their causes..." :—

166. Various powers in fire and other things come to be as a result of their own causes; they are fixed and not always exist.

167. Otherwise, if the established rule [that various powers come to be as a result of their causes] is not accepted,

all their effects would arise [not only from the Lord but] also from them [=fire etc.] at the same time.

"Their" means "of fire etc.". The word "also" (*api*) means "not only from the Lord but" ≪Tib. 192a≫. "The established rule" is that [various powers] come to be as a result of their causes."[24] The Vedavādins say [that] a spider performs actions by nature. [Therefore, according to the assertion of Buddhists, it would always be making webs, and no sustention.] How is it that it does not continually make webs etc. which are its own effects ? [Therefore, it is not a fault at all that one who by nature performs actions does not manifest its powers at the same time.] Then [the author] replies, "...by nature...":—

168. It is not recognized even in the case of the spider that [it] is by nature the cause of [its] thread, for [it] makes [its] web of saliva on account of its greed to eat living beings.

The purport is that the spider itself does not act by nature but on account of "[its] greed to eat living beings" which arises only sometimes from a definite cause.

This [spider] is not always of one and the same nature. Its powers also sometimes appear since they appear as a result of their causes.

(f) *A Criticism of the Theory that Creation by God is without any idea.*

Even if [the opponents say that the Lord] does not act because of compassion nor because of sport, but [He acts] in some way without any idea (*abuddhi*), [the author] says, "...in any way at all" :—

169. If [it is said] that [Puruṣa] acts in any way at all, what is meant by His being possessed of wisdom ? For even a fisherman does not act without aiming at some results.

[If] thus [the Puruṣa thoughtlessly performs actions without any plans], how should thoughtful people pay attention to the words, for [this kind of thing] is not acceptable (even) in the case of the fisherman and other ordinary people ?

"Being possessed of wisdom" (*buddhimattā*) means "being prudent" (*prekṣāvattā*).

"Śanaka"[25] means "fisherman" (*kaivarta*).[26]

(C) *An Application of the Same Method to Viṣṇu, Brahmā and Kāla (Time)*

The author shows that Viṣṇu and the like, who are assumed as creators of the world by opponents, should also be known to have been refuted by this very refutation of *Puruṣa*, (saying), "Viṣṇu, Brahmā and the like..." :—

170. Śauri (Viṣṇu), Ātmaja (Brahmā) and the like who are assumed as creators of the world have also actually been all refuted by this very method.

In the above "Śauri" is Viṣṇu, "Ātmaja" is Brahmā. "Time" which is conceived to be possessed of wisdom by the opponents is comprised by the words, "and the like", as is explained :—

> "Time[27] ripens the beings.[28] Time annihilates the creatures. Time awakes when [people] are deeply asleep. Time is indeed invincible."[29]

"When deeply asleep" (*supta*) means "when people are lying at the time of unification (with the absolute). Other things [like Time], which are assumed by those of slow intellect, are also covered [by the words "and the like"]; so they have all been included.

Here ends an examination of *Puruṣa*.

Notes

1. "Anya" ityādinā. "Anya' is the first word of stanza 153:
anye tv īśasadharmāṇaṃ purusaṃ lokakāraṇam /
kalpayanti durākhyātasiddhāntānugabuddhayaḥ //

2. *Candrakānta*. It is a gem which is supposed to be formed from the congealing of the moon's rays, and to dissolve under the influence of its light.

3. *ūrṇanābha ivāṃśūnāṃ candrakānta ivāmbhasām /*
prarohāṇām iva plakṣaḥ sa hetuḥ sarva-janminām //

This stanza is quoted as a Vedic verse in *Tarkajvālā* as VIII, 17 and is used for the explanation of the *Vedānta* school in the *Prameyakamalamārtaṇḍa* (p. 17b). But it does not exist in extant Vedic literature.

4. *puruṣa evaitat sarvaṃ yad bhūtaṃ yac ca bhāvyam.* (*evedaṃ* instead of *evaitat* in the *Ṛgveda*).

5. The suffix *-vat* indicates all the cases and numbers of the noun to which it is attached (cf. Speyer: *Vedische und Sanskrit Syntax*, Sec. 118, p. 36).

6. *Tattvasaṃgraha*, v. 87 (p. 54) reads:
neśvaro janmināṃ hetur utpattivikalatvataḥ |
gaganāmbhojavat sarvam anyathā yugapad bhavet ||

7. The reading in Dvārikādās Śāstrī's edition: *vyādhidā-* for *ādhidā-*.

7a. The reading in our text : *nārakādiduḥkhitamatvanirmāṇāṃ* should be corrected into *nārakādiduḥkhitasattvanirmāṇāṃ*. The reading in Dvārikādās Śāstrī's edition (Bauddha Bharati Series-1, Varanasi, 1968): *nārakādiduḥkhita-tattvanirmāṇāṃ*. A Tibetan translation: *dmyal ba la sogs pa sdug bsṅal daṅ ldan paḥi sems can sprul bar*.

8. The reading: *anukampānām* must be corrected into *anukampyānām* in consideration of the reading of the *Pañjikā* and Dvārikādās Śāstrī's edition.

9. *Anukampyasattvābhāvāt*. A Tibetan translation : *brtse bar bya ba sems can med paḥi phyir*.

9a. Dvārikādās Śāstrī's edition: *-bhāvāt kim ālambya tasyā* for *-bhāvāt| yasyā*.

10. The reading: *yad eva manuṣyāḥ* must be corrected into *ye deva-manu-* which is the reading of Dvārikādās Śāstrī's edition.

11. Both our text and Dvārikādās Śāstrī's edition read: *apekṣyād eva lokasyotpattes...*, but its Tibetan translation: *ltos nas lhaḥi ḥjig rten du skye baḥi phyir* (=*apekṣya devaloka (e) utpatteḥ*).

12. Dvārikādās Śāstrī's edition: *-kāraṇā* for *-kāraṇe*. A Tibetan translation: *byed pa*.

13. *Aśaktāvasthāyā aviśiṣṭatvāt*. A Tibetan translation: *mi nus paḥi gnas skabs daṅ khyad par med paḥi phyir ro* (=because of being not different from the incapable state).

14. Sic. A Tibetan translation: *blo gros bzaṅ bo*. The theory ascribed to Praśastamati is quite close to that of Praśastapāda.

15. *Parahitārtham* A Tibetan translation: *gshan rjes su gzuṅ baḥi don du* (=*parānugrahārtham*).

16. *Śaktisvābhāvyāt*. A Tibetan translation: *nus paḥi ṅo bo ñid yin paḥi phyir*.

17. The reading: *anugrahaḥ paraḥ kuryād ekāntasukhitaṃ jagad* must be corrected into *anugrahaparaḥ* in consideration of a Tibetan translation: *rjes su ḥdsin pa lhur byed pa naḥgro ba gcig tu bde ba daṅ ldan pa byed do*. Dvārikādās Śāstrī's edition: *anugrahaḥ paraṃ kuryād* for *anugrahaḥ paraḥ kuryād*.

18. Cf. stanza 156.

19. *graṅ ba daṅ dro ba tha dad pa gñis bstan paḥi dṅos po ñid skad cig re re la ḥjig pa ni dus*.

20. Cf. *Sthirabhāvaparīkṣā*, the 8th chapter of the *Tattvasaṃgraha*.

21. Uddyotakara, *Nyāyavārttika ad* IV, 1, 21, p. 463 (ChowkhSS., 1915). Cf. R. Yamada and K. Ito (tr.), *Indo-Shinkan-Shi*, p. 154.

22. *Nyāyavārttika ad* IV, 1, 21, p. 465. Cf. R. Yamada and K. Ito, *op. cit.*, pp. 158 ff.

23. It is discussed in the *Īśvaraparīkṣā*, the 2nd chapter of the *Tattva-saṃgraha*.

24. The reading : *eṣa niyama iti | svahetubalasaṃbhavakṛtaḥ* is

translated in consideration of *ṅes pa ḥdi shes bya ba ni raṅ gi rgyu ḥi stobs kyis byas pa ḥo.*

25. A Tibetan translation: *ña pa.*

26. A Tibetan translation: *ña śor.*

27. Our text lacks this portion which Dvārikādās Śāstrī's edition reads as follows :

kālaḥ pacati bhūtāni kālaḥ saṃharate prajāḥ |
kālaḥ supteṣu jāgarti kālo hi duratikramaḥ || iti |
supteṣv iti pralayakālalīneṣu lokeṣv ity arthaḥ | anyasyāpy evambhūtasya kumatiparikalpitasyāpi grahaṇāt saṃgrahaḥ || 170 ||

28. The reading of the Sde-gde edition: *min pa* is an copying error of *smin pa.*

29. Cf. the theory of the *Kālavādins,* which has been referred to in this present work, Vol. I, Part II, Chapter 1, Section 4.

B. Remarks

In the above translation of the whole of chapter six ("An Examination of Puruṣa") of the Summary of The Truth (*Tattva-saṃgraha*), there are many philosophically important points to be learned from the discussion.

Kamalaśīla says (note to v. 153) that the protagonist of the puruṣa doctrine is a "follower of the Veda" (*Veda-vādin*). In India generally, "follower of the Veda" meant one who took the authority of the Vedic texts as absolute[1] and it is an interesting point, as already noted,[2] that in the "Bodhisattva-Laṅkāvatāra-sūtra Outer-path-Hīnayāna Nirvāṇa Treatise" the "follower of the Veda (*Veda-vādin*) again is presented as one who taught that the world is evolved from puruṣa. Kamalaśīla himself calls the "follower of the Veda" also a "follower of puruṣa" (*Vedavādin* = *Puruṣavādin*). So that generally speaking the Buddhists of that period thought that the central philosophical concept of the Veda was world-evolution from puruṣa. As we have considered in a previous section, Bhavya has also informed us that puruṣa is the fundamental concept of the Vedānta school, and we learn that in the period of both Śāntarakṣita and Kamalaśīla, such was likewise thought to be the case.

As we see through the argumentation of the *Tattvasaṃgraha* above, puruṣa is the world cause and the root and source from which all living things and everything in the natural world arise.

It is a purely spiritual principle which has knowledge (*jñāna*) as its fundamental essence. It is eternal, constant, and unique, and even if all things should be destroyed and return to nothingness, it would continue to exist unaffected. As being the world cause, it has this characteristic in common with the Īśvara postulated by the Nyāya-Vaiśeṣika and other schools, as both Śāntarakṣita and Kamalaśīla admit.

Thus puruṣa as presented here is a different concept from the Lord of the Nyāya-Vaiśeṣika school, but is actually the same as the Lord (Īśvara) taught in the Vedānta school generally. Nonetheless, Śāntarakṣita does not use the term "Lord", (Īśvara), but in his discussion uses mainly the term "*puruṣa*". This fact also shows that there must have been a good many people at that time also, among the Brahmins devoted to the Upaniṣads, or in one section of the Vedānta school, who called the fundamental cause of the world "*puruṣa*". It is frequently mentioned even in the literary works[3] of the period that Vedānta students regarded *puruṣa* as the Absolute, and also in the first chapter of the Māṇḍūkya-Kārikās, *puruṣa* is made the cause of the world evolution.

Between the Nyāya-Vaiśeṣika "Lord" and the *puruṣa* there is the distinct difference, that in the former theory, the various constituent elements of the world are constant and immutable in their fundamental essence, and *Īśvara* uses them *as raw material* to construct the world. This *Īśvara* is thus an entity other than the elements which he uses to form the universe, and in relation to the world creation, he simply plays the part of the efficient (impelling) cause. Whereas *puruṣa* is presented now as both the efficient (impelling) cause as well as the material cause in regard to the world creation. That is, the *puruṣa*, by its own inherent *power* constructs the world, *producing* from within its own self the materials for the world. What it has in common with the Nyāya-Vaiśeṣika "Lord" is only the point of being the active agent, i.e. the efficient cause, which effects the creation, preservation and destruction of the world. (This last point is discussed in detail in Chapter Two, *Īśvara-parīkṣā*, of the *Tattva-saṃgraha.*).[3]

As against that, Śaṅkara later on was usually calling the world-cause "Lord" (*īśvara*) or "Highest Lord" (*parameśvara*), elevating it conspicuously as a philosophical concept. Accordingly we see that on this point too, the early Vedānta philosophy appears to have differed somewhat from the philosophy of Śaṅkara.

Now what is the relation between *puruṣa* as cause of the world and its evolved effects, all the things of the world ? How could the latter be created from the former ? On this problem, Śāntarakṣita alludes to the spider and the thread it spins out of itself, and in the verse quoted from Kamalaśīla, there are in addition the metaphors of the moonstone and water, and the fig-tree and the bud. Now these three metaphors, as already noted, are referred to by Bhavya as Vedānta views.[4] Thus the proponents of *puruṣa* as referred to by both Śāntarakṣita and Kamalaśīla do not differ essentially from the Vedāntins as presented by Bhavya. The *puruṣa* concept also agrees for the most part, except that *puruṣa* as reported by Śāntarakṣita and Kamalaśīla is a step further advanced than that given by Bhavya, since it is completely dissociated from any mythical colouring and is postulated as an altogether abstract principle.

Next we shall look at the refutation by Śāntarakṣita and Kamalaśīla of the idea of world evolution from *puruṣa*. We find that it can be divided roughly into two parts.

First, the reasoning deployed to attack the concept of īśvara in the Nyāya-Vaiśeṣika school can be applied also in the same way to the *puruṣa* concept. For example, something which causes something else to be produced and to arise, must itself have been produced and caused to arise by yet some other thing. *A producer must itself be something previously produced.* Since nevertheless it is stated that *puruṣa* in itself has never been produced, then it can only exist in imagination like lotus flowers in the sky, and does not actually exist at all. So the argument continues. Since these reasons are always put forward whenever they criticize the concept of *īśvara*, we have here only touched on them. In this chapter we shall rather concentrate on the next two points.

Second, is there or not a purpose in the evolution of the world ? If there is, what is that purpose ? Each of these points is examined in detail to show rationally that the assumptions of the thinkers of the time concerning world creation could not be maintained. Of course, similar criticisms can also be applied to the Nyāya-Vaiśeṣika creation theories[5] but in this chapter where Śāntarakṣita is examining *puruṣa*, he argues in special detail. From his discussion we discover that at the time there were the following five theories of the *purpose of creation* prevalent among adherents of *puruṣa*.

The first theory holds that the creation of the world is based upon compassion to living beings. The most difficult point about this view is that at present the suffering and happiness is not equally divided among the beings, but that some, for example gods, enjoy great happiness, while others, for example animals or the beings in hell and so on, are sunk in the depths of pain and sorrow. How can one explain these facts ? The supporters of the theory answered this objection by saying that the *puruṣa* considers the merit or demerit of each living being according to the good or evil deeds it has committed in its past lives, and visits them with retribution or reward in the form of pain or pleasure in conformity with those deeds. So the *puruṣa* cannot be said to be without compassion. This general idea is taught in the *Brahma-sūtra* (II.1.34, II.3.42).

The second theory holds that the creation of the world by *puruṣa* is for the sake of sport. This also was an ancient doctrine, taught for instance in the great epic *Mahābhārata*;[6] it is an idea which existed in the Sāṃkhya-Yoga theory, and later this too is powerfully advocated in the *Brahma-sūtra* (II.1.33), where it is said that the creation of the world was "the mere sport" (*līlākaivalyam*) of *īśvara*. The idea was inherited by Indian thinkers in later centuries, and taught along similar lines by Nanak and Kabir among others.[7] Again the same theory found expression in the Nyāya school in later generations,[8] though it had not been accepted there in the early period. Uddyotakara in the sixth century rejected the view of creation "for the sake of sport" (*krīḍārtha*).[9]

The third view holds that the creation of the world is the fundamental nature (*svabhāva*) of *puruṣa*, in the same way as combustion is the fundamental nature of fire, so that the world is produced as a natural function which ever exists in *puruṣa*. This theory, as Kamalaśīla says, was advocated by Uddyotakara,[10] and also coincides with the position taken on the evolution of the world in the first chapter of the Māṇḍūkya-kārikās.[11]

The fourth theory says that the creation has no definite purpose, that there is no deliberation by *puruṣa*, which simply acts in a particular way on particular occasions. This argument sees no teleological necessity and recognizes no causal necessity, so that it can be said to be a sort of doctrine of chance. It is not clear whether any such theory really was advocated in the orthodox Brahmanical tradition. A doctrine of chance had been advanced by free thinkers in society at large from a time prior to early Buddhism.[12]

For the fifth theory, the doctrine of Praśastamati is cited in the annotated translation of Kamalaśīla (note to verse 163). He sets out two views on the purpose of world creation, though it is not clear which is intended to be his own view. According to the quoted passages in Kamalaśīla, one theory is similar to the first theory noted above, and the other theory is in accordance with the third theory given above but avoiding its logical difficulty. That is, just as spring, summer, autumn and winter succeed each other in regular sequence, so the three powers of *Iśvara* origination, preservation and withdrawal appear in order, and in this way are understood the origination, continuance and dissolution of all living beings in that order.

> The thinker Praśastamati has so far not been identified, except that it has been noted that his words are quoted several times in the *Tattva-saṃgraha* and again he is also quoted alongside Uddyotakara in the *Prameyakamala-mārtaṇḍa*, a philosophical work of Jainism.[13] Accordingly there can be no doubt of his historicity. His dates are uncertain, but judging from the fact that in the reference he is put before Uddyotakara, he perhaps may have been prior to him. As seen from the phrases quoted here, he was well versed in logic, and possibly may perhaps have been of the Nyāya school. Praśastapāda, of the Vaiśeṣika school, who wrote the *Praśastapāda-bhāṣya*, is a different person.

From the above we find that at least five interpretations were in existence about the purpose of world creation by *puruṣa*. While we cannot conclude that all these views were held within the Vedānta school, the first three at least were clearly advocated in early Vedānta.

Looking at these theories of the purpose of creation, we can see that among the thinkers of the time were those who were engaged in considerably advanced speculative thinking, who were not like the previous followers of the Upaniṣads employing themselves in memorizing the texts and accepting them as they stood, but were themselves carrying out varied philosophical investigations into the doctrine of the Upaniṣads. These thinkers, though were superficially and simply "followers of the Veda" (*Veda-vādin*), had in fact *developed into Vedāntins.*

Next we shall look at the logical objections of Śāntarakṣita and Kamalaśīla to the theories of world creation. There are not a few elements common to the attacks on the theory of world creation by *īśvara* put forward in India generally. At the same time refutations of this character had been propounded from very ancient times among the Buddhists themselves. As has already been pointed out,[14] the denial of *īśvara* taught in volume 199 of the *Abhidharmamahāvibhāṣā-śāstra* is for the most part the same as that contained in the *Tattvasaṃgraha*. Accordingly it can be taken that here Śāntarakṣita and Kamalaśīla were compiling and synthesizing, enlarging, amplifying and treating in full the denial of *puruṣa* which had been handed down among Buddhists from quite ancient times.

Notes

1. Rāmānuja has contrasted Vedavāda with Bauddha (ad *BS*. II.2.27, p. 494). And examples are extant in which the *Svataḥprāmāṇyavādin*, i.e. the Mīmāṃsā school, calls itself Vedavādin (*SDS*.XII.220).
2. Cf. No. 2, sec. 4, ch. 1 of the present work.
3. Cf. sec. 6, ch. 3 of the present work.
4. Cf. the previous section.
5. *SDS*. XI.194, ff.
6. *MBh*. XII.308.3 (Calcutta ed. 11468); XII.313.15 (Cal. 11621).
7. Carpentier: *Theism in Mediaeval India*, pp. 488, 477.
8. *SDS*. XII. 156.
9. *Nyāya-Vārttika*. IV. 1. 21.
10. Ibid.
11. Cf. No. 2, sec. 4, ch. 6, vol. III of the present work.
12. *adhiccasamuppannika* (in *Brahmajālasutta*, *Dīgha-Nikāya*, No. 1)= *yadṛcchāvādin*.
13. Praśastamatinā ca—"sargādau puruṣāṇāṃ vyavahāro 'nyopadeśapūrvakaḥ, uttarakālaṃ prabuddhānāṃ pratyarthaniyatatvād, aprasiddhavāgvyavahārāṇāṃ kumārāṇāṃ gavādiṣu pratyarthaniyato vāgvyavahāro yathā mātrādyupadeśapūrvakaḥ" iti. Uddyotakareṇa ca —"bhuvanahetavaḥ pradhānaparamāṇvadṛṣṭāḥ svakāryotpattāv atiśayavad buddhimantam adhiṣṭhitāram apekṣante sthitvā pravṛttes tantuturyādivat"—*Prameyakamalamārtaṇḍa*, p. 75 a.
14. Cf. the present work, sec. 3 p. 194 ff.

Sub-Section 2. *An Examination of Ātman falsely constructed by the Aupaniṣadas* (*Aupaniṣadakalpitātmaparīkṣā*)

A. Translation

	Stanza No.
I. The Theory of the *Aupaniṣadas*	328-329
II. Its Refutation by the Buddhists	
a. A Criticism of the Eternality of Knowledge	330-332
b. A Criticism of the View that It is Impossible to Make any Distinction between Final Release and Bondage.	333-335

I. *The Theory of the Aupaniṣadas*

⩽Tib. 219 b. lines 6 ff.⩾ "Other people"[1], i.e. the *Aupaniṣadikas* who cling to the view of non-dualism (*advaitadarśana*), imagine that *ātman* has earth and the other effects of evolution (*pariṇāma*) as Its forms and the eternal and only one knowledge as its nature. Therefore, showing their own theory, [the author] says, "...eternal...":—

328. Again other people assert that these earth, fire, water, etc. are false appearances of the eternal knowledge (*nityajñānavivarta*) whereas *ātman* has it [=the eternal knowledge] as its nature.

"...has it as its nature" (*tadātmaka*) means "has earth and other effects of evolution as its forms and the eternal and only one knowledge as its nature." "Other people" (*apara*) means "the *Aupaniṣadikas*."

What kind of evidence (*pramāṇa*) is available on this point ? [The author] says, ⩽Tib. 22 a⩾[2] "...the object of perception, etc....":—

329. In this world there exists nothing possessed of the characteristics of the object of perception [from the standpoint of the highest truth]. Therefore, it is observed that this all is the evolution of Consciousness (*vijñānapariṇāma*).

For there do not exist earth and the like which have come to take the characteristics of the object of perception apart from knowledge (*jñāna*)[3] so that they (=earth and the like) may falsely appear since there do not exist atoms (*paramāṇu*) and [their] composites.[4] "Therefore,"[5] it is as a matter of course ascertained that those earth and the like are by nature false appearances of Consciousness (*vijñānapratibhāsa*). "This" (*ayam*) means earth and the like.

II. *Its Refutation by the Buddhists*

a. *A Criticism of the Eternality of Knowledge.*

[The author] rejects [the *Vedānta* doctrine] by [saying], "...their...":—

330. But there is a slight fault in their theory because of [their] assertion of the eternality [of Consciousness], since a distinction of the consciousnesses of colour, sound, and so on can evidently be made[6] [among them].

331. But if [colour, sound, taste, etc.] have the only one knowledge (*ekajñāna*) as their nature, colour, sound, taste and so on which are objects to be known (*vedya*) would manifest at the same time. And if [the Consciousness] is eternal, no change of the state would take place.

"There is a slight fault" (*alpāparādha*) since [like the Mahāyāna Buddhists who assert "Consciousness-only", they] also admit "knowledge-only" (*jñānamātra*) which is reasonable. [Therefore, the important point of their doctrine is not different from ours].

[Question:]—Why is it said that there is such a fault, though thus very slight, in that [theory of the *Vedānta* school] ?

Answer:—"Because of [their] assertion of the eternality [of Consciousness]" (*nityatoktitaḥ*).

[Question:]—"[since a distinction of the consciousnesses of] colour, sound and so on [can evidently be made]." (*rūpaśabdādi...*)

Because it is said that eternality means "to preserve one and the same state" whereas non-eternality is "not to preserve one and the same state." It is not always perceived that the consciousness (*vijñāna*) which manifests colour, sound, etc. preserves one and the same state, but it manifests colour at one time and manifests sound and so on at another time successively. Therefore, if those sound, etc. are by nature manifestations[7] of the eternal and one knowledge, then [they] would manifest at the same time, just as a many-coloured cloth manifests,[8] since the knowledge which by nature manifests them always exists.

If [the *Aupaniṣadas* say] that the change of the state which manifests (various) sound, etc. occurs to the knowledge [itself] successively; therefore, the consciousnesses of sound, etc. would not take place at the same time, [the author] replies, "And if [the Consciousness] is eternal, no change of the state would take place" (*nitye 'vasthāntaraṃ na ca*); since various states are not different from the subject of the state, the subject of the state (*avasthātṛ*, i.e. Consciousness) also perishes and arises like various states, or, it would follow that like the subject of the state various states are also eternal. If [they think, in order to avoid that error, that] various states are different from their subject, then (1) the relationship that these states belong to that subject[9] would not be established, since there is no [relationship that one] helps [the other], and (2) [they would have to accept the two entirely different things, the state and its subject,[10] and so they would] contradict [their own] assumption of the eternal and one Consciousness-only.

Furthermore, is the eternal knowledge-*ātman* (*jñānātman*) (1) established through sense-perception or (2) through inference? (1) Firstly, [the author] shows that [it is not established] through sense-perception ≪Tib. 220 b≫, [by saying], "...colour and the like...":—

332. The knowledge different from the consciousnesses of colour and the like is not perceived. When those [consciousnesses of colour and the like] are different every moment, what exists undifferentiated ?

"Knowledge" (*jñāna*),[11] which has the eternal and only one nature, which is the subject of the states, and owing to which [knowledge-*ātman*] is established through sense-perception, which is not really perceived apart from the consciousnesses of colour and the like which manifest successively. One should retort thus: When it is established that these consciousnesses of colour and the like which are perceived successively perish every moment, what else is undifferentiated ? Since such knowledge-*ātman*, therefore, that has obtained the characteristic of perception,[12] is not [in fact] perceived, [it] is the object to be expressed by [the word], "non-being". This is the purport.

And (2) it is not thought that [the knowledge-*ātman*] is

established through inference. If an inference is possible [in this case], does [this inference] (a) have the nature as the mark [which proves its existence] or (b) [its] result[13] [as the mark][14] ?

(a) Firstly, the nature is not [the mark which proves the existence of knowledge-*ātman*],[15] because the nature of that [knowledge-*ātman*] is not established, since no such subject of attributes (*dharmin*) is established, and even if the knowledge-only be established as the subject of attributes, it is not established that any attribute of it is invariably pervaded by its attribute, "eternality". [In other words, nothing is predicated by "eternality"].

(b) Nor is the result the mark [which proves the existence of knowledge-*ātman*], for it is not reasonable that the eternal [knowledge-*ātman*] serves practical purposes successively or at the same time, for there is no result of that [knowledge-*ātman*], and for it is not accepted that there is any result of something else apart from it.

Therefore, thus there is no means of knowledge with which to prove [the existence of] such knowledge-*ātman*, but there are sense-perception and other [means of knowledge] which negate [its existence]. Thus [the theory that everything is] evolved appearance (*vivarta*) of the eternal knowledge is not reasonable.

b. A Criticism of the View that It is Impossible to Make any Distinction Between Final Release and Bondage.

Furthermore, [by saying]. "...inverted...", [the author] shows that no distinction can be made between final release and bondage in this theory:—

333. [In your theory] there is no distinction between inverted and non-inverted knowledge. Then, how do bondage and final release exist in a man who has only one knowledge as his nature ?

According to him (=the Buddhist) who is of opinion that many consciousnesses, which are different in their continuity-series (*saṃtāna*), which perish every moment, and which belong to each person, function, a distinction between bondage and final release [is] reasonably[16] [made] by dint of the rise of the continuity-series of knowledge, inverted and non-inverted. Final release is attained because through the steps of Yoga practice the pure knowledge arises gradually and the continuity-series of the impure knowledge ceases to exist. Therefore, the effort to attain final release ≪Tib. 221 a≫ bears fruit.

But according to you (=*Aupaniṣadikas*) who are of the opinion that *ātman* has eternal and only one knowledge as its nature, how then do bondage and release exist in a man who has only one knowledge as his nature ? For—(1) if only one knowledge has always the inverted nature, then final release would not be established, since there would be no change of state. (2) If [only one knowledge] is [always] non-inverted, then there would be no bondage, since [it] has constantly the pure nature.

According to us (=the Buddhists), however, it is thought that consciousness (*vijñapti*) is defiled [at one time] and pure [at another time] because of [its] difference in continuity-series. Therefore, a distinction between bondage and release [can be explained] reasonably,[17] as is said in the following:—

> "And it (=consciousness)[18] is defiled and pure, stained and stainless. If it is not defiled, all the embodied ones are those who have already been released. If it is not pure, the effort [to attain final release] would be fruitless."

The [*Aupaniṣadikas*] may say that bondage and release are merely false constructions (*kalpita*) and not true from the view-point of the highest truth (*pāramārthika*), and [therefore, it is not necessary to make a distinction between bondage and release as you assert].

Then, [the Buddhists say] in this case, the origin[19] of false constructions should also be explained. [But your theory cannot explain why the false construction can be established]. On the contrary, in the theory (=Buddhism) that knowledge is non-eternal, [its] origin has already been explained. Therefore, your effort of practice to observe the truth for the sake of attaining final release and of transcending transmigration will result merely in weariness.[20]

This is shown [by saying], "Really...what...":—

334. Really, what can a Yogin destroy and establish by means of the Yoga practice ? Really it is impossible to throw away an inverted view which has it (=eternal knowledge) as its nature.

335. But the knowledge of truth cannot be produced [by the practice], for [it] is always existing because of having it (=eternal knowledge) as its nature. Therefore, [if you are right] this Yoga practice would also entirely be useless.

If a Yogin destroys something or works by practice to observe the truth then his effort will be fruitful. But [in fact] (1) first of all, this effort does not destroy the inverted view, since this inverted view has it as its nature, namely, has the eternal knowledge as its nature. Therefore, [the inverted view] cannot be discarded, for it is impossible to discard [the eternal thing], since the eternal thing is imperishable.

(2) And it is impossible to establish the knowledge of truth through the practice since the knowledge of truth is always existing ["because of having it as its nature"],[21] i.e. because of having the eternal knowledge as its nature. Therefore, this [argument] ≪Tib. 221 b≫ is not right.

Here ends the *Aupaniṣadātmaparīkṣā*.[22]

Notes

1. There is no word "*ātman*" in the Tibetan translation.
2. A Tibetan translation=*yoṅs su gyur pa.*
3. A Tibetan translation=*śes pa.*
4. *Avayavinaḥ* has been understood as a modifier of *asattvāt* according to the Tibetan translation.
5. A Tibetan translation=*de lta bas na śugs kyis.*
6. *Upalakṣaṇa.* This term is generally used in the sense of "the act of implying something that has not been expressed" and "using a term metaphorically" but in the Buddhist texts it is also used in a slightly different sense. Hsüan-Tsang translates the word *upalakṣaṇā* (*Bodhisattvabhūmi*, p. 83, line 8) as "careful observation".
7. *Jñānapratibhāsa.* A Tibetan translation=*śes pa la snaṅ ba* (manifestation in knowledge).
8. *Vicitrāstaraṇapratibhāsavat.* A Tibetan translation=*gos khra bo snaṅ ba bshin du.*
9. *Tasyaitā iti.* A Tibetan translation=*ḥdiḥi ḥdi shes bya ba* (=*tasyaiṣā iti* ?).
10. *-virodhaś ca,* but a Tibetan translation=*ḥgal baḥi phyir ro* (=*-virodhāc ca*).
11. *Avasthātṛ jñānam.* A Tibetan translation=*gnas skabs paḥi śes pa* (*avasthātṛjñāna, tatpuruṣa*).
12. The reading in our text and Dvārikādās Śāstrī's edition: *upalabdhikṣaṇaprāptasya* must be corrected into *upalabdhilakṣaṇaprāptasya* in consideration of a Tibetan translation: *dmigs paḥi mtshan ñid kyir gyur pa.* Cf. *Śabdabrahmaparīkṣā* of the *Tattvasaṃgraha.*
13. The reading: *kāryaṃ vā* must be corrected into *kāryaliṅgaṃ vā* in consideration of a Tibetan translation: *ḥbras buḥi rtags yin graṅ.*

14. Cf. *Tattvasaṃgraha*, vv. 147, 148 and *Pañjikā* on them. This argument is based on Dharmakīrti's logic. He classified the inference into two according to the relationship of the middle term to the major term, that is to say, according as the major premise is either an analytical judgement or a synthetic judgement. For example, in the inference "This is a tree, because of its being a *śiṃśapā* tree", its major premise is an analytical judgement that all the *śiṃśapā* trees are trees; it is called *svabhāvahetu*. On the other hand, in the inference "That mountain has fire, because of being smoky", its major premise is a synthetic judgement that wherever there is smoke there is fire; it is called *kāryahetu*. Here the former inference is named "*svabhāvaliṅga*" and the latter "*kāryaliṅga*". This distinction is applied throughout the whole text of the *Tattvasaṃgraha*.

15. Our text lacks this portion which Dvārikādās Śāstrī's edition reads as follows: *...tathābhūtasya / [kasyacid dharmiṇo 'siddhyā tatsvabhāvāsiddheḥ / jñānamātre ca dharmiṇi siddhe 'pi tasya nityatvadharmeṇa kasyacit taddharmasya vyāptyasiddhe / nāpi kāryaṃ liṅgam, nityasya kramayaugapadyābhyām arthakriyānupapatteḥ; tatkāryasya kasyacid abhāvāt / tadvyatirekeṇāparasya kāryasyānabhyupagamāc ca/tad evaṃ na kaścit tathābhūtasya] jñānātmanaḥ...*

16. *-yuktimatī*. A Tibetan translation—*rigs pa daṅ ldan pa ma yin te* is not right.

17. *Yuktā*. A Tibetan translation=*rigs pa ma yin no* is not right.

18. *Sā* (=*vijñapti* ?)

19. *Nibandhana*. A Tibetan translation—*rgyu mtshan*.

20. *Sa kevalam āyāsaphala eveti*. A Tibetan translation=*de ni ḥbras bu dal ba ḥgaḥ shig tu zad do she bya ba ston pa ni* (it is taught that it produces merely a certain static fruit.).

21. Supplied from a Tibetan translation=*deḥi bdag ñid yin paḥi phyir te* (=*tādātmyāt*).

22. *Ity Aupaniṣadikātmaparīkṣā*. A Tibetan translation =*de kho na ñid bsdus paḥi dkaḥ ḥgrel las gsaṅ ba paḥi bdag brtag pa ste bcu gcig paḥo* (= *Tattvasaṃgrahapañjikāyām Aupaniṣada-ātmaparīkṣā nāma ekādaśaḥ paṭalaḥ*).

B. *Remarks*

When we carefully examine in detail the passages translated above, in which Śāntarakṣita and Kamalaśīla have attacked the Upaniṣad followers, although very briefly, we can come to several noteworthy conclusions. (Hereafter Śāntarakṣita will be abbreviated to Ś., and Kamalaśīla to Kam.)

(1) Upaniṣadic School of the Time

Although there must already have been numerous varied sub-schools existing within Upaniṣadic Vedānta at that time, only the non-dualistic theory (*advaita-darśana*, Kam.) is here presented as the doctrine of the Upaniṣadic school (*Aupaniṣada, Aupaniṣadika*). Thus Buddhists of the time would have thought that the central idea of the Upaniṣad school could be called the theory of non-dualistic monism. Here, as I shall explain later, they agree with the accounts of the Jaina writers Samantabhadra and Akalaṅka. However, the theory of non-dualism referred to is by no means the same as the doctrine of Śaṅkara line of the later period. A general outline of the non-dualism which is attacked here is as follows :

(i) *Ātman* is the original substance of the natural world composed of elements such as earth, water, fire, etc. The basic essence of that *ātman* is *jñāna* — simple knowledge everpresent. That is, Ātman is the knowing self (*jñānātman*). And since it is also said to be the main subject (*avasthātṛ* — as substance or support) of the various conditions of the individuals, in a certain sense it is accepted that the great Self and the individual selves are the same.

(ii) The development of the world from *ātman* is called evolution (*pariṇāma*) and also temporary manifestation (*vivarta*), and both Ś. and Kam. interpret these two words in the same sense.[1] Again, Kam. uses the word manifestation (*pratibhāsa*). Thus the usage of technical words related to world creation is the same as that in both Bhartṛhari and in Śaṅkara (as will be shown later), and the sharp distinction between transformation (*pariṇāma*) and illusory appearance (*vivarta*) in the Advaita later had not yet been established. Or if it had, it was still not influential enough to have impressed itself on the Buddhists.

(iii) Earth etc., the objects of cognition (*grāhya*), do not exist, in the highest sense. Neither do atoms nor their compounds (*avayavin*) actually exist. All things are a development (transformation of consciousness, *vijñāna-pariṇāma*). Here they have used the same technical terms as the Vijñāna-vāda school.

(iv) Although there is in Buddhist philosophy a precise distinction between consciousness (*vijñāna*) and knowledge (*jñāna*), here they are used in the same sense. (Moreover, Kam. gives the word *vijñapti* the same meaning). On this point, there is agreement with Vedānta philosophy in general, whereas the account given by Bhavya, examined in the preceding section, differs.

(v) The appearances of the objects of cognition arise in a successive order, so that everything does not appear at the same time and give rise to confusion. Accordingly, even in non-dualism, there is a conceivable basis for the ordinary world.

(vi) In the highest truth, our bondage and liberation are not established facts. There is originally no difference between them, but one appears as a result of our making distinctions (*kalpanā*).[2]

(vii) Liberation arises by knowledge of the truth (*tattvajñāna*) and for that purpose it is necessary to practise the Yoga training. On this point there is complete agreement with the account given by Bhavya.

(viii) As is clear from the above, the doctrines of the Upaniṣad school here attacked have a great resemblance to those of Mahāyāna Buddhism. That is, as Kam. has argued, they too assert that all things are knowledge-only (*jñāna-mātra*) so that in this fundamental tenet it must be said to coincide with the Consciousness-only theory (*Vijñāna-vāda*) of Buddhism. Moreover, Ś. in his criticism of the Upaniṣad school remarks "there are slight errors in their school"[3], and thus Buddhists themselves admitted *some resemblance to their own doctrines.* So a major part of this theory of the Upaniṣad school was a doctrine which was acceptable from a Buddhist standpoint. This parallels Bhavya's view that the Vedānta had smuggled in the doctrine of the Tathāgata. And when we consider that Akalaṅka, a Jaina writer of the same period,[4] criticizes the theory of Advaita for the same faults as the Buddhist theory, we see that a resemblance between Advaita and Buddhism was admitted at that time in the philosophical world of India generally.

Now if the Advaita theory here attacked had these particular tenets, then in the Vedānta of the period whose theory actually was it, or which line is being indicated ? Kam. calls it *Advaita*, from which fact one would first think of Śaṅkara. However when we examine the above characteristics one by one, we find that there is by no means exact conformity between it and the theories of Śaṅkara in the commentary on the *Brahma-sūtra* (*Brahma-sūtra-bhāṣya*). The Upaniṣad school here presented called the Absolute the knowing self (*jñānātman*), but Śaṅkara in his works calls the Absolute the supreme self (*paramātman*) and the supreme Brahman (*param brahma*), while the individual self is called the conscious-self (*vijñānātman*).[5] And the idea of a transformation of consciousness (*vijñānapariṇāma*) is criticized in detail in a passage where Śaṅkara attacks the Consciousness-only theory (ad *BS*. II.2.28-31).

However, if we follow Śaṅkara, consciousness (*vijñāna*) is another name for mind (*manas*) or the function of apperception (*buddhi*), and is the organ which unifies and controls the cognition and behaviour of the individual being,[6] but is never considered to be the absolute root of all things, nor is it the individual self either. Again, even in the *Brahma-sūtra* II.3.15, which presents in direct opposition the different view of opposing school(s) on *vijñāna* and the views of the author of the sūtra about it, both sides take *vijñāna* as an organ of the individual self. Accordingly, insofar as technical terms are concerned, the philosophy of the Upaniṣad school which is criticized in the *Tattvasaṃgraha* is different from the *Brahma-sūtra*, from its opponents given there, and from Śaṅkara. If one looks for those who in the early Vedānta had asserted that Brahman is consciousness (*vijñāna*) one can cite Bhartṛprapañca.[7] His theories however are by no means similar to the Buddhist theories.

We should perhaps say rather that the theories of the Upaniṣad school presented here are close to those in chapter four of the *Māṇḍūkya-Kārikās*. In the *Kārikās* (IV.47, 48, 50, 51, 52), transformation of consciousness is explained on lines similar to the Consciousness-only theory, and what is more it is thought that knowledge (*jñāna*) is something indivisible from Brahman (*GK*. III.33; IV.96, 99). Of course it cannot be taken that Ś. here has directly attacked the *Māṇḍūkya-Kārikās*. However, I think it can certainly be concluded that there were living, at the time of Śaṅkara or a little before, thinkers who held a view like that of these *Māṇḍūkya-Kārikās*, using similar technical words and with a doctrine very close to the Buddhist, and it was this which Ś. was attacking.

A further point is, that here it is only Advaitins who are presented as "followers of the Upaniṣads", but it cannot necessarily be concluded that only Advaita was then flourishing. As we shall discuss later on, there were then a great many Vedānta philosophers holding views other than Advaita, and mostly quite apart from Buddhists. Again, even what is called Advaita here is not necessarily the same as what may be called the Advaita of the Śaṅkara line, as has already been remarked.

(2) Criticism of the Upaniṣad School.

Now what were the attacks made by Śāntarakṣita and Kamalaśīla against this particular Advaita doctrine ? The criticisms can be roughly divided into two : (i) criticism of the doctrine of the permanence of the knowledge which is the essence of Ātman, and (ii) criticism that if a permanent knowledge is postulated, there would be no distinction between liberation and bondage.

These attacks will later on in the *Śabdabrahmaparīkṣā* of the *Tattvasaṃgraha* be reproduced in substance when criticizing the doctrine of Bhartṛhari. In the following I will put in parentheses the numbers of the verses there which correspond to the arguments here.

(1) Criticism of the permanence of knowledge.

(a) Consciousness as a general principle manifests *in a succession* of forms, sounds etc. as its objects. If consciousness were permanent and simple, it would not manifest in a succession in this way, but would manifest at one time all things of creation. In that case no changes in the phenomenal world could happen.

(b) If one does admit that different conditions in the phenomenal world can arise successively, then according to the Advaita theory, all the conditions would be inseparable from the original subject of the conditions, and there would be birth and destruction, change and transition for it (i.e. consciousness) also (cf. v. 137).

If one denies that, and says that the subject of conditions is permanent, that would amount to saying that all the conditions also are permanent (cf. v. 138). Again if to avoid this difficulty, one takes it that conditions and their subject are separate, one cannot explain how the two can have relations between them; moreover that too would lead to a contradiction with the fundamental tenet of Advaita (cf. note to v. 331, v. 134).

(c) No proofs for the existence of a permanent knowing-self exist, i.e. the contents of our consciousness are produced and destroyed every moment. Accordingly, the knowledge which is permanent, unique and uninterrupted cannot be demonstrated by perception. That is, according to the logic of Dharmakīrti, in order to demonstrate logically the existence of a certain thing, one can do it by the fact that its own essence (*svabhāva*) is its demonstrative reason (*liṅga*), or else, its changing effect (*kārya*) is its demonstrative reason, but in that case, the own essence or the changing effect together cannot exist in the knowing-self. Thus, one cannot assume to know its existence even by comparison (cf. *Pañjikā* on v. 332, vv. 147, 148).

(2) The criticism that a difference between bondage and liberation cannot be established.

Knowledge, which is the fundamental essence of *ātman*, is permanent and immutable according to your theory. Now if knowledge, as the *ātman*, should possess always a fluctuating fundamental essence, liberation could not arise, and, if it should possess a fundamental essence which is unfluctuating and pure, bondage would not be able to exist (v. 333). In this way, in the case of the former, since it is impossible to discard fluctuation, the practice of *yoga* would be of no use, and in the latter case the knowledge of the truth would already be established, thus it would be useless to practise the religious training of yoga (vv. 334, 335. Furthermore, cf. *Pañjikā* on v. 151).

This criticism had been strongly made in ancient times by Nāgārjuna.[8] And Śāntarakṣita has probably once again explained and elucidated it.

Further, as indicated within the parentheses in the foregoing, even against the philosophy of Bhartṛhari, Śāntarakṣita has set forth a similiar criticism. Accordingly, in the early Vedānta school, despite the fact that there were several differences in traditional lines, all these inherently possessed the same logical faults, so Śāntarakṣita thought.

Notes

1. Further, cf. the *Śabdabrahmaparīkṣā* of the *Tattvasaṃgraha.*
2. Cf. *GK.*II,32, and commentaries thereon.
3. *alpāparādha.* This is said for those persons who are very close to their own theory, but have not yet realized the truth. Cf. *GK.*IV.43.
4. Cf., sect. 3, chap 2, of the present work.
5. Deussen; *SVS.*194, Amn. 82.
6. Śaṅkara ad *BS.* II.3.32, II.4.6 (Vol. II, p. 108, line 10).
7. Cf. sect. 3, chapter 7, part 5 of the present work (Vol. 3).
8. "If one supposes that certain mental afflictions really exist for a certain person, insofar as their self essence is concerned, (they) how could (they) be severed ? (For) can a person sever his own essence ?" (*Madhyamaka-Kārikā,* XXIII.24.).

"If one supposes that certain mental afflictions do not really exist for a certain person in their own essence, how could (they) be severed? Can anyone sever what does not really exist ? (Ibid. XXII.25). "In anyone who is already stricken with metaphysical inversion, no metaphysical inversions can arise longer. "(Not yet) afflicted with inversions, all the metaphysical inversions cannot arise." ibid. XXII. 17." Further see, *Madhyamaka-hṛdaya* VIII, 69.

SECTION IX : VEDĀNTA PHILOSOPHY AND BUDDHISM AFTER ŚĀNTARAKṢITA AND KAMALAŚĪLA

1. *Remarks*

Coming to the period after Śāntaraksita and Kamalaśīla, Indian and Chinese Buddhism progressively diverged, and came to develop separately and independently. Works of Indian Buddhism formulated during this period, apart from those related to Esoteric (Tantrik) Buddhism, have for the most part not been translated into Chinese. By now Chinese Buddhism had in the main imported and adopted the important Buddhist ideas, and was setting about establishing a new Buddhism on that basis. Buddhism in India, on the other hand, pursued the tendency to become esoteric (*Vajrayāna*). Works of Indian Buddhism of this period have not yet been adequately investigated, but a comparatively large number of the expository treatises and commentaries composed in this period appear to make reference to the Vedānta school. In the following, we shall try to give some of the works among the Buddhist writings in India during this period which make allusion to the Vedānta philosophy.

1. Avalokitavrata wrote a detailed sub-commentary on the Prajñā-pradīpa-*śāstra* of Bhavya, and in it he mentions Śaṅkara and his doctrine quoting the Vedas as well.[1]

2. Jñānaśrībhadra wrote a great commentary on the *Laṅkā-vatāra Sūtra*. His dates are not certain, but perhaps it may be taken that he was around the time of Kamalaśīla.[2] In that work, he mentions the Advaita doctrine :

"In the *advaita* (non-dualist) doctrine, word should be one with meaning; but word and meaning can be different according to various circumstances, just as to two people suffering from diseased vision the moon appears distorted in various ways."[3]

That word (*śabda*) forms the fundamental essence of all things (*artha*) was strongly asserted by Bhartṛhari, and the idea was also accepted and handed down by Śaṅkara and others. Again, as by a person who has some disease in his eyes, the moon is taken as being distorted in various ways, a person who is affected by ignorance cannot rightly cognize the truth, but adopts various mistaken opinions. This was frequently taught in the original Buddhist scriptures, but Śaṅkara also has adopted it.[4] Accordingly, the idea explained above is in general close to Śaṅkara's theory. Further, Bhartṛhari also has said[5] that Jñānaśrībhadra is a thinker with ideas similar to those of Bhartṛhari and Śaṅkara. These things probably point to the fact that the Vedānta thinkers of the Śaṅkara line had a close connection with Buddhists of that period.

3. Further in the *Kṣaṇabhaṅgasiddhi*,[6] a work by Ratnakīrti, a Buddhist of a later period, there are given the logical theories of a person called Śaṅkara, though it is not at all certain that this is indeed the famous Śaṅkara who was the Vedānta scholar. At least, the theory related there cannot be found in his *Brahma-sūtra-bhāṣya*.

4. The above-mentioned criticism of the Vedānta doctrines in the *Tattvasaṁgraha* of Śāntarakṣita is very interesting. However, no influence from it can be traced in Chinese Buddhism, since it was not translated into Chinese. But it seems that the arguments exercised considerable influence upon later Buddhists in India. For example, in the *Bodhicaryāvatārapañjikā*, which is the commentary of Prajñākaramati (950-1030 A.D.) on the *Bodhicaryāvatāra* by Śāntideva, the Ātman doctrines of various schools are referred to and criticized largely on the basis of the *Tattvasaṁgraha*.[7] The theory of the *Upaniṣad-vādins*[8], which is referred to in one section of the *Bodhicaryāvatārapañjikā*, is in content in accordance with the above-mentioned theory of the Upaniṣadvādins in the *Tattvasaṁgraha* :

"However, the *Upaniṣadvādins* accept (the existence of) one, universal and permanent knowledge, running throughout all living beings. (According to their doctrine) this world which is of earth, water, air, fire etc. manifests as an illusion (*vivarta*) in that (consciousness). And Ātman is no other than its real being.

The objects of external cognition (apprehensibles) namely the various compounds of atoms etc., do not exist as anything capable of being established by valid proof."

Then he quotes verses 118 and 119 of the *Tattvasaṁgraha.*[9] (Generally speaking, the verses quoted in regard to the Ātman doctrines of various schools in this part of the *Bodhicaryāvatāra* are almost all taken from the *Tattvasaṁgraha.*)

The above account therefore cannot be a primary source of information about the Vedānta philosophy of the time, but it shows the fact that Śāntarakṣita's *Tattvasaṁgraha* was regarded as an important text by the Buddhists even in later centuries.

The original manuscripts of philosophical treatises of Indian Buddhism after Śāntarakṣita and Kamalaśīla have almost all been lost, and most of them do not even exist in the Chinese Tripiṭaka translations. Quite a few of them have been handed down in the Tibetan Tripiṭaka, but as these were not published in a critical edition until recently, we have not, as things stand, found it possible to search for many accounts of Vedānta philosophy in the works of the time. And even suppose we could find some, those which might offer positive contribution to the elucidation of the history of Vedānta philosophy are likely to be comparatively few in number. Before then there had been plentiful intercourse with China and the dates of the various Buddhist classics are for the most part clear, but with the cutting off, of the connection with China the dates of Buddhist classics become very vague and conjectural. But it is probably fair to say that the fact that there are references to Vedānta philosophical doctrines in books of the period shows that the Vedānta school *in its own right* was fully active at this time also.

Notes

1. M. Walleser : *DAV.* S. 15.
2. *Nihon Bukkyō Gakukyōkai nenpō,* Eighth Year, article by Susumu Yamaguchi, p. 125.
3. Peking edition (XLII.194a, 8=194b, 7). According to S. Yamaguchi, op. cit, p. 154.
4. *ekaś candraḥ sa dvitīyavad avabhāsate.* (Śaṅkara ad *BS.* vol. I, p. 10, line, 3).
5. Problems relevant to Bhartṛhari will be discussed later on.

6. *Six Buddhist Nyāya Tracts*, ed. by Haraprasad Sastri, p. 57.
7. *Bodhicaryāvatārapañjikā*, p. 452, l. 7 ff. (B. I. ed. by Poussin).
8. *Upaniṣadvādin* is referred to in *Bodhicaryāvatārapañjikā*, op. cit p. 465, l. 7 ff.
9. Translation of these two verses is in the foregoing section.

2. *Bhāskara the Vedāntin in Buddhist Literature*[1]

In Buddhist literature the Vedānta philosophy or the Vedānta school is referred to often, but, insofar as the writer of this paper knows, no name of any individual Vedāntic philosopher is mentioned. Even the name of Śaṅkara, the greatest philosopher, is not mentioned by ancient Buddhists. So it is quite noteworthy that the theory of Bhāskara is mentioned in the *Tattvaratnāvalī* by Advayavajra (11th century), a scholar of later Vajrayāna, and that Bhāskara was regarded as the representative scholar of the Vedānta school. Remarking that there is a danger that the theories of both the *sākāra-vijñāna-vādins* and *nirākāra-vijñāna-vādins* slip into the ambit of the Vedānta philosophy, he says as follows :

Paramārthasan-nitya-sākāravijñāna-samādhau bhagavataḥ saṃsthitavedāntavādimatānupraveśaḥ / sa hi paramārthasan nityaṃ svacid-rūpabrahmābhinnapariṇāmarūpaṃ jagad icchati / tathā coktam—

yad yad vai dṛśyate kiñcit tat tat brahmeti kalpayet /
tato nānyagataṃ cittaṃ brahmaṇy evāvatiṣṭhate //

iti samādhimalaṃ sākāravādinaḥ /

evaṃ nirākāravādināpi nitya-nirābhāsa-niṣprapañca-svasaṃvedanavijñānabhāvanāyāṃ Bhāskaramata-sthita-Vedāntavādimatānupraveśa-prasaṅgaḥ / so 'pi vyapagata-sakalanāmarūpaprapañcopaplavaviśuddhaprakāśānandaghana-nitya-brahmābhyupagacchati /[2]

"When one practises the contemplation of knowledge-with-images as eternal and existent in the absolute sense, he might slip into the view of the Vedāntavādins which is a theology. For he (the Buddhist of Vedantic inclination) accepts that the world is existent in the absolute sense, eternal, and that its essence consists in a development (or manifestation) which is not essentially different from Brahman, the self-knowing. So, it is said (by the Vedāntavādin) :

"Whatever is seen, one should consider it to be Brahman.
Mind does not exist in some other separate thing; it exists in Brahman only.
This is the (possible) spoiling of his contemplation on the part of the one who practises the contemplation (of knowledge)-with-images.
Likewise, for the one who holds to knowledge-without-images, there too is a danger that, in practising the contemplation of the self-cognizant knowledge which is eternal, without manifestations and without phenomenal diversity, he might slip into the view of the Vedāntavādins who adhere to the opinion of Bhāskara. For he also accepts Brahman as eternal, pure, splendour and bliss only, without the defilements of phenomenal diversity consisting of all names and shapes."

The distinction between the *sākāra-vijñānavādins* and the *nirākāra-vijñāna-vādins* was made and adopted by later Buddhist philosophers of India, such as Kamalaśīla (in his *Tattvasaṃgraha-pañjikā*), Mokṣākaragupta (in his *Tarkabhāṣā*) and others. In this connection, Bodhibhadra's definition in his *Jñānasārasamuccayanibandha* may be helpful for clarifying the passage. He says :—

"Here the Yogācāras are of two kinds, (those who maintain that knowledge is) always (endowed) with images (*sākāra*) and (those who maintain that knowledge in its absolute state is) without images (*nirākāra*). Of these, *sākāra* is propounded by Dignāga and his followers. They teach that the images of cognition are by nature dependent on something else (*paratantra-svabhāva*), as is said in the following: The object of cognition is none other than internal image that appears in the guise of an external being.[3]......... They talk only of six kinds of cognitions. *Nirākāra* is taught by Ārya Asaṅga and his followers. They maintain that the images of cognition are by nature representations (*parikalpitasvabhāva*) and are (as much false as) the hair seen by one suffering from partial blindness. Concerning this the following is said: If the object of cognition is accepted as being an external reality there would be no non-conceptual knowledge (*nirvikalpakajñāna*); (but) without it Buddhahood cannot be attained.[4] And again: When non-conceptual knowledge is acquired, no objects ever appear; therefore one must understand the non-existence of the object, and since that is non-existent the content of cognition is also non-existent.[5] They talk of eight kinds of cognition; but some say there is only one kind. This theory of one kind (of cognition) is maintained also by some of the *sākāravādins*."[6]

This distinction has been admitted in traditional Vijñānavāda scholarship of China and Japan also, in which the representative scholar of the *sākāravāda* was recognized as Dharmapāla and the representative tradition of the *nirākāra* has been recognized in the theory of Asaṅga chiefly conveyed by Paramārtha.

Anyhow, the terms *sākāravāda* and *nirākāravāda* in the above-cited passage are used in a way quite different from the current use in Indian philosophy in general, in which *sākāravāda* is maintained by the Sāṃkhya, Vedānta as well as the Sautrāntika, whereas the *nirākāravāda* was held by the Nyāya-Vaiśeṣika, the Kumārila school and probably the Vaibhāṣika.[7] The use of these two terms, derived from the traditional use by later Vijñānavādins, was adopted by Vajrayānists.

From the discussion above, some noteworthy conclusions can be drawn out.

(1) Buddhists were aware of the fact that the teachings of the Vedāntins were quite close to those of the Buddhists.[8] This fact was also admitted by Akalaṅka, the Jain philosopher, in his commentary on Samantabhadra's *Āptamīmāṃsā*, v. 24. Advayavajra followed his predecessors with the same kind of evaluation.[9]

(2) Advayavajra compared the *sākāra-vijñānavāda* to the Vedāntic teachings of Hindu theism, whereas he compared the *nirākāravijñānavāda* to the Vedāntic teachings of Bhāskara. This judgment is justifiable to a considerable extent.

(3) Advayavajra mentioned Bhāskara as the representative Nirākāra Vedāntin, and not Śaṅkara. Śaṅkara, the Vedāntin, is not mentioned even a single time in any Buddhist or Jain philosophical work, whereas Bhāskara is mentioned in this passage and in a commentary on Dharmakīrti's work.[10] The teachings of Advaita Vedānta are criticized in Buddhist works by Bhavya, Śāntarakṣita and Kamalaśīla and in Jain works by Samantabhadra and Akalaṅka. It is likely that this remark that the Vedānta philosophy of the type of Bhāskara is meant holds true with the Advaita theory criticized in the

Dvādaśāranayacakra of Mallavādisūri and Siṃhasūri's commentary on it.

(4) From the above-mentioned conclusion another emerges, namely that it is likely that Śaṅkara's scholarly tradition became influential in the sociological context only in later days. We cannot say from just when, but for some centuries after the demise of Śaṅkara the influence of Bhāskara was stronger than that of Śaṅkara.[11]

Notes

1. This section was originally published in the *Annals of the Bhandarkar Oriental Research Institute*, Golden Jubilee Volume, vol. XLVIII-XLIX, Poona, 1968, pp. 119-122.

2. *Advayavajrasaṃgraha*, edited by Haraprasad Shastri. Gaekwad's Oriental Series, vol. 40, 1927, p. 19. I have cited this passage with emendations by the late Hakuju UI, in his *Daijō Butten no Kenkyū*, pp. 5-6.

3. *Ālambanaparīkṣā*, v. 6.

4. *Mahāyānasaṃgraha*, ed. Lamotte, II, 14 bc.=VIII, 20c.

5. Ibid. II, 14 b.f.=VIII, 20 f.

6. Peking ed. 51, b. 3 ff. I have cited this English translation with slight alteration from Prof. Yuichi Kajiyama's paper, *Journal of Indian and Buddhist. Studies*, vol. XIV, No. 1, Dec. 1965, p. 31.

7. Satkari Mookerjee, *The Buddhist Philosophy of Universal Flux*, p. 77

8. e.g. *Madhyamakahṛdaya* VIII, 60; 78; 91. *Tarkajvālā*, VIII, 79; 87; 91; *Tattvasaṃgraha*, v. 330.

9. Striking enough, the Buddhist Vijñānavādins call themselves "*Advaita vādinaḥ*". *Pramāṇavārttikabhāsya* of Prajñākaragupta, edited by A. S. Altekar. Patna, K. P. Jayaswal Research Institute, 1953, p. 606.

10. For this information I am indebted to Prof. Y. Kajiyama.

11. This fact may correspond with the chronological strata of architectural remains at Shringeri, the headquarters of Śaṅkara's tradition. Only the Śrīcakra and the samādhi of Śaṅkara go back to the time of Śaṅkara. All other monuments and buildings derive from later times, especially from the reign of the Vijayanagara dynasty.

SECTION X : CONCLUDING REMARKS

In the foregoing, we have examined in chronological order the accounts in the Buddhist literature relating to the Upaniṣad and Vedānta schools, and can now draw the following conclusions :

1. During the period of earliest Buddhism, the Old Upaniṣads of the earliest period had already come into existence, and the Old Upaniṣads of the middle period were in process of being composed, and their ideas are reflected in the sacred texts of early Buddhism. One section of the Brahmins of the time took the verses of the Upaniṣads literally, and persons who inquired into the meaning, and tried to extract the underlying sense of them by philosophical inquiry, were very rare. This was the state of things roughly up to the time of King Aśoka (latter half of 3rd century B.C.).

2. Buddhism split into several schools and when it came to the period when these confronted each other, passages of the Upaniṣads seem to have been quoted in theoretical works of Buddhism. By this time the Upaniṣads had already been compiled and attained authority as one section of the Vedic revelation.

However the Upaniṣad followers of the time still took what was written in the texts quite literally, and the Buddhists did not know of any of them who were going further and trying to interpret the true meaning of the sacred texts and formulate philosophical systems. It was rather a Vedānta synthesized with Sāṅkhya philosophy which was generally popular. This was the state of affairs from King Aśoka up to Nāgārjuna (c. 200 A.D.).

3. In Mahāyāna literature which can be thought to have been in existence prior to Nāgārjuna, there is no reference to Vedānta philosophy, so that in this period it probably had not yet become an independent school and did not have general influence in society. Even in the period of Nāgārjuna and Ārya-Deva, almost no change or development in the thought of the Vedānta seems to have been observed. One section of Brahmins of the time, as before, continued to follow the Upaniṣadic texts faithfully, and in the accounts in Buddhist writings nothing appears of any attempt to set up some particular philosophy based on those texts.

4. However in the writings of Bhavya (490-c. 570), there is a quite distinct idea of a Vedānta school which carried on philosophical investigation. Among the views of the Vedānta school described by him, there are to be found primitive theories in their original Upaniṣadic form, but along with them highly developed theories of Ātman, that are indeed varied and numerous.

Since in his work they are discussed as an independent school, it is certain that by the fifth century at latest, among Brahmins who were followers of the Upaniṣads, there were fairly developed philosophical thoughts, and the Vedānta school which they formed was of considerable importance in the intellectual world of the time. But their doctrine was principally that the world evolved from puruṣa or ātman, and no doctrine of Māyā or of non-duality (*advaita*) yet appears. This fact can be confirmed from what is recorded by Dharmapāla who lived at the same period as Bhavya.

5. Then in the works of Śāntarakṣita (c. 680-740) and Kamalaśīla (c. 700-750), there are presented, and refuted, theories of a Vedānta school under the name "Upaniṣad school". The theories of this school are called "*advaita*" but they are not necessarily identical with those of Śaṅkara.

6. Still later, Vedānta theories are similarly referred to in Buddhist works, and in particular it is noteworthy that the advaita theory of the Śaṅkara line is presented. Accordingly, so far as the accounts in Buddhist texts go, the *advaita* theory of the Śaṅkara line spread in general through the intellectual world in India after the period of Śāntarakṣita and Kamalaśīla, i.e. after the period in which Śaṅkara lived.

7. Scholars have frequently noted the fact that one section of Vedānta doctrines has a resemblance to the thought of Mahāyāna Buddhism, and the Buddhists of that time themselves had already noticed the resemblance. and discussed the differences and similarities of the two. However this means in the main that the Vedānta school had adopted Buddhist ideas. It can be taken that Buddhism would have been influenced by Vedānta philosophy in the Mahāyāna Buddhism of the late period. but in the early period of the rise of Mahāyāna Buddhism I believe that in general it was rather the other way round.

CHAPTER V

VEDĀNTA PHILOSOPHY AS SEEN FROM THE SCRIPTURES OF EARLY JAINISM

SECTION I : INTRODUCTION

Jainism is a religion that was established about the same time as Buddhism and developed parallel to it. Its founder was Nigaṇṭha Nātaputta (circa 444-372 B.C.).[1] It is said that he practised spiritual disciplines for a long time and finally awakened to enlightenment and became the Jina ('victorious one'). Therefore this religion is called the teaching of Jina[2] namely Jaina or Jainism. Throughout India, Jainism is taken as a religion with a very close relationship with primitive Buddhism. There are very many similarities of doctrine, legends and terminology. Also its paths of historical development generally spread alongside those of Buddhism. The founder was of the Kṣatriya class as was the Buddha; however this group's development was mainly centred around merchant and artisan guilds.

The Jains did not recognize the authority of the Vedas, the holy book of all Hindus, and did not observe the Brahmins' religious ceremonies. Orthodox Brahmins who inherited the traditional culture of the Indo-Āryans looked upon Jainism as the most formidable of the heretical teachings. The Brahmins classed Jainism along with Buddhism and Materialism (*Lokāyata*) as the three great heretical religious systems (*Nāstika*). Therefore they were at every point in opposition to the various ideals of the traditional Brahmin system.

From the very beginning Jainism premised a denial of the doctrines which the Brahmins had established as a system. They held constantly a critical and aggressive attitude in regard to the other philosophies. As the formation and organization of the great Jain religious following developed with time, there gradually came to be more contact and interchange with the orthodox Brahmin culture, which also was all the time evolving. Even more than Buddhists, the Jains adopted and used whatever they thought might be useful in the propagation of their teaching, including the stories, legends and myths of the traditional Brahmins. At the same time they kept continually attacking and criticizing ever more minutely all philosophical systems not in accord with their own, devising powerful arguments against them. The various philosophical Jain writings are therefore an inexhaustible treasure for philosophical arguments between the various schools in India during the Middle Ages. There has not been much research on Jain literature in the past, and yet for the historian of Indian thought it is the most valuable record that cannot be overlooked. It absolutely must be referred to for tracing the earlier history of thought of the various philosophical schools. This applies specially to that of the Vedānta, where there are very few existing records of the first period. The manner in which Vedānta is reflected and criticized in the Jain writings becomes a very important source for the general study of the history of the Vedānta. Jain writings are undoubtedly highly valuable material to clarify Vedānta thought of the early period, especially since practically none of the early period Vedānta literature is extant today. Again they are most useful for the Middle Age period, as the dates of the various Jain writers are fairly clear. In Buddhism the dates of the various thinkers are generally determined only on the basis of the year of the Chinese translations of the various Buddhist scriptures, and the position is even more obscure for the Brahmin writers. There are however many among the Jains whose period is more or less certain. So the accounts in their writings are an important basis for the reconstruction of the history of Indian thought.

The scriptures of the Jains that refer to Vedānta philosophy can be roughly divided into two main classes : holy scriptures (*āgama* or *siddhānta*) and philosophical writings. Besides, there are innumerable books written by Jains such as biographies of its saints, history, cosmology, ethical writings concerning life among the group as well as worldly life, poems, collections of holy sayings, moral admonishments, and stories. In the strict sense however these have but little relation with philosophical debate. In the following pages, the Vedānta thought which appears in the scriptures and that expressed in the various philosophical writings of the Middle Period will be examined separately in independent chapters.

Notes

1. Hajime Nakamura: *Indo Kodaishi* (History of Ancient India), vol. 2 (Tokyo: Shunjusha Press, 1966), pp. 432 f.

2. Since Buddhism is the teaching of the Buddha, it has come to be called Buddhism (Bauddha, or Buddha's teaching), in the same way Jainism, as it is the teaching of Jina, must be called 'Jinism' (The Teaching of Jina), so it has been asserted, but here we shall follow the usual way of speaking "Jainism".

SECTION II : VEDĀNTA THOUGHT DESCRIBED IN THE EARLY JAIN SCRIPTURES

Jainism was founded[1] around the end of the fifth century B.C. about the same time as Buddhism. About 300 B.C., it started to split into the Śvetāmbara (white-robed) and the Digambara (nude); and about one B.C. more or less, these were clearly divided and stood opposed to each other. Each of these sects relied on their own scriptures; the scriptures of the Digambara are, however, practically all non-extant today. Because of this limitation, there is no alternative but to chiefly investigate the scriptures of the Śvetāmbara. This scripture has forty-five parts in all, but what is of special importance among these are twelve parts which is called 'Aṅga'. The Aṅga scripture is recorded in a special Prākrit[2] called Ardhamāgadhī or Ārṣa, and it is the most important reference for becoming acquainted with the actual conditions of early Jainism. Its records will be relied on in the following paragraphs. It can be generally thought to be formed in the period between the third century B.C. and the beginning of the Christian era.[3]

So far as our present research has gone, the words "Upaniṣad" and "Vedānta" are not found in the Aṅga scripture. In one of the Aṅga works called *Bhagavatī*, the arts and sciences of the time are carefully listed, and of these there are five philosophical schools mentioned : Vaiśeṣika (*baisesiya*), Buddhism (*Buddhasāsaṇa*), Sāṁkhya (*Kāvila*)[4], Lokāyata (*Logāyata*) and the *Saṭṭhitaṃta*.[5] There is no reference to a Vedānta school. So at the time of compilation of the *Bhagavatī* writing, the Jains were not aware of a Brahmin group that specially revered the Upaniṣads, or if there were such an organized independent group, they were not very influential in society.

Ideas that can be regarded as Upaniṣadic or Vedāntic are described in places in the Aṅga scriptures, just as they are in early Buddhist scriptures. Though these descriptions are very brief, they are most important in investigating early Vedānta and its history. An examination of each of these propositions shows that it is expressing some conception found in the Upaniṣads.

(1) *Monistic Development*

In the early *Sūyagaḍaṃga* (1.1.1.9) the following statement is presented.

> "As what was originally one lump of clay appears in various shapes; in the same manner, consciousness (*vinnū*) takes various forms and appears as the entire world (*kasiṇe loe—kṛtsno lokaḥ*)."[6]

This thought has the same conceptual standpoint as the doctrine of Uddālaka which is clearly expressed in the *Chāndogya Upaniṣad* (6.1.4) :

> "Just as one is able to know anything made entirely from clay from one lump of clay so things that are subject to change are names which are apprehended by words.[7] Reality is only the clay."

Being (*sat*), the world principle, compared to the lump of clay, is the absolute spirit in the doctrine of Uddālaka. In regard to this sort of conception there is a close inquiry in the *Sūyagaḍaṃga* (1.1.1.10) :

> "How can one explain the law of retribution of cause and effect, that a person who commits an evil act will later himself incur suffering." If there existed merely the one *ātman* which all humanity held in common, would not the recompensing effect of an act performed by one person be incurred by another, as Ātman is the basis for all good and evil actions ?"[8]

As has been already discussed, the same point was pressed against the Buddhists as well as the Sāṃkhya school[9] and the Vedānta scholar of the early period endeavoured by every means to solve this problem.[10] Again in the same *Sūyagaḍaṃga* (2.1.25) it explains by various similes; "All existence stems from *puruṣa*, and the cause (*kāraṇa*) of all is that Īśvara. Everything in this world has *puruṣa* as its origin as well as its end. By *puruṣa* they are made; from *puruṣa* they are born; by *puruṣa* they are manifested.

All belong to *puruṣa*, and exist on *puruṣa*."[11] *Puruṣa* was originally a word for "man". It came to be used, however, to mean original cause of the spiritual world, the basic body of the universe, and again Īśvara in the thought of the orthodox **Brahmin** system from a very early age. The idea of *puruṣa* as the basic principle of the universe is found in various places in the Upaniṣads.[12]

(2) *Transcendental Theism*

In the *Sūyagaḍaṃga* (2.6.46-47), there is the teaching of the Ekadaṇḍin, which states that good act together with clear intelligence is the cause that makes emancipation possible. It then postulates "invisible, great, eternal, unbreakable, and indestructible *puruṣa*." This is within all living beings and is far superior in all ways, like the moon being superior to the various stars.[13] According to a commentary, this teaching is that of the Vedāntin school. This sort of thought is expressed in various places in the Upaniṣads. The following verses are most similar to it.

"Ātman[14] has no defilements,
Dwells further away than the air,
Uncreated, great, and lives on in eternity.

(*Bṛhad. Up.* IV, 4, 20)

"In truth, this great uncreated Ātman...
There (inside its womb of consciousness)
As governor of all things, ruler of all,
Supervisor of all, it rests.

(*Bṛhad. Up.* IV, 4, 22)

(3) *Phenomenal Illusionism*

Jainism at the time of its first developments divided all the existing philosophical teachings of the time into four classes: *kriyāvādin* (those who admit the action of the soul), *akriyāvādin* (those who do not admit the action of the soul), *ajñānavādin* (agnostics), and *vinayavādin* (upholders of disciplines). The following is one theory of the *akriyāvādins*:

"The sun does not rise, again does not sink.
The moon does not become full nor does it become new.
The whole world is in actuality determined as false.

(*Sūyagaḍaṃga* I, 12, 7)[15]

Thus the *akriyāvādins* denied the various changes in the phenomenal world. It can be seen that there were those who asserted that the whole world was false. The commentator Śīlāṅka (latter half of the ninth century) classified this as a teaching of the Śūnyavādin. There are scholars that support his view, but this is not correct.[16] When Jainism was originating, the Śūnyavāda, that is to say the Mādhyamika school, was not yet established. What is also of interest is that this same thought is clearly stated as one of the heretical teachings in the scriptures of early Buddhism also.

"Thus have I heard. At one time the Buddha dwelled in the country of Śrāvastī in the garden of Jetavana Anāthapiṇḍadārāma.

At the time the Exalted One said to the various bhikkhus: Some people maintain and set forth an opinion like this :

"The wind blows not; the fire burns not; the water flows not.
The arrow does not shoot; pregnancy is not giving birth;
The breast does not give milk.
Whether the sun and the moon sometimes rise, sometimes set,
It is sometimes light, sometimes dark.
No one is able to know.

(Chinese translation of *Saṃyutta-nikāya*, Book 7, 164 teaching)[17] This is also in the *Saṃyutta-nikāya*. (*Saṃyutta-nikāya* XXIV, I. Vo . III, p. 203)[18]

This verse is again given as a heretical teaching in the Chinese translation of the "*Jñāna-prasthāna-śāstra* (Awakening of Knowledge)",[19] the fundamental śāstra of the Sarvāstivādins. This was probably taken directly from the scriptures of early Buddhism and used again without any change. This is also explained by the venerable Vasumitra and Bhadanta[20] who are both well-known scholars of the Sarvāstivādins. For both, it is the teaching of the school which asserts a very minute and eternal soul, namely, the *ātman* as the true substance. Vasumitra interprets the ātman which is asserted by the heretical teachings as "something which is everywhere and which exists and works behind all things."

Bhadanta interpreted it as "a superior function, and something that changes all things." Both regard it as an active being and a fundamental principle which governs everything.

There can be no doubt, however, that this thought was advocated by some scholars during the first periods of Jainism as well as Buddhism, because the Jain scriptures and the scriptures of the earliest Buddhism were teaching nearly the same doctrine. As the various scholars of Hīnayāna Buddhism have commented, this was none other than a tenet of the Brāhmin scholars who assumed the *ātman* as the world principle. There are expressions more or less similar to this even in the Upaniṣads.

"The sun does not shine there, nor the moon, nor the stars—
Nor these lightnings, and much less this fire (on earth) !"
(*Kāṭhaka-Up.*, v. 14)

Practically the same words are in the *Śvetāśvatara-Upaniṣad* VI, 14; the *Muṇḍaka-Upaniṣad* II, 2, 10; and the *Bhagavadgītā*, XV, 6. The light of the phenomenal world is nothing when compared to the absolute light that is Brahman. Again in the *Śvetāśvatara-Upaniṣad* (4.9-10), the natural world was likened to the miraculous power of a god or an illusion (*māyā*); and the God Rudra, the creator of the world, was called a magician or deceiver (*māyin*).

The above quoted extracts on phenomenal illusionism are more or less similar to this thought. These ideas were advocated by one group of Brāhmins at that time, and probably became known to the Buddhists and the Jains. The idea, therefore, that all aspects of change in life and death in the world of phenomenon are not real in the higher sense, already existed at this time.[21] It later was influenced by the Mādhyamika school of Buddhism, and rapidly developed; and finally under that influence, the doctrine of Māyā (Illusion) was formed. Aside from the above, there are more passages in the Aṅga scriptures in which the thought of the Vedānta is stated.[22] A full account cannot be given here because the study of the Jain scriptures is not sufficiently advanced at present.

Notes

1. It has been handed down that Mahāvīra did not originate a new religion at all, but rather revolutionized and developed the religion of a sect called Nigaṇṭha which had been in existence prior to him. The actual conditions of that sect, prior to him, are almost all unclear.
2. However, what has been handed down to the present are 11 sections.
3. On the date of formation of the Jain canon, cf. Walther Schubring:

The Doctrine of the Jainas Described after the Old Sources (Delhi : Motilal Banarsidass, 1962), pp. 57; 73-125.

4. A. Weber: *Über ein Fragment der Bhagavatī*, II Teil, S. 248.

5. Perhaps it points to a Sāṁkhya-yoga theory. Cf. H. Ui, *Indo tetsugakushi*, p. 465. *Ṣaṣṭitantra* is discussed by Emil Frauwallner in his *History of Indian Philosophy*, vol. I (Delhi : Motilal Banarsidass, 1973), pp. 252, 262 f., 388.

6. Some non-Jain teachers said:

"As the Earth, though it is but one pile, presents many forms, so the intelligent (principle, viz. the *ātman*) appears under various forms as the universe." *Sūyagaḍaṃga* I, 1, 1, 9. (Hermann Jacobi's translation).

Jahāya puḍbavīthūbhe ege nāṇāhi dīsai /
evaṃ bho kasiṇe loe vinnū nāṇāhi dīsai // (Vaidya's edition is referred to).

The commentator explains this opinion as the doctrine of the Vedāntins. (Hermann Jacobi: Jaina Sūtras, *Sacred Books of the East*, vol. XLV, p. 237).

7. According to my own interpretation of the word *vācārambhaṇa*, which will be discussed on another occasion. Cf. the Brahma-sūtra. II.1.14.

8. Hermann Jacobi, *SBE*, Vol. XLV, p. 237.

9. Jōyuishiki-ron (*Vijñapti-mātratā-siddhi*), Vol. I, p 4; *Madhyamaka-hṛdaya* VIII, 63; *Tattvasaṃgrahapañjikā* ad v. 151; *Sāṁkhya-Kārikā* 18.

10. *Gauḍapādīya-Kārikā* III, 5; *Madhyamaka-hṛdaya*, VIII, 12.

11. *ahāvare tacce purisajāe isarakūraṇie tti āhijjai* /
...iha khalu dhammā purisādiyā purisottariyā purisappaṇīyā purisasaṃbhūyā purisapajjoiyā purisa abhisamannāgayā purisam eva abhibhūya ciṭṭhanti /

12. Sukhtankar, WZKM. Vol. XXII, 1908, p. 130, n. I. This verse in the *Sūyagaḍaṅga* is said to be reminiscent not only of the ideas but also the manner of expression of Rāmānuja. It can be thought, however, that it has more connections with the Upaniṣads.

13. *avvattarūvaṃ purisaṃ, mahantaṃ saṇātaṇaṃ akkhayam avvayaṃ ca* /
savvesu bhūesu vi savvao se cando va tārāhi samattarūve //
(Interpreted by H. Jacobi, *SBE*, Vol. XLV, p. 417).

14. Most of the time, *ātman* and *puruṣa* are taken in the Upaniṣads as practically synonymous.

15. *nāicco udei na attham ei na candimā vaḍḍhai hāyaī vā* /
salilā na sandanti na vanti vāyā vañjho niyao kasiṇe hu loe //

Based on the edition by P. L. Vaidya. Sukhtankar cites this from another edition as;

vañjhe niie kasiṇe hu loe = vandhyo niyataḥ kṛtsnaḥ khalu lokaḥ.
(WZKM. Vol. XXII, 1908, p. 130, n. 3)

16. Sukhtankar: *op. cit.* p. 130, n. 3.

17. *TT.*, Vol. II, p. 45 a.

18. *kismiṃ nu kho bhikkhave sati kim upādāya kim abhinivissa evaṃ-diṭṭhi uppajjati* //
Na vātā vāyanti na najjo sandanti na gabbhiniyo vijāyanti na candimasuriyā udenti vā apenti vā esikatthāyiṭṭhitā iti //

19. Cited in *TT.*, Vol. XXVI, p. 914 a; p. 1028 c.

[Translated from Japanese into English by Akira Hata]

20. Referred to in the Chinese version of the *Mahāvibhāṣā-śāstra*, Vol. 199 (*TT.*, Vol. XXVII, pp. 995c-996a; cf. p. 1002 c.

21. In the Buddhist scriptures also, this sort of expression is seen. *Udāna*, I, 10, p. 9. Here it is concerned with the state of emancipation. A similar thought is seen in the *Māhābhāṣya*, 3.2.123 of Patañjali and the fact that it is condemned was pointed out by Y. Kanakura, in the journal, "*Shūkyokenkyū* (Study of religion)", Fourth year, 2.3, pp. 151-164. Again the existence of the *ekavādin* which was a kind of a teaching of no-process is pointed out in one of the early Jain scriptures, the *Thāṇāṅga*. (Y. Kanakura, *Indo-kodai-seishinshi*, (Spiritual history of old India), p. 170).

22. In the Tenth Aṅga, the *Paṇhāvāgaraṇaim* (p. 28b) it states:

eko āyā akārako vedako ya sukayassa dukkayassa ya karaṇāṇi kāraṇāṇi savvahā savvahiṃ ca nicco ya nikkio nigguno ya aṇuvalevo tti.

A. Sen interprets this as a saying of the Sāṃkhya school, and Abhayadeva notes it as one of *ātmādvaitavādyādayaḥ*. (A. Sen: *A Critical Introduction to the Paṇhāvāgaraṇāim*, p. 35).

SECTION III. : YĀJÑAVALKYA AND OTHER UPANIṢADIC THINKERS IN A JAIN TRADITION

The ideas of Upaniṣadic thinkers are set forth sporadically in the scriptures of early Buddhism and Jainism, but the names of their expounders are not mentioned individually.[1] The various ideas of individual thinkers of the Upaniṣads could be known only through the Upaniṣads and the corresponding passages of the Brāhmaṇas. However, the *Isibhāsiyāiṃ*, an old Jain text, which came to be known and published some years ago,[2] may give some clues to know more details of the ideas of some Upaniṣadic thinkers.

Yājñavalkya, who is regarded as the greatest philosopher of the Upaniṣads, is mentioned in the 12th *ajjhayaṇa* as Jaṇṇavakka. Let us examine the sayings ascribed to him as follows :

'Having known[3] that as long as there is the desire for the world, so long is there the desire fo wealth[4]; and that, as long as there is the desire for wealth, so long there is the desire for the world, and having known[5] the desire for the world and the desire for wealth [i.e. having annulled them], one should go by the path of the cow (*gopatha*). One should not go by the Great Path (*mahāpatha*). It was said by Jaṇṇavakka, the worthy one (arhat), the ṛṣi, as follows :

"Just as doves, pheasants, and cows take morning-food in this world, even so the sage (*muni*), having entered the sphere of action (*gocara*, the area for begging), should not chat, nor should he be excited[6] [with anger, even if he cannot get food while begging]. (v. 1)

He should seek for food which is pure, as alms with the five beggars (i.e. *śramaṇas*, *brāhmaṇas*, the poor, guests and dogs).[7] What has been obtained by the one who is free from faults has been got in the best way to annul [these defilements]. (v. 2)

He should consider the Way which is in accordance with the essence [of the Act) and which causes fruitful results.

He should consider the result of anger, etc. (*krodha, māna, māyā*, and *lobha*)[8] of himself and of another person." (v. 3)

Thus[9] he is the Enlightened One (*buddha*), the calm one (*virata*), free from evil, the tamed one, fit for liberation, the leader. He will never return to this mundane existence. So I say.'

The thoughts introduced here coincide very well with those of Yājñavalkya set forth in the *Bṛhadāraṇyaka-upaniṣad.*

At the request 'to explain the Brahman that is immediately present and directly perceived, that is the self in all things', Yājñavalkya answered :

'It is that which transcends hunger and thirst, sorrow and delusion, old age and death. The Brahmins,[10] having known that self, having overcome the desire[11] for sons, the desire for wealth,[12] the desire for worlds, live the life of mendicants. That which is the desire for sons is the desire for wealth; that which is the desire for wealth is the desire for the worlds, for both these are but desires. Therefore let a Brāhmaṇa, after he has done with learning, desire to live as a child. When he has done (both) with the state of childhood and with learning, then he becomes a silent meditator.[13] Having done with (both) the non-meditative and the meditative states, he becomes a Brāhmaṇa (a knower of Brahman).'[14]

The attitude of becoming sincere and pure-minded like a child was encouraged by Vedāntins also in later days.[15] In later Mahāyāna also the Five Kinds of Behaviour[16] which should be practised by Bodhisattvas were encouraged, and the Behaviour of the Child is one of them.

Moreover, this ideal has been common to different traditions; it is a universal phenomenon in the history of ideas of mankind. The primordial state of man was compared to that of the child by Lao-tzu.[17] Christ also said :

'Truly, I say to you, unless you turn and become like children, you will never enter the kingdom of heaven. Whoever humbles himself like this child, he is the greatest in the kingdom of heaven.[18]

According to another tradition, Yājñavalkya taught as follows:

'On knowing Him, in truth, one becomes an ascetic (*muni*). Desiring Him only as their world, monks wander forth. Verily, because they know this, the ancient [sages] did not wish for offspring. What shall we do with offspring [they said], we who have attained this Self, this world. They, having risen above the desire for sons, the desire for wealth, the desire for worlds, led the life of a mendicant. For the desire for sons is the desire for wealth and the desire for wealth is the desire for worlds; both these are, indeed, desires only.'[19]

There are striking coincidences between the Upaniṣadic and Jain traditions. Both traditions especially mention as human desires the desire for worlds (*lokaiṣaṇā*) and the desire for wealth (*vittaiṣaṇā*) which are explained as identical with each other. The *Bṛhadāraṇyaka-upaniṣad* mentions the desire for offspring *putraiṣaṇā*) in addition, which is lacking in the Jain text. 'The desire for offspring' is explained as 'taking a wife' (*dārasaṃgraha*) by Śaṅkara[20]. In the later Vedānta school the above-mentioned three constitute the 'Three Desires' (*eṣaṇātraya*), which became an important concept. However, insofar as we can judge from the context of the above-cited passage of the *Isibhāsiyāiṃ*, it is likely that Yājñavalkya did not necessarily fix the 'Three Desires'. In any case, the practice of silence by the sage (*muni*) was encouraged by Yājñavalkya. In this respect also both the Upaniṣadic and Jain texts coincide with each other.

It is not clear what was meant by the teaching : 'One should go by the path of the cow (*gopatha*).' According to the *Bṛhadāraṇyaka-upaniṣad,* King Janaka of Videha granted a thousand cows to Yājñavalkya, and in connection with this the following verses are cited :

'The narrow ancient path (*aṇuḥ panthāḥ*) which stretches far away, has been touched (found) by me, has been realized by me.

By it, the wise, the knowers of Brahman, go up to the heavenly world after the fall of this body, being freed [even while living].

On that path they say there is white, blue, yellow, green and red. That path was found by a Brahmin and by it goes the knower of Brahman, the doer of right and the shining one.'[21]

The phrase: 'to go on the path of (to live on)' (*tena pathā*) is common to both traditions. The teaching: 'to live on alms with detached mind' is conveyed in both the Upaniṣadic and Jain texts as peculiar to the teachings of Yājñavalkya. The thought of *karman*[22] (and of its *vipāka*, fruition) is said to have been propounded for the first time by Yājñavalkya among the many Upaniṣadic philosophers, and this is evidenced by the Jain text.

These facts of coincidence will lead us to the conclusion that although the *Isibhāsiyāiṃ* does not convey the thoughts of Yājñavalkya as a whole, it sets forth some characteristic aspects of his thoughts. Uddālaka, another great philosopher of the Upaniṣads, is mentioned as Addālaa in the *Isibhāsiyāiṃ* (35th *ajjhayaṇa*) : Although the descriptions in the Jain text are fairly detailed, they do not coincide with the thoughts of Uddālaka as set forth in the sixth chapter of the *Chāndogya-upaniṣad*. Only the description of transmigration is somewhat similar :

'In the wide-spread wilderness of transmigration, he harms himself again, and again.' (*cāturanta-saṃsāra-kāntāre punaḥ punar ātmānaṃ parividhvaṃsanti*)

The possibility of liberation by wisdom also is set forth :

'Therefore, in order to annul these (defilements), having acquired the right and perfect knowledge, and having known oneself and another's self, one should act, free from environmental bondages.' (v. 9)

Only this much is the description of the thought of Addālaa (= Uddālaka).

The *Isibhāsiyāiṃ* (4th *ajjhayaṇa*) describes also the teachings of Aṅgarisi or Aṅgarisi Bhāraddāa. Who was he ? The Buddhist *Theragāthā* (219-21) conveys three verses ascribed to Aṅgaṇika Bhāradvāja. At the first glance one might think of correspondence between the two texts. According to the Buddhist text, he was a Brahmin, and practised asceticism, with the Fire God as his deity. However, the passage in the *Theragāthā* is too short to extract any conclusion or identification. This person is not mentioned in other Buddhist scriptures. Rather, do we not have to seek for the counterpart in Upaniṣads ?

According to the *Muṇḍaka-upaniṣad*, Brahmā the Creator, taught the knowledge of Brahman to Atharvan, and Atharvan taught it to Aṅgir. He in his turn taught it to Bhāradvāja Satyavāha. The latter taught it to Aṅgiras. The knowledge consisted of the higher and the lower knowledge.

'Two kinds of knowledge are to be known, as, indeed, the knowers of Brahman declare—the higher as well as the lower. Of these, the lower is the *Ṛg-veda*, the *Yajur-veda*, the *Sāma-veda*, the *Atharva-veda*, Phonetics, Ritual, Grammar, Etymology, Metrics and Astrology. And the higher is that by which the Undecaying is apprehended.

That which is ungraspable, without family, without caste, without sight or hearing, without hands or feet, eternal, all-pervading, omnipresent, exceedingly subtle, that is the Undecaying which the wise perceive as the source of beings.'[23]

The phrases corresponding to the above-cited verses in the *Isibhāsiyāiṃ* are as follows :

'The knowledge by which I know [my] Self overtly or secretly as without beginning or as with beginning is motionless and permanent... The heart of man is deep and hardly to be understood.' (vv. 3; 4)

These phrases do not coincide with the above-cited ones exactly, but convey a similar tone. According to a Jain canon (*Ṭhāṇa* 390 a), there are two surnames, Bhāraddā and Aṅgirasa, in the Kāsava (Kāśyapa) *gotra*.[24] This coincides with the tradition in the *Muṇḍaka-upaniṣad*. Is it not possible to assume that the two persons with different surnames were put together as one person in later days ?

Then the teaching of Jama (Yama) is said as follows :

'The man who is not delighted when there is acquisition and who is not dejected when there is no acquisition—he is the supreme one among men, like Indra [Sayakkau, Śatakratu] among gods.' (*ajjhayaṇa* 43)

We do not find any corresponding phrase in the *Kāṭhaka-upaniṣad* whose teachings are ascribed to Yama. The only phrase which might be taken into consideration is :

'Realizing through self-contemplation (*adhyātma-yoga*) that primal God, the wise man leaves behind both joy and sorrow.' (*Kaṭha-up.*, I.2.12).

In Buddhist literature, on the other hand, Yama is regarded as the god of justice or the judge, and it is not likely that such a teaching is ascribed to Yama. There is a legend that a monk called Yamaka expressed the thought that the ascetic whose mental defilements have been annulled will be reduced to annihilation after death, and that Sāriputta admonished him to give up such a wrong view.[25] This legend does not necessarily conflict with the Jain tradition, but it would be rather difficult to identify Yamaka with the above-cited Jama.

The first *ajjhayaṇa* of the *Isibhāsiyāiṃ* sets forth the teachings of Deva-Nārada, and we do not find in earlier Upaniṣads passages which directly correspond with them. In the *Chāndogya-upaniṣad* (VII. 1 f.), the teachings which Sanatkumāra conferred upon Nārada are set forth, but as a whole they do not correspond with the teachings of Deva-Nārada in the *Isibhāsiyāiṃ*. Similar expressions are as follows :

(*Isibhāsiyāiṃ*)	(*Chāndogya-up.*)
savvato vippamukk 'appā (v. 2).	*sarvagranthīnāṃ vipramokṣaḥ* (VII. 26. 2).
saccaṃ c 'evôvasevatī (*upasevati*), *dattaṃ c 'evôvasevātī*, *bambhaṃ c 'evôvasevatī*. *saccaṃ c 'evôvahāṇavaṃ*...	*eṣa tu vā ativadati yaḥ satyenātivadati* (VII. 16). *yadā vai vijānāti, atha satyaṃ vadati, nāvijānan satyaṃ vadati, vijānann eva satyaṃ vadati* (VII. 17).[26]
savv' atthese samaṃ care (v. 2).[27]	*sarvam āpnoti sarvaśaḥ* (VII. 26.2).

These should be taken as partial coincidences.

From the above investigation the following conclusions are reached :

1. The teachings ascribed to Jaṇṇavakka coincide with the teachings of Yājñavalkya in the *Bṛhadāraṇyaka-upaniṣad*. There is no doubt that the *Isibhāsiyāiṃ* conveys some thoughts and assertions of this Upaniṣadic philosopher. Some sages mentioned in this work may also be the same as those in the Upaniṣads.

2. If this conjecture is right, it means that the *Isibhāsiyāiṃ* conveys various assertions of Upaniṣadic thinkers which are missing in the extant Upaniṣads. They may turn out to be valuable materials for ascertaining the thoughts of some Upaniṣadic thinkers. One point which should be taken into consideration is that the sayings in the *Isibhāsiyāiṃ* do not necessarily

convey faithfully what the Upaniṣadic thinkers taught, for the *Isibhāsiyāiṃ* uses peculiarly Jain phrases and terms.

3. Studies along this line will give some clues to fix the dates of Upaniṣads. It is accepted that the *Isibhāsiyāiṃ* is earlier than the *Suttanipāta* which is probably the oldest scripture of Buddhism. Then it has been made clear that the thoughts of earlier Upaniṣads—which are not necessarily the same as those set forth in extant Upaniṣads—came into existence still earlier than that.

4. In the days when Buddhism and Jainism arose, the distinction between the Āstikas and the Nāstikas based on whether they accept the Veda or not was not conspicuous. There were many homeless recluses or wandering ascetics. The thoughts of some of them were incorporated into the Upaniṣads and were conveyed to posterity. The orders deriving from some ascetics such as Pāsa and Mahāvīra merged into one as Jainism. The order centering around Sāriputta developed as Buddhism. Śākyamuni as the religious leader was ignored by some Jains, for he is not mentioned in the *Isibhāsiyāiṃ*; the representative of Buddhism was Sāriputta in this Jain text. Many other thinkers whose thoughts are set forth in this Jain work have left no sayings nor texts, for their orders became extinct in later days.

5. The Vedānta school which aimed at formulating synoptical and consistent interpretations of various Upaniṣadic passages had not yet been established in the period when the *Isibhāsiyāiṃ* was composed.

Notes

1. Hajime Nakamura: the present work, *supra*.

2. *Isibhāsiyāiṃ*, ed. by Walther Schubring, Nachrichten von der Akademie der Wissenschaften in Göttingen, Philologisch-Historische Klasse, 1942, no. 6, pp. 489-576; 1952, no. 2, pp. 21-52. Cf. Walther Schubring: *Die Lehre der Jainas* (Berlin und Leipzig: Walter de Gruyter, 1935), S. 83. This text is not included in the Aṅgas, but is very old.

3. *āṇaccā*. I adopted Schubring's interpretation of it as *ājñayā* in another passage (p. 31). Schubring thinks that this word has crept in by mistake in this passage (p. 557-8), but we do not think this is necessarily to be assumed.

4. As was pointed out by Schubring, this expression is used in *Āyāraṅga*, Bambhaceräiṃ, 3. 14 ff. Cf. *no logass'esaṇaṃ care*, *Āyāra*, 17.26.

5. *parinnāe*. This term is used in connection with the first *satya* of the Four Noble Truths of Buddhism.

6. The same phrase is used in *Isibhāsiyāiṃ*, XLI, verse 17.

7. Ratnachandraji: *Ardhamāgadhi Dictionary*, p. 335. Schubring (p. 558) says that this explanation is found in *Thāṇa*, but his interpretation of *samaṇa* as *nirgrantha* seems to be too narrow. There must have been those who were not *nirgranthas* among the *samaṇas* of those days.

8. Supplemented from the commentary. These are the fundamental vices according to Jainism. But it is doubtful whether Yājñavalkya virtually admitted these four as a set.

9. The following phrase is repeated as a set phrase always at the end of each *ajjhayaṇa* of the *Isibhāsiyāiṃ*. Concerning its interpretation, cf. my article in *Journal of Indian and Buddhist Studies*, May 1966.

10. The interpretation to take *brāhmaṇa* for 'the one who has realized Brahman' or 'the true Brahmin' is found in *Bṛhad. Up.*, III.8.10; *Chānd. Up.*, IV.1.7.

11. *eṣaṇā*=*kāma* (Śaṅkara).

12. According to Śaṅkara and Ānandajñāna, wealth is two-fold, i.e. of men and of gods (Śaṅkara ad *Bṛhad. Up.*, III.5.1).

13. *muni*. Śaṅkara interprets it as 'the man who thinks': *mananān munir yogī bhavatīty arthaḥ* (ad *Bṛhad. Up.*, IV.4.22). This interpretation is different from the ordinary *Volksetymologie*-explanation deriving *muni* from *mauna* (silence) but it coincides rather with the results of research by modern comparative philology. Mayrhofer connects it with *manyate* (to think). (Manfred Mayrhofer, *Kurzgefasstes etymologisches Wörterbuch des Altindischen* (A Concise Etymological Sanskrit Dictionary, Heidelberg, 1953 f., Lieferung 17, 1963, pp. 654-5). Turner and other scholars think that *muni* is derived from the old form of the verb *muṇāti* (to know) (R. L. Turner, *A Comparative Dictionary of the Indo-Aryan Languages*, Oxford University Press, 1962 f., Fasc. VIII, 1965, p. 588). Moreover, the fact that *muta* is used instead of *mata* in the older layers of the *Suttanipāta* may confirm this conjecture from the other side (*Suttanipāta*, 714 790; 793; 797-8; 802; 812-13; 887; 1086; 1122).

14. *Bṛhad. Up.*, III.5.1. On the interpretation of this passage, cf. *Brahmasūtra*, III.4. 47-50.

15. Śaṅkara ad *Brahmasūtra*, III.4. 50.

16. The Five Kinds of Behaviour are : The Sacred Behaviour, the Brahma Behaviour, the Deva Behaviour, the Child Behaviour and the Sick Behaviour (A Chinese version of the (Mahāyāna) *Mahāparinirvāṇa-sūtra*, vol. 11. *TT*, vol. 12, p. 673 b).

17. *Lao-tzu*, chapter 20.

18. Matthew, 18. 3-4.

19. *Bṛhad. Up.*, IV.4. 22.

20. ad *Bṛhad. Up.*, III.5. 1.

21. *Bṛhad. Up.*, IV. 4. 8-9.

22. *Bṛhad. Up.*, III.2. 13; IV. 4. 5; IV. 4. 3-4.

23. *Muṇḍ. Up.*, I. 1. 4-6.

24. Schubring, *Isibhāsiyāiṃ*, p. 493.
25. *Saṃyutta-nikāya*, XXII. 85, vol. III, pp. 109-17. *TT.*, vol. 2, p. 30 c; p. 31 c.
26. The meditation on Brahman is set forth throughout the teaching.
27. Cf. *savvato virate dante savvato parinivvuḍe.*

P. S. The English translations of passages of the Upaniṣads in this section have been cited with slight modification from S. Radhakrishnan's *The Principal Upaniṣads* (London, George Allen and Unwin, 1953).

SECTION IV. THE VEDĀNTA AS NOTICED IN MEDIAEVAL JAIN LITERATURE

After the compilation of the canonical literature many Jain dogmaticians came to compose diverse compendiums of the doctrine and to engage in philosophical discussion. There are extant a number of Jain works composed especially after the fourth century, A.D. Some of them were written in Prākrit, others in Sanskrit, and quite a few works refer to the Vedāntic thought prior to Śaṅkara. Moreover, it is peculiarly interesting to find some sayings of Jain scholars in which Vedāntic influence can be found. For example, Kundakunda, a Digambara scholar (fourth century, A.D.), said as follows :

> "He who thinks, 'I kill,' and 'I am killed by another' is foolish and ignorant. But the wise never think so."
>
> (*Samayasāra*, v. 262)[1]

This coincides with the following verses of the *Kāṭhaka-Upaniṣad* (II, 18; 19)—as regards the thought at least :

> "This (*ātman*) is unborn, eternal, ever-lasting and permanent; and even if the body is killed, it is not killed. If the killer thinks that he kills (another person,) if the killed thinks that he is killed, they do not know (the truth). This one does not kill, nor is that one killed."

Nearly the same sentences are found in the *Bhagavadgītā* II, 19 and 20. It seems that Kundakunda knew the concept of *ātman* in the Brahmin orthodoxy. With regard to the nature of ātman he asserted that 'intelligence is *ātman*' and that 'without *ātman* intelligence cannot exist.'[2] According to the commentary it seems that he regarded intelligence as a quality (*dharma*) of *ātman*. However, there is no explicit evidence that he was referring to the Upaniṣads or the Vedāntins.[3] This holds true of the works of other Jain scholars in those days. So the extent of their interchange of ideas with, or influence by, the

Upaniṣadic scriptures or the Vedāntins as an existing school is not clear, although they must have known something of the Vedāntic thought of Brahmin orthodoxy.

From the period of about 600 A.D. things came to be different, The *Dvādaśāranayacakra* by Mallavādin (c. 400 A.D.) was commented upon by Siṃhasūri (7th century A.D.).[4] Explanations of the Vedānta philosophy appear in the commentary portion, and they are important for they are prior to Śaṅkara. Non-dualism is discussed. (advaitajñatvadarśanam advaitam, p. 222; advaita, p. 223; advaitavāda, pp. 271; 279; advaita, advaitārtha, p. 288).

Samantabhadra, the great Digambara scholar, explicitly attacked the Advaita theory of the Vedāntins in his work *Āpta-mīmāṃsā* (or *Devāgamastotra*). This work, consisting of 115 verses, is an introduction to the work *Gandhahastimahābhāṣya* which is a commentary on Umāsvāti's *Tattvārthādhigamasūtra*. Attacking and criticizing the theories of other philosophical schools of those days, it tried to prove that the Jain *tīrthaṅkara* was the Omniscient One. It was greatly esteemed in later days, and wielded great influence. Verses 24 to 27 of the work attack the Advaita theory. [The text was edited[5] together with the commentary *Aṣṭaśatī* on it written by Akalaṅka (c. 700-770, A.D. who was approximately contemporary with Śaṅkara]. The verses run as follows :

> verse 24 :
>
> "On the stated, one-sided view of the Advaita theory also our experienced distinction between the agents and the actions would be nullified. Nothing comes out of itself."[6]

[*Aṣṭaśatī*] The uncovering of errors in one-sided views (*ekānta*) on being (*sat*) etc., is what is stated [in the following verses]. If [the Vedānta school] should say, "Well, because we admit the one-sided view of *Advaita* the theory of many-sidedness (*anekānta* or the doctrine of the Jains) cannot be established," [we reply] "That is not right. For [the view of the Vedānta school] contradicts our sense-perception (*pratyakṣa*) and the like. The distinction between the subject of action (*kāraka*) and his action (*kriyā*) is not a mere assumption, but is established for every body through the means of knowledge (*pramāṇa*). But [the Vedānta theory] would be contrary to it. It is, as it were, the same as in the case of the theory of momentariness (*kṣaṇika*, i.e. the Buddhist theory). [If what the Advaitins maintain be right], nothing arises from itself, nor does it arise from anything else, but just as in the case of the person who has slept well (he does not have any experience of birth and destruction). For there is no way that one can understand [Advaitism as it stands). Therefore, the argument (of Advaitism), which contradicts our experience, is not valid. It is exactly the same as the theory of non-self (*nairātmya*) (the Buddhist theory) is not correct. Then likewise the non-dualism also contradicts the sense-perception (*pratyakṣa*) that there exists a difference between the agent and his action.

> verse 25 :
>
> "(In the Advaita theory) there would be no distinction between (good and bad) *karmas*, no distinction between (favourable and unfavourable) rewards, and no distinction between (pleasant and unpleasant) areas. There would exist no distinction between knowledge and ignorance. The same would be true of the distinction between bondage and liberation."[7]

[*Aṣṭaśatī*] For the purpose of attaining (good) fruits one should examine through one's own consideration, Advaitism and other theories which contradict the means of knowledge. For it is not reasonable for (our) thinking to have an understanding of it in different ways. (The non-dual principle) which is free from the distinctions such as merit and demerit, pleasure and pain, this and the other world, knowledge and nescience, bondage and final release, should be rejected by those who act by their own consideration. It is just as the theory of non-self (*nairātmya-darśana,* Buddhism) should be rejected. Therefore, such a discussion has now taken place here.

> verse 26 :
>
> "If the principle of Advaita should be established by means of reason (*hetu*), there must exist a duality (*dvaita*) between reason and what is to be proved (*sādhya*).
>
> If (the principle of Advaita) should be established without reason, why should not dualism too be established from mere words alone ?"[8]

[*Aṣṭaśatī*] What is not established (in any way) should not be adopted by those who wish to gain profit and to discard disadvantage. For example, "the one-sided view of emptiness" (*śūnyaikānta*) (the theory of the Mādhyamika school) should not be adopted. Therefore, non-dualism, i.e., which cannot be established, (should not be adopted).... In this case (the fact that non-dualism cannot be established) will not become a non-established reason (*asiddha hetu*). (Reason for that will be explained:) (1) If the establishment of the principle of non-duality be based upon the reason (*sādhana*), then there would exist the duality of that which is to be established and its reason. Or, in the same way as the principle of non-duality (*advaita*) is established, how is duality not established ? (2) If (although the reason does not exist) one accomplishes one's objective by merely saying it, everything would be established for all. (Accordingly, the theory of non-dualism cannot be established).

verse 27 :

"Without dualism (*dvaita*), *advaita* cannot be established, just in the same way unless reason (*hetu*) exists, fallacious reason (*ahetu*) cannot exist. Negation of anything which has a name cannot exist without (the existence of) that which should be negated."[9]

[*Aṣṭaśatī*] The word 'non-dualism' (*advaita*) points to the ultimate truth (*paramārtha*) which contradicts that which one thinks in his heart, for it is a single word to which a negative prefix is attached. It is the same case with the expression "non-cause" (*ahetu*). In this case the range of applicability (for the negative prefix) is not too broad. (That is, if the prefix 'a' of *advaita* is a negative affix one must not assert that the range of application of the negative affix is too broad). For, the negative affix is related to the negation of a thing as something of such a nature. (Now) it must be thought that in all cases, if there is nothing to be negated, the negation of anything which has the name is not possible. (Therefore, the negation of duality must admit the existence of duality).

So far is Samantabhadra's criticism of the Vedānta theory, and then he begins to attack the Vāiśeṣika and other systems. In the above-cited short passage we find some aspects of early Vedānta philosophy of those days. The Vedānta philosophy which Samantabhadra knew of can be summarized as follows:

(1) The term "*advaita*" is not one which was originally coined by the Jains, and so he must have adopted it from some other theory current in philosophical circles before him. Therefore we are led to the conclusion that the term '*advaita*' originated before

600 A.D. In those days, about 600 A.D., when Samantabhadra lived, there was prominently current a philosophical system called "Advaita".

(2) Considering verse 24, the Vedāntins of those days thought that *brahman* causes the universe by itself (*ekam, asahāyam*), i.e., by *brahman* as the efficient cause, and from itself (*svasmāt*), i.e., from *brahman* as the material cause. There is no reference to the individual self, but, as the theory is called the '*Advaita*,' they must have thought that the individuals come into existence due to the manifestation of *brahman*. The theory was thorough monism. However, the Vedānta philosophy discussed here admits the *emergence* of the whole universe out of *brahman*, and not the non-emergence (*ajati*) of it. In terms of philosophy, their standpoint was the emanation theory (*pariṇāmavāda*), not the illusion theory (*vivartavāda*). This is why Samatabhadra pointed out the impossibility of emergence or coming into existence of the universe on the Vedāntic theory. The Vedānta philosophy in his days, although it was referred to as 'Advaita,' seems not to have set forth the *māyā* theory or illusion theory as was done by the followers of Śaṅkara in later days. Considering the fact that Samantabhadra and Akalaṅka repeat the criticism that 'if we should adopt the assertion of the Advaitins, all the differences of the phenomenal world would be annulled, and all practical life would come to be impossible,' we have to think that the Advaitins of their day though adopting a monistic standpoint, accepted the differences of the phenomenal world, and did not deny them. If the Advaitins then had asserted that all the aspects of the phenomenal world are in reality false and illusory, the Jain scholars would inevitably have made a frontal attack on this assertion, and would not have resorted to such a round-about way of *reductio ad absurdum* (*prasaṅga*). It was possible for both the Jains and the Advaitins to engage in such a controversy because both the parties based themselves on the same presupposition that the phenomenal differences are not false and illusory. Anyhow, it is noteworthy that the appellation *advaita* came into use among the Vedāntins before Śaṅkara.

Investigating carefully the passage of Akalaṅka's commentary on those verses, which is more than a hundred years after Samantabhadra, we can notice the following two features concerning the Vedāntic theory of those days.

(1) Akalaṅka, criticizing the Advaita theory, very often asserts that the Advaita theory commits the same fallacy as the Non-ego theory (*nairātmyadarśana*), and that it coincides with 'the extreme theory of the Void' (*śūnyaikānta*), or with 'the theory of momentariness' (*kṣaṇika*). It seems that the Vedāntic theory of his days which had some relations with Akalaṅka set forth a doctrine which was very similar to that of Buddhist philosophy. This situation is easily understandable, when we consider the fact that he was a contemporary with Śaṅkara and the *Māṇḍūkya-kārikās* must have already been composed. This corresponds exactly with the fact that, in the camp of Buddhism, Śāntarakṣita in the same period said that the thought of the *Aupaniṣadas* differs very slightly from the Buddhist thought.[10]

(2) Akalaṅka interprets '*advaita*' as the highest reality (*paramārtha*); this interpretation is often shared by the Śaṅkaraite Advaitins.[11] It seems that Akalaṅka, knowing the existence of Advaitins influenced by Mahāyāna Buddhists, wrote his commentary on the verses by Samantabhadra, with them in mind.

Next we shall consider the philosophical significance of the criticism by Samantabhadra and Akalaṅka on such an Advaitic theory. The contents of their criticism can be summed up as the following :

(1) Absolute idealism cannot make clear how it is that dualistic differences of the phenomenal world are established. (vv. 24; 25)

(2) Non-duality (*advaita*) cannot be proved by means of logic. (v. 26)

(3) The concept of non-duality as such presupposes the existence of duality. (v. 27)

(4) Practical life cannot be based on a standpoint of absolute monism. (v. 25)

Let us first consider the second point. The Vedāntins also admitted that the one fundamental principle of *brahman* (or *ātman*) cannot be proved by means of logic (the three-propositional or five-propositional argumentation). This is why the Vedāntins emphasize that the absolute can be comprehended only by means of intuition (*anubhava*) apart from logical argumentation. Therefore they resorted to logic only in the cases when they refuted the assertions of the opponents, and did not apply them to the absolute.[12] And the logic they resorted to was characteristically *reductio ad absurdum* (*prasaṅga*) which aimed at pointing out clearly the fallacies or incongruities involved in the assertions of the opponents. This feature is conspicuous in the *Māṇḍūkya-kārikās,* the works of Śaṅkara and Śrīharṣa's *Khaṇḍanakhaṇḍakhādya.* As the resorting by Advaitins to logic is solely for *prasaṅga,* and not for proving the existence of *brahman* as such, the second criticism (v. 26) must be judged to have failed in refuting the Advaitins.

Likewise, the third criticism (v. 27)[13] cannot be regarded as hitting the vulnerable point in absolute monism. Even the Advaitins do not deny duality (dvaita) wholly. They assert only that duality is true from the standpoint of daily experience (*vyavahārāvasthā*),[14] but not from the standpoint of absolute truth (*paramārtha-avasthā*). Therefore duality and non-duality are not concepts directly opposed to each other on the same level; their dimensions are different. Non-duality is thought of from a standpoint which transcends duality. Non-duality is always negative to duality, but duality is established not as the negation of non-duality in the same dimension; but as something which is dependent (based) on the principle of non-duality.

When we consider that the relation of duality and non-duality in the Advaita school is of such a character, we shall be able to understand that the fourth criticism (v. 25) has also gone amiss. The Advaitins admitted the possibility of all kinds of practical activity on 'the standpoint of daily experience' (*vyavahārika-satyatva*), which concept was firmly implanted by them in Brahmin orthodoxy. Their replies to such a criticism seem to be all right so far as they go. Or we may put this way—As such a criticism was directed at them, the post-Śaṅkara Vedāntins came to particularly emphasize the distinction between the standpoint of the absolute truth and that of daily experience. Throughout such controversy the significance of the confrontation between the Advaitic standpoint of transcending logic and the Jain one of esteeming it should be fully considered.

The first item of the Jain criticism exactly hits the vulnerable point in absolute monism. How is it possible that the absolutely non-differentiated, ultimate one principle should develop the variety of difference in the phenomenal world ? If the absolute is utterly undifferentiated and one, it must remain still as one and the same for aeons. Why is it that the aspects of change and transience come into existence ? This criticism was already raised by an opponent in the *Brahmasūtra* II, 1, 24. It was an important problem for the metaphysics of absolute monism. Later philosophers of this school toiled to solve this difficult problem, and finally came to solve it by evolving the principle called 'Ignorance' (*avidyā*) or 'Illusion' (*māyā*). By means of this the Advaitavāda was established, equipped with clear metaphysical theories. But they could not escape attacks by other schools. Later Jain scholars concentrated on attacking this principle of *avidyā* or *māyā*. Hemacandra. the great Jain scholar (twelfth century A.D.) confronted it with the following dilemma :

"If māyā is being (*sat*), then two principles (*brahman* and *māyā*) will be established. (So, the assertion of non-duality is negated).

If māyā is non-being (*asat*), then from whom will the variety of the phenomena come out ?

If you, the opponents, would say that māyā has the power to produce functions, yet how is it possible that a lady is a mother and yet barren at the same time ?" (*Vītarāgastuti*, v. 13)[15]

Such a criticism was already made by Kumārila.[16] Malayagiri, who was a contemporary of Hemacandra, directed the same refutation at the Advaitins.[17] In order to avoid such a refutation by other schools, later Advaitins finally came, as a solution of the problem, to define *māyā* as 'one that cannot be described neither as being nor as non-being' (*sadasadbhyām anirvacanīyam*).[18] So far is our discussion on early Vedānta in connection with the assertions by Sāmantabhadra and Akalaṅka. In the later works after him the Vedānta as an independent school is referred to and introduced with various appellations. Mallavādin (eighth century A.D.), having set forth different opinions of various schools on the problem whether the object of perception (*pratyakṣa*) or of inference (*anumāna*) is a universal (*sāmānya*) or a particular (*viśeṣa*), says:—"The Vedāntavādins think that a universal alone is the object of perception or of inference, for, if a particular should be the object, then both perception and inference would come to be fallacious, because, due to non-duality of *ātman*, everything must be one and the same."[19] The theory that the universal alone is the object of perception and inference was introduced as one of the Vedāntins in Kumārila's *Ślokavārttika*.[20] Bhartṛhari's thought[21] may be near to it. It seems that here Mallavādin set forth the Vedāntic thought as was mentioned above from the standpoint of his own. Śīlāṅka (the latter half of ninth century A.D.) defined the *'Ātmavādin'* as those who think *ātman* to be 'the one whose aspects are the evolution of all the universe' (*viśvapariṇati-rūpa*).[22] Here he must have probably meant the *pariṇāmavāda* in the early Vedānta school. Prabhācandra refers to, and criticizes, the theory of the Vedānta school in his voluminous work *Prameyakamalamārtaṇḍa* (a commentary on Māṇikyanandin's *Parīkṣāmukha*), and a sub-commentary on it says that he refers here to the *Vedānti Bhāskarīyaḥ*.[23] The context here seems to justify the remark of the sub-commentary. So Prabhācandra was virtually attacking the theory of Bhāskara.

Having in view that various opinions are mentioned in these Jain works as the theories of the Vedānta school, it is certain that the Vedānta existed as a school in those days. But in the eyes of the Jains this school was not of much importance in the world. Haribhadra, the great Śvetāmbara scholar (latter half of ninth century A.D.), briefly sets forth, in his *Ṣaḍdarśanasamuccaya*, the teachings of the Six Schools (Buddhism, Nyāya, Sāṃkhya, Jainism, Vaiśeṣika and Mīmāṃsā) and Lokāyata in addition as an appendix, but he does not refer to the Vedānta at all. The *Upamitibhavaprapañca kathā*, a religious story composed in 906 A.D., by Siddharṣi, the Jain author, refers in a passage to the Six Systems[24] which are the Naiyāyikas, Vaiśeṣikas, Sāṃkhyas, Buddhists, Mīmāṃsakas and Lokāyatas, and another set of the six eliminating the Mīmāṃsakas and including the Jains. Anyhow, neither set mentions the Vedānta as an independent school. Considering these facts, it seems that the Jain scholars at large in those days did not particularly esteem the Vedānta as a philosophical school.

But after the tenth century things became different. Probably due to the increase of the social influence of the Vedānta school, this school is very often referred to in the Jain works in this period. It is noteworthy that the Advaita theory of the school of Śaṅkara alone is mentioned as the thought of the Vedānta. In the *Yaśastilaka* composed by the Digambara scholar Somadeva, in 959 A.D., there is a passage[25] where the theories of various philosophical schools are set forth. In this passage the theory o the Vedānta school is set forth as follows :

"Liberation comes about from the destruction of the consciousness of all individual distinctions and of Ignorance, by means of meditation on the highest brahman." (*paramabrahma-darśana-vaśād aśeṣa-bheda-saṃvedana-avidyā-vināśāt, iti Vedānta-vādinaḥ.*)

"In the same way as, when a jar is destroyed, the space in the jar merges into the (great) space, so, every living being, when its body is destroyed, merges into the highest *brahman,*—so say the Brahman-monists." (*yathā ghaṭavighaṭane ghaṭākāśam ākāśībhavati tathā dehocchedāt sarvaḥ prāṇī pare brahmaṇi līyate iti Brahmādvaitavādinaḥ*).

This is conspicuously the Advaita theory of the Śaṅkara school.

In the later days also Hemacandra and Malayagiri attacked solely the Advaita theory, as was discussed above. "The chattering Brahman-philosophers" (*brahma-vādivāvadūka*) referred to by Ratnaprabhā[26] (thirteenth century A.D.) are none but the Advaitins of the Śaṅkara school, saying that "the phenomenal world is false."[27] Therefore, the appellation "*brahmavādin*", which was formerly applied in a wider sense, was here applied chiefly to the school of Śaṅkara.[28] Malliṣeṇa (thirteenth century A.D.) refers to the '*brahmādvaitavādin*'.[29] Malayagiri (twelfth century A.D.) and Abhayadeva (eleventh century A.D.), following the traditional interpretation that the *ātmavādin* is the one who makes an assertion that 'all the universe is nothing but *puruṣa* (*puruṣa evedaṃ sarvam*)', chiefly made efforts to refute the theory of the Śaṅkara school.[30]

Notes

1. According to the Sanskrit rendering in *Sacred Books of the Jains*, vol. VIII, ed. and tr. by R. B. J. L. Jaini, 1930.

2. S. Radhakrishnan: *The Principal Upaniṣads*. New York: Harper and Brothers, 1953. Cf. *Chānd. Up.* VIII, 5; VIII, 10, 2.

3. *The Pravacana-sāra of Kundakunda Ācārya*, together with the commentary, Tattvadīpikā, by Amṛtacandra Sūri, English translation by B. Faddegon edited with an introduction by F. W. Thomas, Cambridge, p. 16.

4. The saying that 'the soul that dies as a man becomes a god or some other being. In both cases the essence of the soul does not disappear nor is it reborn as someone else' (*Pañcāstikāya*, 17) was taken by the commentator for explaining '*Kṣaṇika ekānta*' i.e., Buddhism and '*nitya ekānta*', i.e., Vedānta. However, we are not quite sure whether this passage certainly refers to the Vedānta. (This material is mentioned by Yensho Kanakura in the journal *Bunka*, vol. VI, no. 11, p. 84).

It is said that as a work providing sources for the study of early Vedānta philosophy Dr. Kapadia's introduction to his edition of Mallavādin's *Dvādaśāranayacakra* (4 vols.) is useful. But this has not been available to me. Editions are as follows:

Dvādaśāranayacakra of Śrī Mallavādisūri with the commentary Nyāyāgamānusāriṇī of Śrī Siṁhasūri. Part I of Four Aras. Edited by Muni Caturavijayaji and Lalacandra B. Gandhi. Baroda: Oriental Institute, 1952.

Dvādaśāranayacakram of Śrī Mallavādi Kṣamaśramaṇa with the Nyāyāgamānusāriṇi Commentary by Śrī Siṃhasūrigaṇi Vādi reṣamā Śramaṇa, ed. by Acarya Vijayalabdhisuri. (Śrī Labdhisurishwar Jain Granthamala No. 20 and 26). Chhani, 1948 and 1951.

Dvādaśāraṃ Nayacakraṃ of Ācārya Śrī Mallavādi Kṣamāśramaṇa, with the Commentary Nyāyāgamānusāriṇī of Śrī Siṃhasūri Gaṇi Vādi Kṣamāśramaṇa, Part 1. Edited by Muni Jambūvijayajī. Bhavnagar: Sri Jain Atmanand Sabha, 1966.

Mallavādin, a Śvetāmbara scholar, lived from the end of 4th to the first half of the 5th century of the Vikrama era (Foreword, p. VI). As the Vikrama era begins with 58 B.C., he lived, broadly speaking, in the 4th century A.D. Siṃhasūri, who wrote a commentary on it, belongs to the latter half of the 7th century A.D. (ibid. p. VII. Cf. *WZKSO*. vol. I, 1957, pp. 147-151).

5. The text was edited in *Sanātana-Jaina-Grantha-Mālā* 7, published (together with *Pramāṇaparīkṣā* in a book) by Pandit Pannalal Jain Bakaliwal, Benares 1914. This edition includes not only Akalaṅka's *Aṣṭaśatī* but also Vasunandin's *Vṛtti*. The latter is very helpful for understanding the meaning of the verses, as it tries to explain them literally and faithfully by paraphrasing them. The *Aṣṭaśatī* tries on the other hand to make clear the purport of the verses. In this article the author based his translation chiefly on the *Vṛtti*. Vasunandin is supposed to have lived between the tenth and thirteenth centuries (M. Winternitz: *A History of Indian Literature*, vol. II, p. 577, n. 2).

6. *advaitaikāntapakṣe 'pi dṛṣṭo bhedo virudhyate (=mithyābhavet) / kārakāṇāṃ kriyāyāś ca naikaṃ (=asahāyaṃ) svasmāt (=ātmanaḥ) prajāyate (=utpadyate) //* The words in parentheses have been inserted from the *Vṛtti*.

7. *karmadvaitaṃ phaladvaitaṃ lokadvaitaṃ ca no bhavet / vidyāvidyādvayaṃ na syāt bandhamokṣadvayaṃ tathā //*

8. *hetor advaitasiddhiś ced dvaitaṃ syād dhetusādhyayoḥ / hetunā ced vinā siddhir dvaitaṃ vāṅmātrato na kim //*

9. *advaitaṃ na vinā dvaitād ahetur iva hetunā / saṃjñinaḥ (=nāmavataḥ) pratiṣedho na pratiṣedhyād ṛte kvacit //*

10. *Tattvasaṃgraha* v. 330; *Pañjikā* ad, 1.c.

11. e.g., *advaya ātmā paramārthaḥ* (Śaṅkara ad *Gauḍapādīya-Kārikās*, ĀnSS. p. 9 *l*.8); *paramārthasad advaitam* (*ibid*. p. 128, *l*.1); *advayena ca paramārthasatā 'tmanā* (*ibid*. p. 95, *l*.18): *advaye paramārthasaty ātmani* (*ibid*. p. 97, *l*.13).

12. Only Bhartṛprapañca is an exception to it.

13. A criticism of the same purport was directed against the Vedānta school by Bhavya, the Buddhist philosopher. Cf. The Tibetan version of the *Madhyamakahṛdaya*, VIII, 72.

14. *Sarvadarśanasaṃgraha* (Government Oriental Series I), XVI, l.658.

15. *māyā sati ced dvayatattvasiddhir athāsatī hanta kutaḥ prapañcaḥ | māyaiva ced arthasahā ca tat kiṃ mātā ca vandhyā ca bhavatpareṣām ||* This information was given by courtesy Prof. S. Matsunami.

16. *Ślokavārttika*, Saṃbandhākṣepaparihāraḥ, vv. 82 cd-86 (pp. 662-663)

17. O. Schrader : *Über den Stand der Indischen Philosophie zur Zeit Mahāvīras und Buddhas*. Strassburg, 1902, p. 41, Anm. 3.

18. e.g., Vedāntasāra, 37 (in Böhtlingk's *Chrestomathie*).

19. "*viṣayavipratipattim*" *iti | ihakaścin Mīmāṃsakādibhiḥ pratyakṣasya sāmānyaviśeṣau dvau api viṣayau kalpitau | anumānasya sāmānyam eva viṣayaḥ na viśeṣah | Sāṃkhyena dvayor api viśeṣo viṣaya iṣṭaḥ sāmānyasyābhāvāt | Vedāntavādinā ca sāmānyam eva viṣayo dvayoḥ, ātmādvaitatayā sarvasyaikatvād viśeṣe bhrāntatvād dvayor iti vipratipattiḥ pratyakṣādiviṣaye |* (*Nyāya-binduṭīkāṭippaṇī* of Mallavādin, ed. by Th. Stcherbatsky, *Bibliotheca Buddhica* XI, p. 35). Mallavādin wrote a commentary on the *Nyāyabinduṭīkā* written by Dharmottara who was a Buddhist. It was not unusual for Jain scholars to study heretical (non-Jain) works.

20. *Ślokavārttika*, Pratyakṣasūtra, 114-116, p. 169.

21. *Vākyapadīya*, III, 1, 6.

22. O. Schrader, *op. cit.* p. 41.

23. *Prameyakamalamārtaṇḍa* (NSP. 1912), pp. 17 ff.; pp. 88 ff. Nothing is known about the author of the subcommentary and its authenticity, but it must have been based upon old tradition. This text was published prior to the edition of Bhāskara's *Brahmasūtrabhāṣya* (ChowkhSS. No. 70, 185, 209) published for the first time in 1915 A.D. The author of the subcommentary could not have read Bhāskara's printed text. The identification in the sub-commentary can be justified in the following passage also; *mokṣāvasthāyāṃ caitanyasyāpy ucchedān na kṛtabuddhayas tatra pravartante ity ānandarūpo mokṣo 'bhyupagantavyaḥ.* (*Prameyak.* p. 88) Cf. *paramātmānaṃ pratipadya tenaikībhūtās tasmin brahmaṇi modanta iti.* (Bhāskara ad *Brahmasūtra*, IV, 4, 22. p. 249) Bhāskara's date seems to have been between that of Śaṅkara and that of Prabhācandra.

24. Pp. 661-664 (ed. by P. Peterson and H. Jacobi, *B.I.*, 1899-1914).

25. *Yaśastilaka* (ed. by MM. Pandit Sivadatta, NSP. 1903), part II, pp. 269, 270.

26. Ratnaprabhā's *Ratnākarāvatārikā* ad *Pramāṇanayatattvālokālaṅkāra* of Śrī Vādi Devasūri, part I, p. 34. (*Yaśovijaya-Jaina-Grantha-Mālā*, 22). Ratnaprabhā was a disciple of Devasūri. Cf. Introduction to it, p. 10; Schubring, *Die Lehre der Jainas*, S. 215.

27. *prapañco mithyā, pratīyamānatvāt, yad evaṃ tad evaṃ, yathāśuktiśakale kaladhautaṃ, tathā cāyaṃ, tasmāt tathā.* (*ibid*, p. 34.)

28. Cf. *yad...brahmavādibhir avidyāsvarūpaṃ cādṛṣṭam avādi tad apāstam.* (*ibid.*, part II, p. 156).

29. *brahmādvaitavādino 'vidyā' paraparyāyamāyāvaśāt pratibhāsamānatvena viśvatrayavartivastuprapañcam apāramārthikaṃ samarthayanti.* (*Syādvādamañjarī* ad *Vītarāgastuti* 13).

30. O. Schrader : *op. cit.* p. 41.

SECTION V : CONCLUSION

The above discussion may contribute in making clear the general outline of the history of the development of the Vedānta school.

(1) When early Jainism came into existence, various ideas mentioned in the extant older Upaniṣads were current. They are reflected in the holy texts of the early Jains. The Jains refuted them as heresies, but what is called an Upaniṣad, as a part of the Vedic scripture, is not mentioned at all. It is natural that a specific school called the Vedānta which particularly esteems the Upaniṣadic scripture is not referred to at all. This is the situation up to just before Christian era.[1]

(2) After the compilation of the holy texts, Jain thinkers were engaged in making commentaries on the holy texts, compiling manuals of the doctrine, composing hymns and so on. The interchange of ideas between Jainism and Brahmin orthodoxy must have been considerable, and the Jain scholars were occasionally influenced by the Vedāntic thought. But they did not refer to the Vedānta school as before. Considering the fact that other schools are mentioned in earlier Jain works, the Vedānta school of those days seems to have an almost negligible existence which scarcely attracted the attention of the Jains, and to have not yet achieved the status of what might be called a philosophical school. It seems probable that some Brahmins were handing on and studying the Upaniṣadic scriptures, but beyond that they did not venture to advocate a new theory or to attack the doctrines of other schools. So much for the situation in the period before 600 A.D.

(3) From about 600 A.D., onward some Jain scholars came to deal with the Vedānta with the status of what might be called a philosophical school, and to attack its thought. It seems that the Vedānta as a school gradually came to flourish on the periphery of the philosophical circle, but it was not as influential as other schools in the world. The fact that what is set forth in the Jain works of those days as the theory of the Vedānta is of various kinds makes us understand that various Vedāntic theories were current. It is noteworthy that Śīlāṅka in the eighth century attacked a sort of Advaita theory similar to Buddhism. So much for the situation in c. 600-900 A.D.

(4) In the Jain works after the tenth century A.D., the Vedānta is often referred to and is attacked severely. It is interesting to find that herein only the Advaita of Śaṅkara is dealt with. Although various schools of the Vedānta tinged with sectarian tendency of Hinduism were current in this period, they are not explicitly dealt with. Probably they were of importance only in the respect that they gave philosophical foundations to popular religious sects, and they were given little attention among highly intellectual scholars. In their eyes the school of Śaṅkara alone mattered as representing the Vedānta school. It is likely that we may not trace this tendency to regard the Śaṅkara school as representing the Vedānta very much further back.

This picture that we gain from Jain sources of the historical development of the early Vedānta school and thought is in remarkable agreement with that which we draw by relying on Buddhist sources.[2] Although the Jain materials relevant to this problem are rather scanty, this coincidence reveals that the conclusions gained from relying upon Jain and Buddhist sources confirm each other and are reliable, probably corresponding to the actual history of this school.

Notes

1. H. Nakamura, "Vedānta Philosophy as Seen from the Scriptures of Early Jainism," *Journal of the Oriental Research Institute*, M. S. University of Baroda, vol. VIII, No. 2, 1958, pp. 148-155.

2. H. Nakamura, "Upaniṣadic Tradition and the Early School of Vedānta as Noticed in Buddhist Scripture," *Harvard Journal of Asiatic Studies*, Vol. 18, 1955, Nos. 1 and 2, pp. 74-104.

CHAPTER VI

VEDĀNTA AS IT APPEARS IN THE ORTHODOX BRAHMANICAL LITERATURE

SECTION I. THE BRAHMINS AS TRANSMITTERS OF INDIAN CULTURE

Indian culture developed and attained maturity centering chiefly round the priestly caste of Brāhmins. In India for three thousand years from the ancient past to the present, the major industry has been agriculture, and almost all the inhabitants have been farmers living in small villages throughout the country, following an economic life isolated and feudalistic. The leaders at the center of this farming culture were in fact the Brahmins.

India's fertile and rich soil, its climate of tropical heat and plentiful rainfall, is conducive to quick and bountiful harvests, and further facilitates the task of the farmer, so that in a good many cases little effort is needed to secure food, housing and clothing. Their life was an easy one compared with that of people of some other lands. They did not have to be spurred to earn their livelihood so much, but could subsist without much exertion. Thus the trade in other areas was minimal, and trade was rather in precious, high-priced, or luxury articles. With such a way of life, the warrior or merchant classes were weakened as forces for social cohesion. What unified the Indian people socially, and gave them self-awareness as a single people was rather the priestly caste of Brahmins.

The dependence on the course of nature for the livelihood of the people was particularly great, and it was thought that the rites, prayers and incantations of the Brahmins were essential in cultivation of the land and for avoiding disasters of famine and epidemics. Accordingly the farming people of India had no great respect for merchants, and tended to regard the existence of the warrior (royal) class as useless.[1] even at times classing them with brigands, whereas for the Brahmins they had respect and reverence like "gods on earth". The close connection between the farmers and the Brahmins was firm and unshakable for over three thousand years. Neither the support given to the

Buddhist order by the great king Aśoka, nor invasions of tribes from the North-west, nor the sword of Islam, nor the imperialism of Britain, could produce even a ripple in this historical social tradition. The Brahmins, ignoring utterly the invaders from outside, went on using Sanskrit for three thousand years without change, and reciting the Vedas without altering a letter. Buddhism, with its opposition to the rituals and prayers of the Brahmins, was finally expelled from India. The mainstream of Indian culture is Brahmanical through and through.

No small part of the noble culture which arose in India in the past was from the hands of those outside the Brahmin caste, but it had no stability as a social tradition, and immediately vanished. The weakness of the cultural tradition of the warriors is an example. In the past there existed a brilliant warrior culture in India but practically none of it survived. For instance, it is an indubitable historical fact that in the very ancient past the martial arts were actively studied, but the classics on the martial arts were all lost, and all that has survived is fragments annexed to *religious works* of the Brahmins. Even the great epic *Mahābhārata*, which should be called the national epic of India, was originally a descriptive poem much in favour with the warrior and the masses. But it was later revised and changed so that it ended up as a very Brahmanical work, and only in this way could it survive to the present day. Again it is no secret that great cities were built along the Ganges river, and formidable social power was possessed by the guilds of merchants and artisans. Yet in the whole context of Indian history this was a very insignificant and ephemeral phenomenon. What has survived of their cultural legacy is merely trifling. A great many of the works dealing with industry have also become extinct.

In this situation, we are compelled to take the religious works of the Brahmins as the most important material in investigating the various aspects of Indian culture of the past. Even works in the general cultural field which are not religious have been more or less coloured with Brahmanical overtones, so that in our investigations in the history of thought we can lump together as Brahmanical all the material except works which are Buddhist or Jain. In what follows it is proposed to examine in succession Vedānta thoughts appearing in Brahmanical literary works and religious works, and so help to illumine the history of early

Vedānta thought by these sidelights. The investigation is also very interesting for its own sake as touching the social and cultural significance of Vedānta philosophy.

Notes

1. In the Buddhist texts, when disasters which plague human beings are listed, the evil of a king is frequently listed along with the evil of brigands.

SECTION II: VEDĀNTA PHILOSOPHY IN THE EPIC POEMS

Among the classical works of India's orthodox Brahmins, the oldest are the Vedas, but as these were mostly already in existence *before* any Vedānta school came into being, I must exclude them from consideration here. After the Vedas, what comes up for examination is the two great epic poems of India, the *Mahābhārata* and the *Rāmāyaṇa*.

The *Mahābhārata* is a great epic poem which deserves to be called the national poem of the Indian people. Its title means "the historical poem of the battles of the Bharata tribe" and originally had as the main theme the combats between the five princes of Pāṇḍu and their cousins, the hundred princes of Kuru, who are all thought to be historical persons. But in course of transmission, amendments and enlargements were frequently incorporated, and the popular edition which exists at present is a massive work comprising over 10,000 verses combining the eighteen parts of the original poem with the great supplement of the *Harivaṁśa*. Its origin has been said to be traceable back to the 4th century B.C., but it is supposed that it finally attained its present form around 200-400 A.D.[1]

Thus it came into being over a long period of time, and at least three times underwent a great revision; with the various supplements and expansions, there have come to be great differences between the ancient and the new in each section. In particular, it seems that the appended *Harivaṁśa* was composed last, with its contents and thought reminiscent for the most part of the Purāṇas.

The *Mahābhārata* is a historical poem chiefly concerned with the original battles and devoutly studied by warriors and masses, but when later it came to be added to and handed down by the Brahmins, it came to include a great number of accounts of the mythology, legends, religion, philosophy and legislation of the Brahmins. Of these, the longest one explaining philosophical thought is the twelfth part Śānti-parva, in particular its latter half "on the method of liberation" (*Mokṣadharma*), and in addition to this there are the *Bhagavad-gītā*, the *Anugītā*, and the *Sanatsujātīya*, which are all more or less complete philosophical works inserted into the *Mahābhārata*. Besides these there are not a few sections which are interspersed with fragmentary philosophical thoughts.

The philosophical theories taught in these sections are certainly of many different kinds, even contradictory passages appearing here and there in the course of the work. These sections were originally composed by different writers in different periods, but such disunities and contradictions came to be accepted when they were later inserted and given definite form within the *Mahābhārata*. It is correspondingly difficult to give any brief outline of the various ideas taught in these sections, but if we are asked to sum up briefly the special characteristics which pervade the whole work, we would have to say that its thought is characterized by the Sāṃkhya and Vedānta philosophies. On the question whether this thought resulted from a commingling of the two, or whether it represents a transient stage on the way to the later classical formulations of the two schools, there are differences of opinion among scholars; since it is very difficult to make a brief summing up, I shall not discuss the problem here. However, from among the complex and variegated philosophical ideas appearing in this enormous epic poem, we can list as having exerted considerable influence on the formulation of the Vedānta philosophy of later centuries the theism of the *Bhagavad-gītā*, the doctrine of Sāṃkhya-yoga, and the doctrine of the inner self.

The idea of worship of a personal god has existed in India from ancient times, the tendency appearing markedly already in the *Śvetāśvatara-Upaniṣad*, and reaching its highest tide in the worship of Viṣṇu in the *Bhagavad-gītā*. The God Viṣṇu, as one of the solar gods anciently in the *Ṛg-Veda*, had thereby a special supremacy, and it was held that the paradise where the dead are gathered is bathed in the nectar of his grace. With the passage of time the intensity of devotion to him gradually increased, and in the *Bhagavad-gītā* he is identical with the supreme Brahman taught in the Upaniṣads. Kṛṣṇa, one of the principal characters in the chronicle of the battle, is seen as an incarnation of Viṣṇu. What this scripture stressed is wholehearted faith in the supreme one god; if with devoted love (*bhakti*) one worships and serves the supreme god, by his grace one becomes free from the circle of transmigration, and attains the heaven of the supreme god, dwelling with the highest god without any distinction and living in eternal prosperity and happiness.

Then on the fringe of this central thought, various philosophical theories are expounded. Among them are some which have elements in common with the Sāṃkhya theories and with the Yoga theories, and again there are also others which are identical with what is taught in the Upaniṣads. While there are scholars who believe that those Upaniṣadic theories may have been appended in later centuries.[2] this has not yet received the assent of Indologists in general. At any rate, apart from the fact that it cannot be said that they have been set up on exactly the same basis as the Upaniṣad philosophy, there is the further point that it is taught that all four castes can obtain liberation—the highest beatitude—by the grace of the supreme deity, and on this point the Brahmins, who follow and regard the Vedas (including the Upaniṣads), as absolute and sacred maintained a different position. The *Mahābhārata* accordingly must have originally come into existence from a source different from the Upaniṣads but as it spread progressively among the people, it gradually acquired a definite social authority, finally coming to be considered as almost equal in authority to the Upaniṣads.[3] Vedānta scholars of later centuries have all revered the *Bhagavad-gītā*, and many commentaries and expositions of it have been written. Even Śaṅkara, who did not recognize a personal ruler-god as absolute, wrote a commentary upon it. Nor need we mention the Vedānta scholars of other schools who have emphasized loving faith (*bhakti*) towards the supreme deity. Throughout the Vedānta schools in general of later centuries, this work was revered, together with the Upaniṣads and the *Brahmasūtra*, as the "three authoritative texts" (*prasthānatraya*).

While it may also be said that the Sāṃkhya-yoga theories are taught in the *Bhagavad-gītā*, they are particularly clearly explained in the twelfth part of the *Mahābhārata*.[4] This can be seen as Sāṃkhya doctrine, but with the special point that besides the twentyfive principles taught in the classical Sāṃkhya, it expounded the supreme and unique self as a twenty sixth principle, and this has all the essential qualities of the Brahman taught in the Upaniṣads. This theory had already been proposed in the first century A.D.[5] or perhaps even before that, and throughout the period during which the historical poems came into existence the Sāṃkhya theories, which thus adopted Upaniṣadic ideas, can be taken to have been strongly in favour in Indian society at large. Its influence does not end with the epic poems, but persisted on into the Purāṇa literature, Tantra works etc., and in holy texts and religious writings of Hinduism, so producing a complicated theology. Roughly speaking, those who thought on these lines seem already in the period when the epic poems came into being to have been interpreting the verses of the Upaniṣads in a manner akin to Sāṃkhya. The *Brahmasūtra* strongly rejects the interpretation based on these lines.

In the narrow sense, the Vedānta school came into existence out of this rejection of this kind of Sāṃkhya-style Vedānta. A fundamentalist tendency aiming at elimination of the influence of Sāṃkhya can be found already in the inner self (*adhyātman*)[6] doctrine within the epics themselves. This theory can be called a kind of Vedāntic theory, and according to it, eight principles are recognized, consisting of the five elements, consciousness, intellect, and the individual self (*kṣetrajña*); the supreme Brahman gives birth to the five elements, and afterwards entering into them as the individual self, brings it into being. Such is the doctrine. While there are few characteristics in this theory which are Sāṃkhya-like, still subsequently the *Brahmasūtra* (II.3.15) rejected this theory also.

Besides these, various other philosophical theories were also being taught, and these also were more or less steeped in Vedāntic influence. Even in stories unrelated to philosophy, union with Brahman is considered to be the highest ethical purpose of human life.[7] These philosophical and general world views were influential in later centuries, and contributed to the formulation of the Vedānta, but the philosophers of the epic poems were not themselves consciously philosophers of Vedānta. They say nothing of any Vedānta school. The word "Vedānta" does appear frequently in the epics, where it has the plain meaning, "the secrets of the Veda" comprising either the Āraṇyakas or the Upaniṣads. But it did not carry the connotation of a Vedānta school.[8] In the *Mahābhārata*, four systems of thought (*jñānāni*)[9] have been listed, and these four refer to the Sāṃkhya-yoga, the Pāñcarātra, the Veda's āraṇyaka (*Vedāraṇyaka*)[10], and the Pāśupata.

Their founders are said to be respectively: Kapila for the Sāṃkhya, Hiraṇyagarbha for the Yoga, **Apāntaratamas[11] as the** propagator of the Veda, Śiva for the Pāśupata, and Viṣṇu for the Pāñcarātra schools, but among these it is taught that Viṣṇu is the consummation (*niṣṭhā*). In each of the four schools listed above (or five if we split up Sāṅkhya and Yoga), there was some greater or lesser admixture of Vedāntic thought. But no independent school is referred to as having systematized a philosophy round the Upaniṣads as one section of the Vedas. So it appears that there was not as yet any such well-defined school of philosophy. Again, even the special technical terms of the later Vedānta philosophy had not yet come into being. Viṣṇu as the supreme deity is called the knower, prosperity, truth, and bliss, but is not explained as being of the nature of spirit (consciousness, *cit*); much less does the appellation 'being, cognition and bliss' (*saccidānanda*) appear yet.[12]

Thus even in the most philosophical portions of the *Mahābhārata,* neither is the name of Vedānta school listed, nor is the special vocabulary of the Vedānta philosophy of later centuries employed, so it is probable that no Vedānta school as such had yet come into existence.

Of course, to argue the non-existence of a thing simply because of the absence of extant records is a very dangerous procedure, but in this case the fact that there are no accounts of it in that vast epic poem, which is a gigantic encyclopedia in itself, may be thought to be proof strong enough. However, as we have already mentioned, followers of the "Āraṇyakas of the Veda" were regarded as one group, and since they were referred to as "men of wide knowledge who specialize in the Vedānta" (*Vedāntaniṣṭha bahuśruta*),[13] the Āraṇyakas and Upaniṣads in the Vedic canon were specially looked upon as important at the time, and there perhaps were men who were engaged in commenting on and learnedly studying these works. They would not, however, have gone outside the area of interpreting passages of the sacred texts and making comparative studies, and had not, I imagine, come to formulate a philosophical system as yet. Quite distinct from any such interpretative standpoint were the philosophers of the epic poems, who rather synthesized popular religious works preaching adoration of the gods Viṣṇu and Śiva, the monism of the Upaniṣads, theories of Sāṃkhya and methods of religious training of Yoga, and continued to express freely their own particular original philosophical thoughts.

Further, even concerning the Brāhmaṇa portion of the Vedas, it seems that the same kind of interpretative and scholarly investigation was being carried out actively at that time, and the fact is on record that there were such scholars who were engaged in such studies at that time.[14] Moreover, not even the Mīmāṁsā school is mentioned in the works, and no example can be found of the word Nyāya used in the sense of the learning of this school.[15]

As against the *Mahābhārata,* a conventional and popular poem in clear and simple verse, the *Rāmāyaṇa* is an epic poem composed with rhetorical flourishes in elegant and beautiful style, and should be recognized as the forerunner of pure literature of later centuries. The popular edition which exists now is composed of 24,000 verses. Traditionally it is regarded as the work of the poet Vālmīki, but not all of it was composed by the pen of one poet. It is however generally assumed that its present form was completed from around the 3rd century B.C. to the 2nd century A.D. Its contents are concerned with Rāma, the son of King Daśaratha, whose capital was in Ayodhyā; in order to avoid an internal split within the court, Rāma retired to meditate in the forest, accompanied by his wife Sītā and his younger brother Lakṣmaṇa. The evil king Rāvaṇa snatched away Sītā and returned with her to his stronghold, the island of Laṅkā. With the help of the monkey leader Hanumān at the head of a monkey army, Rāma was able to rescue her by attacking Laṅkā and killing Rāvaṇa, after which they returned home and he ascended the throne—such are some of the vicissitudes related by the epic. This epic poem, insofar as it is a pure literary work, does not in the strict sense seek to present philosophical arguments, and so it has been accepted generally that it has no connection with the philosophy of Vedānta or of the Sāṃkhya school or with the philosophical doctrines of the Yoga.[16] The "speakers about Brahman" (*brahma-vādin*) who appear in the *Rāmāyaṇa* are not meant to be students of Vedānta but scholars who were commentators on the Vedas.[17]

In this work, however, the hero Rāma is so highly respected and worshipped, that he comes to be elevated from the position of a hero to that of the presiding deity. And when we examine it carefully, we find among the words referring to Rāma himself not a few expressions of Vedāntic philosophy. For example, Brahmā says to Rāma: "The entire world is your body" (*jagat sarvaṁ śarīraṁ te*),[18] and also says "You are the past and the future." (*tvaṁ bhūto bhavyaḥ*).[19] The former is an idea emphaiszed in particular by Rāmānuja in later centuries. The latter appeared in the later period of the ancient Ṛg-Veda, and has long been characteristic of the Vedāntic philosophy.[20] Again, Rāma himself is called "he who knows Ātman" (*viditātman*).[21]

Accordingly the purely literary composers of that time who fashioned the epic poem *Rāmāyaṇa*, had also embraced a Vedāntic concept of the absolute deity they worshipped and whose followers they had come to be. And ideas of this kind would also have held sway over the masses of the time.

Notes

1. Hopkins; *GEI.* p. 389: Winternitz: *HIL.* vol. I, pp. 465, 475; Hopkins, *ERE.*, article on the *Mahābhārata.*

2. R. Garbe : *Die Bhagavadgītā,* Einleitung. F. O. Schrader, and A. Hillebrandt also agree to the theory of Garbe. Cf. Winternitz : *HIL.* vol. I, p. 436, n. 2.

3. Since the original name of the *Bhagavad-gītā* was "The *Bhagavadgītā Upaniṣadaḥ*," in a certain sense it itself claimed authority as an Upaniṣad.

4. Hakuju Ui, "*Indo Tetsugaku Kenkyū,* " vol. I, pp. 170-171, "*Indo Tetsugaku Shi,*" pp. 200-202.

5. In the *Buddha-carita*, written by Aśvaghoṣa, it is stated that Ārāḍa Kālāma, when he was asked his teaching by the Buddha after the latter became a religious renunciant taught a kind of Sāṃkhya theory, and as its contents are practically the same as those taught in Part 12 of the *Mahābhārata,*

Aśvaghoṣa may have attributed this theory to Āḷāḍa Kālāma in the light of these verses in the *Mahābhārata* (O. Strauss : Zur Geschichte des Sāṃkhya, *WZKM*. 1913, S. 257-275; Hopkins : Notes on the Śvetāśvatara, the Buddha-carita, *JAOS*, Vol. XXII, 1901, pp. 387-388). Since Aśvaghoṣa was a contemporary of King Kaniṣka (c. 100-150 A.D.), we should probably take it that this Sāṃkhya-yoga theory came into existence in the First Century A.D., or even before that. Further, this passage in the *Buddha-carita* is related by the "*Hongyō jukkyō*" word for word in the same way in the same place, and the "*Kako Genzai Inga kyō*" also mentions a theory practically the same as that in the *Buddha-carita*. Hakuju Ui, *Indo Tetsugaku shi*, p. 202).

6. *MBh*. XII. 194, 248 f, III. 210-213. Cf. Hakuju Ui, "*Indo Tetsugaku shi*, p. 205.

7. Winternitz : *HIL*. Vol. I, p. 380.

8. Cf. Hopkins : *GEI*, pp. 93-94; Carpenter : *Theism in Mediaeval India*, p. 177, n. 2, and Part I, Sec. 1, Chapter 3 of the present work.

9. *MBh*. XII. 351 (349). 1 ff., 64 ff. : Hopkins : *GEI*. pp. 96-97 ; P. Deussen : *Vier Philosophische Texte aus dem Mahābhārata*, pp. 849, 855.

10. However, in *MBh*. XII. 351 (349).64, it has become only Veda.

11. It is traditionally dated that certain persons called him Prācīnagarbha.

12. Hopkins : *Epic Mythology*. p. 208.

13. *MBh*. XIII. 69, 20. Hopkins, *GEI*. p. 94.

14. *MBh*. XII.19, 22, refers to *pūrvaśāstravidaḥ*, saying of him : *kriyāsu niratā nityam dāne yajñe ca karmaṇi*.

15. Hopkins : *GEI* p. 94.

16. Charles Schobel : "Le Ramāyaṇa du point de vue religieus, philosophique et moral." *Annales du Musée Guimet*, tome treizième.

17. e.g., *Rāmāyaṇa* I.12.5 (ed. NSP.)—"interpretes du Vèda" (Roussel).

18. *Rāmāyaṇa* (Publicato per G. Gorresio), VI.102, 26.

19. Ibid. VI.102, 13.

20. Part II, Chapter 1, Sect. 5, Item 2, of the present work, and *Madhyamaka-hṛdaya*. 8.4.

21. *Rāmāyaṇa* (Publicato per G. Gorresio), I.46.13; III.77, 27; VI, 9.9.

SECTION III: VEDĀNTA THOUGHT IN THE DHARMAŚĀSTRAS

In India from early times a great number of law books were composed. They lay down, from a Brahmanical standpoint, structures, customs and daily activities of society, concentrating on such problems as the systems of four castes and the four stages of life (*āśrama*). At first they were written in the comparatively concise *sūtra* style and their contents also were brief and simple, but later on elaborate law books containing also civil and criminal law were produced. These were compiled and edited by the priestly *Brahmins* and the outlook of Brahmanism is clear in them. Among the Buddhist texts the *Vinaya-Piṭaka*, which is one of the *Tripiṭakas*, should be classed as a kind of law book, but this is a legal work applicable only to the order of monks and not to society at large, whereas the law books edited by the *Brahmins* purport to be rules and regulations for society in general, and are completely different in significance from the *Vinaya-Piṭaka*. These law books compiled by the *Brahmins* have been highly regarded as most valuable sources for information about social conditions in ancient India, though on the other hand some scholars assert that they are simply Utopias composed by *Brahmins* of the priestly class, remote from actual conditions of society in ancient India.[1] Thoroughgoing investigation would be needed to clarify the historical and social significance of the Brahmanical law books, but I shall not now enter into this problem. All I would say is, that since these law books are works by the *Brahmins*, they are valuable sources for information about their *thought*. It is needless to say that *Vedānta* thought expounded in them rates highly as revealing an aspect of the history of *Vedānta* philosophy.

Among the ancient law books, it is specially in the *Āpastamba-Dharmasūtra* that Vedānta thought appears. This work has been considered as one section of the *Kalpasūtra* belonging to the *Āpastamba* school, a Black *Yajurveda* school in southern India, and it is one of the oldest extant law books. In I.8.22 and 23 of this work, Vedāntic ideas are explained, particularly in the section called the "*Adhyātmapaṭala*", on which there exists a commentary ascribed to Śaṅkara called the "*Adhyātmapaṭala-vivaraṇa*", which has been published.[2] In presenting the following translation I follow this commentary.

The authenticity of the commentary has been called into question.[3] But in its quotations it restricts itself almost entirely to the ancient *Upaniṣads*, and its literary style resembles that of Śaṅkara. Moreover as a commentary it is far more accurate than the *Ujjvalā Vṛtti* of Haradatta, which is a commentary on the entire *Āpastamba-Dharmasūtra*[4], and since also it is apparent that its author was versed in *Vedic* Sanskrit, it may well be by Śaṅkara. Even if it is not an authentic work by him, I would think that it may be put in the same category—it must, in other words, have been written by a scholar of learning and education similar to Śaṅkara at a period not too far from his.

Āpastamba-Dharmasūtra I.8.22.

1. One should practise the *yoga*[5] concerning *ātman*, which accords with reason and does not distract the mind.[6]
2. There is no higher [goal] than the attainment of *ātman*.
3. In order [to attain to] that *ātman*, we shall quote those sacred stanzas[7] which teach the attainment of *ātman*.
4. All living creatures are the castle of that (*ātman*) which dwells in hiding-places, uninjured and spotless. Those who worship[8] the [*ātman*] which is immovable, abiding in the movable [phenomenal world], become immortal.
5. Abandoning everything which is called the object [of the senses] in this world, a wise man should worship that [*ātman*] which dwells in hiding-places.
6. If one says without attaining *ātman* within himself, "I wish to look for the place [as a clue to] cognizing that good (*ātman*) within the other things." [the teacher tells him], "Serve this advantageous one (*hita*) who is great, whose body is luminous, and who is the lord kept in everything, and not the disadvantageous (*ahita*) without being desirous [of the pleasure of the external world].
7. He, who is the eternal one in all beings, wise, immortal, constant, devoid of parts, soundless, bodiless, touchless, great and pure, is all and is the supreme goal. He is the center [of all]. He is the city intersected with many streets.[9]
8. He, who worships it (=the *ātman*), who always practises the life of the religious mendicant (*prādhva*)[10] everywhere, and who sees [*ātman*], which is difficult to see and subtle, with his mind under control, will rejoice in the heaven.

Āpastamba-Dharmasūtra I.8.23.

1. The wise man who sees all beings within himself, who does not become deluded while pondering, and who sees himself within all beings, is truly a "Knower of *Brahman*"[11] and shines forth in the uppermost world of the heaven.[12]
2. He who is subtler than the thread of the lotus-fibre, keeps on covering all, who is larger than the earth, constant and persists to contain all, is the supreme one, divides himself, different from the knowledge of this world which is identical with the object to be perceived by the senses. All

bodies spring from him. He is the root [of the world]. He is eternal and constant.

3. But the destruction of faults results from the *yoga* here in this existence. Having, eliminated [the faults] which destroy the creatures, the learned one arrives at peace (*kṣema*).
4. Now we shall enumerate the faults which destroy the creatures.
5. [They are] anger, exultation, wrath, covetousness, delusion, hypocrisy, violence, falsehood, gluttony, slander, envy, lust, secret hatred, neglect to control the senses, and neglect to concentrate the mind. The destruction of these [faults] takes place through the means of *yoga*.
6. Non-anger, non-exultation, non-wrath, non-covetousness, non-delusion, non-hypocrisy, non-violence, truthful words, moderate eating, non-slander, non-envy, the distribution of property, alms-giving, uprightness, kindness, tranquility of the mind, control of the senses, peace [with all beings], concentration of the mind, noble conduct [becoming an *Aryan*], warm feelings, contentedness—these are [the virtues] which must necessarily be observed throughout all of the [four] stages of life.[13] He who puts them into practice according to the rules becomes one who goes everywhere.

In the above, *sūtras* 22.4-23.3 are quotations from works of authorities prior to the *Āpastamba-Dharmasūtra*. As the commentator says, they may be citations from some *Upaniṣads* composed before that time, but not found in any extant *Upaniṣads*. But the following are very much like the *Kāṭhaka-Upaniṣad* :

Āp. Dh. S.	*Kāṭhaka-Up.*
22.4, *ahanyamāna*	*na hanyate hanyamāne śarīre* (II, 18) *nāyaṃ hanti na hanyate* (II, 19). (*cf. Chānd. Up.* VIII, 10, 4: *Bhag. G.* II, 19, 20;
4, & 5, *guhāśaya* (=*ātman*)	*eṣa sarveṣu bhūteṣu gūḍhātmā* (III, 12); *guhāṃ praviṣṭa* (III, 1); *guhāṃ praviśya* (VI, 6; 7).*eko devaḥ sarvabhūteṣu gūḍhaḥ*, *Śvet. Up.* (VI, II)

4, *temṛtāḥ* [*bhavati*]	*amṛtās te bhavanti* (VI, 9). *amṛtatvaṃ ca gacchati* (VI, 8). *amṛto bhavati* (VI, 15). *amṛtatvam eti* (VI, 16).
5, *kavi* (=*krāntadarśin, medhāvin, Śaṅkara*) (& 23, 1)	*kavi* (=*medhāvin, Śaṅkara*) (III, 14).
6, *tejaskāya*	*tam eva bhāntam anu bhāti sarvaṃ tasya bhāsā sarvaṃ idaṃ vibhāti* (V, 15). cf. *Muṇḍ. Up.* II, 2, 110; *Śvet. Up.* VI, 14. (cf. the simile of sparks in the *Up.*)
6, *sarvatra nihitaṃ*	*viddhi tvaṃ etan nihitaṃ guhāyām* (I, 14). *sarvabhūtāntarātman.* (V, 10)
6, *mahāntaṃ... sarvatra nihitaṃ.*	*mahāntaṃ vibhum* (II, 20).
7, *nityo vipaścid amṛto dhruvaḥ.*	*na jāyate mriyate vā vipaścin nāyaṃ kutaś cin na babhūva kaścit* / *ajo mityaḥ śāśvato 'yaṃ purāṇo*...(II, 18)
7, *anaṅgo 'śabdo 'śarīro 'sparśaś ca.*	*aśabdam asparśam arūpam avyayam tathā 'rasam* (III, 15).
7, *sa sarvaṃ paramā kāṣṭhā.*	*kāṣṭhā sā parā gatiḥ* (III, 11). *paramā gati* (VI, 10).
8, *dūrdarśaṃ nipuṇaṃ.*	*na hi suvijñeyam aṇur eṣa dharmaḥ* (I, 21). *dūrdarśaṃ gūḍham anupraviṣṭaṃ guhāhitam* (II, 12). (According to Jacob's Concordance the word *dūrdarśa* is used only in the *Kāṭhaka-Up.*)
8, *modeta viṣṭape*	*modate svargaloke* (I, 12; 18).
23.1, *nākapṛṣṭhe virājati.*	*brahmaloke mahīyate* (III, 16).
2, *aṇīyān bisor ṇāyā... varṣīyāṃś ca pṛthivyāḥ...*	*aṇor aṇīyān mahato mahīyān ātmā* (II, 20).

Some of the words, expressions, ideas and so on in the *Adhyātmapaṭala* are also common to other *Upaniṣads*, but as shown above, those identical or similar to the *Kāṭhaka-Upaniṣad* are overwhelmingly conspicuous, in nearly every *sūtra* of the *Adhyātmapaṭala*. It is moreover specially to be noted that the *Adhyātmapaṭala* according to its opening and closing *sūtras*, aims to teach the *yoga* concerning *ātman* (*adhyātmikayoga*), and *Kāṭhaka-Upaniṣad*

II.12 teaches that one should realize the state of final release by means of the *yoga* concerning *ātman* (*adhyātmayoga*). According to Jacob's concordance, this technical term is used only in this passage of the *Kāṭhaka-Upaniṣad*, of all the *Upaniṣads* with which he dealt. From the above facts we must concede a remarkable resemblance between the *Adhyātmapaṭala* and the *Kāṭhaka-Upaniṣad*. This may lead us to the following conclusion :

As already discussed,[14] the *Kāṭhaka-Upaniṣad* was composed during the period 350-300 B.C. by one or more of the new poet-thinkers who had a different standpoint from that of the ancient Vedic theologians, and in the same stream of thought were composed other *Upaniṣads* remarkably like the *Kāṭhaka-Upaniṣad*. At present these are not extant, but a very limited portion of them has been transmitted, as quotations, in the *Adhyātmapaṭala* of the *Āpastamba-Dharmasūtra*. Since the composition of these *Upaniṣads* may have been around the same time as the *Kāṭhaka-Upaniṣad*, the date of the *Adhyātmapaṭala* would be at the earliest 300-250 B.C. The date of the present form of the *Āpastamba-Dharmasūtra* can be neither earlier than that, nor very much later.

So far it has generally been accepted on the basis of George Bühler's[15] study that the *Āpastamba-Dharmasūtra* was composed in the 4th or 5th century B.C. His grounds were as follows : Since the style and use of words in the *Āpastamba-Dharmasūtra* display archaic forms not in accordance with the rules of Pāṇini's grammar, either the author did not know the Pāṇini grammar (about 350 B.C.) or he knew it but did not think it important. The archaic forms of the book are not deliberate, for the irregularities in this text are peculiar to itself alone, and cannot be found elsewhere. The *Āpastamba-Dharmasūtra* (I.2.5.4 et seq.) calls the famous Śvetaketu, who appears in the *Śatapatha-Brāhmaṇa* and the *Chāndogya-Upaniṣad*, a "man of latter days" (*avara*), so it should have been written in a period not too remote from that of this Old *Upaniṣad*. Therefore (concluded Bühler) we may say that the work belongs to the 5th or 4th century B.C.

However these grounds as they stand are weak and flimsy. The fact that the text does not agree with the grammatical rules of Pāṇini does not permit the inference that it was composed prior to Pāṇini. In view of the very nature of *sūtra* works, special usages are to be expected in them. But since it can be taken that by the time of Patañjali (about 150 B.C.), Pāṇini's grammar was relied upon and in general use among scholars, it may be well to judge that this work came into existence prior to that date Again, there is no necessity to suppose that because Śvetaketu is called a "man of latter days", the date of the *Āpastamba-Dharmasūtra* is close to that of the *Chāndogya Upaniṣad*. Pāṇini clearly states that there are two kinds of *Brāhmaṇas*, those of ancient date and those which are new.[16] Kātyāyana (about 250 B.C.) regards as a "man of latter days" the famous Yājñavalkya who appears in both the *Brāhmaṇas* and the *Upaniṣads* and calls him his "contemporary" (*tulyakāla*).[17] For these reasons it is possible to think that there is a gap of several centuries between the *Āpastamba-Dharmasūtra* and Śvetaketu, even though the *sūtra* calls him a "man of latter days". Therefore it is not at all unreasonable to suppose that the *Dharmasūtra* assumed its present form in

300-250 B.C. (or even later than that).[18] But since there seem to be also a great number of old elements in this work, handed down and written before that time but put together finally only in this period, further investigation is required.

The *Adhyātmapaṭala* is systematically arranged. In the first two *sūtras* it gives an outline of religious practice; next it quotes passages from the *Upaniṣads* which expound *ātman*, and it concludes by listing various virtues as a regimen for practice. In Vedic texts various virtues are taught here and there, but we do not find vices and virtues systematically contrasted with each other as they are here. So that even in his listing of the virtues we can observe a *systematic attitude* on the part of the editor of the law book...

Again, the Upaniṣadic passages quoted in the *Adhyātmapaṭala* are not strung together causally, but are all of them concerned with clarification of the nature of *ātman*. Even the *Kāṭhaka-Upaniṣad* which perhaps was composed in the same period as these passages and is also closely connected with, comprises not only this kind of symbolic explanation of the nature of *ātman* but has also various extraneous arguments and not a few somewhat obscure allegorical expressions. This tendency is notable especially in the ancient Upaniṣads. But the *Adhyātmapaṭala* selects and quotes *only* passages which explain *clearly* and directly what *ātman* is. Accordingly we can infer a special attitude or standpoint of the editor from his method of using quotations. He is *selective* in regard to the Upaniṣadic texts, and this attitude or standpoint can perhaps be said to be *Vedāntic*. The *Āpastamba-Dharmasūtra* nowhere refers to any *Vedānta* school, nor was the author himself probably conscious of the fact that such a standpoint is *Vedāntic*. But we can recognize in it the first shoots of the Vedānta.

Since this *Adhyātmapaṭala* explains clearly the nature of *ātman*, it is regarded as important in later *Vedānta*, so much so that it is quoted in their commentaries on the *Brahmasūtra* by both Śaṅkara and Rāmānuja,[19] and, as we have already pointed out, there is even a commentary ascribed to Śaṅkara.

As for the thought of the *Adhyātmapaṭala*, it is on major points almost the same as that of the *Kāṭhaka-Upaniṣad*. Ātman is the essence of all, including not only the human but all varieties of the living being. It is the greatest and at the same time the smallest, hidden in the innermost recess in all individual selves. The fact that all living beings, that is to say, individual selves, are called "walled city" (pur-pura) specially reminds us of Rāmānuja's philosophy, according to which all spiritual beings and the material world constitute the "body" of the Absolute. Ātman as the Absolute is also said by the *Adhyātmapaṭala* to be "good", "eternal", "constant", "great", "pure", "immortal", "intelligent", "spotless", "supreme", "root", "scatheless", "auspicious" "lord" and so on. These attributes are used in the other Upaniṣads as well and are not to be regarded as peculiar to the *Adhyātmapaṭala*.

As to religious practice, it teaches the *yoga* of meditating on and worshipping *ātman*. It calls the state of final release "peace" (*kṣema*). It clearly allows that final release is attained in the present existence. On the other hand, expressions such as "He......will rejoice in heaven" and "The wise man...shines forth in the highest world of heaven" point to the notion that complete release is attained in heaven after death. The *Upaniṣadic* passages quoted in the *Adhyātmapaṭala* are chiefly concerned with the life of the wandering mendicant, but at the end of the section it lays down that one ought to practise the *yoga* of meditation on *ātman* throughout all the four stages of life, i.e. student, householder, forest-dweller and wandering mendicant. Thus in regard to the problem which engaged the attention of later centuries: should one who meditates on *ātman* become a wandering mendicant or is he permitted to lead the life of a householder, the author of the *Āpastamba-Dharmasūtra* does not definitely come down on one side or the other. He must have thought that every member of the *Āryan* society should practise the above virtues.

Why, one may ask, did the author of the *Āpastamba-Dharmasūtra* compose an *Adhyātmapaṭala* of this kind ? It occurs in the course of an account of expiations for transgressions in general, and the author's intention is to enjoin knowledge of *ātman* as the best means by which to purify the mind of those who have committed the various sins.[20] It is therefore clear that in the *Brahmin* society of that time the knowledge of *ātman* was considered capable of purifying the mind. It is to be noticed here that this *Vedāntic* thought is put forward here as the view of the author himself and not merely as a possible view. Even by this time, Vedāntic thought had already become a philosophy of the *Brahmins*.

Among the *Dharmasūtras* in prose it is only the *Āpastamba-Dharmasūtra* that sets forth *Vedāntic* thought. As for the *Mīmāṁsā*, it is referred to in various Dharmasūtras. In *Vāsiṣṭhadharmasūtra* III.20 and *Baudhāyanadharmasūtra* I.1.8 a "*Mīmāṃsaka*" is mentioned together with "one who knows the *Aṅgas*" and "one who recites the works on the sacred law".[21] The *Āpastamba-Dharmasūtra* uses the term *Nyāya* for the knowledge of the *Karmamīmāṃsā*, and follows the *Mīmāṃsāsūtra* not merely in the use of the phrase "one who knows the Nyāya"[22] but also in laying down the same rules.[23] Thus one can suppose that by this time, alongside the Vedāntic tendencies the *Karmamīmāṁsā* was to some extent already established.

In the Dharmasūtras of early days *nyāya* and *mīmāṁsā* were synonymous. But in later days law scholars distinguished between them. In the *Yājñavalkya-smṛti* (I, 3) *nyāya, mīmāmsā* and *dharmaśāstra* were distinguished from each other. According to the commentary *Mitākṣarā*, *nyāya* means logic (*tarkavidyā*). *mīṃāṁsā* means 'examination of Vedic passages (*Vedavākyavicāra*) and *dharmaśāstra* is *Manu* and others,. So, when the *Yājñavalkya-smṛti* was composed, the examination of Vedic passages was regarded as an independent branch of learning, but *Karmamīmāṃsā* and the Vedānta philosophy were not yet distinguished from each other.

Cf. *Mantra-brāhmaṇāny adhītya kalpaṃ mīmāṃsāṃ ca yājñiko 'dhītya vaktraṃ padaṃ smṛtiṃ caicchikaḥ* / *Varāha-gṛhya-sūtra*, GOS.18. 6. p.8.

After the prose Dharmasūtras we have to examine the *Mānava-dharmaśāstra*. It is conjectured that originally simple proverbial sayings in verse were collected, and edited into the present form of the text in the second or third century A.D. In the first and the last (twelfth) chapter, philosophical ideas are taught, but as scholars have pointed out, it is Vedānta philosophy which is mixed with Sāṃkhya and influenced by *Mahābhārata* XII.[24] For these reasons it should be studied in connection with the Sāṃkhya philosophy and the philosophy of the *Mahābhārata*, and I shall no consider it here. But in the *Mānava-dharmaśāstra* there are some references to the learning of the Upaniṣads and when and how it is to be done. I shall examine them here since they give information about the transmission of the Upaniṣads.

> They call that Brahmin who initiates a pupil and teaches him the Veda together with the *Kalpa* and the *Rahasyas*, 'the teacher' (of the latter). (II.140)
>
> A twice-born must learn the whole Veda together with the *Rahasyas*, performing the various austerities (*tapas*) and the vows prescribed by the Vedic rules. (II.165)
>
> He who learns the *Ṛg-veda-saṁhitā* three times with a concentrated mind or the *Yajur-veda-saṃhitā* or the *Sāmaveda-saṁhitā* together with the *Rahasyas* is freed from all sins. (XI.263)

Since it can be taken that the 'secret doctrine' (*rahasya*) mentioned here refers to the Upaniṣads or at least includes the Upaniṣads, the compiler of the *Mānava-dharmaśāstra* holds that the Upaniṣads are to be learned together with the Saṁhitās. Thus the Upaniṣads are regarded as subordinate to the Vedas and have not yet come to be esteemed more highly than the Saṁhitās as they were by the later Vedānta thinkers.

Thus the students studied the Veda (including the Upaniṣads) under the teacher. The Brahmins who taught them had families, wives and children,[25] and so were not wandering mendicants. On the other hand, it is laid down that those who study the Upaniṣads do not directly realize the teaching until, having completed their duties as householders, they have to renounce the world, meditate on *ātman* and focus their attention on the Upaniṣads. For example, the *Mānava-dharmaśāstra* prescribes that the Brahmin who is a forest-dweller, having performed various religious observances (*dīkṣā*), should study the Upaniṣads (*Aupaniṣadīr ātmasaṁsiddhaye śrutīḥ* (*abhyaset,* Comm.). VI.29)

> "A twice-born man who, with concentrated mind, practises the ten-fold law and has paid his (three) debts, may, after learning the Vedānta according to the prescribed rule, become an ascetic (*saṃnyaset*)." (VI.94)

Concerning the wandering medicant, it says:

> "He should always recite the sacred words (of the Vedas) regarding the sacrifice, the sacred words regarding the gods, and the sacred words regarding the *ātman* (*adhyātmika*) taught in the Vedānta (*Vedāntābhihita*)." (VI.83)

According to the *Mānava-dharmaśāstra*,[26] only in the life of the wandering mendicant is the quest for final release through the Upaniṣads possible, and one who has not yet fulfilled his duties as a householder (the 'three debts' i.e. study of the Veda, sacrifices to the gods, and the bringing up of offspring) is strongly forbidden to entertain a desire for final release.

> "After he has paid the three debts, let him turn his mind towards final release. But he who seeks it without having paid (his debts) sinks downwards (=goes to hell)." (VI.35)
>
> "Having studied the Veda according to the rules and having begotten sons according to the sacred law, and having performed the sacrifices according to his ability, he then may turn his mind towards final release (*mokṣa*)." (VI. 36)
>
> "A twice-born man (*dvija*) who seeks final release without having studied the Veda, without having begotten sons, and without having performed the sacrifices, sinks downwards." (VI.37)

He can become neither a forest-dweller nor a wandering medicant without passing through the stages of student and householder. And those stages have to be passed through in successive order (cf. VI.34). Therefore, although he studies the Upaniṣads when he is a boy or a youth, he realizes them after he becomes old and renounces the world. There may be something similar in the way modern man may in his old age quietly appreciate and relish the classical works he studied when he was a boy or a youth.

Such a wandering mendicant had no definite place to live, but wandered about here and there, taking the shade of a tree[26] as his resting-place. There was as yet no idea of a group life in a great monastery. We must therefore conclude that when the *Mānava-dharmaśāstra* was current there had not yet come into existence anything like the later Vedānta school established in great monasteries and, in particular, studying devotedly the Upaniṣads alone. Moreover, the custom of renouncing the world directly without going through the life of a householder, which appeared in later centuries, was not socially admitted as yet.

The social significance of the Vedāntic thought which is seen in the *Mānava-dharmaśāstra* can also be recognized in other law-books. For example in the *Yājñavalkyasmṛti*, one of the most important law-books of India, after the rules of the forest-dweller and wandering mendicant, a philosophical discussion is appended. According to recent studies, the philosophical section is a later addition to this law-book,[27] but in the opinion of its compiler, philosophical speculation on *ātman* is the concern of the wandering mendicant. So on this point it is in accord with the standpoint of the *Mānava-dharmaśāstra*.

As for the philosophy of the *Yājñavalkyasmṛti*, it is in its contents Vedānta blended with Sāṁkhya and Yoga. On this point as well it agrees with the *Mānava-dharmaśāstra*. A detailed examination of this matter must await another occasion. But the statement in the text (III.110) that the Āraṇyaka which Yājñavalkya obtained from the sun god, namely the *Bṛhadāraṇyaka Upaniṣad*,[28] is to be known, should be noted in the context of the history of early Vedānta philosophy. Furthermore, the text says that the *ātman*, which abides like the steady flame of a lamp in the centre of the body, should be realized; if one has realized it, he will not be born again in this world (III.109). The view of *ātman* to be realized as an object as is set forth in the following, is typically a *pariṇāmavāda*.

> "Just as sparks fly out from a heated lamp of iron, so do ātmans (i.e. individual selves) indeed come forth from the (single) ātman." *niḥsaranti yathā lohapiṇḍāt taptāt spuliṅgakāḥ sākāśād ātmanas tadvad ātmānaḥ prabhavanti hi* (III.67)

This is a view of ātman which is widely held in the Vedānta school in general as well as in the Upanisads. And it is just this view which the third chapter of the *Māṇḍūkyakārikā* and Śaṅkara condemn and reject.[29] This portion in the *Yājñavalkyasmṛti*, which probably took shape later than the 4th century A.D.,[30] reveals that such a view of *ātman* was current among authors of the Dharmaśāstras of the time.

A great number of law-books in addition to those mentioned above were written and are extant today, and the Vedāntic thought which is frequently referred to in those texts will one day have to be examined. But the theory that one should practise both knowledge and action (*jñānakarma-samuccayavāda*) can be pointed out as one of the characteristics of the Vedānta thought which appears through the law-books in general. This is the theory that to attain the Absolute Brahman, active religious practices have to be combined with the knowledge which contemplates Brahman, neither of them being of itself sufficient to lead a man to final release. This is what Bhāskara emphasized later, in sharp contrast to Śaṅkara's thought which attaches importance to knowledge (*jñāna*) only. But the tendency towards the former theory had already appeared in the law-books.

> "He who acts thus will become one with Brahman." (*Baudhāyana-dharmasūtra* II.7.13.13)[31]
>
> "Just as (neither) horses devoid of carts nor carts without horses (can carry any load), so are both austerity (*tapas*) and knowledge (indispensible) to the ascetics." (*Hārītasmṛti* VI.10.10).[32]
>
> "Just as the birds fly indeed with two wings, so does one attain the eternal Brahman by both knowledge and action (*jñānakarma*)." (Ibid. VII.10.11)

The similies given here are also used in the *Brahmasūtra* III.4.26.

Thus the law-books agree, in their thought, with the later Vedānta philosophy to a considerable extent, but the influence of law-books upon Vedānta is far greater in respect of the rules of practice and life. The way of the ascetic's practice and life is discussed in *Brahmasūtra* III.4 where the three commentators Śaṅkara, Bhāskara and Rāmānuja refer as its scriptural authority to the *Gautama-dharmasūtra*, the *Āpastamba-dharmasūtra*, the *Dakṣasmṛti*, the *Atrismṛti* and the *Mānava-dharmaśāstra*.[33]

So it seems that it was rather in the field of regulations for the life of the practitioner that the law-books exerted their influence.

Notes

1. See such works as R. Fick, *Die sociale Gliederung in nordöstlichen, Indien zu Buddha's Zeit*. Kiel, 1897 and T. W. Rhys Davids, *Buddhist India*. London, 1902.

2. It is also called the *Adhyātmapaṭalabhāṣya*. *Minor Works of Śaṅkarācārya*, ed. by H. Raghunath Bhagavat (Poona, 1925), pp. 422-435. It is also published in the *Trivandrum Sanskrit Series*.

3. Belvalkar, *Shree Gopal Basu Mallik Lectures on Vedānta Philosophy*, Pt. I, (Poona, 1929), p. 219.

4. The *Ujjvalā Vṛtti* of Haradatta was composed in the 15th century or

about one hundred years earlier than that. Though not extant at present, a previous commentary on the *Āpastamba-Dharmasūtra* was also once in existence (G. Bühler, *Sacred Books of the East*, Vol. II, Introduction, p. xlvii). There are not a few mistakes in Haradatta's commentary on the *Adhyātmapaṭala*. For example, Haradatta reads *idam id, iha id, iha loke* (22,5) as *idam idi, ha idi ha* (Bühler, *op. cit.*, p. 76, n. 5), and this is clearly a mistake and points to the fact that he is not familiar with Vedic usage. Śaṅkara however interprets it correctly. Haradatta's note on 22.6 is also unreasonable as Bühler says, whereas it can be interpreted without so much difficulty on the lines of Śaṅkara's interpretation. In regard to the eightfold *viṣṭapa* Haradatta gives another unreasonable interpretation, based on folketymology.

5. *yogāḥ—akrodhādayaḥ* (Śaṅkara).

6. *niścārika—niścārayanti mano ntaḥsthaṃ bahirviṣayebhya iti naiścārikāḥ krodhādayo doṣāḥ* (Śaṅkara).

7. Śaṅkara says that they are quoted from the *Upaniṣads* of other schools (*śākhāntaropaniṣadbhyaḥ*). Haradatta says likewise that they are quoted from some *Upaniṣads*.

8. *anutiṣṭhanti=mamātmeti sākṣāt pratipadyante* (Śaṅkara). But I have followed Bühler's interpretation of the word as worship.

9. *vaibhājanaṃ puram*. I have followed Bühler's translation based on Haradatta's commentary. Śaṅkara interprets it as "discriminating itself" (*vivekaḥ ātmanaḥ*).

10. *prādhvaṃ bandhanam ātmaikatvarasaprajñatāṃ sthirāṃ bāhyaiṣaṇāvyāvṛttarūpāṃ sarvasaṃnyāsalakṣaṇām* (Śaṅkara).

11. Brahmā. This is a suggestive expression. See my Japanese translation of *Māṇḍūkyakārikā* IV, 85, the present work Vol. III Part 6. Cf. *Chānd. Up.* IV.1.7.

12. *nākapṛṣṭha*. In India it has been thought from the time of the *Ṛgveda* that the entire universe is spherical in shape, so it probably points to the highest place of this sphere.

13. *samayapadānīti / samayasthānānīty etat / avaśyānuṣṭheyānīty arthaḥ /* (Śaṅkara).

14. Cf. the present work Vol. I, Part I, Chapter II, Section I, 1.

15. G. Bühler, *The Sacred Books of the East*, Vol. II, Introduction, pp. xl-xliii. Cf. J. Jolly, *Recht und Sitte*, p. 3.

16. Max Müller, *A History of Ancient Sanskrit Literature* (London, 1859), p. 361.

17. Max Müller, *ibid*, p. 363.

18. According to Hopkins the *Āpastamba-Dharmasūtra* cannot have been in existence before the 2nd century B.C. As for the point that it does not obey Pāṇini's grammatical rules, he explains that Pāṇini's grammar chiefly lays down the usage of the Sanskrit of the North, whereas in the Andhra of the South-East coast ancient linguistic characteristics were preserved until later centuries (Rapson, *Cambridge History of India*, I, p. 249).

19. Śaṅkara *ad Brahmasūtra* II, 1, 1 (Vol. I, p. 421); *ad* I, 1, 17 (Vol. I, p. 121. *ātmalābhān nāparaṃ vidyate—Āp. Dh. S.* I, 8, 22, 2); Rāmānuja *ad Brahmasūtra* II, 1, 1 (p. 399).

20. G. Bühler, *op. cit.*, p. xxix.
21. *The Sacred Books of the East*, Vol. XIV, pp. 20; 144.
22. *Āp. Dh. S.* II, 4, 8, 13. II. 6, 13, 14. Cf. G. Bühler, *op. cit.*, pp. xxvii-xxviii.
23. According to Bühler, what is laid down in *Mimāṃsāsūtra* I, 3, 3-4 is mentioned in *Āpastamba-Dharmasūtra* I. 1, 14, 8-10. (Bühler, *op. cit.* pp. xxviii-xxix
24. G. Bühler, *Laws of Manu*, Introduction, pp. lxxiv, cxiv-cxvii.
25. *Manu* III, 70; 78.
26. *Ibid.* VI, 26.
27. H. Losch, *Die Yājñavalkyasmṛti : Ein Beitrag zur Quellenkunde des Indischen Rechts* (Leipzig, 1927), p. 75 f.
28. M. Winternitz. *Geschichte der Indischen Litteratur*, Vol. III, p. 499.
29. With regard to each of these passages, see my notes on *Māṇḍūkya-kārikā* III, 15 and the present work Vol. II, Part III, Section 5.
30. H. Losch, *op. cit.*, Einleitung, p. xiv-xvii.
31. *evam ācaran brahmabhūyāya kalpate* /
32. *yathāśvā rathahīnaś ca rathāś cāśvair vinā yathā* /
evaṃ tapaś ca vidyā ca ubhāv api tapasvinah //
dvābhyām eva hi pakṣābhyāṃ yathā vai pakṣiṇāṃ gatiḥ /
tathaiva jñānakarmabhyām prāpyate brahma śāśvatam //
(Belvalkar, *op. cit.*, pp. 168-169)
33. Cf. the present work Vol. II, Part IV.

SECTION IV: VEDĀNTA IN THE ARTHAŚĀSTRAS

Alongside of the law books we must take up the *Arthaśāstras* for discussion. The Indian people of the ancient period thought that the three objects (*trivarga*) to be sought for by mankind are *dharma* (virtue), *artha* (wealth) and *kāma* (love or sex). The *Dharmaśāstras* enjoin realization of order in human society whereas the *Arthaśāstras* teach the most efficient means to obtain wealth. The most important and representative example of the *Arthaśāstras* is the *Kauṭilīya-Arthaśāstra* traditionally ascribed to Kauṭilya (or, Cāṇakya), who was the prime minister of Candragupta, the founder of the Maurya Dynasty. It is a guide book for the statesmen, concerned with politics, economics, diplomacy, conduct of life and so forth. It is a valuable source of information about the actual conditions of the ancient Indian society. Not the contents, are from the pen of Kauṭilya himself, but it is supposed that it assumed its present form perhaps in the 3rd century A.D.[1]

Since this work teaches chiefly the artifices and machinations of politics with no discrimination among the various means to an end, it has frequently been compared to the *Il Principe* by Machiavelli, and its central thinking is very utilitarian, realistic and materialistic. It seems that the author was deeply versed in the views of the *Vaiśeṣika* philosophy,[2] so, its contents have almost no connection with the *Vedānta* philosophy. Let us, however, examine the text since there are in it very significant references to the social evaluation of the *Upaniṣadic* learning.

The *Kauṭilīya-Arthaśāstra* in its first chapter (*vidyāsamuddeśa*).[3] recognizes four sciences (*vidyā*) : (1) philosophy (*ānvīkṣiki*), (2) theology (*Vedic* learning, *trayī*), (3) economics (*vārttā*) and (4) jurisprudence (*daṇḍanīti*). Among these sciences the first, philosophy, comprises the *Sāṃkhya*, *Yoga*, and *Lokāyata* (*Sāṃkhyaṃ Yogo Lokāyataṃ cety ānvīkṣikī*). A most interesting point is that it makes no reference to the two schools of *Vaiśeṣika* and *Nyāya*. The later *Nyāya* school asserts that philosophy (*ānvīkṣikī*) is nothing but the *Nyāya* itself. Nevertheless these two schools are not referred to here. This may point to the fact that they had perhaps not yet been fully recognized as philosophic schools. Furthermore, neither the *Mīmāṃsā* nor the *Vedānta* schools are referred to. What is the reason ? It is an indubitable fact that by about the 3rd century A.D., when the *Kauṭilīya-Arthaśāstra* was compiled into its present form, these two schools were already in existence, but the fact that here they are not referred to indicates perhaps that the author of the *Arthaśāstra* did not recognize either of them as schools of philosophy. According to the *Kauṭilīya-Arthaśāstra*, the essence of philosophy is demonstration and investigation through reasoning (*hetubhir anvīkṣamāṇā...*)[4] and it would be difficult to admit that the *Mīmāṃsā* and the *Vedānta* are schools which engage in purely theoretical and philosophical speculation. Both schools regard the *Veda* as absolute and carry out philosophical speculation only in conformity with it. For this reason the *Arthaśāstra* classifies the two schools under *Vedic* study (*trayī*).

If we look more closely at the historical facts, it is a new attitude that the author of the *Arthaśāstra* made philosophy an independent science. Some other thinkers did not accept independence of philosophy itself but regarded it as a special field of theology (*trayī vārttā daṇḍanītiś ceti Mānavāḥ* /

trayīviśeṣo hy ānvīkṣikīti /).[5] The author of the *Arthaśāstra* on the contrary gives the three sciences, *Sāṃkhya, Yoga* and *Lokāyata,* an independent academic status as philosophy, distinguishing them from theology.

It is already seen in the old law books that philosophy may be distinguished from theology. For example, the *Gautama-Dharmasūtra* (XI, 3) says, "[The king] should be fully instructed in the threefold *Veda* and in philosophy"[6] (*trayyām ānvīkṣikyāṃ cābhivinītaḥ*). Accordingly, the tendency to regard philosophy as an independent science had already existed from ancient time, but it is probably the *Kauṭilīya-Arthaśāstra* that particularly emphasized this point. In view of such facts it would seem reasonable that the *Mīmāṃsā* and the *Vedānta* schools which had a close relation with the *Veda* were included in theology (*Vedic* learning).

Therefore, even in this period one group of the *Brahmin* who followed the *Upaniṣads* continued to exist but the author of the *Arthaśāstra* looked upon them not as philosophers but as a group of *Vedic* theologians engaged in logical speculation, since from the viewpoint of the author of the *Arthaśāstra* they were still scholars of exegesis. It is, therefore, not at all surprising that neither *Mīmāṃsā* nor *Vedānta* is mentioned.

The same evaluation is seen in the case of the *Arthaśāstra* scholar, Kāmandaki (6th century)[7]. He also thought that the sciences of the *Mīmāṃsā* and *Vedānta* could be included in the *Vedic* study (*trayī*).[8] Again the view[9] which postulates simply a fourfold science, i.e. philosophy, theology, economics and jurisprudence was accepted by the *Yājñavalkyasmṛti* (I, 310) and the scholars of the *Nyāya* school. Further, as we shall mention later,[10] this putting of the *Vedānta* school under Vedic study was also inherited by the *Nyāya* school. Thus the method of classifying sciences in the *Kauṭilīya-Arthaśāstra* was a model for a long time whose authority weighed on later scholars, by whom also *Upaniṣadic* study was not accepted as an independent philosophy.

Incidentally the fact that the author of the *Arthaśāstra* dismissed *Vedāntic* study as a kind of *Vedic* theology, shows that it was outside his interests. His main concern was with the means by which to strengthen his country and to increase power. It is natural that the kings, politicians, and worldly *Brahmins* who were their advisors, completely unscrupulous in the means they employed to gain their ends, familiar with every possible form of tactics, kept themselves well away from the *Vedānta* philosophy.

The *Kāmaśāstras*[11] also are exactly the same in disregarding *Vedāntic* thought. It has frequently been pointed out that the *Kāmasūtra* (4th century A.D.), the oldest extant text of this kind, is similar to the *Kauṭilīya-Arthaśāstra* in its construction and way of expression. Its author affirms that in order to enjoy sexual pleasure one may violate the moral codes and go so far as to break the law. He asserts that the science of *kāma* can be established as those of *dharma*, *artha* and *mokṣa* can be. So it cannot be supposed that he totally rejects the *Vedānta* which teaches *mokṣa*. However, his concern was perhaps completely apart from the mentality of the *Vedāntic* seekers. He was writing for city-dwellers (*nāgaraka*), debauchees indulging in enjoyments in cities and widely separated from the *Vedānta* philosophy.

From the above facts we could come to the following conclusion: until the period of the 3rd or 4th century A.D., the kings, and wealthy merchants of large cities were absorbed in aggressive warfare in order to increase their power over other countries or busy acquiring vast wealth and property or spending every night in sexual enjoyment and sumptuous banquets. These rulers and influential people of cities did not pay much attention to the *Vedānta* philosophy, and it was in a different social milieu that the Upaniṣads were being handed down and studied.

Notes

1. M. Winternitz, *Geschichte der Indischen Litteratur*, Vol. III, p. 523.
2. J. Jolly, *Arthaśāstra of Kauṭilya* (Lahore, 1923), Introduction, p. 25.
3. Jacobi has already examined this passage ("Zur Frühgeschichte der Indischen Philosophie", *Sitzungsberichte der Presussischen Akademie der Wissenschaften in Berlin*, 1911, p. 732 ff.) (=H. Jacobi : *Kleine Schriften*, Wiesbaden : Franz Steiner, 1970. pp. 547ff.
4. J. Jolly, *op. cit.*, p. 4.
5. J. Jolly, *op. cit.*, p. 4.
6. I have followed Jacobi, *op. cit.*
7. According to the study undertaken by Formichi from the astronomical point of view, Kāmandaki died at the same time as Varāhamihira, who died in 587 A.D., or a little before that. Jacobi has confirmed the theory of

Formichi with the consideration of other data (cf. Jacobi, *op. cit.*). However, Winternitz, *op. cit.*, p. 526 assigns to him the date 700-750 A.D.

8. *aṅgāni Vedāś catvāro Mīmāṃsā Nyāyavistaraḥ |*
dharmaśāstraṃ Purāṇaṃ ca Trayīdaṃ sarvam ucyate ||
Cf. *upāṅgadvitayaṃ caitan Mīmāṃsā Nyāyavistaraḥ*, *Ahirbudhnyasaṃhitā* XII, 12.
9. But *Manu* VII, 43 distinguishes *trayī vidyā* from *ātmavidyā*.
10. Cf. the present work Vol. I, this Chapter, Section, 6.
11. Winternitz, *op. cit.*, p. 540.

SECTION V: WORKS ON NATURAL SCIENCE AND THEIR CONNECTION WITH VEDĀNTA

Of the various fields of natural science in India, medicine was the one with the closest relations with philosophy. The inception of medicine in India can be traced back to the *Atharva Veda* (and the *Kauśikasūtra* appended to it). The early art of medicine appearing therein is quite naive, being strongly coloured by magic, but it did take note of the ways of using medicinal herbs, and again a fair knowledge of the science of dissection is shown. Later on, during the period of the composition of the *Brāhmaṇas*, the art of medicine was continuing a low development, but when the time came which saw the appearance of great cities along the banks of the Ganges, the science of medicine for the first time became an independent study in itself and seems to have made rapid advance. In particular, its development in the period of the Buddha (5th century B.C.) was remarkable, and the names of many noted doctors have been handed down in the Buddhist scriptures, the epic poems and elsewhere. Now medicine became more exact, with the field of the surgeon becoming distinct from that of the physician. Today a good many of the medical treatises are extant, these books not being pure medicine like those of today, but dealing also with the education necessary for a doctor, even going into questions of philosophy and religion. Thus to throw light on the thought of the Indian doctors is an important matter for students of Indian thought generally. On this Professor Dasgupta[1] has already made some substantial contributions, but for our present investigation into early Vedānta philosophy we shall look carefully into the relation of the Ātman doctrine as it appears in one of the oldest medical works, the *Caraka-saṁhitā*, with Vedāntic thought. *Caraka-saṁhitā* is the name of one work of internal medicine. Ātreya was a physician of the fifth century B.C., whose pupil Agniveśa wrote a medical work called *Agniveśa-saṁhitā*; this was later expanded by Caraka to make the work as it exists today.[2] Caraka was a physician of Kashmir, a contemporary of King Kaniṣka, and his dates are perhaps 100-150 A.D.[3]

In the *Caraka-saṁhitā* there are various sections on medicine, but logic is taught as one of the necessary qualifications of a doctor. As Dr. Hakuju Ui has already shown in his critical edition, translation (into Japanese) and study,[4] the work is a valuable source for early Indian logic.

Furthermore, the book also contains valuable philosophical expositions, and it is here proposed to introduce and examine those parts specially relevant to Vedānta. The 11th century commentary by Cakradatta (or Cakrapāṇidatta, Cakrapāṇi, Cakra) is the oldest still extant, and it has been referred to in making the present translation.

The first chapter (*prathama-adhyāya*) of the fourth part (*śarīrasthāna*) of the *Caraka-saṁhitā*, after analysing and describing the mental functions of the individual,[5] describes the existence of a puruṣa which should be called "the human being himself" or "the essence of the human being", in the depths of the individual man (*puruṣa*), and the commentator interprets this as "Ātman".

> "The eternal puruṣa (*ātman*) is without beginning; but the puruṣa (man) who is born by reason of a cause, is the reverse (i.e. has a beginning).
>
> "It is seen that what is (pure) being, without a cause,[6] is eternal; what arises from a cause is the reverse." (IV.1.57)
>
> *anādiḥ puruṣo nityo viparītas tu hetujaḥ //*
> *sad akāraṇavān nityaṁ dṛṣṭaṁ hetujam anyathā //*
>
> "It (pure being) cannot be grasped by being (in the phenomenal world)[7] Eternality does not come from any being (in the phenomenal world).
>
> "It should be known that it is unevolved and unthinkable; the evolved is the reverse." (IV.1.58)
>
> *tad eva bhāvād agrāhyam nityatvaṃ na kutaś cana /*
> *bhāvāt, jñeyaṃ tad avyaktam acintyaṃ vyaktam anyathā //*
>
> "The unevolved is Ātman and is the individual self

(*kṣetrajña*), eternal, all-pervading and immutable. That which differs from it is the evolved. Both of these will be further explained." (IV.1.59)

avyaktam ātmā kṣetrajñaḥ śāśvato vibhur avyayaḥ /
tasmād yad anyat tad vyaktam, vakṣyate cāparaṃ dvayam //

"That which is perceived by the senses is the evolved and perceptible. Again, that which is different from it is the unevolved, grasped through indications (*liṅga*) and beyond the senses." (IV.1.60)

vyaktaṃ caindriyakaṃ caiva gṛhyate tad yad indriyaiḥ /
ato 'nyat punar avyaktaṃ liṅgagrāhyam atīndriyaṃ //

Therefore the Ātman conceived by Caraka should be said to be the essence of human beings. Neither is it grounded on any other principle nor is it limited by time; it is eternal, all-pervading, and immutable, and it should be called pure being (*sat*). Accordingly it transcends the phenomenal world and cannot be understood conceptually, nor perceived by the senses. So the Ātman conceived by him accords with the Ātman taught in the Upaniṣads and Vedānta philosophy. However his Ātman is ever the individual self (*kṣetrajña*), its existence being known by inference from indications (*liṅga*). What are these special indications of Ātman ? Caraka explains as follows .

"Desire, aversion, pleasure, pain, effort, intelligence, firmness, intellect, memory, "I"-consciousness, are the indications of the supreme self." (IV.1.70)

icchā dveṣaḥ sukhaṃ duḥkhaṃ prayatnaś cetanā dhṛtiḥ /[8]
buddhiḥ smṛtir ahaṅkāro liṅgāni paramātmanaḥ //

"These indications are perceived as belonging to one living but not to one dead. Therefore have the great sages said that (these are) the indications of Ātman". (IV.1.71)

yasmāt samupalabhyante liṅgāny etānī jīvataḥ /
na mṛtasyātmaliṅgāni tasmād āhur maharṣayaḥ //

"Truly when Ātman is gone, the body, an empty house without intelligence, is said to be resolved into the five elements (of which it consists), since (it) is not different from the five elements." (IV.1, 72)

śarīraṃ hi gate tasmin śūnyāgāram acetanam /
pañcabhūtāviśeṣatvāt pañcatvaṃ gatam ucyate //

"Though non-conscious, the mind has actions with the supreme (*para*) as its prompter. It is taught that when this all-pervading (Ātman) is connected with the mind, actions belong to it." (IV.1.73)

acetanaṃ kriyāvac ca manaś cetayitā paraḥ |
yuktasya manasā tasya nirdiśyante vibhoḥ kriyāḥ ||

"And since Ātman is conscious, it is called an agent (*kartṛ*). And because it is not consciousness, the mind, though having actions, is not (so) called." (IV.1.74)

"The living beings by their own self (Ātman) lead their own self (Ātman) by the vital airs into all the wombs (man, cow, elephant etc.), for there is no other (such as some Lord)[9] who is the controller of this (living being). (IV.1.75)

yathāsvenātmanātmānaṃ nayati sarvayoniṣu |
prāṇais tantrayate prāṇī na hy anyo 'sty asya tantrakaḥ ||

As we see, the Ātman which Caraka is teaching is an individual at the centre of each individual existence. And it is identical with the Ātman taught by the Vaiśeṣika school.[10] The *Vaiśeṣika-sūtras* were compiled around 50-100 A.D.[11], but since its doctrines would have been established long before that, Caraka would probably have adopted them into his own system.

Then this Ātman doctrine was adopted not only by Śabarasvāmin of the later Mīmāṁsā school, but Śaṅkara also adopted it as it stood, and it formed Śaṅkara's theory of the individual self.[12] However, Śaṅkara, taking this Ātman as the individual self (*jīva*) as in Vaiśeṣika philosophy, thought that the supreme self was essentially opposed to it, while Caraka called the individual self in itself the supreme (*para*) and the supreme self (*paramātman*). Accordingly, on this point the standpoint of Caraka coincides with the Vaiśeṣika theory, and is exactly the opposite of the view of Śaṅkara. The coincidence of the Ātman theory of Caraka with the Vedānta philosophy is in only an extremely limited area. However on the problem of liberation, he emphasized union with Brahman and expresses views similar to Vedānta.

"At the time of this renunciation of the last (*karma*), all sensibility becomes altogether free from representation, knowledge and cognitions, and ceases altogether to act." (IV.1.152)

tasmiṃs caramasaṃnyāse samūlāḥ sarvavedanāḥ |
asaṃjñajñānavijñānanivṛttiṃ yānty aśeṣataḥ ||

"Then the Ātman of living beings which has become

Brahman is not perceived, and having quitted all states, there is no mark of it." (IV.1.153)
ataḥ paraṃ brahmabhūto bhūtātmā nopalabhyate /
niḥsṛtaḥ sarvabhāvebhyaś cihnaṃ yasya na vidyate //
"And the person who knows Brahman goes toward it. An ignorant man cannot know it."
gatir brahmavidāṃ cātra nājñas taj jñātum arhati /

Again in another passage this is said :

"Liberation is cessation. It is the supreme. It is tranquillity. It is the imperishable. It is Brahman. It is final release. Now we explain the path to be followed by seekers after release."[13] *nivṛttir apavargaḥ tat paraṃ praśāntaṃ tat tad akṣaraṃ tad brahma sa mokṣaḥ /*
tatra mumukṣūṇāṃ udayanāni vyākhyāsyāmaḥ. //

Then it goes on to give directions for those who seek liberation, but these do not differ greatly from those generally accepted in India for religious renunciates.

From what we have seen of this doctrine of liberation, there are places where it is like Vaiśeṣika ideas on the subject, but in vocabulary, expression and so on the affinity with Upaniṣadic or Vedāntic doctrine is marked. It has however a very different flavour from the doctrine of liberation as enjoying the absolute bliss and happiness of Brahman as taught by one section in early Vedānta, or from the Vedāntic liberation as taught by Hindu religious sects. Caraka's ideas on philosophy can be taken to have been based on his own medical experience, with which he combined Sāṃkhya and Vaiśeṣika philosophy, and furthermore on the subject of liberation also adopted Vedāntic ideas.

But he did not do more than adopt and accept some Vedāntic ideas and expressions which however do not form the essential part of his thought. What he made the goal was human happiness, and for human beings physical health was very important, also spiritual peace and a trustworthy and moral role in society. These things together would, he believed, promote human happiness.[14] His intellectual tendency is this-worldly—hedonism in the good sense of the word. Thus the life of a wandering renunciate, who rejects all empirical pleasures and meditates on Brahman, he did not altogether recommend. Probably he simply recognized that the enunciate's life was just one of the good ways of life which a man might lead. Thus Vedānta philosophy is not an important element in the structure of his thought, but the fact that he did include it may be taken as showing that in society at the time of Caraka, namely about the second century A.D., this way of thinking was fairly wide-spread.[15]

An immense number of medical works were composed after Caraka, but the investigation of these will have to be postponed to some other occasion. Related to medicine was a kind of alchemy which studied drugs and sought to make an elixir of life, using mercury. This was called the "mercury school" (*Raseśvara-darśana*).[16] A good number of their works are extant and have been published. A clear reflection of Vedānta ideas can be found in them, but these texts are not merely difficult to get hold of but their dates of authorship are unclear, and as it is, thus difficult to decide whether they can be of significance in the study of early Vedānta, their consideration is omitted here.

Works of mathematics, astronomy and astrology were produced in profusion before the eighth century when Śaṅkara lived, and some of them have survived to the present, and have been studied as texts in their own fields, quite apart from philosophical thought. There is in fact no essential relation with Vedānta philosophy. An author may make a salutation to Brahmā at the beginning,[17] and in texts of later centuries to "the god of truth, the supreme Brahman" (*satyā devatā param brahma*).[18] But this is simply following the general custom in India in beginning a work with a salutation to some god.

It could be Brahmā or the supreme Brahman or some other god; sometimes the sun-god Sūrya or Vasiṣṭha[19] are saluted, or again the elephant-headed god Gaṇeśa.[20] For these scientists it could be *any god* who was so saluted, the question of which particular god, it was having no essential connection with the science at all, but depending rather on the faith of the individual scientist himself.

While very occasionally some reference is made to Vedāntic ideas[21] mingled with Hinduism and Sāṃkhya philosophy, it is no more than a mere mention and hardly to be taken as showing any substantial connection.

Notes

1. Dasgupta : *HIPh.* Vol. II, pp. 273-436.

2. However, since Caraka was not able to complete that supplement, a doctor of Kashmir, called Dṛḍhabala, between the 7th and 10th century, later devised and completed a supplement on the latter half of Chapter 17 of the Part 6, and on the two parts 7 and 8., and at the same time, it is said he added some corrections to the first part of Part 6.

3. H. Ui, "*Indo Tetsugaku kenkyu*", Vol. II, pp. 427-431.

4. Ibid, p. 425-471.

5. *Caraka-saṃhitā*, published by Motilal Banarsidass, Lahore 1929, Vol. I, p. 543.

6. According to the commentator, this is said to distinguish puruṣa from "previous non-existence" (i.e. before manifestation—*prāg-abhāva*) which though it has no cause, does not have existence either.

7. *bhāvād utpattidharmakāt tan nityatvaṃ na kuto 'pi bhāvād bhavati nityatvaṃ hi na kuto 'pi bhavati* / (*Cakradatta*)

8. This line is the first half of the *Bhagavad-gītā* XIII, v. 6, except that "*prayatnas*" is "*saṃghātas*" there.

9. According to **Cakrapāṇidatta**.

10. For instance the demonstration of Ātman is the same as that taught in *Vaiśeṣikasūtra* III.2.3, and again the relation between Ātman and will is what is taught in *Vaiśeṣikasūtra* III.2.1.

11. H. Ui, "*Indo Tetsuggaku shi*," p. 178.

12. Cf. Item two, Section 2, Chap. 9, Part 5, of the present work.

13. *Caraka-saṃhitā*, IV, 5, 13.

14. Dasgupta, : *HIPh.* Vol. II, pp. 418-423.

15. The explanations in the passages cited are extremely brief, and cannot be taken as after the establishment of the philosophical schools in later centuries, so that they are probably not a part of the supplementary additions by Dṛḍhabala but from the pen of Caraka himself.

16. Concerning the doctrines of this school, cf. the thesis by Jolly in *Festschrift Windish*, and Chap. 9 of the *Sarvadarśanasaṃgraha*.

17. *Sūryasiddhānta*, *JAOS*, Vol. 6, 1850, p. 145.

18. Cf. the opening passage of the *Bhaṭadīpikā* (ed. by Kern, 1874) by Paramādiśvara, the gloss on the *Āryabhaṭīya*.

19. See the beginning of *Pañcasiddhāntikā* by Varāhamihira.

20. Cf. the salutory stanza in *Līlāvatī*.

21. In *Sūryasiddhānta*, XII.12, it says that Vāsudeva is Brahman, and occupies a position above the 25 truths also.

SECTION VI: VEDĀNTA PHILOSOPHY IN PHILOSOPHICAL AND RELIGIOUS WORKS*

It is needless to say that the Vedānta philosophy has been taken up for discussion far more frequently in the field of philosophy and religion than in any other cultural area, since it is the most important philosophy among the orthodox Brahmanical traditions. For this reason a number of philosophical works in the orthodox Brahmanical traditions, composed before Śaṅkara, constitute most valuable material for throwing light on early *Vedānta.* There are, however, only a few passages in those works which refer to the Vedānta philosophy. The majority of the extant philosophical works of the orthodox Brahmanical traditions were written after the time of Śaṅkara, and in each philosophical school there remain only a few texts written before him. Other religious and theological works, especially those of Hinduism, should also be taken into consideration, but there too, almost all the extant texts were composed after Śaṅkara, though the historical origin of Hinduism itself can be traced back to an exceedingly ancient period. Owing to this paucity of material, passages referring to early Vedānta philosophy are very few in number, far less than what is available from the Buddhist and the Jaina scriptures. However, no matter how scanty the materials may be, they are so important that they cannot be overlooked. In the following, I would like to examine them one by one.

First of all, the *Vaiśeṣikasūtra* (7, 2, 3 & 4) refutes the view that everything is one (*sarvaikatva*), and concludes that the theory that all is one is wrong (*bhrānta*). Here it may be rejecting Sāṃkhya as well as *Vedānta*, but at any rate it is clear that it refutes the monism of the *Vedānta* philosophy.

Moreover, the same text (4, 2, 2 & 3) refutes not only the theory that the body consists of the five material elements but also the idea that the body consists of three material elements—earth, water and fire. As the reason for his rejection the author states: "For the other attributes (*guṇa*) do not appear." The attributes of water and fire do not appear in the dead body. If the body were composed of earth, water and fire, their attributes should appear in the body not only while alive but also after death. But this does not occur. This fact demonstrates that the body is not composed of the three elements, but it has one element, earth as its chief component. This argument is evidently made against the Vedānta school which asserts on the basis of Uddālaka's thought (*Chāndogya-Up.* VI, 3-6) that all things consist of water, fire and earth and the body also is composed of the same three elements (cf. *Brahmasūtra* II, 4, 20-22).

Furthermore, while demonstrating the existence of *ātman*, the *Vaiśeṣikasūtra* refers to an argument of opponents that the existence of *ātman* cannot be established by means of inference but only by means of the *Veda*. Namely, when one touches another person, e.g. Yajñadatta, no sense arises that this *ātman* is Yajñadatta. Therefore, there is no visible mark (*liṅga*) indicating the existence of *ātman*. Again, the fact of tangibility is recognized as common to other things, so that in this point there is no distinction from other things.

> One cannot, therefore, know the existene of ātman through a direct awareness/ For this reason *ātman* has to be known by means of the *Veda* (*Āgamika*, III, 2, 6-8)[1].

Since it is chiefly the *Upaniṣads* that teach the existence of *ātman*,[2] those who attack the Vaiśeṣika view here might be *Vedāntins* following the *Upaniṣads*. The view that *ātman* cannot be established by means of logic but only by means of the *Veda* is what is later emphasized by Bhartṛhari and Śaṅkara.[3] However, since the Mīmāṃsā and the Vedānta schools had not yet been separated at that time, it might well be thought that the *Mīmāṃsakas* are also included among the opponents of the *Vaiśeṣika* school who hold the above view. (It is likely that the *Mīmāṃsā* school at that time had not yet been influenced by the *Vaiśeṣika* philosophy)

Since the *Vaiśeṣikasūtra* took shape in 50-100 A.D.,[4] our examination of the above arguments reveals that a group of Brahmins who regarded the *Upaniṣads* as their absolute authority attacked, and were refuted by, the Vaiśeṣika school in the first century, A.D.

There is no other reference to the *Vedānta* philosophy[5] in the works of the Vaiśeṣika school written before Śaṅkara, but the works of the *Nyāya* school, a sister system of the former, provide information about it which should be examined in order to know the history of the *Vedānta* school. There is no direct reference to it in the *Nyāyasūtra* but interesting information is available in Vātsyāyana's commentary on the *Nyāyasūtra*.

Vātsyāyana accepts the fourfold learning exactly as taught in the *Kauṭilīya-Arthaśāstra.*[6] According to him, philosophy (*ānvīkṣikī*) is the fourth learning (*caturthī vidyā*) which means simply logic (*nyāyavidyā, nyāyaśāstra*). Against the charge that: "Is it not meaningless to construct a philosophical system of the *Nyāya* school by bringing forward doubt (*saṃśaya*) and other items ? For these are covered in the study of right means of knowledge (*pramāṇa*) and objects of knowledge (*prameya*) and they are not separate things." He asserts that "doubt and other items should be brought forward" and argues as follows :

> "If these [items] be not stated separately, this [philosophy] would become merely a study of the inner *ātman* like the *Upaniṣads.* Therefore, philosophy is separately established by means of doubt and other items."
>
> *teṣām pṛthagvacanam antareṇādhyātmamātram iyaṃ syāt, yathopaniṣadaḥ.*
>
> *tasmāt saṃśayādibhiḥ padārthaiḥ pṛthak prasthāpyate.*

Commenting on this, Uddyotakara says:

> "If there be no such items as doubt in philosophy, it would be included in the *Vedic* study like the *Upaniṣadic* study since [it] would be merely a study of the inner *ātman.* Thus the fourfoldness [of the learning] would cease to exist."
>
> *adhyātmavidyāmātratvād Upaniṣadyāvat trayyām evāntarbhāva iti catuṣṭvaṃ nivarteta.*[7]

Thus both Vātsyāyana and Uddyotakara regard the "Upaniṣadic study" (*Upaniṣadvidyā*) or a "study of the inner *ātman*" merely as theology or *Vedic* study and not as philosophy. According to them, it is only learning which gives rise to doubts about every aspect of nature and life and then answers them by means of reasoning which can really deserve the name of philosophy. The *Vedānta* school however attaches importance only to the *Upaniṣads* and dismisses logical thinking. Considering, therefore, that the *Vedānta* is not philosophy in the pure sense of the term, they decline to give the name of philosophy to it. It is clear that on this point as well, these *Nyāya* philosophers hold the same opinion as the author of the *Arthaśāstra.*

In this way the early *Nyāya* philosophers refused to admit the significance or raison d'être of the *Vedānta* philosophy as philosophy. Nevertheless, they could not neglect the social fact that this philosophy was actually gaining strength in the intellectual world of the time.

Referring clearly to the *Vedānta* philosophy in another place[8] of his commentary, Vātsyāyana states and then refutes it as follows :

"Some people think: [final release] is to discard the life which has already been taken on and not to take on a further life. The people who know final release teach that infinity is final release. [It is taught in the scripture that] "*Brahman* is the state without fear, age or death and attainment of peace". In release are manifest the eternal bliss of *Ātman* equally with its glory. When it is manifest, a man is finally released and in peace and bliss. [However), their argument is not reasonable because of the absence of evidence. There is neither sense-perception nor inference nor scriptural testimony with which to prove that in release is manifest the eternal bliss of *ātman* equally with its glory."

"Some people" in the above passage evidently refers to the *Vedānta* school. They consider *brahman* as the absolute principle and final release as manifestation of the eternal bliss (*nityaṃ sukham*)[9] of *ātman* which is one's own nature. Such a concept of final release is one of the characteristics of the *Vedānta* philosophy.

Furthermore, the same work of Vātsyāyana (*Nyāyabhāṣya* ad IV, 1, 41)[10] introduces different theories which classify all things in various ways. One of them is the opinion that:

> "All is one existent, because of the absence of distinction."
> *sarvam ekaṃ sad, aviśeṣāt.*

In his sub-commentary *Nyāyavārttikatātparyaṭīkā* Vācaspatimiśra interprets this as a theory of non-dualism of *brahman* (*brahmādvaita*), quoting the passage which explains *brahman* as one without a second (*ekam evādvitīyam, Chāndogya-Up.* VI, 2, 1) and the one which denies distinctions among beings (*Bṛhadāraṇyaka-Up.* IV, 4, 19). To deny or disregard the distinction among beings, interpreting them as transformations of the one ultimate principle, is one of the characteristics of the *Vedānta* philosophy. Therefore, the theory quoted above may point to a doctrine of the *Vedānta* school.[11]

Vātsyāyana, who was active in 350-400 A.D., could not at that time disregard the *Vedānta* scholars who advocated such a doctrine. Further in the *Nyāyavārttika*, Uddyotakara (550-600 A.D.) refers to views suggestive of the *Vedānta* philosophy in places other than the above-mentioned. For example, he criticizes a theory according to which *ātman*, the individual self which is the controller of individual existence, apportions right and wrong (as the subject which supports them)[12]. This is in accordance with Jaimini's theory which is referred to in *Brahmasūtra* III, 2, 40, and it has been inherited by the later Mīmāṃsakas. It may, however, be possible to regard it as one of the different views presented by the early *Vedānta* philosophers since it is referred to in the *Brahmasūtra*.

Thus in the works of the early *Nyāya* and the *Vaiśeṣika* school the primitive *Vedānta* philosophy of the early period is transmitted and no reference is made to any theory like that of illusory manifestation (*vivartavāda*) of the Śāṅkara school,. Even in later centuries Udayana (10th century), an important scholar of the *Nyāya-Vaiśeṣika* school mentions the name of Bhāskara as one who taught that all things evolved from *brahman*[13] without referring to Śāṅkara. The Śaṅkara school does not seem to have been yet regarded as important in the intellectual world of that time.

Besides the *Vedānta* school, the Sāṃkhya school is the one which exerted the greatest influence upon the history of Indian thought, and a blending and synthesis of the thought of the two schools can often be found in important works of thought in India. The thought of both schools possesses inherently the possibility of being easily synthesized, but the pure classical *Sāṃkhya* school rejects the *Vedānta* philosophy,. Especially the ancient *Sāṃkhya* school which is grounded on the theory of the plurality of *ātman* was not able to admit the monistic tendency of the *Vedānta* philosophy. The former takes up this point of the latter for thorough investigation.

The *Sāṃkhyakārikā* (18), which is the classical text book of the *Sāṃkhya* school, rejects the theory of oneness of *ātman* and advocates its plurality. This argument could be summarized as follows: the existence of many *ātmans* which are mutually different should be admitted, for the activity, function and state of an *ātman* are neither common to those of another nor does a change in one *ātman* take place in another. The same argument is employed when the Buddhists and the Jainas attack the *Vedānta* philosophy. In relation to this argument, the commentators introduce the *Vedānta* thought of that time.

> "According to a theory, the one *ātman* pervades all the bodies just as a string pierces gems although gems are many and the string is one, and just as Viṣṇu shares His pleasure with 160,00 maidens at the same time. So is the one *ātman*. It can pervade all the bodies." (*Suvarṇasaptati*)
>
> "Then certain masters who are *Vedavādins* think as follows: This one single *puruṣa* can be seen in all the bodies just as a string (*sūtra*) pierces [a great number of] gems (*maṇi*). No matter how many gems there may be in this world, only the one string pierces all gems. If so, does the highest *ātman* which corresponds to a string exist in many bodies which correspond to gems or is the one called *puruṣa* perceived in many [bodies] just like the moon reflecting on the surface of water, that is to say, just as one moon is perceived on the surface of rivers, wells, tanks, and so forth ? A doubt arises in this point." (*Māṭharavṛtti*)
>
> "The one single *ātman* is the ruler (*adhiṣṭhātṛ*) in all the bodies just like a string whose nature is to run through [many] gems." (*Gauḍapāda*)

The simile of a string piercing gems is introduced in the *Vijñaptimātratāsiddhi* as well.[14] That of the moon reflecting on the surface of water is frequently employed by the later *Vedānta* school (cf. *Brahmasūtra* II, 3, 50), and such a method of explanation is called the reflection theory (*pratibimbavāda*). Thus the facts show that the doctrine of the *Vedānta* school was known to the *Sāṃkhya* school at the same time and that the relationship between the highest *ātman* and the individual *ātman* was variously explained by the same school. However, *Māṭhara* attributes the theory to a *Vedavādin* and not to a *Vedāntavādin*. Therefore, it is likely that the independence of the *Vedānta* school had not yet been generally accepted. The *Suvarṇasaptati* was composed before 546 A.D. and the other two commentaries were probably written in about 600-700, A.D.[15] It is, therefore, to be noted here that, although it was the period when *Vedānta* philosophers appeared one after another, their view was ascribed to *Vedavādins*.

The origin of the Sāṃkhya school is exceedingly ancient, but its extant texts composed before Śaṅkara are only the *Sāṃkhyakārikā* and its commentaries. They refer briefly to the *Vedānta* philosophy as I have mentioned above and there is no reference to the *māyā* doctrine yet. In the works of the *Sāṃkhya* school, the *māyā* doctrine was called into question only after the time of Śaṅkara. In commenting on *Sāṃkhyakārikā* (9), Vācaspatimiśra attacks the *māyā* doctrine, saying, "It is not possible to say that the notion of the phenomenal world being real is false, for there is no evidence to contradict it."[16]

Now we push on to the Yoga school. Prior to Śaṅkara there are the *Yogasūtra* and Vyāsa's commentary (*Bhāṣya*) on it. But the *Yogasūtra* is not concerned with logical debates, and even in the commentary of Vyāsa there is no place where he refutes the *Vedānta* school. The practice of *Yoga* is common to nearly all of the schools in India, and the Vedānta school also adopts it. Therefore, they probably did not think it necessary to refute the doctrine of the *Vedānta* school.

The *Mīmāṃsā* school has been in a sister relationship with the *Vedānta* school since the time of its establishment, and they claim to be the two great systems of the orthodox Brahmanical tradition. Most scholars of the early *Mīmāṃsā* school belonged to the *Vedānta* school at the same time. One and the same person studied both schools. Therefore, the *Mīmāṃsakas* did not reject the *Vedānta* philosophy (in this connection, see the present work, Vol. II, Part III, Chapter 1 and Vol. III, Part V, Chapter 1). However, in later centuries there arose in the *Vedānta* school a tendency to reject as inferior teaching the *Mīmāṃsā* philosophy which centres round rites. Consequently, the *Mīmāṃsā* school came to reject positively the *Vedānta* philosophy. The eternal existence of the individual *ātman*, from the standpoint of the highest truth, is absolutely necessary and indispensable presupposition on which the *Mīmāṃsā* philosophy can establish their rites. Nevertheless, there appeared a number of philosophers in the later *Vedānta* school who asserted that "the individual *ātman* is real only in the worldly life and unreal from the standpoint of the highest truth." The *Mīmāṃsakas* naturally tried hard to attack this threat to the basis of their philosophy of rites. As the result the *Mīmāṃsā* school came closer to the *Nyāya-Vaiśeṣika* philosophy with regard to the problem of the individual *ātman*.

As far as the extant texts show, it is Kumārila among the *Mīmāṃsakas* who first attacked the Vedānta philosophy. In his *Ślokavārttika* (*Pratyakṣasūtra*, 114-116, p. 169) he introduces and attacks a view, which according to the commentator Pārthasārathimiśra is the theory of the *Vedāntins*. It runs as follows:

> "But other people (= *Vedāntins*) say that [the object of non-determinate knowledge][17] is the highest universality (*mahāsāmānya*), as real substance (*dravya*), namely pure being (*sat*). Thus the theory that sense-perception (*pratyakṣa*) has universality (*sāmānya*) as its object has been accepted" [114].
>
> "[When an objector asks], 'If sense-perception is non-determinative, how can particularities (*viśeṣa*) be cognized ?', it is replied that various particularities are cognized by the determinative faculty of cognition (*savikalpaka-buddhi*). Therefore, some particularities (i.e. individuality) exist only in their respective objects and again, some particularities [such as cowness (*gotva*)] exist in many objects." [115]
>
> "When one does not think of these particularities which are established by [respective] exclusion or agreement, the sense-perception which arises with reference to a cow is not distinguished from that which arises with reference to a horse."[18] [116]

According to the commentary, this argument is refuted in the following stanzas and later again a further argument is mentioned as a theory of opponents, which may also be that of the Vedānta school.[19]

> "[The determinative] cognitive subject (= knower) (*dhī*) superimposes a genus (*jāti*) and so forth [which are different from a thing] upon a thing (*vastu*) which is not a genus itself. Therefore, the subject of cognition is [false] like a mirage (*mṛgatṛṣṇikā*)."[20] [140]

The Vedānta doctrine mentioned here resembles that of Śaṅkara but it is not the same in every respect. For example, it is in accordance with Śaṅkara's philosophy in regarding the Absolute as being but he neither calls it substance (*dravya*) nor the highest universality (*mahāsāmānya*).[21] In these respects the Vedānta doctrine in question is closer to Bhartṛhari's view. At least, what is taught in stanzas 114-116 is all advocated by Bhartṛhari.[22] It also greatly resembles what is mentioned as a *Vedānta* theory by a Jaina scholar Mallavādin.[23] These facts show evidently that a Vedānta doctrine different from Śaṅkara's was prevalent in intellectual circles prior to him.

It is to be noted here that the concept of the highest universality (*mahāsāmānya*) was generally taken in India as the highest concept at the ultimate limit of thought, but in fact was taken only as an abstraction, and was made the essential character of the Absolute by philosophers like Bhartṛhari. Their unique significance in the history of philosophy can be recognized in this respect. However, the idea was not original with these *Vedānta* scholars but had already been taught in the *Vijñānavāda* philosophy of Buddhism. In his *Bodhisattvabhūmi* Maitreya regards the highest universality as a characteristic of the ultimate state and it is understood as attainable by means of non-determinative wisdom.[24] So the influence of the *Vijñānavāda* can here be seen upon the Vedānta philosophy.

In the *Ślokavārttika* of Kumārila there is another place where he attacks the Vedānta philosophy.[25] There he only attacks it without introducing it first, but from what he says one may guess whom he attacks.

> "But an impure transformation could not arise in a pure *puruṣa*". [82cd]
>
> "And, [if one says that living beings are afflicted with suffering because of good and evil *karma* (*dharma* and *adharma*) performed by each individual *ātman*, we reply], such suffering is not reasonable because *dharma* etc., merit and the like are dependent on [*puruṣa*, i.e. *brahman*] itself. Or if they (=merit and the like) start functioning by their own power [at the beginning of the world, they] would exist apart [from brahman]. [If so, the monism of *brahman* could not stand since the creation would not be caused by the desire of the Lord]." [83]
>
> "Further, since [*brahman*] itself is of pure nature and there exists nothing else [but *brahman*], how could nescience (*avidyā*) like a dream and so forth work on that [*brahman*] ?" [84]
>
> "If one says that [*brahman*] is invaded by something else, [his position] would become dualism. [In other words, since two principles, *brahman* and something else, have to be accepted, non-dualism will be discarded]. On the other hand, if [one says that] nescience belongs to [*brahman*]

by nature, [which does not need another principle because of the function of nescience, we reply], nobody would be able to remove it. [And so no final release would be possible]" [85]

"Indeed, if something different [from nescience, e.g. *yoga*, etc.] could arise, natural nescience could come to be destroyed in some places. But for those who regard the only one *ātman* as the means [to destroy nescience] there is no cause [=means to destroy nescience], different [from *ātman*]."[26] [86]

Stanzas 82 and 83 attack the most ancient Vedānta philosophy, especially the theory of transformation (*pariṇāmavāda*), which agrees with the theory of an opponent school in the *Brahmasūtra* (II, 1, 4; II, 1, 34 and 35). So Kumārila is repeating here a refutation of the Vedānta philosophy which had been already made prior to him. In the next stanzas 84-86 he attacks a new form of Vedānta philosophy, i.e. the theory of false manifestation (*vivartavāda*). According to the commentator Pārthasārathimiśra the author refutes the *Ātmādvaitavādins* here. From the stanzas it is clear that those people were of opinion that the absolute *brahman* evolves itself by the power of nescience (*avidyā*), the phenomenal world as its effect being illusory like dream and illusion. Their view is in accordance with the thought of non-dualism. This fact indicates that such a non-dualistic thought has already come into existence before Śaṅkara, since Kumārila lived before him.[27] It is very significant from the standpoint of the history of thought. Kumārila's argument against it hits at a crucial point of non-dualism. This kind of argument is often made in attacking non-dualism in India. The argument in stanzas 85 and 86 resembles that in the *Āptamīmāṃsā* (v. 25) of Samantabhadra, a Jaina scholar, as well and is similar in its idea to what is discussed by Hemacandra when he attacks non-dualism.[28] The principle of nescience which was posited in order to give a firm foundation to non-dualism is in fact the weakest point in this doctrine and the attacks of other schools have been focussed upon it.

As can be seen from Kumārila's arguments, he is no longer regarding the Vedānta school as a sister system of the Mīmāṃsā school. He attacks it as sharply as he criticizes other schools, and we can take it that from his time the two schools came to be separated and antagonistic to each other. Mīmāṃsā scholars after Kumārila likewise reject the Vedānta philosophy. Śālikanātha, a pupil of the Mīmāṃsā scholar Prabhākara who was however an opponent of Kumārila, also attacked nondualism.[29] In much later centuries the Mīmāṃsā school was inclined to adopt the Vedānta philosophy,[30] but before that the two schools seem to have been mutually antagonistic.

We have so far examined the references to the Vedānta philosophy which are made in early philosophical works. We must also deal with the Vedānta philosophy as is seen in the works of Hinduism, the popular religion of India. Since Hindu sects have been greatly influenced by the Vedānta philosophy, it is no doubt certain that Hindu masters have been in close contact with the Vedānta school. However, I will defer a study of the relationship between the two to some other occasion and will now examine only how Hindu works describe the Vedānta school and its doctrine.

The theological works of Hinduism are innumerable, but nearly all of them came into existence in later centuries, with only a few belonging to the same period as pre-Śaṅkara early Vedānta philosophy. The *Purāṇa* literature comes into this category. For example, the *Garuḍapurāṇa*[31] accepts that the *Vedānta* is connected with philosophical discussion. Again in the *Viṣṇupurāṇa* the supporter and ruler of all beings is taken to be the god Viṣṇu, and it is said that Viṣṇu is praised in the *Vedānta*.[32] However, so far as the ancient *Upaniṣads* at least are concerned, one cannot say that Viṣṇu is regarded as the highest Lord. In that case, is it that the author of the *Viṣṇupurāṇa* was acquainted with new *Upaniṣads* which emphasize the worship of Viṣṇu ? Or is he boldly insisting that there is this concept in *Upaniṣads* ? At any rate it is certain that authors of the *Purāṇas* knew that the *Vedānta* (=the *Upaniṣads*) is a special section of the *Veda* teaching a supreme principle. They knew not only that, but also the germ of the new Vedānta philosophy. The *Viṣṇupurāṇa* (V.1) refers to the twofold *brahman* and the twofold knowledge corresponding to it (*dve vidye*), i.e. higher and lower knowledge, and also mentions a branch of learning which enquires into the distinction between the individual self and the great self. It is probable that the *Viṣṇupurāṇa* exercised some influence upon formation of Śaṅkara's thought since he quotes it in his works.[33] Moreover, the *Vāyupurāṇa* reads as follows:

"He who knows the one *puruṣa* is called *Brahmavādin*."[34]
ekaṃ yo vetti puruṣaṃ tam āhur brahmavādinam |

As the *Vāyupurāṇa* probably was already in existence by the 7th century,[35] it can be seen that some people advocated the one *puruṣa* as the world principle before that time. The *Purāṇa* literature has made a great contribution to the establishment of the Vedānta philosophy, but it seems that there are only a few direct references to the *Vedānta* school. Since the religion of the *Purāṇas* is generally for the general masses, they do not seem to have been concerned either to argue with or defend the Vedānta as a philosophy.

Among the Hindu scriptures Itihāsas, Purāṇas, many Saṃhitās of the Vaiṣṇavas and Āgamas of the Śaivas should be taken into consideration, but most of them are unpublished, or if published, difficult to obtain. Here I would like to take up, only the best-known, the *Ahirbudhnyasaṃhitā*, for discussion. This work seems to have come into existence around the 5th century.[36] In 12.3, it enumerates and explains the *Veda* (*trayī*), the *Sāṃkhya*, the *Yoga*, the *Pāśupata*, and the *Sātvata* (= *Pāñcarātra*) as the *five* kinds of doctrinal systems. They are the same as those mentioned in the *Mahābhārata* XII.[37] Therefore, the author of this work, like the author of the great epic, did not admit the *Vedānta* school as a special independent school of philosophy. Although he refers to the *Vedānta* (*Trayyanta*), this means the *Upaniṣads* and has nothing to do with the name of a school of philosophy. He asserts that one can directly (*aparokṣam*) cognize *brahman* by means of the *Vedānta*.[38] On the whole the thought of the *Ahirbudhnyasaṃhitā* itself is remarkably Vedāntic and there are not a few assertions which remind one of Śaṅkara's non-dualism. For example, it admits two kinds of knowledge, higher and lower, and teaches that all *karmans* are burnt up by means of the former.[39] And in the same work the power which covers the highest nature (*paraṃ rūpam*) of the individual *ātman* and the supreme *ātman* is called nescience (*avidyā*).[40] In this respect its similarity to Śaṅkara's philosophy could be pointed out, but it cannot be said to be the same concerning his concept of nescience since, according to him, nescience is not the cause which establishes the pluralistic opposing relationship of the individual selves.

Moreover, the text refers to the *Karma-Mīmāṃsā*,[41] but only as an accessory (*upāṅga*) to the *Vedic* learning and not as the *Mīmāṃsā* as an independent school of philosophy.

However, at the time of Śaṅkara the *Vedānta* school is referred to as an independent school in works of Hinduism as well. In the *Yogavāsiṣṭha*, which was perhaps composed before the 8th century,[42] the *Vedāntavādins*' concept of final release is stated along with those of the *Sāṃkhya* school (*Kāpila*), the *Vijñānavādins* and the Jainas (*Ārhata*).

> "The Vedāntavādin holds that by the general acceptance of the idea 'All this is Brahman', accompanied with calmness of mind and control of the senses, final release is certain".[43]

From this it might be concluded that in this period the Vedānta school was recognized by people generally as a school in opposition to other powerful schools of philosophy.

After the time of Śaṅkara the connection between Hinduism and the Vedānta philosophy became closer and closer and a great number of theological works have been handed down till today. However, since they are outside the scope of the present work, I shall leave them out of the consideration here.

Notes

*This portion was formerly published under the title : "Vedānta Philosophy in Philosophical and Religious Works" in *Umesha Mishra Commemoration Volume* (Allahabad : Ganganatha Jha Research Institute, 1970), pp. 47-64. Here this article has been revised.

1. As for such an interpretation of these *sūtras*, see Hakuju Ui, *Indo Tetsugaku Kenkyū* (= A Study of Indian Philosophy), Vol. III, pp. 487 ff. and p. 520.

2. *tasmāt samyag Upaniṣadāṃ śravaṇāt tattvasākṣātkāra upapadyate, na tu mananapraṇālikayā* (Upaskāra *ad Vaiśeṣikasūtra*, III, 2, 8).

3. The doctrine of Bhartṛhari is to be discussed in Part VII of the present work. *śrutyavagāhyam evedam atigambhīraṃ brahma na tarkāvagāhyam* (Śaṅkara *ad Brahmasūtra* II, 1, 32, Vol. I, p. 502, line 2); [*vedānta-*] *vākyārthavicāraṇādhyavasānanirvṛttā hi brahmāvagatir nānumānādipramāṇāntaranirvṛttā* (Śaṅkara *ad Brahmasūtra* I, 1, 1, Vol. I, p. 36, line 2); *tasmāc chabdamūla evātīndriyārthayāthātmyādhigamaḥ* (Śaṅkara *ad Brahmasūtra* II, 1, 27, Vol. I, p. 496, line 8). In addition to those Śaṅkara's arguments of this kind can be frequently seen in his works.

4. Hakuju Ui, *Indo Tetsugaku Shi* (—A History of Indian Philosophy), p. 178.

5. In addition to the *Vaiśeṣikasūtra*, Praśastapāda's *Padārthadharmasaṃgraha* and the *Daśapadārthaśāstra* were also composed before Śaṅkara but in neither of them any passages can be found which present the doctrine of the *Vedānta* school.

6. Vātsyāyana *ad Nyāyasūtra* I, 1,1, pp. 4-5; 10 (ĀnSS.).

7. *Nyāyavārttika*, p. 12.

8. *Nyāyabhāṣya ad* I, 1, 22, pp. 37-38.

9. *Ibid.*, p. 306.

10. But it is not possible to conclude absolutely that it points to the *Vedānta* school, since it might point to the *Sāṃkhya* school. In the "*Śāstra on the Four Sects in the Laṅkāvatāra-sūtra*" ascribed to Āryadeva such a theory is attributed to the *Sāṃkhya* school : "There are some heretics who say that everything is one... It is the doctrine of the *Sāṃkhya* school that everything is one." (*TT.*, Vol. XXXII, p. 155a.). However, it might be more reasonable to look upon it as pointing to the *Vedānta* school. Furthermore, the theory that everything is the same also appears in the *Upāya-hṛdaya* (Hakuju Ui, *Indo Tetsugaku Kenkyu*, Vol. II, pp. 486 ff.). The same is also said in the *Mahāyānāvatāra* chuan 1: "The doctrine of the *Sāṃkhya* school has a fault in thinking that [everything] is one." (*TT.*, Vol. XXXII, p. 40b.).

11. Hakuju Ui, *Indo Tetsugaku Shi*, p. 478.

12. *ātmaivādhiṣṭhātā dharmādharmayor bhaviṣyatīti* (*Nyāyavārttika ad* IV, 1, 21, Chowkhambā Sanskrit Series, p. 459). Yamada and Itō (tr.). *Indo Kodai Shinkan Shi*, p.147.. (Die Entwicklung der Gottesidee bei den Indern von H. G. Jacobi) Cf. *Gauḍapādīyakārikā* II, 25 and my translation and note on it in the present work, Vol. III, p. 350 (Japanese edition).

13. In his *Nyāyakusumañjali* (2) Udayana says : *sargo brahmapariṇater iti Bhāskaragotre yujyate*, and Govardhana comments on it as : "*Bhāskaras Tridaṇḍimatabhāṣyakāraḥ*" (Aufrecht, *Catalogus Catalogorum*, Vol. . I, p. 793).

14. Cf. the present work, Vol. I, Part II, Chapter 1, Section 3.

15. Hakuju Ui, *Indo Tetsugaku Shi*, p. 473.

16. *prapañcapratyayaś cāsati bādhake na śakyo mithyeti vaditum iti.*

17. *nirvikalpakasya viṣayam*, Comm.

18. *mahāsāmānyam anyais tu dravyaṃ sad iti cocyate |*
sāmānyaviṣayatvaṃ ca pratyakṣasyaivam āśritam ||144||
viśeṣās tu pratīyante savikalpakabuddhibhiḥ |
te ca kecit pratidravyaṃ kecid bahuṣu saṃśritāḥ ||115||
tān akalpayad utpannaṃ vyāvṛttānugatātmanā |
gavy aśve copajātaṃ tu pratyakṣaṃ na viśiṣyate ||116||

In translating the last stanza I read *vyāvṛttyanugamātmanā* (for *vyāvṛttānugatātmanā*), following the reading of the commentary.

19. The commentary reads : *codayati*. The English translator G. Jhā interprets it as *Vedāntic* objection.

20. *jātyādyarthāntaraṃ yasmād atadrūpe 'pi vastuni |*
bhavaty adhyasya dhīs tasmān mṛgatṛṣṇādibhiḥ samā || (pp. 177-178).

jātyādi=jātiguṇakriyānāmadheyāni ("genus and so on" denotes a genus, a quality, action and name), Comm.

21. But this statement is concerned with the *Brahmasūtrabhāṣya* only.

22. To be discussed in the present work, Part VII.

23. *Nyāyabinduṭīkāṭippaṇi* of Mallavādin, ed. by Stcherbatsky, B.B. XI, p. 35.

24. *yā bodhisattvānām anabhilāpyaṃ dharmanairātmyam ārabhya satyāvabodhāya vā satyāvabodhakāle vā satyābhisaṃbodhād vā ūrdhvaṃ prajñā paramapraśamavyupasthānā nirvikalpā sarvaprapañcāpagatā sarvadharmeṣu samatānugatā mahāsāmānyalakṣaṇapraviṣṭā jñeyaparyaṃtagatā samāropāpavādāntadvayavivarjitā madhyamapratipadanusāriṇī, iyaṃ bodhisattvānāṃ tattvānubodhaprativedhāya prajñā veditavyā* (*Bodhisattvabhūmi*, p. 212, lines 12-20). (=The Chinese version of the *Yogācāra-bhūmi*, chuan 43, *TT.*, Vol. 30, p. 528c)

25. *Ślokavārttika*, *Saṃbandhākṣepaparihāra*, vv. 82cd-86 (pp. 662-663).

26. *puruṣasya ca śuddhasya nāśuddhā vikṛtir bhavet* // 82cd //
svādhīnatvāc ca dharmādes tena kleśo na yujyate /
tadvaśena pravṛttau vā vyatirekaḥ prasajyate // 83 //
svayaṃ ca śuddharūpatvād asattvāc cānyavastunaḥ /
svapnādivad avidyāyāḥ pravṛttis tasya kiṃkṛtā // 84 //
anyenopaplave 'bhīṣṭe dvaitavādaḥ prasajyate /
svābhāvikīṃ avidyāṃ tu nocchettuṃ kaścid arhati // 85 //
vilakṣaṇopapāte hi naśyet svābhāvikī kvacit //
na tv ekātmābhyupāyānāṃ hetur asti vilakṣaṇaḥ // 86 //

27. Cf. the present work, Vol. I, Part I, Chapter 2.

28. Cf. *Ibid.*, Part II, Chapter 2, Section 3.

29. In his *Prakaraṇapañcikā* (pp. 154-155) Śālikanātha attacks the *Advaitasiddhānta* by quoting the second verse of the *Tarkakāṇḍa* in the *Brahmasiddhi* of Maṇḍanamiśra. It is a very interesting fact in the history of thought that Śālikanātha attacks Maṇḍanamiśra's non-dualism without criticizing Śaṅkara's (S. Kuppuswami Sastri, 'Further Light on the Prābhākara problem,' *Proceedings and Transactions of the Third Oriental Conference*, Madras, 1924, p. 480).

30. For example, see Laugākṣi-Bhāskara's *Arthasaṃgraha* VII, *Arthavāda*.

31. Cf. the present work, Vol. I, Part I, Chapter 3, Section 1, n. 24.

32. Works by H. H. Wilson, Vol. VII, p. 95; Vol. IX, p. 252; Vol. X. p. 201.

33. Śaṅkara's *Chāndogyopaniṣadbhāṣya* (ĀnSS, p. 280) says : "*tatroktaṃ Paurāṇikaiḥ—'ābhūtasaṃplavaṃ sthānam amṛtatvaṃ hi bhāṣyate' iti.*" This is a quotation from *Viṣṇupurāṇa*, II, 8, 96 (cf. Jacob : *The Vedāntasāra*, p. 76). Further, there exists a quotation from the *Viṣṇupurāṇa* in Śaṅkara's *Gītābhāṣya* as well (cf. A list of quotations at the end of the Ānandāśrama Sanskrit Series edition of the *Gītābhāṣya*).

34. Th. Aufrecht : *Catalogus Codicum MSS. Sanskriticorum Bibliothecae Bodleianae*, Oxonii 1859-64, p. 56b.

35. M. Winternitz, *History of Indian Literature*, Vol. I, pp. 553-554.

36. *Ibid.*, p. 589, n. 3.

37. Cf. the present work, Vol. I, Part II, Chapter 3, Section 2.

38. *antaraṅgaśamādyaṅgabhaktiśraddhāpuraḥsaram /*
Trayyantair brahmavijñānam aparokṣaṃ vibhāvyate // (*Ahirbudhnyasaṃhitā*, XIII, 26)
tasya yo 'vyabhicāreṇa sādhanatvaṃ prapadyate /
hitasādhanam ity uktaḥ so 'rtho Vedāntapāragaiḥ // (*Ibid.*, XIII, 10)

39. *Ahirbudhnyasaṃhitā*, XLV, 18 (but this information is obtained from Schrader : *Introduction to the Pāñcarātra and the Ahirbudhnya-Saṃhitā*, 1916, p. 97).

40. *Ibid.*, XLV, 3-4 (but this information is obtained from Schrader, *op. cit.*, pp. 97-98).

41. *Ibid.* XII, 12.

42. A man called Gauḍābhinanda, who lived in the middle of the 9th century, condensed this work into his *Yogavāsiṣṭhasāra* (S. Konow, *Karpūramañjarī*, HOS. Vol. IV, p. 197). The fact that such a summary work was composed concerning the *Yogavāsiṣṭha* means that it must have won considerable authority at that time. This may indicate that it probably came into existence before the 8th century. However, on the other hand, stanza II, 16, 60 in this work is almost the same as a passage in Kālidāsa's *Kumārasambhava*, but the former may be a quotation from the latter (cf. S. Dasgupta, *A History of Indian Philosophy*, Vol. II, p. 230). Therefore, this work must have been written after the 5th century.

43. *Vedāntavādino buddhyā brahmedam iti rūḍhayā /*
muktiḥ śamadamopetā nirṇīya parikalpitā // (*Sthitiprakaraṇa* 21, 26)

SECTION VII: VEDĀNTA IN PURELY LITERARY WORKS

India is a land of poetry. In all fields of culture, not a few of the important works have been written in beautiful verse. Not only literary and religious works but also pure academic works of philosophy, logic, jurisprudence, politics, mathematics, astronomy, and grammar, in themselves tending to be rather dry, are in verse, often employing highly refined rhetoric. In fact every aspect of Indian life is pervaded by literary arts. However, no matter how excellent this kind of literary production, there is a distinction from literature in the narrow sense since the authors were writing for a different purpose. In the following pages we shall discuss Vedānta referred to as a school in pure literature in the narrow sense.

Among the works composed as pure literature, not a few are written on the basis of Vedāntic thought, but inasmuch as they contain no exact philosophical discussion they differ markedly from works of the Vedānta school itself, which specialize in philosophical arguments or theological interpretations. There is thus no hope of finding in purely literary works any material regarding the details of the philosophical systems of the time. There are however casual references to religious sects, philosophical schools, or their ideas. Although the accounts are mostly short and simple, we may make some guesses from them about the actual situation, characteristic thinking, and social position of the schools of the period. For this reason we shall examine some accounts in literary works in order to see how the Vedānta thought or school appears in the eyes of literary men.

But we shall treat only those literary works which stand in the orthodox Brahmanical tradition. Vedānta philosophy as seen by Buddhist or Jaina literary men will not be considered here since it has already been discussed in Chapters 1 and 2.

Anyone who concerns himself with the literary arts in India first of all thinks of the poet-saint Kālidāsa (400-460 A.D. or c. 410-470 A.D.), a representative poet of India. His drama *Vikramorvaśī*, which is one of his masterpieces and concerned with the love story of King Purūravas and a heavenly nymph named Urvaśī, opens with the following stanza:

> "May He who in the Upaniṣads is called the one Puruṣa, who ever pervades both heaven and earth, who alone is truly signified by the word Lord (*īśvara*) which applies to no other, who is sought for in the heart by seekers of liberation who have controlled breath and mind, and who is easily obtained by means of steadfast yoga of devotion (*bhakti-yoga*), grant you the supreme bliss !"
>
> *Vedānteṣu yam āhur ekapuruṣaṃ vyāpya sthitaṃ rodasī*
> *yasminn īśvara ity ananyaviṣyaḥ śabdo yathārthākṣaraḥ /*
> *antar yaś ca mumukṣubhir niyamitaprāṇādibhir mṛgyate*
> *sa sthāṇuḥ sthirabhaktiyogasulabho niḥśreyasāyāstu vaḥ //*

It has already been asserted by a scholar[1] and is clearly seen in the above stanza that Kālidāsa was a follower of Śiva and followed Vedāntic thought. We may take it that he believed that the Upaniṣads teach one Puruṣa, constant and omnipresent, who is none other than the Lord (*īśvara*); being united with the Lord Śiva through the practice of steadfast *bhakti-yoga*, one can attain final release. *Bhakti-yoga* is to devote oneself to the Lord with fervent faith and is particularly emphasized in the *Bhagavad-gītā*.[2] Therefore, while revering the Upaniṣads, he regards their central concept Puruṣa as identical with the God Śiva. Further, his self-sacrificing loving devotion to the God Śiva derives from the *Bhagavad-gītā* of the Vaiṣṇava sect, so that he is taking a remarkably eclectic and harmonizing attitude. Moreover, in some of his works he praises the God Viṣṇu.[3] What made this non-exclusive attitude possible may have been his fundamental Vedāntic standpoint.

It is known from Kālidāsa's other works that he was quite familiar with Vedāntic thought. In a hymn to the Lord, he says:

> "You are the one alone who, manifesting glory as the three states,[4] have become the cause of dissolution, subsistence and creation."
>
> *tisṛbhis tvam avasthābhir mahimānam udīrayan |*
> *pralayasthitisargāṇām ekaḥ kāraṇatāṃ gataḥ ||*
>
> (*Kumārasambhava* II.6)[5]
>
> "You know yourself through yourself, create yourself through yourself, and you dissolve into yourself through yourself, you who have accomplished all that was to be done."[6]
>
> *ātmānam ātmanā vetsi sṛjasy ātmānam ātmanā |*
> *ātmanā kṛtinā ca tvam ātmany eva pralīyase ||*
>
> (*Ibid.* II.10)
>
> "Salutation to (you who are) first creator of all, then supporter of this all and then destroyer of all, to you whose nature is divided in three ways."[7]
>
> *namo viśvasṛje pūrvaṃ viśvaṃ tad anu bibhrate |*
> *atha viśvasya saṃhartre tubhyaṃ tredhāsthitātmane ||*
>
> (*Raghuvaṃśa* X.16)
>
> "You are all-knowing, unknown (to any other). You are the womb of all, born from yourself. You are the lord of all, having no lord. You are only one, assuming all forms."
>
> *sarvajñas tvaṃ avijñātaḥ sarvayonis tvam ātmabhūḥ |*
> *sarvaprabhur anīśas tvam ekas tvaṃ sarvarūpabhāk ||*
>
> (*Ibid.* X.20)[8]

Thus the concept of the Lord expressed by Kālidāsa is evidently Vedāntic and corresponds closely to that of the Brahman in the *Brahmasūtra,* which was taking shape in the same period as Kālidāsa. He cannot however be counted among the Vedānta philosophers in the strict sense since he himself embraces concepts from Sāṃkhya philosophy and Hindu theology as well as the Vedānta philosophy. Nevertheless it is certain that Vedāntic thought was pretty well known to Kālidāsa and readers of the time who loved his works.

Moreover, a literary figure of the 7th century, Bāṇa, refers to the existence of an Aupaniṣada school. He wrote the *Harṣa-carita* in praise of the virtues of King Harṣa (606-647 A.D.), and one passage records how King Harṣa once went to pay a visit to the saint Divākaramitra in the Vindhya mountains. When the king entered the mountains, religious men, who had come together in the forest from countries near and far, were holding discussions. They leaned against pillars, sat upon rocks, dwelt in small huts wound about with vines, rested in the thickets of the forest, sat in the shade of branches, or crouched down on the roots of large trees. Then in the same passage the following various kinds of religious men are listed.[9] The remarks in parentheses are the notes given by the commentator Śaṅkara. (The dates of this Śaṅkara are not known but as he frequently quotes the *Amarakośa* he must have flourished after the 8th century. He is not the great philosopher Śaṅkara).

Ārhata (= nagnakṣapaṇaka)	Jains
Maskarin (= parivrājaka)	Wandering mendicants.
Śvetapaṭa (—śvetorṇākambalī-vāsas, nagnakṣapaṇabheda)	Jains of the Śvetāmbara white-robed school
Pāṇḍurabhikṣu (according to the commentary, pāṭūrabhikṣu = tyaktakāṣāya)	Wandering medicants who have abandoned Buddhism and returned to Hinduism, wearing a white robe.[10]
Bhāgavata (= viṣṇubhakta)	The Bhāgavata sect.
Varṇin (= brahmacārin)	Students who study the Vedas.
Keśaluñcaka	Ascetics who have pulled out their hair.[11]
Kāpila (Sāṃkhya)	
Lokāyatika (= Cārvāka)	Materialists
Jaina[12]	
Kāṇāda (= Vaiśeṣikatarkajña)	The Vaiśeṣika school.
*Aupaniṣada (= Vedāntavādin)	The Vedānta school.
Aiśvarakāraṇika[13]	the school which asserts that the lord is the cause of the world.

Kārandhamin (=dhātuvādin)[14]	Alchemists
Dharmaśāstrin (=smṛtijña)	Scholars of the Dharmaśāstras
Paurāṇika	Believers in the Purāṇas.
Sāptantava[15]	(see footnote)
Śaiva	The Śaiva sect
Śābdika (=Vaiyākaraṇa)	Grammarians, lexicographers.
Pāñcarātrika (=Vaiṣṇavabheda)	the Pāñcarātra sect.

The above list shows the major schools which existed in the 7th century and the "Aupaniṣada" school listed above seems to indicate the Vedānta school. By that designation a specific school which attaches special importance to, and follows, the Upaniṣads alone is meant, since it is mentioned separately from the students who study the Vedas according to the rules prescribed in ancient times, and is also distinguished from various schools belonging to the Vaiṣṇava and Śaiva sects. It is probable that the Aupaniṣada school had no sectarian colour at that time. (It should be particularly noted that in this passage neither the Mīmāṃsā nor the Yoga is clearly indicated).

The Vedānta school is referred to in another passage of the *Harṣacarita*, which describes in detail the terrible shock to the Court from the death of King Prabhākaravardhana, the father of King Harṣa. It contains the following passage:[16]

"Such was the state of his sacred majesty King Harṣa that he gave up all activities from grief for his father; to him good fortune seemed as a curse, the great earth a great sin, kingship a sickness, property as snakes, a house as hell, kinsmen as fetters, life as infamy, the body as harm, health as blame, long life as the fruit of sin, food as poison, poison as nectar, sandal-wood as fire, love as a saw, heartbreak as prosperity. Round him were sons of ancient noble families who had received the favour of the Court for successive generations, teachers honoured by successive generations of families and whose words were proper, old Brahmins well versed in the sacred scriptures (*śruti*), holy texts (*smṛti*) and history (*itihāsa*), consecrated ministers of the king who were learned and famous, celebrated wandering mendicants who had rightly attained the truth of the inner Self, sages indifferent to pleasure and pain, *teachers of Brahman* (*Brahmavādins*) *who were well versed in declaring out the unreality of birth-and-death*, and believers in the Purāṇas who were skilful in removing sorrow."

In the Sanskrit original this passage displays great skill in rhetoric. In this instance the "Brahmavādin" is listed separately from "wandering mendicants who had rightly attained the truth of the inner Self" and "sages indifferent to pleasure and pain." As the latter two groups clearly refer to the wandering mendicants and sages whose life has been admired and praised from the time of the Old Upaniṣads, the "Brahmavādin" here seems to indicate people who had set up new theories based upon the Upaniṣads. Moreover from the fact that they are said to have taught "unreality (unsubstantiality) of birth-and-death", it is clear that in their opinion the phenomenal world of transmigration is false and non-existent from the standpoint of the highest truth. Therefore we may suppose that they held views close to the Māyā doctrine. As the author Bāṇa flourished about a hundred years earlier than Śaṅkara, we would think that this is an important account which indicates that a view resembling the Māyā doctrine was already prevalent prior to Śaṅkara. The term "Brahmavādin" had existed from exceedingly ancient times, but it does not always have the same specific meaning. Bāṇa interprets it in a very special sense and uses it as synonymous with "Vedāntin". Use of the term in the same sense also occurs in Śaṅkara's works.[17]

As for the Brahmavādins' thought, the idea of the unreality of birth-and-death (*saṃsārāsāratva*) may be considered to be an influence from Mahāyāna Buddhism. In Maitreya's *Bodhisattvabhūmi*[18] the awareness of impermanence and unsubstantiality (*anityāsārasaṃjñā*)[19] is given as one of the concepts which the Bodhisattva should practise. The wisdom which removes the obstacles to the practice of the Bodhisattva is of four kinds, and one of them is "insight into unsubstantiality of *saṃskāras*"[20] (*saṃskārāsāratvadarśana*)[21]. Moreover it is said that:

> *tam bodhisattvo mithyā-phala-dṛṣṭi-kṛtaṃ doṣaṃ laghu laghv eva prajñayā pratividhya sarvasaṃskārāṇām asāratāṃ yathābhūtam pratyavekṣate*[22]

"Then the Bodhisattva, having soon realized through his right wisdom that this wrong view according to which everything is the effect of the Lord would lead one to faults, rightly perceived that all *saṃskāras* are unsubstantial.[23]

The "unsubstantiality of *saṃskāras*" (*saṃskārāsāratva*) in the *Bodhisattvabhūmi* is the same in idea as the "instab``ity" of birth-and-death" of the *Brahmavādins* recorded by Bāṇa. So the

Brahmavādins of that time might have taken in such a thought from Mahāyāna Buddhism.[24]

The statement that the Brahmavādins attended upon the king is worthy of notice. The Vedānta scholars of that time perhaps occupied a very high social position as spiritual leaders of kings and nobles. As I have already pointed out,[25] the Upaniṣads themselves were compiled and handed down by the top levels of Aryan society. It is therefore natural that the Vedānta school which stands in this line also found its believers in the upper levels of society. This feature can be recognized also in the *Brahmasūtra.*[26] And in social position the Vedānta school in the strict sense is opposed to the popular religionists of the Śaiva and Vaiṣṇava sects. Again, the Purāṇas also might have been followed by one section of the upper social level at that time since Bāṇa notes that believers in the Purāṇas also attended upon King Harṣa.

Thus the literary man Bāṇa evidently knew of the existence of the Aupaniṣada school, but we must take note of the fact that those students are described as either wandering mendicants who have abandoned home and given up desire, or ascetics who have retired to dwell in the mountains. For city people concerned with daily affairs in a complex social life, the learning of the Vedānta philosophy was not so important. For instance, in the *Kādambarī* of this same Bāṇa a great many arts and sciences to be studied by young nobles in the cities are listed,[27] but Vedānta study is not among them. Intellectuals in the cities no doubt had a certain leaning towards Vedānta philosophy, but as they first of all had to obtain the practical knowledge essential to their standing as citizens, investigation of the Vedānta may have been considered to be of secondary importance.

Vedāntic thought similar to Bāṇa's is handed down in the lyrical poem *Kirātārjunīya* of Bhāravi (c. 6th century) as well. He also reflected on the impermanence of the world which can be compared to a flash of lightning or waves of water.

> "I do not seek pleasure nor wealth which are unstable like the waves of water. Being afraid of the lightning of impermanence, I do not seek the state of independence of Brahmā."
>
> *na sukhaṃ prārthaye nārtham udanvadvīcicañcalam |*
> *nānityatāśanes trasyan viviktaṃ brahmaṇaḥ padam ||* (XI.66)

Even the state of Brahmā is not free from the wind of impermanence. Therefore he wishes to attain an absolute state which transcends even that. It can only be attained by knowledge of the Absolute. Such a special significance of knowledge is emphasized in other passages as well.

> "For those who wish to approach the highest state of Brahmā which is pure and free from birth-and-death, there arises knowledge, which prevents births, from this (Himālaya)[29] of the sacred texts which drive away darkness."
> *vītajanmajarasaṃ paraṃ śuci brahmaṇaḥ padam upaitum icchatām |*
> *āgamād iva tamo 'pahād itaḥ sambhavanti matayo*[30] *bhavacchidaḥ ||* (V.22)

This stanza differs from the previous one in the way of treating "the highest state of Brahmā" but it might be difficult to find consistency in literary works. Anyway knowledge is looked upon as the only means for final release, and attention should be paid to the historical fact that Bhāravi is already thoroughly conversant with the notion.[31] He also can be regarded as an intellectual forerunner of the Advaita Vedānta philosophy of later centuries.

Again, Bhavabhūti who as a dramatist is as famous as Kālidāsa, also refers to a special Vedāntic idea. He lived perhaps around 690-740 A.D.[32] and may be a senior contemporary of Śaṅkara. In the beginning of his drama *Mālatīmādhava* he makes a noteworthy statement on the social significance of Indian philosophical thought in general.

> "What is the use of speaking out Vedic recitation and the knowledge of the Upaniṣads, the Sāṃkhya and the Yoga, since no merit arises to an actor therefrom ?"
> *yad Vedādhyayanaṃ tathopaniṣadām Sāṃkhyasya Yogasya ca jñānam tat-kathanena kim, na hi tataḥ kaścid guṇo nāṭake.*

Jagaddhara comments on this stanza, "No merit arises to the actor from the recitation of the Veda and the like since they are of no use to an actor."[33]

Vedādhyayanāder nāṭake kaścid guṇo nāsti, teṣāṃ nāṭake 'nupayogāt.

The thought of the Upaniṣads, Sāṃkhya and Yoga is that which is pursued by religious ascetics. On the other hand an actor's professional duty consists in satisfying aesthetic people who seek worldly pleasure. Indian plays in particular are remarkably aesthetic and sensuous, and there are almost no dramas which do not have as their theme intense love, always with a happy ending. Therefore, almost all philosophers and men of religion in India are antagonistic to the theatre. They hate theatre-going and in not a few cases forbid it. The relation between the two groups is of a total opposition. In such circumstances it would be all the more natural that the study of Upaniṣads or Vedānta philosophy should be "of no use" to an actor.

Nevertheless Bhavabhūti himself is quite acquainted with the philosophical thought of the time. He is thoroughly familiar with not only the Yoga[34] but also the Vedānta philosophy. In his work *Uttararāmacarita* he refers to a special Vedānta Philosophy.

He especially emphasizes that the Absolute has Speech (*vāc*) as its nature. He clearly sets forth in his benedictory stanza at the very beginning of this work:

> *idaṃ kavibhyaḥ pūrvebhyo namovākaṃ praśāsmahe /*
> *Vandemahi ca tāṃ vācam amṛtām ātmanaḥ kalām //*
>
> "We ask for this salutation to the ancient poets. We respectfully salute Speech which is the immortal part of *ātman*."

The idea of Speech as the absolute principle can be found throughout this play. For example, in the second act the woman ascetic Ātreyī speaks to the gods of the forest thus:

> "At that time indeed the creator of beings, the lotus-born Lord (Brahmā), approached the sage (Vālmīki) who was brilliant with the light of the Word Brahman and said, 'O sage ! you have realized the Brahman whose essence is speech. Therefore now speak out the *Rāmacarita*. The light of your holy spiritual vision is unlimited. You are the first poet.' Then the holy Prācetasa (Vālmīki) composed the *Rāmāyaṇa* epic which was the first such manifestation of word-Brahman among men."

The passage clearly shows that Bhavabhūti accepts the principle of Word-Brahman (*śabdabrahman*). There is no doubt at all that the concept is very important for him since in the concluding stanza (VII.20) he salutes "the poet who knows Word-Brahman" (*śabdabrahmavit kavi*). But here the word

Brahman does not refer to the metaphysical principle proposed by the Grammarians, but has rather the sense of the mystical power of speech in making possible the composition of the epic. In other words, Brahman is not intended as the Absolute or the world-principle as taught in the Vedānta, but has rather the meaning of mystical power of speech as taught in the Veda generally. Thus it cannot be said that it is Vedānta philosophy that is referred to in this passage. Nevertheless it must also be realized that Bhavabhūti is making an implied reference to it. The "manifestation of Speech-Brahman" (*śabdabrahmaṇo vivartaḥ*) in the above passage is undoubtedly what Bhartṛhari is propounding at the very beginning of his *Vākyapadīya*. Bhavabhūti seems to *parody* the theory of Bhartṛhari. The word *vivarta* is of course a technical term in Vedānta philosophy. He refers to *vivarta* in another passage also.

> "One and the same sentiment of compassion, by reason of different causes takes on different transformations apparently distinct from each other; just so water takes on transformations as a whirlpool, as foam and as waves, but all these are nothing but water."
>
> *eko rasaḥ karuṇa eva nimittabhedād bhinnaḥ pṛthak pṛthag ivāśrayate vivartān /*
>
> *āvartabudbudataraṅgamayān vikārān ambho yathā salilam eva tu tat samagram //* (*Uttararāmacarita*, III.47)

The word "*vivarta*" in this verse is paired with *vikāra* (transformation) and the two have the same meaning.[35] So the word *vivarta* in this case does not mean the false appearance set up by *avidyā* (ignorance) as in the later Advaita Vedānta, but can be taken to have the meaning of "transformation" as in the work of Bhartṛhari and others. A comparison of the relationship between Brahman and its transformations, namely the phenomenal world, with that between the ocean and its waves is often made by Vedānta writers.[36] Vedānta philosophy is again referred to also in the following famous verse:

> "Just as all evolved things dissolve into Brahman (through knowledge), so cloud masses are some-how dissolved by the wind which is like knowledge."
>
> *vidyākalpena marutā meghānām bhūyasām api /*
>
> *brahmaṇīva vivartānāṃ kvāpi pravilayaḥ kṛtaḥ //* (VI.6)

In this way the writer Bhavabhūti takes it as a matter of course that readers of his drama have some elementary knowledge of Vedānta philosophy. Although, as already remarked, he accepts that the mentality of dramatists and actors can hardly be in harmony with the spirit of Vedāntins, the thought of Vedānta could not be overlooked. It may therefore be reasonable to suppose that Vedānta philosophy was widely diffused among intellectual classes in general before Śaṅkara. And it could be said that the Vedānta philosophy handed down by Bhavabhūti is closest to the thought of Bhartṛhari.

Still later, the Vedānta school is referred to here and there in literary works. Stanza 3 at the beginning of the *Mahānāṭaka*[37] (or *Hanumannāṭaka*), which may have been written after Śaṅkara, records[38] that Vedāntins term their Absolute, Brahman:

> "May Hari, Lord of the three worlds, whom the Śaivas worship as Śiva, the Vedāntins as Brahman, the Buddhists as Buddha, the Logicians, clever in the means of knowledge, as the Creator, devotees of the Jaina doctrine as Arhat, and the Mīmāṃsakas as karma, grant you, your cherished desire."

Again, in the beginning of the *Vikramacarita* (or *Siṃhāsana-dvātriṃśikā*)[39] which is a later work, it is said:

> "To destroy all the impediments, salutations to the One (absolute principle) whom the knowers of Brahman-Vedānta (*brahmavedāntavid*) call Puruṣa who is the ultimate fundamental principle, and whom others call the cause of all the beings or the Lord."[40]

And in the Jaina version of this same text, in a passage listing the names of schools whose representatives pay homage to the king, Vedānta students (*vedāntika*)[41] are referred to.

The authors of these literary works are thus aware of the existence of the Vedānta school, and to some extent influenced by its thought. But they do not regard as absolute Vedānta philosophy in the strict sense of giving a special importance to the Upaniṣads. Instead, they admit the raison d'etre of each of the various philosophical systems. But this very attitude taken by them displays a characteristic of the Vedānta philosophy itself—something similar is also found in the philosophical viewpoint of the *Māṇḍūkyakārikā* and the *Vākyapadīya*.[42]

In the above we have presented and examined some passages in purely literary works referring to Vedānta philosophy. It is to be noted that these authors give differing accounts of the Vedānta philosophy, and it may therefore be supposed that previous to Śaṅkara's period of activity a great variety of types of Vedānta was already diffused widely among intellectual people in general.

Notes

1. M. T. Narasimhiengar, 'Kālidāsa's Religion and Philosophy', *IA*, 1910, pp. 236-241. This problem was discussed again recently.

T. K. Gopālaswamy Iyengar : Pre-Śaṅkara Upaniṣadic Philosophy as Expounded by Kālidāsa. *Umesha Mishra Commemoration Volume* (Allahabad : Ganganatha Jha Research Institute, 1970), pp. 179-186. Prof. Iyengar was led to the conclusion that "Kālidāsa does not conceive of māyā as enveloping the Supreme Being nor does he deny the reality of the world......(He was) an ardent advocate of the Upaniṣadic philosophy on the lines of the *śarīra-śarīri-bhāva* which admits unity in spite of diversity, which was later on expounded in detail by Rāmānuja."

2. The term *bhaktiyoga* appears in *BhG* XIV. 26.

3. Cf. M. T. Narasimhiengar, *op. cit.*,

4. According to a commentary, Hari, Hara and Hiraṇyagarbha.

5. T. Gaṇapati Śāstri (ed.), *The Kumārasambhava of Kālidāsa* (TrivSS No. XXVII).

6. *Kṛtinā=kṛtakṛtyena* (*Prakāśikā*)

7. It means that He exists as Brahmā, Viṣṇu and Śiva.

8. Cf. *Raghuvaṃśa* X.16-32.

9. Führer (ed.), *Harṣacarita* (BSS), p. 315 ; English translation by E. B. Cowell and F. W. Thomas. London, 1897, pp. 235-237.

10. According to the interpretation of Cowell and Thomas.

11. According to the *Prabodhacandrodaya*, Jaina ascetics were apparently sometimes referred to in this way (MW).

12. Śaṅkara interprets this as *Bauddha*. He also interprets *Jainaiḥ* as *Śākyaiḥ* in another place (p. 97). However, no example in which "Jaina" is interpreted in a Buddhist meaning is perhaps available anywhere else in Sanskrit texts. Not only in the Buddhist sacred texts in general but also in the *Uṇādisūtra*, the Buddha is called "jina" (cf. Max Müller, *ASL* p. 249) but the designation "*Jaina*" is employed only in connection with Jainism.

13. Śaṅkara glosses this as *Naiyāyika*. However, close connection between the Nyāya and (the doctrine of) the Lord was only conceivable in latter centuries. So it is still doubtful whether one could interpret the term *aiśvara-kāraṇika* in Bāṇa's as pointing to the Nyāya school. The great scholar of the Vedānta school Śaṅkara uses the term *īsvarakāraṇavāda* to mean the Sāṃkhya-yoga theory (Śaṅkara *ad BS* II.2.37-41, Vol. I. pp. 605 line 12; 606 line 10; 607 line 9; 609 line 2) and not the Nyāya school. However, both the Nyāya school and the Vaiśeṣika school did in his time

accept the existence of the Lord. (*Kaṇāda-Akṣapādāditarkaśāstreṣu ca saṃsāravilakṣaṇa īśvara upapattitaḥ sādhyate*, Śaṅkara *ad Bṛhad. Up.*, p. 155).

14. Śaṅkara also gives another interpretation according to which *kārandhamin* means *pāṣaṇḍabheda*.

15. Both Cowell and Thomas translate this term as "adepts in sacrifice requiring seven ministering priests" and give the note : "or containing seven leading types, see Sāyaṇa on *ṚV*. X, 124."

16. *Harṣacarita, op. cit.*, p. 239; English translation, *op. cit.*, p. 162.

17. Cf. The present work, Part I, Chapter 3, Section 4.

18. *Bodhisattvabhūmi*. p. 191, line 11.

19. *Yogācārabhūmi*, Vol. 42 (*TT*. XXX, 523c).

20. *Ibid.* Vol. 39 (*TT*. XXX, 509b).

21. *Ibid.* p. 131. line 9.

22. *Ibid.* p. 130, line 27.

23. *Ibid.* Vol. 39 (*TT*. XXX, 509b).

24. The word "*asāra*" appears also in comparatively ancient Upaniṣads; *kadalīgarbha ivāsāram* (*Maitrī Up.* VI.2). However this too may well be the influence of Buddhist texts (cf. Poussin, *Mvṛ* p. 41, n. 9)

25. Cf. The present work Part I, Chapter 3, Section 2.

26. Cf. *Ibid.* II, 4, 3, 1 ; H. Nakamura, 'The Basic Standpoint of the Vedānta Philosophy', *The Toyō Bunka Kenkyū*, no. 4. june 1957, p. 44 ff.

27. C. M. Ridding (tr.), *The Kādambarī of Bāṇa*, p. 60.

28. Mallinātha interprets this as *mukti*.

29. In the previous verse (V 21) the Himālaya range has also been called *Gaurī-guru*, the father of Gaurī, consort of the god Śiva, and it is regarded as a sacred region and is said to be a source of the uprising of knowledge (*kṣetraviśeṣasyāpi jñānopāyatvād ity āśayaḥ*,—Mallinātha *ad* V. 22)

30. *matayas tattvajñānāni*, Mallinātha.

31. In *Kirātārjunīya* XVI, 32 the "knowledge of truth" (*tattvasya saṃvittiḥ*) is said to destroy "unwisdom" (*apavidyā*). However in spite of the emphasis on knowledge, in another place it teaches that the supreme Lord appears in a manifest form in order to save living beings, out of compassion for them (XVIII, 30).

32. The present work, Part I, Chapter 2, II, B, Section 2.

33. R. G. Bhandarkar (ed.), *Mālatīmādhava*, Act I, p. 16, lines 46, 47.

34. *Ibid.* Act V; *Mahāvīracarita*, beginning of Act III.

35. The word *vivarta*, also used in *Mahāvīracarita* V, 57 and in *Mālatīmādhava* Act I lines 329 and 397 by the same Bhavabhūti can be taken as synonymous with *pariṇāma*, on which see the note by Bhandarkar (p. 18).

36. Cf. Fragment 3 of Taṅka; fragments of Bhartṛprapañca; Śaṅkara *ad BS*, II, 1, 13, Vol. I, p. 456.

37. This work came into being by 850 at the latest (Winternitz : *GIL*, III p. 242)

38. yaṃ śaivāḥ samupāsate Śiva iti brahmeti Vedāntino
Bauddhā Buddha iti pramāṇapaṭavaḥ karteti Naiyāyikāḥ/
Arhannity atha Jainaśāsanaratāḥ karmeti Mīmāṃsakāḥ /
So'yaṃ vo vidadhātu vāñchitaphalaṃ trailokyanātho Hariḥ //
(Aufrecht : *Bodl. Cat.* p. 142b)

39. It is said that this work was composed at the time of King Bhoja of Dhārā in the 11th century to extol his virtues (Winternitz : *GIL*, III, p. 340).

40. yaṃ brahmavedāntavido vadanti parapradhānaṃ puruṣaṃ tathānye viśvodgateḥ kāraṇam *īśvaraṃ* vā tasmai namo vighnavināśanāya (A. Weber *Ind. Studien*, XV, p. 209)

41. A. Weber, *Ind. Studien*, XV, p. 295.

42. For this kind of attitude in the Vedānta school see the present work Part VI, Chapter 3, Section 4, and also the present author's "Confrontation and Conciliation between Differing Philosophical World-views", *Tetsugaku Zasshi*, July 1947, included in "Development of Philosophical Speculation in India" (Tokyo : Shunjusha Press, 1967).

CHAPTER VII

SUPPLEMENT
VEDĀNTA THOUGHT HANDED DOWN BY THE GREEKS

In order to clarify the traces of intellectual developments in ancient India, works from the hands of the Indians themselves should of course be the principal sources of materials, but along with them, accounts by foreigners should, in a certain sense, also be regarded as of considerable value. The works of foreigners travelling throughout India, living there for some time, and actually seeing first hand the life of the ancient Indian people, are particularly valuable in the following two respects:

(1) The accounts of foreigners are put together from a viewpoint different from that of the Indians themselves. The accounts of the Indians themselves frequently mix fact with fantasy, trying to idealize the actual conditions, while the accounts of foreigners for the most part describe the scene as it really was.

(2) The works of ancient Indians are often obscure as to dates of composition, but dates of the works by the foreigners are frequently clear.

Accordingly, the accounts of foreigners on India have their special importance, and among them, perhaps the most important is the account by Megasthenes in particular of things seen and heard in India. Megasthenes was sent to Pāṭaliputra, the capital of the country of Magadha, as an emissary of the King Seleucus Nicator, and it is said, frequently had interviews with the great King Candragupta (founder of the Maurya dynasty) who controlled India at that time. Again, according to the tradition of the historian Arrian, he also had an interview with King Porus (Died 317 B.C.).

The year Megasthenes was dispatched to India is not clear, but perhaps it may have been after a treaty was concluded, and friendly relations were established, between King Seleucus and King Candragupta. In that case, it seems that he probably set out for Pāṭaliputra sometime between 302 and 288 B.C.[1] After returning to his own country, he wrote down what he had seen and heard during his stay in India, and composed a book called "Indian Miscellany" (*Ta Indika*). This work has unfortunately been lost and is not extant today, but in many Greek and Roman works, many fragments of it have been handed down. In fact the knowledge about India of the ancient period (Greeks and Romans) was mainly based upon this work. Therefore, if we carefully examine in detail his works as quoted in the works of later centuries, it should be a contribution to the elucidation of actual conditions in ancient India. In not a few points, his accounts cover the actual state of affairs during the period exactly from the end of the 4th century B.C. to the opening of the 3rd century.

In this work, then, he records the social system of India at that time, and reports the thought of the philosophic sages of that time. According to him, the Indian society of that time was made up of seven classes. Those are, the philosophers (*philosophoi*), farmers, herdsmen, artisans, warriors, officials and counsellors.[2] His theory of these seven strata has frequently been debated among scholars, but we omit these considerations here. For the time being, what we shall here examine is the thinking of the philosopher class out of these seven classes.

According to him, the class of philosophers had the least number of actual members, and yet received utmost respect from society. In this case, this philosopher class could be roughly classified into the Brahmins (*Brakhmanes*) and the Śramaṇas (*Sarmanai*).[3] It is clear that the former represents the name of the Brahmins (*Brāhmaṇa*) and the latter, the name of wandering monks (*śramaṇa*). This corresponds to the fact that in the early Buddhist scriptures and the rock inscriptions of King Aśoka, the Brahmins and Śramaṇas are listed next to each other. Megasthenes has given us a fairly detailed explanation of them which it is not necessary here to discuss point by point. But on the thought of the Brahmins, a short passage of his is so valuable that it cannot be overlooked in the investigation of the history of the Vedānta school. He had the greatest respect for the thought of the Brahmins.

First of all, Clement of Alexandria has recorded the following as the words of Megasthenes :

"And further the author Megasthenes who lived during the

same time as Seleucus Nicator has noted the following in the third chapter of his "Indian Miscellany" (*en tēi tritēi tōn Indikōn*).

"And all that our ancients have taught concerning nature (*physis*) originated with philosophers other than the Greeks, that is with Indians, and was taught by the Brakhmanes and by the people called the Jews in Syria." (*Strom.*I, p. 305. D. Ed. Colon. 1688 = Megasthenes' Fragment XLII).

Therefore, Megasthenes thought that what was taught in general by Greek philosophy had already been taught by the Brahmins of India. In that case, he presents the thought of Brahmins as follows:[4]

"Now, among them (= the Brahmins), a great number of debates have been held concerning death. In the final analysis, they thought that life in this world really is like the child in the womb during the period of its agitation (until it is born), and that death on the contrary is to be born into true life. Then this (= be born into true life) is for the philosopher (the true) happiness, and in order to become firm in readiness for death it was usually believed that practice of extreme asceticism (*askēsis*) is a necessity.

Again, the things that happen to men, whatever they may be, are neither good (*agathon*) not bad (*kakon*). For (supposing that any thing were determined as originally essentially good or bad) people have (in addition) ideas like those of a dream, but it is not the case that by one and the same thing some people are afflicted and others made happy. Nor is it true that the same person is affected variously by the same thing so that he sometimes is afflicted and sometimes made happy by it.

And in regard to nature, what the Indians say is very simple and naive, so he (= Megasthenes) says. And rather than dialectic (*logoi*) they are more advanced in practice (*ergoi*) for their faith is based on many myths. But on many (other) things they hold to beliefs common to the Greeks also. For instance, that the universe arises and dissolves, those people (= Indians) also say. And the universe is a sphere. God who controls and also creates this universe, pervades every part of the whole universe (i.e. is all-pervading). There are distinct principles existent in all things, but the one (the principle) which gives rise to the universe is water. And besides the four elements there exists a fifth which is energy of nature (*physis*) and from this (fifth, energy of nature) the heavens and all the stars (arise).

This (earth) is set in the centre of all. As to seed and spirit, and other things, they (Indians) say the same (as Greeks). As to the immortality of the spirit, the judgment of the dead and this kind of thing, they like Plato have woven myths."

Looking at the theories presented here, we see that there are also some which are common with general orthodox Brahmanism. For example, the addiction to philosophical speculation on death, as well as the great respect for religious and ethical practice, rather than rational speculation on the phenomenal world, can be found in common with the Brahmin philosophers in general. However, the special philosophical theories referred to here coincide for the most part with those taught in the Upaniṣads.

(1) First of all, as regards good and evil from the human standpoint, absolute standpoints are not set up, but only relative ones; an idea which is no more than something often expressed in the Old Upaniṣads (e.g. *Kauṣ. Up.* I.4; *Bṛhad. Up.* IV,3.22; IV,4.23; *Tait. Up.* II,9). And this idea was also adopted in the Vedānta philosophies of later centuries. (In particular, cf. *Brahmasūtra* IV.1, 13-15).

(2) Again in relation to cosmological argument, Megasthenes discovered that the same kind of concepts existed among the Indians as in the Greek philosophers, and his accounts also agree well with the cosmological speculations of the Upaniṣads and broadly of the Veda in general.

(i) The world is first made, and in the end returned to destruction, and has a limited span in time—this concept appears in the Upaniṣads, and later in the orthodox brahmin line it was generally taught, so that it may not be necessary to cite a succession of examples. In Greece also, it had been thought from ancient times.

(ii) Again, the universe is a hemisphere, and the surface of the earth is round—this concept appears already in the Veda-saṃhitā from the very first beginning of the history of orthodox brahmin thought.[5] Not only is it accepted in general in all the Upaniṣads, but Śaṅkara also thought in a similar fashion.[6] Even in Greek philosophy, to say that the universe was a perfect sphere had become a traditional concept. That the totality of things, or the world is a sphere, was perhaps advocated by

Xenphanes,[7] and then it was clearly stated by Parmenides. The latter specifically asserted that "that which exists" (*to eon*) as the fundamental principle of the world, forms a perfect sphere.[8] The students of Pythagoras thought that "the limited is superior to the unlimited"[9], and Empedocles said that all things, during the time of the chaos in the remote past, were a sphere,[10] and the conception that the universe is a sphere is also accepted by Plato[11] and Aristotle.[12]

Further, the Indians in general thought that the earth occupied a position in the centre of the vault of heaven of the sphere, but no such concept had yet been clearly expounded in the Vedic texts.[13] In the literature after the Vedas, gradually there appeared the viwe that the earth is a circle surrounded by a great sea. Therefore, in this point, it is clear that Megasthenes was recording ideas arising after the Vedic texts.

(iii) The idea that the creator of the world remains pervading his creation is a common point of the cosmologies in a great number of Upaniṣads. In Greece it can be said that probably Thales[14] and the early Stoic[15] thought come closest to this.

(iv) The theory that it is water in particular which is the world-cause, is occasionally propounded in the Vedānta literature, and even in the Upaniṣads a trace of it can be found.[16] In Greece it is well known that Thales in particular asserts this idea.

(v) The postulated fifth element, energy of nature, set up in addition to the four elements, can be said to point to the ether (*ākāśa*). Here the Brahmins of that period advanced a step beyond the theory of three elements taught in the *Chāndogya-Upāniṣad* II.2, the *Aitareya-Upaniṣad* V.4, and in the Manu Law Book, I.75-78, and one finds the five elements of earth, water, fire, air and sky. Among these, it was supposed that the ether was the original element.[17] In Greece also, the theory of five elements was accepted by Philolaos and Aristotle and also others.

(3) The idea of seeking immortality pervades the whole of the Vedas, and the idea of a judgment after death also is clearly- and distinctly expounded in the Vedas.[18]

To explain such philosophical concepts by means of mythology (*mythos*) is one of the outstanding characteristics of the Upaniṣads. Megasthenes recognized the resemblance to Plato on this point.

In this way, as we examine the account of Megasthenes, we see that the philosophical theories presented here are for the most part close to those of the Upaniṣads. Megasthenes did not study directly the original works of India, but probably passed on what he heard from the Brahmin scholars and others, and at that time, not only were the Veda-saṃhitās already in existence, but also the early Upaniṣads had perhaps been composed. He also reported on the life of Brahmins who performed the rituals and practised the precepts, but what he has handed down as philosophical theories of the Brahmins, coincides with much of the Upaniṣads. Of course, it can be thought that he was reporting what he heard about the ideas in works apart from the Upaniṣads, but even in that case, such works would naturally take as their basis the ideas of the Upaniṣads, the earliest philosophical works of India.

And so in the fragments of Megasthenes we cannot find reference to the theories of philosophical schools like the Sāṃkhya and Vaiśeṣika, and we must note that there is not a word about Buddhism and Jainism. Judging from this fact, it appears that in the intellectual sphere of the orthodox Brahmins of that time, ideas like those of the Upaniṣads were generally predominant, and on that foundation of such ideas the Vedānta school progressively took distinct form and finally made its appearance.

After the "Accounts of India" of Megasthenes, next most valuable is the "History of the Military Excursions of the Great King Alexander" (*Anabasis Alexandrou*), by Arrianos (c. 95-180), which in volume seven, has an account of India. But it chiefly relies upon Megasthenes, and no fresh material appears which might directly bear on the history of the Vedānta.

Instead one might look at the "Life of Apollonius" by Philostratus. Apollonius of Tyana, a Greek of the first century A.D., was born in Tyana of Cappadocia in Asia Minor, and was a philosopher who belonged to the new Pythagorean school. He set out to India with a companion, Damis, and the account of their travels was later compiled and edited by Philostratus (170-245), and is still extant today. Before this the Greeks who went to India set out chiefly for military, political, diplomatic or commercial reasons but Apollonius' purpose was no such mundane interest but mainly a purely spiritual concern, to acquire the wisdom of the Brahmin philosophers of India. This point has to be specially noted. However, there are many passages where it is doubtful whether the account of his travels does accurately reflect the actual state of things in India of that time, and it has even been doubted whether he ever in fact went to India. However, judging from material discovered recently in India, it seems probable that he did go, and it can be thought that perhaps he may even have influenced Indian thinkers in some ways.[19]

We find in the account that in India philosophy was greatly respected,[20] and that good political policies were carried out on the basis of philosophical wisdom. It is unfortunate that there are no detailed accounts of the philosophical thought of the time, but in connection with the ideas of the Upaniṣads, we may note, for example, the following dialogue. Apollonius was surprised at the mystical power which the great Brahmin Iarchas had a deep knowledge of all things, and asked whether by it the Brahmin knew himself or not. For "to know the self" (*to eauton gnōnai*), as in the case of Greek philosophy was thought in India to be an extremely difficult thing. But Iarchas made an unexpected reply:

> "It is just because we know the self first of all, that we know all things. For unless one first contemplates the self which is in all of us, one cannot get (into the investigation) of this philosophy."[21]

This clearly is the theory "by knowing the self (*ātman*) to be able to know all"[22] as is taught in the Upaniṣads, and the later Vedānta scholars called this by the name of "proposition (promise)" (*pratijñā*). Accordingly we can affirm the fact that in this account influential Brahmins in India around the first century A.D., were devoted to a philosophy of the *ātman* taught in the Upaniṣads, and further that it made a deep impression on a philosopher of Greece.

Notes

1. Cf. J. W. McCrindle : *Ancient India as described by Megasthenes and Arrian*, 1877, pp. 13-16.
2. Fragment I, B. 40 ff.
3. Cf. Fragment I, B. 40 ff.
4. E. A. Schwanbeck : *Megasthenis Indica, fragmenta collegit*, Bonu

1846, p. 137. In addition, Fragment 54 also records something about Brahmins and their Indian philosophy, but this passage is by pseudo-Origen and it is questionable whether he is in fact directly quoting from Megasthenes, and it is omitted from consideration here.

5. In the *Ṛg-Veda* III.55.20 form of heaven and earth is compared to two bowls joined together, and in X.89.4, Indra is said to hold the heaven and earth apart just as the axle supports the two wheels. Further, cf. A. A. Macdonell : *Vedic Mythology*, p. 9.

6. Deussen : *SV.*, p. 257, Anm. 98.

Further, cf. *Āpastambadharma-sūtra*, Adhyātma-paṭala 23, 1. (Part II, Chapter 3, Section 3, of the present work).

7. Zeller : *Die Philosophie der Griechen*, Bd. 1, Apt. 1, p. 661. Deussen : *A. G. Ph.*, II,1, p. 74.

8. Zeller : op. cit. I.1. p. 695. Deussen : *A. G. Ph.* II.1, p. 83.

9. Zeller : op. cit. I.1. p. 458. Cf. p. 521.

10. Zeller : op. cit. I.2. p. 973, Deussen : *A. G. Ph.* II.1. p. 117.

11. Zeller : op. cit. II.1 p. 808, Deussen : *A. G. Ph.* II.1. p. 278.

12. Zeller : op. cit. II. 2, p. 448 : Deussen : *A. G. Ph.* II.1. p. 354.

13. A. A. Macdonell: *Vedic Mythology*, p. 9.

14. Zeller : op. cit. I. 1, p. 263.

15. Zeller : op. cit. III.1, p. 141.

16. On each one of these passages, I have recorded whenever the theories of "the worshippers of water" and of "those who set forth origination from the Cosmic Egg" were investigated. (Part II, Chapter 1, Section 5, Item 2 of the present work.)

17. Further, cf. "those who maintain the theory of origination from ākāśa". (Part II, Chapter 1, Section 5, Item 2 of the present work).

18. Concerning the idea of judgment after death appearing in the Veda, cf. A. A. Macdonell : *Vedic Mythology*, p. 169.

19. Cf. Part VI, Chapter 2, Section 4, Item 3 of the present work.

20. F. C. Conybeare : *Philostratus, the Life of Apollonius of Tyana*, 1917. Vol. I, pp. 196-197.

21. F. C. Conybeare : op. cit, pp. 266-267.

22. Bṛhad. Up. II.4, 5 ; IV.5.6; Chānd. Up. VI.1.3; VI.4.5; Muṇḍ. Up. I.1.3.

II

PART III

SCHOLARS BEFORE THE *BRAHMA-SŪTRA*

CHAPTER VIII

THE CHARACTER AND THOUGHT OF THE SCHOLARS PRIOR TO THE *BRAHMA-SŪTRA*

As already related, after the ancient *Upaniṣads* of the early period came into existence, the tradition which follows them as sacred authority continued on without interruption in an unbroken line. There must have been correspondingly numerous thinkers of the line who advocated special doctrines, but almost no individual names or thought of such schools of the very ancient period have been passed down. As a rough classification of the early Vedānta schools, we can divide them into those prior to and those posterior to the compilation of the *Brahma-sūtra*, and in relation to the period prior to the *Brahma-sūtra*, since no literature at all of the Vedānta school itself has been handed down, it may be said that the thought of the individual thinkers then is, for the most part, unclear. We can only get a general idea from the literature of other fields of the tendency of thought of the Vedānta school during this period. We have, in the previous Part II, considered the tendency in thought which we learned from literary sources, but to know the thought or even the names of individual thinkers is almost completely impossible. In the *Brahma-sūtra*, the fundamental scripture of this school, some of the names of early thinkers have been noted, and not only has their thought been discussed and criticized, but their names have been referred to also in works of other fields. In this chapter we shall take up the examination of the character and thought of these thinkers.

SECTION I : KĀRṢṆĀJINI

The *Brahma-sūtra* (III.1.9) says :

"If it be said that depending upon conduct [in this world, one attains various births], it is not so.

[The word 'conduct' (*caraṇa*) in the sacred passage] refers indirectly [to the remainder of *karma*]. Thus [said] Kārṣṇājini."

And this discussion has been set forth in connection with the following sacred passage :

"Therefore, those whose conduct (*caraṇa*) has been good in this world, may expect to attain some good birth, i.e. the birth of a brahmin, or kṣatriya, or a vaiśya. But those whose conduct has been evil in this world, can expect to attain an evil birth, i.e. the birth of a dog, a pig, or a caṇḍāla." (*Chānd. Up.* V.10.7)

In this verse it is taught that the man who has good and beautiful conduct in this world will, after he dies, be born again as a member of one of the three upper classes, while the man who has ugly and evil conduct will be born again as a very low and mean person or as an animal. Just what relation this verse has to the teaching of the five fires (*pañcāgni-vidyā*), taught in the verse immediately preceding it, was discussed among the theologians of that time. The "Teaching of the Five Fires" is so called because it says that human beings go to the world of the moon after death, and from there fall down and are reborn on the earth, dividing the process into five stages, which, under the pretext of being names for ceremonies and rituals, are called "fires". On this question, a certain theologian has interpreted this sacred verse literally (according to the three commentaries[1] on this *Sūtra*), and has understood that the wherefore of the conditions at the time of rebirth into this world, is based upon the kind of good and evil conduct at the time when one was active in the previous world, and he thought that that is all there was to it. However that may be Kārṣṇājini, so as to relate it to the teaching of the five fires, interpreted this verse in the following manner. According to him, the word "conduct" (*caraṇa*) of the verse should not be understood in the literal meaning of "action" but refers indirectly to the "remainder of Karma" (*anuśaya*)[2].

That is to say, according to the teaching of the five fires, man after death proceeds to the world of the moon, accompanied by his action (*karma*), and after he has received his rewards and punishment there, again returns down to the earth and is born again; while in the world of the moon, he does not exhaust the rewards and punishment of his karma and so nullify it all, as there is still a small amount of karma remaining. Then, it is said that the individual selves accompanied by their remaining karmas return to enter this world, and are born into various conditions, in accordance with whatever remaining karmas they have.

Incidentally, such an interpretation has this difficulty. If one holds that it is in accordance with whatever remaining karma one has when he descends from the world of the moon, that the individual self is born in varying conditions, even a person who had performed good action previously in this world, since he would not be limited to that when he is reborn, need not necessarily be born into a good environment; in that case, the precepts (ethical principles, *ācāra*) of the behaviour taught in the Brāhmanic canon would be meaningless. Against such a criticism he is said to have answered :

> "(It is not meaningless) since (the sacrifice) depends upon good conduct." (*Brahma-sūtra* III,1.10)

That is to say, karma is the motive force which directly causes a person to be born into a good environment or a good position, and "the remaining karma" is based directly on the actual performance of the rituals in the present world, but for these rituals to bring out their effects, the correct performance of conduct in general is necessary. The man who does not perform good conduct cannot obtain good rewards, even if he does carry out the rituals; this is the point. Thus Kārṣṇājini held to the same idea as the verse which says "The Vedas do not purify the man who is devoid of good conduct" (*Vasiṣṭha-smṛti* VI.3)[3]. Then at the same time, we can know that he thought that the rituals are the most important things for human life, and that the ethical precepts are only of the secondary significance, subordinate to the rituals.

Since Kārṣṇājini is referred to in the *Mīmāṃsā-sūtra* (IV.3.17, VI.7.35), as well he was also a scholar of the ritual Mīmāṃsā. And as a scholar of the rituals, his words have also been quoted in the *Kātyāyana-śrauta-sūtra*.[4] Even seen from the *Brahma sūtra*, since Kārṣṇājini was a man who had regarded the rituals, as very valuable, there may be no objection if all of these are thought to refer to one and same person. In that case, since he was a man prior to the formulation of the *Mīmāṃsā-sūtra*, and as he belongs to the period in which the various ritual *sūtras* were being worked on and produced, he must naturally be thought to be prior to the 4th century A.D. But to clarify in more detail the dates of his life is a difficult proposition in the present circumstances.

Notes

1. In translating the *Brahma-sūtra*, I have referred to the three ancient commentaries of Śaṅkara, Bhāskara, and Rāmānuja.
2. "Action" (*karman*) according to Bhāskara.
3. This is quoted in all three commentaries on *Brahma-sūtra* III.1.10.
4. A. Weber : *A History of Indian Literature*. p. 140. Further, his name also appears in *Gaṇapāṭha 'upaka'* in Pāṇini's Grammar.

SECTION II : KĀŚAKṚTSNA

Kāśakṛtsna's views are quoted in the *Brahma-sūtra* (I.4.22). According to the *Bṛhadāraṇyaka Upaniṣad*, the philosopher Yājñavalkya is said to have taught his wife Maitreyī as follows :

> "...'Verily, not for the sake of the husband[1] is the husband dear, but the husband is dear for the sake of the Self. Verily, not for the sake of the wife is the wife dear, but the wife is dear for the sake of the Self. Verily, not for the sake of the sons are the sons dear, but the sons are dear for the sake of the Self. Verily, not for the sake of wealth is wealth dear, but wealth is dear for the sake of the Self. Verly, not for the sake of brahminhood is brahminhood dear, but brahminhood is dear for the sake of the Self. Verily, not for the sake of kṣatriyahood is kṣtriyahood dear, but kṣtriyahood is dear for the sake of the Self. Verily, not for the sake of the worlds are the worlds dear but the worlds are dear for the sake of the Self. Verily, not for the sake of the gods are the gods dear, but the gods are dear for the sake of the Self. Verily, not for the sake of living beings are living beings dear, but living beings are dear for the sake of the Self. Verily, not for the sake of all is all dear, but all is dear for the sake of the Self. Verily,... it is the Self alone that should be seen, heard, reflected on and meditated upon." (*Bṛhad. Up.* II.4.5; cf. IV.5.6).

What is this *ātman* (self) expounded here ? Is it merely an individual self, an individual existence ? Or, is it what should be called the universal Self, the highest Self ? These questions had been discussed among Vedānta scholars from quite ancient times. In the *Brahma-sūtra* (I.4.19 ff.) it has been determined that this *ātman* is not an individual self but the highest Self. In the passage above, however, the word *ātman* at the first glance is explained as though it meant an individual existence. Why is it so ? On this point, there was a difference of opinion among the three thinkers, Āśmarathya, Auḍulomi, and Kāśakṛtsna. The *Brahma-sūtra* (I.4.22) only states : *Avasthiter iti kāśakṛtsnaḥ.* ('Because of the existence', said Kāśakṛtsna.) The three commentators interpret the *sūtra* as follows :

"Because this highest Self also exists as the conscious self (—individual self), it is possible to begin [the conversation with Maitreyī] with the statement of non-difference between the highest Self and the individual self in this way." (Śaṅkara)

asyaiva paramātmano 'nenāpi vijñānātmabhāvenāvasthānād upapannam idam abhedenopakramaṇam.

"(The relation between the highest Self and the individual self) is not the relation between *prakṛti* (= Matter) and the evolved. Nor does the individual self, which is absolutely different, become identical [with the highest Self] in the state of final release. But the highest Self, even before the departure from the body (i.e. before death), exists in the form of the individual self; so (the conversation with Maitreyī) begins with a statement of non-difference (between the highest Self and the individual self). (Bhāskara)

na prakṛtivikārabhāvo nāpy atyantabhinnasya jīvasya muktyavasthāyāṃ abhedāpattiḥ, kiṃ tarhy utkramaṇāt prāg api jīvarūpeṇa paramātmano 'vasthānād abhedenopakrama iti.

"Because [*Brahman*] exists as *ātman* within the individual self which is his own body, Brahman is taught by means of the word indicating the individual self." (Rāmānuja)

svaśarīrabhūte jīvātmany ātmatayā 'vasthite jīvaśabdena brahmapratipādanam.

Since these three ancient commentaries thus give their own different interpretations, we are at a loss to decide which to adopt, but by other criteria we can, I think, ascertain the original meaning of the *sūtra*. First of all, since this passage in the *Brahma-sūtra*, lists the theory of Kāśakṛtsna after relating those of the other two scholars (Āśmarathya and Auḍulomi), we can conclude that this is the finally determined theory (*siddhānta*) adopted by the author of the *Sūtra*. Throughout the entire *Brahma-sūtra*, whenever it lists different theories, it is a definite rule to give the finally determined theory last,[2] and, in this case, that the theory of Kāśakṛtsna is the established theory is also acknowledged by the three ancient commentaries.

On this point the *Brahma-sūtra*, as discussed later,[3] stands on the theory of "difference and non-difference" with regard to the relation of *Brahman* and *ātman*. Since this is accepted in general by present day scholars, Kāśakṛtsna also, whom the *Sūtra*-author followed, must have held the "difference and non-difference" theory in the same way.[4] Moreover, the word *avasthiti* is used in this *Sūtra*. We see in other examples of usages[5] in the *Brahma-sūtra* hat this word is employed in the sense : "it exists conditioned temporally and spatially."[6] Accordingly, in this case, *avasthiti* means that the supreme Self, who transcends temporal and spatial limitations, assumes the form of the individual self, and appears in the empirical world. Accordingly, the individual self is not completely identical with the supreme Self, but is one part of it.

It is, Kāśakṛtsna must have asserted, precisely for this reason, that the above-quoted passage of the *Bṛhadāraṇyaka Upaniṣad* seems to point to the individual self.

An account which supports such a conclusion is to be found in Vācaspatimiśra's subcommentary on the *Brahma-sūtra*. In his subcommentary[7] on *BS*.I.4.22, he states the general view of the Śaṅkara School that Kāśakṛtsna held the theory of non-dualism and then refutes the assertion of those others who follow the theories of Kāśakṛtsna, saying as follows :

Ye tu Kāśakṛtsnīyam eva matam āsthāya jīvaṃ paramātmano 'ṃśam ācakṣus, teṣāṃ kathaṃ 'niṣkalam niṣkriyaṃ śāntam' iti na śrutivirodhaḥ.

"Why would not, however, those [thinkers] who, on the basis of Kāśakṛtsna's view, teach that the individual self is a part of the highest Self, be in opposition to the Śruti passage : "(It is) without parts, without activity, tranquil" (*Śvet. Up.* VI, 19) ?"

According to the further commentary, Amalānanda's *Vedānta-*

kalpataru, "those who follow Kāśakṛtsna's view" points to Bhāskara.[8] On the other hand. in his commentary[9] on *BS* I.4.22 Bhāskara refutes the theory of the *māyāvādins* and then says : "It should be forcibly accepted that the Lord is different from this (individual self), the individual self which is the subject of transmigration being a part of the Lord."

> *tasmād anya īśvaras, tad-aṃśo jīvah saṃsārīti, balād abhyupeyam.*

This would fit in nicely with the account mentioned before. Accordingly, not only has Bhāskara himself admitted in this way that his thought is based upon the theory of Kāśakṛtsna, but such an impartial scholar as Vācaspatimiśra has also acknowledged this fact.

Thus from the above considerations we are able to form the following conclusions :

1. Kāśakṛtsna firmly maintained the assertion that the relation between the supreme self and individual self is one of "non-identity and non-difference", and that the individual self is either a part of the supreme self or is a constitutive element of it (*aṃśa*). This idea is also clearly asserted in *BS*.II.3.43.

2. The thought of Kāśakṛtsna, having been adopted by the *Brahma-sūtra*, was again inherited and developed by Bhāskara. Then, the historical and ideological connection between these thinkers was believed in with considerable conviction in one section of the academic world of the period around the 13th century when Amalānanda lived.

Furthermore, Kāśakṛtsna was regarded as the advocate of the established doctrine of the Vedānta school by all the members of that school even in later centuries. The Vallabha school, for example, also attributed the theory in *BS*.III.2.29, which discusses the relation of the individual self and the supreme self, to Kāśakṛtsna.[10]

In the foregoing, we have examined some aspects of Kāśakṛtsna as one of the Vedānta thinkers, but he was also a grammarian. (As a grammarian, his name has generally been handed down as Kāśakṛtsni.)

In the *Mahābhāṣya*, a work of the grammarian Patañjali (c. 150 B.C.), Kāśakṛtsni, as a grammarian, is frequently referred to, and the Mīmāṃsā which he taught is called the Kāśakṛtsnī, and it is recorded that men who study his work are called "pupils of Kāśakṛtsni" (*Kāśakṛtsnāḥ*).[11] Again, his study of grammar has also been called Kāśakṛtsna.[12] And in the *Vākyapadīya* of Bhartṛhari, it is said that :

> "The *sūtra* : '*tad arham*' (Pāṇini, V.1.117) is not introduced in any other work on grammar."
> (*tad arham iti n'ārabdhaṃ sūtraṃ vyākaraṇāntare*) p. 714. (*Vākyap.*III.14.566.)

Helārāja comments on this : "Neither the students of Āpiśali nor those of Kāśakṛtsni recite this *sūtra*."[13]

Consequently, Kāśakṛtsni, like Pāṇini and Āpiśali, was an editor of the *sūtra* related to grammar, and his work differed from the extant Pāṇinian grammar, and, we can know, had been handed down up to the time of Bhartṛhari.

As this work has not been transmitted to the present time, its contents, system, etc. are not clear, but according to the records of the later grammatical works, Kāśakṛtsni's books consisted of several *sūtras* which are composed of three chapters (*adhyāya*).[14] On certain kinds of problems, this work includes rules which differ from the grammar of Pāṇini. Grammarian students of later centuries have also noticed this fact.[15] Then again, it is known that his work has some points in common with that of Āpiśali.[16]

The date of Kāśakṛtsni's life is not clear, but there is no doubt that he lived prior to Patañjali. And since the *Vārttika* of Kātyāyana has referred to the rules of Kāśakṛtsni's grammar,[17] he should be prior to Kātyāyana. Again, since there are many instances in which he is mentioned together with Āpiśali, it would not appear that he lived in a period too far distant from that of Āpiśali. Āpiśali, according to an account (VI.1.92) by Pāṇini himself, was one of the predecessors of Pāṇini, but Kāśakṛtsni can be supposed to the later than Pāṇini.[18] In which case, we may conclude that he probably lived somewhere around 350 to 250 B.C.

Furthermore, Kāśakṛtsni, as already mentioned, is said in an account by Patañjali to have been also a Mīmāṃsā scholar.[19] As if to confirm this, there has been handed down in a work of the later Vedānta school of limited non-dualism[20] the legend that Kāśakṛtsna was the author of the *Saṃkarṣaṇa-Kāṇḍa*. However, just as the legend that Jaimini is the author of the *Mīmāṃsā-sūtra* and the *Saṃkarṣaṇa-Kāṇḍa*, has not handed down the true facts, this too might amount to no more than a mere legend. That is, it would appear that since the name of Kāśakṛtsna as a famous thinker had been transmitted up until later centuries, there may have originated such a legend spontaneously.

Further, a doubt arises as to whether or not Kāśakṛtsni and Kāśakṛtsna are perhaps different persons but insofar as the two names greatly resemble each other, and as the learning of Kāśakṛtsni[21] has been called Kāśakṛtsnam, and his students are called Kāśakṛtsnāḥ. I think that perhaps later grammatical schools,[22] the Mīmāṃsā school as well as the Vedānta school have referred to Kāśakṛtsni as Kāśakṛtsna. Moreover, both the grammatical schools and the two Mīmāṃsā have an intimate connection as the two important types of the orthodox brahmanical scholarship from ancient times; in many instances the same author has studied both branches of learning, as we shall examine in this work, so that it would appear that there is ample reason to believe both names refer to one and the same person.

Again, Kāśakṛtsna seems to have been also both a Vedic scholar and a scholar of the rituals. The name of Kāśakṛtsna as a Vedic scholar is mentioned together with that of Yāska[23] in a work by Bhaṭṭa-Bhāskara-miśra,[24] and his name is said to appear also in Bodhāyana's *Gṛhya Sūtra*.[25] Again, the name of a scholar Kāśakṛtsni[26] has also been given in the *Śrauta Sūtra* of Kātyāyana, but in the same *Sūtra*, it also refers to a theory by Bādari and that by Kārṣṇājini, both being scholars of the ancient Vedānta school. Even in later centuries, since there were many men who were thoroughly versed in the Vedas and in the rituals in general, and who wrote partial explanatory works on them, we can judge from these facts that there should be no objection to the thinking that either Kāśakṛtsni or Kāśakṛtsna as a ritual scholar was the same person who had the same name as handed down as a scholar of grammar, the Mīmāṃsā, and the Vedānta. In reality, then, he, being chiefly a scholar of the rituals, probably studied the various other branches of learning also.

Notes.

1. *patyuḥ kāmāya*. This probably could be understood as "because of the husband," or "for the sake of the husband." Other phrases also should be interpreted in the same light.

2. Śaṅkara, in his commentary, has sometimes differed from this rule, but in those cases, his interpretation is mistaken. E.g., see the commentary on *Brahma-sūtra-bhāṣya* IV.3.7 ff. Cf. the present work, Part IV. Chap. 3, Sect. 4, I.

4. Thibaut (*Intro.* p. XIX) originally held that Kāśakṛtsna embraced the theory of non-difference (i.e., Nondualistic monism), basing himself upon the sub-commentaries on Śaṅkara's commentary (ad BS.I.4.22) : since then, this assertion has been accepted by Indologists in general, but the supposition is not correct. Insofar as the theory of Kāśakṛtsna in the Sūtra is said to be the finally determined doctrines (*siddhānta*), Śaṅkara and his commentators stressed that Kāśakṛtsna's theory was nondualistic monism, in order to combine it with their own theory.

5. I.2.17; I.3.22; II.2.4; II.2.13; II.2.36; II.3.24; KIII.3.32.

6. Thibaut, *Introduction*, p.C., and Guha; *Jīvātman*, p. 189 hold that this *avasthiti* means "permanent abiding or permanent abode within something," but this interpretation relies too heavily upon Rāmānuja's views. No other example agrees with this usage.

7. Bhāmatī, p. 337.

8. "*Bhāskarasya matam anūdya dūṣayati—ye tv ity ādinā*"—*Kalpataru*, p. 223 (Viz SS).

9. This corresponds to I.4.21 in Bhāskara's *Bhāṣya.*

10. Belvalkar; *Lectures*, p. 167

11. *Kāśakṛtsninā proktā mīmāṃsā Kāśakṛtsnī tām adhīte Kāśakṛtsnā brāhmaṇīti.* (*Mahābhāṣya*, Vol. II, PP. 206; 249; 325). His name also appears in Pāṇini's Grammar, *Gaṇapāṭha* "*Upaka*"

12. *Pāṇininā proktaṃ. Pāṇinīyam / Āpiśalam / Kāśakṛtsnam iti /* (*Mahābhaṣya*, Vol. I, p. 12).

Pāṇinīyam akālakaṃ vyākaraṇam / Kāśakṛtsnam / Gurulāghavam / Āpiśalam duṣkaraṇam / (*Kāśikā* ad IV.3.115) *anyena kṛtā Māthureṇa proktā Māthurī vṛttiḥ / Pāṇinīyam / Āpiśalam / Kāśakṛtsnam /* (*Kāśikā* ad IV. 3. 301).

These materials are from Kshitish Chandra Chatterjee, *Kāśakṛtsna* (*IHQ*. Vol. VIII, 1932, pp. 224-227).

13. *Āpiśalāḥ Kāśakṛtsnāś ca sūtram etan nādhīyate.*

14. *aṣṭakaṃ Pāṇinīyaṃ sūtram / tad adhīyate vidanti vā / aṣṭakāḥ Pāṇinīyāḥ / trikāḥ Kāśakṛtsnāḥ /* (*Candravṛtti* III.1.42).

Pāṇinīyam aṣṭakaṃ sūtram, tad adhīyate aṣṭakāḥ, Pāṇinīyāḥ / daśakāḥ, Vaiyāghrapadīyāḥ / trikāḥ, Kāśakṛtsnāḥ (*Kāśikā* IV.2.65).

Āpiśalapāṇinīyāḥ. "*Pāṇinīyaraudhīyāḥ / Raudhīyakāśa-kṛtsnāḥ /* (*Kāśikā*, VI.2.36).

These are from Chatterjee, *ibid.* See also *Kāśikā* ad V.1.58; Belvalkar; *SSG.*, p. 10.

15. Patañjali, in his commentary on Pāṇini's Grammar II.1.50, says : *kim punar dvigusaṃjñā pratyayottarapadayor bhavatī.* On this Kaiyaṭa has noted as follows : *Kāśakṛtsnasya Pratyayottarapadayor iti sūtraṃ tad vicārayati / Pāṇinīyaṃ tu paścād vicārayiṣyati /*

Again, Ksīrasvāmin, in *Kṣīrataraṅgiṇī* (II.60, S. 114) says that the past particle of the root *śvas* according to the Kāśakṛtsna school is not *śvasita*, but must be *śvasta*. *Kāśakṛtsnā asya* (i.e. the root *śvas*) *niṣṭhāyām aniṭtva āhuḥ / āśvastaḥ / viśvastaḥ /* And in the *Mādhavīya-Dhātuvṛtti* also, concerning the root *śvas*, it is said : *niṣṭhāyām iṭam necchanti Kāśakṛtsnā iti Svāmi-Kāśyapau*. (According to Chatterjee, *ibid*).

16. *Āpiśala-Kāśakṛtsnāyos tv agrantha iti vacanād anyatra Pratiṣedhābhāvaḥ*.—Kaiyaṭa ad V. I. 21.

17. *dvigusaṃjnā pratyayottarapadayoś ced itaretarāśrayatvād aprasiddhiḥ*. (Kātyāyana, ad II.1.51, Vol. I, p. 392), Cf. note 15.

18. Chatterjee, *ibid*., asserts this is based on the passage in Kāśikā ad VI. 2.36. Kāśakṛtsna is mentioned in the *upakādayaḥ, arīhaṇādayaḥ* in *Gaṇapāṭha* of Pāṇini's Grammar, but this will not demonstrate that he was earlier than Pāṇini.

19. However, further investigation is necessary to determine what Mīmāṃsā means in Patañjali.

20. In the work *Tattvavārttika* on the *Śrībhāṣya*, the following verse is recorded as a quote from the *Tattvaratnākara* :

Karmadevatā-brahmagocarā sā tridhodbabhau sūtrakārataḥ / Jaiminer muneḥ Kāśakṛtsnato Bādarāyaṇād ity ataḥ kramāt //

This differs from the traditional theory. On this, Vedānta-deśika, in his work *Adhikaraṇasārāvali*, has explained as follows :

Vṛttigranthe tu Jaiminyuparacitatayā Ṣoḍaśādhyāya upāttā Saṃkarṣaḥ Kāśakṛtsnaprabhava iti kathaṃ Tattvaratnākaroktiḥ / atra brūmaḥ saduktau na *vayaṃ iha mudhā bādhituṃ kiṃcidarhā nirvāhas tūpacārāt kvacid iha ghaṭate hy ekatātparyayogaḥ //*

On such a difference related to the problem of the author, *Śeṣagovinda*, who wrote the commentary on the *Sarvasiddhāntasaṃgraha*, has explained that the *Devatākāṇḍa*, said to be a work by Jaimini, and the work said to be by Kāśakṛtsna are different works. However, no affirmative grounds exist which might permit this interpretation. (These sources come from Chatterjee, *ibid*., and S. Kuppuswami Sastri and P. P. Subrahmanya Sastri: *A descriptive Catalogue of the Sanskrit Manuscripts in the Government Oriental Library*, Madras, Vol. XXVII, 1937. Introd., pp. III-VII).

21. This coincides exactly with the case of the learning of Āpiśali being called *Āpiśala*. E.g., *Āpiśalam adhīte* (Vārttika 3 ad Pāṇini IV.1.14): *Āpiśala-Pāṇinīya-Gautamīyaḥ*. (*Mahābhāṣya*, Vol. III. p. 125).

22. In the Kṣīrataraṅgiṇī written by Kṣīrasvāmin, and in the *Kavikalpadruma*, by Vopadeva, Kāśakṛtsna is listed as the name of a grammarian. (Aufrecht; *CC*. I, p. 103; Aufrecht; *Bodl. Cat*. p. 175 b.)

23. He was a scholar thoroughly versed in the Black Yajur Veda.

24. A Weber : *HIL*., pp. 42, 91.

25. Radhakrishnan; *I. Ph*., Vol. II, p. 433.

26. A. Weber : *HIL*., pp. 139, 140. *Indische Studien* XIII, p. 398; 418.

SECTION III : ĀTREYA

There are frequent injunctions in the *Upaniṣads* to perform the worship (*upāsanā*) related to each branch of the rituals. For example, it is said :

> "One should worship the fivefold *sāman* with regard to rain.
> The *hiṅkāra* is the wind that brings the rain.
> The *prastāva* is the birth of the cloud.
> The *udgītha* is the falling of the rain.
> The *pratihāra* is the lightning and the thunder.
> The *nidhana* is the cessation of the rain."
> (*Chānd. Up.* II.3.1-2)

Here it is taught to meditate and worship each one of the five types of melodies by comparing them to the process of rain, but just who is it that is to perform the meditation ? Should the sacrificer, who pays for the religious ceremony, perform it ? Or must the priest of the ceremony do it ? This problem was discussed among the Vedānta scholars of the early period.

In connection with this problem, Ātreya thought that the sacrificer himself should perform the meditation. For the verse given above goes on to say :

"There is rain for him, and he brings rain for others who, thus knowing, worships the fivefold Sāman with regard to the rain."
(*Chānd. Up.* II.3.2)

Here is taught the effect and reward brought about by this worship. The person who receives this good fortune is generally admitted to be the sacrificer (*yajamāna*), who arranges for the ceremony and employs the ritual priests, so that this worship, also, should be performed by the sacrificer (*BS*. III.4.44).[1]

But the *Brahma-sūtra* next gives a theory of Auḍulomi opposing this. According to Auḍulomi the worship related to the various branches of the ceremonies is to be performed by the ritual priest (*ṛtvij*), and the sacrificer does not undertake it. The worship by loud singing (*udgītha*) or the worship, etc., by the melodies taught in the *Upaniṣads* are comprised within the actual performance of the ceremony, and it is just for the performance of the ceremony, including these melodies, that the sacrificer is giving remuneration to the ritual priest. In the sacred verse quoted by Ātreya, it is taught that the performer of the worship receives the benefits therefrom. So Ātreya held that the one who actually performs the worship must be the sacrificer himself, but since the ritual priest performs the ceremony for the sake of the sacrificer, it is not the least irrational that the one who receives the fruits of the sacrifice be the sacrificer (*yajamāna*), though the one who performs the ceremony is the ritual priest. A comparison of the three ancient commentaries shows that the theory of Auḍulomi is as above.

Although the question of who performs the worship (and meditation) related to the parts of the ritual, is very important, the fact that among the thinkers who considered this point various differences of opinion arose quite soon, should be carefully noted. Incidentally, of the two theories given, the author of the *Brahma-sūtra* rejects the theory of Ātreya, and adopts that of Auḍulomi as correct.[2] Consequently, Ātreya was regarded as in error.

Nothing of his doctrines on the Vedānta has been handed down besides this, but the name "Ātreya" appears also in the *Mīmāṃsā-sūtra*.[3] Consequently, it is evident that he was also concerned with the ritualistic *Mīmāṃsā*, being thus both a Vedic and a ritual scholar. His name is listed in the *Kātyāyana-śrauta-sūtra*, the *Taittirīyaprātiśākhya*,[4] the *Bodhāyana-gṛhya-sūtra*, and the *Bharadvāja-gṛhya-sūtra*.[5] These all probably refer to the same man, who as a ritualist would also have been expert in Mīmāṃsā. But the Ātreya[6] who appears in the Vedas must not only be taken as completely different from this one, but the latter also must be distinguished from the Ātreya (i.e. Brahmanandin), a Vedānta thinker appearing later than the *Brahma-sūtra*.[7] And he is also different from the medical doctor Ātreya, almost universally revered as the founder of Indian medicine.[8]

While the dates of his life are not clear, he was perhaps of the same period as the Kāśakṛtsna considered above, as we may gather from the fact that he is referred to in almost all the same works. At any rate, it would be no great mistake to take it that he lived from 350-250 B.C.

Notes

1. The above follows Śaṅkara and Bhāskara. Rāmānuja also interprets it in the same sense.

2. On this point, the previously mentioned three ancient commentaries are in complete agreement.

3. *Mīmāṃsā-sūtra* IV. 3.18; V.2.18; VI.1.26.

4. A. Weber : *HIL*, p. 241.

5. Radhakrishnan : *I. Ph.*, II. 433.

6. Macdonell and Keith : *Vedic Index*, s.v. Ātreya.

7. Cf. the present work, Part V, Chap. 5.

8. The medical doctor Ātreya lived around the fifth century B.C. (Hakuju Ui, *Indo Tetsugaku Kenkyū*, II, 428). He was probably not the same as the ritualist Ātreya. Indian medicine may have developed independently of the magical arts of ancient India, as a separate branch of learning, and it was remarkably distinct from the orthodox brahmanical theology. There could have been no thoroughgoing agreement between the scientific and rational thought of the Indian medical doctors and the orthodox brahmins' attitude dominated by rituals. And Ātreya is called Bhikṣu Ātreya in Caraka's Work on Medicine *Caraka-saṃhitā*, *Sūtrasthāna*, *adhyāya* 25,V.24, p. 238). As he is called a "bhikṣu", he must have renounced the rituals. Consequently, the ritualist Ātreya should be considered as completely different from the medical doctor Ātreya.

SECTION IV : AUḌULOMI

As already remarked[1], Auḍulomi took, as against Ātreya, the position that the worship in the parts of the ritual is to be performed by the ritual priest, and this is adopted as the finally settled view (*siddhānta*) in *BS.* III.4.45.

In addition, we see elsewhere in the *Brahma-sūtra* (I.4.21) that he also held special opinions even on metaphysical problems. That is to say, there is a doubt, as to the beginning sentences of the *Bṛhadāraṇyaka Upaniṣad* II.4.5 and IV.5.6,[2] whether the *ātman* doctrine is being taught by words which prima facie indicate individual self, and according to the three ancient commentaries, he is said to have given the following answer :

> The individual self differs from the supreme self while it possesses a body, but when a man obtains the clear knowledge by means of the practice and training in knowledge and meditation, dies, leaves the body and obtains complete liberation, the individual self becomes the supreme Self, and so it is that in the (*Bṛhadāraṇyaka-Upaniṣad*) passages given above, the teachings are presented in terms reminiscent of the individual self. Then, the three ancient commentaries all quote the verse :
> "Just as the rivers, giving up their name and form, flow out

> and disappear into the ocean, so the wise, released from name and form, approaches the sacred *Puruṣa*, who is higher than even the highest." (*Muṇḍ. Up.* III.2.8).

And both Bhāskara's commentary and the *Bhāmatī* quote a stanza of the **Pañcarā° school:**

> "Up to liberation, the individual self and the supreme Self are different.
> But when liberated, there exists no distinction, or there is no cause for distinction."

Thus his thought may have had some points in common with these verses. In abstract terms his metaphysical position may be generalized as : "In liberation, there is no difference; in transmigration, there is difference" *muktāv evābhedaḥ, saṃsāre bheda eveti.*[3] Furthermore, this transmigration is not illusory, as with Śaṅkara, but is real (*satya-saṃsāra-daśā*).[4] According to Bhāskara, it is taught that "the absolutely different individual self becomes identical in the state of liberation." (*atyanta-bhinnasya jīvasya muktyavasthāyām abhedāpattiḥ*).

Accordingly, his doctrine was a very special "non-identity non-difference" theory. The theory, as expressed above, does in some respects derive from one of the intellectual strands of the *Upaniṣads*, but it was not adopted as the finally determined doctrine (*siddhānta*) by the author of the *Brahma-sūtra*. The view however did not die out but was again advocated in the seventh century by the Vedānta scholar Brahmadatta.[5]

Moreover, according to the *Brahma-sūtra* (IV.4.6) he is said to have asserted that since the individual self is of the nature of pure consciousness (*citi—caitanya*) when liberated and united with *Brahman*, that *ātman* is as pure consciousness alone. This view is sharply opposed to that of Jaimini (*BS*.IV.4.5). The author of the *sūtra* accepts Auḍulomi's view, but does not regard it as the final doctrine.

Thus the theory of Auḍulomi has been in some cases adopted, and in other cases not adopted, in the *Brahma-sūtra* and does not necessarily agree with the standpoint of the *Sūtra*-author. At any rate, there is no doubt that he was an authoritative Vedānta thinker.

Further, Auḍulomi is also mentioned in the *Mahābhāṣya* of Patañjali.[6] Consequently, he had some influence even in the field of grammar, and it is clear that he lived prior to Patañjali.

Perhaps he lived in nearly the same period as Kāśakṛtsna, Ātreya and the others.

Notes

1. Cf. the preceding section.
2. This passage appears in Section 2, "Kāśakṛtsna," of this chapter. (Cf. p. 7)
3. Ānandajñāna ad *BS*.I.4.21.
4. Govindānanda : *Ratnaprabhā* ad *loc.c.*
5. Cf. Part V, Chapter 12 of this work.
6. ad Pāṇini, IV.1.85,78. Further his name appears in the Pāṇini Grammar *Gaṇapāṭha*, *Bāhū*.

SECTION V : ĀŚMARATHYA

The theories of Āśmarathya appear twice in the *Brahma-sūtra*. The meaning of the saying in the canon (*Chand. Up.* V.18.1), that the supreme Self has a size equal only to the spread of the thumb and index finger, is discussed in the *Brahma-sūtra* (I, 2, 29ff.). In this regard Āśmarathya is said to have asserted that although the Lord has infinite size, He takes on such a size and manifests Himself (*abhivyakti*) to the worshipper in order that the worshipper can perform the worship.

Moreover, according to the *Brahma-sūtra* (I, 4, 20), Āśmarathya asserted in connection with the conversation between Yājñavalkya and Maitreyī (*Bṛhad Up.* II,4,5; IV,5,6), which is taken up for discussion in the *Brahma-sūtra*, that the teaching of *ātman* as a thing "to be seen" should be regarded as a mark (*liṅga*) which indicates that the Upaniṣadic promise (*pratijñā*) : "When *ātman* has been known, this all is known" (cf. *Bṛhad Up.* II 4, 5) can be fulfilled.

According to the commentators (Bhāskara, Ānandajñāna, Govindānanda), his theory is "Difference and non-difference", but they take it that this assertion is in regard to non-difference.

Although the supreme Self and individual self are different principles, the promise that "when *ātman* is known, this all is known" is possible since there are some points which they have in common. If the two were completely different, such a promise, he says, could never be implemented.

"If the individual self and the supreme Self were absolutely different, then the teaching having begun by referring to the individual self in the present passage, and then going on to a conclusion referring to the supreme Self, would be lacking in continuity (i.e. an anacoluthon). Again, the promise (in the sacred text that when ātman has been known this all is known) would not be implemented. Therefore the side of non-difference has been taught first."

Incidentally one may inquire, what difference would there be between the thought of Āśmarathya and that of Kāśakṛtsna who is referred to after him (in *BS*. I.4.22), inasmuch as it may be taken, as already remarked, that they both proposed a doctrine of difference-non-difference ? The details are not easy to follow, but according to Bhāskara (ad I.4.21),[1] Āśmarathya takes it that the relation between the supreme Self and the individual self is the same as "the relationship between prakṛti (=matter) and its evolutes (*prakṛtivikārabhāva*)". Consequently he thinks that the supreme Self is the material cause of the individual self.

Since Āśmarathya is here trying to discover the import of the promise (*pratijñā*), Bhāskara's commentary is, I think, correct. According to the *Bhāmatī* (ad loc.), Āśmarathya compared the relationship of the supreme Self and individual self to that between fire and a spark. In that case, there would be agreement in meaning with the account of Bhāskara. Therefore, although they assert in common a theory of "Difference and non-difference", Kāśakṛtsna and Āśmarathya have some differences in doctrine.

Comparison of the relationship of the supreme Self (or Brahman) and the individual self to the spark which flies out of the fire, has already been taught in the Ancient *Upaniṣads* (*Bṛhad. Up*. II.1.20; *Muṇḍ. Up*. II.1.1; *Maitri-Up*. VI.26, 31). Āśmarathya has accepted this, and the allegory is frequently used by the Vedānta school later. Very early, it is mentioned in the *Brahma-sūtra* III.2.28, the Draviḍācārya fragment 13,[2] the *Māṇḍūkya-Kārikā* I.6, and later, Nimbārka[3] and others still taught the same view. Then, on the other hand, it was criticized as not the true theory of the ultimate reality by the *Māṇḍūkya-kārikā* III.15 and by Śaṅkara.

Āśmarathya, like other Vedānta scholars of the early period, was also an authority on the ritualistic learning and the ritualistic

Mīmāṃsā. His name appears in the *Āśvalāyana-Śrauta-sūtra*[4] and in the *Mīmāṃsā-sūtra* (VI.5.16). And according to Pāṇini's Grammar (IV.3.105), Āśmarathaḥ Kalpaḥ is listed as one example of the new ritual learning on the ritual branch of learning (*Kalpa*).[5] Consequently, a consideration of these facts allows the conclusion that he lived probably in a period not too far separated from Pāṇini.[6]

Notes

1. According to Śaṅkara, I.4.23.
2. Cf. the present work, Part V, Chap. 6, Sect. 1. And *Yājñavalkya-smṛti* III.67.
3. Ghate : *The Vedānta*, p. 32.
4. A. Weber : *HIL.*, p. 242.
5. *Ibid.*, pp. 46, 53, 242.
6. His name also appears in *Gaṇapāṭha, Garga* of Pāṇini's Grammar.

SECTION 6. BĀDARI

Bādari's doctrine is mentioned in four places in the *Brahma-Sūtra* (I.2.30, III.1.11, IV.3.7, and IV.4.10).

First of all, Bādari asserts in the *Brahma-sūtra* (III, 1, 11), as against Kārṣṇājini, that the word *caraṇa* (conduct) in *Chānd. Up.* V, 10, 7[1] previously mentioned should be understood in its primary meaning (*mukhya*).

"Conduct" means not the remainder of *karman* (*anuśaya*) as proposed by Kārṣṇājini, but action (*karman, anuṣṭhāna*); i.e. the "pleasant conduct" (*ramaṇīya-caraṇa*) of the scriptural passage is understood to mean "good conduct" (*sukṛta*), and the "stinking conduct" (*kapūya-caraṇa*) is "bad conduct" (duṣkṛta). Therefore, he thought that according to the good or evil actions performed by a man in this world, that man would either be born in the upper three classes or be reborn in the meanest class or as an animal. However, it was not that he denied the theory[2] of a two-stage recompense, that holds that after death one goes to the world of the moon and there receives the fruits of his *karma*; afterwards, coming back down to this earth one is reborn in any one of several states. He simply asserted that after coming down to this earth, the state received, or the circumstances, is determined by the wherefore of the behavior performed previously on this earth. Consequently, whereas Kārṣṇājini esteemed rituals highly and said that all good works of mankind are merely aids to the realization of the fruits of the rituals, and how the rituals are performed determines the conditions of the future existence, Bādari did not think them so important, but rather seems to have thought that the rituals were included among good actions in general. In the three ancient commentaries the point is not clearly brought out, but we can suppose from the position of that *sūtra* that the *Sūtra*-author probably regarded the theory of Bādari as the final view (*siddhānta*). This has been clearly stated by the sub-commentators (Ānandajñāna and Govindānanda).

Again in the *Brahma-sūtra* I.2.30 the following theory is presented, on the question why in *Chāndogya-Upaniṣad* V.18.1 it is taught that "the Vaiśvānara Self (i.e. the supreme God) one should worship as of the extent of the span between the outstretched thumb and index finger (*prādeśamātra*)." It is taught in this way for the sake of constant remembrance of the supreme God by the heart which is of the extent of the span between thumb and index finger,[3] or by the mind (*manas*)[4] which dwells in the heart. It is said that Bādari advocated this theory.

Moreover, he held unique theory concerning liberation. According to the *Chāndogya-Upaniṣad* IV.15.5-6, when the person who has attained distinct knowledge, passes through various states after death and enters the lightning from the moon, there is a non-human *puruṣa* (*puruṣo 'mānavaḥ*) there, and that *puruṣa*, it is taught, leads the dead human to the *Brahmā*. What kind of thing that *puruṣa* is had been discussed among the theologians of that time. Bādari held that it was "*Brahman* as an effect" (BS.IV.3.7). Again, according to Śaṅkara and Bhāskara, it is the lower *Brahman* (*apara brahma*). Bādari discusses in detail his reason for understanding it as such, but the position he maintains consistently is in summary as follows :[5]

1. He admits the double theory of "*Brahman* as an effect" and "*Brahman* as a cause" (highest *Brahman*). The latter is higher (*para*) than the former.
2. *Brahman* as an effect is also the *Brahma*-world (*brahmaloka*). This has a pluralistic existence, and is expressed by the

plural. Opposed to it, the *Brahman* as a cause is unique and cannot be expressed by the plural.

3. *Brahman* as an effect occupies a place in space, and the man who obtains clear knowledge goes there after death. That is, it can be the goal of progress. On the other hand, *Brahman* as a cause transcends spatial determinations, and it is impossible to progress towards it.

4. *Brahman* as an effect is not *Brahman* itself (*brahman* as a cause), but it is near to it. It has a proximity (*sāmīpya*) to *Brahman* itself. Consequently, one can call it the "*Brahma*-world", by a tentative and analogical expression. Bādari seems to have thought that the "*Brahma*-world" is the highest ideal realm within the world extended in space.

5. When the entire world is destroyed and enters the period of dissolution and returns to nothing (*pralaya*), the world of *Brahman* as an effect returns in dissolution to the highest *Brahman*.

6. Although the individual self who attains the knowledge of *Brahman* remains in the *Brahma*-world, it will dissolve into the supreme *Brahman* together with *Hiraṇyagarbha*, the overseer (*adhyakṣa*) of the *Brahma*-world, when the *Brahma*-world returns to dissolution. According to the three ancient commentaries, this idea is said to correspond in import to the following verse in the *Kūrma-Purāṇa* :

> "When the dissolution of the world occurs, namely, in the final end of the supreme One, all those who have set right their minds enter the highest state (*paraṃ padam*) with *Brahmā*."

In this way, Bādari's thought is very close to that of Śaṅkara in several respects. The twofold *Brahman* which he posited can be thought to correspond to the idea of the supreme *Brahman* (*paraṃ brahma*) and the lower *Brahman* (*apara brahma*) in Śaṅkara philosophy. That the latter becomes the goal of progress, and that the former cannot become the goal of progress, is also the same. Consequently, Śaṅkara holds that the theory of Bādari in the *Brahma-sūtra* IV.3.7-11 is the established theory (*siddhānta*). Of course this is not correct as an interpretation of the *Sūtra*,[6] but the fact that Śaṅkara would go so far as to attempt such an impossible interpretation and conclude that Bādari's view was the final one, should perhaps be adequately noted. In this respect, he can be admitted as the *forerunner* of Śaṅkara.

His thought, however, is by no means completely the same as Śaṅkara's. For example, according to the doctrine of the nondualistic monistic school, one can obtain liberation in the body he was born with even in the present world, and at the time of death, he is completely united with *Brahman*, but Bādari thought that only after death, when one returns to dissolution in the *Brahman* world in the remote future, can he then attain complete liberation. Therefore one must also admit the fact that the *Māṇḍūkya-kārikās* and other works produced in the interim from Bādari to Śaṅkara exerted an important influence.

Further, Bādari asserted with regard to the state of final release that there exists neither body nor sense-organs in the liberated individual self[7] (*BS*. IV.4.10). He is opposed to Jaimini on this point. As already mentioned, he thought that in the ultimate state of liberation the individual self returns to annihilation at the destruction of the world, so that it would presumably be more natural that the liberated individual self could not possibly have a body or sense-organs, and thus he was consistent from beginning to end.

Bādari was not only a singular Vedānta thinker, he was also a scholar of the ritualistic Mīmāṃsā. His theory is mentioned in the *Mīmāṃsā-sūtra*.[8] And his name as a ritual scholar has also been given in the *Kātyāyana-Śrauta-sūtra* (IV.3.18), and the *Taittirīya-Prātiśākhya*.[9] Consequently he too must have been well-versed in the Vedas and the rituals in general, just as other Vedānta scholars of the early period.

While the dates of his life are not clear, he perhaps would have lived during the same period as the thinkers considered in the preceding sections.

Notes

1. On this passage, cf. Section 1, "Kārṣṇājini" (p. 4).
2. This fact is clearly stated in *BS*.III.1.8 ff. (Cf. The present work, p. 256).
3. The theory of Bhāskara.
4. The theory of Śaṅkara. But Rāmānuja interprets it as merely "in order to worship it as a span long."
5. Concerning some proofs which could lead to such a conclusion, cf. the commentary note on the *BS-bhāṣya*. IV.3.7-11 (p. 360 ff.).
6. Cf. commentary on *BS-Bhāṣya* IV.3.7 (p. 368 ff.).

7. According to the *Mahābhārata* XII.335.6-12, the inhabitants of the "White island" (Śvetadvīpa), the ideal land, are held to be apart from all demerit and sin, and to have no sense-organs.

8. III.1.3; VI.1.27; VIII.3.6; IX.2.33.

9. Weber : *HIL.*, pp. 139, 241; Macdonell and Keith : *Vedic Index*, s.v. Bādarāyaṇa.

SECTION 7. JAIMINI

Jaimini has generally been regarded in India as the founder of the ritual Mīmāṃsā school; The Mīmāṃsā teachings are called the theories of Jaimini (*Jaimini-naya*,[1] *Jaiminīya-mata*,[2] *Jaimini-darśana*[3]); and the Mīmāṃsā school is entitled as the school of Jaimini (*Jaiminīya*[4]). Accordingly, any mention of Jaimini at once calls up associations with the learning of the ritualistic Mīmāṃsā, yet he was also, at the same time, a Vedānta thinker, and in this chapter, therefore, we should give some consideration to him in that role.

Notes

1. E.g. *Arthasaṃgraha, maṅgalācaraṇa.*
2. E.g. Haribhadra, *Ṣaḍdarśana-samuccaya*, v. 77.
3. E.g. *SDS*.XII.
4. E.g. the final verse of the *Arthasaṃgraha*, and *Prasannapadā*, p. 523, line 9.

1. *Works*

According to tradition, at least the following three works by Jaimini have been handed down :

1. *Mīmāṃsā-sūtra*
2. *Devatā-kāṇḍa*
3. *Śārīraka-sūtra*

In the following, we shall take them up one by one for examination.

1. *MĪMĀMSĀ-SŪTRA*[1]

According to tradition, Jaimini is the author of the *Mīmāṃsā-sūtra*, and this has been accepted throughout India. However, the *Mīmāṃsā-sūtra* handed down to the present time was not directly written by Jaimini himself. In this *Sūtra*, the name of a scholar called Jaimini is mentioned five times,[2] and for the author of the *Sūtra* to give his own name within a *Sūtra* composed by himself would be unusual. Not only that, in the *Mīmāṃsā-sūtra* VI.3.4, Jaimini is referred to as the supporter of the opponent's objection (*pūrva-pakṣa*) related to the rituals, and is later rejected. Consequently, the compiler of the *Sūtra* is clearly different from Jaimini, and while he respected and relied upon him as an authoritative thinker, he did not follow Jaimini's theories in all respects, but maintained a critical attitude towards them. It is not clear to this day just who the author of this *Sūtra* is. Perhaps it was compiled as a kind of textbook on ritualistic *mīmāṃsā* learning by the *Mīmāṃsā* scholars after the time of Jaimini. Since in the extant *Mīmāṃsā-Sūtra* the names of a great many others besides Jaimini appear, it might be a compendium of their theories—If so, one can suppose that quite a long period of time was necessary for it to assume such a form.

As the *Mīmāṃsā-sūtra* has already been published and its translation also is completed, we shall here omit any explanation of its contents.

As for the commentaries on the *Mīmāṃsā-sūtra*, the oldest extant is the *Bhāṣya* by Śabarasvāmin; there were, however, a great number of commentaries written before that. These have not survived but we know that at least the works mentioned below were at one time in existence :

1. A *Vṛtti* by Upavarṣa.[3]
2. A *Vṛtti* by Bodhāyana.[4]
3. A *Bhāṣya* by Devasvāmin.[5]
4. A *Vṛtti* by Bhavadāsa.[6]

Besides these, it is known that there existed also :

5. A *Vṛtti* by Bhartṛmitra.[7]
6. A *Vṛtti* by Hari.[8]

Of these, No. 5 is thought to be a little later than Śabarasvāmin, and the date of No. 6 appears to be prior to Kumārila—only that much is clear.

Notes

1. This is also called *Jaiminīya-sūtra*, *Mīmāṃsā-śāstra*, and has been named *Jaiminīyaṃ dharma-śāstram* (SDS.XII.1.24).

2. III.1.4, VI.3.4, VIII.3.7, IX.2.39, XII.1.8.
3. See the present work, Part V, Chap. 2, Sect. 2.
4. See *ibid.*, Chap. 4, Sect. 2.
5. According to *Prapañcahṛdaya* (p. 39), Devasvāmin summarized the commentary of Upavarṣa, and wrote an extremely detailed *Bhāṣya* on the *Ṣoḍaśalakṣaṇa-pūrvamīmāṃsā-śāstra.*
6. According to *ibid.*, *loc. cit*, he was later than Upavarṣa, but earlier than either Devasvāmin or Śabarasvāmin. He is frequently mentioned in the works of the Mīmāṃsā school. Cf. V. A. Ramaswami Śastri, "*Old Vṛttikāras* on the Pūrva Mīmāṃsā Sūtras," *IHQ*, Vol. X. (1934), pp. 449-450.
7. See the present work, Part V, Chap. 8.
8. According to G. Jhā, *The Prābhākara School of Pūrva Mīmāṃsā* (p. 127), it is mentioned in the *Śāstradīpikā* X.2.59, 60.

2. *Devatā-kāṇḍa and the Saṃkarṣaṇa-kāṇḍa*

According to tradition, besides the *Mīmāṃsā-sūtra*, Jaimini wrote another work, composed of four parts (*adhyāya*), which discusses the divinity (devatā). This work is also called the *Saṃkarṣaṇa-kāṇḍa*, the *Saṃkarṣakā*, or simply the *Saṃkarṣa*, and is also referred to as the *Devatā-kāṇḍa*, as it discusses the divinity of the rituals.[1] As to the reasons for calling it the *Saṃkarṣaṇa-kāṇḍa*, it is said that this was because it gives in detail what should have been explained, but was left unsaid, in the *Mīmāṃsā-sūtra.*[2]

The nature of this work should be said to be an appendix, and as we shall explain, the early Mīmāṃsā scholars saw there was some connection between the *Mīmāṃsā-sūtra* and the *Saṃkarṣaṇa-kāṇḍa*, and wrote commentaries on both of them.[3] The relation is thus acknowledged generally in India.[4]

As for the commentaries on this work, the following are known:

1. The commentary by Bodhāyana. Bodhāyana wrote a commentary on the *Saṃkarṣaṇa-kāṇḍa*,[5] which forms one part of his *Kṛtakoṭi*. As he combined the *Mīmāṃsā-sūtra* and the *Saṃkarṣaṇa-kāṇḍa* and called it the *Ṣoḍaśalakṣaṇī*, his commentary assumed that the two works formed an indivisible unit. His work has been lost and does not exist today.

2. The commentary by Upavarṣa. Upavarṣa also wrote a commentary on both the *Mīmāṃsā-sūtra* and the *Saṃkarṣaṇa-kāṇḍa*, but it has not been preserved to the present[6] day.

3. The Commentary by Devasvāmin. He may perhaps be the same person who was the author of the commentary

(*Bhāṣya*) on the *Āśvalāyana-śrauta-sūtra*. He also wrote a commentary in 16 chapters on the *Pūrvamīmāṃsā*. A copied manuscript of this work has survived to the present day, which, as a commentary on the *Saṃkarṣaṇa-kāṇḍa*, is the oldest extant one.[7] Since the commentary by Upavarṣa is very complex and difficult for the average person, tradition says that he wrote a very simple version of it.[8]

4. The Commentary of Bhavadāsa. He also wrote a commentary on both the *Mīmāṃsā-sūtra* and the *Saṃkarṣaṇa-kāṇḍa*, but it has not been transmitted to the present day.[9]

5. The Commentary of Śabarasvāmin. This work had already been lost, but it is said to have been extremely simple and brief.[10]

6. The Commentary (*Bhāṣya*) of Govinda. This work no longer exists today.[11]

7. The Commentary by Rājacūḍāmaṇi Dīkṣita. He was an erudite scholar well-versed in all branches of learning, who wrote a commentary on the *Saṃkarṣa-nyāya-muktāvali*.[12]

8. The Commentary by Khaṇḍadeva. He lived during the first part of the 17th century, and wrote a commentary called the *Bhāṭṭadīpikā* on the *Mīmāṃsā-sūtra* and the *Saṃkarṣaṇa-kāṇḍa*, which has already been published. (*The Saṃkarṣaṇa-kāṇḍa with Khaṇḍadeva's Commentary Bhāṭṭadīpikā*. Edited by Rāma Miśra Śāstrī. *The Pandit*, 14 (1892), Nos. 11, 12, pp. 1-32, 15 (1893), Nos. 217, pp. 33-127.)

9. The Commentary by Bhāskararāya. He was the son of Gambhīrarāya Dīkṣita, and lived in the 17th century. He wrote a subcommentary on the *Bhaṭṭadīpikā*, called the *Bhaṭṭacandrikā*.

The last three commentaries listed above comment on each successive *sūtra* in the *Saṃkarṣaṇa*.[13] We see from them that the *Saṃkarṣaṇa-kāṇḍa* had 347 *sūtras*, divided into four parts, and that each part was further divided into four chapters. None of the chapters distinguishes the various sections (*adhikaraṇa*) which may include a number of *sūtras*, but each *sūtra* is taken as one section.

Part *adhyāya*	Chapter *pāda*				Total
	1	2	3	4	
13	15	18	24	27	84
14	41	18	15	30	104
15	25	36	20	14	95
16	13	19	22	10	64
			Grand total		347

This work is generally thought to be a supplement to the *Mīmāṃsā-sūtra* composed of 12 chapters. There are many miscellaneous topics discussed therein, and no general plan of construction is to be found to unify the work.

Concerning the contents of this work, Madhusūdana-Sarasvatī, after saying in the *Prasthāna-bheda* that Jaimini composed the *Mīmāṃsā-sūtra*, says the following :—

"In the same way as this, the *Saṃkarṣaṇa-kāṇḍa* composed of four parts (*adhyāya-catuṣṭaya*) was also written by Jaimini. Now it is generally known by the name *Devatā-kāṇḍa*, but since it describes the ritual of worship (*upāsanā*), it has been included within the ritual mīmāṃsā".[14] Again, we see in the *Prapañca-hṛdaya*, a work resembling the *Prasthāna-bheda*, that it is composed of four parts (*adhyāya-catuṣka*), and combined with the 12 parts of the *Mīmāṃsā-sūtra*, it forms the *Pūrva-mīmāṃsā-śāstra*;[15] while in regard to its contents, it is explained that it chiefly discusses the divine.[16] The *Saṃkarṣaṇa-Kāṇḍa*, has been from olden times esteemed as valuable for its explanation on the divine.

The *Brahma-sūtra* (III.3.43) briefly says that "This has already been explained" (*tad uktam*). Commenting upon it, Śaṅkara says that, if the divinity is each time a different one according to the invocation, the three offerings also are to be different, and then he further says :

"This has already been taught in the *Saṃkarṣa*—The divinities are different from each other on account of their being cognized thus."

("*tad uktam*" *Saṃkarṣe* "*nānā vā devatā pṛthagjñānāt.*")[17]

In any case, the *Saṃkarṣaṇa-kāṇḍa* has a close connection with the *Mīmāṃsā-sūtra*, and it was perhaps edited by the same school at the time of compilation of the latter. The thinkers after Bodhāyana (c. 500 A.D.) insofar as they worshipped it in the same way as the *Mīmāṃsā-sūtra*, may have come to hand it down as a work by Jaimini, just as the *Mīmāṃsā-sūtra* was later attributed to Jaimini. (On the other hand, the legend is also prevalent[18] that the author of this work is Kāśakṛtsna). In any event, there is no doubt that it was ascribed to Jaimini only in somewhat later centuries.

Notes

1. Ānandajñāna and Govindānanda (ad *BS.*III.3.43) note that the *Saṃkarṣa* is the *Devatā-kāṇḍa.*

2. R. G. Bhandarkar, *Collected Works*, II., p. 107. *saṃkarṣa, saṃkarṣaṇa* mean 'brief,' or "summarized." Such a supposition by Bhandārkar can be verified on canonical grounds in the ancient literature also.

pūrvādhyāyacatuṣkeṇa (=*Devatā-kāṇḍena*) *mantravācyā ca devatā / saṃkarṣeṇoditā tad dhi devatākāṇḍam ucyate //*—*Sarvasiddhāntasaṃgraha* I.21.

3. Śabarasvāmin also accepted the existence of a close connection between the two . . . iti *Saṃkarṣe vakṣyati.* (Śabarasvāmin ad *Mīmāṃsā-sūtra* XII.2.11).

4. In the *Prapañcahṛdaya* (p. 39), both works are combined and are called the *Ṣoḍaśalakṣaṇa-mīmāṃsā-sūtra*, which is divided into the *tantrakāṇḍa* and the *saṃkarṣakāṇḍa* (or the *devatā-*), in contrast to the *brahma-kāṇḍa*. There is just one exception in the ancient literature. In *Sarvasiddhāntasaṃgraha* attributed to Śaṅkara, it is stated that the *Devatā-kāṇḍa* belongs to the Uttara-mīmāṃsā, constituting its first half, and that it is by Vyāsa. (As will be remarked later, it was taken that Vyāsa was the same as Bādarāyaṇa).

"The Uttara-mīmāṃsā consists of eight parts, divided into two sections, the Section of Divinity (devatā-kāṇḍa) and the Section of Knowledge (Jñāna-kāṇḍa). The *sūtras* by Vyāsa cover both of them" (I.20).

"Now the divinity in the sacred verse (*mantra*), explained in the *Saṃkarṣaṇa*, is (discussed) in the first four parts. It is truly stated to be the section on divinity" (I.21).

This is against the general view in India, but perhaps the author of the *Sarvasiddhāntasaṃgraha* put it into the Uttara-mīmāṃsā since the devatā-kāṇḍa refers to worship (*upāsanā*) as well.

5. See Frag. 2 of Bodhāyana.

6. See the present work, Part V, Chap. 3, Set. 2.

7. According to V. A. Ramaswami, "The *Saṃkarṣa Kāṇḍa*", (*IHQ*. Vol. IX, 1933, pp. 290-299).

8. *tad api* (*upavarṣabhāṣyam api*) mandamatīn prati *duṣpratipādaṃ vistīrṇatvād ity upekṣya ṣoḍaśalakṣaṇa-Pūrva-mīmāṃsā-śāstramātrasya Devasvāminā atisaṃkṣiptaṃ kṛtam.* (*Prapañcahṛdaya*, p. 39).

9. According to *Prapañcahṛdaya* (p. 39), he appears to be later than Devasvāmin. Further, in Devasvāmin (*Bhāṣya* ad XV.2.1), the following is said :

asmin pāde 'apūrvāt tathā somaḥ' ity ārabhyāpādaparisamāpteḥ. Bhāvadāsam eva bhāṣyam iti.

The source for the latter is according to V. A. Ramaswami, *ibid.*

10. See the present work, Part V. Chap. 9, Sect. 1.

11. See *ibid*, Chap. 13.

12. According to Ramaswami, this work is inserted in Hultzsch, *Reports of South Indian MSS.*, Vol. II, No. 1489.

13. However, in these three commentaries, the text of each *sūtra* is cited for explanation partly; each *sūtra* is not cited as a whole. It has been said that the copy of only the *Saṃkarṣaṇa-kāṇḍa* is extant (R. G. Bhandarkar, *Collected Works*, II, p. 107), but it is not clear whether or not it has been published. Recently V. A. Ramaswami Sastri, in his article given above, has collected and published the verbatim quotations of the *sūtras* in the *Saṃkarṣaṇa-kāṇḍa* in later works. For additional comments on the *Saṃkarṣaṇa-kāṇḍa*, see M. L. Sandal, "Introduction to the English Translation of the *Pūrvamīmāṃsā-Sūtra*" (*SBH. Series*, Vol. I, pp. x-xii).

14. See *Prasthāna-bheda*, p. 6; Ui Hakuju, *Indo Tetsugaku Kenkyū*, IV. 442.

15. *Prapañca-hṛdaya*, pp. 38-39.

16. *Ibid.*, pp. 41-42. Some passages in this published work are obscure; they run as follows :

tathā Devatā-kāṇḍasya prathamādhyāye sarveṣāṃ mantraviśeṣāṇāṃ devatātattva-pradarśane tātparyam iti pradarśitam / dvitīyādhyāye vidhyarthavādanāmadheyānāṃ mantra-devatā-viśeṣatvaṃ / tṛtīyādhyāye devatātattvaṃ svecchāvigrahatvādiguṇa-gaṇālaṃkṛtam / caturthādhyāye devatā phalaṃ satkarmaṇām apavargādhikāriṇas tādātmya-lakṣaṇam apavargaphalam iti /

17. In the Bhāskara's Commentary, there is *tad uktaṃ Saṃkarṣe "nānā devatā pṛthaktvād" iti*, and in Rāmānuja's Commentary, *tad uktaṃ Saṃkarṣaṇe* "nānā vā devatā pṛthakvāt." The published version of Rāmānujas, Commentary has this as a statement from *Saṃkarṣaṇa-kāṇḍa* XIV.2.15.

18. See the present work, Sect. 2 (p. 13).

3. *Śārīraka-sūtra*

Prof. Belvalkar recently published a noteworthy opinion that Jaimini also wrote the *Brahma-sūtra*.[1] Sureśvara's work, the *Naiṣkarmyasiddhi* has been published together with its prose commentary, the *Sambandhokti*, which is also said to have been written by Sureśvara himself. As a response to stanzas I.15 and 17, stanza I.91[2] reads as follows :

adhicodanam āmnāyas tasyaiva syāt kriyārthatā /
'tat tvam asy' -ādi-vākyānām brūta karmārthatā katham //

Then this is commented on as follows :

yad api Jaiminīyaṃ vacanam udghāṭayasi tad api tadvivakṣā 'parijñānād evodbhāvyate. kiṃ kāraṇam / yato na Jaiminer ayam abhiprāya 'Āmnāyas sarva eva kriyārtha' iti / yadi hy ayam abhiprāyo' 'bhaviṣyat, 'athāto brahma-jijñāsā'—'janmādy asya yataḥ'-ity evamādi brahmavastusvarūpamātra-yāthātmya-prakāśanaparaṃ gambhīranyāyasaṃdṛbdhaṃ sarva-Vedāntārtha-mīmāṃsanaṃ Śrīmac-chārīrakaṃ nāsūtrayiṣyat / asūtrayac ca / tasmāj Jaiminer evāyam abhiprāyo-yathaiva vidhivākyānāṃ svārtha-mātre prāmāṇyam evam aikātmyavākyānām apy anadhi-gatavastu-pariccheda-sāmyād' iti.[3]

"And as for the quotation from Jaimini (verse 17), that, too, was based on ignorance of that writer's real intention. For Jaimini did not mean that all Vedic texts are concerned with injunctions to act or prohibitions from acting. If so, he would never have composed the Vedānta Sūtras[4] beginning with "Now, therefore, the enquiry into the Absolute (Brahman)" and "He from whom all this came forth", which are intent solely on proclaiming the true nature of the Absolute as the real, and which amount to a critical exposition of the meaning of the Upaniṣads when taken in their entirety, backed by profound reasoning. But as a matter of fact he did compose them. Therefore we conclude that Jaimini's real belief was that just as the injunctions are authoritative within their own sphere only, so the passages proclaiming the one Self are equally authoritative in theirs, the two classes of passages having both an equal claim to authority in that they deal with matters not previously knowable from any other source."

(Alston's translation : *The Realization of the Absolute*, I: 91, p. 66.)

We see from this passage that Jaimini wrote a *sūtra* entitled the *Śārīraka*, and yet the first two *sūtras* are coincidental with the extant *Brahma-Sūtra*. So, therefore, Belvalkar assumed that the extant *sūtra* by Bādarāyaṇa was formulated based upon this *Sūtra* by Jaimini.[5] While there is something to be said for this assumption, would it not perhaps be better to think as follows ? —As we shall consider in the next section, Bādarāyaṇa is not the author of the extant *Brahma-sūtra*.

The legend which says that he was, came into existence in later centuries. Accordingly, just as the extant *Brahma-sūtra* came to be handed down as a work by Bādarāyaṇa, could there not have been someone who handed down that the extant *Brahma-sūtra* or its prototype was a work by Jaimini ? At present, even prior to Śaṅkara, there were those[6] who regarded Jaimini's theories in the *Brahma-sūtra* to be the final position (*siddhānta*). Consequently it is easy to suppose that they could have handed down the belief the *Brahma-sūtra* or its prototype was a work of Jaimini. Then Sureśvara probably was aware of this fact. However nothing more exact can be said in our present state of knowledge.

Notes.

1. Shripad Krishna Belvalkar, *Jaimini's Śārīraka-sūtra* (*Festgabe für R. Garbe*, S. 163 ff.).
2. BSS. 2nd ed., 1925, II.52.
3. As we cannot now refer to the original work, we shall rely on the article by Belvalkar.
4. The Modern scholar, S. K. Belvalkar, held that the core of the Vedānta Sūtras consisted in exegesis of texts from the Chāndogya Upaniṣad deriving in the first instance from Jaimini. Śaṃkara ascribes them to Bādarāyaṇa, and Upadeśa Sāhasrī XVI.67 suggests he may have identified Bādarāyaṇa with Vyāsa. From the point of view of modern scholarship they are a collection of aphorisms that were frequently altered, added to and re-moulded in the course of time, and are not assignable to any one specific author. Above all, they were probably originally part of the Mīmāṃsaka Sūtras, and Śrī Śaṃkara may well have been the first man to have treated them separately. The previous commentator to whom he refers (Bhagavān Upavarṣa) seems to have treated the two sets of aphorisms as one connected work. Perhaps Sureśvara is here referring back to that tradition. However Hiriyanna points out (Notes to his edition of "Naiṣkarmya Siddhi", pp. 229 ff.) that Śāṃkara too, sometimes speaks of the Mīmāṃsaka Sūtras and Vedānta Sūtras as if they were one connected work, e.g. Vedānta Sūtra Commentary, III.iii.53. (Alston's note)
5. Further, Belvalkar asserted that the theories attributed to Jaimini in the *Brahma-sūtra* have indeed only a relation with the *Chāndogya Upaniṣad*, and he argues that Jaimini wrote a *sūtra* on only that *Upaniṣad*, and later Bādarāyaṇa enlarged it in order to include all the *Upaniṣads*. This argument has rather weak grounds, however. It cannot be said that the arguments of Jaimini are related only to the *Chāndogya Upaniṣads*. See the following chapter.
6. See commentaries on the *Brahma-sūtra*. IV.3.7 ff.

2. *His Personality and Dates*

The name of Jaimini does not appear in the more important Vedic scriptures,[1] but a school belonging to the *Sāma Veda* is called the Jaiminīya school, and it has handed down the works with titles beginning with his name: *Jaiminīya-saṃhitā, Jaiminīya-brāhmaṇa, Jaiminīya-upaniṣad-brāhmaṇa, Jaiminīya-śrautasūtra, Jaiminīya-gṛhya-sūtra.*

Then his name is given in the *Śāṅkhāyana-gṛhya-sūtra* (only in the portion interpolated in later centuries, however), and in the *Āśvalāyana-Śrauta-sūtra* (XII.10), Jaimini is made to belong to the Bhṛgu clan.[2] Again, the name Jaimini also appears in the genealogy (*vaṃśa*) at the end of the *Sāmavidhāna-brāhmaṇa*,[3] according to which he is the disciple of Vyāsa Pārāśarya and the teacher of Pauṣpiṇḍya. And in the *Viṣṇu-purāṇa* III.6.1.4, since he is held to be the teacher of Pauṣpiṃji, this would agree, but since the *Sāmavidhāna-brāhmaṇa* is not an ancient *Brāhmaṇa*, the genealogy probably came into being in later centuries. In the *Viṣṇu-purāṇa* III.4.8.9, Jaimini is mentioned[4] as the man who received the revelation of the Sāma Veda and according to the *Bhāgavata-Purāṇa* XII.6.49 ff. Jaimini is held to be one of the four disciples of Vedavyāsa,[5] while in the *Mahābhārata* I.63.89, he is held to be one of the five disciples of Vyāsa; such accounts, however, do not exist in the Vedic literature. Nonetheless, the fact that Jaimini, like Bādarāyaṇa, has been handed down as belonging to the school pertaining to the *Sāma Veda*, should be adequately noted.

The name of Jaimini does not appear in the *Mahābhāṣya*[6] by Patañjali, and in the great epic poems, he is only known as a saint.[7] In the collection of fables, the *Pañcatantra*, there is preserved the legend that the sage Jaimini, the founder of the Mīmāṃsā school, was trampled to death by an elephant,[8] but in the text translated into Pehlevi in the 6th century, this story has not been included.[9] Further, as a work bearing his name, there is extant the *Jaimini-sūtra*,[10] a work on astrology, and one section (*Āśvamedhika-parvan*) of the *Jaimini-Bhārata*, the Mahābhārata edited by Jaimini, has been handed down to the present, and already published, but nothing can be learned of its author. Hemacandra, the great Jain scholar, remarks that although such wretched Cārvākas (materialists) are truly disgusting nihilists, they are far better than that evil demon Jaimini clad in a mendicant's robes, who lurks in the shades of sacred words of the Vedas.[11] Hemacandra, from his standpoint of non-injury to living things, was highly critical of Jaimini, who had established ritualism as a branch of learning, which offers animals as sacrifices and robs them of their lives. Thus, the name "Jaimini" was quite famous in the history of India's culture, but it is still not clear at all what kind of a person he was. Only the fact seems to be beyond doubt, however, that there lived a historical personage of the name of Jaimini who established the *Mīmāṃsā* study, and who was thoroughly versed in both the ritual learning and the Vedānta doctrines.[12]

The dates of that Jaimini as a Mīmāṃsā scholar are also a problem, but he undoubtedly lived before the compilation of the *Mīmāṃsā-sūtra*. It is evident that this *Sūtra* came into being prior to the *Brahma-sūtra*,[13] and since the *Vaiśeṣika Sūtra*, formulated in c. A.D. 50-100, was in part based upon this *Mīmāṃsā-sūtra*,[14] the latter must be of the same period or even earlier. Moreover, Bādarāyaṇa was more than a generation earlier than this, and Jaimini was even earlier than he.[14] However, he probably was later than the scholars discussed in an earlier section of the present work. In which case, the dates of his life would be c. 200-100 B.C., and I think he could be regarded as of the same period as Patañjali.

Notes

1. Macdonell and Keith, *Vedic Index*, s.v. Jaimini.
2. A. Weber, *HIL.*, pp. 56, 58, 240.
3. *Ibid*, p. 240, n.
4. *Ibid.*, loc cit.
5. According to Festschrift Garbe, S. 164. Further the same is also said in the *Mārkaṇḍeya-Purāṇa*. (Cf. Winternitz, *HIL.*, I. 560).
6. But in the *Mahābhāṣya*, there is reference to the *Mīmāṃsaka*.
7. Hopkins, *GEI.*, p. 97.
8. The unhappy death of Indian sages :

Pañcatantra II, v. 33 (textus ornatior : v. 28) :

siṃho vyākaraṇasya kartur aharat prāṇān priyān Pāṇiner mīmāṃsākṛtam unmamātha sahasā hastī muniṃ Jaiminim /

chandojñānanidhiṃ jaghāna makaro velātaṭe Piṅgalam ajñānāvṛtacetasām atiruṣāṃ ko 'rthas tiraścāṃ guṇaiḥ //

Translation by R. Schmidt :

"Pāṇini, den Grammatiker, brachte ein Löwe um sein theures Leben; den Weisen Jaimini, den Gründer den Mīmāṃsā, zerstampfte flugs ein

Elephant; den Piṅgala, eine wahre Schatzkammor der Verskunde, tödtete ein Seeungeheuer am Meeresstrande : was kümmort sich wüthende Thiere, deren Geist Unwissenheit verhüllt, um Verdienste."

(Cf. O. Böhtlingk, *Indische Sprüche*, I Aufl., v. 3253.)

9. A Weber, op. cit, p. 240, n.

10. *Ibid.*, loc. cit.

11. *Yoga-śāstra* II.38. (According to p. 15 of the translation by Mr. Suzuki).

12. There are scholars who maintain that the author of this *Sūtra* was held to be Jaimini only because the *Mīmāṃsā-sūtra* was formulated by the Jaimini school of the *Sāma-Veda* (see Winternitz, *GIL.*, III.425, Anm. 2). Such a judgment, however, lacks affirmative grounds.

13. See the present work Part IV, Chap. 2. Appendix, Sect. 3 (p 400).

14. Dr. Ui, *ITK*.I.244, 252-253, *ITS* p. 166.

15. See the following section.

3. *His Vedānta thought*

It has been admitted within the Vedānta school from quite ancient times that Jaimini was an authoritative scholar on the Vedānta learning, etc. Not only does his name frequently appear within the *Brahma-sūtra*, but Sureśvara also has handed down, as we discussed earlier, that he was the author of the *Śārīraka-sūtra*. And the Jain scholars hold that both the ritual mīmāṃsā learning and the Vedānta learning developed from Jaimini, and that both schools derive from Jaimini.[1] Consequently, it is acknowledged throughout India that he was an authority on the two Mīmāṃsās. However, his works related to the Vedānta have not been preserved to the present, and only a few of his words are just quoted within the *Brahma-sūtra*. We shall now take up an examination of them.

Jaimini has been far more frequently quoted in the *Brahma-sūtra* than any other thinker who lived prior to that *Sūtra*, even more than Bādarāyaṇa. His views appear clearly under his own name 11 times in the *Brahma-sūtra*. (I.2.28, I.2.31, I.3.31, I.4.18, III.2.40, III.4.2, III.4.18, III.4.40, IV.4.40, IV.3.12, IV.4.5, and IV.4.11). And his name, though not in the *Sūtra* but in the ancient commentary, is mentioned at IV.1.17 also. In three places (I.2.31, I.2.28, and I.4.18), he is listed as a commentator on particular passages of the sacred texts, and in III.4.40 and IV.1.17, the coincidence with the opinion of Bādarāyaṇa is pointed out. In addition, in seven passages, the views of Jaimini are noted as special heretical doctrines, after which the views of Bādarāyaṇa are stated, Bādarāyaṇa being taken as criticizing Jaimini. In the following, we shall summarize his doctrines as they appear in the *Brahma-sūtra*. (Cf. the translation of *Brahma-sūtra-bhāṣya* in the next Part.)

1. Jaimini held a special doctrine which he applied to separate sacred sentences taken from the *Upaniṣads*. For instance in *BS*.I.2.2 ff, he discusses the problem whether the universal self (*ātman vaiśvānara*) taught in the *Chāndogya-Upaniṣad* (V.11.6) means the supreme self (or the supreme deity), and not fire either as divine or as an element. This problem of reaching a conclusion exercised the theologians of that time. A certain scholar proposed that since the word *vaiśvānara* had been used from ancient times in relation to fire, this passage teaches that one should worship "the fire within the abdomen" (*jāṭharāgni*) as a symbol of the supreme self (*BS*.I.2.26). On this, Jaimini did not accept that in this passage it is necessarily the fire within the abdomen that should be worshipped as a symbol of the highest deity; rather, he asserted that there would be no objection if the words "universal fire" (*vaiśvānarāgni*) were interpreted as pointing directly to the highest deity, in accordance with their etymological[2] meaning (*BS*.I.2.28).

2. In the *Chāndogya-Up*. (V.18.1) it is taught that the *Vaiśvānara* self should be worshipped as a span-long (*prādeśamātra*). In Jaimini's understanding the statement is made in the sense of "identification" (*sampatti*) (*BS*.I.2.31). Various things in the Universe are identified with corresponding parts of the human body in the following *Śruti* passage which appears immediately after the above teaching :

"[The heaven] which shines so brightly is truly the head of the *Vaiśvānara* self. [The sun] which has all forms is its eye. [The wind] which has various courses is its breath. Broad and vast [space] is its trunk. [Water] as wealth is truly the bladder. The earth (i.e. the foundation) is its feet. The altar is its breast. The grass on the altar is the hair. The *Gārhapatya* fire is the heart. The *Anvāhāryapacana* fire is its mind. The *Āhavanīya* fire is the mouth." (*Ch. Up*. V, 18, 2). And so an identification of the highest deity with the size of a span is taught in the previous passage as well.

3. Again, some consideration of the individual self is undertaken in the *Kauṣītaki Upaniṣad* (IV.19), and in reply to the question : "where does this person go when he is here asleep?", it is said thet "then the person becomes one with that prāṇa alone."[3] Therefore, in his understanding (BS.I.4.18), this passage is to teach *Brahman* and this is true also of the *Bṛhadāraṇyaka Upaniṣad* (II.1.16-17).

In the three passages given above, there are presented the peculiar interpretations of Jaimini himself on separate sacred verses of the *Upaniṣads*, but from the foregoing items, we can offer the following conclusion in connection with the Vedānta scholar, Jaimini :

1. Jaimini was a commentator scholar thoroughly versed in the *Upaniṣads*.
2. He accepted the existence of a supreme self (or supreme deity, or the *Brahmā*). Since no thought concerning the presiding deity appears in the *Mīmāṃsā-Sūtra*, it has been generally thought in the academic world that Jaimini did not accept a presiding deity, and it may be a fact that he gave little reflection to anything like a presiding deity. Yet, the fact that the presiding deity or the *Brahmā* was taught in the *Upaniṣads* of the same period as he was, I think, admitted by him as a manifest fact.
3. Moreover, he acknowledged that the worship (*upāsanā*) of the supreme deity was prescribed in the Upaniṣadic canon.
4. Ultimately the individual self is none other than *Brahman*. And he thought that during deep sleep, the individual self returns to and enters into *Brahman*, but when it awakens, it returns from *Brahman* to this phenomenal world.
5. He thought that there was no objection to using etymological interpretations (*yoga*) in canonical commentaries. This etymological interpretation differs from the present day linguistic etymology, and was rather like the so-called folk etymology (Volksetymologie).

In the foregoing, we have examined Jaimini's theories mentioned in the *Brahma-sūtra* which are unrelated to those of Bādarāyaṇa, but in the next chapter, we shall take up the consideration of those portions which are mentioned in comparison with Bādarāyaṇa's thought. And the reason is, that both the later Mīmāṃsā school and the Vedānta school arose separately out of the confrontation of the thought of Jaimini and Bādarāyaṇa, and it is particularly necessary to pay regard to this fact.

We can, however, in the light of the foregoing examination, definitely assert that Jaimini was not merely a scholar of the ritual *mīmāṃsā* alone, but was also thoroughly conversant with the *Upaniṣads*, and was also a Vedānta thinker who held peculiar interpretations of his own.

Notes.

1. *atha Mīmāṃsakam brūmo Jaiminīyāparābhidham* // v. 60
Mīmāṃsako dvidhā karmabrahmamīmāṃsakas tathā /
Vedāntī manyate brahma karma Bhaṭṭa-Prabhākarau // v. 61
—Rājaśekhara :*Ṣaḍdarśana-samuccaya*.

Jaiminiśiṣyāś caike Uttaramīmāṃsāvādinaḥ, eke Pūrvamīmāṃsāvādinaḥ, tatrottara-Mīmāṃsāvādino Vedāntinas, te hi kevalabrahma-advaita-vādasā dhanavyasaninaḥ śabdārthakhaṇḍanāya yuktiḥ kheṭayanto nirvācyatattve vyavatiṣṭhante /. . .
—*Laghuvṛtti* by Maṇibhadra (ad Haribhadra : *Ṣaḍdarśanasamuccaya* v. 64, Chowkh. SS., p. 64)

2. On this etymological meaning, see "Deciphering the *Brahma-sūtra*," commentary on I.2.28 (p. 146).

3. See the commentaries on this *sūtra*.

SECTION 8. BĀDARĀYAṆA

It has been held in general in India that the author of the *Brahma-sūtra* is Bādarāyaṇa.[1] And Śaṅkara himself seems to have thought so.[2]

On the other hand, there is also prevalent the theory that the author of the *Brahma-sūtra* was Veda-Vyāsa, that is to say, the same person who has been handed down as the compiler of the Vedic Canon. The oldest instance of this legend appears in the sub-commentary, *Bhāmatī* by Vācaspati-miśra,[3] and later, not only the sub-commentators Ānandajñāna and Govindānanda, but the Vedānta thinkers Rāmānuja, Madhva, Vallabha, Śrīnivāsa, Baladeva, etc., and also the rhetorical scholar Jagannātha-Paṇḍita, have held that the author of the *Brahma-sūtra* is Veda-Vyāsa or Vyāsa who was the author of the epic poem, *Mahābhārata*,[4] and this view came to be held in general in later centuries.[5] They were, on the other hand, aware of the legend that the author was Bādarāyaṇa, so that they thought that Bādarāyaṇa and Vyāsa were the same person. In later works, it is clearly asserted that both are the same.[6] Then Vyāsa came to be regarded as the founder of the Vedānta school.[7]

However that may be, these legends about Vyāsa came into being in later centuries, and Śaṅkara in his *Brahma-sūtra-bhāṣya* never regarded Bādarāyaṇa as the same as Vyāsa, but thought that Vyāsa was only the author of the ancient traditional works (*smṛti*), such as the *Mahābhārata*, etc.[8]

Then, in relation to the popularization of Vedas, a man called Apāntaratamas, who was born by the order of Viṣṇu during the transition period from Dvāpara to Kali, was said to have been born in this world as Kṛṣṇa Dvaipāyana and promulgated the Vedas.[8a] Accordingly, for Śaṅkara, the author of the *Brahma-sūtra-bhāṣya*, Vyāsa was no more than the author of the *smṛtis*, and was entirely different from Bādarāyaṇa. The view that both are the same arose after Śaṅkara, from the movement to attach authority and prestige to the *Brahma-sūtra*.

On the other hand, in the *Upadeśasāhasrī* (I, 16, 67) of Śaṅkara, Vyāsa is mentioned as the authority of the Vedānta.[9] Although he is not referred to explicitly as the author of the *Brahma-sūtra*, it can be understood by implication in this case that Śaṅkara took him for its author.

How the compiler of the *Brahma-sūtra* came to be regarded as identical with Vyāsa, is easily comprehensible. For the definition of the word 'Vyāsa' is "compiler".[10] The man, Veda-Vyāsa, was not an actual historical personage[11] but a mere mythological invention, so that arguments whether he was the same as another or not would be indeed meaningless. But if one should take up the problem whether the scholar who compiled the Vedas or the *Mahābhārata* is identical with the compiler of the *Brahma-sūtra*, it would be well to conclude that they are not the same person. For both the Vedas and the *Mahābhārata* had already been compiled before the *Brahma-sūtra*.

Brahma-sūtra

Further, in connection with the author of the *Brahma-sūtra*, other legends also exist. In the *Skanda-Purāṇa*, quoted by Madhva and Baladeva, it clearly states that Kṛṣṇa, the incarnation of Hari, composed the *Brahma-sūtra*, and no mention is made of Vyāsa.[12] However, this merely amounts to a legend, and has no connection with historical facts.

Moreover, the fact that the *Brahma-sūtra* was authored by Bādarāyaṇa was also acknowledged by Śaṅkara, and although this has been adopted by many Indologists of late, it also amounts to no more than a single ancient legend. In the *Brahma-sūtra*, since there is frequent mention of the theories of Bādarāyaṇa as authority for his own theories, the *Sūtra*-author must have lived after Bādarāyaṇa. It is the same situation as in the case of the *Mīmāṃsā-sūtra*, which similarly cannot be a work by Jaimini. We see in one case in the extant *Brahma-sūtra*, that the *Sūtra*-author first states his own opinion (III.2.38-39) after which there is a passage where he confirms his own theory by the theory of Bādarāyaṇa (III.2.40). And there are places where the *Sūtra*-author confirms the theories of Bādarāyaṇa (III.4.8.17).[13] Again, on the other hand, there are cases where what is given as a theory of Bādarāyaṇa is by no means coincident with the theories of the *Sūtra*-author himself.[14] Therefore it is a definite fact that the present *Sūtra* is not a work by Bādarāyaṇa. Especially, since it is a clear and distinct fact that Jaimini was not the actual author of the *Mīmāṃsā-sūtra*, as we discussed in the previous section, it should seem quite natural that the same also holds in the case of Bādarāyaṇa.[15]

Not only was Bādarāyaṇa the Vedānta thinker upon whom the author of the *Brahma-sūtra* relied the most, he was also perfectly versed in the ritual *mīmāṃsā*. In the *Mīmāṃsā-sūtra*, the name of Bādarāyaṇa is listed five times.[16] The *Sūtra* always quotes his sayings as the theories of an authority, and never tries to attack them.[17] Moreover, Śabarasvāmin also, who wrote the commentary on it, emphasized that the theories of Bādarāyaṇa should be respected.[18]

Bādarāyaṇa means the "descendant of Badara". His name is not mentioned in Pāṇini's Grammar, but merely listed in *Gaṇapāṭha* on it, nor is it mentioned in the Great Epics.[19] However, in *Śāṇḍilya-bhakti-sūtra* 91, his name is given.[20] Further an astronomer[21] called Bādarāyaṇa also existed, but his connection with the expert of the two *mīmāṃsās* is not clear. According to the genealogy of *Sāmavidhāna-Brāhmaṇa*, Bādarāyaṇa was the disciple of a man called Pārāśaryāyaṇa, and further he was the teacher of Tāṇḍin and Śāṭyāyanin. Then, it is said that he was four generations after Vyāsa Pārāśarya, and three generations later than Jaimini.[21] Accordingly, if one allows anything of historicity to this account, it could be supposed without great error, that Bādarāyaṇa lived as much as 100 years later than Jaimini. Then, as we discussed in the previous section, he would have lived prior to the formulation of the *Mīmāṃsā-sūtra*, and since, as seen from the *Brahma-sūtra*, he always either criticized or accepted only compromizingly the theories of Jaimini, and his theories presuppose those of Jaimini, we can be certain that he was later than Jaimini. If we take it that he lived between the time of the compilation of the *Mīmāṃsā-sūtra* and the period when Jaimini himself lived, we can put him from about 100 B.C. to the beginning of the era, namely, a man of about the first century B.C.

We see in the *Brahma-sūtra* that he considered his chief task to be to criticize the theories of Jaimini. Whenever his theories are quoted, the theories of Jaimini are always listed as the object of his criticism. Accordingly in the next chapter we shall discuss his thought by making a comparison with that of Jaimini. Then in that way we shall be able to clarify the fundamental standpoint of the Vedānta school itself.

Notes

1. E.g., *SDS*. XVI.1.64; *Prasthāna-bheda*, p. 6, line 9.

2. In a passage of the commentary on the *Brahma-sūtra* by Śaṅkara (Vol. I, p. 31, line 3), he is called merely *bhagavān Sūtrakāraḥ*, and the *Sūtra*-author is not called Bādarāyaṇa. Again, in I.3.30, II.1.37, he is merely called *ācārya*. However, since it is said in the commentary on the final *sūtra*, *ata uttaraṃ bhagavān Bādarāyaṇa ācāryaḥ paṭhati*, perhaps it might be thought that not only this final *sūtra*, but the entire *Brahma-sūtra* as well, is Bādarāyaṇa's work. In which case, the theory which holds the *Sūtra*-author to be Bādarāyaṇa would have existed before Śaṅkara.
See *Bhāmatī*, *Maṅgalācaraṇa*.

3. Guha, *Jivātman*, pp. 5-6. Radhakrishnan, *I.Ph.*433.

V. V. Mirashi, The Traditional Author of the *Vedānta-sūtras*—Bādarāyaṇa or Kṛṣṇa Dvaipāyana ? (*Proceedings and Transactions of the Second Oriental Conference*, Calcutta 1922, p. 465 ff).

4. E.G., *SDS*., IV, line 31.

5. Cf. *Abhidhāna-cintāmaṇi*, 847; *Trikāṇḍaśeṣa* 2.7.20; *Śabdakalpadruma*, etc. (According to *PW*).

6. Madhusūdana-sarasvati comments on the word *Vedāntakṛt* in the *Bhagavad-gitā* 15.25, and says, "*Vedāntakṛd Vedāntārthasaṃpradāya-pravartako Vedavyāsādirūpeṇa.*

7. Śaṅkara ad *BS*.III.12, II.3.47.

8. Ibid., III.3.32.

8a. *Vedāntasyaiva tattvārthe vyāsasyāpi matau tathā* / (*Upadeśasāhasri* I, 16, 67)

iti praṇunnā dvayavādakalpanā nirātmavādaś ca tathā hi yuktitaḥ / (I, 16, 68)

(ed. by Sengaku Mayeda, Tokyo : Hokuseido Press, 1973, p. 129)

9. Cf. Winternitz, *HIL.*, I.322 n.

10. Annals of the Bhandarkar Institute, Vol. I (1919-20), p. 1 ff (= *Collected Works of R. G. Bhandarkar*, II.419 ff.).

11. Guha, *Jīvātman*, p. 6.

12. According to Dr. Ui, *ITK*, I.141-142.

13. See the next chapter, section 2 (p. 77).

14. Guha (*Jīvātman*, pp. 3-4) firmly asserts that the author of the *Brahma-sūtra* is Bādarāyaṇa, and says that it is by no means strange in India for the author to give his own name in his work and expound in the third person. For, besides Bādarāyaṇa, the same method was employed by Jaimini, Bodhāyana, Kauṭilya and Vātsyāyana (the author of the *Kāma-sūtra*). And not only in the ancient Sanskrit literature, but also in recent writings in the language of India, the same pattern is found, for example, in the works of Nānak, Tulsī Dās, Kabīra, Tukārām, Caṇḍīdāsa, and Vidyāpati. Radhakrishnan (*I.Ph.*II.432) argues in the same way. However, in the case of recent Indian languages the state of affairs is completely different, and in the case of the ancient *sūtras*, on the contrary, insofar as these *sūtras* were not actually written by the persons who were their traditional authors, but the *Sūtra*-authors merely followed the opinions of these persons, it is explicable that they later were regarded as the *Sūtra*-authors. Winternitz admits that in India it is customary for the author to present his own name in his works, but, he asserts, in the *Mīmāṃsā* or *Vedānta- sūtras*, the circumstances are different, that they were written by men of the Jaimini school or the Bādarāyaṇa school, and are not the actual works of these two scholars. (*GIL.* III.425).

15. I.1.5.; V.2.19; VI.18; X.8.44; XI.1.63.

16. Guha, *Jīvātman*, p. 7.

17. *Bādarāyaṇa-grahaṇaṃ Bādarāyaṇasyedaṃ mataṃ kīrtyate Bādarāyaṇaṃ pūjayitum, nātmīyaṃ mataṃ paryudasitum* // Śabara *ad Mīm.* S. I1.5; cf. ad XI.1.64.

18. Hopkins, *GEI*.97.

19. H. Ui, *ITK*, I.143.

20. A. Weber, *HIL.* 243, n. 259.

21. *Ibid, loc. cit., Indische Studien*, Bd.IV.377.

CHAPTER IX

THE SEPARATION OF THE TWO MĪMĀMSĀS

SECTION 1. THE RELATION BETWEEN THE TWO MĪMĀṂSĀS

In the preceding chapter, we examined eight Vedānta thinkers who were prior to the compilation of the *Brahma-sūtra*, and it became clear that nearly all of them were thoroughly versed not only in the Vedānta but the ritual Mīmāṃsā as well. Whereupon, we must now take up our consideration of the relation between the Vedānta and ritual Mīmāṃsā.

The Vedānta thinkers, as previously mentioned,[1] developed a special branch of learning for the sake of elucidating the true import of the *Upaniṣads*, and this fact corresponds nicely to the investigations carried out by the Mīmāṃsā school (*Mīmāṃsaka*) upon the rituals which are prescribed in the Vedas.

In India in general, a division is made of the entire Vedas between the ritual portion (*karma-kāṇḍa*) and the knowledge portion (*jñāna-kāṇḍa*.)[2] The former is the part which explains the rituals of Brahmanism, and corresponds chiefly to the Veda *Saṃhitās* and the *Brāhmaṇas* in general.[3] The latter is that section which teaches the metaphysical speculations concerning all the things in the universe, and corresponds mainly to the *Upaniṣads* (*Vedānta*). However, as already pointed out, the Vedānta school carried out interpretative and scholarly studies on the knowledge portion of the Vedas, and the Mīmāṃsā school carried out studies in the same way as the Vedānta, upon the ritual portion of the Vedas. Moreover, the rules relating to the rituals taught in the Vedas had, in later centuries, become obscure and difficult to understand, and as various Vedic schools made individual compilations of the sacred texts, the explanations relating to one and the same ritual were not necessarily in agreement, sometimes even contradicting one another. So that for the actual performance of the rituals there were not a few cases where it was not clear how to make a choice, and thus the branch of learning called ritual Mīmāṃsā came into being, as an attempt to remove the contradictions and unify the various theories, and further to consider the general rationale of the rituals, and progressively to enter into philosophical discussion about them.[4] Consequently, though their objects of study differ, the Vedānta school and the Mīmāṃsā school are just the same in academic standpoint and method. Both schools have the philosophy peculiar to orthodox Brahmanism, with the words of the Veda being regarded as works of revelation (*śruti*), revered as absolutely authoritative for all knowledge. Then, they share the attitude of seeking to unify and harmonize, from one definite standpoint, all the contradictions and anomalies which exist in the sacred texts. In this sense, the two schools are akin.

Such interpretative learning or systematic investigation related to the Vedas in general, is called the Mīmāṃsā. The word "Mīmāṃsā" had frequently appeared already in the *Brāhmaṇas*, and it meant "the discussion and consideration of doubtful points of the actual performance of the rituals". The learning of this Mīmāṃsā, again, was in ancient times called "*nyāya*". This word, although it was later used as the term for the Nyāya School, in ancient times meant also the theoretical consideration of the rituals,[5] and in the Mīmāṃsā school, *nyāya* was retained as a term for the learning of its own school even in later centuries.[6]

Details of the early Mīmāṃsā are insufficiently known. From a very ancient times, the branch of learning of the Mīmāṃsā appears to have already been admitted as an independent field of study. In the Great Commentary by Patañjali (2nd century B.C.), there is mention made of the "Mīmāṃsā scholars" (*mīmāṃsaka*).[7] Patañjali the grammarian seems to have based himself on learning and scriptures of the early Mīmāṃsā schoo.l[7a]

Then, in ancient times there was some relation to the investigation of the rituals, but later, it also came to be used in relation to the study of the *Upaniṣads*. Thereupon, the Mīmāṃsā of rituals, being investigation into them, was called the "ritual Mīmāṃsā" (*Karma-mīmāṃsā*)[8], and against this, the Mīmāṃsā related to the sacred Upaniṣadic texts was called the "*Vedānta-mīmāṃsā*."[9] Students who were chiefly engaged in the study of the former called it briefly the "Mīmāṃsā school," and those students who were mainly concerned with the investigation of the latter, usually called it briefly the "Vedānta school." The fundamental canon of both schools included the *Mīmāṃsā-sūtra* and the *Brahma-sūtra*, and in the opening passages of these works, since it is determined that the objects of study of the two schools are respectively *dharma* and *Brahman*, the learning of the Mīmāṃsā school was called *dharma-mīmāṃsā*,[10] and that of the Vedānta school was sometimes called the *brahma-mīmāṃsā*.[11] Again, the object of investigation of the latter being also "embodied beings" (*śārīra*), the latter was sometimes also called the *śārīraka-mīmāṃsā*.[12]

In addition, the former was called the prior-mīmāṃsā (*Pūrva-mīmāṃsā*) or the "former mīmāṃsā" (*Prācī Mīmāṃsā*),[13] and against this, the latter was called the "later mīmāṃsā" (*Uttara-mīmāṃsā*).

Such a distinction of "former and latter" was, I think, already established before the time of Śaṅkara. Śaṅkara called the words of the *Mīmāṃsā-sūtra*, the "former section" (*pūrva-kāṇḍa*),[14] the "first section" (*prathama-kāṇḍa*),[15] and the "first instructions" (prathama tantra).[16] In such a case, why was such a distinction of "former" and "later" made in connection with the two Mīmāṃsās ? Various explanations have been proposed. First of all, some scholars suggest that it was because the ritual Mīmāṃsā came into being first chronologically, the vedānta school being established later.[17] However, the assumption is not correct, for as we shall examine in Part II of the present work, the thought of the Vedānta philosophy had been conducted in the Indian intellectual world continued from a very ancient period, and the thinkers prior to the formulation of the *Brahma-sūtra* for the most part studied the learning of both Mīmāṃsās. Accordingly, both Mīmāṃsās had developed in parallel and existed together, and it is difficult to accept a chronological separation of earlier and later. The ancient *Brāhmaṇas* came into being before the *Upaniṣads* in general, and only to this extent can it be said that the ritual Mīmāṃsā must have come into existence first. However, Indians of later centuries were not at all aware of the problem of the earlier or later chronology in relation to the dates of the scriptur.e

A certain scholar maintains that since the men of the upper three castes of Indian culture, after performing the rituals during their stage of life as householder, entered a life of meditation in the stages of both forest-dweller and wandering mendicant, and insofar as the early Mīmāṃsā has a relation to the stage of householder, and the latter Mīmāṃsā is related to the later two stages, they were thus named.[18] However, as we shall discuss later in the present work, since some men within the Vedānta school emphasized the performance of the rituals for a householder, this supposition is not accurate.

Again, it has been suggested that the names are because the earlier Mīmāṃsā is based upon the early portion of the *Brāhmaṇas*, and the later Mīmāṃsā is based upon the later portions. But as there are some of the *Upaniṣads* which are not part of any *Brāhmaṇas*, this presumption is also inaccurate.

Instead, we perhaps should rather understand as follows : The learning of both Mīmāṃsā, combined together, formed the philosophical system of the orthodox brahmins who faithfully followed the Vedas. Between the two, an intimate and close connection existed. In which case, why did the distinction arise between "earlier" and "later" ? The answer seems to be that the Vedānta Mīmāṃsā presupposed the ritual Mīmāṃsā as a precondition. The ritual Mīmāṃsā can be set up without necessarily presupposing the Vedānta Mīmāṃsā, but the Vedānta Mimāṃsā, on the contrary, from the first assumes the ritual Mīmāṃsā as a precondition. This fact is made clear in particular in the *Brahma-sūtra*, III.3.[19] In this sense the two are coupled in the relation of earlier and later.

The basic scripture of the early Mīmāṃsā is the *Mīmāṃsā-sūtra*, and that of the later Mīmāṃsā is the *Brahma-sūtra*, which two works are the respective pillars of the two Mīmāṃsā branches of learning. Between the two works is placed the book called *Devatā-kāṇḍa* or *Saṃkarṣaṇa-kāṇḍa*. This is rarely included within the later Mīmāṃsā, but generally included in the early Mīmāṃsā, to which it forms a supplement.[20] Now, it frequently has been taught that the twenty parts (*viṃśaty-adhyāya*), made up of twelve parts of the *Pūrva-mīmāṃsā-sūtra*, the four parts of the *Devatā-kāṇḍa*, and the four parts of the *Brahma-sūtra*, constitute the *Mīmāṃsā-śāstra*.[21] Since Bodhāyana had already clearly stated[22] that these three books make up the entire Mīmāṃsā learning, such a doctrinal system must have already been in existence during Bodhāyana's time, around A.D. 500 at the latest.

Thus, the Vedānta school arose with a close kinship to the *Mīmāṃsā* school. The pre-*Brahma-sūtra* orthodox brāhmaṇical theologians almost always studied both at the same time. Yet, this simultaneous learning was possible only in the fields of acquirement of objective knowledge or the interpretative academic investigation of the scriptures, and it is impossible to take as equally absolute what is expounded in the *Brāhmaṇas* and the ideas taught in the *Upaniṣads*. Between the thought of the two, there exist some fundamental inconsistencies. Scholars of the two Mīmāṃsās were devoted to and respected both as sacred works, but found themselves in the position of inevitably having to value one of the two over the other within their own minds. Yet, as very little has been handed down, and only the fewest of fragments remain of the compositions and literature of the many pre-*Brahma-sūtra* theologians, there are practically no means for learning their real views. But it can clearly be recognized in the confrontation of Jaimini and Bādarāyaṇa, that they could not have avoided valuing one over the other. We can foresee, in the confrontation of these two men, the later establishment of these two schools.

In the next section we shall examine this in more detail.

Notes.

1. See the present work, Part I, Chap. 3, "Early Vedānta Philosophy."

2. Cf. *Prasthānabheda* (H. Ui, ITK IV.435) Sāyaṇa ad *Taittirīya-Āraṇyaka* X.1 (ED. ĀnSS. p. 698). The doctrine of the two sections (*kāṇḍa-dvaya*) had already been accepted by Śaṅkara and was adopted by his commentators (Śaṅkara ad *BS*.I.1.4, I.53, line 8; ad *Bṛhad-Up*., p. 3). In a work of later centuries, the *Saṃkṣepa-Śaṃkarajaya* I.21.27, the *yoga-kāṇḍa* is set up in addition and it admits three *kāṇḍa* (Deussen, SV. S.20, Anm. 1).

3. Even in the *Brāhmaṇas*, however, the section corresponding to the *Upaniṣads* is the *jñānakāṇḍa*, and it appears to have been thought that the *Śatapatha-Brāhmaṇa* X, "*Agnirahasya*," for example, also belonged to the *jñānakāṇḍa*. Cf. *BS*.III.3.44-52.

4. But with regard to the *Karmakāṇḍa*, however, as a similar systematic study, ritual scriptures (*kalpa-sūtra*) had been composed by the ritual schools in a very ancient period. The compilation of these scriptures was based upon the necessity of performing the rituals, and as the various rules concerning the performance of the rituals prescribed in the *Brāhmaṇas* are related in the utmost minuteness, their nature differs essentially from the *Mīmāṃsā-sūtra* which contains considerations related to the general principles of rituals. In the *jñāna-kāṇḍa*, on the contrary, no section corresponding to the *Kalpa-sūtra* was composed. Not only are both the elucidation of the true meaning of the individual passages in the *Upaniṣads*, and considerations of metaphysical

problems, taught within the *Brahma-sūtra*, but rules related to actual practice are also included therein.

5. See the present work, Part II, Chap. 3, Sect. 3, "Early Vedānta Philosophy," p. 458.

6. E.g., the *nyāya* in the title *Nyāyamālāvistara*, a work by Mādhava, means the learning of the *Pūrvamīmāṃsā*.

7. *Mahābhāṣya* ad II.2.29. This, however, is presumed to be a reference to the scholars of the *Pūrva-Mīmāṃsā*. (Cf. A. Weber, *Indische Studien*, XIII.438, 455).

7[a]. E. Frauwallner, *WZKSO* IV, 1960, S. 92-118.

8. Or, it was also called *vidhivṛtta-mīmāṃsā* (*Pañcapādikā*, p. 33).

9. *Pañcapādikā*, p. 76, line 5. Also called the *Vedānta-vākya-mīmāṃsā* (*Pañcapādikā*, pp. 52, 76). And the *Brahma-sūtra* is called *Vedānta-mīmāṃsā-śāstra* (Śaṅkara ad BS. I.19, line 1; *Pañcapādikā*, p. 41).

10. *Pañcapādikā*, p. 52. Now the *Mīmāṃsā-sūtra* has also been called the *Dharmavicāra-śāstra* (*SDS*.XII.52).

11. Sometimes called the *Brahma-vicāraka-śāstra* also (*SDS*.XV.1.136).

12. Śaṅkara ad *BS*.I.18, line 5; *Prasthānabheda*, p. 6, line 7. The *Brahma-sūtra* itself has also been titled in this way.

13. *SDS*.XII. line 3.

14. Śaṅkara ad *BS*.III.3.1 (Vol. II.p. 360, line 4).

15. *Ibid.*, III.3.1 (II.251, line 14), III.3.33 (II.332, line 8), III.3.50 (II.367, line 8).

16. *Ibid.*, III.3.25 (II.308, line 3), III.4.27 (II.423, line 10).

17. A. Weber, *HIL.*, 239.

18. E. Carpenter, *Theism of Medieval India*, 299.

19. In the article by O. Strauss (*Udgītha-vidyā*, *Sitzungsberichten der preussischen Akademie der Wissenschafte*, *Phil.-Hist. Klasse*, 1931, XIII.243 ff, Berline 1931), this relation is, in particular, made clear.

20. See the present work, Part III, Chap. 1, Sect.7.1., pp. 35-40.

21. *Sarva-siddhānta-saṃgraha* I.17; *Prapañca-hṛdaya*, pp. 38-39.

22. See Bodhāyana, Fragment, No. 2.

SECTION 2. THE IDEOLOGICAL CONFRONTATION OF JAIMINI AN BĀDARĀYAṆA.

As thinkers, Jaimini and Bādarāyaṇa stood in completely different positions in regards to the problem of religious practice. Their fundamental confrontation appears clearest in the *Brahma-sūtra* III.4.1-17. To summarize the positions of these two men, we can state the following :[1]

The thinkers of India have expressed the most desirable thing for mankind, or the ultimate objective of all human action, by the words "the aim of man" (*puruṣārtha*), which Jaimini held to be "the performance of the rituals," but Bādarāyaṇa took it to be "final release". The difference between these practical objectives forms a conspicuous difference in the thought of the two thinkers related to individual problems.

According to Jaimini (or those of his line), the most important essential thing for human beings is the performance of the sacred rituals which the Aryans had performed endlessly from time immemorial, the acquisition of prosperity in the present and future worlds, and the acquiring of good fruits and rewards.

It must be noted that all actions (*karmāṇi*) of human beings are comprised within the rituals in the broad sense. Man ought to perform the rituals throughout his entire life (2). While it is true that the Upaniṣads teach that one ought to know *Brahman*, still even the person who does have knowledge of *Brahman* cannot give up the performance of the rituals. That even the man who has attained clear knowledge of *Brahman* performs the rituals by summoning the ritual priest, is taught in the sacred canon (3).

Therefore, the significance of "knowledge" (*vidyā*) is frequently stressed in the *Upaniṣads*, but why is that ? Jaimini admitted that the word "knowledge" has a twofold meaning, i.e., knowledge and remembrance (worship). As to these two meanings, he thought the following : (1) Since the rituals are prescribed by the Vedas, it is quite proper that an understanding of their contents is necessary in order to perform them. Accordingly, in that sense, knowledge (vidyā) about the contents of the scriptures has significance (6). (2) And the word "*vidyā*" also means remembrance (contemplation), and is used in the same sense as worship (*upāsanā*). It means to sit in meditation and to keep in mind and think about the highest deity or some other sacred object. It, too, is frequently taught in the *Upaniṣads*, but there it is explained as employed to increase the benefit of the rituals. For example, in performing the rituals, if one also performs meditation, the results will be that much greater.

Since a man of Brahmanistic faith both possesses such knowledge (*vidyā*) and also performs the rituals while he is alive, the knowledge and action (*karman*) will accompany his individual self at the moment of his death. The passages in the *Bṛhadāraṇyaka Upaniṣad* IV.4.2 must be interpreted in this sense. Consequently, both knowledge (*vidyā*) and action operate towards bringing about the fruits of the rituals, but in every case, the action of performing the rituals is the most important fact, and the meditation has significance only in the sense of being a supplement (*śeṣa*) to the rituals (4, 5). In the *Upaniṣads* it is taught that one should know the *ātman*, and the fruits of this knowledge are also explained, but these passages are supplementary verses to the ceremonial rules which govern the rituals and should be included among the explanatory passages (*artha-vāda*). They are exactly similar to the exegesis which are the verses explaining the meterials for the rituals, the methods of purification and the ceremonies (2).

The foregoing is the essence of the doctrines of Jaimini and his followers as taught in the *Brahma-sūtra* III.4.2-7. As we may judge from these words, Jaimini does accept the *Upaniṣads* as sacred authority, but in regard to their value, he thinks that they amount to no more than mere supplementary materials to those sections of the *Brāhmaṇas* which teach the rituals.[2]

On the other hand, Bādarāyaṇa emphasized the following three principles (*BS*.III.4.1) :

1. "The aim of human life" (*puruṣārtha*) is liberation. The happiness in this and the future world which can be obtained by the rituals should not really be desired by mankind.

2. Liberation arises from the knowledge of *Brahman*. One should distinctly discriminate between the performance of the rituals and the knowledge of *Brahman*.

Further, in addition in *Brahma-sūtra* III.4.8-17, the *Sūtra*-author agrees with Bādarāyaṇa and refutes the theory of Jaimini. The argument given here was not asserted by Bādarāyaṇa himself, but are the words of the *Sūtra*-author, yet their import is to oppose Jaimini and to approve of Bādarāyaṇa, so that it may well be thought that the author was influenced by Bādarāyaṇa's thought and that Bādarāyaṇa himself also adhered to the type of thought expounded in the passage. According to it, the view of the *Sūtra*-author (or Bādarāyaṇa) can be said to be as follows :—

A clear distinction must be made between the life which endeavours to perform the ritual, and that which concentrates on the knowledge of *Brahman*. It is not possible that the same person can simultaneously perform both. The clear knowledge (*vidyā*) of *Brahman* is not subordinate to the rituals. It is independent of the rituals (17). One should understand in the *Bṛhad-āraṇyaka-Upaniṣad* IV.4.2 noted above, that at the moment of one's death, knowledge accompanies those who have attained clear knowledge of *Brahman*, while action (*karman*) attends those who have performed the rituals, etc., but knowledge and action do not both accompany the same person (11).

It is an indubitable fact that the *Upaniṣads* teach liberation that is different from the rituals. And it is explained there that there is the highest deity (or, *Brahman*), superior (*adhika*) even to the individual self. This is completely meaningless for the subject of ritualistic Mīmāṃsā learning, but it is the Absolute upon which we should rely. Accordingly, the fact that liberation is the true objective of man has authority in the scriptures (8).

Now, if one attains to the clear knowledge of *Brahman*, he will be free from all good and evil *karmas* wrought by his former conduct (16). And even if a man who has once attained the clear knowledge of *Brahman*, later commits such an act in the present world, because of the power of clear knowledge (*vidyā*), the karma of that action will not defile him (14). The man who has attained the clear knowledge of *Brahman* need no longer perform the rituals (14). He forsakes all desires for offspring, property, etc., and leads the life of a wandering mendicant (15). Since this mendicant severs all relations with women, he is also called the celibate, and it is taught in the scriptures that clear knowledge exists in the men who lead such a life (17).

In this way, the systems of Jaimini and Bādarāyaṇa differ in their standpoint on religious practice. Jaimini thinks that to respect the Vedas and perform faithfully the rituals prescribed in the scriptures, is the fundamental duty of the brahmins. And the performance of the rituals, according to Indian social custom, is possible only by a married man leading a householder's life, and requires large sums for expenses. Now the raising of offspring and the unceasing performance of rituals are held to be the sacred duties of the Aryans. Accordingly, the life of religious practice taught by Jaimini is possible only for the layman who is married and has sufficient wealth.

However, Bādarāyaṇa, on the other hand, does not value so highly the significance of the rituals, but rather advocates instead the life of a wandering mendicant. Escaping from the life of a householder, forsaking wife and children, abandoning all wealth and property, wearing old clothes and eating coarse food, passing life wandering and meditating on *Brahman*, and peacefully dwelling in the state of enlightenment—these are his life ideals.

The person who spends his life according to the ideals of Bādarāyaṇa, because he severs all relations with females, is also called the observer of chastity (*ūrdhvaretas*), and, in addition, there is also the forest-dweller, he who retires in seclusion to the woods and forests, and both these ideals are taught in the scriptures. On this point, Jaimini asserted : The scriptures which teach them merely *refer* to those persons who practice such a life. No command is laid down that one should practise such a life. In other words, those verses are not religious precepts. For there are other verses which negate such a way of life. Against this, Bādarāyaṇa asserted the following : Although it is clearly directed in the scriptures that the head of the household should perform the rituals, it is also commanded, in the same way, that one should also practise the life of either a forest-dweller or a wandering mendicant. These verses are not merely references, they are *injunctions* (III.4.18-20).

Bādarāyaṇa, however, did not go beyond asserting that there is equal authority for the life of the forest-dweller or wandering mendicant as for that of the householder, and did not adduce any definite texts as authority for the positive superiority of the forest-dweller or mendicant. This fact is the same as in the passages noted previously (III.4.9-10). Scholars of the Bādarāyaṇa line, as pointed out by those of Jaimini line, have never denied either that the *Upaniṣads* teach that the man who knows the *Brahman* should also perform the rituals, or that meditation is a supplementary stage of the rituals. While the Bādarāyaṇa line admits this, it points out the fact that not everything in the *Upaniṣads* is to the same effect, but that the contrary is also taught, in that there are verses which command that one should abandon the practice of rituals, etc., and it limits itself to saying that in its own theory also, it is equally (tulya) a fact that contrary theories also exist in the canonical authority.

Throughout all of the assertions of the Bādarāyaṇa line, we see that here it is admitted that several mutually contradictory ideas exist in the *Upaniṣads*. In that case, one can no longer depend upon the scriptures in order to determine which among them is to be taken as the authority, but there is no other recourse for individuals than to do it by their own thinking. Then since they thus determine that a particular theory, on one hand, is the true one, and another theory, on the other hand, is provisional, it must be admitted that the Bādarāyaṇa line had already taken up the problem of the confrontation of heterogeneous world theories, which came to be discussed so actively in the later Vedānta school.[3]

At any rate, the life centered about the rituals of the Aryans and advocated by Jaimini, and that of the religious mendicant idealized by Bādarāyaṇa were directly opposite in nature. According to the law-books of the Brahmins, they, or the men of all the upper three castes, are supposed to pass through the four stages of life during their life-time. These four stages are : that of the student. during which he studies the Vedas under a master; then returning home, he marries and becomes a householder, performing the rituals and raising children during that stage; this is followed by the stage of forest-dweller living in seclusion in the woods, and finally, the stage of wandering, spending the rest of his life as a mendicant beggar. Both Jaimini and Bādarāyaṇa admitted that these four stages are explained in the law-books, etc. Then they both also admit equally that a person who has once become a wandering mendicant cannot again become a married householder. On these points they concur (III.4.40). But among these four stages, Jaimini particularly placed stress on the life of the householder, while Bādarāyaṇa valued more the life of the wandering mendicant.

Should one approve of the layman's type of life which preserves the fruits of the labours of the ancestors ? Or, should one affirm the life of the religious wanderer who moves about as the floating clouds and running waters ? This opposition in regard to the actual practice, as stated above, is already acknowledged in the *Upaniṣads*, and the rivalry of these two world-views, moreover, is also recited movingly in the epic poem the *Mahābhārata*.[4] And this confrontation reappears in the logical debate between Jaimini and Bādarāyaṇa here. Both thinkers as orthodox brahmins carrying on the tradition from ancient times, had broad and complete knowledge of the Vedas, and were erudite and thoroughly versed in the two Mīmāṃsās. However, in relation to their attitude towards the life of religious practice, they embraced completely different views. This ideological confrontation later had a deep influence on both Mīmāṃsā schools.

The attitudes of the two towards actual practice, and their differences in interpretation of the scriptures, also appear in other passages in the *Brahma-sūtra*. The acquisition of clear knowledge of *Brahman* was prevalent among men from old, and in this connection, it becomes a problem whether or not the gods also have the qualifications to acquire the clear knowledge of Brahman. The people of India during this time thought that the gods had an existence like humans, being merely superior, but that they still were within the bounds of illusion (*māyā*). In this connection, Jaimini held that the gods did not have the qualifications to acquire the clear knowledge, but against this, Bādarāyaṇa asserted that they did. According to Bādarāyaṇa, the gods, too, desire liberation, and consequently have the potential for release. They can venerate the *Upaniṣads* and also realize *Brahman*. The *Brahma-sūtra* takes Bādarāyaṇa's theory as the final doctrine (I.3.26-33).

This confrontation too was based upon a difference in the fundamental thought of the two men. According to Jaimini, the objective is to attain for oneself, by means of the rituals, a well-being *equal to that of the gods*. The clear knowledge of *Brahman* is no more than an aid in attaining this objective. Accordingly, he may well have thought that the wisdom of *Brahman* was useless for the gods. However, on the other hand, according to Bādarāyaṇa, the union with the absolute, who *transcends even the gods*, is the final objective. Accordingly, even the gods must meditate on *Brahman* in order to transcend their own state.

The idea of *karma*, i.e., that our daily good and evil actions leave behind a residual power which produces reward or retribution in the future, is the same as in other schools in India, and both Jaimini and Bādarāyaṇa accepted it. But regarding the method of realizing the fruits of karma, they differ. Jaimini holds that *dharma* brings forth the fruits, and asserts that this fact not only has the authority of the scriptures, but also is justifiable logically (III.2.40). As explained also in the commentary on that passage, in the Mīmāṃsā school *dharma* is also called "new potential" (*apūrva*), and is a certain residual power which is produced when the rituals are correctly performed, and which give rise later to the fruits of action. In that case, there is the problem that in the case of a man who does not perform the rituals, how would the fruits come about ? On this point, there is no explanation whatsoever in the *Brahma-sūtra*. Against this, Bādarāyaṇa believed that the supreme deity distributes the fruits of pleasure or pain in accordance with the previous behaviour of each individual self. According to him, the supreme deity is the cause (*hetu*) of the bestowal of fruits for the individual self (III.2.38-41). As we have already considered,[5] Jaimini also admitted that a supreme deity or the supreme deity was taught in the *Upaniṣads*, but in his line of thinking, it was thought that a supreme deity or the supreme deity was presupposed only in order to carry out the meditation as a supplementary step in the performance of the rituals, and did not have such an important function. Opposed to this, Bādarāyaṇa gives extremely great importance to the supreme deity. In view of the fact that he held liberation to the objective of humanity, and did not recognize the significance of the rituals as being so great, it must be said to be quite natural. The author of the *Brahma-sūtra*, on this point, follows the theory of Bādarāyaṇa, while rejecting that of Jaimini (II.1.34, II.3.42, III.2.38-39).

In relation to the problem of liberation, Jaimini embraced a theory opposite to that of Bādari. According to the *Chāndogya Upaniṣad* (IV.15.5-6), "the nonhuman *puruṣa*" leads the dead who have clear knowledge to *Brahman*. So it is taught, but just what does this "*Brahman*" mean ? Bādari understood it to be *Brahman* as effect, but against this, Jaimini said it was the supreme *Brahman* (IV.3.12). Jaimini, of course, also admitted such a "*Brahma* as effect" in contrast to the supreme *Brahman* (IV.3.14), but just how he conceived of it is not clear.

Against these two theories, Bādarāyaṇa thought that each of them is partially true. Following the teaching of Śāṇḍilya (*Chānd. Up.* III.14.1), he thought that if he worships *Brahman*, according to what his will is in this world, so will he be when he has departed from this life. That is, if one performs worship with some aim in mind, in that way the aim will be attained. According to the different objects of worship, the fruits also are said to be different. Then, he taught that if one worships one or the other of the two *Brahmans*, but without the use of a symbol (*pratīka*), he will be led to the one he selects. That is, the person who concentrates on the supreme self, will penetrate to that supreme self, and he who concentrates on the *Brahman* as effect, will proceed to that *Brahman* as effect. He asserted that a strict distinction should be made between the worship of symbols, i.e., names, words, meanings, etc. and the worship of *Brahman* (*BS*.IV.3.15-16). Consequently, his view of liberation can be said to be a tolerant compromise between the two theories noted above.

Again, in the state of release, the Vedānta school in general teaches that *ātman* manifests its original essence, and the early thinkers also thought in the same way, but Auḍulomi, on this point, asserted that the *ātman* manifests itself as knowledge alone (*citi*). Against this, Jaimini asserted that the liberated individual self manifests those attributes which are taught in the sacred passage : "Free from evil, free from old age, free from death, free from grief, free from hunger and thirst, whose desire is the real, whose thought is the real, such an *ātman* should be sought "(*Chānd. Up*. VIII.7.1). Jaimini thought that since these attributes originally belong to *Brahman*, the individual self in the state of liberation should have equal attributes with *Brahman*. Against both these theories, Bādarāyaṇa asserted that although *ātman*, as Bādari says, is that which has pure knowledge only as its nature, this does not contradict the theory of Jaimini (IV.4.5-7). Bādarāyaṇa's thought is here again eclectic.

Again, against the assertion of Bādari that neither body nor the organs exist in the liberated person,[6] Jaimini argued that the liberated man must have a body and organs since, according to the *śruti* passage : "He is one, he becomes three, he becomes five, he becomes seven, he becomes nine; then again he is called the eleventh, and hundred and ten and one thousand and twenty." (*Chānd. Up* VII, 26, 2), it is taught that he takes various forms.

Admitting both these theories, Bādarāyaṇa asserted that the liberated man is of both kinds; it is quite optional to have or not to have a body and sense organs (IV.4.10-12). Here again, Bādarāyaṇa demonstrates his eclectic and synthesizing attitude. Thus Bādarāyaṇa adopted a thorough-going syncretic and compromising tolerant attitude towards the problem of liberation. Perhaps the masters advocating the different theories on this problem had so much prestige during Bādarāyaṇa's time, that Bādarāyaṇa found it difficult to make a decision as to which one was most faithful to the holy texts, and here he may have taken a position of inclusion and compromise as presenting the least difficulty in interpretation. This standpoint formed one of the outstanding traits of Vedānta philosophy until later centuries.

Furthermore, this fact may also be interpreted as signifying that Bādarāyaṇa was considerably later chronologically than the other scholars such as Jaimini.

In the foregoing, we have examined the contrasting thought of Jaimini and Bādarāyaṇa, and we can find at the bottom of the assertions of both, a consistent intellectual base for each one of their ideas. Accordingly, the theories attributed to Jaimini and Bādarāyaṇa in the *Brahma-sūtra* could perhaps be thought without much trouble to have originated with just these two persons. Consequently, we can think, there is no need to assume that the names Jaimini and Bādarāyaṇa stand for several different people with the same name.

Furthermore, the doctrines of Bādarāyaṇa have been generally taken as the final theories (*siddhānta*) by the commentators, but *the opinion of the Sūtra-author himself does not necessarily always coincide with that of Bādarāyaṇa*. For example, as we have already related, Bādarāyaṇa respects the life of the one who leaves home to become a wandering mendicant, while the *Sūtra*-author rather encouraged meditation on *Brahman* while performing the rituals as a lay householder.[7] Again, Bādarāyaṇa admitted a twofold *Brahman*, as the supreme and as the effect, but the theory of the twofold *Brahman* is not taught in the words of the *Sūtra*-author himself. Consequently, in such a case, the *Sūtra*-author, it seems, might have quoted the theory of Bādarāyaṇa as merely one of the heretical doctrines. Again, concerning the attributes of the individual self which has been liberated, the theory of Bādarāyaṇa is merely listed as one theory even where the heretical theories are being enumerated (IV.4.5-7), and judging by all appearances, the fundamental relation with the thought of the *Sūtra*-author seems to be very flimsy indeed. However, it may have been certain that in their entirety the thoughts of Bādarāyaṇa are quoted quite frequently by the *Sūtra*-author.

Notes

1. The numerals given within parenthesis in the following are those of the *Sūtra*. Concerning the original of the *Sūtra*, see "An Interpretative Reading of the *Brahma-sūtra*."

2. In exact opposition to the Vedānta schools, there existed at that time men who asserted that *the Upaniṣads are meaningless works.*

anarthakā Vedāntāḥ. na teṣām brahmaṇi pramāṇam ity eta eva Vedoṣarā Vedāntā iti keṣāṃcid udgāraḥ. (*Pañcapādikā*, p. 83).

vidhiśeṣatvābhāve Vedāntāprāmāṇyaṃ manyamānā Vedoṣarā Vedāntā iti kecit. (Ānandajñāna ad *Bṛhad. Up. Vārttika*, p. 72, ad. v. 238).

Upaniṣadāṃ tu Vedoṣaratvenāmānatvāt. (*Ibid.* p. 361, ad v. 66).

3. Cf. the present work : Part VI, Chap. 2, Sect. 4; Part VII, Chap. 4, Sect. 7, and the present writer's *The Problems of Indian Thought* (*Indo Shisō no Sho-Mondai*, Tokyo : Shunjusha, 1967), pp. 205-272.

4. The "Dialogue between father and son" in the *Mahābhārata* XII.175 is especially famous.

Cf. Winternitz, *HIL*, I.417 ff; Hopkins, *Epic Mythology*, p. 34.

5. Cf. the present work, Part III, Chap. 1, Sect. 7.3.

6. *Ibid*, Sect. 6.

7. *Ibid*, Part IV, Chap. 3, Sect. 5, 1.

PART IV

THE BRAHMA-SŪTRA

CHAPTER X

INTRODUCTION

The *Brahma-sūtra*[1] is the fundamental text of the Vedānta school, so much so that the history of the early period of this school can be divided into pre and post-*Brahma-sūtra* periods. The *Brahma-sūtra* has actually become the basis upon which we learn the philosophical thought of the early Vedānta school. Since, however, the style of this work is concise to a fault, omissions in it are many and to interpret the text is not at all easy, academic research on it has not yet been adequately completed, so that I think our immediate task is to advance present studies as much as possible further and try to clarify the ideological content and historical significance of the work itself.

Notes

1. A critical edition of the *Brahma-sūtra* in collation with nine commentaries has been published.—

Brahmasūtra of Bādarāyaṇa. Ed. by Kapileshwara Mishra. Santiniketan, 1930.

An attempt to translate the *Brahma-sūtra* into English with reference to commentaries has been made.—

The Brahma Sūtra. Translated with an Introduction and Notes by S. Radhakrishnan. New York, Harper, 1960.

SECTION 1. OTHER NAMES OF THE *Brahma-sūtra*

The basic text of the Vedānta schools is called the *Brahma-sūtra.* This name may have had its origin in the fact that in the beginning of the opening volume, the enquiry about *Brahman* is proclaimed. Consequently, it has also been called "The treatise for investigating *Brahman*" (*Brahma-vicāra-śāstra*).[1]

Again, since the Vedānta learning, namely, commentary and scholarly research on the *Upaniṣads*, is, as already remarked, called the Vedānta-*mīmāṃsā*, its fundamental canon the *Brahma-sūtra* has been called the *Vedānta-mīmāṃsā-śāstra*,[2] or simply, the *Vedānta-śāstra*.[3] Furthermore, the term *Vedānta-sūtra* has been much in use among Indologists in general, though this term appeared in works of later centuries and cannot be discovered in comparatively ancient literature of the Vedānta school. Insofar as the *Brahma-sūtra* is the basic text of the Vedānta school, recent Indologists have had a tendency to rely upon this term (*Vedānta-sūtra*) for the sake of convenience.

The *Brahma-sūtra* has also been called the *Caturlakṣaṇī* (The Book of Four Sections),[4] referring to the fact that it is composed in four parts (*adhyāya*), and this term contrasts with the *Pūrva-mīmāṃsā-sūtra* which is made up of 12 parts, and is accordingly called the *Dvādaśalakṣaṇī* (The Book of 12 Sections.)[5]

This *Brahma-sūtra*, again, has been called the *Śārīraka-sūtra*,[6] and the *Śārīrakaṃ Śāstram*,[7] or simply the *Śārīraka*.[8] It appears that this title has been in existence from a very ancient time. Both Upavarṣa[9] and Bodhāyana[10] have referred to the *Brahma-sūtra* as merely *Śārīraka*. Insofar as we can discover from the extant literature, the term "*Śārīraka*" may have been the most ancient designation.

Linguistically the name "*Śārīraka*" means "that which has body," or "the self within the body". And insofar as the *Brahma-sūtra* makes that a topic of investigation, it became another name for the *Sūtra* by extension.

Now, what is the meaning of "that which has body" ? On this problem, different theories are held by thinkers even within the same Vedānta school. Śaṅkara does not give any explanation to the meaning of the world "*Śārīraka*," but concerning the import of this work, the *Śārīraka*, he says :

"Others, again and among them some of ours, are of opinion that the individual self as such is real. To refute those holding such theories, who obstruct the way to the complete intuition of the unity of the Self, this Śārīraka has been set forth, whose aim it is to show that there is only one highest Lord ever-unchanging whose substance is cognition, and who, by means of Nescience, manifests himself in various ways, just as a magician appears in different forms by means of his magical power. Besides that Lord there is no other substance of cognition."[11]

That is to say, the thinkers who embraced mistaken opinions thought that this individual self possessed of a physical body is the actual existence in the final sense : but this view is not the true knowledge. In the final truth, the individual self is identical with the highest self or the highest deity. And Śaṅkara thought that it is given the name "Śārīraka" because it is the objective of the *Brahma-sūtra* to clarify this question. So for him, "that which has a body" means the individual self (*jīva*). His disciple, Padmapāda, positively declared that it means the individual self.[12]

However, against this, Rāmānuja thought that "that which has a body" means the highest *Brahman*, and the *Brahma-sūtra* is called the *Śārīraka* because it discusses that. After discussing "the *ātman* consisting of bliss" taught in the Second Part of the *Taittirīya Upaniṣad*, he says :

> "Everything different from the highest Self, whether of conscious or non-conscious nature, constitutes Its body.[13] Therefore, that Self alone is the unconditioned embodied Self. For this very reason competent persons designate this doctrine which has the highest *Brahman* for its subject matter as the *Śārīraka*, i.e. the doctrine of the embodied Self."[14]

Now, which of these interpretations in this case is correct ?

The theory of absolute identity of the individual self and *Brahman* taught by Śaṅkara is contrary to the thought of the *Brahma-sūtra* itself, but the idea that the body of the *Brahman* is the individual self and the physical world, is not clearly taught in the *Sūtra* either. Instead, the word "*śārīra*" (bodied-being) in the extant *Brahma-sūtra* usually means the *individual self,* and in no case is it used to refer to *Brahman*. Accordingly, neither one of the interpretations can be accepted as they stand; it would appear, however, that each of the interpretations has perhaps transmitted a partial aspect of the original meaning. "That which has a body" refers directly to the individual self, but since the individual self, according to the *Brahma-sūtra*, is a part (*aṃśa*) of *Brahman*, the investigation of the basic nature of the individual self would actually be not different from the consideration of *Brahman* itself. And since each individual self belongs to *Brahman*, each physical body is a body for the particular individual self, and at the same time would also have significance as a body for *Brahman* who is the totality of all existences. If one interprets it in this way, it would be no wonder at all, I think, that the entire *Sūtra* is called "*Śārīraka*."

Then, if we note the special nature of this *Brahman*, we shall be able to understand easily also how in later centuries in the two commentators Śaṅkara and Rāmānuja, two completely different interpretations concerning the meaning of the word "*śārīraka*" came to be proposed. Śaṅkara and Rāmānuja each places emphasis on one of the two sides of the "*śārīraka*" concept of the *Sūtra*-author, which are completely different from each other, and understood that that was the meaning of the word.

Notes

1. *SDS*.XVI, line 82. The *Brahma-sūtra* is referred to as *brahma-mīmāṃsā*, (*SDS*.V,1. 5).

2. Śaṅkara ad *BS*.I.19, line 1; *Pañcapādikā*, p. 41.

3. *SDS*.XVI, line 64.

4. Bhāskara ad *BS*. p. 6.

5. Bhāskara ad *BS*. p. 6; *SDS*.XII, line 4. "*Lakṣaṇa*" in this case means *adhyāya*. Therefore this *Sūtra* has also been called the *Dvādaśādhyāyī* (*Prasthānabheda*, p. 6, line 1).

6. *Vedānta-sāra*, p. 1.

7. Bhāskara ad *BS*. p. 5.

8. Śaṅkara ad *BS*. I.3.19 (Vol. I, p. 279, line 1).

9. *Śārīrake Vakṣyāmaḥ*. (Śaṅkara ad *BS*. III.3.53).

10. Cf. Bodhāyana fragment 2. (To be discussed in the third volume of this work).

11. Śaṅkara ad *BS*, I.3.19, Vol. I, pp. 278, line 14-279, line 3.

12. *Śarīram eva śarīrakaṃ śarīrake bhavaḥ śārīrako jīvaḥ / tam adhikṛtya kṛto granthaḥ Śārīrakaḥ /...śārīrakaṃ jīvatattvam adhikṛtya kṛtatvam astīti śārīrakābhidhānam /* (*Pañcapādikā*, p. 40).

13. According to the philosophy of Rāmānuja, all individual selves and all things which are not spirit form the entire body of the *Brahman*.

14. Ad *BS*.I.1.13 (p. 202). Further, Sukhtankar (*Teachings of the Vedānta according to Rāmānuja*, *WZKM*, 1908, pp. 128, 129) asserts that since the learning of the Vedānta is called *śārīraka-mīmāṃsā*, and also since the *Brahma-sūtra* is known by the other name of *Śārīraka*, the *Śārīraka* must indicate *Brahman*.

SECTION 2. THE CIRCUMSTANCES UNDER WHICH THE *Brahma-sūtra* CAME INTO BEING

Prior to the compilation of the *Brahma-sūtra*, diverse theories had existed among the thinkers within the Vedānta school concerning the interpretation of the individual passages of the *Upaniṣads*, and other fundamental metaphysical problems. The *Brahma-sūtra* summarizes, arranges and criticizes these interpretations and theories, organizing them into one system, and thus became the basis for the development of the later Vedānta philosophy. It was thus endeavouring to consider each of the passages in the Ancient *Upaniṣads* which were unintelligible or those parts where doubts existed, and to settle those dubious points.[1] The word "*Sūtra*" originally meant "lengthwise thread" and according to Śaṅkara, this *Sūtra* is like a thread of wreath which binds together the verses of the *Upaniṣads*, which themselves are likened to lotus flowers.[2]

This work in its present form was not written at one time We may assume that to reach its present state it had to go through a great many complicated meandering and tortuous courses. Our inspection of the extant *Brahma-sūtra* will show, for example, that IV.1.18 though composed prior to Śaṅkara was undoubtedly appended to the *Sūtra* at a fairly late date.[3]

In the following, we shall take up a consideration of the circumstances under which the *Sūtra* came into being, until the time it attained its present form.

This work does not discuss in random order the obscure passages in the *Upaniṣads*; it affirms that it treats them in accordance with a fixed system. First of all, let us look at the topics taken up in the Part I, Chapter 1 to Chapter 3. The *Chāndogya Upaniṣad* is quoted the most frequently, and these passages are explained *following the order of the chapters* of the *Chāndogya Upaniṣad*.[4] As indicated in its opening verse, the *Brahma-sūtra* sets up *Brahman* as the Absolute, and considers its primary duty to be the investigation of that, but the *Upaniṣads* by no means teach that only *Brahman* is the absolute. Other things besides are set up as the absolute principle or the world cause, yet the passages, which hypothesize various principles and contain many contradictions, are merely miscellaneously recorded in the texts. Consequently, the *Sūtra*-author, who tries to see *Brahman* as the fundamental principle of the world, necessarily encountered the difficult problem of how to interpret the passages in the *Upaniṣads* which prima facie vary from this. Again, even supposing that there were no contradictions with the idea of *Brahman* as the world-cause, much of the phraseology and explanatory methods in the *Upaniṣads* are very vague in meaning. And the elucidation of the exact meaning of these formed one of the chief duties of the Vedānta scholars of that time. So the *Sūtra*-author, for the most part, interprets and explains that the passages in question mainly from the *Chāndogya-Upaniṣad*, as topics taken up one after the other *in order*, *mean*, in their real intention, that various things which are presented in the respective passages in this *Upaniṣad*, are *Brahman* (or the highest self, the highest deity). He lays it down that one must not understand them as indicating anything else. Then, when he is treating the various passages in the *Chāndogya Upaniṣad*, he also considers incidentally phrases in other *Upaniṣads* related to them. Some of the phrases in the *Upaniṣads* referred to in this connection have some sort of connection with the phrases in the *Chāndogya-Upaniṣad* quoted in the *Brahma-sūtra*, and there are also some cases in which the reason for quoting those passages is not clear to our present-day eyes, and in not a few instances, as we shall point out later,[5] one can admit a clear-cut connection in content. I believe this is an acceptable estimate of the entire Part One of the *Sūtra*.

The sections related to the *Chāndogya-Upaniṣad* are not merely limited to Part One. There are also passages which treat in particular of this *Upaniṣad* in Book II, Chapter 3 and 4; Book III, Book IV, Chapter 2 and 3. In fact, whenever problems common to the *Upaniṣads* are treated, the basis for particular consideration is the *Chāndogya-Upaniṣad*.[6]

The fact that the *Brahma-sūtra* has a close relation to the *Chāndogya-Upaniṣad* seems to have been known also to Śaṅkara himself. Scholars have frequently asserted that the thought of Śaṅkara has the closest connection with the *ātman* theory of Yājñavalkya in the *Bṛhadāraṇyaka-Upaniṣad* in particular. And Śaṅkara's commentary on the same *Upaniṣad* is about two times more voluminous than his commentary on the *Chāndogya-Upaniṣad*. This shows that he greatly esteemed the former. However, in Śaṅkara's commentary on the *Brahma-sūtra*, passages of the *Chāndogya-Upaniṣad* are quoted most often. Furthermore, they are frequently quoted without mentioning the name of the *Chāndogya*, saying that "it is thus said in the *Brāhmaṇas*" (*iti Brāhmaṇam*) or "The *Brāhmaṇas* say . . ." (*tathā Brāhmaṇam*). Moreover, when he quotes the passages of Chapter 6 of this *Upaniṣad*, he merely says, "In Chapter 6, it is said" (*ṣaṣṭha prapāṭhake*).[7] Consequently, pre-Śaṅkara scholars were well aware of the fact that the *Brahma-sūtra* is based upon the *Chāndogya-Upaniṣad*, and Śaṅkara, it would seem, had accepted that tradition.

Considering the facts given above, we can say that the *Brahma-sūtra* was composed within the various lines of the early Vedānta school, and particularly in the school which revered the *Chāndogya Upaniṣad.*

This fact can also be verified from other aspects. The thinkers who are most frequently quoted and followed as being the most authoritative in the *Brahma-sūtra* are Jaimini and Bādarāyaṇa; and these two men, as we have already noted, are said to be men of the school belonging to the *Sāma-Veda*. Consequently, the men of this school had sufficient reason to set up and systematize the doctrines centring about the *Chāndogya Upaniṣad* belonging to that school. (The *Kena Upaniṣad* also belongs to the *Sāma-Veda*, but inasmuch as it is so brief, it probably would not serve as a basis for a doctrinal system.)

Thus, though the *Brahma-sūtra* was indeed based upon the *Chāndogya-Upaniṣad*, in its most important thought it also adopted ideas from the other *Upaniṣads*. For example, in *BS*.I.1.2., the definition of *Brahman* as the primal source which is the creator, preserver and destroyer of the world, is based upon the *Taittirīya Upaniṣad.*[8]

And the theory of the origination of the five elements (II.3.1 ff), also comes from the same *Upaniṣad.*

A consideration of such facts will confirm that the *Brahma-sūtra* author had a definite intention to synthesize, harmonize and unify the thought of all the *Upaniṣads* while remaining true to the *Chāndogya Upaniṣad*. Accordingly the original form of the *Brahma-sūtra* would have been compiled by a school belonging to the *Sāma-Veda*, but it *contained implicitly the possibility of being adopted by other Veda schools also.* Now with the passage of time, and as other Upaniṣadic theories came to be gradually adopted in the *Brahma-sūtra*, this *Sūtra* finally seems to have reached a position as the one fundamental canon common to the many orthodox brahmanical schools.

Moreover, later, as the Vedānta school took definite shape as a school, the necessity arose, on the other hand, *to attack the doctrines of other schools* outside the orthodox Brahmin line of that time. The opponent against which the greatest effort in attack was exerted by the *Brahma-sūtra* was the Sāṃkhya school. The influence of the Sāṃkhya school of that time appears to have been considerable. Of the schools other than the Vedānta, they were most conspicuous in the point that they also took the *Upaniṣads* as their authoritative texts. The verses which the Vedānta school had understood as teaching *Brahman*, they thought, taught the *puruṣa*, the fundamental essence (*pradhāna*) or the results of its evolution. Consequently, the Vedānta thinkers of that period rejected the interpretative standpoint of this Sāṃkhya school, and had to eradicate the doubts concerning the import of the scriptures. Again, since the Sāṃkhya school took the same standpoint as the Vedānta school that the effect is contained within the cause (*satkāryavāda*), the latter was forced to clarify the difference in thought with its own school. Because of these circumstances, a special effort was made in the *Brahma-sūtra* to attack the Sāṃkhya school in particular. Perhaps it was not only the theories of the Sāṃkhya, but of schools in the Vedānta itself which had taken up ideas very similar to the Sāṃkhya, which were included in the attack. Then, again, not only the Sāṃkhya school, but the Yoga school, as well as the others powerful at that time like the Vaiśeṣika School, Buddhism, Jainism, the Pāśupata school, the Bhāgavata school, and the Lokāyata school, were also included in the attack.

Let us look at the section in the *Sūtra* which refutes the other schools. Since the Buddhist theory of Consciousness Only is vigorously attacked, the phraseology of these attacks must have been added after 400 A.D.[9] However, the *Sūtra*, which interprets passages of *Chāndogya Upaniṣad*, must have come into existence far earlier than that. And the eight thinkers mentioned in the *Sūtra* are all men of the pre-Christian era. Consequently, it is impossible that these Sūtras came into being all at the same time. For the *Brahma-sūtra* to attain its present form, it must have passed along a complicated and lengthy course. Dividing the process roughly, it would perhaps be as follows : First Period : Synopses were composed in the schools belonging to the *Sāma-Veda*, centering on the *Chāndogya-Upaniṣad*, and treating of the *Upaniṣads*.

Second Period : Theories of the *Upaniṣads* were taken up in the *Brahma-sūtra* and the entire *Sūtra* was notably enlarged. Further, this *Sūtra* came to be adopted as the synopsis of the *Upaniṣads* for the Veda schools in general.

Third Period : The entire *Sūtra* was unified and revised, logical refutations of other Indian schools were appended, and finally the extant form of the *Brahma-sūtra* came into being.

Generally speaking, the *Brahma-sūtra* was progressively enlarged in these three stages.[10] Of course, we cannot absolutely conclude that this was the case, but there is no doubt that through the passage of time, enlargements and appendices were added slowly. The original of the *Brahma-sūtra* is thus very ancient, and its inception can be traced back to the period of the formation of the *Kalpa-sūtra*. However, there are very few grounds upon which to base a conclusion that individual *Sūtras* were added at a certain stage or at a certain time. There have been scholars who have tried to restore definitely the original form of the *Brahma-sūtra* in the first stage,[11] but the results of their efforts amount to no more then subjective supposition. and beyond saying that the section of attacks on other schools was appended later, it is difficult to come to any definite conclusion. The restoration of the original meaning of the extant *Brahma-sūtra* is a tricky problem indeed and perhaps one must say that determination of its earliest form is impossible at the present time.

Furthermore, only the *Brahma-sūtra* has been handed down to the present time, as a *Sūtra* interpreting difficult passages in the *Upaniṣads*, but just as the *Brahma-sūtra* was compiled in the school revering the *Chāndogya-Upaniṣad*, it has been thought that *perhaps in the same way, sūtras were constructed in the schools worshipping other Upaniṣads*. As Deussen has already pointed out,[12] the Upaniṣadic passages discussed in Part One of the *Brahma-sūtra* are quoted following their order of appearance in each of the *Upaniṣads*. Since we cannot conclude that this is merely an accidental coincidence, it is thought that perhaps similar commentary *sūtras* had previously been composed on the other *Upaniṣads*, and no section of these was adopted in the *sūtra* of the school following the *Chāndogya Upaniṣad*; and when those related passages were joined together and once united, Part One of the *Brahma-sūtra* came into being in its present form.

Accordingly, additional *sūtras* also existed,[13] but insofar as only the *Brahma-sūtra* was adopted and prevalent generally, it alone survived, and the others were lost or not transmitted. It is not clear why the *Brahma-sūtra* alone was able to retain such influence.

Further, insofar as this *Brahma-sūtra* was handed down in secret from master to disciple among a very limited section of *Brahmin* theologians, outsiders, it would appear, were not able to acquire easily a detailed knowledge of its contents. Although the Vedas, the *Upaniṣads*, and the *Māṇḍukya-Kārikās* are quoted in the Buddhist Canon, the *Sūtra* is not mentioned once, and for that its secrecy may have been the reason.

Notes

1. *yatra Vedavākyāt saṃdeho jāyate tannirākaraṇe Sūtrakārapravṛttiḥ.* (Bhāskara ad *BS.*I.3.10).

2. *na / Vedāntavākyakusumagrathanārthatvāt sūtrāṇām / Vedānta-vākyāni hi sūtrair udāhṛtya vicāryante /* Śaṅkara ad *BS.* (Vol.I.36, lines 1-2).

3. Commentaries on Bhāskara deliberately omitted BS.IV, 1, 18 saying : *Brahma-sūtra*, IV.1.18, p. 346.

4. H. Ui, *ITK*, I. 106-107.

5. Cf. the "explanatory notes to the *Brahma-sūtra*," Chap. 2 of the present part, which I could not translate entirely.

6. Even in relation to *Pañcāgnividyā*, for example, the *Brahma-sūtra* and Śaṅkara have followed the *Chāndogya Upaniṣad* (Deussen, *SV.* 389).

7. Deussen, *SV.*32, Anm. 21.

8. Cf. Chapter 2, "Explanatory Notes *Brah*' I.1.2.

9. Cf. the following section.

10. Belvalkar has published a report similar to this, but I was not able to see his manuscript.

11. Belvalkar, *Lectures*, 142-146.

12. Deussen, *SV.* 130-131.

13. It has been handed down that Jaimini wrote the *Śārīraka-sūtra*, and it is said that there was also a *Sūtra* of Draviḍācārya. See the present work, Part III, Chap. 1, Sect. 7.1 and Frag. 15, in Part V, Chap. 6, Sect. 1.

SECTION 3. THE DATES OF THE COMPILATION OF THE *Brahma-sūtra*

Hitherto the academic world has usually followed the general tradition in India that Bādarāyaṇa is the author of the *Brahma-sūtra*, and therefore attempted to date the *Sūtra* by determining his dates. However, as we have already argued, we must take it that Bādarāyaṇa and the compiler of the *Sūtra* are different persons, and therefore this view is unsatisfactory.

But all that can be asserted is that the *Sūtra* was edited in its present form after Bādarāyaṇa, and so the dates of the *Sūtra* must be determined on the basis of other evidence.

The word "*brahma-sūtra-pada*" appears in the *Bhagavad-gītā* XIII.4,[1] but this does not refer to this *Sūtra*, but should be understood as indicating "verses explaining *Brahman*," i.e., writing of the Upaniṣads. In the *Mahābhārata*, the word "*brahma-sūtra*" also appears, but it is either another name for the incantations[2] (*mantra*) or means "the sacred thread"[3] and has no relation to the work so entitled. Now these senses of the word are common in India.

Consequently, clues to determine the dates must be sought within the *Sūtra* itself. Since the *Brahma-sūtra* attacks various schools, e.g., Sāṃkhya, Vaiśeṣika, Buddhism, Jainism, Pāśupata, Bhāgavata, etc., it must have come into existence later than any of these schools. Among them, the Sāṃkhya school, or a form thereof, has almost undoubtedly been in existence as a school from before 300 B.C. The Vaiśeṣika school was established as a school during the first century B.C. Jainism passed through almost the same historical and development process as Buddhism. The Bhāgavata school was established in the 2nd century B.C., and the Pāśupata is equally old.[4] Thus, these schools were in existence from quite olden times, and so no reference made to these schools can serve to ascertain the dates of the *Sūtra*. However since the *Mīmāṃsā-sūtra* is referred to[5] several times in this *Sūtra*, we can affirm that the latter came into being much later than the former. But if we are to try to specify the dates more exactly, we have after all no other recourse than to rely upon the clues related to Buddhism.

We see in the arguments of the *Brahma-sūtra* that the *reductio ad absurdum* (*prasaṅga*) of the Mādhyamika school is frequently used.[6] Since this may be the influence of the Buddhist

Mādhyamika school, the present form of the *Sūtra* undoubtedly came into being after Nāgārjuna. Moreover, since the theories of the Vijñāna-vāda are attacked[7] in II.2.28-32 of the *Sūtra*, it is a certain fact that its compilation in its present form was completed after the rise of the Vijñānavāda. The Vijñānavāda (Yogācāra School), the basis of which was established by Maitreya nātha and Asaṅga, was spread throughout India in general by the activities of Vasubandhu, so that by the time it came to be attacked by other schools, it should be regarded as later than Vasubandhu. Since Vasubandhu lived c. 320[8]-400, we could look upon the year 400 as the earliest date of the compilation of the extant *Brahma-sūtra*.

Next is the problem of determining the later limit of the date. As has already been remarked, inasmuch as the *Brahma-sūtra* has not been quoted in other works of a comparatively ancient period, it is impossible to determine its date by means of quoted passages. But the names of many thinkers who wrote commentaries on the *Brahma-sūtra* are known, and from a consideration of their dates,[9] we find that it is difficult to extend the dates of the *Brahma-sūtra* to a much later century. Accordingly, we can take it that 400-450 is the period during which the *Brahma-sūtra* was compiled in its extant form. Nonetheless, this refers only to the dates when the *Brahma-sūtra* assumed its present form, and the great part of the *Sūtra* must have been in existence much earlier than that. Merely to realize that the thinkers mentioned in the *Sūtra* were men of the pre-Christian era, makes this fact easily apparent. Again the sections of the *Sūtra* which deal directly with verses of the *Upaniṣads*, e.g., I.1-3, III.3, etc., can be taken, for the most part, to have been compiled prior to the Christian era.

Notes

1. The commentary of Ānandajñāna refers to the extant *Brahma-sūtra*, and Garbe (*Bhagavadgītā*, S.140), Guha (*Jīvātman*, p. 19), etc., follow this. Belvalkar (*Lectures*, p. 140) says that insofar as the *ṛṣibhir* in the passage of the *Gītā* is in the plural number, we must take it that a great number of *Brahma-sūtra* were in existence. And Karmarkar (The Relation of the *Bhagavadgītā and* the *Bādarāyaṇa Sūtras*, *ABh.* I, III. 1921-22, pp. 73-79) supposes that this is a reference to a work of the same name which existed before the extant *Brahma-sūtra* came into being, which discussed the relation

between *kṣetra* and *kṣetrajña*, and which came to be replaced later by the extant *Brahma-sūtra*.

However, many Indian commentators, from Śaṅkara on, quote various sentences of the *Upaniṣads* as the "phrases of the *Brahma-sūtra* referred to in the *Gītā*", Nīlakaṇṭha says they are *Brāhmaṇa-vākya*, and Śrīdhara takes them as referring to *Upaniṣad-vākya* or to the extant *Brahma-sūtra*. Again, Hopkins (*GEI*, pp. 15-16), proposes that the word *Brahma-sūtra* here may have the same sense as "*Vedasūtra*" in *MBh*. XII.341.63 which refers to the Vedas in general. Therefore a consideration of the commentators also shows that there is no objection if we interpret this word as indicating, in the Vedas, those Upaniṣadic texts which particularly discuss *Brahman*.

It is impossible that the extant *Brahma-sūtra* was in existence during that period. And on the supposition that the reference is to some sūtras which resemble the *Brahma-sūtra*, Śaṅkara would not have been likely to have given the comment on the work which he does.

2. *MBh*. VII.94.70. Hopkins, *Epic Mythology*, p. 107. Even in this case, however, it seems that there is still the sense of a thread which binds together.

3. Hopkins, *GEI*. pp. 364, 484.

4. According to H. Ui, *ITK*, I.152-153.

5. Cf. the present Part, Chap. 2, Supplement, Sect. 3, p. 398. Furthermore no trace of Buddhist influence can be found in the *Mīmāṃsā-sūtra*.

6. Cf. the present work, Part IV, Chap. 3, Sect. 2, p. 419 ff.

7. Previously, H. Jacobi ("The Dates of the Philosophical *Sūtras*," *JOAS*-. XXXI, 1910, p. 1 ff.) (Reprint : Hermann Jacobi : *Kleine Schriften*. Herausgegeben von Bernhard Kölver, Wiesbaden : Franz Steiner Verlag, 1970, pp. 559-587.) made a study, disregarding the commentaries, of a section in the Sūtra which is by them regarded as attacking the Vijñāna-vāda theories, and asserted that it is not the Vijñāna-vāda which is being attacked there, but the Mādhyamika. Based upon this, he inferred that the formulation of the *Sūtra* occurred in the period between the rise of the Mādhyamika and the Vijñāna-vāda Schools. However, as was discussed in detail by Dr. Ui in his *ITK*, I.152-167, it should be interpreted that the Vijñāna-vāda doctrines are being attacked also. (Concerning this, see "An Interpretative Reading of the *Brahma-sūtra*" on those passages related to this problem.) Stcherbatsky (*The Soul Theory of the Buddhists, Bulletin de l'Académie des Sciences de Russie* St. Pétersbourg, 1919 p. 825, n. 2) maintained that "the fact that Buddhist idealism is mentioned in the *Nyāya-sūtra*, will not serve as demonstrative grounds for the sake of determining the dates of composition. For, in the history of Buddhist philosophy, idealistic opinions and views have frequently appeared." This argument could also apply in the same way to the *Brahma-sūtra*. However, as in the assertion by Jacobi (*Deutsche Literaturzeitung*, 1922, p. 270), it may be well to take it that it was probably after the time of Vasubandhu that the Brahmin philosophers became concerned with such Buddhist tendencies.

8. H. Ui : *ITS*. p. 387.

9. Cf. the present work, Part V, Chap. 1.

SECTION 4. PRESTIGE OF THE *Brahma-sūtra* IN LATER CENTURIES

Because the *Brahma-sūtra* was originally constructed as a commentary on and summary of the doctrines in the *Upaniṣads*, it occupied a position as supplementary to the *Upaniṣads*; nevertheless, with the passage of time, it came to be considered as the basic text of the Vedānta school, almost equal in authority to the *Upaniṣads*. Thus the later Vedānta schools took it as one of the tripartite (*prasthānatraya*), the others being the *Upaniṣads* and the *Bhagavad-gītā*. The thought of the *Brahma-sūtra*, as we shall relate later, does not always coincide with the doctrines in the *Upaniṣads* and *Bhagavad-gītā*, but despite their differences, this *Sūtra* is looked upon as being nearly as important in its own right as the others are.

The founders of the schools, or the important thinkers within the Vedānta school, in most cases wrote commentaries on this work. At first, it amounted to no more than the canon of one sect which revered the *Chāndogya-Upaniṣad*; but later, it became the common scripture for the schools which follow the *Upaniṣads*, and as its authority mounted so remarkably, later thinkers probably were no longer able to ignore this *Brahma-sūtra*.

As commentaries on this work, the *Bhāṣyas* written by Śaṅkara (first half of the eighth century) and Bhāskara (last half of the same century) have been preserved to this day, but a great number of commentaries were composed besides. We may list the more important of them in the following table :[1]

Dates	Author	School	Work	Doctrine
1017-1137	Ramānuja	Śrī-Vaiṣṇava	Śrībhāṣya	Viśiṣṭādvaita
1062-1162	Nimbārka	Nimbārka	Vedāntapāri-jātasaurabha	Dvaitādvaita
c. 1230	Madhva	Mādhva	Sūtrabhāṣya	Dvaita
13th century	Viṣṇu-svāmin	Viṣṇusvāmin	Brahmasūtra-bhāṣya	Dvaita
c. 1400	Śrīkaṇṭha	Śaiva	Śaiva-bhāṣya	Viśiṭādvaita
16th century	Vallabha	Vallabhācārya	Aṇubhāṣya	Śuddhādvaita
?	Śrīpati	Liṅgāyat	Śrīkara-bhāsya	Śaktiviśiṣṭād-vaita
?	Śuka	Bhāgavata	Śukabhāṣya	Viśiṣṭādvaita
18th century	Baladeva	Caitanya	Govinda-bhāṣya	Acintya-bhedā-bheda

In addition to these, many other commentaries on the *Brahma-sūtra*[2] have been handed down.

At any rate, since the founders and scholars of the important schools of Hinduism have commented on the work, the *Brahma-sūtra* is not only the fundamental work of the Vedānta school in the narrow sense, it can also be regarded as a common authoritative text of all the schools of Hinduism. Accordingly, at least superficially, it holds prestige and authority as an important and basic scripture for almost a majority of Indian people.[3] In the 16th century, Madhusūdana-sarasvatī evaluated this *Sūtra* as "the most important among all the *śāstras*, and all other scriptures are ancillary (*śeṣa*) to it".[4] Despite the fact that the contents of the *Brahma-sūtra* itself are vague and obscure, it should be particularly noted that its traditional authority has been strictly preserved as of ever greater prestige.

Notes

1. I have made some minor corrections and amendments to the list given by J. N. Farquahar in *An Outline of Religious Literature of India*, p. 287. In the table given above, Farquahar gives the *Vedāntakaustubha* of Śrīnivāsa, the direct disciple of Nimbārka, but according to Dasgupta, it is a sub-commentary on the Vedānta-*pārijāta-saurabha* of Nimbārka (Dasgupta, *HIPh.*, III.402).
2. According to Aufrecht, C, 1.383-386, there are listed nearly 49 direct commentaries on the *Brahma-sūtra*.
3. Many Brahmins, even today, whenever they perform the *brahmayajña* either as laymen or as priests, chant the first phrase of the *Brahma-sūtra* as one of the sacred texts. (R. G. Bhandarkar, *Collected Works*, I.224).
4. According to the *Prasthāna-bheda*.

SECTION 5. THE STYLE OF THE *Brahma-sūtra* AND THE NEED FOR A RE-EXAMINATION OF THE ORIGINAL MEANING OF THE *Sūtras*

The *Brahma-sūtra*, like the basic texts of the other schools, was composed as a member of the *sūtra* literature. Not only the fundamental canons of the other philosophical schools, but the fundamental scriptures related to revealed rituals, householder rituals, law, grammar, and rhetoric, are also *sūtras*.

The *Brahma-sūtra*, however, aims at conciseness, omits all unnecessary repetition, and reduces as much as possible the number of verses; and in the word-inflections which could not be eliminated and have remained, several meanings are included. Why was such a literary style used ? Although we cannot definitely state the reasons, it would seem that perhaps, on one hand, one reason was to facilitate memorization and recitation, and, on the other hand, the other reason was to transmit the *Sūtra*-author's intention to the reader in an impressive manner. Since all *sūtras* are very abbreviated, it is difficult to understand them directly, but if one pays careful attention to them, he can at least partially comprehend them without a commentary. However, the case is very different with the *Brahma-sūtra* ![1]

It is difficult to understand even a single *sūtra* in the *Brahma-sūtra* without a commentary.[2] The omission of the subject or the predicate in a given sentence is common, and sometimes the most important word without which the passage would be unintelligible is omitted. Each *sūtra* usually consists of two to ten words at the most, and it is rare to find one that is longer. In some cases the *sūtra* is made up of one word.[3] Each *sūtra*, in fact, is composed of a collection of signs, rather than being a sentence in the ordinary sense. Some passages are completely unintelligible, if the sūtras alone are read; therefore, it is impossible to understand the *sūtras* without the aid of a commentary.

A question arises as to why it was only the *Brahma-sūtra* that assumed such an extremely concise form, and the answer aside from the practical reasons for the brevity of *sūtra* literature in general, lies in the esoteric character of Vedānta school. As will be discussed elsewhere, the Vedānta philosophy from the beginning had esoteric tendencies, and in order to prevent outsiders from having access to its teaching a brief and enigmatic style of writing was deliberately used.

Since then, the *Brahma-sūtra* was extremely brief and contained many omissions, making its meaning hard of access, when the research on Vedānta philosophy first began the text was intelligible only by referring to Śaṅkara's commentary, *Brahma-sūtra-bhāṣya*. As a consequence, the thought of the *Brahma-sūtra* was never studied independently but always together with this commentary, and the result was that Śaṅkara's thought became identified with that of the *Brahma-sūtra*. The two were never regarded separately, and the study by Paul Deussen (*Das System des Vedânta.* Leipzig : F. A. Brockhaus, 1883; *The System of the Vedānta*, translated by Charles Johnston, Delhi etc. : Motilal Banarsidass, 1972) represents this tendency. Even among contemporary scholars in India, there are not a few who show the same tendency. The majority of the so-called Pandits, who inherit the traditional scholarship of India, are said to belong to the Vedānta school of Śaṅkara's lineage, and since they regard his commentary as the absolute authority beyond any criticism, they do not consider whether or not it is true to the original meaning of the *Brahma-sūtra.*

If, however, we should read the scriptures of the Vedānta school with such an attitude, it means that the whole history of the Vedānta becomes coloured with Śaṅkara's view and this is not a proper approach to the study of the history of thought. It is inevitable and necessary that we study the *Brahma-sūtra* in itself by separating it from Śaṅkara's interpretation, and this method becomes significantly important as we realize that there are many commentaries on the *Brahma-sūtra* which differ greatly from each other. It may be that the conclusion of the research on the *sūtra* itself, will be that Śaṅkara's views are most valid and the other commentaries relatively invalid, but such a judgment can be made only after a critical study. Uncritically to identify the thought of the *sūtra* and of Śaṅkara without undertaking this research is unscholarly and invalid. Thus, even though we may not be able to obtain final conclusions, we must study the *sūtra* itself, and only after we have made the thoughts of the *sūtra* clear will the significance of Śaṅkara and the founders of the Vedānta schools become evident.

There have been a number of scholars who have advocated the necessity of studying the *Brahma-sūtra* independently of Śaṅkara's thoughts. The most important ones are as follows :

Thibaut : *The Vedântasūtras, SBE.*, Vol. XXXIV, Introduction.

Jacob : *The Vedāntasāra*, (Bombay, 1912), Introduction, pp. vii ff.

V. A. Sukhtankar : The Teachings of Vedānta According to Rāmānuja (*WZKM*, 1908, p. 8ff.).

H. Jacobi, *JAOS*, Vol. XXXIII, pp. 51 ff. (Reprint :

Hermann Jacobi : *Kleine Schriften.* Herausgegeben von Bernhard Kölver, Wiesbaden : Franz Steiner Verlag, 1970, pp. 559-587.)

P. M. Modi : *A Critique of the Brahmasūtra* (III.2.11-IV) (*With special reference to Śaṅkarācārya's Commentary*). Part II : System of the Sūtras (III.2.11-IV). Published by the author, Raopura, Baroda, 1956. (This is a detailed study. I could not see Part I.)

Their studies deserve considerable attention, but they are still fragmentary, although a thorough study poses formidable problems.

Since the *sūtra* is originally very brief with many omissions, a considerable number of words must be added to clarify its purport. The decision to use certain words for the sake of clarification rests solely with the commentator. Sometimes completely different words are added, and the same words are on different occasions interpreted in a directly opposite sense.[4] Consequently, it is possible that directly opposed interpretations are given to the selfsame *sūtra.*

There were other reasons which caused such diversity of interpretation. In some cases, for example, both the view of the opposition (*pūrvapakṣa*) and the arguments (*siddhānta*) of one's own school are presented side by side, and depending upon the standpoint from which a certain *sūtra* is to be interpreted, the commentators reached an entirely different conclusion as to which was which.[5]

Furthermore, some textual differences occurred as the result of different transmissions and this led to an entirely contrary meaning of the expression.[6]

There were also cases whereby the same words of the *sūtra* would be interpreted in directly opposing ways. That is, according to the *saṃdhi* rules of Sanskrit grammar, two words are connected together following certain accepted patterns and they would be pronounced or written together, but in order to understand the term, the words would have to be divided. A single compound or a single sentence may have very different meanings, depending on how the words are separated. In order to avoid such confusion, for example, there exists the *padapāṭha* for *saṃhitās* of the Veda which lays down how the words should be split. In the case of the *Brahma-sūtra*, however, such helpful works have not been passed down; so that there are considerable disagreements in separating out the words, and consequently interpretations differ according to the commentator.[7]

Because of such a situation, the various commentators can easily insert individual philosophical views into the *sūtra*. The views of the commentators on the principal philosophical problems differ greatly from the teaching of the *Brahma-sūtra*, and the commentators show considerable disagreement among themselves.

That commentaries of such diverse import were written on the fundamental *sūtra* is a distinctive characteristic of the Vedānta school. With the other systems, although commentaries also differ on minor problems in their sūtras, glaring differences in interpretation did not arise on basic views. The reason which led to the diverse views on the *Brahma-sūtra* exists within the *sūtra* itself.

There are other reasons that preclude uncritical reliance on the commentaries. Since the authors of the extant commentaries were mainly founders or important thinkers of the various sects of Hinduism, they interpreted the *Brahma-sūtra* to suit their own doctrines. Consequently, such commentaries show influence from ideas outside of the Vedānta school in its narrow sense, and some also incorporated a considerable amount of popular beliefs.

When we fully consider the above situation, we realize the difficulties that await the student of the *Brahma-sūtra*. We must rely upon commentaries to read the *sūtra*, but the commentaries themselves reveal mutual disagreement and in some cases they have drifted away from the original meaning of the *sūtra*. Is then the reconstruction of the basic teaching of the *Brahma-sūtra* possible ? And if so, how can it be fully realized ? We believe that by the following means, we can confirm the import of the *Brahma-sūtra* to a considerable degree :

(1) We must seek all helpful explanations from the various commentaries. The commentaries, especially the older ones, were not written merely out of imagination but were based upon the scholarly transmissions within the school with personal views and changes added. Thus, in attempting to clarify the basic import of the *Brahma-sūtra*[8] the older commentaries must

be studied first. However, other methods must be used at the same time, because the various commentaries reveal mutual contradictions and in some cases all of them show diversions from the original meaning.

(2) We must pay attention to the context, theme, and continuity, by which we can get a fair understanding of what it is that the *sūtra* is attempting to express.

(3) We must also pay attention to the usage of terms in the *sūtra*. Since the *sūtra* is written in a special style, if we pay attention to the usage of terms, we can understand the proper interpretation according to the order in the sentence and the form of ending.

(4) Some words in the *sūtras* have unique and special connotations. Although they are not as recondite as in Pāṇini's Grammar, some technical terms are found (e.g., *pratyakṣa, anumāna, āmanana*, etc.).

(5) We must refer to the comments of other *sūtras* on the same problem and interpret the meaning so that no contradictions arise.

(6) In regards to the words and phrases of the *sūtra*, they should be interpreted as much as possible according to the *sūtra* itself without inserting unnecessary comments as do the existing commentaries.

(7) We must turn to the modern studies on the history of Indian philosophy. The commentators were well-versed in the literature of their age, but they paid almost no attention to the historical development of Indian thought. Therefore, it was almost impossible for the commentators to interpret critically the original meaning of the *Brahma-sūtra*, whereas modern scholars are in the position to reach a more objective conclusion on this point.

If we pay attention to the above, we believe we can clarify the original import of the *sūtra*, even if we cannot expect perfect results from our work.

The remaining problem concerns the choice of proper commentaries for reference. The study of all the commentaries on the *Brahma-sūtra* is not only impossible but also meaningless. The first to attempt the clarification of the original meaning of the *Brahma-sūtra* was Thibaut, who compared Śaṅkara' and Rāmānuja's commentaries and compiled a conspectus of this *sūtra*. (G. Thibaut, *SBE*, Vol. XXXIV. Introduction, pp. xxxii ff.) He was followed by Ghate, who clarified the meaning of the *Brahma-sūtra* by studying the commentaries by Nimbārka, Madhva, and Vallabha, in addition to those of Śaṅkara and Rāmānujá. He also made a comparative study of the chief characteristics of these five philosophers. The results of his research are very interesting and contributed greatly to the clarification of Vedānta thought, but the study discussed only the general outline of the important sections (*adhikaraṇa*) and made detailed analysis of only a few major *sūtras*, giving insufficient attention to the individual remaining *sūtras*. (V. S. Ghate : *The Vedānta, a study of the Brahma-sūtra with the Bhāṣyas of Śaṃkara, Rāmānuja, Nimbārka, Madhva, and Vallabha*, Poona, 1926). Karmarkar also published his comparative study on the various important *sūtras* in the *Brahma-sūtra* by referring to the commentaries of Śaṅkara, Rāmānuja, Vallabha, and Keśavakāśmīrin. He also did not discuss all the *sūtras*. [R. D. Karmarkar : *Comparison of the Bhāṣyas of Śaṅkara, Rāmānuja, Keśavakāśmīrin,* and *Vallabha* on some crucial Sūtras, *ABhI*, Vol. I (1918-1920), pp. 105-127; Vol. II, (1920-21), pp. 23-26].

Among the commentaries used by these scholars, Madhva's commentary is extremely inadequate as a reference for reading the *sūtra*. He makes unreasonable and distorted interpretations of statements from the *sūtras* and *Upaniṣads*,[9] and he often gives scriptural citations of doubtful authority which has led scholars to suspect the possibility of their fabrication by him. It is easy to understand that his dualism (or rather pluralism) is very distant from the ideas of the *Upaniṣads* and the *sūtras*. Madhva's commentary, therefore, may be disregarded in analyzing the basic meaning of the *Brahma-sūtra*, although it is the most important text for studying the philosophy and history of Madhva's own school. Ghate referred to Madhva's work for his study of the *Brahma-sūtra*, but it provided no help in deciphering the *Sūtra*.[10] In regard to the commentaries of Nimbārka, Vallabha, and Keśavakāśmīrin, there is also no necessity to study them, for they were compiled at a much later date and we can recognize interpolations of later ideas.[11]

If our purpose is mainly to clarify the basic meaning of the *Brahma-sūtra*, there is not much significance in referring to the commentaries of the Hindu teachers of later dates. Instead, we should refer to Bhāskara's commentary, besides those of Śaṅkara and Rāmānuja. Bhāskara, who appeared between these two men, wrote a commentary free of Hindu prejudices, and for this reason is very important for the study of the *Brahma-sūtra*. In the following section we propose to reconstruct the original meaning of the *Brahma-sūtra* by referring to the three commentaries by Śaṅkara, Bhāskara, and Rāmānuja, which are also the oldest extant commentaries. Whenever these three works show complete agreement, we may consider it to be the original meaning of the *sūtra*, but when there are disagreements among the three, a very tedious process of research will be required.

In Chapter 2 below we have translated the *sūtras* in their order, according to the original meaning which we reached as the result of our research, and the reasons for our conclusions are included in the notes. The various commentators made very difficult interpretations of relatively unimportant words in the *sūtra*, such as the indeclinables, and attached profound meanings to them. But it is doubtful whether or not the author of the *sūtra* intended to imply such deep connotations, and even if he did so, we have noted the *sūtra* as it is without following any interpretation, unless there was a positive reason for using one particular commentary.

Thibaut, Ghate, and others have discussed in detail the reasons that the additions made by Śaṅkara are invalid. During the time when it was still difficult to break away from the practice of studying the *sūtra* itself and Śaṅkara's commentary together, such an approach may have been necessary and its significance is to be fully recognized. But today when we know clearly that Śaṅkara's commentary is not the only true interpretation, we feel no need to repeat this kind of discussion. Therefore, instead of making critical comments on Śaṅkara's commentary, except in special cases, we have made references to the research of Thibaut and Ghate whenever necessary and have concentrated our efforts on reconstructing the original meaning of the *Brahma-sūtra*. The commentaries, furthermore, elaborate very complicated arguments, but it is doubtful whether or not the author of the *sūtra* went as far as they seem to infer. Rather than introducing extraneous ideas, we have tried to understand the meaning of the words themselves, and limited the addition of further words. We believe that this method is proper to our intention, which is the reconstruction of the original meaning. Based upon such an approach, we shall discuss the thought of the *Brahma-sūtra* in Chapter 3.

Notes

1. Each passage is called a *sūtra*, and all the *sūtras* compiled together is referred to in the plural, *Brahma-sūtrāṇi*.
2. A similar point can be made for the *Mīmāṃsā-sūtra*.
3. For details on the style of *Brahma-sūtra*, see Deussen, *SV*. S. 26-29.
4. See Ghate, *the Vedānta*, p. 47.
5. For examples, see commentaries on 2.3.19 ff. and 4.3.7 ff.
6. For example, 4.3.15.
7. For examples, see the notes on 2.3.17, 25; 2.4.2; and 4.3.15 in "Reading of *Brahma Sūtra*."
8. The works of the other schools have been widely read, quoted and criticized by thinkers of rival schools; therefore, they can be utilized in seeking the original meaning of a text. But in the case of the *Brahma-sūtra* it has never been mentioned in other works; therefore, the commentaries must be first studied in any attempt to seek the original meaning.
9. Ghate, *The Vedānta*, pp. 168-170.
10. Ghate, *op. cit.*, p. 169, mentions six instances where Madhva's commentary is thought to be valid, but it is difficult to consider them as valid interpretations.
11. Ghate and other scholars have pointed out the important parts.

CHAPTER XI

EXPLANATORY NOTES ON THE *BRAHMA-SŪTRAS*

In the following part of the Japanese original work comes a Japanese complete translation of the *Brahma-sūtra*, with critical annotations based upon a comparative study of the commentaries by Śaṅkara, Bhāskara, Rāmānuja and others.

In the Japanese original I translated all the *sūtras* of the *Brahma-Sūtras* into Japanese. But to render them all into English here is unnecessary, inasmuch as some good translations have been published and are now available in the West and India. So this part has been omitted from the English translation of this work.

In the following I propose to comment on some important *sūtras* or phrases relevant to the account of the thought of the *Brahma-sūtra* which will come later.

I.1.2. *janmādy asya yataḥ*

(Brahman is the source) from which origin, etc. (i.e. origin, subsistence, and dissolution) of this (world proceed).[1]

1. Śaṅkara and Rāmānuja refer back to : "*yato vā imāni bhūtāni jāyante, yena jātāni jīvanti, yat prayanty abhisaṃviśanti, tad vijijñāsasva, tad brahmeti*". (*Taittirīya-Upaniṣad* III, 1).

I.1.3. *śāstra-yonitvāt.*

(How is it possible to know that Brahman is the source from which the world proceeds, by which it is maintained and ended ?——) It is because Scripture[1] is the source of knowledge about it.)

1. Scripture (*sāstra*) means the Vedas, especially the *Upaniṣads*. Cf. *śāstra* (*BS.* I, 1, 30; II, 3, 33); *śāsti* (I, 1, 19).

II.1.14. *tad-ananyatvam, ārambhaṇa-śabda-ādibhyaḥ.*

The non-difference[1] of them (i.e. *Brahman* as the cause and the world as the effect) (is known) from words like 'comprehending by word'.[2]

1. The word *ananyatva* is used in Kātyāyana's *Vārttika* (ad I, 1, 69, 8. Cf. I, 1, 39, 2; 56, 10). It means 'that an individual thing does not exist apart

from its genus'. This word is interpreted by Śaṅkara as "*vyatirekeṇa abhāvaḥ kāryasya*", by Vācaspatimiśra as "*na khalv ananyatvam ity abhedaṃ brūmaḥ. kiṃ tu bhedaṃ vyāsedhāmaḥ*". In the light of these interpretations, we are led to the conclusion that the Sūtrakāra insisted not upon identity of the world with *Brahman*, but that the world is inseparable from *Brahman*, for the world as effect has come into existence owing to the manifestation of *Brahman*. On this word, see the following article, M. Hiriyanna : "What is *ananyatvam* ?" (*Festschrift Moritz Winternitz*, pp. 221-224).

2. This word refers to *vācā ārambhaṇa* (*Chānd. Up.* VI, 1, 4). Śaṅkara explained it as follows : *vācārambhaṇaṃ vāgārambhaṇaṃ vāg-ālambanam ity etat*. Following this interpretation many Indologists identified *ārambhaṇa* with *ālambana*. But linguistically this interpretation is unacceptable. It should be understood as 'grasping (comprehending) with word', to which Rāmānuja's interpretation comes close.

—*ārabhyata ālabhyate spṛśyata ity ārambhaṇam* /
kṛtya-lyuṭo bahulam (Pāṇini III, 3, 113) *iti karmaṇi lyuṭ* /

"*vācā*" *vāk-pūrvakeṇa vyavahāreṇa hetunety arthaḥ* / (*Śrībhāṣya*, BSS., p. 400). It is interpreted to the same effect in the *Vedārthasaṃgraha* also. Sukhtankar, *WZKM*, 1908, p. 144 f.). Cf. "Ein Sich-klammern an Worte" (K. F. Geldner : *Vedismus und Brahmanismus*, p. 111); "haftet am Wort" (H. Oldenberg : *Die Lehre der Upanishaden* p. 60, fn. 28). Bhāskara's interpretation is close to that of Śaṅkara—*tadabhidheyaṃ nāmadheyam ubhayam ālambya vāgvyavahāraḥ pravartate "ghaṭena udakam āhara*"-iti. Vidhushekhara Bhattacharya has defended Śaṅkara's interpretation ("Vācārambhaṇam', *Indian Historical Quarterly*, XII, 1936, pp. 342-344), but the difficulty in terms of saṃdhi cannot be explained away unless we take it as *vācā* (instrumental)+*ārambhaṇa*. Incidentally Śrīnivāsa (*Vedāntakaustubha* ad *BS*.II, 1, 14) explains it as *vācā vāgindriyeṇa ārbhyate vyāhriyate* (cited in Bhattacharya's article).

II.3.18. *jño 'ta eva.*

(The self is self is of) intelligence,[1] for this very reason.

1. Many Indologists interpret this as follows :—In this *sūtra ātman* is defined as "*jñaḥ*", not "*jñānam*". This means that the Brahmasūtrakāra did not regard *Ātman* as pure Intelligence itself, but as the basis that has Intelligence as a quality (*guṇa*). In this respect the Brahmasūtrakāra is closer to Rāmānuja than to Śaṅkara. (Thibaut : Introduction, p. LIV; Guha : *Jīvātman*, pp. 167-169 : Ghate : *The Vedānta*, pp. 92-93; Karmarkar : Comparison, *Annals of the Bhandarkar Oriental Research Institute*, vol. I, p. 35). But here Intelligence is regarded as the essence of the individual self. (cf. Belvalkar : *Lectures*,, pp. 163-164). This assumption is corroborated by the statement that the liberated individual self is *citi-mātra* (*BS.* IV, 4, 6-7). Such an assumption is shared by many philosophers and intellectuals.—*smaraṇaṃ tv ātmano jña-svābhāvyāt* (*Nyāya-sūtra*, III, b, 40); *jñaḥ Sākṣīty ucyate nājñaḥ sākṣī hy ātmā yataḥ smṛtaḥ* (*Caraka-saṃhitā* IV, 1, 51 (vol. I, p. 549).

II.3.43. *aṃśo, nānā-vyapadeśād, anyathā cāpi dāśa-kitava-āditvam adhīyata eke.*

(The individual self is) a part[1] (of the Supreme Self) on account of the declaration of difference (of the two) and also the reverse (i.e. that the two are not different), for in some (recensions of the Vedas) (it) is spoken of as being (of the nature of) fishermen, gamblers, etc[2].

1. In explaining this *sūtra* Śaṅkara gratuitously inserts into the phrase the term '*iva*', saying "*aṃśa ivāṃśo / na hi niravayavasya mukhyo 'ṃśaḥ saṃbhavati*". As Śaṅkara maintained the advaita theory, which is against the purport of this *sūtra*, he had to make a twisted interpretation. Bhāskara says :—*tadaṃśo jīvo 'sti / aṃśaśabdaḥ kāraṇavācī / yathā paṭasyāṃśo 'vayavas tantur iti.* In his interpretation the relationship between the individual self and *Brahman* is compared to that between threads and a cloth.

2. Śaṅkara, Rāmānuja and Bhāskara all cite, a phrase of an *Ātharvaṇika Brahmasūkta* : "*brahma dāsā brahma dāsā brahmaiveme kitavāḥ.*"

II.3.50. *ābhāsā eva vā.*[1]

Or (the individual selves) are nothing but 'appearances'.[2]

1. According to Bhāskara and Nimbārka. (Cf. Guha : *Jīvātman*, p. 148). Śaṅkara and Rāmānuja read : *ābhāsa eva ca.* But in Rāmānuja's commentary v.1. (*ābhāsā eva*) also is admitted.

2. Śaṅkara takes *ābhāsa* for 'reflection'. (*ābhāsa eva caiṣa jīvaḥ parasyātmano jala-sūryakādivat pratipattavyaḥ / na sa eva sākṣānnāpi vastvantaram /*). Vallabha follows him. Subcommentaries on Śaṅkara's commentary say that in this *sūtra pratibimbavāda* is meant. Śaṅkara says: "Just as, when one reflected image of the sun trembles, another reflected image does not on that account tremble also; so when one soul is connected with actions and results of actions, another soul is not on that account connected likewise. There is therefore no confusion of actions and results." (Thibaut). Śaṅkara takes this *sūtra* as supplementary to the preceding *sūtra*.

On the other hand, Rāmānuja takes *ābhāsa* for *hetv-ābhāsa*, saying that' 'the theory that the distinction among individual selves is brought about due to *upāḍhi* is wrong' and that "if we adopt such a theory, confusion would occur in terms of experiencing the results of former actions'. Nimbārka follows him. Bhāskara refutes the reading of Śaṅkara's text and also his interpretation.

Then what is the true purport of the sūtra ? Rāmānuja's and Bhāskara's interpretation to take *ābhāsa* for *hetv-ābhāsa* is absurd and far-fetched. (Thibaut : Introduction, pp. XCVII-XCVIII). It is likely that the relationship of *bhedābheda* between the Supreme Self and the individual self is meant by means of the simile of reflections of the image of the sun on the surface of water. Vallabha here warns the reader that the word '*ābhāsa*' in the sūtra is not to be understood to mean 'something absolutely unreal' as in the doctrine of Śaṅkara, but 'an appearance', i.e.,' something apparently the same as or having the appearance of something else, but not quite the same.' (Ghate : *The Vedānta*, p. 105) (*na mithyātvarūpā ābhāsāḥ*). If we interpret this word in this way, this will not be inconsistent with the opinion that the individual self is a portion (*aṃśa*) of the Supreme Self.

II.4.7. *aṇavaś ca.*

And (the organs are) minute[1] (in size).

1. 'minute' (*aṇu*) means 'subtlety' (*saukṣmya*) and "spatial limitation' (*pariccheda*), according to Śaṅkara. Bhāskara's interpretation is more or less on the same lines. Rāmānuja takes '*aṇu*' for spatial (*parimitatva*). The reasons why the organs are minute are explained by Bhāskara:—*utkrānti-śruteḥ, tadānīṃ cānupalabdheḥ* (because Scripture has it that the organs go out of body when one dies, and also because their going out is not perceived.). Rāmānuja adopts this opinion.

III.3.3. *svādhyāyasya, tathātvena*[1] *hi samācāre, 'dhikārāc ca; savavac*[2] *ca tan-niyamaḥ.*

(The rite of carrying fire on the head, mentioned in the *Muṇḍaka-Upaniṣad* III,2,10, is said in connection) with the study of the Veda (of the Ātharvaṇikas), because it is described as such in the *Samācāra*; (this also follows) from the subject-matter of the passage, and from its being limited (to the students of the *Atharva-Veda*) as in the case with the oblations. (Therefore, it is not that a *vidyā* is set forth).

1. Śaṅkara, in his text interprets *tathātvena* as *svādhyāya-dharmatvena*. However, it is *tathātve* in the texts of Bhāskara and Rāmānuja.

Bhāskara explains : *tathātve adhyayanāṅgatve nimittasaptamī tadaṅgatayā*. Therefore it is clear that there was already discrepancy in wording among various texts of the *Brahma-sūtra* by the time of Śaṅkara and Bhāskara and that it is not a question merely of scribal errors.

2. The text of Bhāskara has *salilavat* as the original word, but in his Bhāṣya he comments as if the text had *savavat* as in the other two *Bhāṣyas*.

(APPENDIX) RESULTS OF THE COMPARATIVE STUDY OF THE THREE OLD COMMENTARIES

The comparative study of the three ancient commentaries made for the purpose of reading the *Brahma-sūtra* reveals some interesting results from the philological point of view, and they are summarized below for the benefit of the reader.

SECTION 1 DIFFERENCES IN WORDING OF THE SŪTRAS

We shall begin by comparing the three commentaries in regard to the wording of the sūtra.

We used the ĀnSS. edition for Śaṅkara's commentary, and whenever misprints occurred, we referred to the NSP edition. For Rāmānuja's Śrībhāṣya we used BSS. No. LXVIII (1914), published by Vasudev Shastri Abhyankar. For Bhāskara's commentary we used the ChowkhSS. Nos. 70, 185, and 209 editions, published by Vindhyesvari Prasada Dvivedin. Although it contains many misprints and errors which make for difficult reading, we had no alternative, since this is the only published version of his work. For a comparative research on the wording of the *sūtra*, the published editions of Śaṅkara's and Rāmānuja's works are reliable, since they are critically edited, but we cannot trust Bhāskara's commentary, for the reason given above. In the published edition of Bhāskara's commentary there are many instances in which a sentence is not given as a *sūtra* and yet is discussed as one (I, 1, 31; II, 2, 31; II, 2, 32; III, 1, 27; III, 2, 34). In such cases Bhāskara was commenting upon an independent *Sūtra*, as in the other two commentaries, but it must have somehow been dropped from the extant copy. The wording of the *sūtra* in Bhāskara's work as published also frequently differs from that of the other two commentaries, but the *sūtra* quoted in Bhāskara's own commentary often agrees with the interpretations of the other two (I, 2, 7; II, 1, 32; II, 2, 9 II, 2, 11; II, 2, 16; II, 2, 17; II, 2, 19 first half; II, 2, 22; II, 2, 44, II, 2, 45; II, 4, 5; II, 4, 10; III, 1, 2; III, 1, 23; III, 2, 10; III, 2, 12; III, 2 16; III, 2, 21; III, 3, 3; III, 3, 18; III, 3, 23; III, 3, 41; III, 4, 2; III, 4, 8; IV, 1, 4; IV, 1, 11; IV, 2, 5; IV, 4, 16; IV, 4, 21). There must have been either errors in the original manuscript of the *sūtra* on which the published edition was based, or misprints which crept in during publication. Consequently, in spite of the fact that some wordings of the published edition differ from the other two commentaries, we must leave them out of consideration and proceed on the basis of the other two commentaries.

When we compare the other *sūtras* which appear in the three commentaries, almost all of them show complete agreement. However, there are cases, though rare, where some differences exist, and we shall examine them below.

According to Śaṅkara, the number of *sūtras* contained in the *Brahma-sūtra* is 555, but Bhāskara's and Rāmānuja's totals do not agree with this enumeration. A *sūtra* which is listed in one commentary may be missing in another commentary, as evident in the following chart (+indicates the existence of the *sūtra*, —indicates the non-existence, and the number follows that of Śaṅkara's work).

Number of Sūtra	*Śaṅkara*	*Bhāskara*	*Rāmānuja*	*Text*
1.1.9	—	+	+	pratijñāvirodhāt
1.2.16	—	—	+	ata eva ca sa brahma
2.2.23	+	—	+	ubhayathā ca doṣāt
2.2.38	+	—	—	sambandhānupa-pratteś ca
3.2.15	—	+	—	asthūla...
3.4.46	+	—	—	śruteś ca
4.1.18	+	—	+	yadeva vidyayeti hi
4.3.5	+	—	—	ubhayavyāmohāt tatsiddheḥ

It is clear that additions or omissions of *sūtras* were made as the transmissions became diverse and complex. The above chart shows that among the three commentaries Bhāskara's and Rāmānuja's show relatively greater agreement, but no more than that can be concluded from it.

Even among the *sūtras* which are found in common in the three commentaries, the wording does not necessarily agree and considerable differences can be detected. One of the most significant differences is that frequently when the word "and" (*ca*) occurs in both Śaṅkara's and Rāmānuja's commentaries, it may be missing in Bhāskara's work (1.2.16; 1. 2. 26; 2.1.37; 2.2.8; 2.2.9 : 2.2.14; 3.1.8; 3.2.4; 3.2.18). The word "but" (*tu*) is also sometimes missing only in Bhāskara's work (3.2.27; 2.3.41). The lack of such indeclinables seems to be a characteristic of Bhāskara, but there are exceptions. In 1.3.6, for example, *ca* is found only in Bhāskara and not in the other two commentaries. Thus, we can say that the *sūtras* as transmitted by Bhāskara have the tendency to leave out indeclinables, but this is by no means always so.

Occasionally there are some cases in which Śaṅkara's interpretation is different from those of the other commentaries. For example, *Samavāyābhyupagamāc ca*, BS.II, 2, 13 refers back to the preceding *sūtra* according to Śaṅkara, and on II, 2, 39 he set forth two different interpretations.

In examining the other instances of disagreement in the wording of the sūtra, no significant tendencies can be found. If we should classify the divergences in the wording of the *sūtras*, they are as follows (the differences in the *sūtras* already cited are excluded) :

(1) Instances of agreement between Śaṅkara's and Bhāskara's transmissions, but disagreement with Rāmānuja's :

1.1.25; 1.2.19; 1.3.2; 1.3.23; 2.1.16; 2.1.20; 2.3.17; 2.3.46; 2.3.53; 3.1.16; 3.2.12; 3.3.36; 3.4.7; 3.4.18; 3.4.27; 4.1.12; 4.1.19; 4.2.11; 4.2.21; 4.3.14; 4.3.15; 4.4.8.

(2) Instances of agreement between Śaṅkara's and Rāmānuja's transmissions, but disagreement with Bhāskara's :

1.2.20; 2.1.15; 2.1.35; 2.3.19; 2.3.50; 2.4.14; 3.1.1; 3.1.11; 3.2.5; 3.2.16; 3.3.7; 3.3.16; 3.4.23; 3.4.40 first half; 3.4.43; 4.2.2.; 4.4.6.

(3) Instances of agreement between Bhāskara's and Rāmānuja's transmissions, but disagreement with Śaṅkara's :

1.2.18; 2.1.11; 2.2.19 first half; 2. 3. 25; 2.3.44; 2.3.45; 3.1.24; 3.3.3; 3.3.24; 3.3.36 (*sūtra* appears in commentary); 3.4.18 (*sūtra* appears in commentary); 3.4.24; 3.4.37; 3.4.40 latter half; 3.4.51; 4.4.18.

(4) Instances of total disagreement between all three transmissions :

2.2.19 latter half; 3.1.22; 3.3.2; (3.4.42 shows different passages in Śaṅkara's and Rāmānuja's transmission, and the same passage in Bhāskara's is unclear).

The differences in wording of these *sūtras* are not merely errors in the original manuscript, but they must have existed from a very early period, probably prior to Śaṅkara. (See my "Explanatory Notes on "Reading of *Brahma-sūtra*" 2.3.50 and 3.3.3). Since many of the differences are minor and secondary, and the variations between the sūtras are very few, we may assume that they were established considerably before Śaṅkara and that the later transmitters made few changes.

Next, there are cases in which, though the wording is identical, one commentary would interpret a certain *sūtra* as a single statement, whereas another commentary would divide it into two parts. There are also instances in which two *sūtras* are interpreted as a single *sūtra*. We may group them generally in the following manner :

(1) Instances of transmission as a single sūtra by Śaṅkara and Bhāskara but divided into two by Rāmānuja :

1.3.35; 1.3.38; 1.4.25; 2.1.11; 2.3.6; 2.3.12.

(2) Instances of transmission as two sūtras by Śaṅkara and Bhāskara but considered as one by Rāmānuja :

1.3.3 and 4; 2.1.17 and 18; 2.1.35 and 36; 2.2.1 and 2; 2.3.3. and 4; 2.3.26 and 27; 2.3.34 and 35; 2.4.2 and 3; 2.4.14 and 15; 2.4.18 and 19; 3.2.20 and 21; 3.3.47 and 48.

(3) Instances of transmission as two sūtras by Śaṅkara and Rāmānuja but considered as one by Bhāskara :

1.4.17 and 18; 3.4.23 and 24.

(4) Instances of transmission as two sūtras by Śaṅkara but considered as one by Bhāskara and Rāmānuja :

3.3.35 and 36; 4.2.12 and 13.

The first fact evident from the above is that Śaṅkara and Bhāskara are almost always in agreement concerning the division and combination of words.

There are also some differences in the order of the *sūtras* (2.2.6; 3.2.4; 3.3.31). In this case also Śaṅkara and Bhāskara always show agreement, whereas Rāmānuja differs from them.

Thus the commentaries by Śaṅkara and Bhāskara agree closely on the division and combination of words and on the order of *sūtras*, showing that the attitudes and interpretations of these two commentaries are very similar in nature. We shall now proceed to examine the differences in the interpretations by the three commentaries.

SECTION 2 DIFFERENCES IN THE INTERPRETATIONS OF *Sūtras*

The variations in the interpretations by the different commentaries have attracted great attention of scholars ever since Thibaut first pointed out the fact. But when we consider the work as a whole, the differences are not so great. The greatest differences are between the interpretations concerning the relationship between *Brahman* and individual self and concerning the *sūtras* dealing with spiritual liberation, and while the long commentaries on other *sūtras* vary considerably in the different works, there is general agreement concerning the interpretation of the words of the *sūtra*. We list below only the cases in which differences exist.

Expressions are put in brackets to indicate that they are interpreted differently in the commentaries. Differences as to which sacred text is to be taken as the authority referred to by the *sūtra* are marked by the word Text in brackets. When there is no such note, the differences concern the whole *sūtra*. Different interpretations arising from varied readings of the *sūtra* are not given, as they have been listed elsewhere.

In some cases where there are variations, it is not easy to judge which is the most valid interpretation, but my analysis in the preceding section "analysis of the *Brahma-sūtra*", which has partly been translated in this English version, leads me to conclude that in certain cases (marked S) Śaṅkara is truest to the original in his interpretation, in others (marked B) it is Bhāskara, and in yet others (marked R) it is Rāmānuja.

(1) Instances of agreement between Śaṅkara's and Bhāskara's commentaries, with Rāmānuja's in disagreement:

Book I, Chapter 1—12 R(demarcation of *adhikaraṇa*), 17 (Text'), 18R (*anumāna*), 19 (Text).

Chapter 2—7 S, B (*vyomavat*), 8, 11 S, B (demarcation of *adhikaraṇa*), 25 (*iti*), 31 (*sampatti*).

Chapter 3—1 (*svaśabdāt*), 5 (Text), 6 (Text), 8 S, B, 10 S, B (*ambarānta*), 13 S, B (*vyapadeśāt*), 19 R (*tu*), 22 R (demarcation of *adhikaraṇa*), 23 (Text). 26 (*tadupari*), 32 S, B, 33 (*asti*), 40 (Text), 41 (*antara*), 42 (demarcation of *adhikaraṇa*).

Chapter 4—6 (*trayāṇām*), 9, 10. 10 S, B, (*madhvādivat*), 19, 25 S, B (*ubhaya*), 26, 28 R (*sarve*).

Book II, Chapter 1—2 S, B, 8 S, B (*apītau*), 9, 11, S, B, (*api*), 12 (*śiṣṭāparigraha*), 13 R, 13 R (lokavat), 14 (*ārambhaṇa*), 23 R (*aśmādivat*), 25 R (*loka*), 28 (*ātman*)'.

chapter 2—2, 4, 11 R, 13, 18 S, B, 26 S, B, 27 S, B, 28, 30 S, B (*na bhāvo*), 31 S, B, 36 S, B, 41, 44 S, B, 45 S, B.

chapter 3—2 R, 5 (Text), 7 (*vibhāga*), 10 S, B-12, 13 S, B, 14, 15 (*aviśeṣāt*), 15 (Text) 16 S, B, 27 (Text), 29 S, B, 30 S, B, 31 S, B, 32 S, B, 33 S, B, 37 S, B, 38, 39, 40, 41 (scriptural reference), 46, 51, 52.

Chapter 4—1 S, B, 2 S, B, 3 S, B, 4 S, B, 6, 11, 14 S, B, 15 S, B, 17 (Text), 18 (Text).

Book III, Chapter 1 — 13 (*saṃyamana*), 20, 25.

Chapter 2—1, 2, 3, 5 R, 6, 11, 13 (Text), 14, 16 (interpretation of whole passage and Text), 19, 20, 21, 25 first half, 26, 29, 30, 31 (*sambandhabheda*), 35, 37 (*anena*), 41 (Text).

Chapter 3—2, 4 (Text), 8, 9 R, 10 (*sarva*), 12, 14, 16 S, B, 17, 19, 33 (*tadbhāva*), 34, 37, 38, 40, 41, 43, 44, 50, 51, 53, 54, 55 (*na prativedam*), 57 (*kratuvat*), 65.

Chapter 4—2 (*anyeṣu*), 11, 13, 26 (*aśvavat*), 34 (*ubhayaliṅga*), 35 (interpretation of whole passage and Text), 37 (Text), 44 (Text), 51, 52.

Book IV, Chapter 1—1 (*asakṛdupadeśāt*), 2 S, B, 3, 12 (*tatra*), 13 (*tat*), 14, 17 (*ubhayoḥ*).

Chapter 2—6 (Text), 8 (interpretation of whole passage and Text), 9, 10, 17 (*tat*), 19, 21.

Chapter 3—2, 7 S, B, 8, 9, 12, 13, 14.

Chapter 4—8, 12, 15 (interpretation of whole passage and Text), 18 latter half, 19 (interpretation of whole passage and Text), 20 (Text), 21 (Text).

Total : 175 *sūtras*.

(2) Instances of agreement between Śaṅkara's and Rāmānuja's commentaries and disagreement with Bhāskara's :

1.2.17 (*itara*), 20 (*enam*). 1.3.12 (*anyabhāva*), 29 (*nityatva*).

2.1.22 B(*adhika*).

3. 3. 36latter half. 3.4.36 S, B.

Total : 7 *sūtras*.

(3) Instances of agreement between Bhāskara's and Rāmānuja's commentary and disagreement with Śaṅkara's :

1.1.4 (*tat*),12 — 19. 1.3.12 (*vyāvṛtti*).

2.3.50. 2.4.12 S.

3.1.13 B, R. 3.2.25 latter half. 3.3.24. 3.4.25, 47 (*pakṣeṇa*) B, R, 52 (*evam*).

4.2.3 (*anu*) B. R., 12 B. R. 4.3.15 (*tatkratu*, scriptural reference.

4.4.16 (saṃpatti) B, R.

Total : 22 *sūtras*.

(4) Instances where all three commentaries disagree :

1.2.28 (Vaiśvānara), 32 (*āmanati*) B. 1, 4.22 B.

2.1.7 latter half. 2.2.10, 30 latter half. 2.3.40, 43 (*aṃśa*).

2.4.5 (*gati*), 16. 3. 2. 12, 15, 22. 3.3.11 (*pradhāna*), 13

(*sāmānya*), 28 B, 29, 30, 35 B, 42 (*nirdhāraṇa*), 48. 3.4.16, 40, 43 (*ācāra*), 47 (*vidhyādivat*), 48 (*kṛtsnabhāvāt*), 50 (*anāviṣkurvan*). 4.1.6 (*upapatteḥ*), 18. 4.3.10 (Text), 15.
4.4.18 (Text).
Total : 32 *sūtras*.

There are also cases in which the commentaries by Śaṅkara and Rāmānuja clearly differ, but Bhāskara's position is unclear because of the brevity of his comment (E.g., 4.1.4, 4.1.9, etc.). We shall, however, not discuss these here. Furthermore, even when the three commentaries show general agreement on the connection of the *sūtras*, Śaṅkara and Rāmānuja differ in the division of sentences. These have also been omitted, since they have almost no direct connection with the interpretation of words.

According to the above examination, there are differences in interpretation regarding approximately 236 *sūtras* out of a total of 555 *sūtras*. The differences as to what sacred text (or sacred authority) a *sūtra* is alluding to are basically concerned with the import of the *sūtra* as a whole, and when we leave these cases out of consideration, we find differences remaining for approximately 209 *sūtras*. That is, there are differences over the interpretation of words in approximately one-third of the *sūtras*. However, the differences are mainly over words of lesser importance, and the three commentaries do show general agreement. To discuss the differences between the respective commentaries in regard to the import of individual *sūtras* would mean to discuss almost all of the *sūtras*, and for this reason this matter will not be treated here.

When we study the different interpretations concerning the words in the *sūtras*, we find the commentaries of Śaṅkara and of Bhāskara are closest to each other considering the number of instances of agreement. This is a very important fact. It is generally taken that the two have different philosophical standpoints, Śaṅkara espousing *Advaita* and Bhāskara standing for *bhedābheda* theory, and the fact that these two commentaries, reflecting such opposing tendencies, basically agree suggests an important clue for the study of the original meaning of *Brahmasūtra* and the clarification of the process which led to the different interpretations.

While Bhāskara's interpretation is thus strikingly close to Śaṅkara's, his standpoint is not identical with that of Śaṅkara.

In his commentary Bhāskara frequently rejects the argument that the differentiated aspect of the phenomenal world is "only illusion" (*māyāmātra*). (Bhāskara ad *BS*. I, 2, 12; I, 3, 7; III, 2, 3). At times he also mentions the appellations *māyāvāda* and *māyāvādin,* and is clearly criticizing Śaṅkara's theory. (Bhāskara ad *BS*. II, 1, 14, p. 93 ff; II, 2, 29; IV, 4, 14). In another case he quotes Śaṅkara's commentary on one *sūtra* and criticizes it.[1] (ad *BS*. I, 1, 19; I, 2, 23; I, 3, 10; III, 2, 22; III, 3, 30; III, 4, 26; IV, 3, 14, which according to Bhāskara's enumeration is IV, 3, 13).

In the light of these points, it is clear that though Bhāskara makes interpretations very similar to Śaṅkara, he did not merely copy the latter in writing his commentary, for he maintains a strictly critical attitude to the commentaries of Śaṅkara and of other thinkers[2], while at the same time following traditional views in his own interpretation of the *sūtras*. Since the explanations in the two oldest commentaries, reflecting different philosophical points of view, show overwhelming agreement with each other—much more than with any other commentary—we are led to believe that the instances where there is agreement between Śaṅkara and Bhāskara would be the traditional and orthodox interpretation of the *sūtra*. And in the cases where the two interpretations differ, we believe that Bhāskara's interpretation of the *sūtra*, probably best expresses the original meaning of the *sūtra* irrespective of whether it agrees with Rāmānuja. (For concrete examples, see "analysis, of *Brahma-sūtra*.") Thus, the general conclusion is that Bhāskara's commentary is the most reliable, as far as the interpretation of the words of the *sūtra* is concerned.

Śaṅkara's commentary also generally conveys the traditional views in the interpretation of the words of the *sūtra*. Studies in the past have supposed that Śaṅkara's commentary deviates most from the original import of the *sūtras*, but actually it is only Śaṅkara's ideas that are different from the thought of the *Brahma-sūtra*, and his commentary is very reliable, so far as the words of the *sūtra* are concerned. The only thing is that Śaṅkara inserts unnecessary interpolations and ideas of his own in his commentary. For example, in commenting upon the *sūtra* which treats of the relationship between *Brahman* and the individual self. Śaṅkara interprets the words of the *sūtra* faithfully but always stresses that "this explanation is an explanation from the relative standpoint (*vyavahārāvasthā*) and it is not an explanation from the standpoint of ultimate truth (*paramārthāvasthā*). From the standpoint of ultimate truth, the two are non-different." Such thinking comes from Śaṅkara and is not faithful to the *sūtra* itself. Thus, if we except such extraneous explanations, Śaṅkara's commentary is also very reliable. (E.g., 2.3.40 commentary).

On the other hand, Rāmānuja's commentary has been considered to be very important in the eyes of Indologists ever since Thibaut made a comparative study with Śaṅkara's commentary and published his view[3] that Rāmānuja's commentary is more valid as an interpretation of the *Brahma-sūtra*. But Ghate[4] afterwards reached the conclusion, based upon his studies of the various commentaries, that Rāmānuja's commentary does not necessarily grasp the original meaning of the sūtra and that Nimbārka's views are closer to the *Brahma-sūtra*. If, as Ghate states, Nimbārka, who advocated the theory of *bhedābheda*, is most faithful in reproducing the original meaning of the *sūtra*, we can say that the commentary by Bhāskara, who advocated the same theory several hundred years before Nimbārka, is far closer to the original, although Ghate did not refer to Bhāskara. This conclusion seems to be reinforced by the fact that Bhāskara's commentary is closest in time, to Śaṅkara's work, which latter is the oldest extant commentary.

Rāmānuja's commentary may be close in thought to the *Sūtra*, but it is inferior to Śaṅkara's and Bhāskara's commentaries in regard to the interpretation of the words of the sūtra, and we cannot help concluding that it contains interpretations resulting from frequent emendations made by later scholars. The reasons are as follows :

(1) As we noted throughout the preceding "analysis of *Brahma-sūtra*", only parts of which have been translated in this English translation, and in the list given above. Rāmānuja's commentary differs considerably from the two oldest commentaries which reflect different philosophical standpoints. This is the main reason for the above conclusion.

(2) Furthermore, Rāmānuja's commentary contains quotations from later *Upaniṣads* which are not found in Śaṅkara and Bhāskara, a great number of quotations from the Purāṇa literature,

and a strong colouring of the Viṣṇu faith throughout. However, Early Vedānta Philosophy, as our previous study has shown, has no traces of the various influences of Hindu religious sects. Thus, we may conclude that the above characteristics are additions made by later generations and that they were not adopted by Rāmānuja from ancient commentaries.

(3) In the *Śrībhāṣya* there are many passages which seem to have been taken from the *Vedārthasaṃgraha.* This is partial evidence that the ideas of the *Śrībhāṣya* are fairly far from those of the *Brahma-sūtra.*

(4) The explanations of Buddhist doctrines alluded to in the *sūtra* are most inferior in Rāmānuja's commentary. In his section criticizing Buddhism (2.2.18 ff.), in contrast to Śaṅkara and Bhāskara who use proper Buddhist Hybrid Sanskrit and show good understanding of Buddhist thought, Rāmānuja uses very few Buddhist technical terms and his arguments attacking Buddhism miss the crucial points.

For example the "aggregates due to two causes" (*ubhayahetuka samudāya*) in 2.2.18 is interpreted by Rāmānuja to mean "the aggregates of the elements such as earth. etc. which are made of atoms (*aṇu*)" and "the aggregates composed of body, senses, and objects" (*śarīrendriyaviṣayarūpaḥ samudāyaḥ*), but the interpretation that it is the latter which are the "five aggregates" (*pañcaskandha*), as given by Śaṅkara and Bhāskara, is more valid as an explanation of Buddhism (See notes on *sūtra* 18).

Again, *sūtra* 19 criticizes the Buddhist theory that each *aṅga* of the Twelve Cycles of Causation becomes a cause in its turn. Now Śaṅkara lists the twelve cycles correctly in their order, but Rāmānuja begins with ignorance (*avidyā*) and ends with sensation (*vedanā*), while Bhāskara's commentary also contains many errors.

te cāvidyādayo 'vidyāsaṃskāro vijñānaṃ nāma-rūpaṃ ṣaḍāyatanaṃ sparśo vedanā tṛṣṇopādānaṃ bhavo jātir jarāmaraṇaṃ śokaḥ paridevanā duḥkhaṃ durmanastety evaṃjātīyakā itaretarahetukā Saugate samaye kvacit saṃkṣiptā nirdiṣṭāḥ kvacit prapañcitāḥ (Śaṅkara) avidyā nāma viparītadṛṣṭir anitye nityadṛṣṭir amārge mārgadṛṣṭir iti / tataḥ saṃskambhaḥ skannaḥ (sic.) prādurbhavati rāgadveṣamotherṣādilakṣaṇaḥ pūrvoktaḥ / tataḥ *pravṛttiḥ* / puṇyāpuṇyātmakaṃ karma pravṛttiśabdenocyate / ......tannibandhanaṃ *janma śarīragrahaṇam* / ṣaḍāyatanaṃ ca pañca buddhīndrīyāṇi manaś ca /

ṣaḍāyatanam ucyate ṣaḍvijñānāni / pañcānām indriyāṇāṃ pañca rūpādayo viṣayās teṣu pañcavijñānāny utpadyante / manasas tu taddharmā viṣayās tad evaṃ pramātṛpramāṇa-prameyavyavahārasiddheḥ sarvam upapannam iti / (Bhāskara) (Italics indicates explanations which are especially invalid as Buddhist teaching).

avidyā hi nāma viparītabuddhiḥ kṣaṇikādiṣu sthiratvādigocarā / tayā saṃskārākhyā rāga-dveṣādayo jāyante / tataś *cittābhi-jvalanarūpaṃ* vijñānam / tataś ca nāmākhyāś cittacaittāḥ / *tataś* ca pṛthivyādikaṃ ca *rūpi* dravyam / tataḥ ṣaḍāyatanā-khyam indriyaṣaṭkam / tataḥ sparśākhyaḥ *kāyaḥ* / tato vedanā-dayaḥ / tataś ca punar apy avidyādayo yathoktā ity anādir iyam avidyādikā 'nyonyamūlā cakraparivṛttiḥ / (Rāmānuja).

For the above reason we must say that Śaṅkara's commentary is the most valid. This is also true of his view of the Three Non-created Elements (*ākāśa*, *pratisaṃkhyā-nirodha*, and *apratisaṃkhyā-nirodha*) of Abhidharma Buddhism. Śaṅkara comments as follows :

buddhipūrvakaḥ kila vināśo bhāvānām pratisaṃkhyānirodho nāma bhāṣyate / tadviparīto 'pratisaṃkhyā-nirodhaḥ / āvara-ṇābhāvamātram ākāśam iti /

The above interpretation is a faithful reproduction in Śaṅkara's own words of the Sarvāstivādin theory of the Three Non-created Elements. According to the Abhidharma-kośa-śāstra, *prati-saṃkhyā* means "discrimination" and it refers to an especially pre-eminent wisdom (*prajñāviśeṣa*), that is, undefiled wisdom (*anāsravā prajñā*).[5] According to the Chinese translation, *prati-saṃkhyā* means to "discriminate and master each of the Four Noble Truths." Since the result is "extinction," it is translated as "tse-mieh" in Chinese.[6] (tena prajñā-viśeṣeṇa prāpyo nirodha iti pratisaṃkhyā-nirodhaḥ).[7] Thus, *pratisaṃkhyā* has "freedom from bondage" (*visaṃyoga*) as its essential nature. On the other hand, *apratisaṃkhyā-nirodha* refers to "extinction that is not attained by discriminative knowledge,"[8] that is, an extinction due to lack of conditions which produce origination. As for space (*ākāśa*), the Chinese translation reads, "space has non-obstruction as its nature. Because of non-obstruction, it is found in things (*rūpa*)." ("ākāśam anāvṛtir"......"anāvṛtir" anāvaraṇam......tad anāvaraṇa-svabhāvam ākāśam.)[8] This definition of *ākāśa* is found in Buddhism in general.

Thus, Śaṅkara's explanation corresponds to Buddhist, and especially Sarvāstivādin theory, but Bhāskara interprets it in an entirely different manner.

bhāvahetuko vināśaḥ pratisaṃkhyānirodha ity ucyate / ṣūkṣmaḥ svābhāviko 'nimittako vināśo' pratisaṃkhyānirodhaḥ

This interpretation completely misses the point as an explanation of *pratisaṃkhyā* and *apratisaṃkhyā nirodha*. However, in regard to *ākāśa*, he writes, "*āvaraṇābhāvamātram ākāśa iti*", which is correct, as with Śaṅkara. Rāmānuja, on the other hand, comments as follows on *sūtra* 21 :

mudgarābhighātādyanantarabhāvitayopalabdhiyogyaḥ sadṛśasantānāvasānarūpaḥ sthūlo yaḥ sadṛśasaṃtāne pratikṣaṇabhāvi copalabdhyantaraḥ sūkṣmaś ca yo niranvayo vināśaḥ pratisaṃkhyāpratisaṃkhyā-nirodha-śabdābhyām abhidhīyate tau na sambhavata ity arthaḥ

and he writes on *ākāśa* as follows :

tucchatvena Saugataiḥ pariganitasyākāśasyāpi tucchatā pratikṣipyate / ākāśe ca nirupākhyatā na yuktā /

His explanations differ greatly from those in the Buddhist works. In regard to the Three Non-created Elements, therefore, we must conclude that Śaṅkara's commentary is the most valid, and that Rāmānuja's is most inferior.

For *sūtra* 23 Rāmānuja gives a theory which has nothing to do with Buddhism,[10] and for *sūtras* 26 and 27 Śaṅkara and Bhāskara give very reasonable and appropriate interpretations, but Rāmānuja's commentary falls short.[11]

The same evaluation can be made for their criticism of the *Vijñaptimātratā* theory. Let us turn to *sūtra* 30 for example.

"na bhāvaḥ" vāsanānām upapadyate tvatpakṣe "anupalabdheḥ" bāhyānām arthānām. (Śaṅkara)

vāsanānāṃ "na bhāvo 'nupalabdheḥ" pramāṇābhāvād ity arthaḥ. (Bhāskara)

na kevalasyārthaśūnyasya jñānasya bhāvaḥ sambhavati / kutaḥ / kvacid apy anupalabdheḥ / (Rāmānuja)

Śaṅkara and Bhāskara interpret by supplying "*vāsanā*", a technical term of the Vijñaptimātratā theory, and are true to the ancient transmission of older commentaries, while Rāmānuja seems to have rewritten it, and altered the general sense, although he follows the general meaning of the *sūtra* according to old commentaries.

In comparing the various commentaries on the *Brahmasūtra* sections attacking Buddhism, Śaṅkara's commentary is the most superior whereas Bhāskara's remarks often miss the point, and Rāmānuja's interpretation is even more inferior. We may conclude that Rāmānuja's commentary reflects major tamperings by later thinkers.

The above is our conclusion reached by analyzing one section of the *Brahma-sūtra*, but we can have a similar conclusion for the other sections as well. Although Śaṅkara's commentary is very old and good, it digresses greatly from the original meaning in the treatment of the relationship between *Brahman* and *ātman*, because of the interpolations of his own ideas, However, we believe that as far as the commentary on the words is concerned, taken together with Bhāskara's commentary it is very reliable.[12]

We have studied the interpretations concerning the words of the *sūtra*, but there are also great differences concerning the meaning of the *sūtras*. The principal ones are as follows : 2.2.37 ff., 2.3.19-28, 3.1.13-16, 3.2.1-6, 3.2.11-26, 3.2.27-30, 4. 3. 7-16 etc. When we analyze these *sūtras*, we notice that Bhāskara's commentary is most reliable, and if we follow his interpretation, we can understand the *sūtra* in its original form. The reasons for stating that Bhāskara's interpretation is most valid have been noted for individual cases in the preceding section.

Conclusion

We now conclude our philological investigation of the commentaries from various angles by summarizing our conclusions.

1. There are some differences in the *sūtra* transmitted by Śaṅkara, Bhāskara, and Rāmānuja.
2. Bhāskara's commentary is the closest to the *sūtra* in import, and its interpretation of words is very reliable.
3. Śaṅkara's commentary is also very reliable concerning the interpretation of words, having faithfully inherited the traditional views, but the over-all thought of his work is quite different from the original meaning of the Brahmasūtra.
4. When Bhāskara and Rāmānuja show agreement in the interpretation of individual sūtras and Śaṅkara is different, the latter is usually invalid.
5. Rāmānuja's commentary does not deviate too much from the *sūtra* philosophically, but quite arbitrary interpretations are frequently found in the interpretation of words of the individual sūtras.

Notes

1. On the other hand, Vācaspatimiśra rejects Bhāskara's theory in the *Bhāmatī*, see "Shoki no Vedānta Tetsugaku", Part I, Chapter 2, Topic 2, B, Section 1, pp. 88 ff.
2. There are also instances in which Bhāskara criticizes by quoting from *bhāṣyas* other than Śaṅkara's.
3. Thibaut, Introduction, pp. lxxxvi ff.
4. Ghate, *The Vedānta*, pp. 168-9, 183.
5. *AKV*, p. 16, ll.5-8.

5'. The idea of *devayāna* and *pitṛyāna* was originally relevant to sacrifices. (*Manu*, III, 76).

6. *Kando Kusharon*, (Annotated edition of the Chinese version by Hsuan-tsang of the *Abhidharmakośa*) I, 3-4.
7. *AKV*, p. 16, l. 8.
8. na pratisaṃkhyayā prāpya ity arthaḥ. (*AKV*, p. 17, l. 14).
9. *AKV*, p. 15, ll. 6-11.

The *Abhidharmakośa* (Kārikā I, 5) says :

ākāśam anāvṛtiḥ.

Vasubandhu's own commentary explains :

anāvaraṇasvabhāvam ākāśaṃ yatra rūpasya gatiḥ.

(*Abhidharmakoshabhāṣya of Vasubandhu*, edited by P. Pradhan, Patna : K. P. Jayaswal Research Institute, 1967, p. 3).

Cf. na hy ākāśasyānāvaraṇatvaṃ kadācid apy anyathātvam pratipadyate (*Mvṛ*., p. 271, l. 9); ākāśasyānāvaraṇaṃ lakṣaṇam (*Mvṛ*., p. 129, l.9).

10. See Rāmānuja on 2.2.23.
11. See Rāmānuja on 2.2.26 and 27.
12. According to Ghate (*the Vedānta*, p. 176), Vallabha's commentary shows agreement with Śaṅkara's as far as the wording of the sūtras is concerned, except for special cases.

SECTION 3 VARIOUS TEXTS REFERRED TO IN THE *Sūtra*

We shall now examine the various texts which are referred to in the *sūtra*. Since the wording of the *sūtra* is so brief, it is difficult to tell at first glance what sacred text it is that the sūtra is referring to, and the different commentaries propose various texts. In the considerable number of cases where the three commentaries are agreed on a particular scriptural reference, it is most likely that the author of the *Sūtra* had that one in mind. These cases are listed below :

Scripture Quoted	*Sūtra which contains Quotation*
Ṛg-Veda	II, 1, 36; II, 3, 44 (This, however, may be a quotation from *Chānd. Up.*); III, 1, 13.
Sacred Verses in Atharva-Veda School	II, 3, 43; III, 3, 25.
Kāṭhaka-Saṃhitā	III, 4, 31.
Śat. Br.	I, 2, 5; 26; I, 4, 12; III, 3, 18; 19; 44; 47, 52; 55; IV, 2, 13.
Ait. Ār.	III, 3, 55.
Bṛhad. Up.	I, 1, 30; I, 2, 18-20; I, 3, 10-12; 16; 42-43; I, 4, 11-13; 18; 19-22; II, 1, 22; 26; 30; II, 3, 4; 13; 21; 30; 34; 35;i41; III, 1, 3; 4; 7; III, 2, 1; 22; 39; III, 3, 10, 18; 19; 20; 21; 33; 39; 42; 64; 66; III, 4, 5; 11; 15; 17; 26; 47; 50; IV, 1, 3; 16; IV, 2, 4; 16; IV, 3, 2; 8..
Chānd. Up.	I, 1, 4-9; 20-27; I, 2, 1-4; 7; 8; 13-17; 24-32; I, 3, 8-9; 14-22; 31; 34; 35; 37; (41); 42; I, 4, 10; II, 1, 14; 17; 18; 21; II, 3, 6; 12; 13; 44; II, 4, 20-22; III, 1, 1-11; 17; 18; 21-24; III, 2, 4; 7; 31; 33; III, 3, 7; 9; 10; 18; 22; 24; 26; 39; 55; III, 4, 4; 6; 10; 12; 17; 19; 21; 22; 28; 40; 48; IV, 1, 4; 9; 13; 15; 18; IV, 2, 1-3; 5; 19; IV, 3, 4; 6; 13; 16; IV, 4, 1; 2; 4; 5; 7; 8; 10; 11; 22;
Ait. Up.	II, 4, 14.
Kauṣ. Up.	I, 1, 28-31; I, 4, 16-18; II, 3, 19;; III, 1, 12; III, 3, 10; 26; 27; IV, 3, 2.
Tait. Up.	I, 1, 2; 12-19; I, 4, 15; 26; II, 1 , 17; II, 3, 2-8, 10; 36; III, 3, 11-13; III, 4, 1.
Īśa. Up.	III, 4, 7; 13; 14.
Kāṭhaka Up.	I, 2, 9-12; I, 3, 24; 25; 40; I, 4, 1-7; II, 3, 17; III, 2, 2; III, 3, 14; 15; 34.
Muṇḍ. Up.	I, 1, 6; I, 3, 1-7; I, 4, 27; II, 1, 26; II, 3, 15; 22; II, 4, 9; III, 2, 23; 24; III, 3, 3; 26; 33; 34; III, 4, 8; IV, 1, 13.

Praśna Up.	I, 3, 13; II, 3, 24; III, 2, 31.
Śvet. Up.	I, 1, 11; I, 4, 8-10; II, 1, 26; II, 3; 22; III, 2, 36.
Mahānār. Up.	(= *Tait. Ar.* X) III, 3, 24.
Jābāla School Up. (But not the extant *Jābāla-Up.*)	IV, 1, 3.
Rāṇāyanīya School *khila*	III, 3, 23.
Unknown śruti	IV, 1, 17.
Mahābhārata	II, 1, 1.
Bhag. G.	I, 2, 6; I, 3, 23; II, 3, 45; IV, 1, 10; IV, 2, 21.
Gautama-Dh.S.	III, 1, 8.
Manu.	II, 1, 1; (III, 4, 30).
Dakṣasmṛti	III, 4, 39.
Atri-smṛti	III, 4, 41; 43.
Kūrmapurāṇa	IV, 3, 11.
Mīmāṃsā-sūtra	III, 3, 26; 33; 44; 50; (III, 4, 20); III, III 4, 41; (42).
Saṃkarṣa-kāṇḍa	III, 3, 43.

The numbers in parenthesis indicate probable scriptural references, although the three commentaries are not in agreement.

In the other cases where the three commentaries disagree, we have not speculated on what texts the *Sūtra*-author must have had in mind.

By analyzing the scriptural references on which the three commentaries show complete agreement, we can draw the following conclusions :

1. The *Brahma-sūtra* makes the most reference to the Chāndogya Upaṇiṣad. Accordingly, the conclusion given earlier that the *Brahma-sūtra* was compiled by a certain school which held to the ideas of *Chāndogya Upaniṣad* becomes even more justified.
2. When we study the references to the two huge *Upaniṣads Bṛhadāraṇyaka* and *Chāndogya*, we discover that the *sūtra* makes reference to the former at least 57 times, and to the latter at least 127 times, thus placing a much greater emphasis upon the *Chāndogya Upaniṣad.* However, Śaṅkara's *Brahma-sūtra-bhāṣya* quotes the *Chāndogya* 809 times, while he quotes the Bṛhadāraṇyaka 565 times.[1] When we consider this ratio

with the former ratio, we see how highly Śaṅkara regarded the *Bṛhadāraṇyaka*. (Since the *Brahma-sūtra* itself quotes mainly, the *Chāndogya*, it is only natural that his quotations from it should be greater in number). That he stressed the *Bṛhadāraṇyaka* is further evident from the fact that his commentary on this work is much more detailed in comparison to that on the other, even though the two *Upaniṣads* are of equal length. We can see a difference in attitude between the *sūtra* and Śaṅkara on this matter.

3. The *Brahma-sūtra* discusses the older *Upaniṣads* centered around the *Chāndogya*, and it does not make reference to the new *Upaniṣads*.
4. The practical life of the recluse is based mainly upon the Brahmanical law books (*Dharmasūtras, smṛtis,* etc.). However, it is problematic whether or not the author of the *sūtra* was actually aware of the references which all three commentaries contain.

It may have been the case that an old commentary now lost made reference to a particular passage, which may then have been utilized by all the commentaries.

The *Brahma-sūtra* makes frequent reference to the *Mīmāṃsā-sūtra*, and so we must assume that the author was familiar with the latter, and it is certain that the *Mīmāṃsā-sūtra* was in existence prior to the *Brahma-sūtra* in its present form.

Notes

1. Deussen, *SV*. S.32.

CHAPTER XII

THOUGHT

In the previous chapter, "Analysis of *Brahma-sūtra*", using the aforementioned philological method, we tried to elucidate as much as possible what could be regarded as the primary meaning of the sūtra. Based on the results of that study, we shall next explain the thought of the *Brahma-sūtra*. We propose to restate in clear form what the *Sūtra*-author sought to express, and the fundamental assumptions on which he did so. Therefore, leaving aside the various commentators, Śaṅkara and others, we intend to confine ourselves to those elements that we can conclude to have been the thought of the original author.

The *Brahma-sūtra* itself is a work that aims at a systematic interpretation of the words of the Upaniṣadic scriptures, and the greater part of the work refers to individual passages of the *Upaniṣads*. However, the question of how the *Brahma-sūtra* interprets a particular section or phrase in the *Upaniṣads* is not our present concern; what concerns us is rather the philosophic thought which is postulated in support of the scriptural interpretations. With respect to the meaning of different words or the purport of various sections of the *Upaniṣads*, the *sūtra* makes its own peculiar judgements and gives at times strained and distorted interpretations. That this was done reveals the fact that the author of the *Sūtra* had, as a commentator himself, ideas and a philosophic viewpoint of his own. Especially in regard to philosophically vital problems, such as the relation between the Highest Self and the individual self, or the meaning of liberation, he notes the diverse contentions of the various thinkers and adopts one of them as the established view (*siddhānta*).

Thus the author of the *Sūtra* had a distinctive viewpoint in regard to the differing views existing within the Vedānta schools up to that time. Accordingly, we shall comprehend and state as clearly as possible the philosophic thought that the author of the Sūtra either explicitly expressed or implicitly accepted in relation to the various problems.

SECTION 1 THE HISTORICO-SOCIAL ATTITUDE OF THE *Brahma-Sūtra*

According to Vedānta philosophy, one should regard the knowledge of *Brahman* and the attainment of liberation as the supreme goal of human life. However, according to the *Brahma-sūtra* the cognition concerning *Brahman* was not something that could be conceded to all men. Only members belonging to the three classes of the upper strata of Indian society (that is, the *Brāhmaṇa, Kṣatriya,* and *Vaiśya*) have the right to participate in that teaching, and the *Śūdra,* which is the lowest class, was barred from it (1.3.34-39). Here, the traditional attitude of the established orthodox Brahmin reveals itself in naked clarity. From ancient times it had been taught in the Vedic scriptures that "the *Śūdra* is not qualified to perform rituals",[1] and later the various law books that the *Brahmaṇas* had compiled consistently allow the privilege of hearing, studying, and understanding the Vedic scriptures and the performance of prescribed rituals only to the three classes of the upper strata, and the *Śūdra* was barred from them. The author of the *Sūtra* reasoned that since the Vedic scriptures are kept away from the *śūdra* in this manner, the understanding of the truth which is grounded on the *Upaniṣads* was not possible for the *Śūdra.* Such prescriptions correspond to the sentence in the *Mīmāṃsā-sūtra* (6.1.25-28) that rules, "the performance of rituals is allowed to the three classes of the upper strata only."

Now, with respect to rituals as a social act, it is possible to deny the participation of the lowest class by means of authority, but regarding the knowledge of the Absolute which is a matter of individual, personal awareness, no authority could possibly suppress it. Śaṅkara of a later period also strongly emphasizes the fact that it is impossible to prescribe the knowledge of truth by means of prohibitory rules.[2] For example, even in the Upaniṣadic scriptures, there is the story of Jānaśruti, who, though he himself was not a *Śūdra.* was hailed and scorned with "Oh, *Śūdra* !" and yet attained knowledge of the Absolute. There is also the story of Jābāla, the illegitimate offspring of a lowly servant girl, who was granted initiation because of his scriptural learning. Now, the *Brahma-sūtra* lacked explanations for such cases that existed in the scriptures in order to prove that these people were not members of the lower class, it offered extremely forced and strained interpretations.

In any case, we are able to recognize the distinctive social character of the early Vedānta school that compiled the *Brahma-sūtra* in the fact that they reserved the knowledge of *Brahman* to only the three classes of the upper strata. This trait was transmitted to later periods by the various schools within Vedānta which lacked the sectarian nuance of Hinduism, particularly by the Advaita school of Śaṅkara, but this also came to be severely criticized by the followers of Hinduism. Not a few sages of Hinduism originally came from the lower class and they mostly affirmed that no matter how low the person, were he to worship the Highest God with loving devotion he could be saved without fail through the divine grace of the Highest God. In this respect, the early Vedānta school that compiled the *Brahma-sūtra* stands in clear contrast to some sects of Hinduism.

In this way, the *Brahma-sūtra* restricts those who have the right to participate in the teaching to the three classes of the upper strata. However, even among the qualified, its principal concern was especially with the people of a limited, wealthy upper strata. The *Brahma-sūtra* held that in order to attain knowledge of *Brahman*, rituals were the effective means and urged the performance of rituals.[3] However, it was not an easy matter for the ordinary Indian people of that time to faithfully practice the various rituals prescribed in the scriptures. Aside from the household rituals that were normally practiced in the home, the large scale rituals that were performed by engaging various priests which required considerable time and vast expenses. Thus, even assuming that they were allowed to the three classes of the upper strata, the common mass of people who were pressed by the demands of daily living could not possibly perform these rituals.

There were many others who also never performed the rituals at this time. Could they ever attain knowledge of *Brahman* ? This became a problem, and the *Brahma-sūtra* conceded that even those who do not perform rituals have the qualification to gain knowledge (3.4.36-37). Knowledge will be granted to them, if they perform various kinds of *dharma* (3.4.38). However, the performance of rituals was encouraged, if at all possible (3.4.39). We may conclude, therefore, that the author of the *Sūtra* belonged to the privileged class that could observe the rituals and the stages of life (*āśrama*) prescribed in the Brahmanical law books, and, furthermore, that people in such a status were the objects of the teachings of this *sūtra*. The *Brahmasūtra* in general presupposes the knowledge of rituals and *Karmamīmāṃsā* as normal.[4] Thus, those who do not perform rituals are discussed only secondarily. In short, the *Brahma-sūtra* was compiled by a school which had its basis in a limited, upper strata of Indian society.

The *Brahma-Sūtra* is also a product of pure scholarship and had significance for only an extremely limited group of intellectuals. Such a difficult and pedantic theological work could never catch the imagination and heart of the masses of the people, This work criticizes divergent ideas prevalent at the time, but the criticisms were directed exclusively to academic matters. The attack on Buddhism is a disputation against the philosophical theories of the Sarvāstivādins, Sautrāntikas, Mādhyamikas, and Vijñānavādins, and there is no mention at all of the common folk beliefs and customs of Buddhism. The criticisms against Jainism, Bhāgavata sect, and Pāśupata are directed to their metaphysical theories, and nothing is said of their forms of worship or actual life.

Now, there were many schools which were absorbed in philosophical speculation during that time, but it was the Sāṃkhya school to which the *Brahma-sūtra* directed its major criticism. We can understand Part One of the *Brahma-sūtra* to be mostly criticism of the Sāṃkhya interpretation of Upaniṣadic passages. Part Two, Chapter 1, is mainly devoted to refutations of Sāṃkhya arguments, and Part Two, Chapter 2, 1-10, criticizes Sāṃkhya philosophy by listing its errors. There are also many references to Sāṃkhya theories and rejection of its scriptural interpretations throughout the *sūtra*[5]. Thus, a great portion of the *Brahma-sūtra* is devoted to the criticism of Sāṃkhya, and it is possible to say that it was through this criticism that the Vedānta school established itself as an independent philosophical tradition.

Before the compilation of the *Brahma-sūtra*, the *Sāṃkhya* system was the greatest philosophical school in the Brahmanic tradition. We can trace its scholastic tradition to the ancient past, and it had a marked influence upon the theologies of common faiths. That its existence as a philosophical school was recognized from a relatively early period is evident from the notation in the *Artha-śāstra* of Kauṭilya.[6]

The Sāṃkhya system had an intimate connection with Vedānta school from ancient times. The seeds of the theory of three qualities (*triguṇa*) of Sāṃkhya are found in the older *Upaniṣads* of initial period (*Chānd. Up.* VI). And Sāṃkhya ideas and expressions are clearly evident in the older *Upaniṣads* of the middle and later periods. In the great epic, *Mahābhārata*, and the Codes of Manu, Sāṃkhya philosophy, having the characteristics of Vedānta ideas, is taught. Whether the ideas of the Sāṃkhya which had existed as an independent school from an earlier period influenced these works, or whether the Vedāntic Sāṃkhya ideas established the classical Sāṃkhya philosophy after undergoing critical reflection is a problem that has yet to be solved by scholars. At any rate, the Sāṃkhya system maintained intimate relationships with the Vedānta schools, and they claimed orthodox Brahmanic authority to rival the Vedāntic claims. Thus, the Sāṃkhya system regarded the *Upaniṣads* as their scriptures, and they proclaimed that they were the orthodox inheritors of Upanisadic thought.[7] They claimed that although many things and principles were taught in the *Upaniṣads*, they were nothing else than the principle of *puruṣa* and the fundamental material (*pradhāna*) or their variations taught in the Sāṃkhya system.

The early Vedānta school had to wipe out such Sāṃkhya interpretations and clarify the essential message of the *Upaniṣads*. The *Brahma-sūtra* recognizes that the Sāṃkhya system and its sister school, the Yoga, are based upon *smṛti* (*smārta*, 4.2.21), but that the *sūtra* is based upon *śruti* which is the absolute standard for Brahmanic knowledge and conduct. And they assert that if the Sāṃkhya teaches anything contradictory to *śruti*, it is to be rejected. (2.1.1). For example, the concept of *pradhāna* which is posited as the fundamental material cause of world emanation and taught by the Sāṃkhya system is assumed in *smṛti* (*smārta*, 1.2.19), but it is not found in the scriptures (*aśabda*, 1.1.5) and only inferred (*anumāna*, 1.3.3, and *ānumānika*, 1.4.1) by man through his thinking faculty.

The author of the *Brahma-sūtra* attempted to expel all traces of Sāṃkhya influence from the *Upaniṣads* in a complete and thoroughgoing manner. For example, the masculine form of "unborn" (*aja*) and the feminine form of "unborn" (*ajā*) taught in the *Śvetāśvatara Upaniṣad* IV, 5, are very close to the concepts of Sāṃkhya *puruṣa* and *prakṛti*, when they are seen from an unprejudiced point of view, but the author of the *Sūtra* attempts to efface all such traces of Sāṃkhya interpretation (1.4.8). Consequently, the *Brahma-sūtra* is also guilty of not being true to the scriptures, for its interpretation is based upon a particular philosophical orientation.

Since the primary task of the *Brahma-sūtra* was to expel Sāṃkhya ideas, thus upholding the purity of the *Upaniṣads* and forming an independent philosophical school, its criticism of the other schools are relatively simple. It asserts that the criticism against the Sāṃkhya system can also be applied to the Yoga system (2.1.3), and the Vaiśeṣika system is also criticized,[8] but it states that the Vaiśeṣika is not embraced by people of culture and learning[9] (Besides these, Buddhism (2.2.18-32), Jainism (2.2.33-36), Pāśupata (2.2.37-41), Bhāgavata sect (2.2.42-45), and Lokāyata (3.3.53-54) are also criticized. These were the primary opponents of the early Vedānta school.

The author of the *Sūtra* rejected these heterodox views and attempted to clarify the true spirit of the *Upaniṣads*, always remaining true to the classical ideals of orthodox Brahmanism. He also had to maintain and protect the essential purity of the teachings. Thus, he was very cautious of the possibility of the teaching leaking out[10] to people who lacked the qualifications to receive them or to students of heterodox views, and, therefore, the wordings of the *sūtra* were made as brief as possible, and he stipulated that the teaching be transmitted only from master to disciple, so that access to outsiders would be prevented. There already existed the strict rule[11] that the Upaniṣadic teachings were not to be transmitted to people other than one's eldest son or disciples, and the *Brahma-sūtra* inherited this esoteric character. Such an attitude is extremely narrow even within the orthodox Brahmanic tradition, but here we can see the unique social attitude of the early Vedānta school.

Such a conservative and esoteric character could not be maintained forever. Heterodox interpretations arose for the very reason that the author of the *Sūtra* feared outside intervention and kept the teaching hidden and closed. The result was that the very ideas which the author of the *Sūtra* eliminated came to eventually occupy the *Brahma-sūtra*. How this occurred will be discussed in Part Five.[12]

Notes

1. *Taittirīya-Saṃhitā* VII, 1, 1, 6.
2. Śaṅkara ad *BS.* III, 2. 21 (Vol. II, p. 220, 11.8-10). See also Part Five, Chapter 9, Section 2.
3. 3.4.32-35.
4. See next section.
5. 1.15-11, 1.118, 1.2.19, 1.2.22, 1,3.3, 1.3.11, 1.4.1-13, 1.4.28, 2.3.51, 4.2.21.
6. Section 1, Vidyāsamuddeśa. See Part II, Chapter 3, Section 4.
7. See the various phrases in *Brahma-Sūtra* and *SDS.*, *Sāṅkhya-darśana.*
8. 2.2.11-17.
9. 2.1.12. See also 2.2.17. 2.3.51-53 may also include Vaiśeṣika theories in its criticism.
10. According to the report of Megasthenes, the Brahmin did not relate philosophical knowledge even to his wife, because of such precaution. (Fragment 41, McCrindle : *Ancient India,* p. 100).
11. See Part I, Chapter 3, Section 2.
12. Vol., III of this work.

SECTION 2 PROBLEM OF KNOWLEDGE

There is no need to mention that the *Brahma-sūtra*, compiled by reactionary scholars of the orthodox Brahmanic lineage, regarded the *Upaniṣads* as absolute authority. The *sūtra* advocated the superiority of the scriptures against the limited powers of human thinking. Philosophical speculation and reason (*tarka*), based upon the human capacity for thinking, have no positive basis (*apratiṣṭhāna*), and inference (*anumāna*) is not applicable to metaphysical problems concerning the absolute (2.1.11). This is clearly a criticism against the Sāṃkhya, Vaiśeṣika, and other systems which conducted philosophical activity independently of the Vedas.

According to the *sūtra*, the theories of the Vedānta school are based upon the scriptures (*śabdamūla*, 2.1.27). As far as the knowledge of the absolute *Brahman* or any metaphysical problem is concerned, the Vedic scriptures (*śāstra*) is the source (*yoni*) or basis (1.1.3.). It is only through the scriptures that the knowledge of *Brahman* is possible, for human theories are inapplicable to *Brahman*. Therefore, throughout the *Brahma-sūtra* the basic reason for any assertion is that "it is taught in the scriptures."

This attitude is a chief characteristic of the *Brahma-sūtra*. In 2.1.26, for example, the opponent argues that the emanation and manifestation of the world by *Brahman* cannot be logically established, as follows : (1) If the whole of *Brahman* emanates, it becomes transformed into another, and this means that *Brahman* itself becomes non-existent after world emanation; therefore, *Brahman* cannot be the absolute. (2) On the other hand, only if one part emanates, this contradicts the fundamental proposition of Vedānta philosophy that *Brahman* is not made up of parts. The author of the *sūtra* does not attempt any rebuttal; in fact, he confirms the existence of such a theoretical difficulty in his own viewpoint, and he states that since the student of Vedānta must believe in the scriptures, its view must be accepted, even if there is such a difficulty (2.1.27). The scriptures even had the power to make people abandon philosophical thought.

Such an attitude is not that of a philosopher but of a theologian. Even the idea that one believes because it is irrational is not found in the Brahma-sūtra, for one must believe without any reason. They probably recognized the fact that metaphysical problems could not be clarified by formal logic, and this attitude is prominent in all the schools of Vedānta.

The scriptures on which the *Brahma-sūtra* relied were the *śruti* and *smṛti*. The former are the Vedas, and the latter are the authoritative texts, besides the Vedas, transmitted from ancient times. The former were considered sacrosanct, and the latter had authority secondary and auxiliary to the former.

According to the *Brahma-sūtra*, the Vedic scriptures are permanent (*nitya*);[1] it is an eternal truth which exists by itself, independent of human creation and activity. While the natural world becomes extinct in *Brahman* and then arises from it by undergoing incomprehensibly vast cycles of time, the Vedic scriptures exist eternally beyond any temporal changes of the universe. The Brahmins of the period regarded the Vedic scriptures as esoteric and they memorized it constantly, never putting them down in writing; so it was only natural that they regarded them as transcendental truth which becomes manifest with each recitation. The Vedic scriptures and its scholastic tradition endured through 3,000 years of the history of India which is characterized by the rise and fall of empires at the expense of foreign invaders and the flowering and withering of many brilliant civilizations. The nucleus of Indian culture can be seen in the uninterrupted transmission of Vedic scriptures. "Secular culture is filled with change and vicissitudes, but Vedic culture is permanent and eternal"—this has been the unshakable conviction of the orthodox Brahmin scholar. The eternal nature of the Vedas was not a matter of logic but of faith for such scholars, and therefore the later Mīmāṃsā school, Vedānta school, grammarians, etc., all proposed their philosophical views to theoretically justify this faith.

For this reason, the "words" of the Vedic scriptures were not mere language or sound but the fundamental models for words. And the Vedic scriptures themselves were believed to be the essence of words manifested in the language of man's experienced world; therefore, when the expression "words" (*śabda*) was used in the *sūtra*, it meant the Vedas (1.3.28). Such a view of the Vedas was held in common with the Karma-mīmāṃsā school. (Other names used by the *Brahma-sūtra* in referring to the Vedic scriptures include *ämanana,*[2] *āmnāna,*[3] *upaniṣad,*[4] *darśana*[5], *nigada,*[6] *mantravarṇa,*[7] and *śāstra.*[8] That they refer specifically to Upaniṣadic passages has been mentioned before).

Although there is no specific mention of what constitutes *smṛti*, it was believed to be the writings of ancient sages handed down through the generations, according to the thinking of Indian peoples in general. The *smṛti-s* which are especially referred to include the *Mahābhārata* (particularly, the *Bhagavad Gītā*), the various Brahmanic law books (*Dharma Sūtra*, Codes of Manu, and other *smṛti-s*), and the various *Purāṇas.*[9]

A fact which is noteworthy is that the *Brahma-sūtra* calls the Vedic scriptures direct perception (*pratyakṣa*) and the *smṛti* inference (*anumāna*).[10] In some cases the Vedas are called holy words (*śabda*) in contrast to the inferences or *smṛti.*[11] The reason for this is not clear, but it may be due to the following reason : *śruti* is the direct source of metaphysical knowledge which does not permit room for doubt, whereas *smṛti* is subservient to it; therefore, the relationship is similar to the cognition in daily experience in which direct perception of an object first appears and then is followed by inference. In human cognition errors are not found in perception, but they may exist in inference; likewise, the Vedic scriptures contain no errors but *smṛti-s* may have some. The Karma-mīmāṃsā school described the writings of the Vedas as direct perception.[12]

Śruti and *smṛti* are frequently cited together,[13] but the latter is man-made and contains the possibility of error; therefore, it is utilized when it shows agreement with *śruti* but abandoned when it disagrees with *śruti*.

In this way the *Brahma-Sūtra* regarded the Vedas as *śruti* as absolute authority, but such a view has significance only among the people who held Vedic scriptures to be sacrosanct and it had no meaning for those who doubted the authority of the Vedas. In order to convince the people who did not fully recognize the Vedas of the validity of the metaphysics of *Brahman*, the early Vedānta scholars had to abandon the scriptures and rely solely upon logical argument. Consequently, in spite of the fact that the *Brahma-sūtra* stressed the absoluteness of the scriptures, it also recognized that reasoning (*yukti*), together with the scriptures (*śabda*), could be the basis of true knowledge (2.1.18). The demonstration by reasoning is considered to be just as important as scriptural authority.[14] According to Buddhist terminology, the significance of both scriptural testimony and reasoning were fully recognized. However, among the two the authority of Vedic scriptures was considered to be superior, and this stands in contradiction to the Sāṃkhya, Vaiśeṣika, and other systems which regarded theoretical proofs as fundamental and the scriptures as secondary. The historical background of Vedānta philosophy which basically began as hermeneutics and later developed into philosophical thought has determined the nature of knowledge.

When we consider this standpoint of the Vedānta school which regarded the *Upaniṣads* as primary and logical thought as secondary, we can understand the historical situation that led to the writing of diverse commentaries, often conflicting with each other, on the *Brahma-sūtra* which continued to be regarded as absolute authority.

The philosophical systems of the orthodox Brahmanic tradition possess their respective fundamental *sūtra*, and they also transmit standard commentaries (*bhāṣya*) upon them. Vātsyāyana wrote a commentary on the *Nyāya-sūtra*, Vyāsa on the *Yoga-sūtra*, and Śabarasvāmin on the *Mīmāṃsā-sūtra*, and they were regarded as having absolute authority by posterity in their respective traditions. There is no authoritative commentary on the *Vaiśeṣika-sūtra*, but the *Padārthadharmasaṃgraha* by Praśastapāda, written as an outline of its ideas, has been regarded highly by later ages. The students who belonged to these systems of philosophy almost never denied the authority of these commentaries or expositions. Although these systems were split into subdivisions and although many commentaries and subcommentaries were written, their differences were very minor and concerned only negligible and unimportant matters. The situation differs slightly in the case of the Sāṃkhya system, because its sūtra was probably composed in later ages, but the *Sāṃkhya-Kārikā* by Īśvarakṛṣṇa would occupy a position similar to the *sūtras* in other systems. The contents of the commentaries on this work also differs only slightly, and the situation is identical with the other systems as far as this fact is concerned. Now, when there are only minor variations among the commentaries and only minimal differences among the subschools of other systems, why is it that only the Vedānta school was divided into various subschools whose fundamental philosophical standpoints are completely different. We can find the answer in the scholastic attitudes of the Vedānta schools.

In the case of the other systems of thought the systematization and interpretation of thought were the central concern, and the philosophical standpoint was clear from the initial inception of the school. Each of the schools developed the implications of their philosophical standpoint, and the variations in view among the followers were very small. The scriptures of the *Upaniṣads* were quoted only as corroborative citations. In the case of the Vedānta school, however, the situation was entirely different. All the students of this school were united in their respect for the *Upaniṣads* whose authority was fully recognized socially and historically and in this sense they had a common standpoint, but since they were not united in thought, they had very little in common in philosophical ideas. Since the ideas in the *Upaniṣads* were diverse and many-sided in implication, the philosophical thought of the Vedānta subschools differed as their emphasis on a particular idea differed. Even in the case of a famous statement in the *Upaniṣads*, since there was ample room to interpolate various philosophical interpretations, various tendencies in thought arose in spite of the fact that they were all based upon the *Upaniṣads*.

Thus, the later Vedānta scholars injected their own peculiar interpretations into the *Upaniṣads*. Since a common philosophical tendency existed among the diverse ideas in the *Upaniṣads*, a common element could be recognized in the Vedānta philosophy which developed from them, but this was true only in the case of certain fundamental creeds and great differences existed among the subschools as far as the majority of problems were concerned. The situation in the Vedānta school was directly opposite to that of the other systems, because the philosophical systems were established after the authority of the *Upaniṣads* was secured. Following the formation of the respective philosophical systems within the Vedānta, strained interpretations of Upaniṣadic statements were made to fit the particular system. This was the reason that many and varied commentaries were written on the *Brahma-sūtra*, and the brevity of the phrases was a mere accidental cause which might have accounted for the diverse commentaries. If the cause were only the brevity of sentences in the *Brahma-sūtra*, such significant differences in fundamental interpretations would not have arisen, although variations in expression might have occurred.

Now, since the discussion in the *Brahma-sūtra* is advanced, based upon such an attitude to knowledge, two attitudes result : one is the attitude of the hermeneutic scholar, and the other is that of the apologist who defends the school's standpoint and criticizes the opponent's arguments.

The hermeneutic scholar considers the meaning of certain sections of the *Upaniṣads*, or of the complete scripture. This has been discussed previously. Now, many kinds of contradictory views are found in the *Upaniṣads*, and some are not acceptable to the author of the *sūtra*, but whenever a passage from the scriptures cannot be accepted as it is, it is understood as a parable (the secondary meaning, *gauṇa*).[16] For example, when a wild man is described, "He is a lion," this does not mean that the man is actually a 'lion but that the description is to be understood as a parable (the secondary meaning). When contradictions are found in the various ideas of the *Upaniṣads*, the contradictions are harmonized and attempts are made to justify the meaning of all ideas. Since the Vedānta school from its original inception appeared with the explicit purpose of harmonizing the contradictory views in the *Upaniṣads*, it is not strange that such a synthetic and compromising attitude is found.

The attitude of recognizing the significance of each of the mutually opposing views is shown not only in regard to the theories within the *Upaniṣads* but also in regard to the diverse views which existed prior to the *Brahma-sūtra*. In 3.3.13 and 14 two interpretations concerning a scriptural phrase are given and both are approved as valid. In 3.4.43 also two views regarding the problem of conduct are given, and both are fully recognized. Thus, the author of the *Sūtra* reveals a very eclectic attitude. From this fact we can infer the complex history of this school prior to the *Brahma-sūtra*, and at the same time know that it inherits the philosophical standpoint of Bādarāyaṇa.[17]

Such a hermeneutical approach corresponds to the approach of the *Mīmāṃsā-sūtra* to the *Brāhmaṇas*. The two Mīmāṃsā schools (Karma-mīmāṃsā and Vedānta) have a sister relationship, and the author of the *Brahma-sūtra* was well versed in the Karma-mīmāṃsā learning.[18] The *Brahma-sūtra* does not only mention the *Mīmāṃsā-sūtra* but utilizes the principle[19] of the Karma-mīmāṃsā. Many Mīmāṃsā terminologies[20] are also frequently used, and many parables[21] concerning rituals are quoted.

We shall next turn our attention to the apologetic aspect of the *Brahma-sūtra*. Since each *sūtra* of the *Brahma-sūtra* is expounded against those who hold opposing views, the whole *sūtra* may be regarded as a record of apologetics or disputations. However, the majority are concerned with conflicting views on the scriptures and are not purely philosophical problems. Part II, Chapters 1 and 2, which criticizes the views of other schools, should be considered as purely philosophical disputation. In studying these sections the first thing to be noticed is the frequent use of the method of *prasaṅga* (the terms *prasaṅga* or *prasakti* is used seven times.)[22] This method is to temporarily affirm the opponent's criticism, then to draw a conclusion not desired by the opponent, and thus to point out the error in the opponent's thesis. This was originally used by Nāgārjuna and Āryadeva of Mādhyamika Buddhism, and it is thought that the *Brahma-sūtra* was influenced by them. What is of special interest is that the arguments made by the *Brahma-sūtra* in criticizing the

Sarvāstivādin is identical in content with the arguments developed by Nāgārjuna in criticizing the theory of cause and effect of the Sarvāstivādin.

Sūtra 2.2.20

"Again, (although the Buddhists recognize the causal relation between each cycle of the Twelve Cycles of Causation, it cannot be established). Because when the subsequent (moment) arises, the preceding (moment) ceases to be (since they maintain that everything has a momentary existence only)."

Madhyamaka-Kārikā, XX

15. "If the association (of cause) is non-existent, how can the cause produce an effect ?"
10. "How can (the cause) already extinct and vanished produce an effect which already exists ?"

Sūtra 2.2.21

"If it be asserted that 'even if there is no (cause), (the effect) is produced', this contradicts the assertion (of the Buddhists who recognize the four *pratyaya*). If it were not so, (and if it be asserted that 'when cause exists, the effect is produced' cause and effect) would be simultaneous (and this would contradict the theory of instantaneous extinction taught by the Buddhists)."

Madhyamaka-Kārikā XX

6. "If the cause is destroyed without giving the cause to (the production) of the effect, that effect which is born when the cause has been destroyed is causeless."
7. "If again the effect appears in associtaion with (various causes), it would follow that both that which produces and that which is produced are simultaneous."

Such a method of *prasaṅga* argument can be seen in other sections of the *Brahma-sūtra*, but the *Brahma-sūtra* is more intent on destroying the opponent's assertion and lacks the intent to constructively and logically advance its own philosophical theory. For example, when the opponent criticizes the Vedānta philosophy, the *Brahma-sūtra* answers simply, "That criticism should also be turned against your own theory,"[23] but does not state that it is wrong to criticize the Vedānta philosophy. Perhaps they recognized logic only as an instrument to refute the opponent. Sometimes the *hetu-vidyā* logic is employed,[24] and at other times *pariśeṣa* (3.2.10) is used, but there are times when errors in logical judgment are committed.[25] Logic in itself was not an important problem for the *sūtra*, because *Brahman* could never be grasped by inference or by logic but only by faith in the teachings of the scriptures.

Since pure, theoretical demonstration of philosophical problems were held to be only of secondary importance, whenever philosophical problems were confronted the author of the *Sūtra* relied exclusively on parables, rather than on theoretical discussion, to assert that his ideas were in accord with truth. Among the 555 *sūtras* in the *Brahma-sūtra*, 85 parables are quoted, and 76 of them are found in Parts II and III in which philosophical discussion occurs.[26] It is clear from this that parables played an important role in the formation of the philosophy of the *Brahma-sūtra*.

Notes

1. 1.3.29, 30.
2. 2.4.14, 3.3.34, 4.4.11, see also 1.2.32.
3. 1.4.25, 3.3.24.
4. 1.2.16.
5. 1.1.25, 1.2.11, 1.3.27, 30, 40, 2.1.24, 30, 2.2.15, 2.3.30, 3.1.13, 20, 3.2.21, 3.3.48, 66, 3.4.3, 8, 9, 28, 51, 4.1.16, 4.2.1, 4.3.16.
6. 1.1.25.
7. 2.3.44.
8. See my "Explanatory Note" to BS.I, 1, 3.
9. See Part IV, Chapter 2, Appendix, Section 3.
10. 1.3.28, 3.2.24, 4.4.20.
11. 3.3.31.
12. SDS. XII, 1.12.
13. 1.3.30, 3.1.8. There are many other examples in which *śruti*, *smṛti* are juxtaposed in two *sūtras*.
14. 2.1.36 and 3.2.38-40.
15. Ghate : *The Vedānta*, p. 39.
16. 1.1.6, 2.3.3, and 2.4.2.
17. See Part III, Chapter 2, Section 2.
18. See Appendix to above chapter, Section 3.
19. 3.3.44 and 49.
20. *anvaya* 1.4.9, 3.3.16, and 3.4.50.
    apūrva 3.3.18, and 3.4.12.
    abhyāsa 1.1.12, 2.2.6, and 3.2.25.
    arthavāda 3.4.2.

upasaṃhāra 2.1.24, 2.4.48, and 3.3.5.
codanā 3.3.1 and 3.4.18.
prakaraṇa 1.2.10, 1.3.6, 1.4.5, 3.3.7 and 45, 4.4.3 and 17.
liṅga 1.1.22 and 31, 1.3.15 and 35, 1.4.17 and 20, 2.3.13 and 15, 3.2.11 and 26, 3.3.44, 3.4.34 and 39, 4.1.2, 4.3.4, and 4.4.21.
vidhiśeṣa 3.3.5.

21. *dvādaśāhavat* (4.4.12), *dhāraṇavat* (3.4.20), *kratuvat* (3.3.57), *pradānavat* (3.3.43), *aupasadavat* (3.3.33), *kuśāchandastutyupagānavat* (3.3.26).
22. 2.1.1, 8, 11, 12, and 26. 2.3.32. (For the method of argument of *Brahma-sūtra*, see also Belvalkar : *Lectures*, pp. 154-156).
23. 2.1.10 and 29.
24. E.g., 3.3.7.
25. 2.3.7.
26. For each citation, see S. K. Belvalkar : "Dṛṣṭāntas in the Brahmasūtras," *Harvard Journal of Asiatic Studies*, Vol. I, 1936, pp. 28-32.

SECTION 3 THE ABSOLUTE AND WORLD-CREATION

1. *Brahman in Itself*

In the *Upaniṣads* and by early Vedāntins before the compilation of the *Brahma-sūtra*, various principles were put forward as the absolute, but the *Sūtras* define the absolute as *Brahman*, and declare emphatically at the beginning of the *Sūtras* that it is the study of *Brahman* which is being begun (I.1.1). The *Sūtras* say that although the explanatory passages of the scriptures differ among themselves, they are united in aiming to teach *Brahman* (I.1.4). Here we clearly observe an intention of unifying and synthesizing all the teachings of the *Upaniṣads*.

Brahman was already by them identified with *Ātman*, and this identification was presupposed by the *Brahma-sūtras* as self-evident or universally accepted.[1] *Brahman* as the world-cause is occasionally called Ātman (I.1.6; II.3. 15) which is the same as what is called Inner Self (*adhyātman*, I.1.29) or the Intelligent Self (*prājña*, I.4.5; II.3.29). What is meant by *Ātman* here is not the individual self (*jīva*) as the centre of each individual, but the highest Self (*paramātman*) as the world principle. It was considered to be the central principle which is immanent in and controls all beings. In the *Brahma-sūtras* the absolute is seldom denoted by the term *brahman*, but rather by *paraḥ*, 'the highest one' in the masculine gender.[2] We must take it that evidently the highest Self (*paramātman*) or the supreme Lord (*parameśvara*) is meant thereby. It seems that in the *Brahma-sūtras* these three terms denote the same principle. No trace is noticeable of a difinition between *parameśvara* and *brahman* such as was made by Śaṅkara. It is to be noted carefully that the absolute was always understood as a personal existence.

Brahman as the supreme self is regarded as an intelligent or spiritual substance, different in character from the non-intelligent, material world (II, 1, 4). It is presupposed in various passages that *Brahman* is a spiritual principle which can be called pure intelligence (I, 1, 5; I, 1, 9; I, 1, 10; III, 2, 16). *Brahman* is pure being as well as pure intelligence. It can be called simply 'being' (*sat*, II, 3, 9). Therefore *Brahman* is the unity of being and intelligence as the absolute.

Nearly all the characters which can be supposed of the absolute are ascribed to this *Brahman*. *Brahman* has unlimited extension (*āyāma*) in terms of space; it is omnipresent (*sarvagata*, III, 2, 37). Its endless (*ananta*, III, 2, 26), and is called 'plenitude' (*bhūman*, I, 3, 8). It is without parts (*niravayava*, II, 1, 26), and without form (*arūpavad*, III, 2, 13). It is eternal, and is called imperishable (*akṣara*, I, 3, 10; III, 3, 33). *Brahman* in itself is undifferentiated (III, 2, 11). There occurs no increase or diminution of its qualities (III, 3, 12). It is difficult to describe it positively in terms of words; it can be expressed only negatively (III, 2, 12)

On the other hand, *Brahman* is at the same time the world-cause, and it is said that all the attributes (*sarvadharma*) of the world-cause can be applied to *Brahman* (II, 1, 37). The characteristics "truth, knowledge and endlessness," set forth in the *Taittirīya-Upaniṣad*, II, 1 can be applied only to *Brahman* (I, 1, 15). Following some other Upaniṣadic passages it is called 'light' (*jyotis*, I, 1, 24; I, 3, 40), and is compared to illumination of a (*prakāśa*, III, 2, 15, 25). The essence of *Brahman* is bliss (*ānanda*, III, 3, 11; 13); it is the cause of joy in individual existence (I, 1, 14). The scriptural passage in which *Brahman* is defined as nothing but 'happiness' (*sukha*) is to the same purport (I, 2, 15); 'the *Brahman* which consists of bliss' set forth in the *Taittirīya-upaniṣad* must be regarded as denoting *Brahman* (I.1, 12-19). The various qualities (*guṇa*) set forth in the teaching of Śāṇḍilya (*Chānd. Up.* III.14), such as having true desires (i.e. his desires are always fulfilled, *satya-saṃkalpatva*), are possible only in *Brahman* (I.2.2). Accordingly it becomes clear that the composer of the *Sūtras*, in contrast to Śaṅkara, thought that *Brahman* possesses pre-eminent qualities. However these qualities, which transcend our limited capacity of thinking and are possible only in the absolute, must have been regarded as not inconsistent with the above-mentioned negative expressions about *Brahman*, nor with the fact that *Brahman* itself is without any distinctions.

In this sort of way, positive descriptions of *Brahman*-in-itself are set forth, and *Brahman* is considered to be the subject or basis (*pradhāna*) of these essential characteristics (III.3.11). The technical definition of the true nature of *Brahman* as 'being, intelligence and bliss' (*sac-cid-ānanda*), stressed by later Advaitins, was not yet established, but the concept is already discernible in the *Brahma-sūtras*.

Notes

1. 1.1.12, 2.1.27-28.
2. 2.3.41 and 46, 3.2.5, 11, and 31, 3.3.52, 4.2.15, 4.3.10 and 12.

2. *Brahman as the World-Cause*

At the beginning of the *Brahma-sūtras* it is clearly declared that *Brahman* is that from which the origin, subsistence and dissolution of this world proceed (I, 1, 2). All the world comes into existence out of *Brahman* at the beginning of an immensely long cosmical period called *kalpa*, and thereafter it subsists, being controlled by *Brahman*; at the end of the cosmical period it is reabsorbed into *Brahman* again, and everything is brought to annihilation.[1]

It is certainly noteworthy that at the beginning of the *Brahma-sūtras* this theory is declared in defining *Brahman*. In the Philosophy of Śaṅkara, *Brahman* as the world-cause is clearly distinguished from *Brahman* in itself, i.e. the highest *Brahman*, whereas the composer of the *Sūtras* thought that to be the world-cause was an essential characteristic of *Brahman* in itself. Therefore the composer of the *Sūtras* did not distinguish between the two *Brahmans*, i.e. the highest *Brahman* and the lower *Brahman*.[2] It is a basic proposition presupposed throughout the *Brahma-sūtras* that *Brahman* in itself is the world cause.[3]

This *Brahman*, being the only cause for the origination of the world, is compared to the womb, and is called the 'womb' (*yoni*) of the universe (I.4, 27). It is also called 'the undifferentiated' (*avyakta*), for it is the potential principle of development for the whole world, but has not yet developed it (III, 2, 23).

The *Sūtras* assert repeatedly that the source of the origination and reabsorption of the universe must be something spiritual.[4] If it lacked the power of intelligence (*jña-śakti*), the origination and development of the universe would have been impossible (II, 2, 9). In general, the functions of origination and development are brought into action by intelligence (II, 2, 3). It seems that the composer of the *Sūtras* thought that a non-intelligent substance, being just a thing, could be modified in shape, but could not develop. This is a refutation of the assumption of the Sāṃkhya school of the fundamental material principle (*pradhāna*) as the world-cause.

Then, what is the origination of the world out of the intelligent cause, as set forth in the *Brahma-sūtras* ?

The composer of the *Sūtras* thought that the physical world could not have been without its causes. It is accepted in experience that only when there exists a cause, does there occur a concrete result (II, 1, 5). Adopting this universally admitted principle, he inferred that there must have been a cause for the whole world, and assumed *Brahman* as the world-cause. As *Brahman* is the ultimate cause, postulated at the limit of the process of tracing back from result to cause, it is quite impossible that it in turn should depend on some more fundamental or ultimate cause (III, 2, 31). It is the ultimate; it can be called only 'being' (I, 1, 9; II, 3, 9).

By the term 'cause' we understand various meanings. First, *Brahman* is regarded as the material cause (*prakṛti-upādāna*)[5] of all beings. It seems that this notion was derived directly from the thought of Uddālaka in the sixth adhyāya of the *Chāndogya Upaniṣad*. As *Brahman* is the material cause of all beings, when we know *Brahman* as the *cause*, we come to know the essence of the beings. In this sense is established as true the promise[6] (*pratijñā*) of the scripture. 'Through the cognition of one thing everything else, even if previously unknown, becomes known' (I, 4, 23, cf. II, 1, 19-20).

At the same time *Brahman* is the operative cause for forming all things. *Brahman* is said to be the creator (*kartṛ*) of the world.[7] The reflection[8] (or willing) of the Self is declared in a passage of the *Upaniṣad* as follows : "He wished 'may I be many, may I grow forth' and finally he created the world." Reflection is possible only for an intelligent being which has a personality. Considering such a passage as this, we are led to the conclusion that the scripture must have regarded *Brahman* or *Ātman* as a personal principle. Therefore the reflection or volition on the occasion of world creation by *Brahman* is the operative cause of world creation—such was the assertion of the *Brahma-sūtras*. In this sense *Brahman* was in the *Brahma-sūtras* regarded as the agent or subject of action with positive volition, and not a static, calm, inactive being. Śaṅkara regarded Brahman with such active character as the Lord (*Īśvara*), and distinguished it from *Brahman* in itself, but the *Brahma-sūtras* itself did not distinguish between the two. It seems that the *Sūtras* identified it with *Brahman* as the material cause. *Brahman* as such a personal principle must be entirely different from the fundamental material cause (*pradhāna*) postulated by the Sāṃkhya school as the world-cause. The *Sūtras* emphasise that their fundamental material cause, being a material principle, could not be endowed with such mental functions as reflection (I, 1, 5).

Moreover, for *Brahman* to establish the various aspects of the phenomenal world, we must admit the existence of the various forms of the phenomenal world. The *Brahma-sūtras* regarded the formal causes of world creation as words (*śabda*, I, 3, 28). 'Words' here are not mere sounds or language, but the prototypes of words which engender them and bring into existence all things in the phenomenal world. For example, a cow as an individual is established on the basis of the word 'cow'. It was supposed that the words which exist latently in *Brahman* become manifest at the time of world creation and establish all beings in their respective forms. And the words as the metaphysical principles of such a significance were identified with the sacred words of the Veda which transcend human words. The idea of the origination of the world from the primordial words was set forth from ancient times among orthodox Brahmins, and was elaborated later by grammarians like Bhartṛhari and by Vedāntins like Śaṅkara.[9]

An action or activity of an intelligent being is in general initiated to fulfil a certain purpose. World creation is an activity of *Brahman* in itself. Then what is the purpose of world creation ? Here the problem of the final cause of world creation comes to be discussed. The opponent says (II, 1, 32). "*Brahman*" is the one who has fulfilled all his desires.[10] His self-sufficiency is vouched for by the Scripture. So you must admit absence of motive on his part, and you must admit absence of any purpose for activity." To this objection the composer of the *Sūtras* replies : "The creative activity is a mere sport of *Brahman*, such as we see in ordinary daily life. It is without reference to any purpose" (II, 1, 33). Such a thought was adumbrated in the later of the old *Upaniṣads*[11] but is expressed here quite explicitly. To assert that the creative activity is mere sport is to negate explicitly any purpose of world creation. So the creative activity is the nature of the absolute, and its purpose cannot be explained. Just in the same way as sport is to enjoy chance, so the creative activity of *Brahman* is a marvellous chance which cannot be explained by any universal rule or principle. It might be called an absolute chance or primordial chance. If we have to find some purpose, then the purpose is the origination and development itself, and there exists no other purpose (*artha*) (1.4.3).

So far the significance of the statement that *Brahman* is the world-cause has been discussed from the four sides. With regard to the above-mentioned four causes, *Brahman* in itself is the cause in any case; there exists no other cause besides him. *Brahman* in itself as *causa sui* originates and develops. In our empirical knowledge of the world it is difficult to find any instance of one and the same principle acting as all the above-mentioned four causes, but it seems that he, composer of the *Sūtras*, thought it quite reasonable, for the considered *Brahman* to possess all powers (*Sarva-śakti*, II, 1, 30).

Things being so, the creative activity is nothing but the self-development of *Brahman* itself, the 'making itself' (*ātmakṛti*) on the part of the Self (I, 4, 26). This idea was derived from the sixth chapter of the *Chāndogya-upaniṣad*, and the creative activity in this sense is called 'modification' (*pariṇāma*, I, 4, 26). It is clear that here the standpoint of the 'modification theory' (*pariṇāma-vāda*) is adopted. (Incidently the term '*Vivarta*', used by later Advaitins to contrast with this, is not used in the *Brahma-sūtras*.)

The fact that the *Brahma-sūtras* adopted the modification theory means that it took up the standpoint of the doctrine of the actual existence of an effect in the cause (*sat-kārya-vāda*, II, 1, 7). That is to say, an effect exists latently already in its cause in one or other form prior to its appearance; when it comes to be seen patently, it comes to be called an 'effect' (II, 1, 16). This is vouched for in the scriptures, and is proved by means of reasons (II, 1, 17-20). This view of cause and effect is common to the Sāṃkhya philosophy, and is in sharp contrast to the doctrine of the non-existence of an effect in the cause prior to its appearance (*asat-kārya-vāda*), as held by the Nyāya-Vaiśeṣika and other philosophical systems.

Considered from such a view of cause and effect held by the *Brahma-sūtras*, *Brahman* as the world-cause and the world as the effect are not different (*ananya*, II, 1, 14).[12] All entities are nothing but *Brahman*. Nothing can exist apart from *Brahman*. *Brahman* is indeed the totality of all things (I, 1, 23).

Then, what is the difference between cause and effect, which are generally considered to be two different concepts ? According to the *Brahma-sūtras*, effect in itself is not different from cause; when a cause, having undergone some limitations, comes to display different modifications, it is called an 'effect'. For example, clay is a cause, and jars, dishes etc. which are its modifications, are its effects. These effects are in themselves nothing but the cause; various modes as effects are nothing but 'comprehension by word' (*vācārambhaṇa*, II, 1, 14).

Brahman should be spoken of only as 'being' (*sat*). According to the above-mentioned principle of cause and effect, from *Brahman* as being, must originate a world identical as being. Origination or development is no more than transformation of pure being into manifold being. Thus the *Brahma-sūtra* itself considered the phenomenal world to be reality, something true, and neither an illusion nor a mere subjective appearance. Its standpoint is extremely realistic. In this respect it was the reverse of the standpoint of Śaṅkara or of some early Vedāntins who preceded him. We must conclude that the māyā theory is not propounded in the *Brahma-sūtras*.[13]

This thought of the *Brahma-sūtras* was derived from some Upaniṣadic passages, now brought to a clearer form in it. However, in some older *Upaniṣads*, a theory to the opposite effect also is propounded, according to which the whole world originated from non-being (*asat*).[14] This theory, which is contrary to the above-mentioned ontological principle, could not be accepted literally by the *Brahma-sūtras*, which held that origination of being from non-being was impossible.[15] The difficulty with the scriptural texts was got over in this way : when non-being is declared by them to be the world-cause, this is not non-being in the literal meaning of the word, but the names and forms (*nāma-rūpa*) of the phenomenal world in their undifferentiated, primordial state prior to world creation, are merely figuratively or tentatively called 'non-being.'[16] Such an ontological standpoint is just the reverse of that of the Nyāya-Vaiśeṣika school.

Considering the fact that the *Brahma-sūtras* took *Brahman* to be the world-cause as such, we are led to the conclusion that the concept of *Brahman* in it must have been a considerably advanced and logically thorough-going one. There is no trace in the *Brahma-sūtras* of the concept of *Brahman* in a personified form (*puruṣa*) though world creation from the *puruṣa* had been set forth in the *Veda-saṃhitās* and the *Upaniṣads*, and furthermore the Buddhists, Jains and literati in general ascribed to the Vedāntins a theory of world-creation from *puruṣa*. According to the *Brahma-sūtras*, *Brahman* is without organs (*karaṇa*, II.1.31), and accordingly without body. The *Brahma-sūtras* abandoned the traditional notion, held by some early Vedāntins and Śaiva theologians, that various phenomena of the world each correspond to some part of the body of the supreme God. Neither is the theory that the whole world is the body of *Brahman*, as was held later by Rāmānuja, explicitly mentioned.

Notes

1. 1.4.25, 2.1.8.
2. *Sūtra* 3.3.59 states that the effect of the various forms of meditation (and consequently knowledge, *vidyā*) taught in the *Upaniṣads* are all the same. From this point also we know that two types of *Brahman* were not considered.
3. 1.1.11, 1.1.18, 1.4.14, 2.1.27, 2.1.37.
4. 1.1.9, 1.1.10, 2.2.1.
5. 1.4.23. See also 2.1.19-20.

6. *Chāndogya-Upaniṣad* VI, 1, 4-6; *Bṛhad. Up.* II, 4, 5.

7. 1.4.6. This derives from the teaching in *Kauṣītaki-Upaniṣad* IV, 19.

8. Abhidhyā. 1.4.24 (See also 2.3.13, *abhidhyāna*). Sūtra 1.1.5 mentions the word *īkṣati* in the creation story of *Chāndogya-Upaniṣad* VI, 2, 3.

9. Śaṅkara ad *BS.* I, 3, 28.

10. *Māṇḍūkya-Kārikā* 1.9.

11. "*Brahman* wanders in the three states (waking, dreaming, sleeping) in one step and (wanders) in the highest state (fourth state) in three steps. The two states of great self are to enjoy truth and illusion." (*Maitrī-Up.* VII, 11, 8).

12. 3.2.30, 3.2.32, 3.2.36.

13. Although the word *māyā* is found in *sūtra* 3.2.3 and even though it is used in the sense employed by Śaṅkara, it refers to the various things experienced in dreams by the individual self and not to the things in the external world during the awakened state. Thus, we may be able to confirm the fact that the author of the *Sūtra* did not embrace *māyāvāda*. On the other hand, if we interpret *māyā* as the supernatural power of *Īśvara*, according to Rāmānuja, it is all the more irrelevant to *māyāvāda*. *Vācāraṃbhaṇa* (2.1.14) and *ābhāsa* (2.3.50) also do not teach *māyāvāda*. See my explanatory notes to these *sūtras*.

14. *Chānd. Up.* III, 19, 1; *Taitt. Up.* II, 7.

15. 2.2.26 and 27.

16. 1.4.15, 2.1.17.

3. *The Rationality of the Development of the World*

The *Brahma-sūtra* discusses in detail how the development of the phenomenal world from *Brahman*, the cause is possible. The essential nature of *Brahman* has been described in (1) above, but it may be summarized as in the definition of the later Vedānta schools—being (*sat*), knowledge (*cit*) and bliss (*ānanda*). Since these attributes of *Brahman* are opposed to the facts of experience in the world, the *Brahma-sūtra* takes up the problem of explaining the contradictions :

I. *Brahman* is pure being and undifferentiated. How can such an undifferentiated, absolute principle be the cause of a multifarious phenomenal world ?

II. *Brahman* is pure knowledge and spirit absolute. How can it evolve the material world of nature ?

III. *Brahman* is an ideal state, to be described as pure bliss. How should it manifest the pain, sorrow and unhappiness in our human world ? These weaknesses were all pointed out in the criticisms of Vedānta philosophy by the various schools of the time.

In regard to the first objection, it was specially an attack from a mechanistic standpoint that was made : it would be irrational that the plurality of phenomena should be manifested by development from a world-cause absolute and undifferentiated. Just as many instruments are necessary for creating anything, so a plurality of causes would be required for world-creation. Thus, it is necessary to posit many co-operating causes of various kinds (2.1.4).

This criticism probably originated from the combination theory (*ārambha-vāda*) of Nyāya-Vaiśeṣika tradition.[1] The author of the *Sūtra*[2] argues against it, stating that world development is possible from *Brahman* alone. He answers by giving the analogies of milk which when left quite alone nevertheless of itself turns into curd, and the gods, who are able to manifest diverse things in their respective worlds without recourse to external means or instruments. This answer, which first merely takes an example from daily experience and transfers it to a metaphysical problem, is inadequate philosophically. It is rather too naïve an answer to the question of how pure being could develop multifarious phenomena. Further one cannot say that the two analogies given are necessarily on the same level. That the milk becomes curd is a natural phenomenon and no more, but the creation of things by a god is rather an act based upon the will of the god. Judging from the fact that he lumps together these two analogies in spite of their difference of import, it appears as though the author of the *Sūtra* had no definite view on the point, but probably merely a vague idea that it is possible for a pure, absolute being to manifest the diverse things of our phenomenal world. Since the *Brahma-sūtra* is concentrated mainly on showing that the variety of absolute principles taught in the *Upaniṣads* comes down to one *Brahman*, probably such other philosophical problems were not matters of deep concern.

Later, philosophers were to devote every effort to resolving this problem. Various attempts can be traced in early Vedānta schools but it was Śaṅkara who attempted to resolve the difficulty by distinguishing the pure *Brahman* in itself from the agent of world-creation—*Īśvara* conditioned by nescience (*avidyā*) and *māyā*. It seems that some such solution had been considered from ancient times. If the undifferentiated *Brahman* develops to manifest the world of differentiation, then *Brahman* possesses the two contradictory natures of undifferentiation and differentiation. The *sūtra* denies this (3.2.11) and states that *Brahman* does not possess a twofold characteristic (*liṅga*). The author probably conceived *Brahman* in itself as always being non-differentiated, and of a different category from the developed aspect characterized by differentiation. Thus, the *sūtra* itself does not distinguish the Highest *Brahman* (*param brahma*) from the lower *Brahma* (*aparam brahma*).

As to the second objection, *Brahman* is pure knowledge. As explained previously, *Brahman* is called being (*sat*), but this being is identical with knowledge and spirit (1.1.9). The objector points out that, *Brahman* which is spiritual and nature which is material are different in essence (*vilakṣaṇa*). Generally speaking, there must be a clear distinction (*viśeṣa*) between the spiritual and the material. Thus, it is impossible for a spiritual *Brahman* to produce a non-spiritual, material world[3] (2.1.4). The Sāṃkhya philosophy was also aware of this theoretical difficulty and asserted that the material can be born only from the material, thus establishing a dualistic world-view with the pure spirit of *Puruṣa* on one hand and the primary material of *Prakṛti* on the other. The author of the *Sūtra* meets the criticism, by saying that this is nct a real problem; there are concrete examples in the world where material things are born from spiritual existence. For example, hair and nails are born from man. There are also cases where the spiritual is born from the material. For example, insects and others are born from cow-dung. Since we have such concrete examples, there is nothing irrational about the material world being produced by the spiritual *Brahman* (2.1.6).

However if the notion of origination from things of completely opposing nature is accepted, will it not amount to falling into a doctrine that the effect is not already in the cause, thus contradicting the fundamental law of causation already explained. To this the author of the *Sūtra* simply answers that it is not a lapse into that doctrine, but gives no reason in support.

On the other side, there arises a further question, regarding dissolution (*apīti*). When the phenomenal world returns to *Brahman* and reaches dissolution, is not the impure aspect of the phenomenal world transferred to *Brahman* ? The answer is that this is impossible. It is as when jar and dish are broken and return to the dust, their forms are annihilated (2.1.8-9). The author of the *Sūtra* relies only upon analogies and does not attempt philosophical clarification concerning these criticisms. Thus, the Vedānta scholars of later ages had to direct their efforts to resolve these difficulties. Śaṅkara established his principle of ignorance (*avidyā*) to explain the process of the spirit becoming the non-spirit, and Rāmānuja claimed that the material world is also the body of *Brahman* and has existed from the beginning.

As to the third objection, the question arises that if the Absolute *Brahman* as the sole cause created the world, why did it create such an imperfect world ? Questions arise similar to those which are found in the theology of the West : The reality of the world is that some individuals are enjoying pleasure and happiness, while others are experiencing pain and suffering. Why did *Brahman* create such a world of inequality ? Even the more fortunate ones know some degree of pain and suffering. Why did *Brahman* create a world filled with such unhappiness ? Does not the Highest God have the defects of unfairness (*vaiṣamya*) and cruelty (*nairghṛṇya*) ? In reply the author of the *Sūtra* states : the Highest God created the conditions of each individual self, dependent (*apekṣā*) upon the good and bad acts of the actions (*prayatna*) of that individual in the previous creation. Consequently, it cannot be said that the Highest God is cruel, just because the individual self experiences pain to some extent, or that there is unfairness, because of inequality of pain and pleasure among individual selves (2.1.34; 2.3.42).

But another question arises, as follows : It is said that the Highest God creates certain effects dependent upon the good and bad acts of the individual self in the past, but since the individual self did not exist prior to the creation of the world and thus could not then be responsible for any act, there can be no distinction of good and bad acts. Therefore, there would be nothing to determine the effects.[4] In response to this the *sūtra* states : The criticism is not valid, because *saṃsāra* is beginningless (2.1.35-36). The prevalent idea in India was that the world underwent creation, subsistence, and dissolution, and the period from creation to dissolution was known as *kalpa*. This process was repeated eternally. Judging from the above reply, there must have been a view prevalent that some part of the *karma* committed by the individual self before absorption in *Brahman* resulted in effects in the next *kalpa* or world creation. This meant that the individual self could have different conditions of existence in former and subsequent *kalpas*. This appears to contradict *sūtra* 2.1.36, which is based upon the scriptural passage, "The creator made the sun and moon as previously" (*Ṛg-Veda*, X, 190, 3), but that was probably applicable only to the cyclical creation of the natural world and not to the destiny of individual selves.

At any rate the attempt to use the law of *Karma* to solve the problem of individual sufferings in a *Brahman*-created world is a special point of the philosophy of *Brahma-sūtra*. At the same time the Highest God was not an absolutely free personal god, because he is dependent upon external factors for world creation. Since he merely allocates the karmic effect appropriate to the individual self, his function was that of an automaton. He is a stern god and not a god of grace; he is a god who makes possible individual action, bondage, and liberation and is the basis of all things, but merely acts as a mechanism and does not positively encourage either good or bad acts on the part of individual selves. This god merely abides (*sthiti*) without doing anything in particular (1.3.7), for the spiritual liberation of individual self is dependent upon the religious discipline and practice of the individual. The burning *bhakti* worship of later Hindu sects is not seen in the *Brahma-sūtra*.[5]

Notes

1. The Jain scholar, Samantabhadra, also issues a similar criticism. See Part II, Chapter 2, Section 3.
2. 2.1.24-25. See also 2.1.31.
3. A similar argument is found in *Śloka-vārttika*, Sambandhākṣepa, 82. See Part II, Chapter 3, Section 5.
4. A similar argument is found in *Śloka-vārttika*, Sambandhākṣepa, 83. See Part II, Chapter 3, Section 5.
5. G. Thibaut stresses the influence on the *Brahma-sūtra* of Bhāgavata thought which begins with the *Bhagavad-Gītā* (Introduction, pp. cxxvi-cxxvii), but this is due to the fact that he is affected by Rāmānuja's commentary, for the *Brahma-sūtra* actually criticizes and rejects the Bhāgavata doctrines.

4. *The Development and Dissolution of the World*

The concept of development of the world from *Brahman* and its establishment does not mean that the whole world is immediately manifested, but that there is a set pattern and order. That is, from *Brahman* arises space, from space air, from air fire, from fire water, and from water earth, so creating the five elements[1] (2.3.1-12). This order follows that in the *Taittirīya Upaniṣad*, but the *sūtra* discusses in detail the opposing view that space does not arise from some other fundamental principle. Since space is called *ātman* (*Tait. Up.* 1, 7, [1]), the immortal (*amṛta*, *Bṛhad. Up.* II, 3, 3), etc., in the older *Upaniṣads* and regarded as identical with the absolute principle, there must have been thinkers, during the time the *Brahma-sūtra* was compiled, who believed that space was the world-cause. The author of the *Sūtra*, however, reduced space to just another element. Space as conceived by him was not just empty open space, but a principle that made possible spatial dimension, and it was thought to be something like the element ether.

In the formation of the five elements in this order, the Highest God creates them by residing in the elements and having the desire of creation (*abhidhyāna*) (2.3.13). It is for this reason that each of the five elements is able to produce the succeeding element in the proper order. The Highest God is thus the indwelling spirit or inner controller (*antaryāmin*), itself ruling all created objects from within (1.2.18).

In explaining the formation of the natural world after the development of the five elements, the *Brahma-sūtra* adopts the tripartite (*trivṛtkaraṇa*) theory of the *Chāndogya Upaniṣad*, 6. According to this theory, the natural world is formed by the union of three elements—earth, water, and fire—but the proportions of the three differ according to each individual thing. For example, the earth which we know through experience is composed of the elements of earth, water, and fire, but the element of earth is dominant and for that reason it manifests the characteristics of the earth element, and so too is called "earth" : The same holds true for the other two elements. It is on this basis that a distinction between earth, water, and fire in the actual world is possible.[2] All other objects that we experience in life are also combinations of these three elements. In the case of human body, for example, flesh, faeces, and mind are composed of earthly nature : urine, blood, and breath are made of water; and bones, marrow, and speech consist of the nature of fire. This view is based upon the idea found in *Chāndogya-Upaniṣad,* 6.5.1 and, but it should be understood as meaning that a particular element is dominant (2.4.21). In this way the formation of name and shape (*saṃjñā-mūrti-kḷpti*) of the various things in the phenomenal world takes place, and the agent who performs this function is always *Brahman* (2.4.20).

Thus the author of the *Sūtra* followed the *Taittirīya Upaniṣad* in recognizing the five elements of earth, water, fire, air, and space, but as far as the formation of the natural world was concerned, it seems that he considered earth, water, and fire to be the material cause, following the *Chāndogya-Upaniṣad,* and rejected air and space as constituent elements. Here again we have evidence of the eclectic attitude of the *Brahma-sūtra,* but philosophically it lacks rigour. As a result, the later Vedānta scholars developed this standpoint further and advocated the theory of quintuplication (*pañcīkaraṇa*) which states that all five elements contribute to the formation of the natural world.

The natural world thus formed is material, and neither mental nor spiritual (2.1.4). Therefore, it has no spontaneous activity; each element has residing in it a god a *devatā* who rules (*abhimānin*) it. The belief of the time was that gods, who are spiritual beings, were hidden behind material things and made possible their movements (2.1.5, 2.4.14).

The different objects which have been transformed (*vikāra*) into the phenomenal world are distinct from each other, and they are limited in some way. Only *Brahman* is without limitation, and there is nothing else that is not limited. In this fashion the things in the phenomenal world are produced (2.3.7). That is, they are limited by time and are impermanent, and furthermore the phenomenal world is incomplete and impure (2.1.8).

However, the external objects experienced in our daily life were never thought to be illusory. This is clear from the ontology of the *Brahma-sūtra* given above, and also from its criticism of the Vijñāna-vāda theory that compares the external objects to be like the experiences in a dream (2.2.28-30). The view is thus very different from that of the *Māṇḍūkya-Kārikā* (especially

Chapter 2 and following) and of the Advaita school, even within the same Vedānta tradition.

The world that has developed is dependent and formed upon *Brahman* the world-cause. All things are dependent (*adhīna*, 1.4.3) upon *Brahman* prior to development in their primitive state, and also after that. Nothing is distinct (*avyatireka*) from *Brahman* (2.3.6), and *Brahman* controls (*praśāsana*) all things (1.3.11). That is, it must fulfil the office (*adhikāra*) of supporting the world (4.4.18), and therefore *Brahman* is called "the support of heaven, earth, and others" (*dyu-bhv-ādy-āyatana*, 1.3.1), the lord (*pati*) of all things (1.3.43), "the support of all things up to space" (*ambarāntadhṛti*),[3] and the power of control and rule is called the "greatness" (*mahiman*, 1.3.16) of *Brahman*. *Brahman* is also likened to an embankment (3.2.31), since it maintains order among all things and prevents their confusion. These doctrines are all taught in the older *Upaniṣads*, and the *Brahma-sūtra* accepts them completely.

This Brahman also resides within (*antarabhāva*) all things (3.2.20), so it is identified with the inner controller (*antaryāmin*) taught in 3.7.1 of *Bṛhadāraṇyaka Upaniṣad* (1.2.18-20). Since *Brahman* is the inner controller, the scriptures command us to worship *ātman* (4.1.3).

This Highest God also controls the law of cause and effect.[4] It grants an effect of pleasure for the good acts of individual self, and links unfavourable effects to evil acts. Thus, this Highest God was viewed by the Brahmins of the period as the supreme being who controls the distribution of justice in the world. The author of the sūtra follows Bādarāyaṇa on this point.[5] The bondage and liberation of the individual self is said to be dependent upon the Highest Self (*para*, 3.2.5).

It was believed that the phenomenal world developed from *Brahman*, continued for an extremely long period of time, and then returned to *Brahman* to become extinct. The various elements return to *Brahman* in inverse order to that of the creation of the world (2.3.14). That is, earth enters water, water enters fire, fire enters air, air enters space, and space enters *Brahman*. The various individual selves also return to *Brahman* and attain a state of complete rest.

The cycle of creation, subsistence, and dissolution of the world was believed to repeat itself endlessly. This is called "recurrence" (*āvṛtti*, 1.3.30). The cycle has continued from the beginningless (*anādi*) past, and it will continue to the endless future. And the world which repeats this endless recurrence is the same (*samāna*) in name and form (*nāma-rūpa*) in each *kalpa* (1.3.30). The individual self continues its beginningless *saṃsāric* wandering through the countless recurrences (2.1.35). Since the older *Upaniṣads*, including the Vedic scriptures in general, do not teach the idea of recurrence and posit an infinite nothingness before world creation, this world view of the *Brahma-sūtra* must have been under the influence of Buddhist scriptures and the *Purāṇas*.

Notes

1. Such an order of creation is mentioned as the theory of a certain non-Buddhist school in Āryadeva's "Refutation of the Twenty Heretical Teachings on Nirvāṇa." See Part II, Chapter 1, Section 4.
2. 2.4.22. See also 3.1.2.
3. 1.3.10. See also 1.3.16.
4. 2.3.42, 2.1.34. 3.2.38 and 39.
5. See Part III, Chapter 2, Section 2.

SECTION 4 THE INDIVIDUAL SELF

1. *The Relationship Between the Individual Self and Brahman*

What is the relationship between the individual self and *Brahman*? This is one of the principal problems in Vedānta philosophy, and the different interpretations may be said to have caused the formation of the various sub-schools. The *sūtras* which discuss this problem, therefore, should be especially studied.[1] According to one *sūtra*, the individual self is clearly defined as being a part (*aṃśa*) of *Brahman* (2.3.43). The various commentaries (2, 3, 45) state that this is based upon a passage in the *Bhagavad Gītā* (15.7), as follows : "An eternal part (*aṃśa*) of myself has become the individual self in the world of living beings." Another *sūtra* (2.3.43) states that the individual self is different (*nānā*) from *Brahman* but at the same time not different. From this we see that the *Brahma-sūtra* took the standpoint of what was called *Bhedābheda* by later thinkers.

What, then, does it mean to say that the individual self is a "part" (*aṃśa*) of the Highest Self ? The *Brahma-sūtra* is saying at the same time that *Brahman* "has no parts" (*niravayava*) (2.1.26). This appears to contradict the former statement, but *aṃśa* and *avayava*, both translated as "part", have different connotations. *Avayava* implies a part of definite size, and itself capable of quantitative division, whereas *aṃśa* is a part which is the point conceived as the ultimately minute, the constituent atom of matter so to say. The former has size and is divisible, but the latter is without size and indivisible. This part (*aṃśa*) has some characteristics in common with the whole, and the whole also inheres in the part, though there are certain characteristics of the whole not contained therein. When we consider these two terms in this manner, the statement that the individual self is an *aṃśa* but not an *avayava* of *Brahman* is not contradictory. Thus, while the individual self is none other than *Brahman* in its essential nature,[2] it is not completely identical with *Brahman*. *Bhedābheda* should be understood in this sense.

When we view this relationship from the standpoint of "non-difference," all individual selves are *Brahman* just as they are. The song in praise of *Brahman* in one of the schools of *Atharva Veda* that even fishermen, slaves, and gamblers are none other than *Brahman* is interpreted as bringing out this point (2.3.43). The *Brahma-sūtra* itself teaches that the relationship between *Brahman* and individual self is non-distinction (*avaiśeṣya*) (3.2.25), but it does not teach the complete identity (*tādātmya*) advocated in *Advaita*. The *sūtra* does not clarify what it means by "non-difference", but the common qualities are probably spirituality, subjectivity, and permanence.

Although from this standpoint the individual self and *Brahman* are not different, they are separate and distinct from other standpoints. The *sūtra* emphasizes the distinction (*vaiśeṣya*, *bheda*) between *Brahman* and individual self (1.2.8, 2.1.22). The Highest Self is the principle which makes possible the activity of *ātman* as the individual self (2.3.41); consequently, the relationship of ruler and subject exists between the two. While *Brahman* has the power to create, maintain and dissolve the world, the individual self has no such powers (1.1.16). *Brahman* is the *ātman* consisting of the bliss (*ānandamaya*), but the individual self has no such quality (1.1.16 and 17). *Brahman* possesses the quality (*dharma*) of "transcending all evil" (*Chānd. Up.* 1.6.7), but the individual self has no such quality.[3] Furthermore, the various attributes of *Brahman* taught in the doctrine of Śāṇḍilya do not apply to the individual self (1.2.3). The individual self receives pain and pleasure as the consequence of his *karmic* acts, but the Highest Self does not experience such effects.[4] (1.2.8, 2.1.13, 2.3.46).

What is of particular interest is that the author of the *Sūtra* himself explicitly states that his theory is not that of Advaita. In *Sūtra* 2.1.21 the following question is raised : Since the *Upaniṣads* frequently teach that the embodied self (individual self) and *Brahman* (highest self) are not different, if *Brahman* himself created this actual world filled with sufferings, did he not bring undesirable effects upon himself ? This does not accord with an omniscient and omnipotent *Brahman*. The *sūtra* answers this by quoting from the scriptures and stating that since *Brahman* transcends (*adhika*) the individual self and the scriptures teach the difference (*bheda*) between the two, it is not true that *Brahman* has created undesirable results for himself.

There are many other *sūtras* which stress the difference between the individual self and the highest self.[5] The *sūtras* also frequently comment upon the opposition between the highest self and the individual self, for the individual self is often referred to as "the other" (*itara*)[6] in contrast to the highest self, and in some cases the highest self is called "the other."[7] They were considered to be in an opposing and contrasting relationship. There is also an instance where the individual self and highest self are ranged together as "dual ātman" (*ātmānau*) (1.2.11), but naturally they are not taken as on an equal basis, for the highest self is superior (*adhika*) to the individual self (2.1.22, and 3.4.8).

Even in spiritual liberation the individual self never becomes completely identical with the highest self, for even after liberation the individual self does not possess the power of creation, and the freedom of the liberated depends upon the *Īśvara* (4.4.17 and 18). It becomes equal to *Brahman* only in the matter of what it enjoys (4.4.20). Both the bondage and liberation of the individual self originate from *Brahman* (3.2.5).

Since the *Brahma-sūtra* clearly distinguishes between the two in this way, its philosophical standpoint is radically different from that of Śaṅkara.

From the above discussion there is no doubt that the *Brahma-sūtra* took the *Bhedābheda* standpoint, and the *Sūtra* gives many anlaogies to make the hearer understand the point. The relationship between the Highest Self and individual self is compared to that between the torch as a source of light and the light (*prakāśa*) it emits (3.2.25 and 28, 2.3.46). The light at its source is concentrated, but it becomes dispersed in various directions. Since they have different extensions, they are not identical; but inasmuch as both are luminous, they are identical. The relationship may also be likened to that between the sun itself and its images reflected in water (3.2.18, see also 2.3.50). The images are different from each other and also from the sun, but since they all reflect the same sun, they are identical. The analogy of the serpent is also given,[8] which is sometimes stretched out and at other times coiled. Although the form differs at various times, the fact that it is a serpent is always the same.

The reason which led the author of the *Brahma-sūtra* to establish such a theory may be understood as follows : various theories are found in the *Upaniṣads* concerning the relationship between the individual self and the Highest Self, sometimes teaching that they are different and at other times that they are identical. Due to this diversity, the *Bhedābheda* theory was established as a synthetic theory. The author of the *Sūtra* himself makes this explicit.[9] He gives various arguments to establish this point, and here again we see the eclectic attitude of the author of the *Brahma-sūtra*.

Notes

1. Formerly Ghate made a remarkable contribution on this problem.
2. See 1.1.26.
3. 1.1.20, 1.3.18.
4. Such an idea is already taught in *Mahābhārata* and *Viṣṇu-Purāṇa* See my notes on *sūtra* 2.3.47.
5. 1.1.19 and 21, 1.2.4, 5, 6, 12, 17, 20, 22, 1.3.2, 5, 7, 20, 42.
6. 1.1.16, 1.2.22, 1.3.18, 2.1.21.
7. 2.3.21.
8. 3.2.27. This analogy is also used in the *Vākyapadīya* (III, 7, 105, p. 246).
9. See 3.2.27.

2. *The Various Characteristics of the Individual Self*

The individual self is sometimes called *ātman*, but since the term *ātman* is sometimes used to refer to the Highest Self, the individual self is particularized by such terms as the embodied self (*śarīra*),[1] the ruler (*adhyakṣa*),[2] or the individual soul (*jīva*).[3] These names refer to the facts that the individual self possesses a body, rules over the body and sense organs, and is the principle of life.

The *ātman* as individual self is our own self (*sva*, 1.1.9), and it can never be abandoned (1.1.8). Even though one tries to abandon *ātman*, it is none other than the one who is attempting to do so. No matter how much one negates ātman, it is found beyond the negation. Thus, the individual self is believed to be located in the innermost part of the individual (3.3.35).

The individual self is permanent (*nitya*), does not newly arise, and does not disappear.[4] It is eternal, being neither produced nor annihilated. The creation and extinction of the world applies only to the material, natural world, and not to the individual self. When the world becomes extinct, the individual selves enter a state of inactivity and rest,[5] but never lose their individual existences.

This individual self is the agent of cognition, and it is called the knower (*jña*, 2.3.18). Neither intelligence nor spirit was directly regarded as in itself the individual self; rather were they considered to be the essence of the individual self.[6] These two have to be taken as distinct concepts. The spiritual nature alone was believed to be inadequate for ātman to exercise the function of cognition, and union with intellect (*buddhi*) was thus necessary.[7] However, the spiritual nature is essentially an aspect of *ātman*. The Lokāyata materialists postulated that spirituality belongs to the body and that there is no *ātman* separate from the body, but the *Brahma-sūtra* emphasizes that the *ātman* exists separately from the body and that the spiritual nature does not belong to the body.[8]

The *ātman* as the individual self is the agent of activity, being considered to be the actor (*kartṛ*, 2.3.32). This was probably asserted in total opposition to the *Sāṃkhya* theory that the *puruṣa* as the pure spiritual principle is inactive. In another section the author of the *Sūtra* states that *ātman* is the agent which makes possible all kinds of activities (*kriyā*, 2.3.36). Since it is essentially active in nature, it moves about freely in the body.[9] As to cognition (upalabdhi), the individual self perceives both what is desirable and undesirable for itself, and as to activity, it actualises both what is desirable and undesirable, not being restricted to one side in any way (*aniyama*, 2.3.37). Thus, on this point the individual self cannot be said to be omnipotent. The individual self takes in (*upādāna*) the functions of the various organs within itself during sleep (2.3.35). The experience of *samādhi* is also based upon *ātman*. Thus one of the chief characteristics of the Brahma Sūtra is that *ātman* has activity as its essential nature, but Śaṅkara almost completely disregards this fact.

Of course, for the *ātman* to manifest these activities it must unite with intellect (*buddhi*), sense-organs, and functional organs, for the ātman alone is incapable of them. Since the individual self unites with the body, including the various sense organs, the injunctions and prohibitions taught in the scriptures become possible (2.3.48). The body is a means to realize action. The activities of the individual self, on the other hand, are also dependent upon the supreme lord (*para*, 2.3.41). But the agent of action is always *ātman* and never intellect (*buddhi*) and the like (2.3.38).

The *ātman*, however, is not always engaged in some kind of activity. Since the *ātman* requires union with the various organs for activity, it becomes an agent when it unites with the organs but not when it is disconnected from them. This is similar to the carpenter who becomes an agent of work when he has tools in his hand but not without them. Thus, in deep sleep ātman is not an agent (2.3.40).

No volitional act or conduct of the individual self ever disappears, for it inevitably entails some result. It was believed that morally good acts would entail good results in future and evil acts would bring about evil results. This idea is common to all sects of Hinduism, the individual self has to experience the consequences of its acts (1.3.7). The individual self which acts and which is visited with the consequences of its acts is always that one same individual self (3.2.9). The individual self always maintains its individuality and is never interchangeable with other individual selves. Although the different individual selves possess the same qualities, since they are united with their respective bodies and are not connected with other bodies, each individual self undergoes only the consequences of its own acts. The effects of *karma* are never confused (2.3.49) As the principle which guarantees non-confusion of *karmic* effects, some thinkers had postulated unseen power (*adṛṣṭa*), resolution (*abhisaṃdhi*), the place of *ātman* (*pradeśa*), etc., but these are all rejected as invalid (2.3.51-53).

Thus, the action and the experience of its result are possible only by union with the body, and so the body is the most important element in the existence of an individual self. It is for this reason that the individual self is called the embodied self (*śarīra*). Expressions such as birth and death are applicable only to the body, and they have nothing to do with the individual self. We speak of birth and death only because the body exists, and the individual self itself is neither created nor extinguished (2.3.16). But the individual self undergoes *saṃsāra*; that is, it escapes from the body at death, progresses, and then returns to a body[10] (2.3.19). And this process of *saṃsāra*, the recurrence of birth and death, is repeated until the individual self gains knowledge and attains spiritual liberation.

The essential nature of this individual self that is in the process of *saṃsāra* is hidden (*tirohita*). Two reasons are given for this, but no final decision as to which is true is made : one states that it is the wish of *Īśvara*, and other that it is because of the connection with the body (3.2.5-6).

Finally, the discussion in the *Brahma-sūtra* concerning the size of the individual self is also noteworthy. There were three views that were generally prevalent in India concerning the size of *ātman*. (1) Extremely great in size : the *ātman* is extremely great and pervades all existence. (2) Extremely small : the ātman is infinitesimal. (3) Same in size as the body : the ātman possesses the same size and weight as the body. Among these the third view is that of the Jains primarily, and it is rejected by the author of the *Sūtra* (2.2.34-36). The views of the *sūtra* itself on this matter are given in 2.3.19-32, but the import is interpreted variously by the different commentators. After our critical examination of this point in the previous chapter,[11] we may conclude that the *ātman* is infinitesimal in the state of *saṃsāra*, and it is all-pervasive in the state of liberation, because it transcends all bondage. It is believed that later thinkers stressed just one of these aspects at the expense of the other. The theory of many essentially all-pervading *ātmans* is rejected by the author of the *Sūtra* (2.3.53).

Notes

1. 1.2.3, 1.2.20, 4.2.12.
2. 4.2.4, 4.3.10.
3. 1.1.31, 1.4.17.
4. 2.3.17. See also 2.2.42.
5. See previous section, 3.
6. See my notes on sūtra 2.3.18 and also sūtra 2.3.28.
7. See 2.3.29 and the following.
8. 3.3.53 and 54.
9. 2.3.34. See also *Bṛhad. Up.* II, 1, 18.
10. See *Kauṣītaki-Up.* I, 2.
11. See 2.3.19 and 29.

3. *The Structure of Individual Existence*

The individual self which is active and experiences pain and pleasure in the state of *saṃsāra* does not exist in isolation but in combination with the body and the various organs.

(1) *The Various Organs*

The various organs are called *prāṇa* in the *Brahma-sūtra*, continuing the usage of the *Upaniṣads*, and it is a synonym of *indriya* as used in Indian philosophy in general (2.4.17).

A difference of opinion exists between the author of *Brahma-sūtra* and his opponents concerning the number of organs. The opponents speak of seven organs (2.4.5), based upon scriptural statements such as "Seven *prāṇas* originate from it," (*Muṇḍ. Up.* II, 1, 8) and "The *prāṇas* which exist in the head are seven." (*Tait. Saṃ.* V, 3, 2, 5). What the seven refer to is unclear, but according to Śaṅkara's commentary, they comprise both eyes, both ears, both nostrils, and mouth. As against that, the author of the *Sūtra* lists eleven organs (2.4.6.), as follows : the five sense organs (sight, hearing, smell, taste, and touch), the five functional organs (speech, hands, feet, excretory and reproductive organs), and mind (*manas*). The list of eleven organs was probably based upon the common view prevalent at the time (especially in the Sāṃkhya theory);[1] while the *Brahma-sūtra* is an exegetical work, it shows traces here of efforts to establish a logical philosophical system.

Among these organs, "mind" is the central organ which integrates the cognitive and functional apperceptions, and it is identical with what is called "intellect" (*buddhi*).[2] The mind however is only the central organ and never the cognitional or functional subject. It remains merely an organ; the subject is always *ātman* (2.3.38, 39).

There is also mention of another theory[3] which would allow an organ called *vijñāna*, but this is rejected by the author of the *Sūtra* (2.3.15).

Now these organs are always united with the individual self, which is therefore called that which posesses *prāṇa* (*prāṇavat*).[4] The various organs are material[5] in nature, composed of the three elements of fire, water, and earth (2.3.15). The organs are also born from *Brahman*, identical with the elements (2.4.1), and their size is infinitesimal (*aṇu* 2.4.7), meaning that it is subtle (*saukṣmya*) and spatially limited (*pariccheda*).[6] This description as "subtle" implies that the subject of discussion is not the organs of various shapes forming parts of the body but the latent function of these organs. In the language of Buddhism, the discussion concerns not 'material organs' but 'organs in the ultimate sense.'[7]

The various organs perform the function of instruments or means of the individual self, but the activities of the organs themselves are controlled by the various gods of nature. It is under their control that the organs display their activities (2.4.14). This means that the gods which govern natural phenomena (earth, water, etc.) also control the various organs (eyes, nose, etc.). It is not thought however, that the gods thereby incur any of the effects of the *Karma* performed by the individual self (2.4.15). This is a very distinctive idea which was taken up by later Vedānta scholars, such as Bhartṛprapañca,[8] Śaṅkara,[9] etc.

(2) *Chief Vital Breath*

Besides the various organs, the *Brahma-sūtra* recognized a principle called Chief Vital Breath (*mukhya prāṇa*). The sūtra calls it "the chief" (*śreṣṭha*, 2.4.8), but it is not an organ (*indriya*, 2.4.11 and 17), for their characteristics are different (*vailakṣaṇya*, 2.4.19), as is indicated clearly in the scriptures (2.4.18).

This Chief Vital Breath arises from *Brahman*, as do the various organs (2.4.8), and it belongs to the individual self (2.4.10). For this reason the individual self is called the "bearer of vital breath" (*prāṇabhṛt*, 1.3.4). This Chief Vital Breath has neither an object of perception nor an object of action (2.4.11); it is attached to the individual self, maintains its life as a living being, and makes possible its activities. And it possesses five functions (*pañcavṛtti*) as follows : breathing in (*prāṇa*), breathing out (*apāna*), continuing breath (*vyāna*), ascension at death (*udāna*), and digestive function (*samāna*). Thus, it is neither simply air (*vāyu*) nor mere activity (*kriyā*, 2.4.9). Its size being infinitesimal (*aṇu*), it cannot be seen with our eyes (2.4.13).

(3) *Body*

The individual self is also united with the body. The *Brahma-sūtra* recognizes two kinds of bodies : one is the gross body which we experience in the present life, consisting of the three elements,[10] fire, water, and earth, and having significance as an instrument of the activities of individual self; and the other is the subtle body which cannot be perceived by our senses. The latter receives detailed attention in the *Brahma-sūtra*.

This subtle body is infinitesimal and escapes along a *nāḍī* at the death of the individual and destruction of the gross body (4.2.9). It does not perish when the gross body is destroyed (4.2.10); as long as the individual self is in *saṃsāra*, it is attached to this, which thus is the basis of *saṃsāra*. It perishes only when the individual enters into *Brahman* (4.2.8). The characteristic of this subtle body is progress; that is, it makes possible movement from one life to another life (3.3.30). Itself so subtle that it cannot be perceived by the physical senses, at the same time it is called the unmanifested (*avyakta*) because it can manifest other gross bodies in future (1.4.2).

Then, how can the existence of this subtle body be demonstrated ? As long as the individual self undergoes *saṃsāra*, there must be a basis which makes possible the continuation of *saṃsāra*. Since the individual self possesses characteristics in common with *Brahman*, though they are not completely identical, it is irrational for the individual self to be the basis of *saṃsāra*. For this reason, a subtle body was postulated. As the mark (*liṅga*) of the existence of subtle body, the *Sūtra* mentions the warmth of the body (4.2.11). When man dies, the warmth thereupon vanishes, but the gross body continues to exist and does not disappear at all. Its shape, weight, etc., remain. Consequently, warmth is not the part of gross body but the part of subtle body. At death, the subtle body thereupon escapes, and consequently the body warmth also—this was the idea.

In regard to the gross body, the major problem in the *Brahma-sūtra* is its connection with the individual self. According to the *sūtra*, the individual self is infinitesimal, but the body occupies space and has extension. How can a thing without extension become related to a thing with extension ? The author of the *Sūtra* believed that the *ātman* as individual self resided in the heart, that is, in a special place within the body (*avasthiti-vaiśeṣya*).[11] In the same way the Highest Self also resides in the heart of man,[12] and thus the individual self and highest Self co-exist within the heart.[13] This notion of the Highest Self appears to contradict the idea of its universal pervasion, but it was probably believed that since the individual self is a part (*aṃśa*) of the Highest Self, the statement that the individual self exists in the heart was also applicable to the existence of the Highest Self. The idea that the *ātman* exists within the heart was already in the older *Upaniṣads*,[14] and the *sūtra* merely reproduced the idea.

The *sūtra*, furthermore, believed that *nāḍīs* led from the heart to the various parts of the body, and that the man of knowledge escaped from the body by going through the 101st *nāḍī* and thus reaching union with *Brahman* (4.2.17). This also follows the teachings of the older *Upaniṣads*.[15] The *nāḍīs* also possess an important significance for the individual self bound to *saṃsāra*, because it enters the *nāḍīs* and achieves union with *Brahman* in the state of sleep (3.2.7). This idea also is found in the older *Upaniṣads*.[16] (These *nāḍīs* originate in the heart, but it is different from either the blood veins or the nerves. The ancient Indians visualized *nāḍī* as an extremely subtle tube in the human body, filled with liquid matter and possessing the above characteristics. Some later *Upaniṣads* and Yoga works expound the theory in detail.)

(4) *Conclusion*

Thus, the structure of individual existence conceived by the author of the *Sūtra* is as follows :

A. Individual Self

B. Limitations (in later language, *upādhi*)

1. Senses—11
   sense organs—5
   functional organs—5
   mind
2. Chief Vital Breath (five functions)
3. Body
   (a) gross body
   (b) subtle body
4. *Karma* which has not yet produced any effects (latent state)

Notes

1. Śaṅkara states that this is based on the passage, "There are these ten *prāṇa*-s in *puruṣa*. *Ātman* is the eleventh" (*Bṛhad. Up.* III, 9, 4), but to take the text in this way would be merely a personal opinion of the author of the sūtra.

2. According to Śaṅkara and Bhāskara, from 2.3.29 on, *buddhi* is referred to as an organ.

3. This is identical with the *adhyātma* theory taught in the *Mahābhārata*. See 2.3.15.

4. 2.4.15 and 16.

5. A view existed from ancient times that the various organs were not made from elements (*bhautika*) but were transformations of *ātman* (*ātma-vikāra*). (Sureśvara : *Bṛhad. Up. Vārttika*, p. 1730, v. 36). The *Brahma-sūtra* probably asserted the material nature of organs against such a view.

6. See my Explanatory Note to *sūtra* 2.4.7.

7. Śaṅkara also recognizes this fact. *vṛttimātrasya karaṇatvopapatteḥ*. (Śaṅkara ad *BS*. Vol. II, p. 111, 112 ff.).

8. Part V, Chapter 7, Section 3, 2.

9. Śaṅkara ad *BS*. II, 4, 14.

10. See previous section, 4.

11. 2.3.24, 4.2.17. See also 1.3.14.

12. 1.2.8, 1.3.25.

13. 1.2.11 and 12.

14. *Chānd.-Up.* VIII, 3, 3; *Bṛhad. Up.* IV, 3, 7; V. 6; *Praśna-Up.* III, 6; *Tait. Up.* I, 6; *Kāṭhaka Up.* II, 20; III, 1; IV, 6; VI, 17.

15. *Chānd. Up.* VIII, 6, 6; *Kāṭhaka-Up.* VI, 16; *Praśna-Up.* III, 6; *Muṇḍaka-Up.* II, 2, 6.

16. *Chānd.-Up.* VI, 8, 1; VIII, 6, 8.

4. TYPES OF INDIVIDUAL EXISTENCE

Although the essence is the same, there are very many differences in the individual selves appearing as such by association with particular bodies, sense-organs, and so on. The *Brahma-sūtra* classifies the various individuals, namely, the lives, into four types (3.1.21).

(1) *jarāyuja*[1] (viviparous, such as human beings[2])
(2) *aṇḍaja* (oviparous, such as birds)
(3) *svedaja* (creatures born from moisture, such as lice)
(4) *udbhijja* (creatures born from a sprout, such as trees)

This classification is based upon the *Aitareya Upaniṣad* (5.3), but the *Chāndogya Upaniṣad* (6.3.1) states that "Truly in these creatures there are only three types of birth. That is, birth from egg, womb, and sprout." The omission of birth from moisture clashes with the former view, but the *Brahma-sūtra*[3], states that birth from moisture is included in that of a sprout, which means that the author of the *Sūtra* considered the lower level of life born from moisture to be close to vegetable life. Of the four types of birth, that from moisture and sprout originate without any sexual relationship, as is generally accepted in the world (3.1.20). Among human beings also the ancients, such as Draupadī and Dhṛṣṭadyumna, were also said to be born without conception.

This classification into four types of birth existed before the *Brahma-sūtra* in India,[4] and it is not peculiar to the Vedānta school.[5]

In another section (2.3.16) life is categorized into what moves (*cara*) and what does not move (*acara*). (Śaṅkara glosses as *jaṅgama* and *sthāvara* respectively.) This classification corresponds to the concepts of animal life and vegetable life, and it is used commonly in the various schools in India.

The concept of living beings that the people of India held is reflected in this method of classification. The following two characteristics are to be especially noted :

1. Human beings are recognized as one type of creature and included in those born from the womb, but they are not given a special category. This idea is radically different from Western thought of the Middle Ages and before, in which human beings were considered apart from living beings in general; the Indian

view is closer to modern concepts of life. The Indians, however, had the bare concept of human beings as beings *born* and *having* life and they did not reach this conclusion as the result of analysis of the phenomena of biology.

2. There is a recognition of the spiritual essence in creatures in general. Spirit was thought to exist not only in human beings and animals in general but also in vegetable life. That vegetable life possesses spirit is frequently emphasized in India.[6] They believed, however, that the manifestation of spirit in vegetable life is incomplete, whereas the spiritual capacity is highly developed in human beings.

Since spirit is thus recognized in all living beings, they should all have an individual self, but it is the individual self of man that is the exclusive concern of the *Brahma-sūtra*, Man (*manuṣya*) has the qualifications to uphold and practice the teachings of the scriptures (1.3.25), though among men the untouchables of the *śūdra* caste are excluded. This meant naturally that sub-human lives such as animals and plants also had no qualifications to gain knowledge of *Brahman*. However, there are different opinions concerning the qualification of gods for knowledge of *Brahman*. How, then, were the gods conceived in the *Brahma-sūtra* ?

The gods are ranked higher than men (1.3.26). They possess bodies, but they can manifest a number of forms by their supernatural powers. Thus, when sacrificial offerings are made to the same god (for example, Indra) at various places simultaneously, that god appears at the different places at the same time (1.3.27). Such a god can create all kinds of things without recourse to external means or instruments (2.1.25). Furthermore, the various gods that rule natural phenomena also control the various organs of man (2.4.14). These gods, should also be considered as individual selves (1.1.21). The gods therefore, simply possess spiritual powers superior to those of men, but apart from that they are neither absolute nor supreme.

In regard to the question of whether or not these gods can follow the ordinances of the holy texts,[7] Jaimini asserted that a god cannot himself be an agent who worships; therefore, gods do not qualify for knowledge of *Brahman* (1.3.31). But Bādarāyaṇa believed that gods have the qualification to follow what is laid down in the holy texts. According to him, the gods have the desire (*arthin*) and the capacity (*sāmarthya*) for spiritual liberation (1.3.26). Thus, the gods also have the qualifications for knowledge of *Brahman* (1.3.33). Thinkers of the Mīmāṃsā tradition believed that the gods were mere figureheads controlled by rituals, but Bādarāyaṇa declared that the gods were part of the *saṃsāric* world and would eventually gain liberation. The *Brahma-sūtra* affirmed the latter view as the established theory.

Since the author of the *Sūtra* did not include these gods in the above classification, he must have thought of some other special classification for them apart from the four forms of existence already mentioned.

Notes

1. This is Śaṅkara's reading. *Aitareya Up.* has *jārūja*.
2. For actual examples, see the various commentaries.
3. The *sūtra* does not give any reason for this, but Śaṅkara explains that the reason is that both those born from moisture and from a sprout appear from earth and water alike.
4. See also *Mahābhārata* XII, 312, 5 (C. 11594)); *Manu* I, 43-46.
5. The *Suśrutasaṃhitā*, I, 23, however, recognizes these four types for animals, and gives fireflies, frogs, etc. as examples for birth from a sprout.
jaṅgamāsv api caturvidhā jarāyujāṇḍaja-svedajodbhijjāḥ /
tatra paśumanuṣyavyālādayo jarāyujāḥ / *khagasarpasarisṛpaprabhṛtayo 'ṇḍajāḥ* / *kṛmikīṭapipīlikāprabhṛtayaḥ svedajāḥ* /
indragopamaṇḍūkaprabhṛtayaḥ udbhijjāḥ / (Guha : *Jīvātman*, p. 55).
6. As an example of such a view :
sukhaduḥkhayoś ca grahaṇāt chinnasya ca virohaṇāt /
jīvaṃ paśyāmi vṛkṣāṇām acaitanyaṃ na vidyate /
—*Mahābhārata*, XII, 184, 17.
7. Śabarasvāmin ad *Mīmāṃsā-Sūtra* VI, 1, 4 ff. states that only human beings have the qualification for rituals and it denies the qualification to other beings.

5. *Consciousness*

According to the *Brahma-sūtra*, the state of individual self can be roughly divided into life and death. The state of life, furthermore, can be divided into three kinds : waking state, dream state, and sleeping state. Among these nothing special is said concerning the waking state.

The dream state is a transitional state between waking and deep sleep, and it is called the intermediate state (*saṃdhyā*) (3.2.1). The *Brahma-sūtra* takes up the problem of the validity of the varied experiences in dream. The opponent argues that the varied creation experienced in the dream state is true and that the creator or the shaper (*nirmātṛ*) is the Highest Self (3.2.1-2). As against this, the author of the *Sūtra* states that everything experienced in the dream state is nothing but *māyā* (*māyāmātra*). Whether *māyā* is interpreted as the "illusion" of Śaṅkara and Bhāskara, or as the "mystic power of *Īśvara*" of Rāmānuja, the author of the *Sūtra* states that experiences in dreams do not have the validity of those in waking because things experienced in dream do not fully show their real nature (3.2.3).

Next is deep sleep, which means absence of dreams (3.2.7) and absolute peace (*saṃprasāda*, 1.3.8). The individual self is thought to go into *Brahman* in deep sleep (1.3.15). That is, the individual self returns to *nāḍīs* in the sleeping state, and it returns to *ātman* through it (3.2.7). Thus, since *ātman* is the place of deep sleep, one is awakening from ātman when one returns to the waking state (3.2.8). The individual self before deep sleep and the individual self after sleeping are one and the same (3.2.9).

These three states had already been treated in the older *Upaniṣads*, but the state of fainting is also recognized here in the sūtra. The *sūtra*, however, states that it is not necessary to take it as an independent state of consciousness, because it pertains partly to death and partly to deep sleep (3.2.20). The fainting state had been disregarded in the *Upaniṣads*, and it came to be considered for the first time in the *Brahma-sūtra*.

SECTION 5 PRACTICE

1. *Practice in Life*

The socio-historical background of the *Brahma-sūtra* determines its theory of practice in life, which is centred on the scriptures and is extremely conservative in nature. The scriptures are the standard of conduct for man, and he should follow what is taught in the scriptures and not practise what is prohibited

(2.3.42). What, then, is the scheme of life that is encouraged in the scriptures ?

A contradiction exists in the *Upaniṣads* concerning the fundamental problem of what constitutes the scheme of life. The contradiction is inherited by the later generations, and it can be clearly seen in the opposition between Jaimini and Bādarāyaṇa, as discussed earlier.[1] In contrast to Jaimini, who stressed the importance of fulfilling the responsibility of a householder by raising children and performing the rituals, Bādarāyaṇa praised renunciation, abandoning family and property, and pursuing the life of a recluse. The *Brahma-sūtra* follows Bādarāyaṇa on this point. The opening verses of Part III, Chapter 4, explicitly assert Bādarāyaṇa's theory and reject Jaimini's view. The scriptures frequently teach the life of a recluse, and this is interpreted as an injunction (*vidhi*) by the scriptures, rather than as a mere statement (3.4.20). And it is further declared that the knowledge (*vidyā*) of *Brahman* can be gained in the life of a recluse (3.4.17).

Those who pursue the life of a recluse have cut off all relationships with women, therefore they are called "the chaste ones" (*ūrdhvaretas*), and the *Brahma-sūtra* often mentions and praises such a life. And they also do "not need to be concerned with the lighting of the fire and so on" (3.4.25). They have abandoned all secular usages, and must observe the disciplines especially prescribed for the life of a recluse. The *sūtras* discuss in detail the importance of chastity. The recluse must cut off all relations with woman and meditate exclusively on *Brahman*, and no one who is vowed to celibacy may revert to family life with a wife (3.4.40). Thus no return to the life of a householder was recognized.

It is not difficult, however, to imagine that there were some recluses who broke the vow of chastity. The problem of whether expiation is possible or not when the vow has been broken is discussed in the *Brahma-sūtra*. According to one theory, already taught in the Brahmanical law books,[2] there is no way to expiate the sin of breaking the vow of chastity. Although a method of expiation is prescribed for students of Vedas who break the rules of chastity, there is no way of expiation for the corruption (*patana*) of a recluse (3.4.41). According to another theory, however, the breaking of chastity by a recluse is a minor sin, and it can be expiated, just as the students of Vedas can perform expiatory ceremonies after having eaten meat or honey (3.4.42). The *sūtra* mentions both views, but regardless of whether it is a major or minor sin, the recluse who breaks his vow of chastity is looked down upon with disdain and ostracized by discriminating people. This was taught in ancient scriptures and it is also the contemporary practice (3.4.43). The eclectic attitude of the author of *Brahma-sūtra* is evident in the treatment of expiation.

There seem also to have been considerable restrictions concerning food. The recluses of the period appear to have been strict followers of the principle that "When the food is pure, the mind is pure" (*Chānd. Up.* VII, 26, 2) (3.4.29). Any kind of food was allowable when facing death from starvation, but only then, and ordinarily the choice of food was limited (3.4.28). Gluttony was prohibited, as well as drinking liquor (3.4.31). The restrictions on food seem to have applied ideally not only to recluses but also to householders.

In this way the *Brahma-sūtra*, following the ideas of Bādarāyaṇa, praises the pure life of the recluse and asserts that the knowledge of *Brahman* results from such a life, but it also states that rituals are necessary for the perfection of knowledge (3.4.26). The ceremonies, such as *agnihotra* and others, that should always be performed, are conducive to spiritual liberation (4.1.16). In other passages it is stated that duties in the various stages of life (*āśrama-karma*) should be fulfilled, and, according to various commentaries, these include the rituals. They should also be performed by people who do not desire liberation, but since they help (*sahakārin*) the production of knowledge those who seek liberation must observe them[3] (3.4.32-33). Therefore there are two types of people who perform the rituals—householders who perform them as part of the duty of their stage of life, and those who perform it as contributing to the production of knowledge—but in either case, rituals are compulsory. (3.4.34). Finally, the performance of works such as rituals will ensure their performers that they will not be overpowered by passions (or sin) (3.4.35).

The *Brahma-sūtra* was aware of the view that when animals are killed for sacrifice in them, ceremonies are thereby impure (*aśuddha*) and as a consequence those who have performed them will be reborn as herbs, etc., in the next life (3.1.25). Yet the author of the sūtra emphasized the importance of ceremonies for orthodox Brahmins. This point is to be especially noted. Although the true reason for encouraging the performance of rituals is not clear, their advocates honoured the life of the householder whose duty it was to perform them, and this naturally conflicted with the view of those who praised the life of a recluse. Even though the former believed that after having completed the period of the householder, one should become a recluse to attain liberation, they differ sharply from the thought of Śaṅkara and his followers in their estimate of the value of the householder's period of life.

Other practices required for the realization of wisdom include the mastery of calmness (*śama*), self-control (*dama*), repose (*uparati*), patience (*titikṣā*), contemplation (*samādhi*), and faith (*śraddhā*)[4] taught in the *Bṛhadāraṇyaka Upaniṣad*, 4.4.23. They are known as auxiliaries (*aṅga*) to knowledge, and they "have necessarily to be accomplished" (*avaśyānuṣṭheya*) for its realization. The scriptures, therefore, clearly enjoin (*vidhi*) this point (3.4.27). Silent meditation (*mauna*) is also enjoined as being conducive (*sahakārin*) to knowledge (3.4.47).

The *sūtra* states that these works, such as rituals, etc., are duties and teaches various kinds of practices, but those who cannot perform the works stipulated for the various stages of life (*āśrama*) in the *Brāhmaṇas* because of poverty and other reasons, will be blessed with knowledge, as long as they practice good works in society. But the performance of duties belonging to one of the stages of life is even more superior (*jyāyas*) (3.4.36-39).

To sum up, we can say that the author of the *sūtra* considered three types of people to have the qualifications for knowledge :

(1) The recluse who renounces family and property, does not perform rituals, lives a life of poverty, and concentrates his thoughts solely on *Brahman*.

(2) The head of a household who performs the rituals and practices meditation on *Brahman*. He is the head of a relatively wealthy family and has wife and children.

(3) People other than the above two who for reasons of poverty, etc., are unable to follow any of the stages of life (*āśrama*) prescribed in the *Brāhmaṇas*, but who always practise good acts and think of *Brahman*.

Among the three, the third type is given as a mere supplementary addition, and the sūtra is mainly concerned with the scheme of (1) and (2). The first type was especially emphasized by Bādarāyaṇa and this fact is inserted into the *sūtra*, but the *sūtra* itself explains the second type in greater detail. Thus while the third type was recognized only out of necessity and it was the first or second type which was recommended, still it was thought that any of them would suffice, and one at any rate of the stages of life (*āśrama*) must be followed (3.4.49). The attitude of the author of the *Sūtra* even on the problem of the practice in life is extremely eclectic and full of understanding.

In later ages the tradition which emphasizes the first type became more influential and comes to form the orthodox view-point of the Vedānta school. Gauḍapāda and Śaṅkara belong to this tradition. In contrast, the tendency to emphasize the second type of life developed later into the so-called "theory of combination of knowledge and works" (*jñānakarma-samuccaya-vāda*), since the view is that both the performance of rituals and the knowledge of *Brahman* are essential. The life of the third type became separated from Vedānta in its narrow sense and became a powerful force in the various sects of Hinduism.

Notes

1. See, Part III, Chapter 2, Section 2, pp. 66 ff.
2. All three commentaries state that it is mentioned in *Atri-Smṛti*, VIII, 11.
3. Such an idea is already found in *Bṛhad. Up.* IV, 4, 22.
4. Deussen, *SV.* p. 85. cf. *Vedāntasāra*, § 17-23.

2. *Meditation*

There are various types of practitioner among the followers of the Vedānta school, such as householders, recluses, those who perform or do not perform the rituals, but all must meditate on *Brahman*, regardless of what kind of life they pursue. Meditation on *Brahman* is an indispensable requisite for attaining liberation.

The author of the *Brahma-sūtra* believed that the main purpose of the *Upaniṣads* is to teach meditation. Critics are mentioned in the *sūtra* who propose that meditation on the *Udgītha* (*Udgīthavidyā*) is a mere glorification which is subservient to rituals and that the stories in the *Upaniṣads* are for the sake of *pāriplava* of the horse-sacrifice (*aśvamedha*), but the author of the *Sūtra*[1] rejects these views and argues that they are all for the purpose of teaching meditation (3.4.21-24).

Various terms are used as synonyms of meditation, such as reverence (*upāsana*), cognition (*vijñāna*), and knowledge (*vidyā*).[2] Other synonyms include concentration (*dhyāna*, 4.1.8., *dhī*, 3.3.33), contemplation (*dṛṣṭi*, 4.1.5), and awareness (*buddhi*, 3.2.33). The concept of meditation, therefore, contains all of these connotations, and all of these terms may be translated into English as meditation. The *Upaniṣads* frequently teach the importance of meditation as the practice of constantly thinking of a sacred object. The *sūtra* interprets it as directing one's mind (*ceto'rpaṇa*) (1.1.15).

The manifold and complex descriptions of meditation in the *Upaniṣads* led to the necessity of examining each form of meditation, clarifying their respective significances, and pointing out the similarities and differences between the various meditations. This problem is discussed in detail in *Brahma-sūtra*, Part III, Chapter 3, and since it has been introduced already in the previous chapter on "The analysis of *Brahma-sūtra*," I shall here only indicate the principles on which the examination of various meditations were based.

In spite of differences in minor matters among the explanations of the diverse forms of meditation prescribed in the *Upaniṣads*, these do not affect their essential unity. Even in the various meditations with the same purport, there appear some differences in minor matters (3.3.2-4). One and the same meditation may also be transmitted through different Vedic schools, of the Vedas, as for example the *Śāṇḍilya-vidyā* attributed to the hermit Śāṇḍilya, and the *Vaiśvānara-vidyā* which teaches the worship of the universal self. Though transmitted in different schools, it is the selfsame meditation and the explanations concerning the auxiliaries may be collected together.[3] A certain form of meditation transmitted in one school may be at the same time practised in another school (3.3.56). Two forms of meditation transmitted as separate within one school may also be actually the one and same meditation.[4]

On the other hand, there are cases where similar descriptions of two different meditations may not necessarily refer to the same meditation. Similarities in explanatory words (*śabda*) or designations (*saṃjñā*) in two different places does not always mean that the same meditation is being discussed.[5] For example, the meditation *Udgītha-vidyā* taught in *Bṛhadāraṇyaka Upaniṣad* 1.3, and that taught in *Chāndogya Upaniṣad* 1.2 are not necessarily identical.[6] There are cases where a particular meditation taught in one passage may consist of two different forms of meditation.[7] Various meditations teaching different attributes, of the same object of meditation (such as *Īśvara*) must also be different (3.3.58).

Now, the author of the *Sūtra* interpreted the complex and manifold varieties of meditations taught in the *Upaniṣads* to be mainly meditation upon *Brahman*. Even in the numerous cases where the *Upaniṣads* do not specify *Brahman* as the object of meditation, they can be interpreted as referring to *Brahman*, for the following reasons : since it is very difficult to meditate upon the absolute at large, some clue to it is needed, and therefore the *Upaniṣads* teach that meditation should be made on the *gāyatrī* metre (1.1.25), on something very small (1.2.7), or on the fire in the body (1.2.26). But even in the case where meditation thus relies on a symbol, *Brahman* is the ultimate goal of meditation (*īkṣatikarman*).[8] The various specifications of the size of *Brahman* are also merely for the purpose of meditation (3.2.33).[9]

For the preceding reasons meditation is to be conducted on a temporary symbol (*pratīka*) as *Brahman*, and it would be erroneous to take *Brahman* as the individual symbols. The basic principle is that the superior reality is to be meditated upon by means of that which is inferior (4.1.5).

Furthermore, the various forms of meditation on *Brahman* are one and the same, and no essential difference among them exists (3.3.1). Thus, the distinction of "higher knowledge" (*parā vidyā*) and "lower knowledge" (*aparā vidyā*) made by Śaṅkara was not entertained. Since the *Brahma-sūtra* differentiates between *Brahman* and the individual self, it does not seem to have recognized any significance in worshipping the individual *ātman* (4.1.4).

Various forms of meditation other han that on *Brahman*

were also taught in the *Upaniṣads*. The meditation, for example, on the members of the sacrificial acts, such as *Udgītha*, etc., were meant to free from hindrance (*apratibandha*) the operation of the rite and to increase its effectiveness.[10] And this *Udgītha* meditation was not limited to any special school but was to be performed equally by them all (3.3.55). There was a difference of opinion between certain thinkers (Ātreya and Auḍulomi) as to whether the worship in regard to certain sections of the rite should be undertaken by the sacrificer or by the priest, but the author of the *Sūtra* follows the latter view and states that it should be the priest.[11]

In the meditation on *Brahman* it is necessary to select (*vikalpa*) and practice only one of the numerous meditations, and there is no necessity to practise more, for the results do not differ (3.3.59). In contrast the meditations conducted for special ends may be practised together or singly, because the effects differ (3.3.60). The worship of the various parts of the sacrificial rite are never practised together.[12]

In order to conduct such meditation one must sit quiet (*āsīna*) because one is unable to unify the thought unless one is so (4.1.7). Its effect is that both the mind and body become steady (4.1.9). It is believed that the contemporary practitioners used to sit in the lotus or half-lotus posture, and that they did not subscribe to the peculiar distorted postures of the later *Yogins*. No special time, place, or direction to face were prescribed by the author of the *Sūtra*; Any place would do provided that concentration of mind (*ekāgratā*) was possible there (4.1.11). Practitioners of this kind of meditation were by the *sūtra* distinguished from *Yogins* in general (3.2.21).

When such meditations were repeatedly practised there would soon be a direct perception of *Brahman* in a state of ecstasy (*saṃrādhana*).[13]

Since the *sūtra* (4.1.1) states that the meditation on *Brahman* must be repeated, it is clear that it did not teach 'sudden attainment.' And since it teaches that meditations have to be continued until death (*prāyaṇa*), it is also clear that even after the intuition of *Brahman* meditation was to be repeated (4.1.12). The knowledge (*vidyā*) obtainable as the result of meditation on *Brahman* was not necessarily assured in this life; if there were no hindrances (*pratibandha*), knowledge could be gained, but if there were hindrances, it would arise in the next life (3.4.51). Thus, the practice of meditation even into the next life came into consideration.

When *Brahman* is perceived directly through the practice of meditation, all the sinful deeds previously performed will dissolve, and no *karma* committed thereafter will cling to the individual self (4.1.13).[14] In the same way neither would good deeds cling to the individual self, and they too would dissolve at death (4.1.14).[15] Although on the rise of knowledge there is dissolution of sinful and good deeds, this is only in respect of those sinful and good deeds which have not yet begun to produce (*anārabdha*) their effects, and the sinful and good deeds which have already produced some effect cannot be dissolved by knowledge. That must await the exhausting of the effects of the deed and its natural extinction thereby. That is, the complete extinction of the deed and its effects occurs when they have been exhausted by means of "experience" (*bhoga*) and the body is completely extinguished. Thus, spiritual liberation occurs only after death.[16] Now, since knowledge does not necessarily appear in the present life, as has been explained, complete liberation is realized in the life following the one in which knowledge was born (3.4.52).

At any rate the author of the *sūtra* recognized the quite unique spiritual power of the knowledge of *Brahman*. And those who realized this knowledge could walk the path of gods after death and achieve union with *Brahman*. Although many forms of meditation on *Brahman* are taught in the *Upaniṣads*, it is said that man can practise any one of them and by it walk on the path of gods (3.3.31).

This concludes our discussion on the meditation taught in the *Brahma-sūtra*. Its chief characteristic is that the content of meditation is very concrete and of definite form; one might say that the meditation and *samādhi* are within the field of differentiated forms. This is probably due to the fact that they derive from the varied forms of meditation in the old *Upaniṣads*. Such practices of meditation formed the orthodox tradition in early Vedānta philosophy, but people who opposed this tradition began to appear, and this opposition reached a peak with the idea of *asparśayoga* in the *Māṇḍūkya-kārikā*.

Notes

1. However, he did not state that everything taught in the *Upaniṣads* was for the purpose of meditation. Sometimes, the teaching is for the purpose of destruction (*abhicāra*) (3.3.25).
2. See Bhāṣyas on 3.3.5.
3. 3.3.5, 10, 33, 34, and 39. But sometimes they are not applicable to other cases (3.3.11-13).
4. 3.3.19, 35, 36, and 38.
5. 3.3.7, 8, and 24.
6. 3.3.6-9.
7. 3.3.20-22, 43.
8. 1.3.13, 1.2.4 and 7, etc.
9. 1.2.7 teaches that it should be worshipped as something extremely small and at the same time extremely big.
10. 3.3.42 and 4.1.18.
11. 3.4.44-46, and see also Part III, Chapter 1, Section 3, pp. 18 ff.
12. 3.3.61-66.
13. 3.2.24-25. The intuition of *ātman* is also taught in 1.1.30.
14. See also 3.4.14 and 16. Such a thought is also found in *Chāndogya Up.* IV, 14, 3; V, 24, 3; *Muṇḍaka Up.* II, 2.8.
15. In *sūtras* 3.3.26 and following it states that at the time of departure (*sāṃparāya*) by escaping from the body the man of knowledge abandons all *karma*. And according to his desire (*chandatas*) he gives his good and evil karma to others. The others inherit (*upāyana*) them. After being freed of good and evil *karma*, the progression (*gati*) on the path of gods takes place. This explanation contradicts the argument that knowledge leads to the cessation of good and evil *karma* and also the idea that *Karmic* retribution applies to the individual self, but perhaps 3.3.26 and following should be understood as an explanation of *Chānd. Up.* VIII, 13; *Muṇḍaka-Up.* III, 1, 3; *Kauṣ. Up.* I, 4, etc. The author of the *sūtra* seems to have recognized this merely as a transmission of a certain school (see 4.1.17). So a difference between the scriptures and the author of the *Sūtra* is also evident here.
16. 4.1.15 and 19.

SECTION 6 TRANSMIGRATION AND RELEASE

1. *The Soul after Death*

The *Brahma-sūtra* doctrine of the soul after death concentrates on the exposition in the *Chāndogya Upaniṣad.*

When a person dies, first the function of speech becomes quiet and merges in the mind. In the same way all other sense faculties merge into the mind. Next, the mind merges into the principal Vital Air (*mukhya prāṇa*), and the Vital Air merges in the individual self. Then the individual self with the Vital Air merges into the elements *(bhūta)* (4.2.1-5). These elements are so subtle that they cannot be perceived by the senses, and they become the seeds for the formation of a future body. That is, they form a subtle body. Of the subtle elements, the most powerful *(bhūyas)* is water (3.1.2). The individual self is enveloped *(saṃpariṣvakta)* in this subtle element, escapes from the former body, and enters some other, new body (3.1.1). Thus, the various elements, the various senses,[1] and the vital air, form in a latent condition, the basis of transmigration, and supported by them, the individual self passes to other bodies. Although the *ātman* can escape from the tangible gross body, it cannot do so due to the condition of being an embodied self *(śarīra)*.[2]

The process of escaping from the body is identical for both the wise *(vidvas)* and the unwise *(avidvas)*, but thereafter they follow completely different paths. This is expounded by means of a unique interpretation to the theory of the path of gods and path of ancestors, set out by the *Chāndogya Upaniṣad* (5.10).

Those who have not gained knowledge, even though they have performed the good works of sacrificial acts, etc., ascend to the lunar world by the path of ancestors *(pitṛyāna)*.[3] The path of ancestors is the path that leads to the lunar world, according to the *Chāndogya Upaniṣad*, passing through the smoke of the body's cremation, then through night, the half month of the waning moon, the six months of the southern course of the sun, and the world of ancestral spirits. The author of the *Sūtra* evidently affirmed this view.

Among the stages of the path of ancestors, passage through the cremation smoke, ancestral world, and lunar world is intelligible inasmuch as they occupy space; but night, the last half of the month, and the six months' southern course of the sun are temporal things which do not occupy space. The whole idea seems strange to modern man, but it derives directly from the thinking found in the *Brāhmaṇa* literature. The theologians of the *Brāhmaṇas* believed that abstract concepts and temporal concepts all possessed substance, and therefore they treated them on the same level as material objects in space. According to their way of thinking, night, the last half of the month, and the six months' southern course of the sun are expressed as though they had material reality, and some of the Upaniṣadic philosophers could not abandon this way of thinking. Thus it came down directly to the author of the *Brahma-sūtra*.

In the lunar world, the individual soul undergoes the *karmic* effects of action in this world and after undergoing *karmic* effects the individual self descends to this world, led by karma (*anuśaya*) (3.1.18). When it descends, it passes through residual ether, air, smoke, mist, cloud, and rain to reach the earth, then enters plants such as rice, barley, etc., and when they are eaten, it enters a male body, resides in the spermatozoon, enters the womb, and becomes a body (*śarīra*), that is, it is born into this world as a human being or an animal,[4] as taught in the *Chāndogya-Upaniṣad*. When the *Chāndogya Upaniṣad* teaches that the individual self "becomes ether, etc.," in the process of descending to earth, it means that it becomes similar in nature (*sābhāvyāpatti*) to ether, for it would be impossible for it to become identical with ether, etc. (3.1.22). The time that the individual self resides in each state is very brief (3.1.23), although the *Brahma-sūtra* does not mention any particular length of time. The stages of the descent are all controlled by individual selves of their own, and the descending soul stays only temporarily in each sphere, controlled by the self of ether, wind, smoke, etc. as the case may be (3.1.24).

In case of birth on earth, the *Chāndogya-Upaniṣad* teaches that those of pure conduct are born into the *Brahmin*, *Kṣatriya*, or *Vaiśya* castes, those of impure conduct are born from the womb of a dog, pig, or cāṇḍāla, and those who are evil-doers fall into a third place and become tiny insects (5.10.7). The *Brahma-sūtra* acknowledges this view, and it considers as standard Bādari's theory that the differences in birth result from actions in this world.[5] Thus, the effects of the good and bad deeds performed in this life would first be experienced in the lunar world, and then they would determine the type of birth after descent to this world; the concept is therefore of a two-stage effectuality of *Karma*. It was believed that endless repetition of *saṃsāric* life was kept going by this kind of experiencing the effects of *Karma*.

On the other hand, the author of the *Sūtra* states (1.2.16) that "those who have heard the *Upaniṣads*" (*śrutopaniṣatka*), those who have gained knowledge of *Brahman*, approach *Brahman* by means of the path of gods (*devayāna*). In the *Ṛg-Veda* the path of gods had meant the channel whereby the gods of heaven went to and returned from the sacrificial site, or the way by which the spirit of the dead ascended to the place of the gods, but here it was taken as the path by which the liberated individual self could reach *Brahman*. The theory of the path of gods was also based primarily on the *Chāndogya-Upaniṣad*. At death after the individual self embraces the various sense faculties, principal vital air, and the subtle elements, light shines at the top of the heart, which is the dwelling place (*okas*) of individual self. This light illumines the passage of the path of gods, and the individual self which has acquired knowledge of Brahman contemplates the path he should take by the power of knowledge (*vidyā*) and, embraced by the highest god that resides in the heart, escapes from the body through the 101st *nāḍī* (4.2.17). The self then goes to the world of *Brahman*, enveloped in a subtle body as he advances on the path of gods (3.3.30). The consequent journey is patterned on the description in the *Chāndogya Upaniṣad*, combined with ideas from the *Bṛhadāraṇyaka Upaniṣad* and *Kauṣītaki Upaniṣad*. It can be taken that the scheme of the stages of the path followed by the author of the *sūtra* was as follows :

(1) Flame (*arcis*) from cremation (*Brahma-sūtra* 4.3.1)
(2) Day
(3) The half month of the waxing moon
(4) Six months' northern course of the sun
(5) Year (*abda*)
(6) Wind (*vāyu*) (Wind is not mentioned in the *Chāndogya-Upaniṣad*, but it is found in the *Bṛhadāraṇyaka*, and so this addition is made.) (4.3.2)
(7) Sun
(8) Moon
(9) Lightning (*taḍit*)
(10) Varuṇa's world (Addition from *Kauṣītaki-Upaniṣad*) (4.3.3)
(11) *Brahman*

In the above process the individual self after escaping from the body, follows the rays of the sun until it reaches the sun (4.2.18). When an individual self quits the body at night, it would seem impossible for it to follow the rays of the sun, since these are not observable. It is, however, stated that a connection between the *nāḍī* and the rays continues as long as the body exists (*yāvaddehabhāvin*). Therefore even though the sun's rays are not observable at night, the individual self does follow them in its ascent to the world of the sun (4.2.19). One who has knowledge, even if he dies when the sun is in the southern course, ascends to the sun (4.2.20). The stipulations in *smṛti* concerning the proper time of death apply to *Yogins* and not to everyone (4.2.21).

The lights listed above are not simply roadsigns and places of experiencing *karmic* effects, but also guides (*ātivāhika*) on the path (4.3.4). Since the individual self advancing on the path of gods does not possess a body, the senses do not function and it lacks perception (*vyāmoha*), so the lights act as guides for it (4.3.5). After entering the world of lightning, "the person who is not a man" guides the individual self and takes him into the world of *Brahman* (4.3.6). *Brahman* is the home of the emancipated (*muktopasṛpya*) (1.3.2.), though its nature was understood differently by Bādari, Jaimini, and Bādarāyaṇa (4.3.7-16). The author of the *Sūtra*, however, seems to have believed that irrespective of these differences of view *Brahman* which is entered would be an ideal realm of bliss. In the next section we shall consider what that realm might be.

As to the path on which the evil-doers must travel, it was identified as a "third place" different from the path of gods or path of ancestors. From this path the evil-doers are born as minute living organisms, without the necessity of conception[6] (3.1.18).

Notes

1. See also 3.1.13.
2. 4.2.12 and 13.
3. See also 3.1.7 ff. and 3.1.17.
4. 3.1.22-27.
5. See Part III, Chapter 1, Section 5 (p. 27 ff.). Cf. *Kauṣītaki-Up.* I, 2.
6. Suffering in hell after death is also taught in 3.1.13 ff. Śaṅkara accepts this as the finally established theory (*siddhānta*), but Bhāskara and Rāmānuja see it as a prima facie view (*pūrvapakṣa*).

2. *The Realm of Spiritual Liberation*

The *Brahma-sūtra*, following Bādarāyaṇa, declared that it is liberation attained by knowledge that is the purpose of man (*puruṣārtha*) and criticized Jaimini's theory of omnipotence of sacrificial acts. Thus, for the author of the *Sūtra*, liberation was the ultimate goal which is the supreme meaning of life.

Spiritual liberation is union (*yoga*) with *Brahman*, and it means to be at rest in the source of our existence.[1] It was believed that the fullest realization would be attained when the individual self, having attained knowledge, went forward on the path of gods after death and achieved ultimate union with *Brahman*. That is, the individual self would go forward on the path of gods and merge, together with the various sense functions and subtle elements, into the highest *Brahman* (4.2.15).

According to the *sūtra*, the individual self achieves union with *Brahman*, who is called the "highest light" in the *Chāndogya Upaniṣad*, and thereby manifests (*āvirbhāva*) its real nature (4.4.1). Such an individual self is one whose real nature has been manifested (*āvirbhūta-svarūpa*, 1.3.19). That is, he is liberated (*mukta*) and has transcended all bondage.

When union with *Brahman* is achieved, the individual self becomes "without distinctions" (*avibhāga*) (4.2.16). This means that the liberated individual self exists indistinguishable from the Highest Self.[2] Yet as each individual self maintains its uniqueness even in the state of liberation,[3] this was not thought to be an absolute coming to unity. The state of liberation, therefore, does not at all mean the extinction of individual self. In that state it still has the function of discriminatory awareness. Liberation is quite different from the state of deep sleep or death where the discriminative function is lacking (4.4.16). The liberated self can actualize his desires by mere will (*saṃkalpād eva*) : if for instance he should desire to see his fathers, he can at once meet them by merely thinking about them[4] (4.4.8). The liberated self is without a lord (*adhipati*), for he himself is his own lord and anything he wishes he can realize (4.4.9).

There is a difference of opinion as to whether or not the *ātman* of a liberated man possesses body and senses, but the author of the *Sūtra* takes the eclectic theory of Bādarāyaṇa (4.4.12-14). According to this view, the liberated man can either take a body or not take one, as he pleases. If in the liberated state a bodily form is not taken then, as in the sleeping state, no desires arise in him; but when a bodily form is taken, desires arise as in the waking state. Furthermore, the *ātman* of the liberated man may adopt not only one bodily form, but can enter into several bodies, just as the flame of a lamp in one corner can illuminate all directions (4.4.15). The individual which has attained such a liberation experiences infinite blessings and joys in *Brahman.*

The emancipated one thus possesses lordly powers equal to those of *Īśvara*, except that it does not possess the ability to control the creation, support and dissolution of the world (*jagadvyāpāra*) (4.4.17). Such are the functions of *Īśvara* alone, and the liberated one's lordly powers are equal to his only in the sphere of enjoyment. The lordly powers of the liberated one, therefore, are not unlimited and absolute, for his powers are derived from *Īśvara* (4.4.18).

The liberated one resides within *Brahman* in this way, and it will never return to this world (4.4.22).

This, of course, does not mean that all those who have gained knowledge attain liberation and depart for the world of *Brahman.* Those who have been entrusted with an office (*ādhikārika*) by *Īśvara* remain in this world as long as it takes to fulfil that office (*yāvad-adhikāram avasthitiḥ*, 3.3.32). The *sūtra* does not define what constitutes such an office, but Bhāskara says that it is to bless and save the world (*lokānugraha*) and Śaṅkara says that it is to spread the Vedas (*Vedapravartana*). Thus, very special individuals, even though they have knowledge, remain in this world of *saṃsāra* for the sake of the others, but almost all remain at rest in the world of *Brahman*, never to return to this world. The basis of the practice is, in the *Brahma-sūtra*, what must be called individual self-interest; the ideal of the *Mahāyāna bodhisattva*, who elects to remain in the world of *saṃsāra* for the liberation of all beings, finds no recognition here. The view of liberation presented in the *Brahma-sūtra* corresponds to the social context already discussed.

The above is a general outline of the view of liberation held by the author of the *Sūtra*, and from the standpoint of the history of Vedānta philosophy we can pick out a number of interesting characteristics.

(1) Liberation in the *Brahma-sūtra* is an ideal realm where,

still as an individual, man acquires every conceivable lordly power, realizes all desires, and enjoys bliss. The details of the description of this realm of liberation are almost unparalleled in the writings of any Indian school. In the other schools, and in fact in Vedānta itself, liberation is generally expressed in terms of negations and denials; the *Brahma-sūtra* account of it is very positive and concrete.

(2) This realm of liberation is to be achieved after death, and it cannot be reached in this present life. The attainment of the world of *Brahman* is the ultimate liberation, and no other forms of liberation exist; thus the liberation conceived by the author of the *Sūtra* is only of one type. There is no idea of such distinctions of later Vedānta as liberation in this life (*jīvanmukti*), gradual liberation (*kramamukti*), and ultimate liberation. The teaching which emphasizes attainment of liberation and peace by realizing the highest *Brahman* in the midst of this changing world of birth and death was not yet clearly evident in the *Brahma-sūtra*. The belief that liberation is going to a good world after death shows an affinity with the older *Upaniṣads* of earliest period, and with the Jain doctrine.

(3) When we study the different theories of the various teachers about *Brahman* as the goal to which the liberated self goes (4.3.7-16), all the teachers accept two aspects : the highest *Brahman*, and *Brahman* as the effect. Bādarāyaṇa agrees,[5] but the author of the *Sūtra* merely mentions it as one view, and does not himself seem to distinguish these two aspects of *Brahman*. He followed exclusively the teaching in the *Chāndogya-Upaniṣad*, conceiving of the one *Brahman* as the ultimate goal. The explanation of liberation also has only the one aspect. If we examine the various accounts of *Brahman* given in the *sūtra*, we do not find the double aspect postulated. This is another point on which the author of the *Sūtra* seems to have held ideas different from those of Bādarāyaṇa.[6]

The above concludes the examination of practice as found in the fundamental text called the *Brahma-sūtra*. The practice of the Vedānta school underwent great transformation in later ages. Even the Advaita orders founded by Śaṅkara, in later times organized communal life for its many followers in huge monasteries, and there were incidents of armed clashes with other orders. Thus, the practical life of the Vedānta school was quite different in later ages, but in the early period the ideal was as has been described above.

Notes

1. 1.1.19 and 1.1.7.
2. See 4.4.4.
3. See 4.4.12 and following.
4. This is already taught in *Chānd. Up*. VIII, 2.1.
5. See Part III, Chapter 2, Section 2.
6. Bādarāyaṇa and the author of the *sūtra* also do not necessarily agree in their attitude towards the significance of rituals. See Part IV, Chapter 3, Section 5, 1.

INDEX

B

C

E

L

R

T

U